Some Are Smarter Than Others

The History of Marcos' Crony Capitalism

Ricardo Manapat

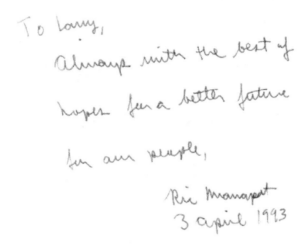

To Larry,
always with the best of
hopes for a better future
for our people,
Ric Manapat
3 april 1993

"Kina Papa at Mama"

Preface

The present book is the expanded and updated version of a 40-page pamphlet published under the same title in September 1979.

The original work was published at a period long before exposes of Marcos and crony wealth had become fashionable and was a time when such an endeavor was fraught with danger.

In spite of the great risks and the financial difficulties accompanying its publication, the pamphlet was successfully reproduced and distributed by the Kasapi (Kapulunganang mga Sandigan ng Pilipinas), a political group active since the late 1960's. Using a dilapidated mimeographing machine and donated supplies, volunteers were sequestered for two weeks at the residence of Renato Tanada and were not permitted to leave until they had reproduced and collated 2,000 copies of the pamphlet. Members of the Kasapi as well as other friends took care of thedistribution. As a safety precaution for the two authors of the original study, a dis-information tactic was employed and a note was added that the pamphlet was theproduct of company researches on the status of its business competitors. The aim was to mislead the martial law regime into looking for the corporate research arm of a leading company rather than an underground political group.

The 1979 study was an unprecedented success. Although the political conditions permitted dissemination only through informal channels, the pamphlet experienced extensive distribution since other concerned individuals and institutions reproduced the study on their own. Within a few weeks, the work had already circulated widely in Manila. Major newspapers in Asia, the United States, and Europe soon followed suit and cited the study in numerous articles. Concerned groups overseas reproduced the study and continued its distribution. The pamphlet took a life of its own. An excited public nicknamed it The Octopus, a reference to the two-headed octopus drawn on the the cover of the mimeographed pamphlet. An article from Mr. & Ms. describes the general reaction to the now-classic expose

. . whose xeroxed copies were passed in the Philippines surreptitiously from one hand to another and discussed in whispers and bated breath and gleaming eyes because it revealed the shameless greed of the Marcoses and their coterie. .

The greatest compliment came from Ninoy Aquino, who, speaking while still incarcerated in Fort Bonifacio, called the 1979 monograph "the most explosive document to have rocked Manila."

But despite the positive reception we were clearly conscious of the limitations of the original study. The research had been hurriedly done in a span of two months and the writing was carried out within a few weeks. The subjects of the study were discussed superficially, while many cronies were never even mentioned. We thus promised to come out with an updated and expanded version.

A further limitation of the original work was pointed out by Luis Tame, the old Huk Supremo. While the work was receiving praises from many quarters, Taruc was the only one who offered constructive criticism. He pointed out that, while the work had the value of identifying the properties of Marcos' cronies, it failed to show how Filipinos had become poorer in the process of wealth accumulation. We thus again promised to try to improve the work in this regard.

This book then comes as a way of fulfilling these promises. While the present work has its obvious imperfections, it hopefully has improved upon the original work both in terms of its coverage and social and political perspective.

When Ninoy Aquino asked us in 1980 how long it would take to finish this updated version, we naively gave the answer as "around two weeks." We slightly miscalculated our timetable. We required more than 1 1 years of research and writing

to do full justice to the topic. Since we had already clearly established the pattern of cronyism in Marcos' regime with our 1979 study, it was no longer necessary to engage in further sensationalism. In our judgement, it was far more important to present a thorough account by setting the events in their proper historical and political context. We hope that the present book proves to be worth the wait of those who expected the book to come out much earlier.

Our motivation in coming out with this book was to document what we believed to be the central aspect of Marcos' regime. It was not our aim to malign the individuals mentioned in this study. Our purpose was purely historical in nature, and individuals were mentioned only insofar as their activities shed light on the history of the period. Our aim is best expressed by borrowing the words of Emile Zola:

> *As to the men I accuse, I do not know them, I have never seen them, I feel neitherresentment nor hatred against them. For me they are only entities, emblems of social malfeasance.*

The reader is cautioned that the book may appear tedious in certain parts but for the dedicated researcher much gold may be unearthed through the diligent patience of the quiet mole.

Acknowledgements

This book would not have been possible without the help of others. Of the individuals who contributed most to this book, the assistance of the following have been essential: Papa and Mama who have been extremely supportive of my work from the very beginning; Rafael Cecilio who painstakingly edited the drafts of the manuscript and saved me from many errors; Dennis O' Leary who shared many ideas, supplied much research, and helped shape the book through many invaluable discussions; Orlando Rivera who was very charitable with his time and helped me solve the many computer problems I encountered in writing this book; Jonathan Barnett who kindly gave me the equivalent of some 20 free days during the first quarter of 1990 which permitted me to work on important sections of this book; Taka and Baby who helped work on a Japanese translation; Maria Estela Barrientos Barquin who worked on a Spanish translation; Jojo, Lulu, and Tita who helped acquire important newsclippings and performed other important errands; Huges Savaille who gave invaluable advice; and a good friend, who for the moment shall be known as Mr. X, for designing the cover and providing important advice on the intricacies of the production of books. The help of the following individuals is also acknowledged: Teddy Yabut, Maria Dolores Vasquez, Margarita Valte, Karen Tafiada, Sara Schlaudecker, Dr. Ciriaco Sabilano, Stephanie Robisson, Eleni Pappas, Richard Pichler, Jennifer Morgan, Rolando Montiel, Jean Molesky, Gina Michael, Karen Marcos Paramo, Atty. Luis "Booty" Jose, Gerardo Esguerra, Cecilia Bofill, Ricardo Bravo, M6nica Beyruti, Gerrnelino and Cynthia Bautista. Other individuals have equally provided help but have preferred to maintain their anonymity. The individuals whose help is acknowledged in this book are not in any way responsible for its contents. Whatever mistakes, limitations, or liabilities the book may have are solely mine.

Some Conventions

Certain conventions have been followed for convenience.

Aside from a few exceptions, all transactions are denominated in dollars. Transactions originally denominated in pesos were translated into dollars by using the average exchange rate for the particular year the transaction took place.

Certain shortcuts have also been used. References to Mijares and Doherty mean the following: 1) Primitivo Mijares, The Conjugal Dictatorship, (San Francisco: Union Square Publications, 1976), and 2) Fr. John Doherty's Interlocking Directorates, an updated and yet-unpublished version of his 1979 Preliminary Study of Interlocking Directorates. Other references are properly indicated in the endnotes. References to the SEC generally mean the Securities & Exchange Commission of the Philippines. References to the United States SEC are explicitly stated. The Far Eastern Economic Review has been generally shortened as Review. Acronyms have also been used for selected institutions frequently mentioned in the text:

COA — Commission on Audit

DBP - Development Bank of the Philippines
EO — Executive Order
GSIS - Government Service Insurance Corporation

KBL - Kilusang Bagong Lipunan, the Marcos political party
LOI - Letter of Instruction
NDC - National Development Corporation
NIDC - National Investment & Development Corp.
(investment arm of the PNB)
NEDA - National Economic Development Authority
NFA - National Food Authority
PD - Presidential Decree
PNB - Philippine National Bank
SEC - Securities & Exchange Commission

Quotes

*I may have committed many sins in my life, but I can tell you
stealing is not one of them.*

— Ferdinand E. Marcos,
in an ABC TV Nightline interview
with Ted Koppel, 4 April 1986

There is no such thing as a secret in Manila.

—— Benigno Aquino Jr.,
reflecting before his fateful return
to the Philippines.

Beware of history, for no secret can be hidden from her.

— Gregoria de Jesus, widow of Andres Bonifacio
Mga Tala ng Aking Buhay at mga Ulat ng Katipunan, (Manila: 1932).

TABLE OF CONTENTS
Abstract of Chapters

The first chapter sets the tone for the rest of the book by attempting to give an idea of the magnitude of the wealth Marcos and his cronies enjoyed. The spending behavior of the Marcos family is contrasted with the poverty of the rest of the country. It is argued that wealth and poverty are the cause and effect of each other.

II. THE DEVELOPMENT OF CRONY CAPITALISM - *Page 66*

The regime of Marcos and Imelda was not a temporary aberration from the historically established patterns of political and social behavior. The ostentation of Imelda and the corruption of Marcos merely represented in a most developed form the two anti—social traditions of the country's social and political elite. Attempts are made to go beyond ordinary notions of corruption as a way of explaining cronyism as the defining trait of Marcos' regime, It is suggested that the phenomenon of cronyism under Marcos be viewed as the use of state power for private interests.

III. THE RELATIVES AND CRONIES – *Page 91*

Every major economic activity was controlled by the First Family, their relatives, or cronies. These relatives and cronies acted as either as Marcos nominees or on their own behalf in key corporations and drew money from government, private, and international sources. The national coffer, the resources of private banks. international loans from multinational banks, and aid money from the US and Japan were placed at the disposal of Marcos' money-making network. Corporations owned or manned by cronies were provided extremely liberal government incentives, selectively granted tax exemptions, assigned lucrative government contracts, granted monopolies and captive markets through presidential decree. given easy and privileged access to credit from local and international financial institutions, and monopolized access to valuable market information available only to the government. When these methods did not suffice, military force was used as a factor in economic competition.

This chapter presents case studies of selected cronies by outlining the activities of the following: Benedicto. Floirendo, Enrile, Cojuangco, Elizalde, Silverio, Cuenca, Velasco, Disini, Lucio Tan, Yao, Gapud. Roman Cruz, the Enriquez and Panlilio families, Bienvenido and Gliceria Tantoco, the Romualdez and the Marcos families.

IV. THE OVERSEAS EMPIRE - *Page 365*

The Marcos family and their friends built an overseas empire which rivals the magnitude of the assets of the biggest multinational corporations. Sophisticated techniques of money laundering were used to hide and transport assets out of the country to amass fortunes in Swiss bank accounts, US real estate, as well as properties in other countries. While the previous chapter documented how wealth was extracted, this chapter discusses how the wealth was transferred overseas. -

V. IN LIEU OF A CONCLUSION: Of Typewriters and Flags – *Page 460*

Efforts by the Aquino government to recover Marcos' wealth have had dismal results. The reasons for the failure in the recovery efforts are analyzed in this chapter.

Chapter I

THE WORSHIP OF BAAL

*I must confess that once upon a time his family and my family
were oligarchs. But we are reformed oligarchs... The Romualdez
family has been in office for many years, and thank God
there is a family that is willing to serve the country... Thank God
they know how to make money. Otherwise, if Marcos did not
have money before, what experience would he have to
make this country prosper? The United States is ashamed it
is rich. Why should we be ashamed? We have some gifted
members of the family. Good. They want to serve the people.
Wonderful.*

—— Imelda Romualdez Marcos [1]

*walla, sabre tam tarima depino, estd el magnifico
piano de cola de un precio exorbitante, y mas
precioso aun esta noche, porque nadie lo toca.*

*('"...over there. on top of a platform made of pine, is a
magnificent grand piano, exorbitantly priced, and
still more expensive this evening because no one plays it.")*

Our translation. Jose Rizal, Nali Me Tangere,
(Berlin: Berliner l3uchdruckerei-Acticn-Gcscllschaft, 1886), p. 3.

A clue to understanding the history of Marcos' crony capitalism may be found in a little—known and almost-forgotten event in Philippine local history. The story never reached the headlines in the Marcos~controlled press, but since it was one which was played out many times in different variations throughout the years of Marcos' reign, the story serves as a metaphor for understanding much of what has happened in recent Philippine history.

THE CITY OF MAN

Several months after martial law was declared in 1972, the Marcos government embarked on a massive program to attract foreign tourists. Part of the nationwide tourism effort was a cleanliness campaign headed by Imelda Marcos to get rid of the various forms of litter that cluttered the city of Manila and its suburbs. Her ultimate aim was to reorganize the whole metropolitan Manila area into one great super-city which she would head as governor. And perhaps as an oblique reference to Saint Augustine, she proposed to call her new dominion the City of Man.

There was not much success in cleansing the city streets of garbage nor in dredging the stenching small rivers and canals which slither throughout greater Mantle. There was, however, partial success in one aspect of the cleanliness campaign. The achievement lay in clearing selected areas of Manila and its suburbs of several squatter communities which were not only eyesores for foreign visitors but were also an uneasy reminder to those who passed by the slum areas in their air-conditioned cars that not all was well in the world which they lived.

We are familiar with the story of one of these poor communities, and it's through the story of this community that we start our exposition of the history of Marcos' crony capitalism.

CONSTITUTION HILL

In preparation for the visit of Prince Juan Carlos de Borbon, squatter families living near the area of Intramuros, the Walled City built during Spanish colonial times, were forcibly evicted from their hovels and dumped in an isolated suburb of Quezon City. The place was called Constitution Hill.

At that time the place was used as the garbage dump of Quezon City. Close to a thousand families were relocated to the area and left to fend for themselves. They were totally cut off from their traditional means of livelihood. Access to public transportation was a walk of several miles on a dusty trail, and commuting to work would have eaten up a good part of their daily earnings. There was no water, no electricity, and no sanitation system. There was only famine, desperation, and death. One cannot imagine a more hostile environment to live in than to be beside tons of garbage. Drinking water had to be fetched from hand pumps several miles away and carried by hand. The community had to endure the stench and eat inside mosquito nets to fend off the hordes of flies which feasted daily on them, their food, and the Quezon City garbage. During the first few weeks of this painful diaspora, children died by the dozens because of exposure to the elements and the lack of potable water.

A member of this community writes:
Almost all of us were left in shock with the events. The first thing that we asked ourselves: why did fate bring us here? Is this a dwelling for men? A fetid dump. You first had to get into a mosquito net before you ate, because the gigantic flies came in roves [2].

There is some irony to the name of the lace. It was called Constitution Hill because it was there where the post-war Republic had planned to relocate the legislature. The name was testimony to the hope that the place would be a wellspring whence the rule of reason and law would flow to guide and nurture the young Republic. But instead, what the relocated families encountered was a huge mountain of garbage and the rusting, decades-old steel frame of the planned edifice towering over them. The community saw something ominous in this dilapidated, inanimate structure. Parents strictly prohibited their children to go near it. They all instinctively felt the hostile and alien character of this silent structure, as if it were a sleeping monster which would one day wake up and devour them.

There is an old Filipino adage which, roughly translated, says that a drowning man will grasp anything even if it be the blade of a knife. Somehow the community survived their initial trial. The garbage dump was covered with soil, and they were able to rebuild their homes in small neat rectangular plots, using banana trees as fences to separate each lot. With the help of the sisters of the Religious of the Virgin Mary (RVM), the community was able to clear a hectare of land and plant rice. A school and a basketball court followed.

But all was short-lived. After more than five years of wielding absolute power, Marcos felt he needed to organize a legislature which would pass laws and legitimize his regime. Preparations were thus made to quickly resume construction to complete the legislative building within a few months, a move which again affected the community of Constitution Hill. It started with the demolition of the shanties of 120 families on March 1977 to make room for the construction of the Batasang Pambansa Legislative Building. Six people died then: an aged person, and five children. They were without shelter for three days and two nights. The succeeding months of 1977 saw the working perimeter of the construction site slowly expand and eat up the adjacent houses, sometimes by twenties, and sometimes by tens, as ad happened during Christmas day of that year.

The residents tried to fight the demolitions in court. They put together their meager savings to get the courts to issue an injunction against the further destruction of their homes. They argued that they were there only because Marcos people had dumped them there, that this would be the second time they would uprooted be from their homes by the national government, and that they were willing to pay for the land they occupied from whatever small savings they had managed to eke out. They lost all the cases. There were powerful economic and political interests at work at both the national and local levels. At the local level, the Mayor of Quezon City, Adelina Rodriguez, was eager to get rid of the community of Constitution Hill because the value of the nearby real estate subdivisions she and her family owned through ADEZ would go up as soon as the area was rid of "squatters" [3]. At the national level, it would have been quite a politically embarrassing situation for the Marcos government to have a community of tuberculars and malnourished children merely a few hundred yards away from the plush parking spaces of Prime Minister Virata and other the highly-paid legislators. The contrast would have been too stark and would have caused some uneasiness. The whole idea behind the Marcos-controlled legislature was to provide legitimacy for the regime, but these efforts at legitimation would be powerfully undermined by the picture of poverty and the suffering of the hundreds of families who lived nearby.

The methods employed by the government were merciless. Officials from the Quezon Ci Mayor's Office and the National Housing Authority called a meeting to inform the people that the rest of their homes would soon be demolished. When the meeting was finished, a woman from the community, Veronica Campo, stayed on in the meeting place. A certain Lourdes Vergara from the Social Welfare Services of the Mayor's Office and a Lieutenant Atienza from the Integrated National Police, along with other government officials, took turns in berating the woman. At around

4:00 o'clock that afternoon, the woman died of a heart attack, leaving two orphans. One was two years old, the other seven months.

There was a further mass demolition of the remaining 400 homes on 6 June 1978. The team from the Quezon City Mayor's Office and the National Housing Authority did not bring any court order or any legal paper authorizing the demolition. What they brought was a complement of 300 Quezon City policemen and Metrocom troopers, four fire trucks, and machine guns mounted on top of army jeeps. General Karingal of the Integrated National Police announced over the bullhorn: "You will now be demolished. You were warned that you would be allowed to stay only until June 5. You were warned that after this date, the place will be clean."

No one was spared. Officials from the City Engineer's Office and the National Housing Authority, two government bodies which were supposed to provide housing for low-income families, were leading the demolition. Some of the men from these offices even took advantage of the situation by stealing from the homes they demolished. One Willy Albia, a resident of Constitution Hill, pleaded with the demolition teams to wait until the next day before they razed his house, explaining that he had a child who was running a high fever. His pleas were ignored.

What were formerly the homes of 400 families became a gigantic pile of wood by the evening. People slept under boards which used to be the walls of their modest dwellings. The crying of children was everywhere. Pain and despair were written in the faces of the men and women.

For four days and three nights, no one could say that he had a home. Within these four days children started to get sick, and by the time the community was able to put up make-shift dwellings, four children had died.

The community of Constitution Hill was totally dispersed: Sister Alfonsa, the nun from the Religious of the Virgin Mary who had been living and working with the community for tears as a volunteer and community organizer, was hauled off to court by Vergara. Because she built a school for the children, the nun was slapped with charges of erecting an illegal structure by the authorities. The sewing machines which the nun used to instill skills in the women of the community were "confiscated" by employees of the city government and were later sold for personal gain. In place of the community of Constitution Hill now stands the Batasang Pambansa Legislative Building where laws legitimizing the regime of Marcos were passed. The place where a school for poor children once stood was blanket by a cement parking lot for the Marcos legislators.

Through this short account, we can see themes which will help us understand how Marcos' crony capitalism worked. We encounter two main sets of actors. On one hand, we have the power wielders who brazenly exercised their prerogatives at the national and local levels. And on the other, we have their victims, the majority of whom live in poverty, are malnourished and sickly, are poorly housed, and are constantly under abuse. A major theme of this book, this chapter, is to contrast the disparity between the lives of the members of these two groups. A subsidiary theme, one which we shall point out whenever the occasion permits, is how the two opposites of wealth and poverty were held together during the Marcos regime. Here is where a supporting cast of actors make their appearance: the legitimators who justified the regime in different ways. This special group provided the theoretical schema through which Marcos' crony capitalism was justified, passing laws favoring the economic interests of those close to Marcos, controlling the courts, monopolizing the media, corrupting the accounting and law professions. The predatory behavior of those who wielded power during Marcos' regime was made possible by the professionals who prostituted their trade to help legitimize the actions of Marcos. And when the irrationality and injustice of these legitimations became transparent and were challenged, military force was used to keep the system functioning. Our account of Constitution Hill is therefore not merely a historical curiosum but serves as a theoretical paradigm, a political looking glass, holding the clue to an understanding much of recent Philippine history.

WEIGHED IN THE BALANCES AND FOUND WANTING [4]

The poverty and hardship experienced by the residents of Constitution Hill represent in microcosm the great suffering endured by the majority of Filipinos.

When Marcos became President in 1965, approximately 13.4 million or 39% of the population could not meet the minimum requirements for food, clothing, and shelter. By 1975, after ten years of his leadership, the number rose to a staggering 20.5 million or 48% of the population.

Studies conducted by government agencies revealed similar trends in Metropolitan Manila. Researches undertaken by the Food & Nutrition Research Council (FNRC) and the Development Academy of the Philippines (DAP) showed that 23.5% of families living in Metro-Manila in 1965 could not meet the minimum requirements for food, with the figure rising to 34.1% in 1971. In the rural areas, the figure was 49.2% in 1965, increasing to 64% in1971.

The same researches indicated that we would have a considerably higher figure on poverty if we considered other basic necessities aside from food. If we were to include clothing and shelter in our calculations, then 49.2% of all families living in Metro-Manila would have been below the poverty line in 1965, with the figure increasing to 59.0% in 1971. In the rural areas, the figure would have been considerably higher, 81.1% of families in 1965, increasing to 83.0% in 1971.

These figures mean that at least 16 million Filipinos, constituting nearly half of the population, were below the food threshold and could not meet the minimum food requirements in 1971. If other needs were included in our considerations, the poverty line would be considerably higher, rising to 26 million people, covering 69% of the population of 1971.

Statistics from the Food & Nutrition Research Council, the National Census & Statistics Office, and the Central Bank showed that a family of six living in Manila in 1974 needed $6.00 per day or $168 per month to meet subsistence requirements in 1974. But by 1979, after a series of increases in the prices of basic commodities, the Annual Report of the Ministry of Social Services & Development (MSSD) admitted that at least 15 million Filipinos, roughly constituting 30% of the population, were earning only $34.00 a month or 20% of what was required to decently meet the 1974 food requirements.

Anywhere from 69.9% to 84.3% of households in the Philippines are poorly fed. If the food threshold is based on a diet of rice, dried fish, sweet potato tops, and margarine, then 69.9% of all households are below this threshold. If the basic diet is expanded to include rice, dried fish, coffee, milk and vegetables such as eggplant, mongo, papaya, and other cheap Filipino vegetables, then 84.3% of total household would not be able to meet these standards [5].

The dramatic increase in poverty during the first and second presidential terms of Marcos led the Food & Agriculture Organization (FAQ) to rank the Philippines in 1974 as one of the top five countries with the worst mal-nutrition rates in the world. The ranking was made by calculating the number of persons who consumed less than the daily 1,600 calories needed to sustain a body in complete rest.

The trend in poverty continued throughout the years of Marcos' rule and was reflected 1n various nutrition studies by different institutions.

Seventy-eight percent of Filipino pre-school children were suffering from various degrees of malnutrition in 1976, according to a survey of the Philippine Nutrition Program of the Food & Nutrition Council. The survey, called *Operation Timbang* [6], covered 4.1 million children and determined that 3.2 million of these preschoolers were malnourished. Permanent damage to brain cells, stunted physical growth, impaired eyesight, and extremely poor condition of the teeth were among the effects of malnutrition as enumerated in the survey.

The Minister of Public Health, Clemente Gatmaitan, gave similar figures for the following year. Citing the results of a 1977 nationwide project of the Ministry of Public Health where preschool children were weighed, Gatmaitan stated that 78 out of 100 pre-school children were found to be suffering from malnutrition.

As of December 1978, 5,116,753 children in 75 provinces and 61 cities of the Philippines had been tested. The survey showed 78.58% or four-fifths of the children were malnourished and only 21.41% could be considered normal. The 1978 study further broke down the figures:

100.00%	**Total**
45.72%	lst degree malnutrition
26.35%	2nd degree malnutrition
6.52%	3rd degree malnutrition
21.41%	Normal

The inadequacy of the Filipino's diet is also reflected in a 1982 nation-wide survey by the Food & Nutrition Research Institute (FNRI) and a 1984 poll by the Ministry of Agriculture & Food (MAF). The FNRI disclosed that daily meals of the average Filipino household are deficient in basic nutrients such as protein, Vitamin A, thiamine, riboflavin, calcium, ascorbic acid and iron. The MAF survey, based on food consumption patterns of varying types of communities throughout the country, showed that the actual food consumption in 1984 provided only a part of the minimum food requirements: 91% of the required energy intake, 43% of proteins and minerals needed; and 54% of the required level of regulating foods. This level of food consumption made the Philippines the second lowest in Asia, next only to Bangladesh, which is considered the poorest nation in the region.

BUTTER-BALL ECONOMICS

The curious thing with most of these government studies is not so much what they say as what they all conveniently gloss over.

Most of the Marcos technocrats believed that the poverty and the hunger that the Filipino experienced was caused by low food reduction levels and by the demands made by a rapidly growing population. Prime Minister Cesar Virata, for example, warned with the naivete characteristic of most technocrats that, unless production levels increase to meet the needs of a growing population, "Filipinos may have to give up one meal a day, "a remark which reflected total ignorance of the already desperate conditions of Filipinos. The viewpoint of most technocrats was that the people themselves were to blame for their poverty due to their poor productivity and their proclivity to pro-create.

The fact is that the Philippines has enough natural resources to feed her population and has been producing more than enough to adequately feed every Filipino since 1974. According to a study made by the National Council on Integrated Area Development, while the country's population in 1981 was an estimated 54.7 million, the actual net food supply produced in this year could have adequately fed 62 million people. The country's land resources alone, if fully and properly utilized, could have provided food for as much as 126.5 million people in 1981, which is more than twice the estimated population that year.

A paradox arises. If enough food is produced to feed every Filipino, why do millions starve?

The key to understanding this paradox is to be found not in the economic theories of Wharton-educated Prime Minister Virata but in his wife's home economics. Sometime before Virata made his gloomy admonition about "giving up one meal a day," his wife was filmed in the papers as complaining about the difficulty of finding Butter Ball brand turkeys in the Philippines. For her, local grown turkeys were not good enough to celebrate the American holiday of Thanksgiving.

At the banana plantations owned by Antonio Floirendo, a close Marcos associate, bananas are produced solely for the export market, which are principally Japanese. Cavendish bananas which do not fit the specified size for expor, although otherwise perfect, are either thrown into the sea or given to Angus cattle for feed. Workers are forbidden to eat these discarded fruits; they are strictly for the consumption of the cattle. Select cuts from the butchered cattle, in turn, are given as gifts to the Marcos family or other friends and associates of Floirendo.

While the majority of the population live in famine, the children of the affluent families in the cities indulge themselves with "junk food." A study of the Philippine Normal College Research Center found that the daily consumtion of junk food by city school children averages three bottles of soft drinks, six pieces of candy, two packs of Cheese Curls, and five pieces of pastries [7]. Nutrition is indeed a problem in the Philippines.

Poverty is more meaningfully viewed when seen not only in absolute terms but also how poor the poor are *relative* to the other sectors of Philippine society. Since enough food is being produced to feed everyone, the existence of famine is clearly related to the problem of wealth and income distribution. No one would have to live in hunger if food were equally distributed. Poverty can be eliminated if incomes and wealth were more equitably distributed.

There have been very few studies on the state of income and wealth distribution during the Marcos regime. But the studies that have been made show a high degree of inequality. If the mean income of the highest 20% were compare with the lowest 20%, one would come up with a ratio of 6.07 in 1961. This ratio skewed further to 14.65 in 1971. This means that the entrepreneurs and managers in the economy, who belong to the top 20%, were earning at least 15 times more than their counterparts in the lowest 20% who engage in manual work and labor doing menial jobs for a living. A country as rich in its natural resources as the Philippines can meet the basic needs of its populace if the productive and distributive mechanisms of the economy are owned and used by the many rather than by the few.

IN LIEU OF OLYMPIC RECORDS

The extreme poverty and malnutrition experienced by Filipinos are further compounded by poor health, a deficient health system, the lack of a proper sanitation system, inadequate clothing and housing, a neglected educational system, and the lack of employment opportunities.

The Philippines has the highest rates for whooping cough, diphtheria, and rabies in the world. It also has one of the highest rates for leprosy. It has the highest rates in the entire Western Pacific Region for tuberculosis, schistosomiasis, and polio.

According to the National Institute of Tuberculosis, around 17 million Filipinos or 32.4% of the total population suffer from tuberculosis. This means that the Philippines has one of highest tuberculosis infection rates in the world, accounting for 40% of all tuberculosis deaths in Southeast Asia.

Approximately 5% of the population in 1984, or roughly over 2 million Filipinos, suffered from diabetes, but barely 1% receive medical attention [8]. The Philippines has the third largest number of blind people in the world, and as of 1983, there was an estimated 17 million who suffered from some correctable form of eye defect.

Eighty-eight out of every hundred Filipinos suffered from tooth decay in 1977, With the ratio rising to 97 for every hundred in 1982, according to surveys by the Bureau of Dental Health Services.

The majority of the diseases and deaths are from causes which can be easily prevented. According to one source, contaminated water causes 80% of diseases [9]. The leading causes of death over the past 20 years, on the other hand, were diseases directly attributable to poverty and malnutrition. Four of the ten leading causes of deaths were from communicable diseases such as pneumonia (16.2%), tuberculosis (10.9%), gastroenteritis (8.3%), and bronchitis (2.5%), according to figures released by the Disease Intelligence Center of the Department of Public Health in 1974. Of the total 283,975 Filipinos who were reported to have died that year, 42.3% were due to these four communicable diseases. This means that of the 780 Filipinos who died every day in that year, the deaths of some 330 could have been prevented.

Mental disorder, avitaminosis, and other diseases caused by malnutrition have since joined these four communicable diseases as top health concerns.

Figures from the United Nation's Children's Fund (UNICEF) are more alarming. According to the UNICEF, 200,000 Filipino children die every year because of diarrhea and communicable diseases. This means a figure of 400 children a day. Calling the situation a "silent emergency," officials from the UNICEF likened the toll to a fully-loaded jumbo jet crashing every day.

The number of babies who die before they reach a full year was 51.7 deaths for every 1,000 in 1978. This ratio rose to 61.8 in 1981. This is a rate higher than those found in neighboring countries such as Vietnam, Hong Kong, Malaysia, Singapore and Thailand [10]. Many of these deaths were due to pneumonia, gastroenteritis, bronchitis, avitaminosis and other nutritional deficiencies. Malnourishment has made the population extremely susceptible to these diseases.

It is highly possible that the figures on infant mortality are actually higher than those which have been quoted, since a great majority of these deaths occur in remote villages and are unrecorded.

Of the children who do survive, man suffer from some degree of mental retardation, caused by the inadequate food intake of conceiving mothers. Every year, some 30,000 Filipino babies enter the world already suffering from the disadvantage of some form of mental deficiency. About 10% of adolescent Filipinos suffer from some mental handicap due to poor nutrition during their youth [11].

PERVERSE PRIORITIES

The death of numerous infants, caused mostly by communicable diseases and dehydration from diarrhea, could easily have been prevented by very simple methods. Dehydration from diarrhea can be corrected by oral rehydration, and communicable diseases can be fought with massive immunization. A media information campaign educating the poor in basic hygienic techniques and other inexpensive corrective methods of combatting disease can curb the death rate in no time. But throughout the years of the Marcos regime, the media efforts of the government have been focussed on a different area.

Minister of Information Gregorio Cendana purchased audio-Visual equipment worth $20 million for useless media projects, and the equipment was left to rot in the National Media Production Center (NMPC) offices. The equipment was an assortment of 16mm film projectors and slide sound masters rom the United States, and Betamax recorders and monitoring sets from Japan. The film and slide projectors from the US were bought in 1979 to equip the information/cultural markets that Cendana and Mrs. Imelda Marcos planned to call *agoras*. But not a single "agora" was ever constructed, and not more than a hundred of the projectors were distributed to the mobile audio-visual vans of the regional offices of the NMPC. The remaining 1,000 film projectors and the same number of slide projectors were left in the Quezon City studios of the NMPC. The Japanese equipment, 1,300 Betamax recorders complete with monitoring sets, were acquired a year later through a loan from the Japanese government. The 1980 loan amounted to ¥1,100,000,000 or almost $8 million to be paid starting 1991. Three hundred of these video machines were parceled to various municipal mayors close to the ruling KBL party [12]. The rest of the Japanese equipment were again left in the Quezon City 0ffices of the NMPC. It was later claimed that most of the equipment were destroyed in a fire, but other sources said that they were sold for personal gain [13].

Aside from an inadequate information and education system to combat disease, the entire health care system itself has an absolutely perverse set of priorities. Despite the prevalence of malaria in the rural areas and the existence of some 20,000 victims of leprosy, only $539,885 for antimalarial drugs and only $28,311 for leprosy medication were spent in 1980. In that very same year, more than $3,805,535 was spent on pimple and acne medication. We know of cases where teen age daughters of the very rich would go in great alarm to their favorite dermatologist whenever a pimple threatened to erupt before a coming party.

The same imbalance is reflected in the distribution of medical and health professionals. In the rural areas, seven out of ten Filipinos die without seeing a doctor. Some 350 rural municipalities or one-fourth of the total are without doctors. The other fourth, representing 370 municipalities had only one doctor per municipality. This represents a ratio of one doctor for 9,000 residents.

Again, the problem is not one of supply but of adequate distribution. Seventy percent of rural Filipinos die without ever seeing a doctor not because of the scarcity of competent health professionals, but because only 3% of total physicians devote themselves to public health. Sixty-eight percent of doctors emigrate to work abroad, representing a drain of hundreds of millions of dollars in training [14]. The remaining 29% devote themselves to lucrative private practice, serving the affluent Manila elite. Not only are these doctors able to quickly recover their investment in their medical training, but they also are able to buy mansions at the most exclusive subdivisions and cap their achievements with several cars. We know of one doctor from one of these subdivisions who had six brand-new cars and a van. They were not all for his use, however. One car was for himself, and the rest were to be shared by his wife and his five daughters. Documents recovered from Malacanan, the Philippine presidential palace, show that Marcos himself had a retinue of eight doctors to attend to his needs, each retained at $2,500 a month.

The pattern is the same for other health professionals. There is only one dentist per 24,000 persons. And while there is only one nurse available for every 27,700 people, the Philippines continues to export 88% of her nurses [15].

DESIGNER HOSPITALS

But the Marcos family was never remiss in recognizing the medical problem. Ferdinand Marcos who always claimed excellent health when he was in power took, without payment, five kidney dialysis machines from Manila hospitals for his personal use. Papers recovered from the Office of the President show that he spent over $60,000 in medicine and medical supplies in 1984 and $70,000 in 1985. When Marcos was finally forced to flee, he left behind in Malacanan a mini-hospital, complete with the most modern medical equipment, worth an estimated $250,000.

The typical hospital in the Philippines, however, is not as well-equipped. A 1980 survey of health facilities showed that most are substandard. Eighty percent of medical centers, seventy percent of emergency hospitals, and thirty percent of general hospitals did not meet minimum requirements [16]. All of the hospitals in the Philippines, with the exception of the most expensive ones, are overcrowded. The hospital bed to population ratio is 1:650 [17]. Overworked doctors at the Philippine General Hospital (PGH), a public hospital frequented by the poor, can hardly meet the demands placed by the influx of indigent patients. It is not uncommon for a patient to receive inadequate treatment at the PGH because of lack of medicine and medical supplies. There have been many occasions when doctors at the PGH have had to perform an operation without the benefit of anesthesia. There are times when there are simply none available.

But Imelda Marcos could not be accused of being inattentive to the health problems of the people she loved dearly. She built several designer hospitals: the Philipine Heart Center, which is the only one in Asia; the Lung Center; the kidney Center; *Lungsod ng Kabataan* or Children's City, the only one of its kind in the world; and the Research Institute for Tropical Medicine. These institutions, constructed at great cost, were equipped with the latest medical equipment and could rival the best hospitals in the affluent countries. But these specialized designer hospitals were not the ones needed by a population whose medical needs were more basic. Most of these hospitals failed to give adequate medical services to poor patients.

At the Philippine Heart Center (PHCA), one of the pet hospitals of Imelda, the director, Dr. Avenilo Aventura, received a huge salary, while his room was equipped with an anteroom, a bar with an upright piano, and a big television projector. The PHCA allotted only 50 out of 250 beds for charity patients, while the rest were for patients who could afford to pay the high fees.

Early in 1986, right before the Marcoses were ousted, the Lung Center had only one patient, while at the Quezon Institute, a hospital frequented by the poor suffering from tuberculosis, many patients were sharing small beds.

Imelda also organized the Nutrition Center of the Philippines (NCP). The NCP receive donations from foreign countries and institutions, including New Zealand, UNICEF (United Nations International Children & Educational Fund), WHO

(World Health Organization), USAID (the United States Aid for International Development), and local drug manufacturers such as Abbott Laboratories, Bristol Myers, and Mead Johnson. Donations from these groups amounted to $6 million. Another $4.2 million donation to the NCP was received from two Middle Eastern countries. According to NCP employees, parts of these donations, especially those which came from the Middle East, were diverted to Imelda's personal account in London and were later used to buy diamonds. NCP employees also raised questions regarding the wealth of Florentino Solon, the Marcos' Minister of Health and NCP Director. When he headed NCP in 1976 his statement of assets and liabilities indicated that he had a net worth of $7,400. By the time the Marcos regime ended in 1986, he owned two houses at Merville Subdivision, a lot in the Ayala Alabang Subdivision, two houses in Cebu City and the Argao Beach Resort in Cebu.

One of the relatively unknown projects of Imelda Marcos was the Research Institute for Tropical Medicine (RITM) in Alabang, Muntinglupa. The institution was organized with the cooperation of the Japanese government and was given formal status through Executive Order No. 674, dated 25 March 1981, defining it as an institute for the development of basic and applied research program for tropical medicine in the Philippines. The Japanese International Cooperation Agency (JICA) constructed and equipped the institute, by including an 80-bed hospital complete with an intensive care unit (ICU) and operating rooms. A research foundation created to support the activities of the institute included as its incorporators Ambassador Eduardo Cojuangco, businessman Lucio Tan, Presidential Legal Adviser Manuel Lazaro, all of whom were close associates of Marcos.

But the impression created by the RITM is that it was organized to benefit Japanese research rather than Philippine health. Of the 1030 admissions in the hospital, 815 or 79.1% were treated as research patients. It claimed that the institute's research program was supervised by the Ministry of Health, but results of the five years of studies made by local scientists were never published. Instead, the research was merely turned over to the Japanese in return for aid grants. It is not certain that the indigent patients of this institution were ever informed that they were not receiving standard and tested treatment but were being subjected to experiments commissioned by the Japanese.

CASAS DE CARTON

Que triste se oye la lluvia, en los techos de carton
Que triste vive mi gente, en las casas de carton...
Que alegre viven los perros, en la casa del explotador
Usted no lo va a creer, pero hay escuelas de perros
y les dan educacion.... [18]

According to most conservative estimates, one out of every five Filipinos live in the urban areas without decent housing. Other studies point to a higher percentage and indicate the ratio to be one out of every three Filipinos.

The Philippines, in fact, holds the distinction of having the largest slum area in Southeast Asia, the Tondo Foreshore Area of Metro-Manila, a community of some 180,000 residents making up 27,000 families, living in about 184 hectares of land reclaimed from Manila Bay. The Philippines has had this distinction since the start of the first presidential term of Marcos in 1965.

Slum areas like the Tondo Foreshore Area and Constitution Hill are found all over the Metropolitan Manila area where people live in a constant state of poverty, malnutrition, congestion, filth, disease, crime and violence.

Families live in hovels made out of scrap pieces of wood and corrugated carton patched together. Some of these homes are so small that one has to crawl to get in. Most of these families have five or six children. Crowning the roofs of these shacks would be pieces of corrugated tin salvaged from the garbage dumps, causing continual leaks during the rainy season. Earthen floors are commonplace, while some of these homes are built on stilts over the stenching *esteros*, or stagnant city marshes, which serve as convenient receptacles for garbage and human waste.

These families, habitually referred to as squatters, numbered 105,000 in Metropolitan Manila in 1963, two years before Marcos assumed the presidency. There was a slight increase of almost 10% to around 115,000 in 1973, a year after martial law was imposed. By 1975, three years later, squatter families grew to 200,000, representing an increase of almost 100%. A seminar on urban problems in 1975 estimate the number of slum dwellers not by the number of families but by individuals, and according to the data presented in this seminar, there was an estimated 1.3 million slum dwellers in 1975 in the Metropolitan Manila area or about a third of the total urban population of 4 million.

It appears that the dramatic increase in slum dwellers in Metropolitan Manila is a direct consequence of government policy rather than by accident. Urban slums were tolerated and allowed to grow by government authorities since the late 1960's. These slum areas were viewed by both the local and national government officials as a source of votes easily bought by empty promises. The second factor which encouraged the growth of slums was the heavy construction of hotels and other infrastructure in the early and mid-1970's. One may even assert that the massive construction projects launched by the Marcos government and the companies owned by Marcos' cronies during this period required the existence of these urban slums as a source of cheap labor.

The dilapidated houses of more than 6.5 million Filipinos or 15% of the population in both the urban and rural areas pose a sharp contrast with the living quarters of the pets and other animals which have found favor with Marcos and his cronies. In the residence of one such crony in the expensive New Manila district of Quezon City, for example, air conditioned kennels are provided for a collection of pure-breed dogs. This idolatry of Baal in different genera is not an isolated case. Marcos himself issued a presidential decree proclaiming a remote South China Sea island near Palawan as a game preserve for African animals. In reality, the island of Calauit, 275 miles southwest of Manila, became the private hunting ground of his only son, Ferdinand Jr. The original inhabitants of the island, 120 families of poor farmers and fishermen, were forced from their homes to make way for the giraffes, zebras, elands, impalas, gazelles, waterbucks, and topis imported from Kenya. The animals were bought at government expense and cost $30,000 a month to maintain.

During his 1982 state visit to the US, Marcos, Imelda, and their entourage stayed at the Waldorf in New York. Marcos took the presidential suite, Imelda the royal suite, while the rest were booked in 20 smaller ones in the Waldorf Towers and an additional 30 thirty rooms in the adjacent Waldorf-Astoria. The bill ran to $109,500 for six nights, a tag which still excluded the expenses for food, taxes, and tips for the bellhops who carried their 800 pieces of luggage. This amount could have built many low-cost houses for poor Filipinos.

For their own personal upkeep, the Marcos family maintained houses by the dozens and spent by the millions each year. Apart from Malacanan Palace, the official residence of the First Family were a chain of houses, mansions, and buildings throughout the Philippines and overseas. The furnishings in these places were priceless *objets d'art* and *objets de venue*.

A count of their residences approximated the number to be close to fifty. This number is limited to the houses for the personal use of immediate members of the Marcos family and does not include the other houses and mansions owned by their relatives and cronies. Neither does this number include the houses, mansions, estates, and commercial buildings in which are scattered in foreign countries and continents [19].

Several of these houses were in Baguio, the favorite summer resort ofrich Filipinos due to its mountain elevation and plentiful pine trees. Here, in the City used by the American colonial government as its summer capital at the start of the century, the Marcos family and their friends held no less than 69 titles, some as real estate, others as residences. Some nine residential homes in Baguio belonged to the Marcoses. Each of the Marcos children had their own house, and each house had its own name. There was the Wigwam House for Ferdinand Jr. (Bongbong), the Fairchild House for Imee, the Hans Menzi House for Irene. Aside from these places for the three children, there were also several others: the Lualhati residence, a two-storey house held for the Marcoses by a crony named Jose Y. Campos on the same road as Bongbong's place; the Banaue Inn which is at the back of Campos house; and the Mansion Guest House, which is the official summer residence of the President. These residences, ranging from one to six hectares in size, were situated in the choicest areas of the city and had spectacular views of the scenic Mines View Park mountain range. After Marcos' downfall, visitors to these houses were at a loss for words to describe the furnishings and could only say that they were "beyond their wildest imagination in riches."

Residences of the First Family also dotted Metropolitan Manila, among them houses in districts such as Makati, Paranaque, Pandacan and San Juan. Each of the three children again had his respective house in the choicest suburbs, with each house and district reflecting the personality of the occupant: Wack-Wack Subdivision for Imee, Forbes Park for Irene and Seaside, Paranaque for Bongbong. In the provinces, they had one in Mariveles, one in Cavite, and a number in Leyte and Ilocos Norte, the home provinces of Imelda and Ferdinand.

Funds for the construction, renovation, and maintenance of these houses came directly from the budget of the Office of the President. Malacanan spent $3.2 million in 1984 and $10.5 million in 1985 for the upkeep and maintenance of these houses. Light, water, power, and gas alone amounted to $1.7 million in 1985. These figures are conservative estimates since they cover only those expenses which the Commission on Audit (COA) was able to verify.

The expenses of the Marcos family in 1985 for the upkeep of their homes alone would have been able to feed 8,000 starving families of six for a whole year. This is equivalent to providing food for a small town of 48,000 people for a whole year.

In Ilocos Norte, Ferdinand Marcos' province in the country's northwest, a magnificent mansion called the "Malacanan of the North" was constructed beside a breathtakingly beautiful lake.

In Tacloban City, the capital of Leyte, Imelda erected a shrine to the Sto. Nina (Infant Jesus), as well as a museum in Calle Real, on the very spot where the Quonset hut that served as her impoverished home once stood [20]. The center piece of the shrine is an image of the Madonna and Child made up of hundreds of Japanese pearls, framed against a background of crimson velvet. Instead of Side altars, the shrine has 13 guest rooms on the side, with each room housing an illuminated scene from Imelda's life. One with Libyan leader Mohammar Gadhafi. On the second floor are the Marcos' living quarters and two reception halls. Among the Imelda mementos displayed in one hall is a huge painting depicting her ethereally rising from the sea, holding a clam shell containing her children's faces, with her husband in the background watching her from a distance. The estimated value of the shrine and the hundreds of different items in it was quoted at $27 million.

In the nearby town of Olot, also in Leyte, the Marcoses had their own million-dollar private seaside resort. The resort was constructed in 1974 so that the Marcoses could personally entertain the participants to the Miss Universe contest being held in the Philippines thaty ear. The place has around a dozen houses and guest cottages, an Olympic-size swimming pool just above the beach, a pelota court, and a 45-hectare, 18-hole golfing green. The Marcos "rest house" had 23 rooms; the guest house for their military aides had 20. During its construction, bermuda grass for the whole resort and the golfing green was flown in from Manila using C-140's of the Philippine Air Force.

NIETZSCHE IN PRINCETON

Poverty also severely affects the educational system. As of 1977, there were more than 4 million youths, aged 15 to 21, who wanted to go to school but could not because of poverty [21]. The attrition rate in the field of education is extremely high. The following table, constructed from 1978 data, shows that for every 100 pupils who start school, only 39 reach Grade VI [22], and only 4 reach fourth year high school:

Number	Status
100	start Grade I
36	drop out before reaching Grade IV
39	go as far as Grade VI
7	enter first year high school
4	reach fourth year high school [23].

The Bureau for Women & Minors revealed in a 1979 survey that while the legal minimum age for employment is 15 years, children start working as early as seven, the age for a mission for the first grade in the Philippine public school system. Rene Ofreneo, a Philippine labor specialist, estimated that in 1976 there were about 3 million children below 10 years who were out of school. Data from NEDA revealed in 1976 that 6 million youths, between the ages of 10 and 19, were out of school. One of every 3 unemployed persons is an out-of-school youth.

Those who manage to stay in school have to deal with the low quality of public education. Facilities are very inadequate, and teachers, although dedicated, are overburdened and paid low wages. A survey of the public school system shows the following ratio of books to students:

    Primary Grades   1: 9.8
    Intermediate   1: 115
    High School   1: 85

At best, there was one book for every eight students. It was further revealed that of the books surveyed, 79% were 5-10 years old. While students suffered from the lack of books, there was much mismanagement and waste of resources which could have produced more and better books for the public school system. A high official of Marcos' Ministry of Education, who was a reputed chronic gambler, continually lost great sums of money to the textbook publishers with whom he habitually gambled. The sums which he lost could not have been covered by his modest salary as a government servant. Another example of the waste of resources can be seen in some cases of publishing engaged in by officials of the Marcos government. The Metro-Manila Commission printed 10,000 copies of books on taxation written by its Finance Commissioner, Mauro Calaguio, while only 2,000 copies were needed. The books cost Metro-Manila $92,000. Imelda also engaged in this type of publishing. In Imelda's East 66th Townhouse in New York, at least four hundred copies of her book *Towards a Human Order* were found unused and were eventually thrown away. The books, published with Philippine government money, were expensively bound and printed on special heavy-pound paper. They were to be given out as promotional material during Imelda's address to the UN.

When school opened for the academic year 1985, the last year of Marcos' rule, enrollment dropped by almost half a million. Because of the economic crisis which was sweeping the nation, only 17% of those who could be in college were actually enrolled [24].

But government funds were never lacking when it came to paying for the Princeton University education of Marcos' eldest daughter, Imee. She was not a government scholar, but government funds from the Philippine National Bank were used to pay for her tuition of $4,445 a semester. Juan Saavedra Castro, a highly respected corporate lawyer from Puerto Rico who volunteered to help recover money stolen by the Marcoses, says that checks for Imee's Princeton tuition fees came directly from government accounts. Saavedra pointed out that "funds to cover those checks came from either treasury warrants or money of the bank.... The bank was literally paying for those checks as there were no funds behind them."

The Marcoses opened at least 15 bank accounts in the US at this time under false names. Some of these accounts were used to fund Imee's studies at Princeton and Bongbong's studies at Wharton, each of whom received a monthly allowance of $10,000.

In the 18th century Princeton estate that was bought for Imee to stay in while she studied, the-book-to-student ratio is dramatically reversed. In the second floor library of the house, hundreds of books lined the walls. Together with *Seduction: A Swinging Game For Swinging Couples*, an adult parlor game which requires the participants to strip, were classics in their field, such as Walter Kaufmann's study on *Nietzsche*, Joseph Campbell's *The Mythic Image,* and H.W.Janson's *History of Art.* Dennis O'Leary, who was assigned to take care of the Princeton property for the new Aquino overnment, commented on the books: "If Imee had read at least half of the books in that library, she would already be very well educated." The books, unfortunately, give the appearance of not having been read; cards from the parlor game, however, do show some signs of slight use [25].

Like many Filipino public school children who drop out of the primary grades, Imee also never finished her degree at Princeton. She later enrolled at the College of Law of the University of the Philippines, but not without some controversy. After Manila newspapers reported that she graduated with honors from the UP College of Law, the student council demanded from Edgardo Angara, the university President appointed by Marcos, that he produce an official file on her academic record, since it appeared that Imee never had the proper qualifications to enter the school and that her name never appeared in the first of approved graduates nor among the candidates endorsed for graduation by a committee. The inquiry from the student council was never answered.

"WE ARE REFORMED OLIGARCHS"

From what can be gathered from partial documents, Marcos, Imelda, and their children spent $68 million in the last two years of his reign. At least $11 million of this amount appears to have been spent on clothes, paintings, antiques, handicraft and other items. This amount breaks down into $6.8 million in 1984, $4.2 million in 1985, and $676,945 in the first two months of 1986. The nature of the rest of the expenses are a little more difficult to determine since many purchases were done on a cash—and-carry basis and receipts are not available.

From the receipts and records recovered from Malacanan and other places after their downfall, one can get an idea of the consumption behavior of the Marcoses.

In April 1983, Imelda spent $90,000 in one day, buying antiques in Vigan, Ilocos. Vigan is a very old town known for its historic Spanish colonial houses. Among the things she bought were an antique matrimonial bed and a conference table.

Again on a single day, Imelda purchased sheets worth $10,340 from Pratesi, an Italian linen store on Madison Ave., New York [26].

Another receipt, one of the many found scattered on the grounds of the residential Palace when Marcos fled by helicopter, was from the Nina Ricci Boutique in Paris, showing Imelda spending the equivalent of $27,222 for 22 items in June and July 1970.

Handwritten notes of Imelda's personal secretary show that the lady spent $4.5 million from May through July on a trip to New York in 1983 [27].

On Milan Hilton stationery, a family friend who signed herself as "Baby," wrote to Imee Marcos:

I am sending you a suitcase full of goodies thru Manila. I hope you find time to wear all the clothes... So far, I 've spent $3,717 out of the $5,000 set aside for clothes [28].

The items included a $142 Valentino jogging outfit and a $270 raw-silk jacket by Armani. The "goodies" cost a total of $4,874.

When it came to the wedding of the youngest of the Marcos children, no receipts were necessary to visualize the magnitude of the expenses. Irene, the youngest and the relatively more reserve of the three children, wanted a quiet, 17th-century style wedding in a small town. The preparations started with thousands of men, including Philippine soldiers, working to renovate and redecorate Sarrat, Ilocos Norte, Marcos' hometown. The 204-year old Santa Monica church where the ceremonies took place was completely renovated by 3,500 especially-contracted workers [29]. Old houses were torn down and rebuilt in the old Spanish colonial style, while streets were paved in red brick and strewn with thousands of flowers and potted shrubs. Specially designed carriages from Austria and horses from Morocco were imported so that the bride and her entourage may parade the town. Paper flowers were pinned on branches when plants did not bloom in time, supplemented with fresh ones flown in from Hawaii [30]. Expenses for the wedding were estimated at $10.3 million [31].

There was a distinctly Imelda touch to the preparations. A new international airport, complete with special runways for jumbo jets, was constructed, and the Philippine Air Lines (PAL) scheduled 24 extra flights to Ilocos Norte to ferry the special foreign and local guests, estimated to number 5,000. Specially chartered buses were also made available to make the 400-kilometer trip between Manila and Ilocos Norte. Two days before the wedding, Marcos inaugurated a huge 6 government-owned resort complex, complete with a 126-room first-class hotel, constructed out of the Ilocos sand dunes to accommodate the privileged friends and guests. Costing $10.5 million, it is an elegant massive brick structure perched on an endless beach, but since the June 1983 wedding, it has been perennially empty of Visitors [32].

General Fabian Ver, Marcos' Chief of Staff, built a handsome burgher's residence. Gowns for the wedding were made by noted Italian designer, Renato Balestra, and the three sets for Imelda and her two daughters totaled $309,420.00. Imelda's Blue Ladies, the nickname for her ladies-in-waiting, gave 21 pairs of brand name shoes as wedding presents. The whole event was televised at the cost of no less than $6 million [33].

BASIC NEEDS

Such expenses were common fare for the Marcoses. The traditional concept of basic needs as comprising food, clothing, and shelter took on a new meaning.

Food, hotel accommodations, and transportation expenses totaled $2.4 million in two years. The breakdown:

$1.1 million 1984
$1.3 million 1985
$212,691 January and February of 1986.

The Marcos family spent at least $3 million for clothes in their last two years in power. Some pieces of clothing, especially those made by the more popular local and foreign couturiers, cost $2,000 to $2,500. Materials for gowns of the Marcos women ranged from $400 to $500 each.

Imelda was able to bring the contents of 67 of her clothing racks when she fled the presidential palace, but some 55 racks filled with clothes were left behind. Among the apparel that remained in these racks were 15 mink coats, 6 silver fox stoles, a swan—feathered gown, a dress studded with Russian diamonds, a selection of fitted bullet-proofed vests, a bullet-proof bra, five shelves of Gucci handbags, and a collection of 200 identical black girdles from Marks & Spencers of London. One dress was carefully embroidered with silver thread, which was estimated to have taken at least 6 months to make.

A partial list of the clothes Imelda left in Malacanan [34]:

Pairs of Shoes (and slippers)	*1,060*
Floor length gowns	*508*
Dresses	*427*
Handbags	*888*
Scarves	*464*
Handkerchiefs	*664*
Pairs of Sunglasses	*71*
Parasols	*65*
Mink coats	*15*
Swan feather gown	*1*

These figures include only clothing items found in the presidential palace and do not include the wardrobe in other residences. US Customs officials chose not to give an inventory of the clothes Imelda brought with her when she came to the US.

People assigned to do inventories in the other Marcos residences were so overwhelmed by what confronted them that they conducted the inventories by the crate rather than by individual item. They encountered crates of watches, rosaries, expensive figurines, cufflinks, personalized golf balls. Fifteen more fur coats, worth $25,000 each, were found in the refrigeration section of the Manila Mandarin Hotel.

Imelda bought expensive perfume not by the ounce but by the gallon. In her New York Olympic Towers condominium, for example, one of the items was a gallon of *Mitsuoko* by Guerlain. Similar large jars of French perfume were found in presidential palace, all turned upside down in special dispensers, so that Imelda would not have a hard time perfuming herself.

American television initially reported that 5,000 pairs of shoes were left by Imelda in Malacanan. A New York Times article corrected this count and pegged it at 1,060. But 1,800 more pairs were later found in one of Imelda's houses in Leyte, bringing the figure to 2,800. Among the shoes that were left was a battery-equipped pair that glows in the dark. Imelda is also known to own a diamond-studded pair of shoes, but this pair has disappeared.

Marcos and his cronies owned a huge fleet of cars, ships, and airplanes. There were at least 101 vehicles and 119 aircrafts and ships identified after they left. Some of these were government-owned vehicles that they appropriated for their personal use.

Among the aircrafts and vessels of Marcos were a $5.5 million yacht, 15 ocean liners, and some 52 helicopters, airplanes, and executive Jets. The aircrafts included a Dassault Brequet Falcon 50, 3 Gates Learjets, 4 Beechcraft Superking Air 200's, 3 Cessna Citations, 3 Cessna Stationairs, a four-seater Modney, a Bell jet-ranger, a Turbo Brush S2RT34.

The presidential yacht, the RPS *Ang Pangulo,* is a 17-cabin, 2,700 ton vessel which has a medical clinic, a piano bar, and a helipad so roomy that it was used by Marcos' three children as an outdoor disco. Used brlefly by General Douglas MacArthur during his visit to the Philippines in the 1960's, the ship itself is estimated be worth around $5.5 million, while the accessories would be worth around $300,000. The yacht was purchased using Japanese funds which were originally established as reparation for damages inflicted on Philippine property during the Second World War.

Among the luxury cars were a $75,000 Mercedes Benz 600 limousine reserved for Marcos, a Rolls Royce and a Cadillac for Imelda, and dozens of Mercedes Benzes for her brothers and sisters. A partial list of the luxury cars: two Rolls Royces, several Cadillacs, Lincoln Continentals, Masseratis, Mercedes Benzes, Mitsubishi Pajero, Chevy Caprice, Nissan Patrol, Nissan Laurel 200, two Nissan Presidents, two Toyota Land Cruisers, two Range Rovers. Among the Cadillacs were a Bubble Top, a Convertible, two Fleetwoods. Among the Mercedes Benzes were 280's and at least two 600's. About 30 of the 40 Mercedes Benzes assigned to the Office of the President have not been recovered. One of the Rolls Royces was a gift to Imelda from Moroccan royalty, but most of the other cars were purchased with funds from dubious sources without paying the usual 300% tax on imported cars.

Imelda also had a personal bus she used during her political trips. The bus had 14 armchairs, two beds, a kitchen, and a bath [35].

REIFIED RELATIONSHIPS

Imelda related to the world in totally reified terms -- human relationships were equated to the exchange of material things. Multimillion dollar buildings and apartments, whole art and antique collections, jewels, clothes, and shoes were purchased with complete abandon. The friendship and the loyalty of friends, the attention of her children, and the affection of her male companions were seen as something to be acquired -- an object of purchase, either with cash or some other bribe masquerading as a gift.

Imelda gave away around $70 million worth of gifts between 1983 and 1984. Her private notebooks recorded some of these expenses and showed that she usually gave $3,000 in cash for birthdays, weddings and wedding anniversaries. Whenever her children were involved, the amounts were usually larger. She gave, for example, $6,600 and $6,000 to grandchildren Borgy and Alfonso during the Christmas of 1984. Envelopes were usually marked either "from FL's or PFM's vault" -- that is to say, from the private vaults of the First Lady or President Ferdinand Marcos.

To her husband, she gave more. One of the US Customs agents who checked the baggage of the Marcoses as they entered the US in 1986 testified that one of the suitcases contained 24 bricks of gold with the inscription: "To my husband on our 24th wedding anniversary" [36].

She also gave out jewelry, watches, cufflinks, and rosaries to her guests. For her not so important visitors, she gave Casio calculator and Alba quartz watches, but for her more esteemed friends, she gave out $350 dollar Cartier watches, which she bought by the hundreds. One receipt shows a delivery of 963 pieces of Elgin watches. Thousands of expensive rosaries were purchased for her daughter's wedding in 1983. Some of the more lavish cufflink sets cost nearly $5,000 each.

She gave huge tips to the people who waited on her. She gave $550 tips for waiters of Hyatt and Via Mare, two places she frequented in Manila. After a 1985 Valentine's dinner party at the Misono at the Hyatt, she gave a $1,100 tip to the waiters, musicians, chefs, and sous chiefs. The bellhops of the Waldorf-Astoria would receive $50-100 bills each time they entered her suites.

Some of the gifts and handouts were astutely calculated to bring political returns. When one of her sisters, Lourdes, died in December 1983, Imelda gave out almost $540,000 to the 5,000 squatters herded by local government officials to attend the wake at the Malacanan chapel. Each of the slum dwellers who attended the wake received an envelope containing $100, while the local government officials who herded them received bigger sums.

Envelopes containing $60 to $600 in cash were regularly given to local government officials who visited Imelda at the presidential palace. She doled out $144,000 in wrist watches and other items to her supporters from the KBL, the Marcos political party, during the legislative eleations in 1984. During the presidential elections which ousted the Marcoses from power, Imelda gave out $300,000 in watches and other gifts during the campaign. Over $108,000 in imported handbags, shoes, perfumes, and wrist watches were given to her Blue Ladies and their friends during this campaign.

She was extremely generous when it came to her more special friends. To them she gave jewels, mansions, and other expensive items. or the special friends she invited to stay with her at the presidential palace, she would leave jewels, mostly pearls, in their rooms for them to take, just as ordinary mortals are left with towels and bibles in hotel rooms. When all but her special friends had left during one of the all-night parties at her East 66th townhouse in New York, she invited them into one of the rooms of the 30-room building and scattered pearls and jewels on the floor and got them to scramble for the little glistening things.

She "lent" money to her friend George Hamilton to buy a "lavish mansion in Beverly Hills and a plantation house in Mississippi" [37]. A whole gang of Filipino carpenters and handymen were brought in from the Philippines to work on the Beverly Hills mansion. Hamilton, who attracted Imelda's attention after he played the role of the vampire in the movie *Love at First Bite*, claimed that he got $5.5 million in 1983 from Gliceria Tantoco, a close friend of Imelda, to make a movie. The movie was never made [38].

Filipino conductor Redentor Romero, who at one time was close to Imelda and paid tribute to her in his book, *An American Affair*, later revealed to Philippine government authorities that Imelda gave gifts to Van Cliburn, another one of her close friends, and to his mother. Romero claimed that among the many gifts which Imelda gave to Van Cliburn was an expensive white Steinway concert and piano, which was delivered to the Carlyle Hotel in New York or Van Cliburn's birthday in 1979. Romero also revealed that Imelda gave Van Cliburn's mother a big, beautiful furnished house in a New York suburb.

Romero, who belongs to some international circles of musical artists, likewise claimed that Imelda helped Rony Rogoff, a New York-based Israeli violinist and frequent visitor to Malacanan, acquire a 1715 Stradivarius violin. Romero asserted that the violin, known as the **Alard Baron Knoop**, was acquired in 1980 for $350,000 [39].

Whenever she travelled abroad, Imelda always brought gifts with her. The Marcoses commissioned American artist Ralph Wolfe Cowan to paint life-size oils for Presidents Carter and Reagan and their First Ladies, and tried to present these as gifts to the White House. The White House demurred, saying that these portraits were too expensive to be considered as gifts. *Time* quoted reports of a $60,000 emerald necklace given by Imelda to Nancy Reagan [40], but the item never appeared in the list of official gifts to the White House and no further confirmation has been available beyond scanty newspaper references. Reports from the COA stated that more than $10.1 million from the Office of the President were spent on gift items relating to state visits between 1984 and February 1986. She brought along various expensive Philippine handicrafts such as jusi and pina cloth, mother-of-pearl picture frames, flower arrangements, jewelry boxes, and Philippine shells worth over $1 million during her 1984 and 1985 trips abroad. Imelda brought $215,000 worth of gifts during her 1985 Moscow trip, $323,000 for her tri to Rome and the Vatican, perhaps thinking the Soviets required less gifts than the Holy See.

ALL THE PERFUMES OF ARABIA

The Marcos family spent at least $1.6 million for flowers in their last two years in power, according to the COA. The flower purchases, paid from the budget of the Office of the President, are broken own as follows:

$1.1 million 1984
$666,405   1985
$91,730   in the first two months of 1986

The flowers were delivered to Malacanan Palace and the homes of the Marcos children in Wack-Wack, Forbes Park, and Seaside, Paranaque. The disco pad at the presidential palace also got its share. On one occasion, Imelda ordered 500 flowers costing 10 each for her trips to New York and Morocco. And when she went to Moscow in October 1985, she brought nearly $27,000 worth of flowers, some of which were rare tropical orchids. A journalist commented that Imelda "wanted the Muscovites to sample sampaguita and tropical orchids amid the hoariness of a Russian autumn."

Not included in the COA report on flowers were the purchases Imelda made when she was abroad. On her trips, she would spend $5,000 a day on flowers. When expatriate Filipinos took over her East 66th Townhouse in New York, one of the receipts they found scattered on the floor was a bill for $40,000 for flowers. Rafael Cecilio, an exiled Filipino who was part of team which took over Imelda's Townhouse and encountered the bill for the flowers, says,

> the $40,000 bill for roses found at the East 66th St. Townhouse represented
> expenses for the month of April. She always ordered $5,000 worth of roses on
> her first day of stay and $1,000 for every day thereafter as long she was around.
> This reminded me of Lady Macbeth's despair that "all the perfumes of Arabia"
> could not wash her hands clean.

As I read these accounts of Imelda's expenses on flowers, my thoughts carried me back to the time when I used to work in one of the slum areas in Quezon City. This slum area was near Constitution Hill, a place where I also worked for almost two years. I remembered an event on one happy Sunday afternoon. This was many, many ears ago, almost two years before I left the Philippines to go into exile in 1980. There was a wedding in the community. Despite their poverty, everyone was happy and looked forward to celebrating the event in whatever way their circumstances allowed them. It was there where I witnessed a most touching, human scene: colored plastic drinking straws were retrieved from the garbage, patiently cleaned, and woven into artificial flowers for the bride, and used to adorn the humble surroundings.

CASH IN SUITCASES

The COA reported that during the last two years of the Marcos regime, chartered flights of the Marcoses on the Philippine Airlines (PAL) amounted to $2.7 million. These expenses included Mrs. Marcos' trips to the US and Europe as well as junkets of their friends, including George Hamilton.

Airfare, however, was the least of the expenses associated with Imelda's trips abroad. The biggest ones involved the sprees which she engaged in where she would buy, not single items, but buildings and expensive condominiums, and whole collections of art and antiques and jewelry. She once tried to buy the PanAm building in Manhattan carrying cash in a van and several suitcases but was unsuccessful in the attempt.

To finance these trips, she would dip her fingers in the national coffer. One and a half million dollars from Philippine intelligence funds were used to finance some of Imelda's trips to New York and the Caribbean. To cover the shopping expenses she would incur in one of her trips to New York, hundreds of thousands of dollars from the New York branch of the Philippine National Bank (PNB) were delivered to her hotel room at the Waldorf-Astoria in an attache case by bank officials. In one single year, she spent $1.4 million for limousine service for her trips around New York. It would have been cheaper to buy the limousines that she used. The bill was again footed by the New York branch of the PNB [41].

The Marcos family brought with them 12 suitcases and attache cases, 22 bulging crates, a larger wooden crate, a foot locker, and carton diaper boxes stuffed with valuables when they fled Malacanan on February 1986 and found sanctuary in Hawaii. The containers, transported out of the country by two C141 transport planes supplied by the US Air Force, had more than $7 million worth of cash and valuables [42]. The baggages contained cash, certificates of time deposits totalling billions of dollars, real estate deeds to land holdings in the US, stock certificates, gold bullion, antiques, art objects, and jewelry. One of the boxes contained a pocket calculator and $1.2 million in pesos freshly printed by the Philippine Central Bank. Other crates, including the box of *Pampers* diapers carried by Imee, contained expensive jewels and antiques. When US Secretary of State George P. Shultz and White House chief of staff Donald T. Regan were shown the inventories of the trove brought by the Marcoses, they were "disgusted" by the gaudiness they saw, according to reports.

BIGGEST BUYER

Imelda shopped so much that one could call her treasure trove to be the best in the world. For example, she spent $10 million on "confidential" trips to two undisclosed destinations, possibly the Seychelles and Nairobi, Kenya, around 1984 (43). She instructed her London staff to withdraw $10.2 million from one of her London bank accounts for her "pocket money" and took along some friends from the US on the trips. It is believed that she bought $4 million worth of diamonds.

When she visited Tokyo in November 1985, Imelda bought natural South Sea pearls worth ¥100 million ($555,560) from a Tokyo jeweller. And after a trip to China, the list of Chinese *objets d'art* she took home ran to many pages.

New York was Imelda's favorite. She frequented classy Fifth Avenue jewelers such as Bulgari Jewelers, Van Cleef & Arpels, Cartier, Fred Leighton, Harry Winston, the latter a concern which specializes in the "rare jewels of the world." As early as the initial years of her husband's first term as president, her shopping sprees at Tiffany's in New York caused a sensation due to her lavish spending. It is known that she bought a pair of sapphire earrings from Van Cleef & Arpels for $1,250,000 in April 1982. [This pair is still unaccounted for.] Another known purchase was for a $100,000 diamond and ruby necklace from the same store [44]. Another purchase was for a selection of antique jewelry costing $234,000. Jewelry purchases in November 1984 amounted to $411,746 for emeralds, rubies, and one 519 carat sapphire [45]. An article in a Middle Eastern magazine on the international jewelry business stated that Imelda figured prominently within the select Circle of international buyers and sellers of expensive jewelry:

> *Even amongst this exotic circle, there is a further level of jewellers able to cater for a range of buyers whose wildest demands can reach $10 million-15 million for only one set of Sparklers. These include... Harry Winston of Geneva, Laurence Giraf, Gerard Joalliers and, perhaps the most powerful of them all, (Robert) Mouawad. Their clients include such names as Saudi Entrepreneur Adnan Kashoggi, UAE ambassador to London Mahdi al-Tajir, the Saudi royal family, and the Philippines' Imelda Marcos (reported to be the biggest buyer of them all over the past 15 years) [emphasis ours].*

Not only did Imelda shop at these stores but she also actually wanted to buy one of them. The same article on the international jewelry business mentioned Imelda as one of the potential buyers of Tiffany & Co. when Avon Products put it up for sale for $135.5 million in August 1984. Other reports linked Imelda to diamond mining operations in South Africa via a corporation based in London.

The woman also had jewelry specially designed for herself. Some of her notebooks contain sketches of designs she wanted to be made, with the stones meticulously specified. Orders for these pieces of jewelry were by the dozens. Receipts for rubies belonging to Imee costing $64,000 were among the things found in the presidential palace after they left. Chairs made of solid silver were in one of their houses. After loading two cargo planes of the US Air Force with their belongings, Imelda left behind 2,142 pieces of jewelry in the Malacanan vault.

Rene Knecht, an international socialite and hotelier, describes Imelda's jewelry collection:

> *She has an incredible collection of jewelry. According to a major jeweller I know in Beverly Hills, she was the largest buyer in the world in the late 1970's. And her collection is really one of the finest. Certainly better than most queens. She had a necklace made of diamonds, of flawless diamonds which came from Winston, and this cost $16 million about 5 or 6 years ago [46].*

Aside from the two caches of jewels Imelda brought with her to Hawaii and those left at the residential palace, other collections have turned up from other places. A few months after the Marcoses fled the Philippines, a Greek-American from California, a Demetrius Roumeliotedes, was apprehended at the Manila International Airport trying to take out $11.6 million worth of jewels. He claimed that they were on consignment from Foo Hang Jewelry of Hong Kong, but the authorities believed the collection to be Imelda's. At the Dasmarinas residence of Imee, 30 suitcases were found, 10 of which contained jewelry which was so numerous that it took three full days to complete inventory [47]. There have also been reports that the wife of another former Southeast Asian leader, now in exile in California, is keeping $700 million worth of jewels for Imelda.

We are therefore aware of four to five different jewelry collections. These would be those left in Malacanan, the collection taken into exile in Hawaii, the ones left in Dasmarinas, the set intercepted at the Manila International Airport, and if we are to believe the reports, the ones being kept for Imelda in California.

PAMPERS BOXES IN EXILE

When she left for exile, Imelda carried parts of her jewelry collection using expensive luggage such as Gucci and Louis Vuitton designer baggages. She also had personalized luggage with the number 777 on them, Imelda's "lucky number." The Hawaii collection included items such as tiaras, broaches, earrings, necklaces, bracelets, rings, cufflinks and chokers made of gold, silver, diamonds, emeralds, rubies, sapphires, pearls, and amethysts. More than 15 pages of the 23-page inventory of their baggage were listings for jewelry. A Washington Administration official who saw the jewelry and art objects brought into Hawaii said that their total value is "incalculable" [48].

Among the 408 or so pieces of jewelry the Marcoses brought into Hawaii were a belt costing $5,530, 70 pairs of jewelled cufflinks estimated at $149,575, and 75 watches worth $90,000. One air of gold cufflinks with emerald stone and diamonds was appraised by US Customs to be worth $3,280. The watches were by Seiko, Rolex, Van Cleef & Arpels, and Cartier. There was a $7,500 man's gold Rolex, a $4,745 Patek Philippe Geneve gold bracelet watch, a lady's Choppard Geneve gold watch worth $6,470, and a $500 table clock from Cartier.

Other pieces of jewelry from the Hawaii collection were three tiaras, two diamond-studded combs, 60 sets of pearl necklaces and Chokers, 35 rings, 30 sets of earrings, scores of brooches, and bracelets.

The tiaras alone were worth nearly $136,000. One of the diamond-studded tiaras was appraised at $30,500. The most expensive of the tiaras, studded with diamonds and pearls "from Catchpoole and Williams, 510 Oxford St., London, England," was estimated at $58,286. A $18,835 gold crown had diamonds and 22 pearls.

One brooch carried eight emeralds and diamonds and was valued at $768,910. A diamond-studded haircomb was worth $44,410.

A set of diamond earrings with a diamond hair comb of about 20 carats was valued at $65,495. A necklace with 5 large sapphires, diamonds and 7 small sapphires was pegged at $376,990. A coral set consisting of one necklace, a diamond ring, and a pair of diamond earrings cost $4,830. Some pieces of the jewelry were unused and still had their price tags on them, such as one jeweled bracelet showing a tag of $12,000.

Also included in the loot was a box of pearls, which when spread out covered a 12 feet by 4 feet table [49]. The pearls were fresh-water, multi—strand baby, Mabe, baroque, mother-of—pearl, and black.

The most expensive listing was for a whopping $1,487,415 for a matching set of "one bracelet, one pair of earrings and one brooch consisting of sapphires, rubies, diamonds."

A partial list of the jewels Imelda attempted to bring out of country is included in an appendix.

Accompanying the jewels was a Philippine national treasure, a three-foot tall ivory antique statue of the *Sto. Nino* (Infant Jesus) covered with diamonds and other precious stones, complete with a hammered silver mantle and a diamond necklace [50].

Buddy Gomez, the Philippine Consul in Hawaii, said that some of Irnelda's jewels are being kept in five "big size" safe deposit boxes at the Kapiolani branch of the First Hawaiian Bank. According to Gomez, Imelda has "all her crown jewels and she has been wearing them alternately." What she may be missing now are her marbles.

THE EAST 66TH TOWNHOUSE

We were able to visit only three of the many houses the Marcoses owned. These are the 30-room, six-story East 66th Townhouse, and the condominiums on the 43rd Floor of the Olympic Towers, both in New York City, and the Princeton Estate in New Jersey [51].

The *objets de vertue* left behind *after the Marcoses already took what they considered valuable* were enough to boggle the imagination. We can only imagine the original contents of the two houses we visited and what was contained in the rest of the estimated 50 or so other houses spread over the tri-state area of New York, New Jersey, and Connecticut [52].

After two 18-wheel trailers drove off with the most valuable contents of the East 66th Townhouse a few days after the downfall of Marcos, the remaining contents of the place still had many valuable items which auctioneers were able to later sell for over $1 million.

The East 66th Townhouse was a vast repository of *objets de vertue* from different countries and historical eras. It contained Chinese antiques, Italian pieces from the Renaissance and other periods, expensive antique furniture from different English and French courts. The Townhouse also contained many rare books, art works, and expensive contemporary items from auction houses. Many of the rooms had elegant and antique crystal chandeliers, porcelain vases, and trees made of semi-precious stones. The kitchen stocked hundreds of gold-plated China and cases of sterling silver cutlery.

Most of the 17th and 18th century European furnishings came from the collection of Fan Fox and Leslie Samuels, well-known New York philanthropists. Imelda bought the whole Samuels collection after she unsuccessfully tried to buy the Park Avenue apartment which housed the items. The co-op board, afraid of the potential complications that could arise with Imelda as a tenant, refused her $10 million application for the place. Imelda settled for the contents instead. Sotheby Parke Bernet, which was holding the auction for the items, cancelled their projected two-day sale when Imelda bought entire collection. Sotheby's had set the starting bids for the whole collection at $4 million, but Imelda preempted the auction when she bought all the items with a $6 million check. She also bought all the 5,500 catalogues Sotheby printed to accompany the auction and undertook to pay Sotheby's commission so the Samuels estate could keep the entire $6 million.

Among the books in the library was a morocco-bound first edition of *Courses de testes et de Bague* by Charles Perrault, Imperial Folio, published in Paris, 1670, stamped with the coat of arms of Lou1s XIV. The estimated price: $4,000-5,000. There were many first or rare editions of Shakespeare, Dickens, and other authors. An auction record was set when the hand-illustrated 1903 Anne Hathaway 20-volume edition of the complete works of Shakespeare was sold for $5,250, topping the previous record of $5,000. Horace Walpole's 28-volume *Works,* described by the catalogue as "containing the Letters, Memoirs of George II, III, Catalogue of Royal and Noble Authors, and Anecdotes on Painting, each a first edition, bound uniformly in 8vo in full blue calf with gilt stamping," was estimated to be between $1,000-2,000. Charles Dicken 5 *Works,* extra-illustrated, large-paper, 4tos, with full red morocco mosaic inset binding, gilt-tooled and wit satin endpapers, was rated between $3,000-4,000.

More than a thousand pounds of monogrammed embroidered silk and satin sheets, bearing the initials of Imelda, were also left behind, with some pieces still in their packages.

Imelda's canopied bed, estimated at $9,000, had for its cover the throw of Czar Nicholas II and Czarina Alexandra. Possibly produced for the imperial coronation of 1896, the throw is made of Imperial Russian lace and cotton velvet. Embroidered with Romanov eagles, it ears the cipher of the Czar and the Czarina.

There were *four Steinway* pianos and an antique harpsichord. Two of the *Steinways* were ebonize concert grand pianos, one was parlor grand piano, and the other was a console. These pianos were bought reportedly all at the same time by her secretary, Vilma Bautista, with a $120,000 check. Van Cliburn made music history by winning the Tchaikovsky piano competitions in Moscow, but his virtuosity would certainly have been tested had Mrs. Marcos asked him to play these pianos all at the same time. All the pianos were in an almost-new condition. The concert and pianos were later sold for as much as $27,000. The George II inlaid mahogany harpsichord by Baker Harris, London, dated 1763, had an estimated value of $15,000.

There were so many items in the Townhouse that 772 items were later auctioned off. Scores of crystal candle holders in unopened boxes were discovered in a closet. There were dozens of pieces of Steubensware, valued at $200 apiece, on top of a kitchen cabinet. Fruit trees, handcrafted from turqouise and carnelian, and other porcelain objects abounded. There were Moroccan wool carpets. A four-foot tall camel sculptured from natural seashells was sold for $2,000. A 19th century shepherd's glass crook, valued at $2,000, was found behind some vases on a mantle. Rafael Cecilio, cited earlier in connection with the flowers, further attests:

> There was a gold n found among the debris by one of the young volunteers who helped clean the Townhouse in preparation {or the big auction. I took it from him and had it appraised by Ken Lindsner of Sotheby's. I was informed that it was a Bulgari pen and was between $1,500 and $2,000.

In the sixth floor discotheque was a sofa with some throw pillows. Among the inscriptions embroidered on them: "*Nouveau riche* is better than no rich at all," "To be rich is no longer a sin, it's a miracle," "Good girls go to heaven, bad girls go everywhere." The pillows were later bought for $700 by the owner of the Hard Rock Cafe, saying that he planned to exhibit it in his London and New York branches.

The various *objets de vertue* covered a wide panorama of world history and culture. There was a fine Portuguese 19th century olive and pink needlework estimated to be between $1,500 and $2,000. There was a rare small South German jewel casket from the Renaissance made of metal and iron around the 1550's. There was also a Continental Baroque oak frame bench from the 1650's with open padded arm rests. A pair of Regency black-painted and gilt-side chairs with grisaille, cushion seat, painted crest rails, rope-twist splat, and ring-turned legs made around 1810 was estimated to be between $2,000 and $2,500. Among the many chandeliers in the house was a highly important 10-light air in neoclassical style made of clear crystal, green glass baluster stems, and gilt metal, estimated to be between $8,000 and $10,000. There were twenty antique wall mirrors from various European periods.

Imelda was also a hoarder of Chinese art, as mentioned earlier. Among the things that were left in the Townhouse were traces indicative of a greater haul. There was a porcelain brush pot with hand-painted foolion from the Tao-kuang Period. A polychromed biscuit figure of a deity found in good condition represented the Late Ming Dynasty for an estimated $2,000 to $3,000. There was a Chinese export porcelain salmon ground bough pot mounted in a Louis XVI-style ormolu made around 1810 which was estimated to be around $2,000. From the Ching Dynasty were a cobalt-glazed porcelain bowl with gilt decoration, made around 1820, and an enameled porcelain bottle vase with floral and leaf sides, with the base bearing a false mark of the *Ch'ien-lung*. A Chinese divider, worth around $80,000, is known to have been in the Townhouse, but it was not among the items recovered.

Chinese art of John Widdicomb was also represented by a Ming style rosewood extension top dining table carved with low relief chinoiseries costing between $3,000 and $5,000, a fine set of 12 Ming style mahogany frame dining chairs costing between $2,500 and $3,500, and a rosewood Ming style altar table with a low relief landscape carving estimated to be between $1,000 and $1,500.

The Italian pieces were either from or patterned after the renaissance, baroque, rococo, and neoclassical cultural perlods.

Made in the style of the Italian renaissance were:
° brass and cast iron fire tools with wrought iron and brass style irons;
* low table composed of mixed woods and 16 and 17th century elements.

From the Italian baroque period were:
° walnut bench, circa 1600, $1,000;
° walnut side table, circa 1650, $900;
° carved wood frame side table;
° oak low table on a trestle base;
° wood frame table with a marble plat on trestle base;
* a pair of carved oak frame armchairs on spiral turned legs, $1,500;

From the Italian rococo period were:
* a gilt and polychrome *verve egiomise* wood frame wall mirror, circa 1750—
   60, $2000-3000;
* a pair of Italian rococo 5—light carved gilt-wood sconces, circa 1800,
   (damaged);
* a mid-18th century rococo walnut settee (bears a label *Au Cabinet de Mr.
   Delamothe et son Hotel eu avignon anciermement chez le Marquis de
   L'Eipine.),* 33000-5000;
° a carved giltwood console table with heavy conforming Sienna marble top,
   circa 1750, $8000-10000.

From the Italian neoclassical style:
* carved giltwood wall minor, circa 1790, $2000-2500;
* parcel gilt and painted side table with marble plat. circa 1790, $2500-3,500;
* carved gilt-wood wall minor, circa 1790, with urn finial and leafy guilloche
   sides, $3000-$5000 (good condition);
* a pair of good Italian gilt-wood 10—light wall candelabra each in the form of
   a split leaf-carved urn, $2500- 3,500;
* neoclassical carved and gilt-wood wall mirror, circa 1790, with crest of mask
   flanked by two winged griffins, $1,000-1,500;
* a carved gilt-wood wall mirror, circa 1790, $2000-2500.

Objects representative of the courts of various English Kings and other expensive items were part of Imelda's Townhouse collection.

Among them were a set of four Regency black japanned and gilt high-lighted side chairs, circa 1810, with pierced back rests and cane seats on sabre legs. The set, mentioned in Cescinsky's *English Furniture of the Eighteenth Century*, was estimated between $3000 and, $4,000. There was an English Regency rosewood lyre form music stand, circa. 1820, and a pair of English 19th century brass and irons on spur feet, together with two brass hand cast iron fire tools.

A Victorian satined wood musical bird cage with a feathered automaton bird was thought to be between $1,500 and $2,000.

An English 19th centu Chippendale scroll-end camel-back settee, carved mahogany frame upho stered in a beige blend, with matching bolsters was estimated to be between $10,000 and $15,000.

A pair of London sterling silver krater form wine bottle coolers by *Paul Starr*, circa 1810, was among the more expensive items found. Once the property of George Augustus Henry, First Earl of Burlington, the wine coolers, crested with the arms of Devonshire impaled by those of Northampton, had an estimated value between $25,000 and $35,000.

From the English courts, were a James I oak frame joined stool, circa 1690; a Wilham IV carved gilt-wood wall mirror, circa 1830; and a Queen Anne style faux-marble enameled pier glass.

From the collection of George I objects were:
* a rare carved gilt-wood frame and gesso side table with a quarter veneered agate top, on cabriole leg ending in acanthus carved feet, $8,000—10,000
* a good pair of walnut frame open armchairs circa 1730, upholstered in a green velour, on cabriole legs ending in pad feet, later sold for $22,000.

From George II:
* a mahogany oval drop leaf table on cabriole leg, with shell-carved knees ending in ball and claw feet, circa 1750, $10,000—12,000;
* a carved giltwood side table, rectangular carcass with a deep pierced skirt supports a conglomerate plat, scroll-carved cabriole leg ending in hairy paw feet, circa 1750, $15,000-20,000;
* a carved giltwood and gilt gesso wall mirror, dentil-molded pediment centered by a draped mask, corbelled rectangular borders, circa 1740, (candle-arms of a later date), $5,000-7,000;
* a mahogany oval drop leaf table on cabriole leg with shell-carved knees ending in ball and claw feet, circa 1750, $10,000-12,000.

From George III:
* a giltwood mirror, circa 1770, with swan's neck and flower finial, once owned by a Lord Wilton of Oxfordshire, sold for $35,000;
* a rare and important side table, marquetry and parquetry rosewood, and giltwood and gesso side table, circa 1780, with molded paterae apron on square tapered paneled leg, ending in block feet, sold for $42,500;
* a mahogany frame double pedestal writing table, circa 1800, with an arched apron with fitted frieze drawer above the three drawers in each pedestal, $l0,000-12,000;
* a tall case clock, made inlaid mahogany and with fret carved arched hood, with two train movement with 12" dial face, circa 1780, made by Emonds, Brentford, $3,000—5,000;
* a pair of carved gilt-wood and gesso oval wall mirrors, laurel gadrooned and with Prince of Wales feathered crests (damaged), circa 1790, $1,000-1,500;
* a rare carved gilt-wood pier mirror, formerly from Lord Wilton, Ditchley Park, Oxfordshire, with swan's neck crested centering a leaf and shell finial, circa 1770, $35,900-40,000;
* important mahogany five pedestal dining table with reeded edge, turned supports with splayed legs ending in brass toecaps and casters, circa 1775, $30,000-40,000;
* a fine carved and giltwood mirror, in a rectangular frame with pointed crest and carved rockeries and architectural elements, circa 1775, $15,000—20,000;
* an English mahogany canterbury on caster feet, circa 1790.

The French were equally represented in various pieces of furniture from the periods of Louis X and Louis XVI.

There was a rare carved walnut cabinet made between 1590 and 1610. The cabinet, between $12,000 and $15,000, is in two parts with four doors and two drawers carved with floral scrolls and masks, complemented by a overhanging cornice and on a block base.

Among the other pieces was a pair of Louis Philippe cut glass and ormolu two tier compotes. Another item was a 19th century oval centerpiece estimated between $1,500 and $2,000. Having three parts with bronze doré borders in rocky form frame inset mirror plats, the central section bears two finial of tritons atop sea shells. The stub feet which form the bottom are made of Mahogany.

From the period of Louis XV are the following items:
* a carved giltwood frame wall mirror with cartouche and leafy swag crest, $2,000-3,000;
* a 19th century marquetry inlaid and ormolu mounted Tulipwood and Kingwood bureau plat, $10,000-12,000;
* a fine style acajou console table with grey marble plat, on cabriole leg with leaf carved knees ending in leafy feet, $5,000-7,500;
* a pair of ormolu fireplace chenets, circa 1750, with putto finials, $2,000-3,000;
* a pair of beechwood bergeres upholstered in a champagne velvet, $1500-1800.

From the period of Louis XVI:
* a stained and carved beechwood *bergere a'orerlies*, upholstered in brown leather, circa 1790, $l,500—2,000;
* an ormolu mounted porphyry krater form urn, $1200-1500;
* a very good gilt-wood console with marble plat, circa 1780, $3,000-5,000;
* a set of four carved gilt-wood ribbon tied wall trophies, circa 1780, $2,000-3,000;
* three carved gilt-wood wall trophies, circa 1770, $1,000—1,500;
* a good style-canape upholstered in a white brocade;
* a fine carved and painted oak regulateur by Balthazar, Paris, circa 1770, $3,000—5,000;
* a French 19th century style cartouche form wall mirror,
* a pair of bronze doré fireplace chenets with putti finials, $500-2,000;
* a carved and gilt wood naval wall trophy,
* an ormolu mounted white marble mantle clock by Lepaute, circa 1780, with an urn finial and on toupie feet;
* a good carved and painted *lit dejour* (day bed), with a Guilloche carved frame on tapered and fluted leg, circa 1780, $3,000-4,000.

An account of the purchase of an antique table from Stair & Company, a well-known New York antiues concern, gives us an idea of how Imelda went about buying the items found in the Townhouse. According to a New York art and antiques appraiser:

Mrs. Marcos was there one afternoon at 5:00pm and saw a beautiful, enormous George III mahogany dining table. It was 20 feet long... She told them, "I'm having a dinner party at 7:00. Can you have it delivered by then ?" The table cost $45,000, and when the sales people said they couldn't make the delivery in two hours, she offered them $5,000 extra. That bonus was paid and the table came on time for the dinner party [53].

MALACANAN AND GUEST HOUSES

Other Imelda dwellings were equally ostentatious.

The Malacanan palace, a stately Spanish colonial mansion which dates back to the late 18th century, also housed a considerable fortune. Apart from the Spanish chandeliers and gilded mirrors which date back to the Spanish colonial regime, the place also contained art from different countries and eras. One room boasted of numerous Chinese trees and flowers made from semi-precious stones, while another had in its alcoves large porcelain vases from the Ming and Ching dynasties. In another place, a small table displays a marble head, said to be a Michelangelo. Among the old leather-bound books are volumes from the library of Maria Theresa, the 18th-century Austrian empress.

Imelda's bedroom, the size of a mini-football field, had a grand piano, a Bosendorfer from Austria. The bed, crowned with a Spanish-style canopy, was customarily covered with delicate pina cloth. A large walk-in vault for valuables was nearby.

Since Malacanan was in the San Miguel district, a very old part of Manila, two ancestral homes were acquired in the area to serve as "guest houses." One home, built by the Eugsters, probably a Spanish family which has since returned to Spain, was constructed more than a hundred years ago and is referred to as the Goldenberg Mansion, named after more recent owners. Imelda is known to have referred to his house as the "big antique." It is the office of the Marcos Foundation and also houses a trove of European furniture and other expensive furnishings. It contains Imelda's collection of excavated porcelain and pottery from different periods in Philippine history, Ban Chieng prehistoric pottery from Thailand, as well as rare Filipiniana books. A second 15-room equally historic house beside the Goldenberg mansion, called the Teus house, was also acquired as a guest house and contained a huge collection of Spanish, Italian, Dutch, Russian, and English antique silverware. The English sets were made by famous English master silversmiths from the 18th and 19th centuries such as Benjamin Smith, Digby Scott, Simon Pantin, Paul de Lamerie, and Paul Storr.

Apart from 30 expensive wine coolers, the collection consisted of an "assortment of antique tea and coffee service, jugs, bowls, ewers, baskets, dishes, goblets, salt cellars, and entire dinner sets" [54]. Christie's, Manson & Woods, the well-known international art and antiques dealer, was asked to appraise and later auction of the Silverware found in these guest houses. International auction records were set in the ensuing January 1991 sale.

A major auction lot was the Egremont Service, a collection of more than 100 pieces of dinner silverware made by Paul Storr, the master Silversmith who worked in London during late 18th and early 19th centuries. Storr made the set in 1806-7 for George, 3rd Earl Egremont (1751-1837). Christie's initially appraised the lot at $600,000, but it fetched $1.76 million, a record for a Paul Storr lot [55].

Another important set was the Craven service, a set of more than 100 pieces made by Sebastian & James Crespell between 1766-1772 for William, 6th Baron Craven. The Christie's catalogue quoted a 1794 book, *The Whig Club*, which talked about the 'unblushing profligacy" of Elizabeth, the baron's lady who doubled as the mistress of the Margrave of Anspach [56]. The lot was appraised at $130,000-$180,000.

Among the other items were the following:
* three pairs of wine coolers, pair of unique soup tureens, covers, and stands by Paul Storr
* Hassell silver, a rare engraved work done by Lamerie in 1736, estimate: $250,000-$350,000
* four fine candlesticks made by Lamerie in 1731, estimate: $180,000-$250000
* two cake baskets by Lamerie, estimate: $60,000-$80,000 and $80,000-$120,000
* four wine coolers made by Philipp Rundell for Sir Richard Sutton in 1819, estimate: $180,000-$250,000
* a pair of George III silver-gilt wine coolers made in London in 1808 by Benjamin Smith, estimate: $70,000-$100,000
* a pair of George III silver-gilt wine coolers, made in London in 1804 by Digby Scott and Benjamin Smith II, and in 1810 by Benjamin Smith II and James Smith III. estimate: $70900-$100,000.
* a pair of Regency silver-gilt wine coolers made by Paul Storr (london, 1813) was estimated at $120,000 but was sold for $288,000.
* 8 a pair of Geo IV silver-gilt Warwick-vase salts made by John Bridge (London 1828), estimate: $5,000-$8,000
* a set of four Regency Ormolu wine coolers on stands, appraised at $40,000 but sold [or $143,000.
* a pair of George III silver wine coolers and stands, appraised at $80,000 but sold for $115,500.

The silver collection racked in $4,451,350 -- a record for the highest price for a single-owner collection. The previous record set was for $2.39 million in 1986. The auction was described as the "best silver sale that Christie's ever had in New York" [57].

OLYMPIC TOWERS

The remnants at the Olympic Towers condominium (641 Fifth Ave.) were estimated at $150,475, according to a pre-auction inventory and appraisal conducted by Sotheby's. These were Russian and silver works of art, malachite furniture and hardstone ornaments. Among the more notable items were a Paul Storr tea urn, a Sevres part dinner service, and two beautiful Faberge pieces.

The silverware that was left were the following:
* a Paul Storr George 1V silver-gilt two-handled cup and cover, London 1823, $6,000-8,000;
* a pair of George II fluted bowls, David Willaume, London 1728, S8,000-12,000;
* a seven piece French silver tea and coffee service, Lucien Tesson, Paris, late I9th century, $3,000-4,000;
* a Regency silver-gilt and alabaster inkstand, London 1820, $1500-2000;
* a pair of polish silver table candlesticks, $800-1,200;

* an eight piece silver and pink enamel partial dressing set in fitted box, Cartier, $800-1,200;

The inventory organized the remaining items according to the rooms they were found. In the green-striped maid's room were the lollowing:
* a large 15-inch faberge silver and malachite jewel casket, Moscow, circa 1885, $12,000-18,000;
* a nine-inch Faberge carved nephrite and silver-gilt dish, Moscow, circa 1900, $4,000-6,000;
* a 10-inch pair of Viennese enamel trumpet-shaped 19th century vases, $3,000-5,000;
* a 20-inch German silver and malachite elephant 19th century obelisk, $3,000-4,000;
* a 16-inch Continental malachite and ormolu ewer, circa 1900;
* a pair of 17.5 inch Chinese 'jade' trees, $3,000-5,000;
* another 10.5 inch Chinese 'jade' tree in a hardstone and gilt metal pot, $3,000-4,000;
* a 9-inch malachite compote on a plinth, circa 1900, $2,500-4,000;
* a 7.5-inch malachite ash tray;
* a 6-inch malachite table cigarette box;
* a 14-inch Cloisonne enamel vase filled with enamel flowers;
* a 16.25 inch gilt-bronze and glass table mirror, circa 1900;
* a 5-inch malachite and silver cube lighter;
* a 7-inch carved jade table ornament;
* a onyx cigarette box, circa 1900;
* a 28.5 inch cloisonne enamel and hardstone pot of flowers, circa 1900, $3,000-4,000.

In the dining room were:
* a 9-inch pair of eastern European large teapots;
* an 11-inch pair of flight and bar: armorial fruit coolers and covers, circa 1805;
* a regency style mahogany three-pedestal dining table, $4,000-6,000;
* a set of ten Chippendale style mahogany dining chairs, $2,500-3,500;
* a pair of Chinese blue ground cloisonne planters;
* a pair of Japanese cloisonne jardinieres with hardstone peony plants, $15,000-20,000;
* a pair of bohemian green overlay glass lustres.

In the living room were:
* a George 1 carved giltwood side table with agate top (from the Samuels Collection), $6,000-8,000;
* an Eastern carved sandstone head;
* a Continental ormolu and circular malachite table, $2,000-3,000;
* a brass and malachite kidney-shaped two tier table, $2,000-3,000;
* a malachite and brass low table, $1,000-1,500,
* a curved giltwood satyr form low table with malachite top, $2,500-3,500;
* four small cloisonne planters with hardstone leaves, $1,000-1500;
* a pair of Chinese peach ground hexagonal porcelain lamps;
* an Italian neoclassical fruitwood armchair,
* Green ground kerman carpet, $1,000-1,500;
* a pair of ormolu mounted glass candelabra, $1,000-1,500;
* a cloisonne inset small table.

In the pink bedroom was a Chinese carved rose quartz vase mounted as a lamp, and in a closet was a pair of carved hardstone grape vine lamps estimated between $1,500-2,000.

In the foyer were:
* a Queen Anne style mahogany double chair-back settee with needlepoint seat, $1,000-1,500;
* a carved white marble figure of a putto with dogs;
* a white stone console table;
* a Louis XVI-style white painted fauteuil.

Imelda's condominium provides a magnificent view of Manhattan. Three adjacent condominiums were bought in the 43rd Floor of the Olympic Towers in Fifth Ave. The walls were torn down to make a huge apartment covering about a quarter of a Manhattan city block, with views of Manhattan from three of the four sides of the building. On the south side, one is a little higher than the steeples of St. Patrick's Cathedral, allowing a view of the rest of Manhattan, including the Empire State building and the twin towers of the World Trade Center. On the east side, one may notice the odd architecture of the building of Citibank, whose eager loans to the Philippines made most of this luxury possible, and farther along are the outlines of the borough of Queens. On the north side, one has a grand view of Central Park, but Harlem and the Bronx are hidden. If Imelda had bought one more apartment in this floor (they had others in other floors), she would have covered the last side on the west, where she would have seen, staring at her a big bold red electric billboard, the numbers for a Fifth Ave. building a couple of blocks away: 666.

But this kind of reminder was unnecessary. It was sufficient that she could peer down at the people visiting St. Patrick's. From this distance, though, it is difficult to notice that among the many colorful figures parading in Fifth Ave., is an elderly blind man, stationary most of the day, while at other times led by a guide dog, selling pencils from a begging cup made of tin. On his cap which he wears during hot summer days is a small cardboard sign asking, "How am I doing, Mayor Koch?"

In this rarefied atmosphere, one senses something artificial, almost surreal, in the surroundings. One grasps for a handle, a guide post to orient one's self. Scouting the surroundings for a mooring, one notices the gigantic electronic billboards from two sides of the Newsweek building, seemingly so near at this height, but the incoherence persists: the boards are out of sync and announce different time and temperature readings.

NAIF

Imelda's hands stripped the aesthetic from art and debased great masterpieces into mere objects to be acquired. This was done in a manner rarely seen in the world of art, qualifying her to be a most philistine collector.

Imelda collected art in the same way she bought perfume, wrist watches, and anything else with a price tag -- by the gallon, by the hundreds, by the legion, guided perhaps by a perverse interpretation of the Hegelian insight that quantity turns into quality.

Imelda amassed a pile of masterpieces from both Filipino and international artists. She treated the Manila Metropolitan Museum as her personal gallery and used the East 66th Townhouse and the Olympic Towers condominium as depositories of the pieces she accumulated.

Among the Filipino masterpieces associated with Imelda are works by Amorsolo and Manansala, both highly esteemed Filipino artists. GSIS chairman Roman Cruz, who is known to be close to Imelda, acquired 24 paintings by Amorsolo and Manansala, worth many millions, through the government body he headed. Records show that these masterpieces art were transferred to the offices of the COA, which was headed by Commissioner Tantuico, who was also close to Imelda. Authorities have encountered difficulties in tracing these paintings.

Imelda also liked to collect naive art, like the work of Polish artist Nikifor, and she also had a collection of 191 naifs by Yugoslav farmers, 120 Russian icons, and 207 pieces of Russian lacquerware [58]. Imelda also collected American art, such as those by Grandma Moses and Andrew Wyeth.

Fourteen 10-foot Cowan oil portraits were left in the East 66th Townhouse. Among these were portraits of Pope John Paul II, Ronald Reagan, Nancy Reagan, and joint portraits of Jimmy and Rosalyn Carter which the Marcoses had commissioned. Ferdinand Marcos had our portraits, while Imelda had three. The Marcos family, the parents of Imelda, and one of the Marcos daughters were also the subject of separate 10-foot oil paintings. One of the Marcos portraits was entitled *The Triumph of Courage*, and another showed Marcos beside a carabao. Two of the Imelda portraits were given the titles *The Triumph of Purity* and *The Triumph of Beauty*. Each Cowan painting with one subject costs $14,000, and an additional figure in the same frame brings an added $4,000. This would mean that the Marcos Family portrait cost at least $34,000. Receipts for other Marcos-commissioned Cowan portraits were later found. These had King Hassan ("two finished portraits") and King Fahd and Crown Prince Abdullah as their subjects, but these were not among those found in the Townhouse.

Imelda started collecting art in the early 1980's and bought most of them either through her close associate, Gliceria Tantoco, or through Mario A. Bellini, a prominent art dealer from Florence. She also dealt heavily with the Hammer Galleries at 33 West 57th Street, New York. An employee of the Hammer Galleries describes a typical transaction with Tantoco:

We rarely dealt directly with Mrs. Marcos. Mrs. Tantoco was obviously her adviser and intermediary in most transactions. She was a toughie, and always insisted on a discount. So when they saw her coming, most galleries automatically raised their prices 25% and then gave a discount of 15% or 17%. Basically my feeling was than they weren't that knowledgeable about art. They didn't know the market but they knew that whatever price was quoted, they wanted a discount. They consistently overpaid for everything sometimes as much as ten times the going rate.

According to some sources, the actor George Hamilton was with Imelda in some of these New York shopping trips for art and antiques [59].

An art dealer familiar with Imelda's purchases describes one particular transaction with the Hammer Galleries in May 1983. Tantoco called the Hammer Galleries, saying that she wanted a "big collection of paintings by one artist." The Hammer Galleries sold her 52 paintings by Paul Gobillard, a little-known impressionist, for $273,500. "It was a nice way to get rid of paintings you didn't want," the dealer said.

The following is a list of some items Imelda bought from the Hammer Galleries:

Fra Filippo Lippi	*Madonna and Child*	$700,000
Pierre Auguste Renoir	*Juenes Filler uas Bord de L'eau*	$475,000
Pierre Au te Renoir	(unidentified)	$475,000
Maurice Utrillo	*LA Maison Blanche*	(included in preceeding)
Claude Monet	*La Pluie*	$365 00
Camile Pisarro	*Jardin de Kew, Pra de la Serre*	$420,000
Paul Gauguin	(still life portrait)	$1.5 million
Paule Gobillard	52 painting	$273,000
Grandma Moses	18 paintings	$700,000
Andrew Wyeth	*Moon Madness*	$300,000

According to the *New York Times*, which examined the receipts from Hammer Galleries, Mrs. Marcos bought 77 paintings from the Hammer Galleries for $4.61 million. One of the receipts read: "Above prices are special prices authorized by Dr. Armand Hammer for Mr. and Mrs. Marcos." It was also reported that some of these paintings were flown to the Philippines on the private plane of Dr. Hammer.

The Hammer Galleries is owned by the brother of Dr. Armand Hammer, one of the richest men in the US and the chairman of Oriental Petroleum, a company which has engaged in oil exploration in the Philippines.

The Hammer brothers are also connected with the Knoedler Gallery at 19 East 70th Street, New York, another art dealership which has extensively dealt with Imelda. One of the items bought from the Knoedler Galle was Paolo Caliari Veronese's *City of Venice Adoring the Christ Child* for $465,000. Another purchase from the same gallery was for Francisco de Zurbaran's *The Holy Family*, purchased for $250,000. According to one art dealer familiar with the sales of Knoedler, Imelda bought about six Old Master paintings and several Impressionists from the Knoedler for an amount close to $5 million.

A Hammer associate enumerates some of the items Imelda bought while her retinue of guards and shopping companions waited outside the galleries: "Grandma Moses, Utrillo, a couple of French impressionists. A Monet footbridge, I think, and possibly a Vlaminck. About the same time, I heard that Knoedler sold them some Old Masters for about $2 million." Frank Ashley, a spokesman for Dr. Hammer, would not comment when queried by reporters [60].

Another who closely dealt with Imelda was Mario A. Bellini, a well-known art dealer in Florence, described by the New York Times as "the dean" of the city's antique dealers [61]. Bellini, who heads his 200-year old family art business, acknowledges that he was "very friendly" with Imelda. Four checks were issued to

Bellini's wife, Adriana, between July and October 1983. The checks were issued in "full payment for Michelangelo painting" which totalled $3.5 million.

The money was for a portrait entitled *Madonna and Child*. Imelda apparently was led to believe that this was indeed a Michelangelo, and she was known to have remarked to Jack Tanzer of the Knoedler Gallery in 1983 that she had a Michelangelo in her Townhouse. But there is only one Michelangelo painting known to exist, according to Everett Fahy of the Frick Collection, and this is the *Tondo Dani*, which hangs in the Uffizi Gallery in Florence, Italy. Two Manhattan art dealers said Imelda approached a law firm at a much later date to get back the money spent on the painting [62].

According to Italian authorities, the Madonna and Child, although not by Michelangelo, is still a valuable piece of art from the school of Michelangelo. Magistrates in Florence slapped Bellini with three sets of charges on 12 September 1988, citing the exportation of valuable art work, and are holding the *Madonna and Child* as evidence.

Bellini was also responsible for selling Imelda 75 Old Masters paintings, which were kept at the Manila Metropolitan Museum. The paintings covered the period from Trecento to the Renaissance and the 18th century Venetian school. Among the names associated with this collection are major figures of Italian art: Titian, Canaletto, Raphael, Boticelli, among others.

The most important piece was an early Raphael, *St. Catherine of Alexandria*, one of the few works by the master left in private hands. The preparatory drawing for this painting is in the Baron Edmond de Rothschild Collection at the Louvre. The painting, estimated to date to circa 1503, was formerly in the Contini Bonacossi collection in Florence. Estimated by Christie's at $800,000, it was bought for $1.65 million in the January 1991 auction by the Italian government, which plans to exhibit it at the Ufizzi Gallery, Florence [63].

From the Venetian Renaissance was Titian's Portrait of *Giulio Romano*, estimated at $300,000 but sold for $1 million. *Christ Among Doctors* and *Miraculous Drought of Fishes*, examples of the mature style from 1550's of Jacopo Robusti, Il Tintoretto was estimated $ 100,000-$ 150,000 each [64].

From the 18th Century were several paintings by Canaletto, the Venetian master. One painting, *Prato della Valle*, was valued at $30,000 but sold for $250,000.

A list of these Italian masters and other art works is included in the appendix.

Other Imelda purchases which Bellini handled were bought from Marco Grassi, a Manhattan art dealer. More than $3 million was paid to Grassi for El Greco's *Coronation of the Virgin*, Francois Boucher's *Apotheosis of Aneas*, and Francisco de Zurbaran's *David and Goliath*. El Greco's *Coronation of the Virgin*, whose preparatory sketch of the same title is displayed in the Hospital of Charity in Illescas, Spain, later sold for $2.1 million, much higher than the $300,000 pre-auction estimate made by Christie's [65].

Imelda kept the more valuable paintings in her East 66th Townhouse and Olympic Towers apartment, while the less valuable ones were stored at the Manila Metropolitan Museum and other houses in Manila. When the Marcoses fled the Philippines, most of the pieces were spirited away from these places. Marco Grassi, commenting on the pieces from the Old Masters collection left in the museum in Manila says, "It is really peculiar that the really good pieces did not appear in the museum." Some paintings by Filipino artists were later discovered in a beach resort several hundred miles south of Manila [66].

Imelda reserved the best of her art collection for her Manhattan East 66th Townhouse. A Hammer gallery employee, delivering "six or seven" Grandma Moses paintings to the Townhouse, witnessed the collection of the masters side-by-srde with the 10-foot Cowan paintings of the Marcoses: "It looked like a warehouse, with boxes everywiiere... There was a lot of art around. I remember *Head of A Woman* by Picasso, a van Gogh, a Renoir, but dominating everything were portraits of them [Ferdinand and Imelda] at the top of the stairs. They were in apotheosis, coming out of clouds an sun rays like gods coming down from heaven."

Within three days after the Marcoses fled the Philippines, the paintings were spirited away with the other *objets de venue*. What was left were a few minor pieces and the name plates for the frames which once held the master works. Among the minor paintings that were left were a set of four late 18th century or early 19th century French military watercolors, and a pen and ink grisaille drawing *Rustic Cottage with Figures* attributed to J.B. LePrince (1734-1781), costing around $2,000-3,000.

From the brass plaques, the following canvasses, oils, and watercolor paintings once hung in the Townhouse:
Pablo Picasso - *Head of a Woman* - (1954), around $400,000
Vincent Van Gogh - *Peasant Woman Winding Bobbins* - watercolor, $100,000
Henri Matisse - *Head of a Woman* - oil canvas
Fra Filippo Lippi - *Madonna and Child* - (c.1460), now in Italy
Paul Cezanne - *Landscape, Aix-en-Provence* - oil on canvas
Francisco Goya - *La Marqueza de Sta.Cruz* – (circa 1805)
Edouard Manet - *Mary Laurent a la Violette* – (1878) Pastel on linen
Edgar Dégas - *Danseuses S'Habillant*
Edgar Degas - *Trais Danseuses* - c.1889), signed lower left
Piet Mondrian – *Eucalyptus* – (1910), oil on canvas
Claude Monet - *L'Eglise a la Seine a Vérheuil* – (1881), oil on canvas
Claude Monet - *La Pluie* (signed, lower left) - oil bought from Hammer
Francois Boucher - *The Apotheosis of Aneas* - canvas, signed 1747
Peter Brueghel, the Younger - *Adoration of the Kings* – oil, signed 1617
Paul Gauguin – *Fruits*
Frans Hals – *Portrait of a Young Man* - signed with Hals monogram
Frans Hals – *Portrait of a Young Woman* - signed with Hals monogram
Peter Paul Rubens – *The Virgin and Child* – (Cumberland Madonna)
Alfred Sisley - *La Baie de Langland, le Rocher* – oil on canvas
Maurice Utrillo - *La Maison Blanche* (signed) – (c.1914) oil on canvas
Anthony van Dyck - *An Apostle* (St. Simon) – oil on canvas
Paolo Veronese - *The City of Venice Adoring the Christ Child* – oil on canvas
Francisco de Zurbaran – *David and Goliath*

The Olympic Towers also contained parts of Imelda's collection, but Marcos associate Floirendo had more time and success in removing the valuables and traces of the paintings once housed in the place [67]. Our paintings from Olympic Towers were later found in a Hackensack, New Jersey warehouse in the possession of Floirendo. Two were originally from Metropolitan Museum of Manila, while the other two were from the Malacanan Presidential Palace. They were appropriated and made art of the furnishings in the Olympic Tower apartment which Floirendo held for Imelda. The Hackensack warehouse so yielded an elaborate gilt frame with label indicating it once held a Goya.

What was inadvertently left in the Olympic Towers was *Sweet Peas* by Henri Fantin-Latour. It was found wrapped in a blanket under the maid's bed. The canvas, depicting peas in a vase, was painted by Fantin-Latour in 1888, and bears the signature *Fantin* on the top eft. The painting is included in the *Catalogue de l'oeuvre complet de Fantin-Latour* published in Paris in 1911 by Mme. Fantin-Latour. A sale by Christie's of London on 14 July 1933 and participation at the 1984 Summer Exhibition of the London Royal Academy form part of the provenance of the painting [68].

A judge prohibited top Manhattan galleries and auction houses from disposing of the art and jewelry believed to be connected to Imelda shortly after the Marcoses fled. The May 1986 order from the judge specifically listed seven paintings. Among the galleries and auction houses mentioned by in the order were the William Doyle Galleries, the Marlboro Galleries, the Hammer Gallery, Christie's, and Sotheby Parke Bernet Inc. These places were also ordered to turn over their receipts and invoices associated with the purchases of Imelda.

These records and others found in Manila indicate that Imelda bought no less than 251 pieces of art. Of these 101 have been found, but 150, comprising the most important ones, are missing. Among the missing ones are three paintings attributed to Pablo Picasso - *Fruit Dish, Bottle and Guitar; Reclining Woman; and Head of a Woman,* which we mentioned earlier. Three paintings by Degas were also missing. There have been reports which indicate that Imelda has been trying to unload some of these paintings. A Monet part of the *Japanese Footbridge series*, works by the Belgian surrealist Magritte, and a Chinese horse from the Tang period from her collection of Asian art are among those mentioned as being offered. The London flat of J .V. Cruz, a former newspaper correspondent close to Marcos, is known to house a self-portrait of British painter Francis Bacon with a possible market value of 500,000 pounds ($700,000) [69].

PYRAMID OF SACRIFICE

What we have attempted to do in this chapter is to describe the poverty and wealth that was created throughout the years of Marcos' rule. Not all the pertinent materials were available. Data on poverty and the general social conditions of the people were usually suppressed or manipulated to reflect the government point of view, while information on the consumption patterns on the Philippine elite, especially the segment associated with the Marcos regime, was concealed with great zeal because of the scandal this type of behavior would have caused. There were areas therefore that eluded the net we cast. But inspite of the great gaps in the data available, we believe we have sufficiently shown the disparity in the life styles of the two sets of actors whom we set out to depict.

There were times when the extremes of poverty and wealth drove us into anger, frustration, and despair. There were times too when it all had a surreal effect. There were times when our accounting of the properties tempted us into incredulity and disbelief. The accumulation of wealth went beyond ordinary human needs, and even beyond what has been normally considered luxurious, that it acquired a perverse, unreal character. Our consciousness became saturated at seeing accounts of so much wealth that we had to temporarily suspend belief in order to cope with the massiveness of what confronted us.

But the reader is assured that our account is factually accurate. For people who have other cultural backgrounds and are not familiar with the Philippines, and also for future generations who might be tempted to dis-believe what is contained in these chapters, the sources used in writing this book are properly indicated in the footnotes.

But those who suffered most directly from the avarice and the pillage of the Marcos regime had a coping mechanism far different from the intellectual suspension of belief. A friend of mine from Constitution Hill sold his blood to hospitals twice a week in exchange for rice for his family. Some begged in the streets. Others scoured the garbage dumps for food, broken glass bottles, and other pieces of scrap that could be recycled. Still others were forced into prostitution. These were the women who worked under the euphemisms so popular in Manila: hostesses, hospitality girls, waitresses, taxi dancers, sauna bath attendants, sexy and a-go-go dancers, and other similar categories that American television loves to periodically show. Some went the way of crime.

As of 1976, there was an estimated 50,000 women in the Philippines who earned their living as prostitutes, according to the *Far Eastern Economic Review*. In Metro-Manila alone, there were at least 25,000 Filipinas, mostly from 20-25 years old, who were employed as "hospitality girls," according the 1977 data of Bureau of Women & Minors of the Department of Labor.

In a single day in 1978, 1,105 beggars were apprehended in Metro Manila. There were 15,000 persons in Metro Manila who depended on begging as a means of livelihood, according to 1977 data from the Bureau of Rehabilitation of the Department of Social ervices & Development.

What Marcos and his wife have done was to stretch our understanding of what is possible within the range of human experience. It was difficult for the mind to conceive the idea of the world as a globe until Magellan circumnavigated the earth. The intellect can sometimes refuse to function when it encounter events which our psychological makeup presumes impossible. It is only in practice that consciousness becomes fully convinced of what is real. This Is the abominable legacy which Marcos and Imelda has bequeathed to mankind: the dubious distinction of extending the range of human experience by showing in practice how much poverty, famine, and deaths were caused to accumulate one of the richest treasures history has known. Ferdinand Marcos, during some of his boasting moods, would say that he was the namesake of Magellan and would continue to draw parallels between himself and the great Portuguese navigator. The only similarity between them is that they have opened us to two radically different worlds.

Our account of Constitution Hill served as our point of departure for our brief exposition. It was a useful way of introducmg the themes of this book. Apart from showing the great chasm that divides the two sectors of Philippine society, it was also a useful way of introducing the themes in the next chapters. Poverty and wealth are not merely two different things but are *related to each other in a causal manner.* While in we tended to be generally *descriptive* in this chapter, we hope throughout the rest of the book to show *the mechanism* used by Marcos and his cronies to amass wealth and cause the poverty of the people and the underdevelopment of the economy.

We know of a man who worked the good part of his life as a laborer. He did not have much schooling because his father had been a peon too and could not afford to send him to school. He started working as a laborer in his late teens. He retired as a laborer when he reached sixty. This was a period in his life to which he had been looking forward. He deposited all of his life savings and his retirement pay with Banco Filipino. There was a run on the bank a couple of months after. He lost all of his savings. The bank owners blamed Marcos' Central Bank Governor, Jose B. Fernandez, for wanting to take over the bank; the Marcos government countered that the owners mismanaged the bank. Whatever the reasons for the dissolution of the bank, what matters at this level of analysis is what hap ened to the multitude of small depositors as a consequence of the paper shuffling of a few highly-placed individuals.

Imelda built many multimillion buildings and hotels. Each of these edifices have their own story. One, the Film Center, has a articularly gipallin history behind it. Imelda impulsively decided to build the Film enter or an international film festival to be held in Manila. Very little planning and preparations were made and the project proceeded at breakneck speed, with laborers feverishly working around-the-clock to meet the hurriedly-imposed schedule. Due to the haste, whole floors collapsed during construction, buryin scores in the quickly-drying cement and other debris. Work did not stop. The laborers were left buried alive in the cement. The project had a timetable to meet. An article from Film, a film review publication of the Lincoln Center in New York, recounts the events of that night:

> This Film Center is the only **palais du festival** which is also a mass mausoleum. Workers had been manning round-the-clock shifts for several months in order to finish the building in time for the opening of the first MIFF [Manila International Film Festival] in 1981 when, shortly before 3:00AM. on 17 November, the roof collapsed. More than 200 persons were buried under fast-drying cement. A security blanket was immediately imposed; nothing could be done until an official statement, minimizing the accident, had been prepared. Ambulances were not permitted access to the scene of the disaster until 9hours after the cave-in. (Later, there were bitter accusations from survivors that they had been given little help in digging out co-workers.) **Orders were given to slice in half those caught unconscious in the quick-drying porous cement.** Had they been dug out or drilled out whole, construction would have been further delayed. This graveyard shift claimed well over a hundred lives [70].

These were poorly-paid laborers who toiled without any insurance or benefits. Most of them had no security of tenure and could be easily fired because construction companies preferred to hire contract workers who could be expediently laid-off.

In the same complex as the Film Center is the Philippine Plaza Hotel. This too was an Imelda creation. It was in a $2,000-a-day suite of this hotel that Imelda chose to spend her first days in the Philippines after she ended her US exile on November 1991. Again hardly known to most were the sacrifices exacted to construct this luxury hotel. In one incident, workers, again facing a deadline, fell several stories to the concrete pavement below as their gang plank gave way. More deaths occurred when the newly-cemented ceiling of the gigantic ballroom fell. As poor supports were used, the cement ceiling gave way before it was totally dry, killing the laborers who were sleeping in the construction area that night. The precise number of victims in these accidents is not known since the events were again hushed. When electricians of the hotel do maintenance work, they encounter in nooks and crannies of the hotel's ceiling, beside the accumulated dirt and grime, small crosses with the names of some the victims etched on the walls, humble tokens of fellow-laborers to those who perished in the pyramids of sacrifice.

In the end, we are left with the question of why and how such behavior was possible, staring at us, demanding an answer. What was Lady Macbeth trying to hide with all her perfumes? And what in her soul was she trying to see with her twenty antique wall mirrors? We have pondered over these questions many times, an after considering many alternative explanations, we tend to concur with the perceptive remark of Tasio, the old philosopher in Jose Rizal's novel Noli Me Tangere, when speaking of the social gatherings in the Philippines during the previous century, he says

> i'Alegrarse no quiere decir cometer locuras!... Es la insensata orgia de todos los anos! Ytodo Ipor qué? Malgastar el dinero, cuando hay tantas misertas y necesidades! Ya! camprendo, es la orgia, es la bacanal para apagar las lamentaciones de todos! [71]

Some view the raw competitive process which produces poverty as an inevitable part of the process of natural selection. But this viewpoint is wrong. What is at work in producing poverty are not natural causes but social and historical ones. We refuse to accept as an immutable forum the process where all the cards are stacked against the person from the time of conception in the womb through the time the person dies, haunted by unemployment and hunger at each and every moment of his unhappy life.

There is a relationship between how one half dies and how the other half splurges. There are many things which have already been eradicated in other countries in the last century but are still sadly prevalent in the Philippines today. Child labor, tuberculosis, and leprosy are examples. Many of tiie social ills that we related early in this chapter are preventabie. The provision of adequate nutrition, the organization of sanitary living conditions, and the introduction of hygienic practices would effectively eradicate many of the diseases and early deaths. overty, disease, and the resultin early deaths are not the natural, pre-ordained state. They are the result of the particular way the social and economic system is organized.

There is both truth and much irony in one of the last letters Marcos wrote as president. On the eve of the February elections which led to his downfall, a letter on Malacanan official stationary was sent to the electorate. The letter announced a tax cut, saying thank you

> ...for the sacrifice you must make in contributing your share from your hard earned money... Your taxes have enabled us to be fed, dressed and housed much better than before.

Octavio Paz [72] and Peter Berger [73] in different books both discuss the Aztec pyramid in Cholula, Puebla as the clue to understanding the history of Mexico. The pyramid was a sacrificial platform where the Aztec riests placated the gods with offerings of human blood. If blood were not offered, the universe would fall apart. Three distinct groups operated within this schema: the great mass of people who offered their lives to the sacrificial cult of Quetzalcoatl, the priests and intellectuals who provided legitimation and meaning to the sacrifice, and the upper classes who benefitted from the rituals. The analogous mechanisms of sacrifice and the corresponding "butter-ball" theories of legitimation by Marcos professionals is what will concern us in this book. We shall hopefully then be able to show in historical detail the insight contained in the following Chinese folk poem:

> Chi Chen Taoist Temple is a fine place
> Fir and pine trees grow in the stone courtyard.
> Rip up the stone flagging and look,
> They are growing on the backs of the poor.

Endnotes

1. Quoted in Seth Mydans and Richard Vokey, Newsweek, 13 September 1982.
2. Our translation from the original Tagalog account written by one of the members of the community. Published in mimeograph form and privately circulated in 1977.
3. The acronym was formed from the Mayor's name, Adelina Rodriguez.
4. "Thou art weighed in the balances, and art found wanting." *Daniel,* 5:27.
5. Alcestis S. Abrera, "Philippine PovertyThrcsholds," and Leonardo Sta. Romana III, "Indicators of Economic Well Being" in Mahar Mangahas ed., *Measuring Philippine Development: Report of the Social Indicators Project,* The Development Academy of the Philippines, 1976.
6. *Timbang* means weight.
7. *Daily Express,* 22 April 1984.
8. *Bulletin Today,* 3 February 1984.
9. *Business Day,* 73 August 1980.
10. *Bulletin Today,* 14 January 1984.
11. *Daily Express,* 12 March 1985; Bulletin Today, 18 August 1985.
12. The New Society Movement, Marcos' political party.
13. An inventory uncovered similar equipment left by Cendana in the facilities of the Maharlika Broadcasting System (Channel 4). The inventory included 5,000 color TV sets and Betamax machines, prompting a media person to comment "Cendana was in a lot of businesses and buy and sell must've been one of them." *Business Day,* 12 March 1986.

14. A survey conducted by the University of the Philippines in 1970-71 showed that one-third of graduates of Philippine medical schools since 1908 have emigrated.

15. *Times Journal,* 25 October 1980.

16. *Daily Express,* 7 May 1980.

17. *Daily Eiqrress,* 7 May 1980.

18. *"How sadly the rain falls on the cardboard roofs/ How sadly my people live in cardboard homes... / How happily the dogs live in the house of the exploiter/ You will not believe it/ But there are schools where they educate dogs..."* Our translation of some lines from a Venezuelan folk song sung by Ali Primera.

19. We shall discuss the overseas properties of Marcos and his cronies in this introductory chapter only cursorily. We shall reserve a fuller study of their overseas properties in Chapter V where we analyze their overseas empire.

20. "Imelda often spoke of her poverty but only to close relatives," says a biography by Carmen Navarro Pedrosa. "She described how her mouth would water whenever she saw neighbors who had margarine with their bread for breakfast."

21. *Times Journal,* 10 August 1977.

22. The primary grades end with the sixth grade in the Philippine public school system

23. Bemabe B. Paguio, *Daily Express,* 26 May 1978.

24. *Business Day*, 12 June 1985, *Bulletin Today,* 21 July 1985.

25. Among the reading materials Marcos brought with him when he left the Phili pines were *Stag, Hustler, Penthouse, Playboy; The Sensous Man, The Corporal Sexecutive, Sex and the over-Fifties.*

26. *Time,* 31 March 1986.

27. *Time,* 31 March 1986.

28. *Time,* 31 March 1986.

29. *Time,* 31 March 1986.

30. *Time,* 31 March 1986.

31. *Time,* 31 Match 1986.

32. *Time,* 31 March 1986.

33. Robert Manning, "The Marcos Mafia: Crony Capitalism Meets popular democracy," *The New Republic*, 25 June 1984.

34. Seth Mydans, "The Shoes: 1,060 Pairs, Not 3,000," *New York Times,* 9 February 1987.

35. *Time,* 31 March 1986.

36. *New York Times,* 27 April 1990.

37. "In Search of the Marcos Millions," PBS broadcast over US TV on 26 May 1987.

38. Hamilton claims that he repaid the money. "I was able to use a portion of the money for expenses but ultimately paid it all back." It appears that Hamilton repaid the initial $5.5 million with a second $6 million loan. The source of the second loan is not known. Judge Keenan in the New York trail of Imelda stopped the prosecution from questioning Hamilton concerning his financial dealings with Tantoco.

39. Rogoff has denied this connection, but Romero reiterated the circumstances surrounding the purchase and said that he stands by the statement he has made to Philippine government authorities.

40. *Time,* 31 March 1986.

41. We shall cover the methods by which money was transferred abroad and used to buy overseas property in more detail in Chapter IV, where we discuss their overseas empire.

42. According to the US House Armed Services Committee, the total cost of moving the Marcos family out of the Philippines amounted to $858,417. The shelves and clothing racks at Andersen Air orce Base in Guam and Hickam Air Force Base in Hawaii were stripped by the Marcoses who chalked up $206,899 in expenses. Among the expenses were $19,971 for long distance calls; $10,555, soap, toothpaste, hair curlers; $630, cosmetics; $2,500, shoes; $1,792, luggage; $3,500, men's socks, belts, underwear; $1,437 for lingerie, hosiery, and underwear.

43. Earlier "official" visits to Iraq, Mexico and US in 1981 came to a bill of around $800,000.

44. *Time,* 31 March 1986.

45. *Time,* 31 March 1986.

46. "In Search of the Marcos Millions," PBS broadcast over US TV on 26 May 1987.

47. *Business Day,* 14 April 1986.

48. *Washington Post*, 25 March 1986.

49. *Financial Times,* 25 April 1986.

50. *Financial Times,* 25 April 1986.

51. We discuss these properties more fully in Chapter IV when we cover the overseas properties of the Marcoses. In this chapter we focus on the *objets de venue* that found in these places.

52. There were other houses in other states. These are discussed in Chapter IV.

53. William Sherman, 'The Marcos Collection,"*ARTnews*, October 1990.

54. Angel Irlandez, "$20 Million Imelda Loot Sale," *Philippines Free Press,* 16 February 1991.

55. Angel Irlandez, "$20 Million Imelda Loot Sale," *Philippines Free Press,* 16 February 1991.

56. Christie's, Magnificent Silver, January 1991 auction catalogue.

57. Angel Irlandez, "$20 Million Imelda Loot Sale," *Philippines Free Press*, 16 February 1991.

58. *FarEastem Economic Review,* 29 September 1988.

59. Reuters New Service, 16 May 1990.

60. Recovered invoices indicated the followin art dealers as also havin transacted business with Imelda: James II Galleries, $6,354; Stair & 0., $292,735; Kentshire, $280,000; Wood Export, $5.5 million for "Russian icons"; John Van Lynn, $3,052 "fee in looking for antiques."

61. Rita Reif, "The Grand Antiques Shops of Florence," *New York Times,* 14 April 1900.

62. It is primarily on Fahy's opinion on this painting that some journalists hastened to judge Imelda's collection as consisting of fakes without actually seeing them, glossing over the purchases of paintings which are obviously genuine. Closer research revealed much value to the paintings. Ian Kennedy, a senior vice president and board member of Christie's who heads the firm's Old Master's Paintings Department, later commented on the paintings: "I do know that there are a lot of rumors about the poor quality of these paintings, but when I saw them I was agreeably surprised" [William Sherman, "The Marcos Collection," *ARTnews,* October 1990]. The Silver and the Old Masters collection was initially appraised between $6-10 million, but the January 1991 auction brought in more than $20 million. Of this amount, almost $14 million was for the paintings. After the auction, Christopher Hartop, another senior vice president at Christie's said, "We knew the sale would be strong, but we were surprised how strong it was" [Angel Irlandez, "$20 Million Imelda Loot Sale," *Philippines Free Press,* 16 February 1991]. Latest opinion thus seems to contradict the initial assessments. In any case, our concern here is the amount that Imelda has spent to acquire these items. There seems to be no question concerning this point.

63. Angel Irlandez, "$20 Million Imelda Loot Sale," *Philippines Free Press*, 16 February 1991.

64. Angel Irlandez, "$20 Million Imelda Loot Sale," *Philippines Free Press*, 16 February 1991.

65. Zurbaran's *David and Goliath* was estimated to be worth $500,000-$700,000.

66. Kagayonan sa may Dagat Beach Resort in Padang, Legaspi City.

67. We will look at the questionable circumstances under which property from the Olypmic Towers was taken in Chapter V.

68. The painting was later auctioned for $400,000.

69. A more organized effort to dispose of the art works from the Townhouse involved Adnan Khashoggi, the Saudi arms dealer who is a close friend of the Marcos family. Khashoggi's involvement with the Marcoses is discussed in Chapters IV & V.

70. Elliott Stein, "Manila's Angels," *Film,* (Published bimonthly by the Film Society of Lincoln Center.), Vol. 19, No. 5, September-October 1983, pp. 48-55. Emphasis ours.

71. 'To engage in merriment does not mean to engage in stupidity!... It is the insensate orgy of the ages! And all for what? To throw away money when there is so much misery and need! Yes, I see it now, it is the orgy, it is the bacchanal to blot out the suffering of all!" Our translation. Rizal, *Noli Me Tangere*, p. 162.

72. Octavio Paz, "Critique of the Pyramid," *The Other Mexico*, (New York: Grove Press, 1972.)

73. Peter L. Berger, *Pyramids of Sacrifice*: Political Ethics and Social Change, (New York: Basic Books, Inc. 1974.)

CHAPTER I

APPENDIX A: ART WORKS

The following is the inventory of art works Imelda purchased as compiled by government investigators. The list is not complete. For example, it does not include Picasso's *Reclining Woman,* Peter Paul Ruben's *Virgin and Child*, or Rembrandt's *Portrait of a Man*. We have also taken the liberty of correcting the first name of Degas which the inventory incorrectly listed as Edouard. Please refer to Chapter V for a discussion of the attempts to recover these paintings.

ITALIAN

Alessandro Botticelli, Florence, 1444-1510
    Madonna and Child, Tempera on panel, 37x29cm
Alessandro Magnasco, Genoa, 1677-1749
    Christ Heals the Cripple, Oil on canvas, 93.5x70.5cm
    St. Jerome, Oil on canvas, 73x58.5
    Mother with Child, Oil on canvas, 40x30cm
    Couple of Farmers with Children, Oil on canvas, 40x30cm
Amadeo Modigliani
    Jeanne Hebuteme, Oil on canvas, 51x22.15
Amico Di Sandro, Florence, 15th century
    Virgin and Child, Tempera on panel, 58x58cm
Andrea Della Robbia
    Madonna and Child, Terracotta relief, 40.5x23, including frame.
Andrea Di *Bodiaiuto*
    Enthroned Madonna Surrounded by Saints, Tempera on panel, 66x67cm.
Andrea Di Niccolo, Siena, 1440-1514
    St. Agostino, Tempera on panel, 161x54cm
    St. Biagio, Tempera on panel. 161x54cm
Antonio Giovanni Canaletto, Venice, 1697-1768
    La Piazetta of Saint Marcus Square, Oil on canvas, 66x104cm
    Padua Landscape with Prato dello Valle, Oil on canvas, 42x85.5cm
    View of the Grand Canal in Front of Saint Marcus Square with the Doggia Palace, Oil on canvas, 66x104cm
    The San Marco Basin with the Island of San Giorgio, Oil on canvas, 61x99cm
    The Departure of the Bucentaur on Ascension, Oil on canvas, 44x73cm
    Portico of a Venetian Palace, Oil on canvas, 128x93cm
    The Grand Canal with the Rialto Bridge, Oil on canvas, 63x88cm
Benvenuto Di Giovanni, Siena, 1436—1518
    The Coronation of the Blessed Virgin Mary, Tempera on panel, 97x58
Bernardino Funagai, Siena, 1460-1516
    Resurrection with Two Angels, Tempcra on panel, 42x62cm
Filippino Lippi, Spoleto, 1457-1504
    St. Julian and the Martyrdom of St. Catherine of Alexandria, Tempera on panel, 135x18cm
Fra Filippo Lippi

Madonna and Child (1460), Oil on panel, 20x12
Francesco Guardl, Pitigliano, 1702-1778
Imaginary View with Marine Life, Building and Arch of Triumph, Oil on canvas, 35x49cm
Piazza San Marco, Oil on canvas, 51x94cm
Parade of Allegoric Floats in the Piazza San Marco, Oil on canvas, 67.5x91.5cm
Caprice with Small Bay in a Lagoon, Oil on canvas, 43x56.5
Inside a Harem, Oil on canvas, 44x61cm
Capricio, Oil on canvas, l0x18cm
Triumph of a Roman Warrior, Oil on canvas, 70.5x52cm
Basin of San Marco, Oil on canvas, 18x32
Antonio and Francesco Guardi
At the Drinking Through, Oil on canvas, 85x113cm
Francesco Zuccarelli, Pitigliano, 1702-1788
Landscape with Shepherd, Oil on canvas, 56x74cm
Landscape with Shepherdess, Oil on canvas, 56x74cm
Hillside Landscape, Oil on canvas, 78x118cm
Landscape, Oil on canvas, 64x83cm.
Francesco Zugno, Venice, 1709-1787
Death of Cleopatra (1752), Oil on canvas, 120x87cm
Meeting of Rinaldo and Armida, Oil on canvas, 116x86cm
Friend of Pietro delln Francesca, 15th century
Saving of Napoleone Orsirti Fallen From a Rock, Tempera on panel, 38x68cm
Gaspare Diziani, Belluno, 1639-1767
Heracles, Deianeira, and the Centaur Nessus, Oil on canvas, 78x98cm
Giacomo Amigoni, Naples, 1682-1752
Bacchanal, Oil on canvas, 64x82cm
Gianantonio Guardi, Venice, 1699-1760
Temperance (1739), Oil on canvas, 155x122cm
The Fortress, Oil on canvas, 155x122cm
Giandomenico Tiepolo, Venice, 1727-1804
The Minuet, Oil on canvas, 79x109cm
Bust of Bearded Oriental Man with Turban, Oil on canvas, 72x54cm
Bust of Bearded Oriental Man, Oil on canvas, 65x45cm
Giovanni Antonio Boltraffio, Milan, 1467-1516
Madonna with Child, Oil on panel, 40x30cm
Giovanni Battista Crosato (Giambattista), Venice, 1685-1757
Salome, Oil on canvas, 63x108cm
Giovanni Battista Piazetta (Giambattista), Venice, 1692-1754
Greedy Child and Miserly Old Woman, Oil on canvas, 45x38cm
Giovanni Battista Pittoni (Giambattista), Venice, 1687-1767
Holy Family, Oil on canvas, 38x49
Giovanni Battista Tiepolo, (Giamhattista), Venice, 1696-1770
Portrait of a Bearded Man, Oil on canvas, 48.2x38cm
Madonna with Child Among Saint Anthony, Saint Francis, & Saint Ludwig of Toulouse, Oil on canvas, 51x31.5cm
Portrait of a Young Man, Oil on canvas, 48.2x38cm
Giovanni Bellini (signed: Joannes Bellinus P.), Venice, 1430—1516
Madonna with Child, Oil on panel, 75x57.5cm
Giuseppe Zais, Agordo, 1709-1734
Open-Air Minuet, Oil on canvas, 122x145cm
Large Landscape with Figures, Oil on canvas, 280x372cm
Landscape, Oil on canvas, 71.5x85cm.
Landscape with Figures and Small Bridge, Oil on canvas, 46x60cm
Jacobo Del Sellaio, Florence, 1441-1493

Nativity, Tempera on panel, 78x45cm
Jacopo Tintoretto, Venice, 1518-1594
　　Miraculous Catch, Oil on canvas, 93x101cm
　　The Wise Men at the Temple, Oil on canvas, 43x101
Leandro Basseno, Basano, 1557-1622
　　Deposition, Oil on canvas, 52x34
　　Interior of a Farmhouse, Oil on canvas, 97x132cm
Lippo Memmi, Siena, 1285-1368
　　Altarpiece of Five Saints, Tempera on panel, 220x200cm
Luca Carlevaris, Udine, 1663 - Venice, 1730
　　Piazza San Marino: Looking Toward the Procuratorate, Oil on canvas, 63x37
Marco Ricci, Belluno, 1676 - Venice, 1730
　　Tempest, Oil on canvas, 100x114cm
Michele Marieschi, Venice, 1696-1743
　　Landscape with Village, Oil on canvas, 73x97cm
　　Imaginary Landscape, Oil on canvas, 73x97cm
Neri Di Bicci, Florence, 1419-1491
　　Large Majesty (1460), Tempera on panel, 190x117cm
Paolo Veronese
　　The City of Venice Adoring the Christ Child, Oil on canvas, 39.75x55.75
Pietro Longhi, Venice, 1702-1785
　　The Charlatan, Oil on canvas, 62x51cm
　　The Fortuneteller, Oil on canvas, 62x51cm
Pseudo - **Pier Francesco Fiorentino**, 15th Century
　　Virgin with Child Blessing the Battistino, Tempera on panel, 65x37cm.
Raphael (Raffaello Sanzio), Urbino, 1483-1520
　　St. Catherine of Alexandria, Tempera on panel
Rosalha Carriera, Venice, 1675-1757
　　Half Figure of a Young Woman, Pastel on paper, 53x43cm
Sano Di Pietro, Siena, 1406-1481
　　St. Catherine of Siena, Tcmpera on panel, 50x33cm
　　St. Berdardino ofSiena, Tempera on panel, 50x33cm
Sebastiano Ricci, Belluno, 1676 - Venice, 1730
　　Last Supper, Oil on canvas, 65x101cm
Segna Di Buonaventura, Siena, 1298-1326
　　Majesty, Tempera on panel, 183x96cm,
Titian (Tiziano Vecellio), Pieve dc Cadore, 1487-1576
　　Giulio Romano, Oil on canvas, 102x87cm

FRENCH
Albert Marquet
　　Algerian View
Auguste Renoir
　　paintin of undetermined title
　　Jeunes Filles au bord de L'eau, Oil on canvas, 12.75x16.5
Bonnard Pierre
　　Baignard Au Grand-Lemps (1899), 14.5xl7
Camille PIssaro
　　Jardin De Kew Pres Dela Serre, 21.25x25.5
Claude Monet, 1840-1926
　　Rain, Oil on canvas, 24x29
　　L'Eglise at La Seine a Vetheind, Oil on canvas, 23x28.5
Edgar Degas
　　Danseuse S'habtllant, Pastel, 25.5x18.5
　　Trois Danseuse ($860,000), Mixed media, 375x3l,75

Le Petit Dejeuner a la Sortie du Bain, Pastel, 121cmx92cm
Edouard Manet
Mary Laurent a la Violette, Pastel on linen, 22 x14
Francois Boucher
Apothesis of Aeneas
L Aube, 17.5x10
Henri Fantln Latour
Sweet Peas, 24x20.5 w/antique frame
Rosa Tremieres (Hollyhocks), Oil on canvas, 28.5x23.5.
Henri Matisse
Head of Woman, Oil on canvas, 25.5x19.25
Maurice Utrillo
La Maison Blanche, Oil on canvas, 25.63x235
Paul Cesanne
Aix-En-Provence, Oil on canvas, 18.3x21.7
Paul Gauguin
Still Life with Idol, Oil on canvas, 18.25x15
EM?
Woman sitting with and flower on lap beside a sitting dog
Portrait of a woman holding a pencil
Paule Gobillard
Jeune Femme Au Piano, Oil on canvas, 21.5x18
Jeane Femme En Rouge, Oil on canvas, 22x18
Paysage Du Midi, Oil on canvas, 15x18
Panier de Pains, Oil on canvas, 15x18.25
Cope De Fleurs, Oil on canvas, 15x18.25
Jeune Femme A la Robe Rouge, Oil on canvas, 21.5x18.5
Jeune Fernme Au Chapeu, Oil on canvas, 21.75x18
Lecture Au Jardin, Oil on canvas, 16x21.25
Vase De Fleurss, Oil on canvas, 22x18
La Visite, Oil on canvas, 19.5x24
Vase De Fleurs, Oil on canvas, 16.15x13.25
Nu Endormi, Oil on canvas, 215x25.5
Vase de Fleurs, Oil on canvas, 14.25x12.5
Vase De Fleurs, Oil on canvas, 15x13
Nature Marie, Oil on canvas, 6x8
Portrait De Petite Fille, Oil on canvas, 25,5x21
Jeune Femme S'habillant, Oil on canvas, 26x21.5
Jeane Femme Au Chignon, Oil on canvas, 29x23.75
Jeane FernmeA La Robe Rose, Oil on canvas, 32x35
La Conversation, Oil on canvas, 25.5x32
La Contre, Oil on canvas, 18x15
Bord De Mer, Oil on canvas, 9.75x13.25
Vue D'Assise, Oil on canvas, 15x18
Le blesnil, Oil on canvas, 18x15
Roses Tremieres Au Mesmil, Oil on canvas, 15x18
Pnysage Du Midi, Oil on canvas, 15x18.25
Paysage, Oil on canvas, 18x15
Portrait De FemmeA L'evenluil, Oil on canvas, 18x13
FemmeA La Rose, Oil on canvas, 16.25x13.25
Mme. Valery a Dinard, Oil on canvas, 16.25x13
Bord De Mer, Oil on canvas, 13x16.5
Clair: Matin Aux Bruyeres, Oil on board, 16.5x10.5
Paysage, Oil on canvas, 10.75x14
La Tonnelle, Oil on canvas, 11x14

Vase De Fleurs, Oil on board, 11.5x14
Le Trais Pommes, Oil on canvas, 9.5x13
An Salon, Oil on canvas, 36x23.5
Nature Morte, Oil on canvas, 18x21.75
Fleurs Et Fruits, Oil on canvas.
La Tasse De The, Oil on canvas, 28.5x23.5
Vase De Fleurs, Oil on canvas, 25.5x21
Le Demier Essayage, Oil on canvas, 39x38
Jeane Femme Tricotant Pres d'Une Fenetre, Oil on canvas, 18x215
Nu Se Coifiant, Oil on canvas, 24x19.5
Femme Au Chapeau, Oil on canvas, 24x19.5
Paysage De Cagnes, Oil on canvas, 13x9.5
Le Jardin Fleur, Oil on canvas, 15x18.5
Le liameau, Oil on canvas, 13.5x18
Au Bord De La Mer, Oil on canvas, 13x16.25
Panier de Fruits, Oil on canvas, 19.5x25.5
Vade Fe Fleurs, Oil on canvas, 5.5x21.5
Jeane Femme Tricotant Pres De La Ferrctre, Oil on canvas, 21.5x18

SPANISH
El Greco
Coronation of the Virgin
Francisco Goya, 1746-1828
La Marques de Sta. Cruz, Oil on canvas, 49.75x81.75
Francisco Zurbaran, 1598-1664
The Holy Family, Oil on canvas, 32.75x24
David and Goliath
Pablo Picasso
Head of a Woman (1954), Oil on canvas, 65x54cm
Fruit dish, Bottle and Guitar (1914), Oil on canvas, 92x73cm

FLEMISH AND DUTCH
Dirk Hals,
Interior with Musicians and Backgammon Players (1628), Oil on panel, 30.13x53.75
Frans Hals
Portrait of a Youn Man, Oil on canvas, 65x49cm.
Portrait of Young Woman
Gerrit von Honlhorst, Holland, 1590-1656
The Seduction, Oil on canvas, 41.75x 54.38
Jan Brueghel the Younger
Allegory of Venus at the Forge of Vulcan (1628), Oil on panel, 165x28.38
Allegory of Earth with flora Surrounding Patti and Satyr, Oil on panel, 16.5x28.38
(companion piece of preceeding)
Jan Cossiers, 1600-1671
Jesus Crucrfied, Oil
Jan Gnifier
Extensive Winter Landscape Skaters and Village, Oil on panel, 14x19
Jan Stun, Leiden, 1626-1679
Merry Making in a Dutch Garden, Oil on panel, 25x 18.5
Jan van Bylaw
A Musician, Oil on canvas, 39x33
Peter Brneghel the Younger
The Adoraa'on of the Kings (1617), Oil on panel, 15.25x225
Peter van Schendel, 1806—1870
Bay with the Torch, 35x295cm

Piet Mondrian, 1872-1944
  undetermined title, paintng with yellow, white and blue.
  Eucabpals, Oil on canvas, 51x41cm.
Sir Anthony van Dykc, Antwerp, 1599 - London - 1641
  An Apostle (Saint Simon?), Oil on canvas, 109x89cm.
Vincent van Gogh, 1853-1890
  Peasant Woman "finding Bobbins, Water Color, 13x16.5

OTHERS
Abraham Janssens
  Peace and Abundance Binding the Arrows of War, Oil on canvas, 152x120cm
Barent Avercamp
  Winter Pleasures with a Horse-Drawn Sleigh near Kampen, Oil on panel, 12x21
Casper Netscher
  Young Woman wk}: a Parrot, Oil on panel, 34x27cm
David Teniers the Younger
  A Rugged Hilly Landscape with Elegant Figures and Monks at a Grotto, Oil on canvas, 163x229cm
Francis Bacon, English
  Self Portrait (1963), Oil on canvas, 165x145cm
  Masmrbaa'on
Marcellus Koflermans,
  Glanficau'on of the Virgin (1559), Oil on panel, 48x48
Rene Magritte, Belgium
  La Lumiere des Coincidence (1958), 10x 12.5
Unsigned
  SL Peter or Paul, Oil on canvas, 35x25

CHAPTER I

APPENDIX B: PARTIAL LIST OF JEWELS

The following is a partial list of Imelda's jewels. it re resents only the jewels inventoried by US Customs officials in Hawaii when she entered the US after Marcos' downfall. Parts of her collection must have been kept elsewhere since some jewels Imelda is known to have purchased are not reflected in the inventory. The total of the estimates for these jewels is $3,351,296.00. It is important to note that the prices here are merely estimates made by US Customs authorities. A New York jeweler familiar with both the New York and European jewelry market was of the opinion that these estimates were on the low side.

$44,410.00	diamond—studded hair comb
$18,835.00	gold crown with diamonds & 22 mabe and cultured pearls
$376,990.00	necklace with 5 large sapphires, diamonds, & 7 small sapphires
$768,910.00	emerald broach with 8 emeralds and diamonds
$47,105.00	tiara with mabe pearl center, diamonds, & rubies
$1,487,415.00	set of bracelet, earrings, broach of sapphires, rubies, diamonds
58,286.00	6—pearl tiara with diamonds (Catchpole & Williams, London)
$305,500.00	4 tiaras with diamonds, (1 4k diamond in center)
$140.00	4 gold settings
$2,745.00	pair of diamond earrings in gold setting
$2,960.00	twined 7-strand double-chocker freshwater pink/white pearls, 14k white—gold & 14kt yellow gold diamond chip clasp

$405.00	chocker, multi-color stone, pearls, rope tie
$325.00	antique chocker porcelain set w/stones & pearls
$7,120.00	multi-strand baby pearl double chocker w/2 ea barrel clasp onyx w/yellow gold & set w/diamond
$935.00	chocker &stmnd seed pearl 4 gold, 4 white w/14k yellow gold set w/diamond clasp
$9,160.00	multi-strand baby arl chockerw/ 2 each 14k yellow gold set w/ ruby & diamonds
$1,770.00	necklace 11~stran white cultured pearls, small 4-section gold dividers
$1,300.00	chocker 10—strand pink cultured pearls, small w/ 18k yellow gold clasp, broach clasp flower shape set /w petals of polish stones w/pink corals & diamonds
$2,500.00	pearl pendants set w/diamonds & amethyst on silver chain
$1,380.00	chocker fresh water pearls 20~strand w/14k yellow gold clasp set/w multi rubies, sapphires & diamonds
$2600.00	3—strand pearl necklace 7x75 w/pendant and clasp 18k set w/rubies, emeralds, sapphires & diamonds
$2,265.00	Necklace 8—strand freshwater pearls w/14k gold clasp set w/rubies
$500.00	9 pieces antique gold bracelet set w/24k pearls
$2,980.00	freshwater pearl necklace 12-strands w/14k yellow gold clasp set w/diamonds
$1,310.00	bracelet freshwater pearls 4-strands white and 6—strand pink w/14k yellow gold clasp set w/diamonds
$465.00	14k gold bracelet set w/37 pearls
$750.00	necklace freshwater pearls 9—strand w 14k gold clasp set w/9 pearls
331,485.00	8-strand freshwater pearl necklace w gold clasp in flower design consisting of pearls & diamonds
$2,420.00	hair comb, same design as clasp
52,420.00	broach, same design as clas
$250.00	hand-cut crystal chocker W Silver clasp
$2,500.00	cultured arl necklace 2-strand 7mm w/silvcr clasp
$790.00	pearl nec lace 2-strand 14k white gold clasp set w/diamond
$1,700.00	antique necklace gold color metal (unknown)
$750.00	freshwater pearl chocker 12—strand w/14k white gold clasp w/diamonds
$195.00	pair of mabe pearl culflinks, 14k yellow gold
$60.00	pair of pearl earrings
$160.00	pair of pearl w/diamond 14k yellow gold cufflinks
$235.00	mabe pearl ring and earrings, 14k yellow gold
$345.00	set (tux-3 studs 2 cufflinks) pearl w/diamonds
$250.00	set ring matching earrings mabe pearl 14k
$525.00	antique bracelet 18k mabe pearl and paradox $5,400.00 27 loose strung black pearls strand
$1,575.00	5-strands black pearl temporarily strung $1,350.00 9-strand temporarily strung, blue pearls 65 mm $1,040.00 8-strand temporarily strung blue pearls, 6.5-75 mm $1,050.00 5-strand temporarily strung blue pearls 8x8-5mm $1,450.00 10-strand temporarily strung blue pearls, 7-5mm
$1005.00	3-strand temporarily strung blue pearls, 8x8-5mm
$450.00	3-strand temporarily strung blue pearls, 8x8-5mm
$390.00	3-strand temporarily strung blue pearls, 7x6-5mm
$420.00	2-strand temporarily strung, 8x8-5mm
$330.00	1-5 strand temporarily strung blue pearls 8-5-8mm
$875.00	7-strand temporarily strung blue pearls 6-5-7mm $1,000.00 1-strand permanently strung pearl w/silver clasp 8.5mm
$270.00	2-strand temporarily strung pearls, 7-7-5mm $1,575.00 9-strand temporarily strung pearls 7-7-5mm
$1,560.00	13-strand temporarily strung, 8mm
$2,760.00	4-strandtemporarily strung, 9mm

$2,250.00	6-strandtemporarily strung, 7-5-8mm
	3-strand temporarily strung, 8-8-5mm $1,000.00 8-strand
	temporarily strung, 6-5-7mm
$990.00	2-strandtemporarily strung, 8mm
$2,375.00	19-strand temporarily strung, 6-5-7mm
$1,140.00	6-strand temporarily strung, 7-5-8mm
$1,650.00	11-strand temporarily strung, 7-5-8mm
$450.00	3-strand temporarily strung pearls, 6-6-5mm
$375.00	5-strand temporarily strung pearls 5-5-6mm
$250.00	2-strand temporarily strung pearls, 6-5-7mm
$1,275.00	3-strand temporarily strung, pearls, 7-5-8mm
$240.00	2-strand temporarily strung pearls, 7-7-5mm
$990.00	2-strand temporarily strung pearls, 8-8-5mm
$500.00	2-strand temporarily strung pearls, 7-7-5mm
$560.00	2-strand temporarily strung pearls. 8-8-5mm
$500.00	2-strand temporarily strung pearls. 7 7-5mm $1,530.00 10-strand
	temporarily strung, mixed pearls $1,500.00 6-strand temporarily strung 8-85mm pearls
$720.00	3-strand temporarily strung, pearls, 8-5-9mm
$560.00	2-strand temporarily strung pearls. S-S-5mm $2,475.00 5-strand
	temporarily strung pearls. S-8-5mm
$620.00	2-strand temporarily strung pearls. 65mm $1,230.00 3-strand temporarily
	strung pearls, S-S-5mm
$450.00	3-strand temporarily strung pearls. 7-7-5mm $1,875.00 5-strand
	temporarily strung pearls. S-S-5mm
$750.00	2-strand temporarily strung pearls. S-8--5mm
$770.00	4-strand assorted-size pearls temporarily strung necklace
$590.00	3-strand temporarily strung peart bracelet
$270.00	2 necklaces, temporarily strung
$225.00	120 loose pearls, mixed sizes
$1,010.00	16 loose pearls, mixed sizes
$225.00	48 loose pearls, mixed sizes
$1,020.00	130 loose pearls, mixed sizes
$355.00	assorted pearls
$750.00	pair of yellow gold broach w/diamond pendant
$210.00	silver diamond earrings
$70.00	pair *at* yellow gold carnngs w/3 pearls each
$70.00	yellow gold nng w/3 pearls
$95.00	yellow gold pearl amethyst brooch
$60.00	pearl and diamond pendant
$20.00	gold chain 750
$265.00	black coral/diaraond earrings A nng
$12.00	4 pieces costume-jewelry necklace
$6.00	2 pieces costume jewelry necklace
$60.00	1 yellow gold nng w/ 1 white, 1 black pearl
$5.00	1 side only pearl yellow gold earring
$20.00	9 pieces yellow gold bell shape spacers
$65.00	13 pieces black pearls
$50.00	Raymond Weil Genieve quartz wristwatch
$75.00	Seiko quartz wristwatch brown strap men's
$75.00	Gucci quartz wnstwatch
$70.00	men's black onyx nng, 14k gold
$75.00	men's Gucci quartz watch
$185.00	pearl on black coral cufflink matching studs
$135.00	pearl on mother *at* pearl cufflinks w/rnatchtng studs
$100.00	diamond cufflinks w/matching studs
$90.00	blue sapphire gold cufflinks
$235.00	pearl w/diamond cufflink w/matching studs
$265.00	diamond black, onyx 14k yellow gold cufflink
$260.00	Cabashon amethyst cufflinks

$170.00	mabe pearl cufflinks
$170.00	same as above
$50.00	pearl cufflinks w/matching studs
$200.00	ruby small diamond cufflink w/matching studs
$200.00	4 boxes containing cufflinks
$190.00	14k yellow gold cuf flinks with 9 rubies each
$50.00	pair white gold and pearl cufflinks
$200.00	pair of gold cufflinks
$200.00	pair of gold w/diamond chips cufflinks
$210.00	pair gold w/diamond chips cufflinks
$250.00	gold cufflinks with matching tie clip
$285.00	pair of cufflinks with matching studs
$50.00	pair mabe pearl cufflinks
$245.00	pair of gold cufflinks
$145.00	pair 14k yellow gold pearl cufflinks w/matching studs
$425.00	gold cufflinks w/matching gold ring
$75.00	pair of cufflinks w/ 4 small stones of ruby, sapphire, and emerald
$450.00	pair of gold ruby w/diamond cufflinks
$75.00	pair of cufflinks
$165.00	pair of pearl cufflinks w/matching studs
$50.00	pair of cufflinks
$335.00	pair of gold cufflinks w/Cabachon amethyst stone
$2,295.00	pair of sapphire w/diamond cufflinks
$80.00	2 pearl bracelets
$50.00	1 pearl bracelet
$630.00	pair of Cabachon amethyst cufflinks
$720.00	pair of 14k yellow gold bird shape diamond/ruby necklace
$2,715.00	14k yellow gold w/dinmond chips necklace
$65,495.00	diamond earrings w/diamond hair comb, approx. 20 cts
$145.00	pair of gold cufflinks
$75.00	Chandler gold pocket watch
$190.00	gold w/diamond chips
$375.00	gold w/diamond ring, broach, earring quartz
$600.00	4-strand small pearls
$185.00	broach & chain gold tennis racket w/diamond w/one stud
$25.00	gold necklace
$230.00	Cabachon cufflink
$90.00	gold w/gold engraved brochure
$525.00	gold broach w/multi colored stones w/ matching earrings
$720.00	gold and diamond bracelet
$240 00	5 matching broach, gold w/diamond and quartz 4-leaf clover
$1,115.00	2 broaches: 1) white stones diamonds, amethys, emeralds, and 2) diamonds and white stone
$200.00	cufflinks, enamel on gold
$260.00	gold bead necklace
$125.00	gold pocket watch
$10,350.00	gold and diamond bracelet
$285.00	topaz cufflink set
$170.00	gold and enamel cufflinks
$7,600.00	pearl, gold, emerald, diamond necklace w/ matching earrings
$4,425.00	multi-stone & crystal necklace w/diamonds with pair of emerald, ruby, diamond earrings
$1,885.00	gold and multi-stone necklace w/ matching earrings & ring
$635.00	gold chain w/scissor A knife pendant
$55.00	gold bracelet w/peart

$650.00	gold chain w/14k bullion block
$150.00	mother of peart w/diamond bracelet & matching ring
$280.00	white gold, green & white jade broach
$220.00	gold w/green stone
$130.00	gold ring w/6 pearls
$425.00	men's gold ring w/amethyst
$260.00	men's gold ring w/aquamarine
$1,212.00	gold ring w/emerald & diamonds
$610.00	gold ring w/ruby A 2 diamonds
$5,670.00	ruby & diamond earrings, gold setting
$625.00	gold bangle bracelet
$75.00	Longine watch gold color, men's
$250.00	Cartier watch
$250.00	same as above
$1,305.00	Chopard Geneve, women's gold watch & band diamonds & rubies
$2,500.00	Chopard Geneve men's gold watch
$115.00	18k Mop/red enamel, w/diamond chip butters
$2330.00	gold Cartier watch w/gold bracelet
$25.00	Alba quartz watch
$50.00	lady's watch w/black strap
$7,695.00	18k gold Rolex watch w/black face

Chapter II

THE DEVELOPMENT OF CRONY CAPITALISM

Government is the great fiction, through which everybody endeavours to live at the expense of everybody else.

— Frédéric Bastiat, Essays on Political Economy, 1872 [1]

Civil govemment, so far as it is instituted for the security of property, is in reality instituted for the defence of the rich against the poor, or of those who have some property against those who have none at all.

— Adam Smith, Wealth of Nations, 1776 [2]

No vacila el mas timido gobemante en dictar una ley que ha de producir la miseria y la lenta agonia de miles y miles de subditos, prosperos, trabajadores, felices lal vez, para satisfacer un capricho, una ocurrencia, el orgullo...

— Jose Rizal, El Filibusterismo, 1891*

("The most timid ruler will not hesitate to impose a law that would cause the misery and slow suffering of thousands and thousands of prosperous, hard-working, and perhaps happy, subjects to satisfy a whim, a fancy, vanity..." Our translation. Rizal. Fl Filiburtcrismo, (Game, 1891), p.249.)

TWO TRADITIONS

The profligacy associated with Imelda is not new. Members of the economic and social elite in the Philippines flaunted their wealth long before Marcos took power. There is historical evidence that members of the local elite engaged in needless spending and crass exhibitionism even as early as the previous century.

Some of the accounts of how wealthy Filipinos of the previous century spent their money and amused themselves reveal how they were equally capable of the appalling behavior we usually associate with Imelda. There is an account, for example, of how a rich plantation owner and his wife visited the Paris World Fair in 1889 and later went on a shopping spree. The couple bought so many items that they later had to charter a whole ship to transport the merchandise from Europe to the Philippines. There is also the story of how a rich opera afficionado loved to listen to the performances of a visiting Italian opera company and imported European orchestra so much that he would buy all the empty seats in the house to assure that the performance would begin on time. The same person was also reported to have clapped so enthusiastically during the perfprmances that he accidentally dropped his 7-karat diamond ring while gesticulating. It is said that he did not even bother to bend down and look for the ring in t e dark. Another wealthy plantation owner from Silay, a town in the sugar-rich province of Negros, maintained his own orchestra so that he could fisten to music whenever he wanted. His cousin from the neighboring city of Iloilo retained his own private soprano and tenor so that he could fall asleep during his siesta as he listened to their singing. An account of the how a wealthy family from the province of Batangas conducted its summer Sunday picnics relates that servants would be sent ahead and would be charged with preparing the picnic grounds by paving it with Persian carpets and chairs imported rom Vienna. During the picnic proper, servants waited upon the family members, while violins played in the background [3].

Much of the behavior of some members of the wealthy classes in the previous century was so totally out of taste that it was often the subject of ridicule. The characterization of Dona Victorina and Dona Consolacion, two totally unsavory society matrons, in Jose Rizal's novels *Noli Me Tangere* (1887) and *El Filibusterismo* (1891) [4] was an attempt to document this tasteless behavior. While these two novels by the Philippine national hero were primarily directed against the abuses of the Spanish friars who controlled the country, they also contained many critical observations about how Filipinos conducted themselves. Rizal's description of Dona Victorina, a wealthy but pretentious woman, and Dona Consolacion, a politically powerful town harlot, portrayed the insecurity, deceit, and gaudy self-indulgence of the society matrons who commanded wealth and power but were completely without breeding. Some of these women from the upper classes wore so much jewelry yet carried themselves totally without refinement that Spanish friars derisively called them *bestias cargada de oro* (beasts laden with gold).

The elite at the turn of the century was equally ostentatious. There is an existing receipt, dated 11 February 1909, belonging to a certain Dr. A. Bautista Lim for a banquet costing 1,100 pesos [5]. The banquet was held at the *Club Filipino,* an exclusive private club for the Spanish-speaking elite, and was catered by *Gran Hotel y Restaurant de Francia,* a French restaurant in Escolta, then Manila's commercial center. The banquet for 75 people included 17 bottles of French champagne, 18 bottles of white wine, 17 bottles of red wine (St. Emilion), as well as other drinks [6]. The average cost for each guest amounted to almost 15 pesos. This was an extraordinary amount. A normal meal at an ordinary Chinese restaurant, consisting of soup, one viand, an unlimited amount of rice, plus two sticks of cigarettes in lieu of dessert, cost only 10 centavos. Given that the ordinary worker at this time earned around 70 centavos for a day's work, the cost for each guest during this banquet was roughly the equivalent of a more than a month's wages of the average laborer. Assuming that he did not have to eat and spend for other necessities, the average laborer would have had to work a total of six and a quarter years to be able to throw such a party for a single night.

There is an account that a wealthy man in the 1930's would occasionally heat his coffee by burning 100.00 peso bills under the pot. The man was related to a Philippine president by marriage and was the heir to a vast fortune made from sugar plantations in the province of Iloilo. While such eccentric behavior may not have been practiced by all members of the elite, it certainly does show the extreme steps certain individuals took to prove their wealth to other people.

Emerging from trauma of the Second World War and savoring the political independence granted by the United States, members of the elite indulged themselves during the period immediately following the war. In the late 1940's and in the early 50's, local elites from various provinces tried to outdo each other in flaunting their wealth. The Mancomunidad Pampanguefia, a social circle composed of wealthy families from Central Luzon, held parties and social gatherings expressly to parade the latest in fashion. The parties were carefully engineered so that the national dailies could publicize in detail the apparel worn by the socieiy matrons. The newspaper articles from this period meticulously describe what the more socially prominent matrons wore, including the prices each woman paid for their formal gowns. As recorded in the newspapers of this period, the price of these dresses were between $2,500 and $5,000 [7]. What did these amounts mean in the late 1940's and the 1950's? In the Philippines, it meant that the laborer from the Central Luzon plantations of these families had to work the equivalent of more than 12 years to be able to earn enough to buy one of these gowns. Since agricultural workers in the Philippines earned $1.60 a day in the 1950's, this meant one of these $5,000 gowns represented the equivalent of 3,125 working days or more than 12 years of labor [8].

It is therefore easy to understand why agrarian unrest festered in the provinces of Central Luzon. An agrarian rebellion developed, led by the Huks, a peasant organization which ha been at the forefront in the struggle against Japanese military occupation. To attract members, all the Huks had to do was to clip the newspaper accounts of these parties and post them in the barrios Without further comment. The glaring inequality was self-evident.

The elites from other provinces were not to be outdone. The Ilongo families from the sugar-producing provinces of the Visayas region had their own social gatherings. They had the Kahirup, asocial circle largely composed of the wealthy Negrense fimilies from the sugar—rich island of Negros. To this circle belongs the economically powerful and politically influential clans such as the Lopez, Montelibano, Ledesma, and Lacson families which exerted a major influence in the pre-Marcos political scene. They engaged in a form of social competition with the elites of other provinces and ribbed the Pampanguenos from Central Luzon for having wealth but not knowing enough about flaunting it.

The situation was again not different in the 1960's and in period right before Marcos imposed martial law in 1972. The advent of the jet plane ave members of the elite a way to alleviate their boredom. One practice of the very rich at this time was to take quick plane trips to Hong Kong, arrive in time for lunch, shop for a few hours, and then go ack to Manila on the same day [9]. Trips such as these represented the beginnings of the Filipino version of the jet-set society which Imelda later brought to unimagined heights.

The high point of social extravagance prior to the Marcos dictatorship is considered by many as the birthday celebration of Eugenio Lopez Sr. in 1968. Don Eugenio, as he was reverently referred to by many of his contemporaries, was possibly the richest man in the Philippines prior to Marcos' regime of plunder. He had many interests, among them sugar plantations, newspaper and television companies, and the national electric utility. Since it was reputedly due to his monetary support that aspirants to the Philippine presidency succeeded, he was considered by many as the patron of Philippine presidents. This birthday party was the grandest social event at this time. His friends from the royalty of Europe were invited. A jet was chartered from San Francisco to transport the guests coming from the US. The guests feasted on beluga caviar, which was plentiful, and drank to their hearts content the expensive champagne which freely flowed from a large specially-designed fountain. A well-known band, imported from the US for the event, entertained the guests. It is said that it was this party that gave Imelda her ideas of how to live and spend.

As members of the traditional elite continued to engage in ostentatious behavior, other Filipinos became critical of such needless spending. The Lopez party, for example, became the object of much criticism before, during, and after the affair. Since plans for such an expensive bash were publicized earlier, student activist groups, as well as other socially concerned individuals, were able to stage a picket near the Lopez part to protest what they considered to be socially irresponsible behavior. The demonstrators, many of whom were seminarians from the Divine Word Seminary and students of exclusive private schools, were later roughed up and dispersed by the police and hosed down by the Manila Fire Department who considered the picket to be an irritant to what was dubbed as "the party of the century." The demonstrators were bitter with the authorities for using force to disperse them and were very disillusioned with what they perceive to be the duplicity of the elite as represented by Raul Manglapus, a Filipino politician related to the Lopez family through marriage [10]. Manglapus had earlier encouraged the demonstration in the name of social reform but had attended the party as one principal guests of the evening.

Since criticism of the behavior of the affluent continued to mount during this time, a respected member of the elite offered an apologia by way of making distinctions between the rich in Philippine society. This particular millionaire, who was equally rich but was not known to lapse into scandalous spending as did the other members of the elite, posited that the rich in the Philippines were divided into three groups, which he termed as the working, the profligate, and the idle rich. He argued that those who worked to acquire their wealth should be spared from the criticisms levelled at the other typesof wealthy Filipinos [11].

It was in this atmosphere of social ferment and political questioning that Marcos declared martial law, assumed dictatoria powers, and instituted crony capitalism.

Our discussion of the historical development of crony capitalism started with a brief survey of how the economic and social elite flaunted their wealth because it places the whole matter in context. Many condemn Imelda's lavish spending for the wrong reasons. Some criticize her not for the great amounts that she spent but because her humble or poor origins prevented her from making tasteful or socially proper purchasing decisions. Most of members of the Philippine elite berate her precisely on the grounds that she was *nouveau riche* and did not have any breeding. Our short discussion of the past spendin habits of membersof the Philippine elite was important because it showed that the scandalous purchases that Imelda indulged in were nothing more than a faithful continuation of these practices. This assertion might prove to be slightly disconcerting to those who are predisposed to look for a new element in Imelda's behavior and develop novel theories concerning her spending habits. The only thing to be pointed out is that there is nothing new, and the only revolutionary conclusion is that Imelda was totally faithful to Philippine elite's tradition of ostentation, of unabashed self-indulgence, of what Thorstein Veblen, the eccentric economist who wrote the acerbic *The Theory of the Leisure Class*, called *conspicuous consumption* -- objects are bought and consumed not because they are needed but because they are a status symbol for one's opulence [12].

A second pattern can be discerned within the chaotic flow of events in Philippine history. This second theme is more important than the previous category of conspicuous consumption because it is the defining trait of Marcos' crony capitalism.

The central characteristic of Marcos' crony capitalism was the use of political power for material gain. This is the most coherent and consistent explanation possible of what occurred in the Philippines during Marcos' rule. Everything that happened during Marcos' time, including the ostentatious behavior of Imelda discribed in the previous chapter, presupposed the abuse of political privilege. To write the history of Marcos' crony capitalism is to document the concrete instances where governmental office was abused for material and personal gain.

The motif of corruption, however, is again not peculiar to Marcos' rule. In the same way that Imelda was merely aping the profligate behavior of the traditional elite, Marcos likewise was merely continuing the long-standing tradition of corruption in Philippine politics. Marcos' corruption was not an aberration from the normal political traditions of the Philippines but was merely the best developed example of that tradition. Corruption, graft, cronyism, patronage, the abuse of political office, and the use of government and state power to further personal ends are the defining characteristics of mainstream Philippine political institutions. Clean government, efficient, positions and promotions based on merit, public service, socially responsible behavior are the exceptions in public office.

One of the earliest examples of the abuse of political privilege for private gain dates back to at least the beginnings of the last century with the practice of the *indulto de comercio* (permit to do business) under the Spanish colonial administration. The *indulto de comercio* was a permit granted to the colonial administrator, the *alcalde mayor*, to engage in business in the province under his jurisdiction. The *alcalde mayor* ruled the provinces for the Spanish crown, acting as provincial governor, judge and interpreter of laws, and general colonial administrator all at the same time.

The position of *alcalde mayor* was a coveted one because the *indulto de comencio* assured substantial wealth to those who were lucky enough to get it. The post of *alcalde mayor* was viewed more as a commercial venture than an administrative post. Aspirants saw the job as a quick way of enriching themselves. The candidates purchased the position from the colonial government. Given the prospects of having complete administrative control over a province, plus the right to conduct business, the prospective *alcalde mayor* was happy to promise a fraction or the whole of a year's salary, or draw a loan, to pay for the position. Since the post was for a fixed term of six years, the natural tendency for the successful *alcalde mayor* was therefore to try to recover his capital in the shortest possible time, pay his debts, and go back to Spain a rich man.

A book describing the conditions in the Philippines in 1810, *Estado de las Islas Filipinos en 1810*, written by a Spaniard, Tomas de Comyn, and published in 1820, related, among others, the extreme corruption that went along with the post of *alcalde mayor* and the *indulto de comercio*. It stated that even servants of the governor, barbers, and ordinary sailors who had no knowledge of the law and administrative affairs manage to land these public posts and were guided only by their "own boisterous passions."

Another book, *Informe Sobre el Estado de las Islas Filipinos en 1842*, written two decades later by another Spaniard, Sinibaldo de Mas, discusses in more detail how the post of alcalde was obtained:

> Upon my arrival at Manila, I asked a very respectable Spaniard who had been in the country for many years about what happens in the provmces. He replied to me: "You know that the alcaldeships are reported to be worth 40,000 or 50,000 duros, and he who seeks one of these posts very earnestly has no other object or hope than to acquire a capital in the six tears the government confers them. Before going to his province, he borrows 8,000 or 20,000 duros from one of the church corporations at such and such a per cent. Besides, he has to pay an interest to those who act as bondsmen for him, both to the government for the royal treasury, and to the church corporations which supply him with money. "

The *alcalde* established a monopoly of credit and trade in the province under his jurisdiction the moment he assumed his post. His political power gave him great advantage over his local competitors. Sinibaldo de Mas, for example, mentioned that no action would be taken whenever thefts would be committed against the competitors of the *alcalde* since the misfortunes of his competitors translated to his obvious advantage. There were reports of instances where the thefts were sometimes even instigated by the *alcalde* himself. Control over local lending was established, and money was lent at usurious rates. A monopoly over the trade of the province's produce was also instituted, leavin the *indio* [13] no other alternative but to sell his products to the *alcalde* or is representatives. Abuses went unchecked by the central colonial government Because of the difficulties of communication and transportation.

Tomas de Comyn summarized effects of the indulto de comercio and its abuse by the *alcaldes*:

> Without examining the inconvenience which may arise from their ignorance, it is yet more lamentable to observe the consequences of their rapacious avarice, which the government tacitly allows them to indulge, under the specious title of **indultos de comercio** . . .
> and these are such that it may be asserted, that the **evil which the indio feels most severely is derived from the very source which was originally intended**

for his assistance and protection, that is, from the alcaldes of the provinces, who, generally speaking, are the determined enemies and the real oppressors of their industry. It is a well known fact, that far from promoting the felicity of the provinces to which he is appointed, the **alcalde** *is mlusively occupied with advancing his private fortune, without being very scrupulous as to the means he employs to do so; hardly is he in office than he declares imself the principal consumer, buyer, and exporterof every production of the prvince.... These miserable beings carry their produce and manufactures to him, who directly or indirectly has fixed an arbitrary price for them. To offer that price is to prohibit any other from being offered -- to insinuate is to command -- the* indios *dare not hesitate -- he must please the* **alcalde***, or submit to his persecution; the alcalde is thus free from all rivalry in his trade...*

Sinibaldo de Mas gave concrete instances of how the *alcalde's* control over trade gave him tremendous opportunities to advance his position at the expense of the *indio*. When the *indio*, for example, delivered rice to the *alcalde*, a larger measuring standard would be used than the one normally employed in the market, wit the effect of undercounting the *indio's* produce. With the case of indigo, another product mentioned by de Mas, some other pretext would be found, such as poor quality and dampness, which would be used to justify a lower price. Sinibaldo de Mas, for example, wrote that

In the province of m---, Don ----, while **alcalde mayor***, was in collusion with the manager of the wine monopoly and they practiced the following. The harvesters came with their wine but were told that it was impossible to receive it. There was a conflict amongst themselves, or they had to return to their village. Then they were told that, if they wished to deposit the wine, they would have to put it in certain jars which had been provided in the storehouse and pay such and such a rent until the administration could introduce it. The harvesters, who needed the money, thereupon sold the wine to the agents of the* **alcalde** *at any price at all in order to return to their homes.*

The power to tax the population also became a great opportunity for the *alcalde* to profit, as Tomas de Comyn shows in his account of how taxes were collected:

The government, desirous of conciliating the interests of the natives with that of the revenue, has in many instances commute the payment of the poll-tax into a contribution in produce or manufactures. A year of scarcity arrives. This contribution then becomes of much higher value than the amount of the tax The payment in produce consequently becomes a loss and even occasions a serious want in their families. They implore the **alcalde** *to make a representation to the government that they may be a allowed to pay the tribute for that year in money. This is exactly one of those opportunities, where, founding his profits on the misery of his people, the* alcalde *can in the most unjust manner abuse the power confided to him. He pays no attention to their representations. He is the zealous collector of the royal revenues; he issues proclamations and edicts, and these are followed by his armed satellites, who seize the harvest, exacting inexorably the tribute, until nothing more is to be obtained.*
Having thus made himself master of the miserable subsistence of his subjects, he suddenly changes his tone -- he is the humble suppliant to the government on behalf of the unfortunate **indios** *whose wants he describes in the most*

pathetic terms, urging the impossibility of their paying the tribute in produce. No difficulty is experienced in procuring permission for it to be paid in money. To save appearance, a small portion of it is collected in cash, and he pays the whole amount to the treasury, while he resells the whole of the produce (generally rice) which has been before collected at an enormous profit.

Our historical excursion into the system of *indulto de comercio* was necessary because it was this system which set the precedent on how those who worked in the government would view public office. It served as the model of behavior for Philippine government functionaries. The work ethic and cultural environment within which Philippine government officials, those elected as well as those a pointed, would later operate was defined at this time. When the modern day Filipino politician runs for elective office, it is not because he is on a social crusade to reform the country. It is because he sees the office he aspires for as an opportunity to enrich himself. He locates wealthy financiers who will bankroll his election expenses and accumulates capital for his election bid. Contributors give to his campaign fund not because they believe in his stated program of government but because they are businessmen who are eager to gain contracts and concessions from the government should their chosen race horse win the elections. Some businessmen play safe and hedge their bets by gambling on all the horses in the race. The politician who wms then uses his office to hand out favors to his financial supporters to repay his debts. Relatives and friends of his supporters are given choice positions in his administration, largesse is distributed in the form of government contracts, and the politician uses his new office to make money or his reelection bid.

Our summary of the descriptions of Tomas de Comyn and Sinibaldo de Mas of the practice of *indulto de comercio* and the behavior of the *alcalde* was therefore not merely an academic exercise but a historical attempt to understand how the work ethic of the Philippine bureaucracy developed. When Sinibaldo de Mas describes how the alcalde calculates his every move in terms of ersonal gain, he could very well have been describing the typical Filipino politician of this century:

> *Finally as he who had come to be an **alcalde**, has had no other object than to acquire wealth, every matter which does not contribute to that object, such as the making of a bridge, or road, the prosecution of evil doers, or any occupation purely of government or justice, distracts and troubles him. On the contrary every means of attaining his end appears to him fitting and good... But to tell the truth, it is not to be wondered that the **alcaldes mayores** work without much scruple. In the space of six years they have to pay their passage from and to Spain; to satisfy the high interest on the amount which their alcaldeship as often cost them; and besides they make their fortunes.*

Lest the accusation be made that the description has been unduly harsh, it should be pointed out that Filipino politicians themselves concur with what has been said about them. Aspirants to political offices have always campaigned against the "graft and corruption" of the incumbent. Should these aspirants win the election on the promise of reforming the government, they would invariably find themselves at the receiving end of the very same criticisms of graft and corruption when election time came anew. The individual faces associated with political offices regularly changed, but what remained constant was the historically and socially defined behavior which assumed that government work was an adventure in personal enrichment rather than a mission of public service.

General Emilio Aguinaldo [14], the first president of the country, made no qualms in claiming public funds as his personal property. it will be recalled that the Spanish colonial government attempted to break the momentum of the revolution by entering into the *Tratado de Paz de Biak na Bato* (Treaty of Peace of Biak na Bato) in 1897, where substantial sums of money were offered to the ilustrado leadership of the revolution if they agreed to stop hostilities against Spain. Four hundred thousand pesos were to be given to Aguinaldo upon his departure for Hong Kong, two hundred thousand was to be given after the surrender of a stipulated number of arms, and two hundred thousand more was to be given after the *Te Deum* was sung at the Cathedral of Manila and the *Palacio Real* in Madrid and an amnesty was declared. While claims would later be made that this money was going to be used to buy more arms to continue the revolution, it is clear that Aguinaldo considered the money as personally his. When three decades later he was asked to render an accounting of the money, Aguinaldo wrote in an open letter in 1929:

> *Hago presente que la cantidad dc P400,000.00 **me pertenecian exclusivamente**, de ocuerdo con las condiciones del Tratado de Paz de Biak na Bato. Sin embargo, impulsado por el deseo de salvar nuesrra Patria de su estado de vasallaje, inverti dicha cantidad en la reanudacion de la Revolucion, conquistando para nuestro pueblo sus mas preciadas libenades. Ysi a pesar de nuestros sacrificios y de los resultados felices de aquellos revoluciones, todavia exigen detalles de su inversion, estoy dispuesto a accederto, a condicion de que **se revelen antes los misterios ocultos de la inversion de muchos milliones de pesos para la campafia por la Independencia** [15].*

The letter contains two significant points.

The first is the direct admission that Aguinaldo considered the 400,000 pesos he received as his personal property: **me pertenecian exclusivamente** (belonged to me exclusively). While Aguinaldo claims that this was a condition of the treaty, it appears that this was more of an eager intepretation on his part rather than an explicit clause in the documents. When he was asked by a companion to account for the 400,000 pesos, Aguinaldo quickly skipped Hong Kong and went to Singapore to avoid a subpoena and make an accounting. No adequate accounting has ever been made [16]. This is an early example of how the Filipino politician never made a clear distinction between the public coffer and his private pocket.

The second crucial point in the letter is Aguinaldo's counter-attack, which is equally revealing. He says he is willing to make an accounting of the money provided that a similar accounting be made of the millions spent in the campaign for independence. It was a direct allusion to the "independence missions" to the United States headed by Sergio Osmefia, Speaker of the Philippine Assembly, and Manuel Quezon, the majority floor leader [17]. The numerous "independence missions" Quezon and Osmer'ia headed were nothing more than costly trips to the US where they engaged in self-aggrandizement and indulged themselves. Considerable sums were spent at these junkets at the country's expense. After Aguinaldo's counter-attack, questions stopped about how the 400,000 pesos was spent.

Quezon, who later served as president from 1935 through 1944 while the country was still under US Commonwealth status, became well-known for his campaign cry "I prefer a government run like hell by Filipinos to a government run like heaven by Americans." While most Filipinos like to think that this slogan was a statement of nationalism, it was in reality an attempt to mask the corruption occurring within the ruling Nacionalista Party, one of the two major political parties in Philippine politics [18]. It was an attempt to hide the corruption within the government by pandering to the anti-American feeling and the aspirations to independence during the Commonwealth period. Claro M. Recto, one of the few genuine nationalists to serve in Congress during this time, later noted that

> The issue of anti-Americanism was so popular that it made the electorate overlook the ten years a corrupt administration the so-called anti-Americans had been giving the people and which had all but ruined the country [19].

Soon after the United States granted political independence to the Philippines after the war, giving the Filipino politician a free rein to abuse his office and run the government "like hell," there were many calls to clamp down on the rampant corruption in the government. The President of the Philippine Senate at that time, Jose Avelino, a key figure in the Liberal Party, the second of the two traditional political parties, adamantly objected to any investigation of corruption in the administration of President Quirino in 1949. The objections of Avelino were recorded by a Filipino journalist:

> Why do you have to order an investigation, Mr. President? If you cannot permit abuses, you must at least tolerate them. What are we in power for? We are not hypocrites. Why should we pretend to be saints when in reality we are not?

A similar indiscretion was committed by Carlos P. Garcia, who served as President from 1957 through 1961, when he rhetorically asked, "Is it wrong to provide for one's old age?"

These quotes have since become a classics in Philippine politics since they came straight from the horse's mouth. The tradition continued with each and every presidential administration in power from the time of political independence in 1946 through the time Marcos became president in 1965. Each presidential candidate routinely accused the incumbent administration of "graft and corruption" and got elected on his pledge of cleaning the government. Marcos' rule was the culmination of this tradition.

THE MARCOS PRESIDENCY

It was with the typical election promise of the Filipino politician that Marcos conducted his campaign for the presidency in 1965. Presenting himself as a social reformer, Marcos boldly stated in an interview with *Life* magazine:

> The first and most essential thing is to stop corruption in government, especially in customs and tax collections. They're bleeding this country to death. It's not easy, but it can be done. What it takes is strong leadership at the top. Once the tremendous powers of the president are properly applied, this country can start up very quickly. Once the government collects all its revenues, we will have

enough fimds for development and progress. We have plenty of blueprints.
What we need now is action [20].

Such rhetoric and double-talk were an integral part of Marcos' olitical style. While campaignin on a platform of clean government, he ha by then already become one of t e country's worst politicians.

Marcos already had a dark past even before he was involved with any government office. He had been convicted beyond reasonable doubt for the murder of Julio Nalundasan, a political opponent of his father, in 1939 [21]. While he claimed to be a guerilla hero during the war and to have been awarded more medals than any other Filipino soldier, later research has shown that these claims to the medals are false and that Marcos in fact may have collaborated with the Japanese [22]. After the war, claiming that he had led a guerilla unit against the Japanese occupation army and that he had supplied cattle to starving American and Filipino troops, he applied for military back pay and compensation for the cattle, but his claims were found to be fraudulent by the US Army [23]. Marcos also reportedly smuggled arms to the forces of Sukarno who were then fighting the Dutch in Indonesia [24].

As a member of the Philippine Congress, first as congressman and later as president of the Senate, Marcos was able to generate great quantities of money with relative ease.

The principal way through which Marcos acquired money as a member of Congress was through the control he exerted over the black market for foreign exchange and the importation of goods into the country in 1963. Marcos authored a law which placed restrictions over the import of goods to the country. Those who wanted to import goods had to secure an import license. Marcos managed to control the granting of these permits, which he later peddled to importers. It was reported that he charged a fee of $5,000 from every businessman who wanted an import license in the early 1960's. Marcos was also able to control the black market for dollars. Businessmen who needed the foreign exchange and could not acquire it from the Central Bank, largely due again to Marcos' control, had to go to him directly to purchase the dollars. A former member of Marcos' cabinet describes Marcos' activities at this time:

> *...Marcos was the lord tong [bribe] collector of every sizeable import license Approved by the Central Bank. He had full time staffs both at his office in Congress and at his residence at San Juan, Rizal to process, follow up and receive cumshaw [bribes] from grateful businessmen... [25]*

On one occasion, when the approval of import permits was being held up by another official of the Central Bank, Marcos went to the official personally and held a gun to his head.

> *So terrified was the bank official that, when Marcos burst into his office and pointed a gun at his forehead, the poor man lost no time in resigning from the bank and emigrating with his family to the United States [26].*

Marcos became a millionaire within a very short time because of this scheme. It was this money he accumulated using his congressional position which allowed him to gain Imelda's hand in such a short time. Marcos showed Imelda his vault, proposed marriage to her even when she was then engaged to another man, and the two got married within 11 days [27].

> ...the Marcos fortune in millions of cold cash was displayed to Imelda before her marriage to Ferdinand. So smitten was Marcos with Imelda that to inveigle her to accepting a dinner date he asked two ladies then with Imelda to come along. On the way to the restaurant, Marcos made some excuse to stop by his bank and invited the three ladies to step inside the vault. As later recounted by one of the witnesses, Imelda's eyes nearly popped out beholding all that cash, not in pesos, but in good old American dollars... Where did Marcos get all that cash since he was neither an industrialist, businessman nor financial wizard with stocks and bonds but was supposed to be an underpaid Filipino congressman? The Marcos family was so poor that by Ferdinand's own account he nearly did not graduate from college because he could not take his final examinations for lack of tuition money. The Marcos biogrpphy relates that it was to get this tuition money from his grandparents that explained Ferdinand's hurried trip to his hometown coincidentally at the time of the Nalundasan murder [28].

Imelda received an 11-karat diamond ring -- one karat for each day she was courted by Marcos. Had she waited a few more days, she surely would have received a more expensive ring, but Imelda could wait no longer. She immediately fell in love with the rich congressman, and marriage came swiftly. After their 1954 wedding, Marcos, now armed with an invaluable political asset, a former beauty queen for a wife, quickly improved his standing in Congress. He became an influential senator and later served as Senate President. By the early 1960's, he was already developing detailed plans for the 1965 presidential elections.

Marcos aaquired the presidency through the successful manipulation of public opinion. inaccurate biography was commissioned, largely dwelling on his spurious heroic war exploits, and it was peddled to Filipino voters and the American intelligence agencies which clandestinely oversaw and guided elections in the former colony. The book, *For Every Tear a Victory,* was published by McGraw-Hill in 1964, in time for the presidential elections the following year. Leonard Saffir, president of the Overseas Press Club of America and executive vice president of the New York public relations firm of Porter/Novelli, recalled the times he served as the New York public relations consultant of Marcos and Imelda in an open letter in the New York Times. Saffir wrote to Imelda as she was about to face trial in New York for racketeering charges:

> *3 November 1988*
> *Dear Imelda Marcos:*
>
> *Welcome back to New York City, where it all started for Ferdie and you some 25 years ago, when he sought the Phflrpine presidency.*
> *The two of you never gave New York its proper place in Filipino history. In fact you won the presidency by denying right down to election day the existence of our "New York strategy. "So now that you're here again, this time to face racketeering charges in Federal district court, it's time to set the record straight.*

*By the way, I hope that don't mind my calling your husband Ferdie. That's what you both asked me to call him back in 1962 in Manila, when we sat around your dining room table mapping out plans to fulfill his dream of becoming president. How refreshing it was for me at that time to hear you talk out democracy in Asia and to listen to your pledge to clean up the graft and corruption that had existed in your country ever since it won its independence. It seems like only yesterday when you, Ferdie and I paraded around the streets of New York visiting every editorial board that would see you. You and Ferdie gave interviews to every journalist I came with who had an interest in your country. It wasn't easy then. After all, Ferdie was a relatively obscure senator... Remember those young women at Finch College in New York City who were moved to the edges of their seats with Ferdie's dynamic talk about life in the Philippines? Well it all worked. You made headlines back in the Philippines. Every word you uttered in New York was on the front pages of your country's newspapers. But we both really know what ultimately defeated your opponent, the incumbent President, Diosdado Macapagal. It was Ferdie's biography, **For Every Tear a Victory** written by the best selling author Hartzell Spence and published by Mchw-Hill in New York in 1964.*

Never in world history has a political campaign been conducted on one issue – a book - as it was in your case, in 1965. Everyone in the Philippines read it. There were editions covering every language. And for those who couldn't read, but could still vote, there was the movie made from the book. Mr. Spence made Ferdie a hero, just as you orchestrated it.

You probably know, by now at least, how the Central Intelligence Agency bought everything in the Spence book, hook, line and sinker. After all, Mr Spence was a much-respected journalist.

In fact, I ourgovemment agencies, as well as most of ourmost important newspapers, treated For Every Tear a Victory *as gospel. The CIA even turned against the candidacy of the former Vice President, Emmanuel Pelaez, who was opposing Ferdie at the time. Instead, our intelligence folk started pushing Ferdie.......let the record show that* For Every Tear a Victory, *the book that won Ferdie the presidency of the Philippines, the book the two of you have always maintained no involvement with, wil go down in history as e world's most successful vanity publishing venture. I'll never forget that Ferdie threatened to have me killed if I revealed that he paid Mr. Spence $15,000 to write the book and guaranteed the sale of 10,000 copies to McGraw-Hill.*

I kept your secret because I believed in him. And what you don't know is that I ke tthe secret even after two agents of Mr. Macapagal offered to buy my story for $50,000....[29]

There was a continuous effort to manipulate public opinion throughout the years of Marcos' rule. Disinformation was among the most important tools Marcos employed. Every detail which was leaked to the pubhc was a calculated step at acquiring either a specific political or commercial objective, or a better image of Marcos.

Even Marcos' golf games became an opportunity for disinformation. Dindo (MI) Gonzalez, who has been writing newspaper columns on golf for more than 35 years, recalled the games be played with Marcos in the 1950's. Gonzalez claimed that Marcos acquired the reputation of being the best golf-playing world leader because he had his caddies lower his golfing card scores and bodyguards would move the balls nearer the hole when no one was looking: "with so many of his bodyguards trailing, he always seemed to get a good lie and seldom, if at all, found himself in a rough." According to Gonzalez, Marcos' bodyguards

> ..kept the ball not only in play, but, I suspect, also kicked it nearer the hole aftera shot. Thus, Marcos' handicap drop d from 14 to 10, and he became known as the chief executive with the lowest handicap in the world.
> ...It stopped being pleasant when he became president... He didn 't feel good when he lost. He would say., "Well, you won this time, but wait till next time. I'll get you. " We used to tremble when he said that, because we were never quite sure what he meant (30)

THE 1972 MARCOS COUP AND CRONY CAPITALISM

Marcos declared martial law in 1972 when his second and constitutionally last term as president was about to end.

He initially tried to extend his rule by attempting to manipulate the Constitutional Convention of 1971 which had been meeting to consider changes to the country's charter. He maneuvered to get the convention to consider a shift to the parliamentary system so that he could then rule the country as Prime Minister even when his term as President had already expired. Delegates to the convention were bribed to support the proposals calling for a change to the parliamentary form of government. Benjamin "Kokoy" Romualdez, Imelda s brother, Fe Roa-Aqumo-Gimenez, the confidential secretary of Imelda, and Lydia Nicasio, the niece of Kokoy's wife, were believed to have acted as Marcos' conduits to the constitutional convention delegates. It was claimed that Marcos had 170 of the delegates in his payroll and had been providing the equivalent of $86,000 a mont for regular monthly salaries and bribes which were distributed to the heads of important committees and voting blocks within the convention [31].

The imposition of martial law in 1972, however, proved to be the more efficient route towards extending his rule.

Masking his power grab with the language of reform, Marcos claimed that he declared martial law to save Philippine society from the extreme left and extreme right elements he portrayed to be threatening the political order. He declared himself to be leading a "democratic revolution" where the political center would meet the threats of the extremists from the left and the right. He promised to establish a "New Society." The "democratic revolution" of the "New Society" would also consist in breaking the privileges of the traditional oligarch and would initiate what he termed to be the "democratization of wealth."

The established patterns of wealth and power were indeed transformed. But the changes which came with martial law belied the rhetoric of democratization and reform. The exact opposite occurred. In a relatively short period, power and wealth became concentrated in the hands of Marcos and Imelda, their relatives, and their closest friends.

The plunder of the nation began the moment martial law was declared. Unprecedented looting of the country's natural resources and wealth ensued.

Marcos and his cronies exerted a vise over the national economy until it came under their total control or became their private possession. The term and larceny is inadequate to describe the magnitude of what transpired during the reign of theft.

The pillage started with the silencing of opponents. Members of the political opposition, politicians as well as students and grass roots organizers, were jailed, some undergoing torture and savage beatings which eventually led to death. The media was closed down. This was to ensure that martial law policies would not meet any opposition. When the media was finally allowed to open, it was only because Imelda's relatives and Marcos' friends already owned or controlled the major newspapers and television and radio stations.

Marcos ruled by presidential decree. Congress was abolished. The congressional building was turned into a museum housing Egyptian artifacts. The Supreme Court tolerated the dictatorship since Marcos had been able to skillfully staff it with appointees who were beholden to him. The head of the Supreme Court, Chie Justice Enrique Fernando, went around publicly carrying Imelda's parasol to shield her from the sun.

The public sector of the economy was controlled by placing trusted technocrats in key government positions. Cabinet ministers followed Marcos' and Imelda's wishes unquestioningly. Government projects were implemented not because they provided public services but because they were sources of kickbacks. The private sector of the economy was sliced into different spheres of influence. Each partition was handled by a relative, a close friend, or a trusted crony. Each company, every industry, all sectors of the economy, provided that they were sources of money, became the object of greed and eventual acquisition. The whole economy came to be divided into different fiefs managed by relatives and cronies who regularly shared their earnings with the dictator.

The country's entire financial system was placed at their disposal. Monetary policy was formulated and conducted on the basis of the benefits they would bring to the industries and companies Marcos and his friends owned. As in the case of the Supreme Court justices, Marcos appointed only those who were loyal to his interests to the posts of Central Bank Governor and Finance Minister. The Central Bank governors who served under Marcos -- Gregorio Licaros, Jaime Laya, Jose Fernandez -- and Finance Minister Cesar Virata prided themselves as apolitical "technocrats" but displayed absolutely no independence from the dictator's monetary and financial policies. Equally subservient managers were assigned key posts in government-owned banks, making it easier for the dictator and his friends to bleed the country's treasury dry through questionable loans to their companies. Private banks were placed in the hands of the cronies, sometimes by forcing the owners out through changes in banking requirements, at other times by more persuasive forms of coercion. These moves assured that the new oligarch would enjoy easy and privileged access to credit from local and international financial institutions. Credit, however, would be routinely denied to other private businesses whenever these businesses became the object of takeovers. As soon as the owners relinquished their businesses to Marcos and his associates, the financial squeeze would ease.

The country's principal export crops, coconut, sugar, banana, and tobacco, was placed under the control of the most trusted cronies. Monopolles in the production, milling, local marketing, and international trading phases of these industries were created through a series of presidenti decrees, resulting in extreme poverty for the agricultural workers in these industries and great wealth or the few who benefitted from the monopolies. The decrees establishing monopolies over the export crops were replications on a grander scale of the practice of *indulto de comercio* which granted a business monopoly to the Spanish *alcalde* and permitted him to cheat and underpay the lowly indio for the rice, wine, and indigo he brought to market. The sections on Benedicto, Floirendo, Enrile, and Cojuangco in the next chapter show in detail how this was done.

Trading monopolies over the country's main imports were established as well. Trusted members of Marcos' cabinet were given charge over the trading of the country's most essential imports such as rice and oil. While the stated rationale for such trading monopolies was to acquire cheaper imports, the exact opposite occurred. The gains from trade were enjoyed solely by those who administered the trade.

While the constitution expressly prohibited conflicts of interest on the part of government officials in at least two provisions, these prohibitions were ignored. The relevant constitutional provisions covering conflicts of interest are the following:

> *No Senator or Member of the House of Representatives shall directly or indirectly be financially interested in any contract with the Government or in any franchise or special privilege granted by the Congress during his term of office. [Article VI. Sec. 17.] The heads of departments and chiefs of bureaus or offices and their assistants shall not, during their continuance in office, engage in the practice of any profession, or intervene, directly or indirectly, in the management or control of any private enterprise which in any way may be affected by the functions of their office; nor shall they, directly or indirectly, be financially interested in any contract with the Government, or any subdivision or instrumentality thereof [Article VII. Sec. 11., par 2.]*

But many of Marcos' cabinet members and top officials organized their own corporations to expressly contract services and supply products to the departments and ministries they headed in blatant disregard for these provisions. Marcos condoned, and even instigated these practices, because he stood to gain from them as well.

Marcos and his cronies used many other techniques to enrich themselves. The country's natural resources, such as its mines and forests, were given to the cronies to exploit. Special levies were instituted on many products, but these government-imposed levies were never subjected to later audit. Extremely liberal government incentives and tax exemptions were selectively granted to corporations owned by favored individuals. Relatives and friends were awarded lucrative government contracts. Captive markets were created through presidential decree to benefit the corporations owned by Marcos cronies. The stock market was manipulated through false public announcements by the government. Bribery, kickbacks, extortion, theft, graft, and the malversation of public funds, already an underground tradition within the Philippine government bureaucracy, were centralized under the dictatorship. Access to valuable market information, normally available only to the government, became an important factor in economic competition in favor of those who were favored by the overnment. And when these methods did not suffice for the purposes of Marcos and his friends, military force was occasionally used as a factor in economic competition.

Fortune magazine, reviewing Marcos' performance, assessed his regime in the following terms: "Marcos' principal economic achievement in 15 years in power has been to help his friends and relatives build giant conglomerates" [32]. Marcos' "democratic revolution" was neither democratic nor a revolution. It is more appropriately described as a coup or counter-revolution where Marcos sought to turn back the attempts at social reform in the early 1970's by perpetuating himself in power and enriching himself and his associates. The next chapter details the methods Marcos and his cronies used to enrich themselves.

The Marcos coup altered the historically established role of the traditional oligarchy and other political and economic patterns in Philippine life. The power of the old oligarchy which depended on export crops and other privileges granted during Spanish colonial rule was irrevocably broken. A new elite was formed from the patronage of the Marcos government. Some members of the old elite, such as the Yulo and Elizalde families whose interests were largely in the sugar industry, chose to collaborate with Marcos to preserve their traditional enclaves of privilege. Other members of the elite were dislodged from their positions of power and were ultimately annihilated because they could not weather the competition from Marcos and his cronies.

From the dissolution of some of the old social forces and the coalescing of new ones emerged a new set of actors which form the new oligarchy spawned by the Marcos coup. Rev. Fr. Joaquin Bernas S.J., one of the country's leading experts on constitutional law and former Provincial of the Society of Jesus, summarized these developments:

> *Political power has become much more concentrated now than before martial law. In other words, martial law did indeed neutralize some segments of the old oligarchy, but only to make possible the entrenchmertt of a chosen segment of that same oligarchy and some new accretion: [33].*

The new elite was nothing more than a large subset of the old oligarchy Mr. Marcos promised to dismantle at the onset of martial law and the "new accretions" who formed the Marcos *nouveau riche.* Some alliances within the old oligarchy were destroyed only to create newer and stronger alliances between the old elements and the new crooks. To this tightly-knit group of *nouveau riche* belonged Rodolfo Cuenca, Herminio Disini, Ricardo Silverio, Antonio Floirendo, and others whose wealth depended on the patronage of Mr. Marcos. The next chapter documents the rise of this new set of oligarchs and details the methods they used to accumulate their wealth.

That there have been changes in the elite structure since the September 1972 coup and that there have been new additions to the favored few in Philippfine society are allegations which were not denied by Mr. Marcos. He himself attested to this in a speech he gave on 19 September 1975 on the occasion of the third anniversary of the September 1972 takeover. So naked had been the power grabs of some of his cronies that Mr. Marcos himself had had to admit that his so-called "New Society"

> is giving birth to a new government elite, who resurrect in our midst the privileges we fought in the past, who employ the powers of high office for their personal enrichment...There are new sores that are emerging...There has arisen massive opportunities for graft and corruption, the misuse of influence, opportunities which are now being exploited within the government service... Among some of the poor, there is still the nagging fear that they have again been left behind, and that we have liquidated an oligarchy only to set up a new oligarchy... the dramatic gains of the past three years have ironically intensified natural appetites for finery and show, for lavish parties, flashy cars, mansions, big homes, expensive travel, and other counter-productive activities.

When Marcos was dogged by criticisms of corruption, his loyal suporters rushed to his defence. Cesar Virata, who served as Marcos' Finance Minister and later as token Prime Minister of the dictator, outrightly denied that Marcos stole government money: "That is not true. There are rumors about that. But that is not true" [34]. Another loyal supporter, Oliver Lozano, a lawyer from Marcos' home province of Ilocos Norte, defended him by saying that charges of corruption cannot be true because of Marcos' "character and upbringing, his adherence to simple living, his thrift, discipline and deeply religious nature" [35]. President Reagan also nobly came to the defense of his beleaguered friend and said "the information I've always had was that he was a millionaire before he took office."

Marcos' income in 1960, six years before he became resident, was $17,000, according to the tax return he submitted. In the two ecades that he served as president, he is approximated to have received $250,000 in official salary [36]. This income, although already relatively large in terms of Philippine standards, could not by any means support the life style and expenses we described in the previous chapter. This by itself constitutes prima facie evidence of violation of the country's anti-corruption laws, Republic Acts 1379 (18 June 1955) and 3019 (Anti-Graft and Corrupt Practices Act, 17 August 1960). Section Two of Republic Act 1379 clearly applies in this case:

> Whenever any public oflicer or employee has acquired during his incumbency an amount of property which is manifestly out of proportion to as such public officer or employee and to his other lawful income and the income from legitimate acquired property, said property shall be presumed to have been unlawfully acquired.

But Marcos and Imelda, together with their associates, were never successfully prosecuted under this statute. Opposrtion members of the parliament tried to have Marcos unpeached, charging him with

> Taking undue advantage of his office and his authoritarian powers, in connivance, conspiracy and collusion with, and/or for the benefit of the immediate members of his family, close relatives, high government officials under his direction and control, and trusted associates and cronies, directly or

indirectly enriched himself in office, amassing an enormous fortune by raiding the public treasury, plundering the nation's wealth, taking over business enterprises of political opponents, creating public monopolies which he placed in the hands of trusted cronies and, in gross violation of Philippine foreign exchange laws, diverting most of such ill-gotten wealth to foreign countries... [37].

Marcos' supporters in the parliament successfully killed the impeachment move.

The magnitude of economic crimes Marcos and his friends committed were totally unprecedented that these crimes are not as yet recognized in statute books, according to one constitutional lawyer. He was of the opinion that the traditional leg definitions of racketeering, and larceny, robbery, and theft are inadequate to describe what occurred during Marcos' regime. The chairman of the US House Foreign Affairs subcommittee on Asia and the Pacific called Marcos' rule a "kleptocracy." The 1986 Guiness Book of World Records lists Marcos as the biggest alleged thief. Other records which were cited along with Marcos' was Sylvester Stallone, who made the most money for a motion picture, Dolly Parton, who made the most for a single concert, and a duck in Avlesbury, England, for laying the most number of eggs. The duck laid a total of 437 eggs in 463 days, of which 375 were consecutive lays before it died of exhaustion on 7 February 1986, the day of elections which ousted Marcos.

Officials of the Aquino administration attempting to describe Marcos' crony capitalism resorted to such terms as "hidden wealth," "unexplained wealth," "ill-gotten wealth," etc. These are rather feeble and ineffective attempts to describe a social phenomenon which has little precedent or parallel in history. "Hidden" wealth is a logical contradiction. The idea of wealth implies a great amount of property and therefore something which is displayed or flaunted. Our previous discussion of conspicuous consumption shows that wealth is anything but hidden [38]. "Unexplained" wealth shows historical ignorance. There is nothing inexpicable about wealth. It is the result of social and historical events. Marcos wealth is completely explainable through history, but officials of Mrs. Aquino's administration, largely ignorant of the details of Marcos' operations, have insisted on using the obscurantist terminology. "Ill-gotten" wealth is a trap set by priests and lawyers. It is an attempt to elevate the issues into sterile scholastic discussions of what is morally or legally right ad nauseam and preempt a concrete understanding of events.

Classical political economy has made us conscious of the importance of analyzing the workings of the state for an understanding of the economy. This intellectual tradition rightly pointed out that it was only through an analysis of the interaction of the state and the economy that society could be adequately explained. A key category of this intellectual tradition was that of *ursprungliche Akkumulation,* of original or primary accumulation. The term, usually mistranslated as primitive accumulation, was used to describe the crude and brutal manner through which the state intervened in the economy to extract surplus from the English working class and produce capitalism in England.

Taking a cue from the classical economists, Marcos' crony capitalism is best explained through a historical analysis of the concrete ways of how wealth and power interacted to produce a new elite. Analysis of how government or state power was used to further the wealth of the individuals, families, and economic groups close to the Marcos family not only avoids the earlier mentioned pitfalls but also provides us with a most consistent and coherent approach to the history of Marcos' crony capitalism.

Such an approach allows us to have a broader view of corruption than what has normally been associated with the term. Minoru Ouchi, a Senior Research Fellow at the Institute of Developing Economies in Tokyo who specializes on corruption in developing countries, views corruption as more than just the isolated acts of individuals but as occurrences which take place within the context of the workings of the state. Ouchi's observations on corruption place much of what happened during Marcos' rule in their appropriate context. Calling for a wider interpretation of the phenomenon of corruption than the traditional legalistic notions, Ouchi writes:

> It would also go beyond the conventional concepts of political corruption based on the nineteenth century liberal statism, ideals of free enterprise, instrumental bureaucracy and fair elections which were supposed to cleanse public life of political corruption. The optimism of liberal statism has not been substantiated. Corruption has not been eliminated; on the contrary, it has been transformed and legitimized. Free enterprise has led in time to the concentration of wealth and power in the hand of a few privileged individuals and groups in business and industry. It has concomitantly given them considerable power and a tight hold over the public bureaucracy. This, in turn, has enabled them to secure and protect their privileged position through special legislation, tax exemptions, public subsidies, the acquisition of public property for private benefit and access to publicly financed investments and loans. Dominant economic interests, political parties and public bureaucrats work together to promote private concerns to the detriment of both possible competitors and the general public welfare. The parties involved scrupulously comply with the law. They claim that as long as they allow prescribed procedure there is nothing wrong if they obtain special treatment. Clearly, they gain unfairly and discriminate against otherm members of society. Corruption occurs systematically, openly, and under the guise of legality. It forms part of the unconscious routine of white-collar workers. Yet, such sophlstlcated, institutionalized and legitimately discriminatory use of power and influence is not considered corruption within prevailing conventional definitions.... Older, legalistic forms of corruption have been superseded in fact by a far broader, more pervasive and insidious erosion of the norms of public conduct. What ismore, the well-bein and progress of the less-privileged is being threatened by the untrummeled spread of these newer forms of corruption throughout the world...[39] (emphasis ours).

The powers of the state were completely indentified with the prerogatives of private individuals and particular groups during the Marcos regime. What has hitherto been considered as individual acts o corruption are more appropriately viewed as actions where Marcos and his cronies did not make any distinction between public office and private interests. Guilt over corruption is hardly possible when one sincerely believes that the state is one's property. One recalls the spirit of Louis XIV, the French monarch to whom the words *l'état, c'est moi* (I am the state) are attributed, when Imelda implicitly considers the state to be her personal property as the following account reveals:

Suggestions that she and her husband accumulated money through kickbacks make her openly furious. She once told Malcarian reporters - which included myself and disenchanted former martial law propagandist Primitivo Mijares - that in their positions she and her husband could easily borrow money from any bank in the world or from rich personal fiiends in the intemational jet set. Whyy, if she'd only run for the presidency, she said, she'd easily have $100 million as pledged by Cristina Ford! And she tried to drive home her point by saying that through the presidency, they could legitimately make money since they could have advance information on government actions and decisions which are useful in business [40].

Gerry Spence, the wily lawyer from Wyoming who represented Imelda against federal racketeering charges in New York in 1990, used precisely this line of reasoning in his defense of the Marcoses. On 3 April 1990, the first day of the racketeering trial, Spence argued in his opening statement that Marcos could not have broken any law since "he was the law" [41]. Spence contended that even Marcos' shipping of money to Switzerland was legal because of this reason. The argument was totally consistent with the way the Marcoses behaved while in power [42]. Marcos, also a crafty lawyer, made sure that whatever he did was legitimized by laws or presidential decrees. Questions of legality or the lack thereof become totally academic when analyzing Marcos' crony capitalism.

A 1984 study on the economic conditions in the Philippines claimed that at least 688 presidential decrees and 283 presidential letters of instruction which "represent one form or another of intervention in the economy" had been issued. These presidential decrees and letters of instruction are examples of the concrete ways through which state power was used to mtervene 1n the economy and create wealth for a select group. According to the 171-page report, the purpose of these presidential orders were

the issuance of exclusive rights to import, export or ecploit certain areas,
the collection of large funds, which are then privately controlled and
expropriated, and the preferential treatment of certain firms for purposes of credit
or credit restructunng [43).

One decree was a special law where Marcos gave himself and his associates blanket immunity for whatever they did in office. The decree was entitled "an act providing for the preservation of public order and the protection of individual rights and liberties during periods of emergency and the exercise of extraordinary owers." The Public Safety Act, dated 12 September 1980 but released to the national assembly only on 13 January 1981, granted immunity to Marcos, his cabinet, "and all other public officers for acts performed in office." It stated that "the prime minister shall be immune from suit from all official acts done during his tenure in office and all officers and employees who followed and executed his lawful order."

These presidential pronouncements provided legitimacy to the actions of Marcos and his cronies. It allowed them to elbow their competitors, tap into the national treasury, and organize their respective conglomerates with a legal facade. These decrees provided a political and legal canopy under which Marcos and his associates could accumulate their wealth without hindrance. What would normally be illegal was legitimized as legal. Thus, when Marcos was under intense criticism for his overseas properties, the presidential palace sought refuge under this canopy and speciously argued "...so long as the acquisitions are legal, nobody can question the owner's right to these properties..."

While the previous chapter described how wealth was spent, this chapter and the next one discuss the origin of this wealth and how it was generated through the use of state power. Our purpose is not rimarily to issue moral and legal judgements but principally to provide the historical research upon which such judgements may be later made.

Endnotes

1. *Essays on Political Economy,* Part III, "Government."
2. Adam Smith, *Wealth of Nations* (1776), ed. Cannan, Book V, Ch. 1., Pt. II, p.2D7.
3. These anecdotes are found in Francisco, Mariel Nepomuceno, and Arriola, Fe Maria, *The History of the Burgis* (Quezon City: GCF Books, 1987).
4. These two novels, masterpieces of literature, considerably helped create a national consciousness and the groundwork for the revolution against Spam.
5. To translate this amount into dollars would be deceptive. At this time, soon after the annexation of the Philippines, the American colonial administration was in a quandary as to how to relate the Philippine peso with the American dollar. The American colonial administration later arbitrarily decided to give the Philippine peso the same exchange rate the Mexican peso had at that time and pegged the Philippine peso at the exchange rate of 2:1 in relation to the dollar. It is therefore more meaningful if we related 1,100 pesos in 1909 not to the dollar or any other international currency but to the level of earnings of the ordinary Filipino during this period. The Philippine peso remained pegged to the dollar at the 2:1 ratio until the 1960's. The process by which the early American military administrators decided to define the peso-dollar ratio would be an interesting historical study in international monetary policy for future scholars.
6. Together with the European wines were entries for Whisky and soda. This indicates how the Philippine elite was quickly assimilating American tastes after the Philippines was colonialized by the United States 1n 1898.
7. Between 5,000 and 10,000 pesos.
8. This is on the assumption that the laborer did not have to spend for food, taxes, and other necessities, and that everything earned was saved.
9. This is from an actual account made by one of the participants.
10. Manglapus was a Senator who faced an unprecedented move to have him unseated for alleged violations of the Philippine Election Code. He also served as Foreign Minister. His stint as Foreign Minister of the Aquino administration has been marred with bungling the negotiations over the US military bases in the country and accusations of hiring a mercenary to assassinate opponents of the Aquino government.
11. I encountered a most fascinating bookstore in the old section of Madrid, in Plaza de San Martin. The walls of the bookstore, *Luis Bardon*, named after its proprietor, are lined up with books from different centuries from floor to ceiling. It is an unbelievable treasure trove of old books.
As Iwas browsing over the collection of books on the Philippines covering the 17th, 18th, and 19th centuries, Sr. Bardon kindly recalled the visits of two men we mention in this chapter: Eugenio Lopez and Manuel Quezon. He recalled, still with a bit of surprise after several decades had already passed, the visits of Eugenio Lopez. Bardén related how Lopez would buy up all of the old books on the Philippines in the store, even if he already had already bought revious copies of other editions. These books would later form part of the Lopez Memorial Museum. The Lopez Museum, which specializes in Philippine colonial

history, is a most important contribution to Philippine culture. In contrast with the previously mentioned anniversary party, this kind of spending had a clear cultural value.

12. Veblen's discussion of conspicuous consumption is found in Chapter IV of *The Theory of the Leisure Class.*

13. The term *indio* was used the Spanish to refer to the local inhabitants.

14. A cousin of Emilio Aguinaldo, Baldomero Aguinaldo, served under the general's forces during the revolution against Spain. Baldomero held the powerful position of Auditor of War and was responsible for providing his cousin with the justification for the execution of Andres Bonifacio, the plebeian hero whom General Aguinaldo viewed as a threat to his leadership. A person who played a prominent role in Marcos' dictatorship was Baldomero Aguinaldo's grandson, Cesar Aguinaldo Virata. Virata, mentioned several times in this book, consistently defended the regime's oppressive economic policies as the dictator's Finance Minister and later token Prime Minister. While one was involved in a mock trial and a political execution and the other was a Marcos functionary, Baldomero Aguinaldo and his grandson Virata in reality played analogous roles. They were the legitimators who provided the theories to justify the pyramids of sacrifice.

15. "I declare that the amount of P40000000 belonged to me exclusively, in accordance with the provisions of the Treaty of Peace of Biak na Bato.

However, motivated with the desire to save our country from its condition of bondage, I invested the said amount in the renewal of the revolution, winning for our people their most precious liberties.

And, if despite our sacrifices and the happy results of those revolutions, details of that investment are still sought, I am willing to do so, on the condition that the hidden mysteries concerning the investment of many millions of pesos for the campaign for independence be first revealed."

Translation and emphasis ours. 'The Money of the Revolution," Philippines Free Press, 7 September 1929.

16. However the money may have been disposed is secondary to the central point that Aguinaldo considered the funds as his personal property.

Aguinaldo initially deposited the 400,000 pesos with the Hong Kong & Shanghai Corp. Bank on 2 January 1898. Two days later, he withdrew 200,000 pesos and deposited it with the Chartered Bank of India, Australia, & China at 2% interest. The account increased by 18,582.90 pesos from further funds received from the revolutionary forces in the Philippines between 6 January and 16 February. Aguinaldo also asked the other revolutionary leaders to send him the second payment of 200,000, saying that he could invest it at 8.5% interest. (However, the second installment of 200,000 pesos from the Spanish government was not sent but was divided amongst other leaders, with Pedro A. Patemo, the negotiator of the treaty, getting P89,500 on the 11th and 12th of January 1898.)

A cache of arms was indeed bought with part of the 400,000 pesos. The arms, however, never reached the Philippines but was later used by Sun Yat Sen in China. Aguinaldo also left 67,000 pesos with the American Consul in Hong Kong, Rounseville Wildman, for the further purchase of arms, but this too never arrived. The "second [shipment of arms], unhappily for the insurgents, did not [arrive] and Wildman never explained why. Nor did he reimburse Aguinaldo the 67,000 pesos given to him in good faith." Teodoro Agoncillo, *Malolos: The Crisis of the Republic*, (Quezon City. University of the Philippines, 1960), p.128.

These two disbursements are the only known significant expenses from the 400,000 pesos. How the remainder of the money was spent remains a mystery. It is known that Aguinaldo kept careful track of the funds. He was described as having exercised an "iron hand over disbursements, every one of which was meticulously and scrupulously noted down in his account book" (Malolos, p.61).

It would have been relatively easy for Aguinaldo to declare how these funds were disbursed. It is therefore surprising for Aguinaldo to dodge the question concerning the disposition of the 400,000 with the claim that it was personally his.

An equally interesting question is what happened to the 67,000 pesos Aguinaldo left with Wildman, the Amerimn consul in Hong Kong, a significant amount in 1898. Moreover, Felipe Agoncillo, one of the leaders of the revolution, claimed that a rich Filipino named Maximo Cortes had given Wildman 10,000 pesos because the consul "promised him to write to the Admiral not to bombard his real estate in Manila," a story believed by the gullible Cortes (quoted in *Malolos,* p.141).

17. I initially thought that the second part of the letter referred to the other leaders of the revolution against pain rather than the "independence missions." I am indebted to Fr. John Schumacher, SJ. for correcting me and saving me from an interpretative error on this point.

18. It was as a member of the Nacionalista Party that Marcos would later become president.

19. Quoted in Renato Constantino, *A Past Revisited,* p. 329-330.

20. George de Carvalho,"A Dirty Campaign on the Corruption Issue," *Life*, 26 November 1965, Vol. 59, No. 22.

21. The conviction was later overturned by the Philippine Supreme Court under questionable circumstances.

22. Marcos at one time claimed that he was only one medal shy of equalling the number of medals received Audie Murpy, the highest decorated soldier of the Second World War. The actual number of medals that Marcos has claimed varied over the years, and most of the claims have been found to be spurious. Marcos' accounts of his activities during the war contained many inconsistencies, especially his accounts of his encounters and imprisonment with the Japanese. Marcos' father, Mariano, was later executed by Filipino guerillas as a Japanese collaborator. Before his death, the father admitted to a US Army commander that he had been recommended to the Japanese by his son, Ferdinand.

23. Mijares, p.244.

24. Mijares, p.262.

25. Mijares, p262

26. Mijares, p.262.

27. Imelda's fiancé at that time still thought that he was engaged to Imelda, only to later find out from the newspapers that she had already gotten married to Marcos. From a personal account of Karen Tanada, the niece of Ariston Nakpil, the former fiance of Imelda.

28. Mijares pp. 259-60.

29. Leonard Saffir, "Imelda and Ferdie - Really Took Me In," *New York Times,* 3 November 1988.

30. Quoted in William Branigin, "By Hook or by Slice," *Washington Post*, 30 March 1986.

31. Marlen Ronquillo, 'The Woman Behind the Con-Con Doleout," *Philippine Daily Inquirer* 17 May 1986; Ronquillo, "170 Con-Con Delegates at Marcos' Beck and Call," *Philippine Daily Inquirer,* 18 May 1986.

32. *Fortune,* 27 July 1981.

33. "Some Reflections on Eight Years Under Martial Rule," speech delivered on 19 September 1980, to the Bishop-Businessmen's Conference.

34. *Business Day,* 13 June 1986.

35. Quoted in William Branigin, "Another Slow Night at the Marcoses," *Washington Post,* 26 July 1986.

36. Lindablue Romero, "Papers Show FM Wealth Ill-gotten," Philippine Daily Inquirer, Gene Orejana, "OSG Bolsters Graft Case vs. FM, 28 Others," *Malaya,* 2 July 1986.

37. The impeachment resolution was filed on 13 August 1985.

38. We have to add to this the epistemological imposmbility of discussing anything which is hidden.

39. Minoru Ouchi, *Political Corruption and Japanese Corporate Donations*, (Tokyo: Institute of Developing Economies, March 1979).

40. Ruben Cusipag, *Philippine Times (*Chicago), 16-31 December 1975, quoted in Mijares, p.259.

41. This is the modern parallel of the Divine Right of Kings. The idea of the absolute power of the national leader also exists in the American political tradition when the executive branch intervenes in the normal political process in the name of "national security." These executive interventions, difficult to challenge, range from the withholding of information from the public to even the administration of justice. In area of American constitutional law, this is termed as the political question doctrine, the theory that the some issues cannot be judged by the courts bemuse they are committed to another branch of the government and are therefore incapable of judicial resolution.

42. Consistent but spurious.

43. *An Analysis of the Philippine Economic Crisis*, June 1984, 171 mimeographed pages.

Chapter III

THE RELATIVES AND THE CRONIES

I never figured crony to be a bad word.

> — *Rudolfo Cuenca, as noted in the Wall Street Journal, November 1983.*

I know President Marcos very well and deserve his support.

> - *Ricardo Silverio, as quoted in Fortune, 27 July 1981*

En Filipinas es cosa sabida que para todo se necesitan padrinos, desde que uno se bautiza hasta que se muere, para obtener justicia, sacar un pasaporte o esplotar un industria cualquiera.

> — *Jose Rizal, El Filibusterismo, 1891* *

> **("It is well known in the Philippines that one needs a godfather for everything, from the time one gets baptized to the time one dies, to obtain justice, apply for a passport, or to start any business." Our translation.   Rizal, El Filibusterismo, p.229.)*

ROBERTO BENEDICTO

THE PREDECESSOR

A century before Marcos or organized his network of cronies, small landowners and settlers in the island of Negros complained to the Spanish colonial government about the injustices they and other unfortunate families suffered at the hands of those with an "insatiable desire to possess" [1]. The complaint, lodged with the Superior Civil Governor in August 1876, protested the "evils which accompanied the acquisition of lands in Negros."

The controversy centered on Don Teodoro Benedicto who usurped the lands of original settlers in the island with the help of some local officials. Don Teodoro, born in 1835 to a Chinese mestizo family in Jolo, started as a petty cloth merchant but later became a Negrense landlord after purchasing Hacienda San Bernardino in La Carlota. He soon gained notoriety in the area because of the manner through which he expanded his properties.

The complainants charged that Benedicto increased his land holdings through deceit and force. A total of 7,000 hectares in the La Carlota district was acquired in this way. An "immense property" on slopes of Mount Kanlaon was annexed through

> the expulsion from his properties of poor indios who had from time immemorial cultivated small plots of coffee and cocoa sufficient to cover the cost of their basic necessities...

Benedicto "usurped" an additional 2,600 hectares in Barrio Bungayin, Isabela which were also cultivated by the same settlers. Don Teodoro likewise booted out the inhabitants of the entire barrio of Antipolo in Pontevedra. He perpetrated another significant land grab, covering approximately 1,600 hectares, in Barrio La Castellana, Pontevedra. The natives in these areas were ejected from their properties, forcing them to "quietly retreat to the mountains with their families where they are relegate to a miserable life."

Benedicto was able to get away with these crimes because he had corrupted the *gobemadorcillo* [2] of Pontevedra by appointing him as his encargado (foreman) in the farms. Since the gogernadorcillo was on Benedicto's side, ejecting the settlers was easy. A testimony of a landowner at that time claimed that the gobernadorcillo had sent armed men to occupy the farms and that the owners "were driven off with violence" when they refused to vacate their lands. In public hearings conducted by Spanish colonial authorities on March 1877 on Benedicto's claim to Hacienda San Bernardino, the testimonies recounted how Benedicto's armed men evicted the settlers from their land and expropriated "all their properties, even the harvest." Benedicto's methods left the poor "without recourse." A total of 21 settlers were expelled in the San Bernardino area alone. These were families who had migrated from neighboring Antique during the 1850's and 1860's and had cleared the lands to establish small plots from one to 18 hectares. The holdings of this group totalled 256 hectares. The government prosecutor who reviewed the case recommended that it be brought to trial with the Negros Court of First Instance, saying that

> in the investigation of the methods employed by Don Teodoro Benedicto for the acquisition of lands, there is criminal liability on his and his accomplices' part...

ROBERTO BENEDICTO

Roberto Salas Benedicto, a descendant of Don Teodoro born on 17 April 1917 in La Carlota, Negros Occidental, continued the tradition of tyranny as one of Marcos' earliest and most trusted cronies.

He was Marcos' classmate and fraternity brother at the University of the Philippines law School. The two developed an early friendship, and it is said that Benedicto treated the struggling Marcos to sandwiches while both were in school. The association continued even after both graduated from law school in 1939.

Although he is not a relative, he became part of the small Marcos circle in Malacanan and was one of the few with complete access to the President's private quarters. Benedicto became the dictator's favorite golfing partner. Largely as recognition of his loyalty to the dictator, he was showered with government sinecures and control over the choicest plums of economic activity. An ambassadorship, a government bank chairmanship, and control over the country's top export form part of the largesse Benedicto enjoyed.

At the height of his power, Benedicto's empire consisted of no less than 85 corporations, 106 sugar farms, 14 haciendas, other agricultural lands, 17 radio stations, 16 television stations, two telecommunications networks, seven buildings, ten vessels, and five aircrafts. Two of the planes, a Britten Norman and a Beechcraft Superking Air, were priced at $4 million. Residential lots and houses in Ermita, 14 hectares of real estate in Bacolod City, a penthouse in Kanlaon Towers, Pasay, 13.5 billion shares in Oriental Petroleum held through Piedras Mining, and membership shares at exclusive golf and country clubs such as Wack-Wack, Canlubang, Alabang, and Marapara. The golf and country club shares alone were estimated at $491,000 [3]. These were the properties that Benedicto considered as loose change. His overseas properties included a sugar mill in Venezuela, a trading company in Madrid, bank deposits, mansions, and limousines in California, apart from other properties in Japan and the US. His deposits in Swiss banks alone was estimated to be $200 million [4]. Rafael Salas, Marcos' executive secretary and Benedicto's cousin, estimated in 1983 that this old Marcos pal had a net worth of $800 million [5].

In return for the favors he received from Marcos, Benedicto served the dictator in a number of ways. On the political front, Benedicto worked as chairman of Marcos' KBL party for Western Visayas [6] since it was organized in 1977 and delivered sizeable votes for Marcos' candidates in subsequent elections. But the more important service Benedicto rendered for Marcos was as a most trusted front and as associate in many corporations and business deals. Benedicto was anointed a Marcos "front man" early in the dictator's career of plunder and was even given a special Power-of-Attorney to deal on behalf of Marcos. The Power-of-Attorney, signed on 14 October 1976, gave him broad powers to act on behalf of Marcos, including the authority to receive payments, manage properties, and run business affairs. Benedicto is also known to have acted on behalf of the Marcos Foundation, a private trust which manages some of Marcos' assets. In one instance, he represented the foundation and attempted to secure a Marcos chair in the Fletcher School of Diplomacy at Tufts University through a donation of $1.5M in 1977 [7]. Benedicto also helped open the first of what was to be many of Marcos' Swiss bank accounts.

When the Marcos government fell, Benedicto fled into exile with Marcos. He is now managing his large overseas interests and is believed to be travelling with a South American passport.

BANK CHAIRMAN AND JAPANESE AMBASSADOR

Recognizing Benedicto's value, Marcos, as soon as he was elected in 1965, appointed the man chairman of PNB, the most important and largest state-owned bank. Benedicto headed the PNB from 1966 through 1970, during which time he secured huge loans for corporations which he or other administration-blessed colleagues (e.g., Rodolfo Cuenca) owned. According to our sources in the shipping industry, Benedicto used his position to acquire vessels for his shipping company, Northern Lines, by securing PNB-guaranteed loans for the ships. The bank also heavily financed Benedicto's sugar industry. His interests in the media and entertainment field likewise received large funding from the state bank [8].

After PNB, Benedicto was given the ambassadorship to Japan. This position was as strategic as the PNB chairmanship since it allowed Benedicto to develop high-level contacts in Japan and consequently acquire large loans, corner war reparations money, and in general receive financial and technical assistance from the Japanese for his corporations and the companies owned by other cronies. He served as Ambassador to Japan from March 1972 through November 1977.

The first step in Benedicto's crony diplomacy lay in currying the favor of important Japanese corporations and politicians. Marcos and Benedicto went through great lengths to gain the goodwill of the Japanese, sacrificing the economic interests of their own country. One blatant example was the ratification of the controversial Treaty of Amity, Commerce and Navigation between the two countries. The pact was a bilateral agreement which granted Japan a "most-favored-nation" status. The treaty has been under scrutiny by the Philippine Senate for 13 years but was never ratified because many felt that it would give Japan undue advantage in using the country's natural resources. Even Foreign Secretary Carlos Romulo, a usually servile Marcos cabinet minister, managed to speak out against the treaty:

> Today, from the Philippine's point of View, this treaty demonstrates the disadvantage and the vulnerability of the developing economy that is the Philippines... We have seen that in the absence of imitations, the operation of the most-favored-nation clause can work against the interest of our people, because it in effect it discriminates in favor of an economic power which has overwhelming means to take advantage of it. We have seen how, in effect, the Philippines will have to hand over to the Japanese any privilege or concession granted by the Philippines to third countries [including ASEAN] in exchange for reciprocal benefits -- benefits which Japan does not have to grant to the Philippines [9].

Soon after he abolished the Philippine Senate and assumed dictatorial powers, Marcos ratified the treaty by presidential decree. Because of the controversial nature of the treaty and the manner it was ratified, the Marcos government tried to promote it to the public. Ambassador Benedicto began expounding on the need for economic cooperation between Japan and the Philippines. In a speech delivered before a group of Japanese businessmen, Benedicto tried to sell the idea that Japan needed a stable and long-term supply of raw materials while the Philippines needed technical and financial assistance, quoting Marcos as saying that "our respective economies complement each other" [10]. Benedicto added that the country was "leaving no stone unturned to attract foreign investors from other countries and particularly from Japan" [11]. As recognition for what Benedicto had done or Japanese interests, the emperor conferred upon him The Order of the Rising Sun, one of Japan's highest honors, for his "contributions to international friendship."

But Marcos and Benedicto had ulterior personal motives in promoting the treaty and encouraging Japanese investments in the country. Mijares wrote that the treaty was ratified only after Benedicto had already made arrangements to personally benefit from it:

> *The 24-man Philippine Senate would not ratify the treaty for 13 years in view of the widespread fear that it would hand over to Japan on a silver latter what the former enemy country sought to win by force of arms during World War II, i.e. the economic damnation of the Philippines. Ratification by presidential decree of the trade treaty came after Benedicto had cornered all deals with prospective Japanese investors in the Philippines [12].*

Benedicto's position as Ambassador to Japan placed him in the unique position to know what areas of investment in the Philippines interested Japanese businessmen. This foreknowledge, coupled with his Malacanan connections, consequently allowed him to arrange highly lucrative joint-venture operations between Japanese corporations and his own companies. He concluded joint ventures with the Japanese for the construction of several of his sugar mills. Benedicto's position also gave him control over the $550 million in Japanese war reparations money the Philippines was to receive and ensure that these funds would be used by Marcos corporations.

THE PHHLEX DEBACLE

While he owned or gained control of dozens of large corporations after he served as ambassador, it was the sugar industry which formed Benedicto's economic empire. Sugar, an important industry since Spanish colonial times and a major export crop since the late 1800's, enabled *hacenderos*, or sugar plantation owners. (13}, to amass fortunes that made them economically and politically powerful. With the help of Marcos' decrees and financing from the Japanese, Benedicto was able to wrest control over this industry from the hacenderos and lord over it during Marcos' regime. Control over sugar, which accounted for 27% of the country's total dollar earnings, was achieved through presidential decrees which gave Benedicto a monopoly over the international marketing, the financing, the milling and planting aspects of the industry.

The monopoly started as early as 1974 when the government tried to take advantage of the steadily rising price of the commodity in the international market. The sharp increase in the international price of sugar, which jumped from $0.04 per pound in 1970 to a high $0.65 in earl 1974, made sugar exports achieve a record value of $737 million, but it also led to the indiscriminate hoarding of the commodity from the domestic market. Hacenderos and sugar traders preferred to hoard and smuggle the commodity to overseas markets rather than sell it domestically at the prices set by the government. The Marcos government in turn use this temporary chaos in the local market as its rationale in organizing the Philippine Exchange Co. (Philex), a government body that would take charge of all the international trading of sugar for local hacenderos.

Philex was initially a subsidiary of the PNB and was managed by Panfilo O. Domingo, a close Benedicto associate, but authority over Philex and its trading activities was later turned over to the Philippine Sugar Commission (Philsucom) which Benedicto headed after coming back from Japan.

Philex took charge of exporting and shipping all sugar bound for the US and other markets, virtually nationalizing the trading of the commodity. It bought sugar from local producers at a low price in order to make gigantic profits in the international market. In this period, the PNB and Philex bought sugar at $19.75 per *picul* (14) and sold it to the US at $69.25, resulting in initial profits amounting to $700M [15].

From the very beginning, the status of Philex and the profits it generated was the subject of much controversy. The presidential decree authorizing the operation of Philex stated that the profits were to paid to a special fund "subject to the disposition of the president for public purposes." Neither the term "public purposes" nor the circumstances under which the funds could be "disposed" were clearly defined. Some quarters, especially those reprepresenting the interests of the hacenderos, argued that Philex was merely their trading agent and therefore all profits generated from international sales should be handed over to them. This issue was never adequately addressed, and when the government trading body finally folded up, the profits likewise vanished.

It was estimated that Philex made $403 million from its trading operations, but contrary to expectations, the company reported a loss of $292 million when it finally folded up [16].

Philex encountered major difficulties as soon as it started operations. The international price of sugar crashed to $0.12 per pound by mid-1975 and bottomed out weeks later at $0.07. The sudden plunge caught the Marcos government by surprise. Philex had expected that the high price of sugar would continue to rise and hoarded sugar in anticipation of higher prices. But it grossly miscalculated the trends and missed the peak [17].

The costs of Philex's speculation were high. Apart from misreading market trends, Philex aggravated the situation by the primitive manner it speculated in the international sugar futures market. Philex placed the futures market with the actual, physical inventories of sugar by hoarding it in warehouses instead of trading in the international commodity markets. This crude strategy resulted in disaster. Much sugar solidified in the warehouses while the Marcos government held back from selling. And when Philex decided to resume sales in February 1975, much of the sugar had deteriorated and was unfit for the market, while the sugar that could still be used was sold at a great loss. Estimates of the losses from this debacle approximated $71.4 million in actual costs and some $600 million in potential revenues.

The following is a description of the effects of the marketing blunder:

The industry was caught with a tremendous inventory of stocks. Sugar overflowed in the warehouses, the pelota courts, swimming pools, and churches. There were problems in marketing, financing, and quality deterioration. Up to now, no official accounting of losses has been made. The boom had turned into a crisis. Production had to be cut drastically. Farms stopped harvesting and planting. Marginal farms were abandoned. Some laborers were hired only two or three days a week to cut production costs. The federation of sugarcane planters reported the burning of 462 hectares of sugar plantations between January to May-end 1977. Some fires were set by workers who had not been paid their wages. The poor became poorer [18].

TIGHTER CONTROL: PHILSUCOM AND NASUTRA

Partly to cover for the mistakes of Philex and partly to have tighter control over the industry, Marcos issued a decree creating the Philippine Sugar Commission (Philsucom). The new body took over Philex and other government agencies dealing with sugar and was granted additional powers over the industry. Philex, the Philippine Sugar Institute, and the Sugar Quota Administration were automatically abolished, and their functions, with their assets and liabilities, were absorbed by the new body. PD 388 creating the Philsucom declared it

..the policy of the state to promote the integrated development and stabilization of the sugar industry so that it can properly discharge its economic and social responsibilities and contribute its share in the development of the national economy [19].

Philsucom was given blanket authority over the sugar industry. The most important power granted to Philsucom was to "act as the single agency engaged in the buying and selling of sugar." This provision meant a monopoly over the most important export crop of the country [20]. Among the other powers of the sugar body were equally important functions:

* determine the prices at which sugar is to be bought and sold at the international and local markets;
* take over any mill or refinery that is delinquent in its financial obligations or has been deemed inefficient by the body;
* organize affiliate corporations;
* enter into contracts and borrow money from local and foreign sources.

Other powers included all-embracing provisions which authorized the Philsucom to "establish policies pertaining to all phases of the industry" and "perform any other functions that may be deemed necessary in view of its purposes." Philsucom was also authorized to "promulgate rules and regulations" to implement the enabling decree, charge levies to finance its operations, and impose penalties to parties which failed to follow its regulations.

An additional decree, PD 1192, was later penned, providing Philsucom broader powers. Among the added functions were

* exclusive control over the marketing cooperatives traditionally controlled by the hacenderos;
* authority to invest its funds in any activity related to sugar production and trading;
* powers to issue bonds and securities which were fully guaranteed by the government;
* tax-free importation of materials and equipment by Philsucom and its affiliates [21].

These two presidential decrees provided the legal foundation for the complete control over the sugar industry. The euphemism used was the "vertical integration of the industry." The Philsucom then created a new trading arm, the National Sugar Trading Corporation (Nasutra), to take exclusive charge over the international and domestic sugar trading. Like its predecessor, Philex, Nasutra was the only corporation allowed to trade in the commodity. Nasutra also had the power to determine the amount sugar that would be allocated for export, domestic, or reserve use [22].

Benedicto headed both Philsucom and Nasutra with other cronies. He served both as president and chairman of Nasutra, and the corporation was registered under his name with the SEC with a paid-up capitalization of $672,000 and an authorized capitalization of $13.4 million. Jose A. Unson, another Marcos associate, served as vice-chairman, while the directors were other Marcos friends such as Fred Elizalde, Armando Gustilo, and Jaime Dacanay.

One of the first controversial steps that Nasutra took was to cover the "trading losses" Benedicto and company had incurred in the hoarding debacle. Nasutra was authorized to borrow $376.3 million for this purpose. The "trading expenses" of Philex of $48.4 million was also reimbursed. No official explanation was ever given why such payments were made by Nasutra. And while the government was reimbursing these losses Benedicto had incurred, port duties amounting to $85 million which Philex had failed to pay were waived. Philex's loan interest payments amounting to millions were likewise written off [23].

Benedicto and his associates took advantage of their positions by milking the sugar industry at each opportunity they had. The methods they used involved manipulating the trading and pricing policy, stealing from industry inventories, smuggling of goods and raw materials, control over the mills, financial coercion of competitors, and the use of the military to massacre workers who protested against their working conditions.

TRADING AND PRICING POLICY

The trading and pricing policy Nasutra adopted was a repetition of the confused policies and trading errors earlier committed by Philex. Nasutra's strategy was to generate trading profits for itself and the international sugar trading companies owned by Marcos and his cronies at the expense of the national interest.

Nasutra bought sugar from hacenderos at a *composite price* it unilaterally set. The composite price was defined as the average of the prices of export, domestic, and reserve sugar. By setting the composite price far below the export price [24], Nasutra was a le to generate multimillion profits for itself supply by acting as the trader for the industry. The presidential decrees authorizing Nasutra as the industry's sole trader assured a monopsomy [25] which dictated the prices.

Representatives of the sugar industry decried Benedicto's scheme as confiscatory since sugar was being taken from them with neither proper compensation nor previous consultation regarding the rates. Nasutra, for example, set the composite price at $0.113 per pound for crop year 1980-81 [26]. The prevailing market price at this time, however, was about $0.27 at worst. The industry was clearly getting less than half of the market price. Even if one made allowances for a lower domestic price, the difference was too great. Whenever the international price of sugar changed, the composite price would likewise be adjusted to maintain the Nasutra profit margin. While, for example, Nasutra sold at $63.70 per picul in the 1979-80 period, it bought at $18.16; when it sold at $40.05, it paid $14.20 [27]. Within less than three years of operations, Nasutra generated profits amounting to $700 million (28).

Apart from underpaying the industry, it appears that Benedicto was also cheating the Central Bank by under-invoicing the value of the sugar he shipped abroad. Calling Benedicto a "thief," Hortensia Starke, a native of Negros Occidental who opposed Benedicto's policies, explained how Benedicto under-invoiced sugar exports:

> I have with me papers showing that in many shipments, Benedicto cheated the Central Bank by misdeclaring the real value of the sugar which he shipped abroad. For instance, this invoice of Nasutra dated 28 October 1980 shows a unit price of $0.155 per pound for a total amount of $153,115.20 FOB value. There is, however, another Nasutra invoice of the same date showing the unit price of the raw sugar as $0.27 per pound. The price difference of $0.115 per pound, when multiplied by the quantity of sugar shipped, comes up to $113,600. This represents only one shipment. During the good years of sugar in 1980-81, when 41 sugar mills were operating. There could 50 shipments each year. If we multiply $113,600 by 50, the total amount would be staggering [29].

Apart from its control on pricing, Nasutra engaged in other questionable trading practices.

An unnecessarily long marketing chain from the actual producer to international markets was established to increase trading profits. This led to greater mark-ups and a consequent redistribution of income from the actual producers to Marcos-favored paper traders. To further increase its profit margin, Nasutra deducted trading costs from the price they paid to the hacenderos. For example, a trading charge of two to three cents was levied for every pound of sugar to be exported, the sum amounting to millions over the years.

Among the other anomalies were delays in paying the hacenderos. This permitted Benedicto to earn extra interest on the money. The move also allowed Benedicto to use later exchange rates in computing the peso equivalent for sugar exported. This tactic had the effect of undervaluing the exports and the pesos to be paid to the hacenderos since later exchange rates were generally lower, with the peso continually depreciating in relation to the dollar.

Apart from squeezing the industry through low prices for sugar and appropriating mills for their use, Benedicto engaged in inventory manipulation, smuggled the commodity, evaded taxes, and procured loans which were never paid.

Trading errors reminiscent of the earlier Philex debacle also characterized Nasutra's international trading practices. Comments made by Ambassador Benedicto concerning trade with Japan are relevant and revealing:

> ...of the 2.5 million tons of sugar that Japan imports yearly, only l00,000 tons comes from the Philippines, and always at a low price. How many sugarmills have been bought by the Philippines from Japan? Nine sugar mills producing about 500,000

tons a year. Why this disproportionate importation, when the Philippines is your natural source of sugar due to our geographical nearness and Japan is a natural market for Philippine sugar for similar reasons [30].

But what Benedicto neglected to point out was that Japan imported sugar from other countries because the Philippines did not enter into long-term contracts when the world price of the commodity was high. This is a variation of the earlier Philex fiasco. As a consequence of this mistake, Japan secured her long-term sugar contracts with Australia (31). This left the Philippines with no long-term contracts, forcing her to sell significantly lower when the international rates later plummeted.

Benedicto's ranting about the lack of trading reciprocity between the two countries may be viewed within a more appropriate context. Benedicto's reference to nine sugar mills bought from Japan was really an attempt to secure markets for the mills which he personally owned. These mills, bought with credits from Japanese war reparations money, ultimately became Benedicto's property or were under his direct control, and the public criticism of Japanese trading policy was nothing more than an attempt to secure markets for the sugar coming from his mills.

OVERSEAS TRADING

When world sugar prices again began to pick up in 1980 [32], Marcos and Benedicto devised yet another money-making scheme.

The Marcos government, through Philsucom, announced that it committed the Philippines to sell 400,000 tons of sugar in the next four years at $0.22 per und1 to an "unnamed buyer" [33]. There was an immediate howl from the hacenderos. When the long-term contract was announced in September 1980, the prevailing world price was already $0.30 per pound. Furthermore, there were definite signs that the international price would further increase [34].

As more facts about the deal came to lightt, it was discovered that Philsucom had committed itself to sell not 400,000 tons over the next four years as originally announced but a staggering 2 million tons. This amount constituted 50% of the projected sugar production for the next four years [35]. An average of 500,000 tons a year for the next four years were to be sold at average price of $0.235 cents a pound; the world market price when the deal was finally arranged was $0.40?

Hacenderos and millers sued in court to prevent Philsucom's announced sale and called the scheme "confiscatory" [36]. The class suit filed with the Supreme Court further argued that the deal was premature since international sugar prices were rising.

The Marcos government countered the suit with a massive propaganda campaign defending the deal. Benedicto himself publicly justified the scheme by insisting on the wisdom of "a conservative pricing policy in exports" and assured the hacenderos that there was still a reasonable margin" of profit left for them [37]. Benedicto's cohorts within the sugar industry also joined the propaganda efforts. Full-page ads endorsing the deal appeared in the Marcos controlled papers. These ads were sponsored by Benedicto-controlled organizations. The Association of

Integrated Millers, the Negros Oriental Planters Association, and the Asociacién Agricola de Bais y Tanjay Inc. praised Benedicto for his "professional and businesslike stewardship of sugar agencies. The Philippine Sugar Association, an organization of sugar mill owners, lauded Benedicto for is "exemplary and successful handling of the many difficult situations" and his "very professional approach" to the international marketing of sugar. The National Sugar Trade Union (NSTU) praised Marcos, Benedicto, Philsucom, and Nasutra for their "efficient and effective management" and thanked "Almighty God Our Father" for the policies of Marcos and Benedicto in the sugar industry [38]. The NSTU ads ran at the cost of $2,800 per day [39]. Inspite of all the space devoted to justifying the scheme, not one of Marcos-controlled newspapers ever mentioned that there was a major suit pending in the Supreme Court against the deal [40]. Critics pointed out that these organizations, like the price of sugar, were controlled by Benedicto.

Benedicto's reasons for committing to such an unreasonable contract became clear when the identity of the "unnamed buyer" was exposed. The "unnamed buyer" was no more than a small group of corporations and individuals who all had close connections with Marcos:

> *After several months of rumor and speculation over the identity of the foreign buyers, President Ferdinand Marcos named them as SuCrest, (Czarnikow)-Rionda and a Mr. Chan, all of New York; and ED. and Farr Mann of London. Industry sources claim SuCrest is owned by Antonio Floirendo, the Mindanao banana magnate, and that he and other brokers buying export sugar are close to the Marcos overnment. Chan is believed to be Jose Mari Chan, who is in partnership with Ramon Nolan, both of whom are also known to the president. Their trading company, Guimaras, is in the same building as Sugar Brokers, believed to be a trading house run by Philsucom chairman Roberto Benedicto [41]*

By selling cheaply to international trading corporations owned or controlled by Marcos and his cronies, profits would be realized not at the Philsucom-Nasutra end but at the New York end where the ultimate destination of the profits could be easily concealed. In the jargon of international business, this is known as transfer pricing, a practice where prices within the marketing chain are adjusted so that profits can be realized in the most convenient places. Philsucom and Nasutra sell cheaply at the world market, sacrificing the interests of the Philippine sugar industry and its workers, so that the international sugar trading corporations connected with Marcos and Benedicto could realize huge profits at the dollar end. (Please see the next section on Antonio Floirendo for more details.)

To assure a more efficient way for transferring profits from the Philsucom-Nasutra side to the trading corporations based in New York, Benedicto and Marcos organized a formidable network of corporations and individuals within the international sugar market [42]. Apart from Jose Mari Chan, Ramon Nolan, and Floirendo who have been mentioned earlier, the other individuals and professionals in the international trading of sugar with known links to Benedicto and Marcos were:

> *Leandra Vasquez - an exiled Cuban who originall worked as a sugar trader in Manila. When Nasutra was founded, he served as Nasutra Marketing Adviser and was directly responsible to Roberto Benedicto for trading the total export requirement of the Philippines. Vasquez, though granted Filipino citizenship by*

Marcos, later became a US citizen, and finally opted for Spanish citizenship, the latter move largely facilitated by a substantial investment in the Basque region of Spain. Vasquez figures prominently in many of Benedicto's overseas operations and would have intimate knowledge of the Marcos-Benedicto schemes.

Jake Vergara - has had a very long association with Benedicto in both the banking and sugar industries. He was head of the Philsucom office in Tokyo and also served as the PNB Vice-President and agent in Japan. Vergara has reportedly played a key role in making arrangements with banks and sugar buyers so that the actual amount of money generated through sugar trading did not reach the Philippines.

Fidel Rosales - a trusted Benedicto friend who served as treasurer of both Bequel Corp. and Cielo Verde Corp, two sugar corporations associated with Benedicto.

Danny Rosenbloom - an employee of Farr Mann, an international sugar trading house which has also been mentioned in connection with the long-term sugar contracts of the Philippines. Rosenbloom initially worked in Manila and later in Miami, Florida. He enjoyed a very close relationship with Benedicto and is considered a key figure in theMarcos-Benedicto sugar conspiracies.

Tommie Zita - is the nephew of Mrs. Benedicto. After receiving his MBA from New York University, Zita worked briefly in an insurance firm in New York. Despite his lack of knowledge of the sugar industry, he was appointed by Benedicto to head the strategic New York Office of the Philippine Sugar Commission and Nasutra, presumably because he could be trusted to carry out his uncle's orders. Zita is known to maintain accounts with Bankers Trust.

Among the international corporations owned by or are associated with Benedicto are:

Czarnikow-Rionda Inc. - a major international sugar trading firm with offices at 120 Wall St., New York. Worth $68 million, this firm was reportedly bought by Benedicto in 1982 with the help of Leandro Vasquez. Czarnikow—Rionda was one of the sugar brokers which held the lucrative four-year contract.
Bequel Corp. NY - an offshore corporation based in the Netherlands Antilles. Bequel purchased 100 voting stocks of Czarnikow-Rionda in March 1980.

Cielo Verde Corp. - bought all non voting stocks of Czamikow—Rionda. Leandro Vasquez was chairman of this corporation, with Joseph Fraites as president.

Rionna de Passe Ltd. - another sugar trading company associated with Benedicto, Rionna de Passe is a Bequel-owned subsidiary in London

Tilden Commercial Alliance Inc. - based in Roslyn Heights, New York financed some of Czamikow-Rionda's activities.

Phil. Sugar Trading Corp. (Philsutra) - a sugar trading corporation with offices in New York, 4 World Trade Center, Suite 520, with Benedicto as president and Zita serving as manager.

No accounting on how sugar was sold in the international market was ever provided by Nasutra, but later studies of the trading firm show substantial unreported earnings. One US account was discovered as having $5.09 million in 1984. Researchers report that this "amount was simply lodged in a suspense account titled advances from various accounts." Latest estimates of Benedicto overseas earnings through sugar trading indicate that over $4 billion earnings abroad were unreported. These funds, representing profits from sugar trading over a 10-year period starting in 1974, were handled by Tommie Zita through the Philsutra [43]. These funds are missing.

The $4 billion was generated through trading in international markets based in New York and London. No study has ever been done on how the New York and London offices operated nor where the money went. After the collapse of the Marcos government, Mrs. Aquino inexplicably appointed Fred Elizalde, a known Marcos and Benedicto associate in the sugar industry and long-standing member of Nasutra's board, as officer-in-charge of the industry [44]. Mrs. Aquino also inexplicably promoted Jake Vergara to executive vice-president of the PNB.

THE MONOPOLY AND SMUGGLING 0F SUGAR

Public resentment against Marcos' and Benedicto's control over the sugar industry led to calls for the dismantling of Philsucom. To deflect the growing criticism of his tight control over the sugar industry, Marcos formally ended the trading monopoly on 15 March 1984.

But the formal announcement did not diminish Benedicto's and Philsucom's grip over the industry. New regulations and conditions were promulgated. Hacenderos claimed that the new regulations strengthened rather than weakened Benedicto's stranglehold over the industry. The new conditions stipulated that all those who wanted to export sugar through Nasutra must enter into five-year contracts committing all of their produce to this trading body.

The move placed the hacenderos in a bind. For almost a decade, all of the international sugar trading had been done by the government, and time was needed to develop new contacts in the international sugar market. Benedicto, however, wanted the hacenderos to immediately decide on long-term contracts with Nasutra or promptly disassociate themselves from the government body. The problem of the hacenderos was aggravated by a glut m the international market. Nasutra would not give them any share of the long-term contracts it had earlier won at relatively better prices. And taking further advantage of the international glut, Nasutra tried to sow fear amongst the hacenderos by stating that not all of the those who applied with Nasutra would be accepted. Another method of coercion was to remind everyone that it was Benedicto's Republic Planters Bank (RPB) which controlled all of the credit and financing for the industry. Anyone who needed to plant for the next season and required credit had to go through Benedicto's bank. Financing could be, and was, withdrawn from the hacenderos who did not play the game [45]. A combination of selective advances to favored hacenderos and payment delays for others was also used to maintain the loyalty of the hacenderos. All of these moves were designed to force the hacenderos to continue using Nasutra as their trading agent even after the legal foundations of the monopoly had been formally rescinded.

Another method of financial coercion was later devised by Benedicto and his associates. The new tactic not only allowed them to cow the hacenderos but it also permitted them to generate money through rather dubious means.

Officials of Philsucom and other individuals close to Benedicto engaged in smuggling operations and illegally imported sugar into the country. According to a complaint filed with the legislature in 1985 (46), a total of 287,237 metric tons of raw sugar, valued at $54.4 million and a landed cost of $ 135 million, was smuggled into the country by Unson and Jaime Dacanay, individuals close to Benedicto. The two serve as Nasutra's executive vice-president and vice-president respectively. The complaint alleged that the commodity was brouht into the country in 18 shipments from 16 December 1983 through 9 Marc 1984 and were unloaded in the Guimaras island terminal, a location which was under total control of Benedicto. Charging Benedicto, Unson, and Dacanay with the crime of economic sabotage, the complaint alleged that the three used the name of Nasutra to import the sugar and later dumped it into domestic market at a profit of $20.7 million.

A further 30,000 metric tons was smuggled from Brazil in 1985 despite the oversupply in the local market. The Brazilian sugar, cheaper than the domestic prices, gave Benedicto enormous profits because of increased sales.

The effect of the massive dumping was to depress domestic sugar prices, creating extra pressure on the financially strapped hacenderos to capitulate and hand over trading to Nasutra. It was estimated that the illegal importation cost the overnment $46.2 million in customs tax and $16.2 million in sales tax, totalling $62.4 million.

Nasutra later claimed that the imported sugar was to be reexported, but there was no record certifying the said claim. On the contrary, existing paperwork seemed to indicate that the sugar was intended for local consumption.

Thus, while Nasutra was overshooting the US sugar quota at this time, implying that some of the produce could have been reassigned to the local market, Benedicto and company were illegally importing sugar:

> While we were importing sugar, Nasutra overshot the US sugar quota for the six-month period, October 1983 to March 1984. Nasutra was supposed to ship 199,125 short tons of sugar; it shipped over 200,000 short tans instead. For demurrage alone (or the fee for detaining the ships beyond the time allowed for unloading because the terminal is too small for the volume being unloaded), the cost to government is estimated at $10,000 per ship per day [47].

In view of these moves, it is instructive to recall earlier and equally self-serving moves of Nasutra which sacrificed interests of local consumers in the name of profits.

When prices picked up in the international market in late 1981, Nasutra stopped delivering to the local market, including the Kadiwa government stores in Metro-Manila, in order to fill two ships or the export market. This move resulted in severe sugar shortages. Sugar which had been imported for local consumption were also reexported so that Nasutra's long-term contracts with Marcos' and Benedicto's international trading corporations in New York could be met. The reexport of imported sugar merely to meet the demands of these trading companies resulted in huge losses on the part of Nasutra and the government.

But when prices slumped in during the first quarter of the following year, these very same Marcos-Benedicto-Floirendo-owned trading corporations and their affiliates breached their long-term contracts with the Philippines and refused to take the delivery of sugar at the contract price of $0.22 a pound. There was no incentive on the part of Nasutra to compel these international trading firms to honor their contracts since both ends were controlled by Marcos and Benedicto. It has been estimated that this breach of contract resulted in a decline of $241 million of export earnings from January through March in 1982, compared to same period in 1981 [48].

Given these highly questionable policies, there is therefore tragic irony in the assessment a government publication gave Philsucom at this time. After enumerating all the achievements of the sugar body, the publication summed up the benefits it has brought by saying, "for the sugar industry, the creation of Philsucom couldn't have come at a better time."

CONTROL OF THE MILLS

Benedicto's control over the industry extended to ownership and tight supervrsron over the country's most important sugar mills.

Control over the mills came in the form of cornering the financing and ownership of new refineries, regulating the production of competing companies, and outright takeover or closure of other mills through presidential decree.

The erratic behavior of the international market provided an excellent opportunity for Benedicto to take control over these mills. When the price plummeted in 1975, Benedicto, citing PD 385 which provided for automatic foreclosures for delinquent mortgage payments, used the occasion to foreclose the small or marginal sugar mills that defaulted in their payments.

But the Philsucom-mandated foreclosures were merely a way for Benedicto to personally benefit from the crisis. Benedicto, using his contacts with the PNB, arranged to "manage" these foreclosed mills for the state bank. A good example was the Pampanga Sugar Milling Company which had defaulted on its payments. In spite of a purchase offer from another company, the PNB awarded Benedicto the management of the mill, thus assuring him of continuous funding from PNB:

> Benedicto concentrated on the foreclosed sugar mills. He was more crude in his operations. He simply entered into contracts with the PNB for the management of the sugar mills. By an arrangement, Benedicto assured himself of continuous funding of his management by the PNB. In one case, Benedicto took over the management of the foreclosed Pampanga Sugar Milling Company (Pasumil). This despite the fact that a French-backed Filipino corporation had offered to buy the Pasumil and relieve PNB forever of sinking in more in the enterprise [49].

The Benedicto takeovers of the mills were later given presidential imprimatur with the promulgation of a decree organizing the Philippine Sugar Corp. (PSC) on 14 November 1983. PD 1890 provided that the PSC be jointly owned by Philsucom (65%) and the PNB (35%) and allocated it $450 million in government funds as its authorized capitalization. The new body, headed by Benedicto, had the authority to float bonds of up to $540 million to finance "the acquisition, rehabilitation and expansion of sugar mills, refineries, and other facilities" [50].

Thus, while the hacenderos were reeling under the blow of low international prices, Benedicto busied himself taking over the foreclosed mills, armed with presidential decrees and government financial backing, in the hope of better sugar prices in the future.

The next step Benedicto took to control the country's milling capacity was to engage in a frenzy of sugar mill construction. Armed with presidential decrees and Japanese financing, Benedicto undertook the construction of several new refineries. It was his attempt to increase domestic production by 40%.

Given the vagaries of the international market, where there were wide and sudden swings in the demand for sugar, the wisdom of such an ambitious program and the intentions of Marcos and Benedicto in pursuing it are suspect. The stated rationale for expanding the country's milling capacity was, in the words of a government publication, "to sell refined sugar directly to importing countries instead of merely supplying foreign refineries with raw sugar."

But succeeding events belied this assertion. The industry suffered from a continually depressed market and a consequent low capacity utilization of the new mills. Millers were in fact later encouraged to branch out to other areas to alleviate the recession within the industry. In one instance, Benedicto and his cohorts, armed with presidential muscle, forced a competing mill, Victoria Milling, to limit its production to 50% of capacity, resulting in a loss of $10.7 million.

More importantly, sugar for the most art was exported not as a refined product but in its raw form, contradicting the initial rationale for the massive modernization program for mills and refineries.

Exporting unprocessed sugar and constructing new mills while there was a slack in demand may appear contradictory at first, but are perfectly logical within the context of how the Marcos cronies operated. Corporations were organized and managed not as legitimate business ventures but as activities to generate quick money regardless of their long term consequences.

Sugar was exported unprocessed despite idle mills because Marcos at this time had just acquired a multimillion dollar sugar refinery in the US through Antonio Floirendo (see section). This sugar company was one of the beneficiaries of the controversial long-term contracts which sold Philippine sugar at give-away prices.

The flurry of sugar mill construction was due to the opportunities that these new projects resented for kickbacks. Industry sources claim that all of the 10 sugar mills built from 1972 through 1976 were overpriced by as much as 100% [51]. In one case, a mill costing $13 million was estimated to have been overpriced by $10 to $15 million. The same industry sources also pointed out that there were discrepancies between the actual cost of projects and the letters of credit opened in favor of agents [52]. The overpricing for the 10 mills generated between $50 million to $75 million.

It is significant that all of these mills were constructed with financing the Export-Import Bank of Japan Benedicto had arranged with while serving as Ambassador to Japan. It is also significant that the construction of these mills were carried out by a select group of Japanese corporations which were beneficiaries of Marcos projects in other occasions. Of the ten mills, eight were built by Hitachi Zosen and later sold to Marubeni Co., while the two others were built by Mitsubishi Shoji, Tomen, and Kawasaki. But while the initial financing came from the Japanese Export-Import Bank, the debt was finally assumed by the PNB which issued the letters of credit for the construction of 10 sugar mills. Financing for these mills represented an increase of $508 million in the country's foreign debt [53].

The case of the Bukidnon Sugar Company (Busco) is illustrative. Busco, located in Paitan, Quezon, Bukidnon, is one of the more important sugar refineries in the country. it is the first to apply mechanized farming to its operations and is the biggest sugar refinery plant in the Visayas and Mindanao area.

Initial funding for Busco came in 1974 in the form of $60 million in credits from Marubeni Iida Co., Tokyo, and Marubeni-Benelux, the Japanese equipment suppliers for the sugar central. Further financing came from the Japanese Expor-Import Bank, which provided 80% of Busco's financing. These credits were backed with guarantees from the PNB.

Benedicto's role was central. The funding from the Japanese was arranged by Benedicto using his position as Ambassador to Japan. The Philippine side was represented by Silangan Investment & Managers, a finance company chaired by Benedicto. Guarantees for the Japanese credits came from the PNB, the state bank where Benedicto was formerly chairman and had left trusted people to do his bidding. The recipient of the loan, Busco, had for its directors Benedicto and other Marcos people such as Jose L. Africa (chairman), Nieto (president), Jose R. Zubiri Jr. (executive vice-president), a former member of the KBL and Marcos' parliament [54]. Busco received further support from Philsucom which Benedicto also headed.

Construction of the refinery started with the eviction of members of the Manobo tribe, in Philippine cultural minority, from their ancestral lands in 1975. The Philippine constabulary and Busco security guards forcibly ejected the Manobo tribesmen from their lands, and the rice and corn lands which were used by the tribe as their source of livelihood were then converted to Benedicto's sugar lands [55].

Busco was constructed at an overprice. industry sources pointed out that mills with a daily ca acity of 6,000 tons such as Busco were built for 30% less. The principal buil in contractor for the project was the Construction & Dovelopment Corp. of the Philip ines (CDCP), a company which typically overpriced its contracts. The CDCP was run by Rodolfo uenca (see section), who also served as director of Busco.

in the end, Busco accumulated $30 million in debt. The PNB was again left holding the bag. Busco's could have paid for its liabilities with earnings from two profitable years. The revenues generated during the 1976-77 and 1984-85 cro years amounting to $38 million could have covered these obligations. nstead, Benedicto and company chose to pilfer the funds and leave the PNB to assume its liabilities. Busco owed the PNB a total of $122 million as of 30 June 1985, representing principal and accumulated interest charges.

Other groups which dealt with Busco were also stiffed. The Bukidnon Sugar Planters Association, whose 1,500 members dealt with Busco, claimed that their hacenderos were owed millions and were suffering huge losses because of Busco's non-payment. The planters claimed that the company had become Benedicto's "milking cow" [5].

Busco also exploited labor. It imported workers from the neighboring islands of Negros and Panay who were desperate for work and paid them starvation rates. Instead of paying full wages, the seasonal workers were paid using the piece-rate (pakyaw system for the back-breaking work of weeding the land and planting the seedlings. For every 1,000 seedlings of sugar planted, each worker was paid the equivalent of $0.32 cents.

A partial list of the mills, refineries, and farms that Benedicto owned and controlled Within the sugar industry and other agri-busmess enterprises:

> RSB Farms
> Republic Sugar Dev. Corp.
> Calinog-Lambunao Refinery
> Bukidnon Sugar Mill
> Upsumco Sugar Mill
> Davao Sugar Central
> Universal Mollasses Corp.
> Bulk Terminal Integrated Sugar Co.
> Guimaras Bulk Terminal
> 2,000 hectare farm, Hacienda Silangan, Bukidnon
> 9 sugar farms totalling 786 hectares in Ma-ao town
> two plantations totalling 127 hectares, Silay City, Negros del None
> three haciendas in Pontevedra, Negros Occidental
> 14 plantations in Negros Occidental
> 2,300 hectares including a 700-hectare coffee plantation in La Carlota City [57].

These Benedicto-owned farms, mills, and refineries also benefitted from government help by cornering for themselves the benefits and incentives that was intended for the whole industry. The tax exemptions for the importation of machinery and the tractor an agricultural equipment pools organized with Philsucom funds, for example, were not equally distributed within the industry but were used for the sugar mills and refineries that Benedicto and other Marcos cronies owned.

OTHER ASPECTS OF PHILSUCOM OPERATIONS

Control of the country's milling system meant control of the supply of sugar. Control of the mills made it a relatively easy task to manipulate the quedan, the system where hacenderos would turn over a percentage of their sugar produce to the mills in exchange for its processing. The inventories of these quedans were manipulated so that they would not reflect the actual transactions.

Hacenderos complained that Nasutra had not paid them $27 million by 1984 for their sugar. Another report made a year before Marcos' fall claimed that the trading body had overstated its advances to hacenderos by $67.2 million [58]. Proceeds from exports, totalling 300,000 metric tons of sugar valued at $118.2 million, were also withheld by Nasutra [59].

A study of Nasutra operations after Marcos' fall showed that the physical inventories of sugar were inconsistent with the outstanding quedans and with balances as recorded in its books. Another report showed that Nasutra failed to remit payments worth $2.7 million to banks during its last year of operations. The amount were for the quedans and bills payable representing the sugar delivered to Philsucom and Nasutra since March 1985 [60].

There were other ways through which the sugar inventories were manipulated.

One method consisted in providing an inaccurate reading of the sugar content of the raw produce. Chemists analyzing the sugar at the centrals and mills were often bribed by Benedicto's men to give a false reading of the actual sugar content, permitting lower prices.

Another tactic was to declare stocks of sugar as "deteriorated." This method of inventory manipulation started as early as the organization of Philsucom in 1977. According to a PNB report, 1.5 million tons of sugar worth $324 million were passed from Philex to Nasutra when the earlier sugar body was dissolved in favor of Philsucom (Nasutra). It was later claimed that this stock had deteriorated and was written off. But sources in the sugar industry believe that this stock was later sold illegally. Nasutra in any case ended paying for these stocks using loans from PNB and other local and foreign sources (61).

This practice appears to have been quite common within Philsucom. As late as a few months before Marcos' downfall, for example, Armando Gustilo, chairman of Nasutra Executive Committee who enjoyed close links to the dictator, declared 1.2 million piculs of sugar as "deteriorated". The stock, originally bought at $16.12 er picul, was sold at $4.84 and later resold at $10.75. Figuring prominenty in this deal was DAE Marketing Corp., a company owned by Antonio Lupingco, known to be close to the Marcos family [62]. The funds from the sale of this "deteriorated" stock, amounting to $9.7 million, was supposed to go to a special fund, but the money is missing.

It is believed that the unaccounted sugar stocks were later smuggled out of the country, earning unreported revenue for Benedicto and his associates.

During the occasions when Benedicto and his associates did report their exports, they did so without paying the proper taxes. According to customs authorities, Nasutra defrauded the government of $132 million in penalties and charges of customs levy on every ton of sugar exported since 1984, making it first in a list of tax delinquent corporations compiled by customs officials [63]. In a collection suit filed against Nasutra, with company directors named as respondents, customs authorities claimed that Nasutra owed the governimerit $108 million, $132 million if interest is included, in unpaid customs levies.

Nasutra also owed the Bureau of Internal Revenue $1.04 million in taxes by the end of 1984, according to the Commission on Audit. This amount represents the money Nasutra withheld from sugar centrals and mills. Nasutra automatically deducted this amount from the proceeds of export sales of sugar before paying the hacenderos for the sugar they turned over to Nasutra. But rather than remit the money to the Bureau of Internal Revenue, Nasutra deposited it in a "trust fund" at Benedicto's Republic Planters Bank. Money from export taxes and other sources that went into this "trust fund" has been estimated to be around million. Apart from the claims of Nasutra officials that the funds were indeed deposited into this "trust fund" at Benedicto's bank, there is no other indication as to where the funds actually went, with the full amount of $30 million missing.

Philsucom was created with the aim of promoting the "integrated development and stabilization of the sugar industry." it may be said that this aim was successfully carried out insofar as this "development" created billions in the hands of a new sugar elite led by Marcos, Benedicto, Floirendo, and their associates.

But while great wealth was enjoyed by a few, the whole sugar industry stagnated, its workers labored under inhuman working conditions, consumers endured high prices, and the country lost major opportunities.

Although Nasutra was created by presidential decree and operated as a government monopoly, it was never subject to the normal procedures of governmental audit. *The billions generated from its operations were never at any point subject to audit by government auditors.* However, a confidential 1985 government report on the sugar industry, which Marcos presumably ordered so as to keep track of Benedicto's earnings, reported major discrepancies in Nasutra accounts. inter-office accounts of Nasutra totalling $161 million could not be reconciled with available documents. It also found that Nasutra had under-reported its profits from 1978 through 1983 by $430 million.

Another source claimed that the trading corporation failed to account for $150 million in revenue from September 1979 through June 1984.

Industry sources estimate that the sugar industry lost $150 million from the rice-faring policies of Benedicto from 1974 through 1982 [64]. Benedicto and company were estimated to have generated an estimated $550 million from the anomalies committed through their activities in Nasutra and Philex [65]. The figure is possibly a low estimate. Given these figures, there is great irony in the work of government publication concerning the role of the trading body:

> *The establishment of the Nasutra as the trading arm of the sugar industry has proved to be another boon both during the critical years and until sugar's resurgence in the international market.*

The outstanding foreign obligations of Nasutra amounted to $155 million when it folded up. These represent loans from international banks such as Bankers Trust, Chemical Bank, American Express. These liabilities were assumed by the Philippine government. This clearly contravened Nasutra's stated aim to "properly discharge its economic and social responsibilities and contribute its share in the development of the national economy."

WORKERS EN THE INDUSTRY

To appease the anger of the hacenderos and other members of the traditional sugar oligarchy at the existing policies, the Marcos government exempted the sugar industry from paying the minimum wage and other allowances stipulated by law. This resulted in the further deterioration of the already miserable living conditions of the more than 500,000 laborers in the sugar industry.

Surveys of the economic situation of sugar workers reveal their desperate plight. These surveys of the wages of both the resident workers (*dumaans*) and migrant workers (*sacadas*) consistently showed that their average wages were at starvation levels even during the milling season when wage rates were generally higher. The following table is constructed from the results of two different surveys:

Average Dolly Household income of Sugar Worker.
$0.55 per day   during off-milling season
$0.72 per day   during milling season [66]

Average Dolly Household income of Sugar Worker:
$0.89 per day   during off-milling season
$1.05 per day   during milling season [67].

These rates were not only well below the prevailing minimum wage but were also not enough to cover the absolute minimum in food requirements. It was pointed out that at these rates...

...about one—fourth of the workers could not afford basic requirements even during the milling season when work was available for almost everyone. The number increases during the off—season. Significantly too many workers reported no upward change in their income during the sugar boom. Little wonder why 50% of them felt that there would be no change in the next five years [68].

Workers in the industry endured these miserable working conditions because of the constant threat of losing their livelihood. Work was not only seasonal but was also difficult to get, especially during the times when the industry was in a slump. In 1985, the last year Benedicto and Marcos controlled the industry, 400,000 sugar workers in the island of Negros were facing starvation. The sugar mills had closed down. No funds were forthcoming for the planting of sugar cane.

A few years before these surveys were done, a Jesuit priest lived and worked with the migrant sugar workers for a few months. The following is part of his account on the living and working conditions of the sacadas:

*There were 200 of us - men, women and children staying in two adjoining **cuartels**.*

There was not a single toilet. There was only one source of water- on old pump. Here everyone did his or her washing, bathing, laundering. We had no blankets, no mosquito nets. For food, three times a day we were served rice - the cheapest, driest, coarsest, most unappetizing I have ever tasted. Many of the grains were unhusked, and there were pieces of gravel to be found among the grains of rice. Rough rice and dry fish, that was all. No liquid, no vegetable, a diet which gave no delight and no strength. Yet strength is needed for the sacada's work. At 3:30 am, the lights come on, and by 5:00 am, the sacadas have trudged, barefoot, through the one kilometer which separates the cane fields from the quarrels. The sacada's work is cutting and loading. This is easier said than done. The work of cutting is monotonous - the same endless ending of the entire body, the same strong cutting strokes of the **espading** *with one hand, the same grasping and jerking and piling up of the sugarcane by the other hand. The work is also very exacting. It saps away one's strength in a very short time. Added to this is the discomfort of wearing thick, close-necked, long-sleeve denims (to protect oneself against cuts and rashes from the gilok and the leaves) under the heat of the burning sun. But the sacada must continually keep on working, since, if he is to eat, he is supposed to cut tons of sugarcane. The sacada must now load the sugarcane. He bends down, grapples with his pile of 25 to 35 canes, and then, under this heavy burden, navigates his way through the field to the railroad tracks where he dumps his load into the bagon. Then the sacada goes through the whole process again and again until all the sugarcane he has cut is completely loaded into the railway cars [69].*

This is a description of the living and working conditions of the seasonal workers in the sugar industry. The millions that Marcos and Benedicto raised through the sugar industry was made possible by the toil of these people. While Benedicto earned millions through his control of the industry, workers in his Busco plantation were paid $0.32 cents for every 1,000 seedlings planted.

When these workers complained about their plight to the Marcos government, they were threatened and beaten up by hired company goons and soldiers. One such occasion directly involved one of Benedicto's closest associates, Armando Gustilo, chairman of the Nasutra Executive Committee and president of National Federation of Sugarcane Planters. The Escalante Massacre, named alter the place where indiscriminate shooting by the military on 20 September 198 took place, resulted in 27 dead and more than two dozen wounded among the protestors. Although Gustilo denies being present during the massacre, his Mercedes Benz was photographed at the Escalante municipal hall on the day of the shooting and is known to have been in close touch with Brigadier General Isidro de Guzman, commander of the Regional Unified Command VI, immediately before and after the shooting. Gustilo, denying any involvement, appeared on TV, saying

I was never in Escalante... the issue is not whether some people were killed or not. The dead are dead, not merely because of the soldiers. They are dead because they were induced and incited to make moves against the government.

It is important to keep these things in mind when reviewing Marcos' and Benedicto's policies in the sugar industry. They serve to remind us that behind the billions that were raised in the industry were the sacrifices of the hundreds of thousands of sugar workers.

This also helps us see the complaints of the hacenderos in their proper context. While the hacenderos kept on complaining about government policies in the industry, proclaiming themselves as the *nouveau poor*, there was really a bias in policy against the workers in the industry. Whenever the export prices dipped, it was the workers who suffered most, not the hacenderos. It was just that the hacenderos, having the advantage of education and money, were able to articulate their position better than the poor unschooled sugar worker. The cost of a decrease in the export price of sugar was automatically passed on to the workers by the hacenderos in the form of massive layofis, lower real wages, and exemptions from the government from paying the minimum wage and other legally required benefits.

Yet, as the studies cited above indicate, increases in the export price were never passed on to the worker in the form of higher wages.

The hacenderos asked, and received, from the Marcos government exemptions from the coverage of four presidential decrees which granted increases in the minimum wage, the monthly allowance, and the monthly emergency living allowance.

The law also provided for a Social Amelioration Fund (SAF) to finance "bonuses" and seem-economic projects for about 600,000 mill and plantation workers in the sugar industry. Researches show that half the workers never enjoyed their social amelioration bonus. The Rural Workers Office of the Ministry of Labor was charged with managing the funds. The fund, estimated to be $100 million covering crop years 1970 through 1985, is missing.

An earlier law, dating to the 1950's, also provided that $0.50 for every picul of sugar produced be set aside for the sugar workers. it was a token amount, but it amounted to millions over the years. The fund was estimated to be at $17 million as of 1960. Over the last our decades, hacenderos have never paid the workers from this fund nor accounted for it.

So when hacenderos complain that Benedicto and Marcos bilked them of their produce, we should equally remind ourselves of how these hacenderos behaved with regard to their workers prior to, during, and after Marcos' regime. Benedicto merely turned the tables on them and for once they were on the losing end.

The hacenderos always contended that Nasutra was merely their agent so that all the trading profits should have gone back to them. Using this argument one can further say that, since it was through the back-breaking work of the laborer in the field that sugar was produce, the earnings should have likewise been plowed back to the poorly-paid worker. In any case, the distribution of the benefits should have been more equitable.

BANKING ENTERESTS

Benedicto also had substantial interests in the banking industry, including ownership of the Republic Planters Bank (RPB), the state-designated private bank for the sugar industry.

Nine months after the Philsucom was established, Benedicto, realizing the importance of controlling financing within the sugar industry, took over the Republic

Bank from Roman and Roxas families. A presidential decree was then issued on 11 May 1978 designating the reorganized bank, Republic Planters Bank, as the depository of the sugar industry. Benedicto was named chairman, with M. Consing serving as president. Victor Ortega, the Marcos-designated Vice-Governor of La Union province and nephew of Benedicto, served as secretary. The newly reorganized bank was to be initially named Republic Savings Bank so that its acronym, RSB, would coincide with Benedicto's initials, but prudence finally won out and the bank was christened Republic Planters Bank.

The effect of organizing the new bank was to further weaken the control of the hacenderos and other sectors of the traditional sugar oligarchy. The PNB, established in 1916 to help Filipino sugar mills during the American colonial administration, had a tradition of favoring sugar interests over the other agricultural sectors. By designating a new bank under Benedicto's control as the commodity bank of the sugar industry, an efficient stranglehold method was devised.

It was a fairly simple matter to control sugar production, especially the harvest of competitors within the industry, by controlling the crop loans. Since the hacenderos could not approach other banks for financing anyone who needed money for the next planting season had to be in the good graces of the Marcos administration. This served as an effective deterrent to criticism of Marcos' and Benedicto's policies. A government publication rationalized this financing monopoly:

> This banking system enables the sugar-industry to avoid fierce competition from private commercial banks and even government lending institutions. Ambassador Roberto S. Benedicto, chairman of Philsucom, noted that the emergence of Republic Planters Bank 1978 as the bank of the sugar industry, was an important strategic decision during that period.

Apart from control over the industry through selective financing, Benedicto was also able to raise money through the RPB because of the support it received from the government. Further government support of Benedicto's RPB came in the form of presidential LOIs. When the Central Bank slapped huge penalties on the RPB for failing to meet reserve requirements in 1983, Marcos came directly to Benedicto's rescue and issued LOI 1330 wiping out the penalties against the bank [70]. The LOI, issued on 6 June 1983, directed the Central Bank to condone the penalties and corresponding interest on the "reserve deficiencies on sugar loans on Republic Planters Bank." While Marcos rationalized his move by stating that sugar was an essential industry, the move had the effect of undermining the efforts of the Central Bank to control the money supply at a time when the country was in deep financial crisis (see Chapter IV).

The Central Bank was further instructed to extend loans to the RPB at subsidized rates. The Central Bank was forced to lend capital to the RPB at the *nominal rate of 4% interest*. Benedicto used these funds to finance his sugar mills and other interests or later reloaned this money to other parties at market rates. This effectively constituted a subsidy for the RPB and other Benedicto companies.

The RPB was also authorized to collect a "welfare fund" from sugar transactions. This amount was automatically deducted not from the composite price but from the price of sugar in real terms, thus allowing for a greater amount of deductions. The purpose of the "welfare fund" was never explained nor the funds accounted for.

During the financial crisis of 1983, the total deposits of RPB dropped 24% and its liquid assets fell from $78.5 million to 39.4 million, a drop of 50%. This meant that RPB, which had total assets of $413.2 million as of June 1984, had a ratio of 0.09:1 between its liquid and total assets. These figures indicate that Marcos and Benedicto were busy moving their money out of the country during the financial crisis of 1983, precipitated by other Marcos cronies. Marcos at this time issued another order to the Central Bank directing it to treat the overdrafts of the RPB as loans, permitting the RPB to freely issue checks which the Central Bank would then treat as a loan.

Other banking interests of Benedicto included the Traders Royal Bank in Manila and California Overseas Bank in Los Angeles.

Benedicto also managed Traders Royal Bank for the Marcos family. It appears that this bank was owned and used by the Marcoses to funnel funds to secret overseas accounts. Imee Marcos had no less than $8.6 million in this bank when Marcos was deposed in 1986 [71]. Marcos himself had $60 million in deposits and treasury warrants. The principal stockholder of bank was FEMII — an acronym for Ferdinand Edralin Marcos Investments (72), with Benedicto overseein the interests of the Marcoses. Traders Royal Bank had tie-ups with Crédit Suisse and Royal Bank of Canada. These tie-ups, especially the one with Crédit Suisse, are meaningful in light of Benedicto's activities to set-up Swiss bank accounts for Marcos [73]. The TRB was a very lucrative venture, reporting profits of $2.45 million for the first half of 1984, partly because it was the bank used by Marcos to stash his take from local gambling casinos (see next section). Benedicto's associate in the sugar industry, Jose Africa, served as chairman of the bank, with Dominador Pangilinan as president. Benedicto's wife, Francesca, had interests in both the Traders Royal Bank and the Republic Planters Bank.

Benedicto also owned the California Overseas Bank of Los Angeles, with real estate investments worth $7 million and total assets of $133 million. Using his Swiss accounts, he purchased the bank between 1975 and 1976 with an initial investment of $2 million of shares. Among those who served as the directors of the bank were the following individuals, most of whom are close Marcos associates: Rodolfo T. Arambulo, Miguel V. Gonzalez, James I. McNally, Dominador R. Pangilinan, Pag-asa San Agustin.

Benedicto at one time owned 100% of the preferred stock and 88% of the common stock of the bank and also had a personal account with the bank amounting to $3 million.

SHEPPTNG AND TRANSPORT SERVICES

Benedicto also owns several shipping lines and other transport-related Companies.

Although his name did not appear on the company papers of Northern Lines, it was widely known in shipping circles that Benedicto was the owner of this large shipping firm and that he held his main office in the Northern Lines building (74). Northern Lines, the largest among the many shipping lines Benedicto owned, was the company designated by Nasutra to carry the country's sugar to the US and Japan. The monopoly he enjoyed in transporting sugar exports meant increased costs and less earnings for the industry. The shipping agent of Northern Lines is Ragus Trading Corp. Ragus, which has offices at 560 Lexington, N.Y., is also believed to be connected to Benedicto and Leandro Vazquez.

Aside from his control of the sugar industry, Benedicto also tried to consolidate the management and influence of the sugar bulk-handling terminals, transport systems, and allied facilities.

Among the shipping and transportation-related companies owned or controlled by Benedicto are

> Republic Transport & Shipyard Co. a lighterage and repair service for ships and barges in Iloilo, registered with the SEC on May 1979.
> Davao Bulk Corporation, registered with the SEC on April 1977.
> Visayan Maritime Academy - a nautical school
> International Forwarders Inc.
> BM-AMCI - trucking for hauling canes, fertilizers, raw and refined sugar
> Molave Bulk Carriers
> Aklan Bulk Carriers
> Coron Bulk Carriers
> Ecija Bulk Carriers
> Marapara Shipping Co.
> Negros Stevedoring Co. - domestic lighterage service
> Fuga Bulk Carriers
> Among the many ocean-going vessels Benedicto owned are:
> Don Salvador II + Don Hortencia + Dona Corazon + Dona Paz + Dona Magdalena + La Carlota + Dona Isabel + Don Pablo + Dona Pacita + Don Herman + San Jacinto.

Benedicto also owned a maritime school, the Visayan Maritime Academy, whose personnel he sometimes used as security.

HOTELS AND GAMBLING

Benedicto also ventured into the entertainment industry, carving niches in hotels and state-supported gambling activities.

The Benedicto entry into the hotel industry again provides clear examples of how government resources were abused for private gain.

After the previous owners were eased out of the Riviera Hotel in 1971, Benedicto took over and renamed it the Holiday Inn Hotel. The creditors of the original owners, the government-owned Development Bank of the Philippines (DBP), had appraised the hotel to be worth 17.8 million but sold it to the New Rivrera Hotel Dev. Corp. for $16.3 million. The charter of the DBP expressly forbids it to incur such losses, but the government bank nevertheless gave Benedicto a $1.5 million windfall by declaring the amount as "uncollectible receivables" [75]. Typical of the way the Marcos cronies operated, the hotel was again milked by Benedicto. While the hotel was appraised at $17.8 million, the DBP again bent backwards and granted loans which far exceeded legal limits. A total of $281 million had been lent by DBP by the time Benedicto decided to get rid of it in 1982. Here is a situation where Benedicto buys a hotel at a $1.5 million discount, borrows money from the government an amount more than twice the collateral, and later dumps the hotel on the government's lap, getting away with $10.3 million.

Other related interests of Benedicto include the Kanlaon Towers Corp. which owns the Kanlaon Towers Hotel, the Bayview Plaza, and an expensive condominium which occupies a whole block in Legaspi Towers in the rich neighborhood of Makati.

Benedicto was one those who benefitted from the few gambling casinos legalized by the government.

He entered the gambling business in 1975 when he purchased a $4M vessel and opened the floating casino for the Manila Bay Enterprises, a firm which operated this ship as a casino. The paperwork for the ship's purchase was done through the Peninsula Tourist & Shipping Corp. This firm was run by Reed Clarke, chairman of Czarnikow-Rionda Trading, and was believed to be a paper corporation which served as an adjunct of Norther Lines. Harry Ernest McMullin, an American from Los Angeles married to Benedicto's first cousin, Vilumin, is also believed to have had a hand in the purchase of this ship and other Benedicto vessels.

The casino earnings were supposed to be turned over the government and used for public works projects. A private firm, Pagcor (Philippine Amusement & Gaming Corp., a government-funded private firm (see section on Romualdez), managed the money which was supposed to be turned over to the government. But government officials were continually rebuffed whenever they attempted to study Pagcor's books or withdraw the money [76]. The proceeds were instead with the Traders Royal Bank [77]. Precise figures on casino earnings were kept secret, but it is clear that the gambling operations raked in a lot of money. One account reported $83.7 million as the annual earnings for 1982. The gambling proceeds were reported to comprise as much as 26% of Trader's total deposits, but no interest has been paid on this amount [78].

MEDIA AND TELECOMMUNICATIONS EMPIRE

The small radio station that Benedicto ran before martial law was transformed into the Kanlaon Broadcasting System, a gigantic tri-media empire covering 3 TV channels [79], 15 radio stations, and a national newspaper, the *Daily Express*. The nucleus for this network came from the privately owned ABS-CBN (80). Under the guise of "national security," the military first took over the facilities on 8 June 1973. They were later turned over Benedicto, with a purchase option offered to Kokoy Romualdez, Imelda's brother, with the provision that the "leases" and compensation to the previous owners would be "reasonable" and determined at a later time [81]. The network was then expanded by Benedicto with heavy borrowings from the PNB.

The *Daily Express*, together with the television and radio stations, served the voice of the Marcos dictatorship, as well as generating income for Benedicto. Benedicto assigned Enrique Romualdez editor of the paper, thus ensuring that it would carry the viewpoint of the regime. Nemesio Yabut, the mayor of Makati, donated an empty lot to the paper to propitiate Marcos after he had killed the dictator's half-brother in a turf war [82].

The Kanlaon Broadcasting System, which had the only full color TV channel in the country (Channel 9), was initially headed by Benedicto's adopted daughter, Kitchie, but was later taken over by Marcos' eldest daughter, Imee Marcos-Manotoc.

Benedicto expanded his media interest by acquiring inter-Continental Broadcasting Corp. (IBC) which operated five television stations, including Channel 13 in Manila, and nine radio stations in Manila and the provinces. The Radio Philippine Network (RPN) was added to the media conglomerate, which included eight television stations and seven radio broadcasting stations in the provinces. Sining Makulay, a cable TV network, was also part of Benedicto's media empire.

The media empire of Benedicto likewise benefitted from many government incentives. Marcos specifically penned a series of LOI's granting special favors to two of Benedicto's companies, Nivico, a TV manufacturing firm, and the Banahaw Broadcasting Corp. (BBC), which formed a part of Benedicto's Kanlaon System.

Marcos issued LOI 640 on 15 December 1977 empowering Banahaw to import $3 million worth of TV transmission epuipment and associated facilities without paying taxes or tariff duties. The LOI also allowed the importation, again tax-free, of $15 million worth of knocked adown l2-inch black and white TV sets over the succeeding five years. The presidential order also permitted Banahaw to contract a local company to assemble the TV sets and sell them to the market, with the proviso that these sets would be sold to the rural areas and at a lower price.

The LOI further directed government ministries to enter into a cooperative venture with Banahaw Broadcastin Corp. in marketing these TV sets. The ministries of Public information, National Defense, Education and Culture, and the National Media Production Center were instructed to use the sets for their public information and educational projects, thus assuring Banahaw of a large captive market.

Marcos issued another letter of instruction in 1982, LOI 640-A, extending the scope and duration of the earlier order. The revised presidential order no longer limited the imports to 12-inch black and white sets. The new instructions directed government ministries to contract with Banahaw "on matters pertaining to peace and order" and distribute the Benedicto TV sets in countryside areas where rebellion was fomenting.

The two letters of instruction were designed to (provide cheap, tax-free parts and assure a captive market for Banahaw an Nivico, the firm contracted to assemble the TV sets.

Because of the tax breaks enjoyed by Nivico, it was able to sell 12-inch black—and-white TV sets for $130, while its competitors who had to pay duties and taxes on imported parts sold their sets for $175.

The blatant patronage led to a lot of criticism. The Consumer Electronic Products Manufacturers Association (CEPMA) claimed that it could sell for $110 what Nivico sold for $130 if its members were given the same tax-free privileges. The CEPMA also complained that the Nivico-assembled sets, while originally intended for the rural areas, turned up in Manila, thus unfairly eating into their market.

Critics claimed that Nivico negated the principal aim of Electronics Local Content Program, which provrded for reduced tariff on raw materials to encourage local manufacturing. Nivico imported only finished parts [83] and was merely assembling Japanese-made parts. The practice violated a Board of Investments (BOT) requirement that a certain percent of finished products must contain domestic components.

It was also pointed out that a new firm, Nivico, was being allowed to enter into an "overcrowded industry," an area where no new entrants were to be permitted. The question was further raised why the presidential orders were being implemented through a new firm which was just an assembler, instead of already-existing TV manufacturers, which were better equipped to meet the technical requirements needed for this venture. Nivico was incorporated in December 1977, the same month LOI 640 was issued, and only started operations in June 1978 [84].

The criticisms centered on the identity of the owner of Nivico, a "prominent industrialist" from Negros island who had remained unnamed all throughout the controversy. The issue was fully discussed in all the newspapers, with the exception of the *Daily Express,* the Benedicto newspaper. The reason for all the residential favors became clear when the personality behind Nivico surface: Benedicto was both chairman and president of Nivico Phil. Inc., a joint-venture with Victor Co. of Japan.
Benedicto was also part of the conspiracy involving several Marcos cronies to monopolize the telecommunications industry through the Philippine Overseas Telecommunications Corp. (see section on Enrile). Among the telecommunications companies Benedicto owned were Eastern Telecommunications and Oceanic Wireless Network, with other Marcos cronies such as Jose Africa and Manuel Nieto having interests in the latter company. Benedicto also purchased major shareholdings in Cable & Wireless Ltd, a London-based firm.

MEAT CARTEL

Benedicto, together with other Marcos associates such as Luis Yulo, also created a "meat cartel" in an attempt to control the importation, distribution, and feed-supply of the country's cattle. This cartel involved the Philippine Integrated Meat Corp. (Pimeco), Phil-Asia Food Industries, and the Yulo King Ranch. The first two companies were directly associated with Benedicto and his confederates, while the third involved Geromino Velasco (discussed later in this chapter).

The Pimeco, organized by Benedicto with Luis Yulo and Peter Sabido, benefitted immensely from government support in the form of huge loans and a government-decreed monopoly over the trading of imported cattle and meat [85].

Backing for Pimeco was also provided through Philbai Int. Pty. Ltd, a government-owned company which imported livestock and meat. Philbai, organized in 1979 throu EO 572, was registered in Australia with a capitalization of A$25,000 dollars, the money drawn from the funds of the the Philippine Bureau of Animal Industry [86]. Philbai imported Australian cattle into the country which Pimeco later distributed. Both Pimeco and Philbai were headed by Peter Sabido, the latter firm run with the help of an Australian named Linden Prowse, a close Sabido associate. Money from Philbai is known to have funded pasture lands of the Sabido family in Australia [87]. Philbai was also charged of contracting freight for the imported cattle at a considerable overprice and of paying an annual "service ee" of A$120,000 dollars to an unnamed consultant in Manila [88]. Around A$1 million dollars were missing when auditors checked the company in 1986. Philbai was also getting letters of credit opened under its name from the Bureau of Animal Industry even when it was not actually importing cattle or beef [89]. The actual importer was the Yulo King Ranch owned by Marcos associates Velasco and Yulo.

Pimeco, typical of the way many crony corporations operated, chalked up huge debts with such as Traders Royal Bank and the GSIS. While its aid-up capital was only $68,000, its debts to the GSIS reached $4.6 million (90), a clear violation of the law.

Completing the meat cartel was Phil-Asia Food Industries Inc., a company dubbed as the first large-scale soybean processing plant in Southeast Asia. The aim of Phil-Asia was to process soya beans into cheap high-protein food and meet all the feed requirements of country's livestock and poultry industry. Plans were later made to also control the importation of soybeans. The company was incorporated by Benedicto in 1975 and was again run by Peter Sabido.

The Phil-Asia plant, publicly inaugurated by Marcos in 1975, was built in Tabangao, Batangas at the cost of $43.7 million, a clear overprice. The giant received heavy financing from government institutions such as the NFA, DBP, NIDC, the latter the investment arm of the PNB, which all sunk in a total of $40 million. By 1986, loans from the DBP had already amounted to $52,696,203, largely representing foreign currency loans with the US Exim Bank [91]. Commodity loans from the World Bank totalled $43 million, in addition to another $5.25 million obligation to the NFA.

There was one problem, however. Nobody ever bothered to plant the soya beans. An attempt was made to foreclose the plant, but it was discovered that the company's assets had by then been degenerated to only $13.4 million. Alan Mauricio, the firm's spokesman, claimed that the above-cited figures were incorrect and that "there is nothing anomalous in any of the transactions done by the company." He did not elaborate further. Apart from Benedicto and Sabido, others involved in the Phil-Asia scam were Luis Yulo and DBP governors Don M. Ferry, Rafael Sison, Jose R. Tengco, Cesar C. Zalamea.

OTHER GOVERNMENT DEALS

Benedicto, with the help of Marcos government ministers, also attempted to corner other services to the government.

Collaborating with Velasco, Benedicto arranged for the overseas purchases for the entire Philippine National Oil Company (PNOC) and got huge commissions from these deals (see section on Velasco).

Integral Factors Corp. (IFC), another Benedicto corporation, controlled the provision of insurance for the government sector. While government offices were supposed to insure with the GSIS, a special presidential decree ordered all major government offices to use the services of Integral Factors. Roman Cruz, chairman of the GSIS, gave Benedcito's firm an exclusive and extremely profitable contract to act as sole and exclusive agent of GSIS with respect to the insurance requirements of the government. Integral Factors in turn reinsured the policies with the GSIS, earning a fat profit in the process without undertaking any risk. But despite these arrangements, the

IFC, in blatant breach of its fiduciary duty as agent, did not make any formal accounting nor did it make any regular remittance of the millions of pesos in premiums it received in trust for the GSIS and was able to obtain a very profitable 'float' or temporary use of government funds... [92].

Among those Integral Factors insured were the sugar exports for crop year 1985-1986, PNOC tanker voyages, and virtually a non-life insurance operations of the GSIS on most government-owned properties. Benedicto received a premium of $25 million through this monopoly in 1985, the last year of its operation.

Another major Benedicto project which involved Velaso and other government officials was the Planters Products Inc. (PPI). Benedicto's group acquired the firm from Esso Standard Fertilizer and Agricultural Co. in 1970 and renamed it Planters Products. The PPI received heavy financing and incentives from the government and grew to be the largest local fertilizer firm, accounting for 3% of all local fertilizer sales.

The PPI was assured of its market from the very beginning since a Marcos letter of instruction issued in 1974, LOI 178, decreeing that all fertilizer users in the country were to be stockholders of the firm. The Marcos order provided for the distribution of 90% of the company's shares of stock to Filipino farmers. Under the Capital Stock Ownership Plan, a farmer acquired a share of stock each time he bought a bag of fertilizer from an authorized PPI dealer or outlet. This program had been singled out by Marcos as a "milestone in the democratization of wealth under the New Society".

This Marcos decree, however, was in reality designed to assure a captive market for the PPI and had the bizarre effect of making the farmers subsidize the firm. Named to the board were Benedicto and arcos ministers and associates:

Arturo Tanco Jr.(Minister of Agriculture)   Chairman

Alfredo Montelibano	Vice-Chairman & President
Panfilo O. Domingo (Chairman of PNB	Director
Geronimo Z Velasco (Chairman of PNOC)	
Roberto S. Benedicto (Chairman of Philsucom)	
Jaime Laya	
Armando Gustilo	
Miguel Zosa	
Ambrosio Lumibao	
Manuel Ortega	

It would appear that this august list of non-farmers would have had to buy tons of fertilizers under the Capital Stock Ownership Plan in order to occupy these positions. Alfredo Montelibano, the president of PPI, was a close associate of Benedicto and had substantial investments everywhere. He formerly worked with the Lopez family but defected when Marcos took over the interests of this family (see section on Romualdez).

While lip service was paid to controlling the price of fertilizers, a government subsidy assured the PPI of its profits. Through the Fertilizer and Pesticide Authority (FPA), a "cash subsidy scheme" was devised where the PPI was paid the difference between the controlled price and the full cost of production and/or importation *plus guaranteed mark-ups.*

Although the PPI was supposed to operate on a no-loss no-gain basis, acting mere as a service to the country's farmers, its 1980 Annual Report indicated a 72% increase in net profit after taxes, an increase from $1.8 million in 1979 to $3.09 million in 1980. Of this amount $1.75 million came from the sale of fertilizers.

While the PPI was registering record profits, farmers were burdened with skyrocketing fertilizer prices. Many studies showed a major factor in the poverty Filipino farmer was the uncontrolled price of fertilizer inputs. While the government claimed to stabilize the prices of fertilizers and other inputs, prices of these products continued to rise. One study estimated that the price of fertilizer inputs rose 300-400% since the PPI came into the picture (93).

Another stud on ricelands in the province of Laguna showed that, while $3.55 was needed to fertilize one hectare of riceland in 1966, $57.60 was required in 1981, a 16-fold increase [94]. In just one year, the price of fertilizers were adjusted four times, doubling the cost from $7.30 in July 1983 to $14.20 in October 1984 [95].

But while the prices of the inputs used by the farmer in production continually rose, generating profits for the PPI in the process, the government kept a tight price ceiling on farm produce, further driving the farmer into poverty.

The PPI predictably claimed losses when it folded operations. Its debts of $50 million were assumed b the government. This amount included foreign loans incurred by the firm. A person familiar with the operations of PPI, however, intimated that "not losses reported in the books reflect actual losses."

To pay for this amount, the government, under the direction of Prime Minister Virata, held the country's farmers liable and devised a plan where the country's farmers would pay for the debts incurred by PPI. Were they not after all the stockholders of the firm? The government plan required the country's farmers to pay an additional $0.55 more for every bag of fertilizer they bought. The levy, instituted in June 1985, aimed at raising capital to pay for the debts of PPI. An observer described the levy as

> *a prohibitive pricing mechanism, an unnecessary additional financial burden and a monstrous liability for the importers and farmers to bear this period of tight credit.*

PARTIAL LIST OF PROPERTIES

A partial list of properties of Benedicto's associates:

Jose Unson has interests in Republic Planters Bank, Armour-Dial, GA Machineries.

Jose Africa has interests in Republic Planters Bank and Traders Royal Bank, where he served as chairman. He also has interests with Eastern Telecommunications, PLDT, Busco. He also served as director of two Cuenca lumber companies, Sta. Ines Plywood and Sta. Ines Melale. Africa also had interests in Hotel Enterprises (Hyatt Regency, together with other Marcos people such as Collantes, Romeo Espino, Troadio Quiazon, and Roman Cruz.

Below is a partial list of corporations which Benedicto owned or had major interests:

ABS-CBN TV Stations
Agrid Ford Universal Equity Corp.
Ago-Industrial & Commercial Security Agency
Association of Integrated Millers
Banahaw Broadcasting
Belgor Investments Corp.
Cable & Wireless Ltd.
Caries Fishing Inc. 00
Carruf Agricultural Corp.
Celebrity Sports Plaza
Computer Research System Inc.
Coron Bulk Carriers
Davo Bulk Corporation
Eastern Telecommunications Phil. Inc.
Ecija Bulk Carriers
Express Commercial Printers Corp.
Far East Managers & Investment Corp.
FEMII building in Aduana
Fuga Bulk Carriers
Holiday Inn
Integral Factors Inc.
Inter-Continental Broadcasting Corp. (IBC)
Ireland Bulk Carriers
Kanlaon Broadcasting System
Kanlaon Towers
Lapay Development Corp.

Malibu Ago usiness
Mar-anao il Resources
Marapara Shipping Co.
Marinduque Minin & Industrial Corp.
Mindanao Nickel ining Co.
Molave Bulk Carriers
National Sugar Trading Corporation
Negros Stevedoring Co.
New Riviera Hotel Dev.
Nivico Phil, Inc.
Northern Lines
Oceanic Wireless Network Inc.
Overseas Bank of California, Los Angeles
Peninsula Tourist & Shipping Corp.
Phil-Asia Food Industries Corp.
Phil-Asia Manufacturing Corp.
Philippine Daily Exp/1:55
Phil. ugar Trading rp.
Philippine Consultancy Systems Inc.
Piedras Mining
Philippine Integrated Meat Co. (Pimeco)
Planters Products Inc.
Philippine Overseas Telecommunications Corp. (POTC)
Radio Philippine Network (RPN)
Republic Planters Bank
Republic Sugar Develo ment Corp.
Republic Transport & hipyard Corp.
Republic Transport & Stevedoring Corp.
Silangan Investment and Managers Inc.
Sining Makuiay
Strachan & MacMurray Ltd., Iloilo
Traders R0 I Bank
Universal uity Corp.
Universal Molasses
Visayan Maritime Academy
Visayan Packing Corp.

Endnotes

1. Material for this episode is from Alfred W. McCoy, "A Queen Dies Slowly: The Rise and Decline of Iloilo City," in *Philippine Social History: Global Trade and Local Transformations*, (Quezon City. Ateneo de Manila University Press, 1982)
2. Roughly equivalent to mayor.
3. *Philippines Free Press,* 8 December 1990.
4. *Philippines Free Press,* 8 December 1990.
5. *Philippines Free Press,* 8 December 1990.
6. This covers the provinces of Iloilo, Capiz, Aklan, Antique, as well as Negros Occidental, the native province of Benedicto.
7. While Tufts University officials initially agreed to establish a Marcos chair in exchange for the donation, strong protests from the student body and an almost unanimous opposition from the faculty ultimate forced its cancellation.
8. Mijares, p.137.
9. Quoted in Rodney Tasker, "Let's have more tangible economic cooperation," *Far Eastern Economic Review,* 10 March 1978.

10. Excerpts of speech delivered at the Japan Productivity Center, Tokyo, reported by a UPI news article and reprinted in the *Times Journal and Daily Express* on 7 March 1974.

11. *Daily Express*, 7 March 1974.

12. Mijares, p.194.

13. The Spanish *hacendero* is used in the Philippines to denote the owner of hu 6 tracts of lands and plantations. In some areas the term *propietario* is also employed, but it is hacendero which is invariably used within the sugar industry. The strictly correct term would be *hacendado*, a term denoting ownership of *haciendas*, rather than *hacendero*, which signifies the owner of the land who works industriously on it. Maria Moliner's *Diccionario de uso del espariol* defines *hacendado* in the sense of *propietario* or one who owns the land ("se aplica al que posee una hacienda o haciendas"), while *hacendero* is a term denoting a hard-working landowner ("se aplica a la persona que se preocupa de su hacienda y la hace prosperar"). *Hacendero* would therefore be a contradiction in terms since landowners in the Philippines do not work their land. *Hacendero* might have been an archaic form of *hacendado* which has since exited from common usage, excepting feudal Philippines. A Spanish dictionary published in 1866 by one D. Ramon Campuzano which I chanced upon in the rastro (flea market) in Madrid lists both *hacendero and hacendado*. This dictionary defmes *hacendero* in a manner which clearly reveals it feudal character: "El que procura con aplicacion los adelantos de su casa y hacienda."

14. The picul, though a standard of measurement prevalent in Asia, has varied in value from country to country:

Philippines	144 pounds
Japan	132.03 pounds avdt
Malaysia, Hong Kong	133.3 pounds avdt
North Borneo, Sabah	180 pounds

The variation implies that the picul was perhaps initially a measurement of volume before Westerners transformed it into a measurement of weight.

15. "Whither Go The Burden and Boon of the Sugar Industry?" *Nassa News*, January 1981, p.17.; Sheilah Ocampo, "Cracks in the Sugarbowl," *Far Eastern Economic Review*, 1 May 1981.

16. Ray S. Enano, "Revival of Nasutra, Philex cases urged," *Manila Times*, 19 March 1986.

17. It should have been obvious to the Marcos government that the price of sugar was artificially high and could not have been sustained for a long period. The cronies and the technocrats at the service of Marcos surely must have been aware of the almost simultaneous expiration of two important treaties and related US legislation which gave Philippine sugar an advantage in the international market. The US Sugar Act, which guaranteed a fixed export quota for Philippine sugar, and the Laurel-Langley Agreement, which reduced tariff on Philippine goods entering the US, both expired in 1974. The International Sugar Agreement, which regulated movement of international sugar prices, also expired at this time, leaving the forces of the market to determine the international price of sugar. These, plus the accumulation of international sugar stock to more than twice ideal level and the growing use of sugar substitutes, could not have possibly escaped the attention of the Marcos government. Yet they persisted in holding on to their stock until the price fell and the stocks deteriorated. Greed blinds.

18. "Whither Go The Burden and Boon of the Sugar Industry?" *Nassa News,* January 1981, p.18.

19. Although the creation of the agency was formally announced in 1977, the enabling presidential decree, PD 338, was actually prepare much earlier and signed on 2 February 1974. This implies that crony control over the sugar industry had been contemplated for a very long time. When Philsucom began operations on July 11, 1977, government publications used the terms "activated" and "implemented" to conveniently gloss over the early planning of Philsucom.

20. Sugar was later replaced by coconut as the chief export crop.

21. Italics ours. The decree was promulgated on 2 September 1977.

22. In the parlance of the sugar industry, these categories are respectively labeled as A, B, C stocks.

23. Sheilah Ocampo, "Cracks in the Sugarbowl," *Far Easiem Economic Review*, 1 May 1981.

24. The rationale was that the higher export price would subsidize the domestic market. But as it will be later shown, Benedicto did not hesitate to sacrifice the interests of local consumers when profits were to be made. Some quarters might point out that since the composite price was the average of three different prices, it necessarily was lower than the higher export price. This is not denied. What needs to pointed out, however, is that the composite price was unilaterally set by Nasutra and the rates it dictated to the industry clearly showed that Nasutra was interested not in subsidizing the local market but in generating trading profits.

25. A monopsomy is a situation where a buyer controls the market. A monopoly is a situation where the seller controls the market.

26. "Gov't Set Composite Price," *Bulletin Today,* 17 September 1980. The composite price for 1979-1980 was roughly $0.10 per pound.

27. Some have pointed out that at these prices planters were actually selling sugar to Nasutra at prices less than what the law obligated them to sell to Nasutra. There were promises to provide "price differentials" where the sugar industry would be reimbursed for favorable export prices, but Nasutra still found a way to hold on to its wide margin. While there were promises of "price differentials," Nasutra made deductions to the "differentials" they were supposed to give back to the industry. In 1979-80 alone, Nasutra deducted an estimated $366 million that from these export price differentials. A further complaint was that these reimbursements were not equitably distributed but rather favored the cronies in the sugar industry.

28. According to a court petition filed against Philsucom and Nasutra by representatives of the sugar industry on 29 December 1980.

29. Privileged speech to the Batasan on 12 November 1990, quoted in *Philippines Free Press,* 8 December 1990

30. Rodney Tasker, "Let's have more tangible economic cooperation," *Far Eastern Economic Review*, March 10, 1978

31. Rodney Tasker, "Let's have more tangible economic cooperation," *Far Eastern Economic Review,* 10 March 1978.

32. It was $0.0811 per pound in 1978, rising to $0.25-$0.30 during the 1979-80 crop year.

33. Leo Gonzaga, "A Storm In The Sugarbowl," *Far Eastem Economic Review*, 13 February 1981.

34. Leo Gonzaga, "A Storm In The Sugarbowl," *Far Easrem Economic Review*, 13 February 1981.

35. *Nassa News*, Ibid.,p.19.

36. Petition of hacenderos against Philsucom and Nasutra on 29 December 1980.

37. Leo Gonzaga, "A storm in the sugarbowl," *Far Eastern Economic Review*, 13 February 1981.

38. "Prayer and Thanksgiving," *Bulletin Today*, 4 January 1981.

39. *Nassa News.* p.19.

40. The only exception was the relatively independent *Business Day*.

41. Sheilah Ocampo, "Cracks in the Sugarbowl." *Far Eastern Economic Revi*ew, 1 May 1981. Please see also the next section on Floirendo.

42. It was reported as early as 1985 that Benedicto had purchased a multimillion sugar trading company in the US. *Mr. & MS.*, 22 February 1985.

43. "Nasutra failed to report 54 billion earnings abroad," *Manila Times,* 31 July 1986.

44. Caram, former member of parliament, claims that Fred Elizalde, named officer in charge, did not make a report about the two offices abroad.

45. When another Marcos crony attempted to muscle in into the sugar industry, Benedicto secured the support of the hacenderos by threatening to pay less for their sugar and withhold crop loans. Benedicto's concurrent position of chairman of Philsucom, Nasutra, and RPB gave him absolute powers within the industry.

46. By former Assemblyman Fermin Caram.

47. *Mr. & Ms.,* 13 March 1984.

48. Leo Gonzaga, "Phil. Sugar Earnings Plunge," *Far Eastem Economic Review*, 14 May 1982.

49. Mijares, p.194, 242.

50. Business Day, 5 December 1983.

51. Oscar Quiambao, "Marcos, Benedicto in Mill Kickbacks?" *Philippine Daily Inquirer*, 14 April 1986.

52. Oscar Quiambao, "Marcos, Benedicto in Mill Kickbacks?" *Philippine Daily Inquirer*, 14 April 1986.

53. It also increased PNB's total exposure to $13 billion. "Nasutra to account for P127B," *Manila Times*, 13 April 1986.

54. Benedicto's Silangan itself invested in Busco by buying $1,000 common shares of stock valued at $0.15 a share.

55. It is rather ironic that, when the sugar industry was later caught in a recession, the government tried to encourage other hacenderos to shift from sugar to rice and corn.

56. *Business Day*, "Busco Official seeks PNB audit," 22 October 1986. Zubiri, Busco's executive vice-president, while denying anomalies, later said "I am willing to face the music."

57. *Business Day*, 9 June 1986.

58. *Far Eastern Economic Review*, 31 October 1985.

59. Ray S. Enano, 'Revival of Nasutra, Philex cases urged," *Manila Times*, 19 March 1986.

60. Ellen Gallardo, "Nasutra owes P2.2 billion," *Philippine Daily Inquirer*, 11 March 1986.

61. Sheilah Ocampo, "Cracks in the Sugarbowl," *Far Eastern Economic Review,* 1 May 1981.

62. *Daily Express*, 22 July 19%.

63. Ellen Gallardo, "Nasutra owes P2.2 billion," *Philippine Daily Inquirer*, 11 March 1986.

64. "Nasutra to account for P127.B," *Manila Times*, 3 April 1986. Another source estimated that Benedicto's control resulted in $1.2 billion to $1.5 billion in losses to producers from 1974 through 1983.

65. Ray S. Enano, "Revival of Nasutra, Philex Cases urged," *Manila Times*, 19 March 1986.

66. *The Sugar Workers of Negros*, commissioned by the AMRSP (Association of Major Religious Superiors of the Philippines)

67. Institute of labor and Manpower Studies, Ministry of Labor, *Report On Living And Working Conditions Of Sugar Plantation Workers In Negros And Iloilo* (1976). *The Wall Street Journal* reported an average of only $0.81. When the government-controlled *Times Journal* reported these figures (12 July 1980), it did so under the title "More, Better Deals For Sugar Workers." Despite the grim figures, the article dared to use such a title.

68. Nieves R. Confessor, "Study of the Working and Living Conditions in the Sugar Industry," *Philippine Law Review,* Vol.2, No. 4, 1977.

69. Arsenio Jesena, "The Sacadas of Sugarland," distributed in mimeographed form.

70. *Philippines Free Press*, 8 December 1990.

71. *Philippines Free Press*, 8 December 1990.

72. *Philippines Free Press*, 8 December 1990.

73. Please see Chapter IV for the activities of Credit Suisse.

74. Benard Wideman, "Filipino Shipping: Sailing Close to the Wind," *Insight,* April 1979.

75. *Far Eascem Ecormmic Review*, 30 June 1983.

76. The money was once transferred out of Benedicto's bank and turned over to the government, but this only lasted a week, with Marcos promptly intervening and ordering the money back to TRB.

77. In Marcos' haste to leave the country, $14 million in casino deposits were left with Traders Royal Bank. A separate account worth $2 million was in name of Stanley Ho, a known gambling figure in Asia. *Philippines Free Press*, 8 December 1990.
78. Guy Sacerdoti, "Dedicated Followers of Fashion," *Far Eastern Economic Review*, 15 October 1982
79. RPN, BBC, and GTV 4.
80. Mijares, pp. 208, 365.
81. Mijares, p.119.
82. Mijares, p.51.
83. "A Question of Privilege," *Far Eastern Economic Review*, 6 October 1978.
84. The plant opened in Santo Nino, near Bacolod City, with an authorized capital of P4 million, of which only P1 million was paid-up.
85. *Business Day*, 31 March 1986.
86. *Business Day*, 29 April 1986; *Malaya,* 29 April 1986.
87. Around $400,000 Australian dollars were used to finance two pasture leases covering 300,000 hectares, Jubilee Downes and Nerimah Downes, both 2,000 miles away from Sydney. The pasture lands were in the names of Roberto Sabido, Peter's father, and an Australian, A. Nicolas. The money was given as a "loan" to Sabido. *Business Day*, 29 April 1986.
88. Freight cost more than the price of the livestock. Philbai also accused of making unjustified advance payments to its shippers. *Business Day,* 29 April 1986
89. *Business Day*, 29 April 1986; *Malaya*, 29 April 1986.
90. *Philippines Free Press*, 8 December 1990.
91. *Philippines Free Press,* 8 December 1990.
92. *Philippines Free Press*, 8 December 1990.
93. Ofreneo, *Capitalism in Philippine Agriculture*.
94. *Ibon,* 15 December 1981.
9S. *Bulletin Today*, 29 October 1984.

ANTONIO FLOIRENDO

Antonio 0. Floirendo started his career as a car salesman in Davao City in the late 1940's. He sold Ford vehicles and parts in the southern island of Mindanao as his main source of livelihood.

He was able to overcome these modest beginnings by slowly and shrewdly cultivating his connections with ruling politicians, starting from the administration of President Carlos Garcia in the late 1950's. He perfected the art of currying the favor of politicians during the 20-year rule of Marcos and used it to Join the select group of Marcos cronies.

At the height of his economic power, Floirendo held one of the biggest banana plantations in the world, fronted for Marcos in a New York-based international sugar trading company, served as Imelda's dummy in many multimillion real estate deals in New York and shell corporations based in the Netherlands Antilles. He is now a multimillionaire with interests in agri-business, real estate, banking and transportation. A high point in this former car salesman's social climb was the marriage of his son, Antonio "Tony Boy" Floirendo Jr., to a Filipina who had earlier won the Miss Philippines and Miss Universe titles.

Beyond serving as a business associate of the Marcoses, Floirendo is also a close friend who catered to their personal needs. When the Marcoses were in Davao, they stayed at the Floirendo mansion in the mammoth banana plantation Floirendo owned. The estate has a magnificent house, complete with a pool and waterfall. They threw lavish parties for the First Family and flew down planeloads of guests, food and drinks, and entertainers from Manila, right in the midst of deplorable living and working conditions of the plantation workers. Wealthy and politically prominent, Floirendo figured as one of the more faithful businessmen in Imelda's back-up group of Filipino industrialists. He was one of the leading contributors to or never-ending projects. He was also a regular member of Madame's entourage in her trips abroad and invariably underwrote a good portion of her traveling expenses. When Mrs. Marcos visited New York in October 1985 to speak during the 40th anniversary of the United Nations, Floirendo was part of her caravan. In this trip, Floirendo was feted as Guest of Honor in one of the dinners with Mrs. Marcos as a reward for his services to the Marcos couple.

Although he came from the northern province of Ilocos, Floirendo played a pivotal role in Marcos' political plans in southern Philippines, especially in Mindanao. He contributed greatly to Marcos' 1965 and 1969 presidential campaign funds. It was in Floirendo's Nenita Stock Farm in Toril, Mindanao, the biggest and most modern piggery in Asia, where Marcos launched his 1969 presidential campaign for southern Philippines. Imelda personally graced this launching, singing love songs to the voters while the pigs brayed in chorus. Because of his effectiveness in delivering votes for areas, Floirendo was named the KBL campaign manager for Mindanao and charged with creating victories such as the controversial candidacy of his protege Luis Santos for Mayor of Davao in January 1980, or that of his own brother-in-law, Rodolfo del Rosario, who ran as KBL candidate in May 1984. It was largely through Floirendo's efforts that Corazon Aquino lost by 23,000 votes in e province of Davao del Norte in 1986.

Floirendo was one of the most powerful individuals in Mindanao during the Marcos reign. A barrio in Davao was named Antonio Floirendo through presidential fiat. Floirendo also at one time attempted to have the controversial Luis Santos named governor of an integrated Metro-Davao so that this associate could wield greater political power. In the province of Davao, Floirendo had more influence than the mayors -- he even swore them to office. His wishes were followed without question. When the national roads were being built in Davao, he had them go through his banana plantation to facilitate transportation of his men and goods. This greatly inconvenienced the public, who have had to travel a few more kilometers to reach their destination. Since he also had a private piggery and cattle farm, he had the public slaughterhouse built near his plantation, far from the town centre, forcing people to bring their livestock farther to be slaughtered. This extra journey consequently raised the price of meat to an artificially high level for the people of Davao City while he enjoyed home-grown choice meat cuts. Floirendo served these choice cuts to the Marcoses when they visited and also gave them away as presents to his close friends.

Due to his strong economic and political hold over Davao, Floirendo was greatly resented by the local populace. After the election of Floirendo's hand-picked mayoral candidate in January 1980, the ensuing celebrations in the city of Davao were bombed. The bomb killed a young singer who had been hired for the affair and severely wounded Edith Rabat, one of Imelda's blue ladies, who had to undergo plastic surgery in the US. Floirendo was unable to attend that event, but this incident and other consequent threats forced Floirendo and his family to go on an extended trip to the US and Europe. Ever since this incident, members of the Floirendo family travelled only by helicopter within the province, with security provided by the military.

When newspapers published reports of his holdings, Floirendo ranted that the articles made

> ...the outright assertion that I, without really being the actual owner of the several properties mentioned, specified, or alluded to in the articles, have allowed myself to be used as a "dummy" for some other person or persons alluded to...

Claiming that the reports were "clearly malicious, false, and untrue," Floirendo complained that they had "illegally, falsely, maliciously, and criminally" attacked his "honesty and integrity, virtue, and reputation for the sheer purpose of exposing [him] to public hatred, ridicule, and contempt." Floirendo viewed the reports as implying that he had violated currency, foreign exchange or internal revenue regulations "or worse, 'economic sabotage', a virtual and unmistakable imputation of treason."

Given the strong reaction on the part of Floirendo, it then behooves us to look at his record with some degree of detail.

START IN CAR DEALERSHIP

Floirendo was able to quickly build his small company into the biggest automotive dealership in Mindanao. His Davao Motor Sales Co., organized in 1947, was soon followed by the Mindanao Motors Corp. in Cagayan de Oro in 1949 and the Valley Motor Sales in General Santos, Cotabato in 1975. Floirendo's carefully cultivated connections enabled him to monopolize the sale of vehicles to government offices in Davao and quickly made him the biggest automotive dealer in the south. Soon, advertisement from Floirendo corporations began to tout his automotive dealerships as a "mighty network" specializing in Ford vehicles in Mindanao.

Floirendo's interests in the automotive industry have since branched out from Mindanao. SEC documents show that he organized United Motors & Equipment soon after the imposition of martial law to engage in the buying and selling of cars and trucks. One of Floirendo's later corporations is Metro-Manila-based Anflocars, registered with the SEC on July 1979 with an authorized capitalization of $3 million. Anflocars was to be the main distributor of Ford vehicles in Metro-Manila; the ultimate aim was to become one of the biggest car exchanges in the country. Financing for the cars sold by Anflocars was provided by another Floirendo corporation, Unifmance, registered with the SEC in June 1978 with $3 million authorized capitalization.

TADECO

The major turning point for Floirendo came when he successfully parlayed his connections with Marcos into a lucrative undertaking with the United Fruit Company, the agri-business giant which virtually controlled the economies of Central American "banana' republics.

After the United Fruit encountered the specter of land expropriation in Guatemala. in the 1950's, it tried to diversify the locations of its plantations to protect its substantial investments. One of the areas the company considered was the fertile lands of Mindanao. The province of Davao del Norte was especially targeted because of the fertility of the soil and its relative accessibility. The original scheme, concocted in 1964 during the time of Marcos' predecessor President Diosdado Macapagal, called for the creation of a dummy for United Fruit, the Mindanao Fruit Co. (Minfruco).

The front company would lease 8,000 hectares from the government-run Mindanao Development Authority (MDA) at a nominal fee of $0.85 per ton of bananas exported annually. Alejandro Melchor II, who then headed President Macapagal's Project Implementation Agency (PTA) and later served as Marcos' Executive Secretary, tried to keep the scheme from the public eye because the project was in direct violation of the 1935 Philippine Constitution and Philippine corporate law which explicitly prohibited land acquisition over 1,024 hectares. Another reason for the secrecy concerning the project was that the land in question was not frontier land to be developed but a thriving modern penal colony. Prisoners from the Davao Penal Colony (Dapecol) had planted and were cultivating thousands of coffee, cacao, coconut, and rubber trees. The place was the largest abaca plantation in the Philippines.

Inspite of the secrecy surrounding the deal, Lorenzo Tanada, one of the country's most respected Senators, was able to expose it and chair a Senate Blue Ribbon Committee investigation into the matter. In an open letter to President Macapagal, Senator Tanada complained:

> One might understand, though not sanction or condone, the alienation of large tracts of virgin land to foreign entities for the latter to pioneer and develop, but it is incomprehensible why a fully operational agricultural estate -- a penal colony at that, should be offered on a veritable silver platter to aliens [l].

The uproar following Tanada's expose forced the proponents of the plan to temporarily retreat until a more favorable political climate could be found. The much-criticized plan was finally implemented soon after Marcos' second presidential term.

The scheme gave Floirendo a central role in the project when it was implemented. The key party was no longer the Minfruco and United Fruit but Floirendo's Tadeco (Tagum Agricultural Dev. Corp). Minfruco and United Fruit in the meantime would provide technical and marketing assistance but the principal operator in the deal would be Tadeco [2].

The contract between the Bureau of Prisons and Tadeco was formalized in 1969, with Floirendo signing for Tadeco as its president and general manager. The deal allowed Floirendo to take over government land and use prisoners from the nearby Dapecol as laborers.

Tanada's fears of delivering a modern, reductive agricultural penal colony to private interests thus materialized. Inspite of glaring violations of the constitution and Philippine law, a private corporation succeeded in acquiring huge tracts of prine agricultural land. Industry experts credit the arrangement to Floirendo's political connections:

> The infiltration of Philippine land by a US banana company was said to have been officially approved through the influence of a man who is head of Tadeco and who also happens to be a close friend of President Marcos, Antonio Floirendo [3].

Floirendo was officially the president of Tadeco, but it is widely known that he was a front for Marcos. Our sources indicate that Marcos got up to 80% of the profits from the operations of Tadeco. Rodolfo del Rosario, Floirendo's brother-in-law, was vice-president and later took over the position of General Manager. Del Rosario also served Marcos as a KBL assemblyman and later as Minister of Natural Resources.

Tadeco already had the title to 1,024 hectares since 1949, the maximum amount of land a corporation could legally hold under the constitution. The takeover of Dapecol land allowed Tadeco to dramatically increase its hectarage. From the additional 171 hectares it was awarded in 1969, the company was able to expand to 4,504.57 hectares in 1976, representing a 317% increase over a seven year period. LOI 790 penned in 1979 further allowed an increase of 25 percent for Tadeco (4). Of the 5,000 hectares originally allocated for the use of the Dapecol, 4,758 hectares were absorbed by Tadeco, leaving only 242 for the pen colony [5]. Total Tadeco holdings, including the original property, reached 6,000 hectares. This made Tadeco the biggest contiguous banana plantation in the world (6). Its center of operations is Floirendo's stronghold in Panabo, Davao del Norte.

Tadeco grows bananas under contract with United Brands, the new name assumed by United Fruit. Most of Tadeco's produce is exported to Japan and the Middle East through American and Japanese transnational trading companies such as the Far East Fruit Co. (Tokyo), United Fruit Japan, an Chiquita Int. Trading Corp. (Citco-Hong Kong). The bananas are marketed under the Chiquita label.

Tadeco was able to sell its bananas cheaper than any of its Philippine competitors due to the favorable arrangements it received. Tadeco was able to acquire or lease government land at incredibly cheap prices and was allowed to hire prison labor at exploitation rates.

Government lands were leased far below the going rate. While its competitors were being charged $40 a hectare, Tadeco paid a mere $5.60. This means that it had to pay only 14% of the rates other plantations had to pay [7]. But inspite of the already low rates Tadeco enjoyed, it was reported that the company never paid the fees to the government from the time it entered into the contract with the Bureau of Prisons in 1969 until the fall of Marcos in 1986 [8]. This represents 17 years of unpaid rent on almost 6,000 hectares of land.

LAND USURPATION

Government support for Tadeco has not been limited to the acquisition of land. It had extended to all sorts of assistance, such as the building of special private roads at public expense, the use of government equipment to build housing facilities, and the use of the military to usurp the land from its occupants. At Marcos' behest, a special smooth road was built straight to the shipping dock so that Tadeco's bananas would not be bruised in transit. Construction was done at government expense. This gave Floirendo tremendous advantage over other banana growers who had to either make do with existing roads or build new ones at their own expense [9]. The final result of this Marcos largesse were smoother looking bananas which sold better in the international market. In addition, government agencies like the Ministry of Public Highways provided help to this private Floirendo concern. As one resident in Tadeco recalls:

> ...when this plantation was just starting, all the government equipment like trucks, cranes, and bulldozers were used here. I know, because they all bore the sign: FOR OFFICIAL USE ONLY [10]

When Floirendo acquired Dapecol land, portions of it had already been long occupied by settlers such as native Ata tribesmen, poor settlers, and former prison inmates who had been released and had chosen to stay in Mindanao. Floirendo used a variety of methods to dislodge them. These methods ranged from buying or leasing the land from the small farmers at prices dictated by Tadeco to outright coercion and terrorism with the help of military units and Floirendo goons. The Ata tribesmen were the first to go, being driven from their original homelands and reservation to the high-lands. The settlers and former inmates were next. Amado Resurreccion, a resident of the area who suffers from the handicap of an amputated arm, recounts how the residents in the area were driven from their and:

> I am head of one of the ejected families. In the whole barrio, I was the last to leave. Because I knew that what they did to us was wrong. Tadeco gave us notice in May 1977, and after three months the people were forced to leave.
> ...We came in the early 50's. I, in 1953... We planted everything; we were the ones who cleared the forest, but not one of us was able to own the land. Up there, they had connections; that is why the land was awarded to them...
> Now they succeeded, and what they did was frighten us. A! the time when people were being ejected, one of the residents was beheaded. They sent a lot of PC (Philippine Constabulary) here, Task Force Pagkakaisa and the Army, CHDF (Civilian Home Defense Force), 57th striking force, and Panamin [11]. The people were afraid. They did not know who will be liquidated next. Some did not sleép in their houses for fear.
> ...I did not leave then. I went to the provincial commander, Colonel Bulusan. I brought to him our petition, signed by the residents in our Barrio, and asking not to do this to us. I also went to DAR and PACLAP. But nothing happened.
> All of them are friends. They are helping one another. They will just push a button and call each other over the telephone and they already understand each other. They will tell you they are doing everything possible. I found out that Floirendo and Col. Balusan are together in this. For instance, the two of them, together talked with me. They fetched me from our house. In a jeep. Then I was brought to Floirendo's oflice. Floirendo said: If you want to be paid you must have your house and improvements assessed by the govemment. (It's funny because those who assessed here were engineers of Tadeco.

I have lived here a long time and I know all their engineers.)
...When Floirendo talked to me then, I thought to just give up because it was already Floirendo. If I would be liquidated, or if they don't give me anything for my house and crops - I would not be able to do anything. They gave me P1,500 for my house and P800 for my crops. When I built that house I spent P2, 000. And I am lucky because I received something. Others did not get a single centavo. Even to just help them build another house.
...Now we are just making butsi and maruya which we sell to the workers. This is where we get our livelihood. We also plan to go back to Bicol. Maybe life is better there. I know that the government has a lot to do with Tadeco. When this plantation was just starting all the government trucks and cranes were used here. And of course, they are using Dapecol land. Marcos knows this. He knows everything that happens here. Even Enrile, all of them up there....[12].

It has been difficult to arrive at an accurate number of the families evicted by Tadeco. In one place alone, in Barrio Tibungol, one account estimates that about 700 families were ejected in August 1977. A study on the Philippine banana industry describes this particular barrio after all of the houses, including the community chapel, were bulldozed by Floirendo's men:

...there is no sign of life here. No children can be seen playing in the yard, no women gossiping at the doorstep, no farmers plowing the soil. There is no sign of what former residents estimate as "the 700 or so families 'that once filled this barrio with laughter and smoke rising from their kitchen fires in the early mornings. Every single house has been bulldozed, including the chapel and the small purok (hut) where meetings were held and where people flocked to tell their tales. Even the backyard gardens were demolished....[13].

Everything was cleared. Only the coconut trees planted by the former residents were spared. When the coconut trees bore enough fruit and fetched profits for Tadeco, they would be hewed down to make way for the ipil-ipil plantatign of NEST Farms, a sister company of Tadeco also owned by Floirendo.

WORKING CONDITIONS

The contract between Floirendo and the Bureau of Prisons permitted him the further advantage of prison labor at starvation wages.

While Tadeco claimed that it utilized prison labor to rehabilitate convicts and prided itself as being the only institution or business enterprise to do so [14], evidence suggests that Tadeco's reasons were far from magnanimous. While this "rehabilitation" program was aimed ostensibly to uplift the morale of the prisoners by giving them a chance to be productive, the reality was that it provided cheap, exploited labor for the plantation.

The *colonos* or members of the Dapecol prison colony are given the hardest jobs in the plantation – harvesting, hauling, and drainage work. *Colones* have been used in Tadeco since 1971 and comprise aroun 25% of the workforce in the plantation. They carry bunches of bananas weighing as much as 50 kilos over great distances. The bananas have to be carefully and delicately handled lest they be bruised and be considered unfit to be sold in convenience stores in New York or to

Japanese consumers. Workers are severely punished if they accidentally bruise the bananas.

All of the workers in Tadeco, prison and non-prison labor alike, faced harsh working conditions, but the prisoners suffered the most cruel treatment. The prisoners have to wake up at 3:00 am. to make the 3:30 check-in and often have to work overtime during the peak season. Most of the prison laborers have deformed backs due to the heavy loads. There was no security in employment as it was common for workers to be dismissed summarily.

Plantation operations posed health hazards for all laborers. Workers were sometimes accidentally sprayed with the chemicals intended for bananas as they are packed. Workers exposed to these chemicals often developed bruises and other wounds. Tadeco medics dismissed these wounds as "allergic reactions." Flu, pneumonia, and other respiratory diseases were also widespread. Many got sick with tuberculosis after a year's work. That 80% of the patients at the Dapecol hospital were workers m Tadeco is an indication of the extreme hardship faced by the workers [15].

Living conditions were sub—standard. There was no proper sanitation. The bunkhouses were overcrowded. In one case, as many as 24 women shared one small room. The abysmal living conditions posed a sharp contrast to the specially cushioned refrigerated trucks and refrigerated ships which had been designed to transport bananas to overseas markets.

One worker summarized the attitude of the Tadeco management concerning the situation of the workers:

> They do not care about our condition, as long as the next day we are strong for the work in the plantation or in the packing plant. Our life is designed for these bananas [16].

Over and above the already below substandard wages, laborers were forced to sign that they had been paid the legal wage. Their daily pay was furthermore subjected to deductions for meals and a "trust fund". It was calculated that the prisoner was left with $0.22 a day after all of the deductions [17].

Aggravating the problem of the workers is the *vale* system. In this system, credit to the plantation store is given in lieu of wages. This results in a system where the workers buy goods only at the plantation store at fixed prices. Since food is inadequate for the back-breaking work to which they are subjected, prisoners often sell their vale coupons at a discount in order to get a little cash for extra food to supplement their rations. The effect of this system is that the prisoner and other plantation workers are forever in debt despite their hard work.

The contrast between the working and living conditions of the plantation workers and the luxury Floirendo enjoyed was rather a stark one. While Floirendo had his own private executive jet to take him to New York to confer with United Brands officials, Tadeco workers dwelt in hovels and died slow deaths.

Rodolfo del Rosario defended Tadeco's lease by saying that the land in question "was a swampy, undeveloped area that we had to fix up at our own cost." But the truth was that the land that Tadeco took over was already a flourishigg penal colony, as Tanada had pointed out, or were already occupied by cultural minority tribes or homesteaders. The lands that Tadeco took over had thriving banana, sorghum, rice, and abaca plantations in the area which were the product of the work of the indigenous population, settlers, or prison labor. Not only did Floirendo take over thousands of hectares of land without paying rent but he also deprived hundreds of families of their homes and livelihood. This enabled Tadeco to take advantage of all the improvements the previous occupants had already done.

OTHER BUSINESSES

Floirendo also branched out into other areas to complement his interests in banana production. He schemed to acquire a monopoly over the production of boxes for packaging bananas. The manufacture of these boxes, which were originally imported from Japan, was another tempting source of revenue. Among Floirendo companies which complemented his banana business were his trucking and shipping companies. He had two small shipping lines, AOF Shipping, registered in May 1976, and Millennium Shipping, registered in April 1979. Panabo Truckin & Services, registered in Davao in une 1967, and the San Vicente Terminal & Brokerage Services, registered in Panabo, Davao in November 1976, were also Floirendo companies.

Other interests included an 8% equity in FNCB (First National City Bank) Finance. He also owned or had interests in other companies such as OLASHAR, Pioneer Trading & Supply Co., Rizal Commercial Banking Corp., Purefoods. Davao Timber is controlled by Ernesto del Rosario, another brother-in-law. ANFLO Corp. is the management firm organized to handle Floirendo's interests.

Floirendo also owns 18,000 hectares in Biliran, Leyte.

OVERSEAS

The day before Marcos' downfall on February 1986, members of Floirendo's family fled the Philippines on a Tadeco-owned Cessna Citation II plane bound for Brunei. Rodelfo del Rosario claimed that Floirendo was somewhere in Europe, but this was only one of many other possible places where Floirendo could have gone.

Floirendo counts among his overseas properties a mansion in Hawaii and expensive condominiums in New York. Some of these New York condomimums are alleged to be held by Floirendo for Imelda, while others are said to be held by shell companies which have links to Floirendo and Imelda. Floirendo also is a director of a shell corporation based in the Netherlands Antilles, Ancor Holdings N.V. This corporation has been named in a New York law suit as a holding company for properties owned by Imelda Marcos.

Floirendo owns a mansion in Makiki Heights, Honolulu. He acquired it in March 1980, paying $800,000 in cash and signing a note for the remaining $200,000. The mansion, known as the Helen Knudsen estate, is located at 2442

Makiki Heights Drive and is directly across the Tantoco house where the Marcoses live in exile. It was valued at $1 million in 1985.

Floirendo and Imelda purchased three adjacent condominiums in the Olympic Towers at 641 5th Ave., New York. The walls of all three condominiums were torn down so as to form a gigantic L-shaped apartment a panoramic view of New York City [18].

Another set of Manhattan properties owned by Floirendo are two expensive east side apartments purchased on December 1982. These are units 11-A and 11-C at St. James Towers in 415 East 54th St., New York. These were bought by Sugarbush Corp. NV, a shell company based in the Netherlands Antilles, but it was Floirendo's brother-in-law, Rodolfo del Rosario, who signed for the papers. Rosenman, Colin, Freund, Lewis and Cohen, a law firm which had been used by Marcos associates on different occasions, took care of the legal aspects of the purchase. The shell corporation gave del Rosario and Floirendo full power-of-substitution through a special Power-of-Attorney. This effectively meant that Floirendo organized a shell corporation to front as the formal owner of the apartments and that this front had in turn given Floirendo and del Rosario legal power to act on its behalf. This arrangement made any attempt to legally recover these apartments difficult.

SUGAR BROKER

Starting 1976, Floirendo extended his interests to the international trading of sugar in New York. He started as a high-level broker between a leading transnational in the sugar industry and the Marcos government, earning large commissions for his services. Floirendo later bought out the sugar transnational and organized his own international sugar trading company personally involving Marcos and Imelda.

After the colossal marketing blunders committed by the Marcos government in the international sales of sugar (19), Philex, the agency charged by the government to sell sugar at the international market, entered into a five-year contract to sell up to 650,000 metric tons of raw sugar to Sucrest Corp, a company based in New York. The contract, signed on 24 March 1976 and extending until 1981, had a value of $1 billion over the five-year period.

The contract was extremely skewed in favor of Sucrest since it provided many generous terms to the transnational but did not guarantee any profits for e Philippine sugar industry. Sucrest was able to secure guarantees that it *first deduct refining and administrative costs and secure a fixed rate of profit firm the deal before money was finally paid to Philex for the sugar* [20]. Under the terms of the Philex Agreement, Sucrest would pay an initial amount to Philex at the time of shipment, but the contract also provided that the fees would be later adjusted to reflect the price of *refined sugar, Sucrest operating costs, and a guaranteed profit for the company.* What the Philex Agreement therefore guaranteed was that Sucrest could *adjust the price of raw sugar* it paid the Philippines should there be any adverse fluctuations in the international price of *refined sugar.* Sucrest's *1977 Accoumant's Report* was very clear on this matter:

The Division's operating results depended primarily upon difference between the cost of raw sugar and the selling price of refined sugar.

Two different markets, that of raw and refined sugar, were therefore linked to each other to assure Sucrest of a fixed rate of profit. The price at which raw sugar was bought had no relation to either the costs of producing it or to local market conditions; it was instead dependent on assuring Sucrest a predetermined rate of profit. Should the international price of refined sugar fall, Philex would reimburse Sucrest an amount that would assure the sugar transnational a constant, predetermined rate of profit. The risks in this case is assumed not by the trader, as is usually the case, but by the producer. Since the risk of price fluctuations was assumed by the Philippine sugar industry, Sucrest was always assured of a profit.

Another factor in determining the price paid by Sucrest for raw sugar was the operating expenses it incurred. Sucrest was allowed to deduct operating expenses from the price it paid for the raw sugar. This clause opened the possibility that many expenses could be classified as "operating costs" merely to force a lower price paid for raw sugar. These points are well documented in Sucrest's *1977Accountant's Report:*

> *A fixed payment is made at the time of shipment which is subsequently adjusted so that the ultimate cost of raw sugar to the Division is based upon actual refined sugar selling prices, less substantially all costs and a profit margin to the Company of a constant percentage. The economic effect of the Philex Agreement is to remove from the Division's operations substantially **all market risk** with respect to sugar inventories. Under the terms of the Philex Agcement, the Division's operations should approximate the fixed profit margin called for in the agreement based upon the actual refined sugar selling prices after deduction of applicable costs.*

This arrangement has led to a perverse situation where the seller ended up owing money to the buyer. Because of the arrangement that Sucrest was able to wangle, Philex, the seller, was indebted to the buyer, Sucrest, by $24 million within the first year of the start of operations. The *1977 Accountant s Report* documents the debt:

> *By virtue of the initial fixed payments against shipments of raw sugar and the adjustment thereof upon the sale of refined sugar under the Philex agreement, the indebtedness of Philex to the Company on May 28, I 977 was approximately $25,000,000, secured by a standby letter of credit of its parent, the Philippine National Bank, in the amount of approximately $24,000,000.*

Sucrest Corp. was able to acquire such a huge long-term contract under very lucrative terms since it had enlisted the services of Floirendo, who took on the role of broker, in its dealings with the Marcos government. An investigative report described the role of Floirendo in the multimillion dollar

> *He opened the doors of the Malacanan Palace and introduced company officials to President Marcos, who approved the contract. Former Sucrest officials say that Mr. Floirendo was retained because of his close ties to Mr. and Mrs. Marcos. "Without Tony Floirendo," says a former senior Sucrest official, "there would have been no Sucrest deal with the Philippines" [21].*

A former senior official of Sucrest who had close dealings with Floirendo was further quoted as saying he always believed that Floirendo "was acting as an instrument of the Marcos family" [22].

A clause in the brokerage agreement between Floirendo and Sucrest provided that brokers fees would be based on the amount of raw sugar bought from the Philippines. It was therefore in Floirendo's interest to sell as much sugar possible irrespective of its price. The lower the selling price of raw sugar, the better for Sucrest and Floirendo, since it meant a bigger profit margin for the sugar transnational and bigger broker's fees for the Marcos crony. The strategy therefore consisted merely in trying to sell as much sugar as possible to Sucrest, regardless of its benefit to the Philippine sugar industry. The more sugar sold, the greater the broker's fees. Floirendo accumulated approximately $1,169,000 in fees from Sucrest in 1977, according to company papers with US SEC. The *1977 Accountant's Report* again documents this arrangement:

> In connection with the Philex Agreement, a brokerage and agency agreement was entered into, pursuant to which fees, used on the volume of raw sugar shipped, are paid by the Sweetener Division out of its profit margin to a Philippine businessman who aided in the negotiation of the Philex Agreement and is providing continuing services relating to said shipments. The Company believes such fees (aggregating approximately $1,169,000 in 1977) are in line with those generally prevailing for such services.

Apparently not all of the members of the board of directors of Sucrest were aware of the arrangement with Floirendo. A respected auditing firm, S.D. Leidesdorf & Co., raised questions concerning the arrangements, saying that both the brokerage and agency agreement with Floirendo were not

> disclosed to them in timely fashion and it is unclear whether timely disclosure of such agreement had been made to the full Board of Directors, and because the payment of potentially large sums was involved, Leidesdorf requested that the Board of Directors make an investigation thereof to determine whether corporate funds had been or were to be used for illegal or questionable payments [23].

A company investigation was made, but Floirendo refused to answer the detailed questionnaire prepared by the law firm hired to do the inquiry. The Federal Trade Commission also investigated the deal, but we are not aware if its findings were ever made public.

What we have here was the pawning of national interests so that a Marcos crony could receive gigantic commissions. Floirendo did not have any experience in the trading of international sugar, and neither did he have any connection with the Philippine sugar industry prior to the Sucrest deal. The only reason why Floirendo was chosen to be Sucrest's broker was because of his close association with Marcos, which assured the acceptance of the conditions of the contract even if its provisions did not benefit the sugar industry and its workers. The profit of Sucrest, and Floirendo's commissions, were assured by Philex, and that was all that mattered.

REVERE SUGAR CORPORATION

After he secured his $1.2 million commission, Floirendo changed his money-making strategy. Realizing that he would make more as owner rather than broker, Floirendo bought Sucrest's Sweetener Division, the Sugar Refining Corp. of America (SRCA), the following year [24]. All three Sucrest-SRCA facilities in Chicago, Brooklyn, and Massachusetts were acquired. Two properties were sugar refining facilities, covering 19 acres in Charlestown, Massachusetts, and 16.5 acres and buildings in Brooklyn, New York. The Chicago location was a facility leased primarily for offices. These properties were bought for $11.8 million and renamed Revere Sugar Corp. The price tag not only transferred the Sucrest-Philex contract to Revere, but it also gave Floirendo the rights to Sucrest's existing large accounts receivables.

The formal ownership of Revere is divided between Floirendo, his United Motors, and two Netherlands Antilles companies which are also linked to him. The stocks are distributed in the following manner:

United Motors & Equipment Co.	1%
Antonio Foirendo	9%
Sweetco Holdings N.V.	40%
Sucor Holdings N.V.	50%

The two Netherlands Antilles shell companies are known to be owned by Floirendo. According to papers filed with t e State of Delaware, the state where Revere was incorporated (25), the renamed company has among its directors Floirendo and Rodolfo del Rosario. Floirendo is listed as Chairman of the Board and Chief Executive Officer. Irwin Jay Robinson, a lawyer who has represented Marcos associates on different occasions, is listed as Vice President of SCRA, while Diosdado Ordonez, another Floirendo associate, is listed as Secretary with address at 210 Clay Ave., Lyndhurst, NJ. Sweetco invested $11.2 million into Revere during the period of acquisition and recapitalization.

Marcos was clearly a hidden partner in Revere. Rolando Gapud, a key Marcos financial adviser who specialized in takeovers of corporations for the dictator, played an important role in the Sucrest buyout, providing financial advice to Floirendo throughout the negotiations. Among documents later recovered were some letters of Floirendo to Marcos. One was a cover letter to a report on the operations of Revere, while another talked about a possible Internal Revenue service investigation of the company.

An aspect of Floirendo's purchase of Sucrest deserves close attention since it is particularly instructive of how Marcos and his cronies conducted business. Prior to Floirendo's purchase of Sucrest, Philex withheld the payment of $11.7 million to the sugar company [26]. Questions concerning the formula to calculate the cost of raw sugar was mentioned as the reason for withholding the payment when Philex requested a renegotiation on November 1977, but evidence suggests that the real reason was to exert pressure on Sucrest to sell its interests to Floirendo. Philex could have chosen to question the terms of the contract at a much earlier time, but it scrutinized the contract only after Floirendo cashed in on his commissions and was ready to buy Sucrest.

Of the $11.7 million withheld as payment, Sucrest still classified $8.2 million as part of its accounts receivables, and it tried to claim the balance of $3.5 million by clarifying the formula used to compute costs of raw sugar. But this matter was resolved only when Floirendo finally owned Sucrest. Company papers clearly show that the $11.7 Philex withheld was the main factor in the turnover of Sucrest. The consequent sale agreement between Floirendo and Sucrest provided that claims sought by Sucrest would be honored and that Floirendo would also "purchase" the Sucrest receivables due from Philex. From the *1977 Accountant's Report* we find the frank admission that the $11.7 million in receivables was indeed a factor in the sale:

> *No assurance can be given that these matters will be resolved on a satisfactory basis. However, as set forth in Note L, the Company has entered into an agreement (which has been delivered in escrow pending fulfillment of certain conditions by each of the parties thereto) to sell the Sweetener Division, subject to the shareholder's aproval and the receipt of the content of Philex. The agreement provides for the pure use by the buyer off the receivable due from Philex, subject to audit by the Philex auditors, as well as the aforementioned favorable adjustment sought by the Company.*

This was in effect corporate blackmail. Since Philex was nothing more than a Marcos creation and was manned by dummies, it is safe to presume that it would meet Sucrest's claims only on the instructions of Marcos and Floirendo. If Sucrest was not sold to Floirendo, then Philex would withhold payments to Sucrest. But if Sucrest did accede to Floirendo, then Floirendo would take over the receivables which would then be promptly paid by Philex. This was clearly the implicit condition in the negotiations. The Sucrest officials who hired Floirendo as their broker initially banked on Floirendo's association with Marcos to land their deal. But it was this very same close association that allowed Floirendo to gobble them up.

A closer look at the figures is equally revealing. Since he was payin $11.75 million for Sucrest but stood to receive $11.7 million in receivables it meant that Floirendo had to shell out only $50,000 in cash to acquire the multimillion sugar transnational. The Sucrest receivables were guaranteed by the Philippine National Bank in a stand-by letter-of-credit, implying that Floirendo was assured of getting the money.

The change of status from brokers to owners of a major international sugar company allowed Marcos and Floirendo a new income generating scheme. The new strategy called for the Philippine Sugar Commission to sell 2 million tons to Revere over the next four years. This amount constituted 50% of the projected Philippine sugar production for the period in question. What was more scandalous was that the price was set at $0.22 per (pound, while the prevailing world price was already $0.30 per pound, with definite signs of going up further [27]. Teofisto Guingona, a businessman active against the Marcos dictatorship, explained the scheme:

> *Sugar experts forecast steady rising prices for the next few years -- perhaps to more than $81 per picul. Yet Philsucom [Nasutra] has agreed to sell 400,000 metric tons, representing 50% of total exports for crop year 1980-8l, to a US-based sugar refining, Sucrest Co. (Revere Corp) an entity owned by a Filipino Antonio Floirendo. The price agreed is $0.22 a pound or roughly $27 per picul. This seems a staggering*

arrangement, considering that the present world price is already over $54 per picul, and considering further that the purchaser is another wealthy Filipino who, with his American allies, can simply turn around, refine sugar and sell at tremendous profits [28].

This scheme enabled Marcos and Floirendo to buy a gigantic amount of sugar from local Filipino producers cheaply and sell at the higher international market price. This meant a huge profit margin since sugar was bought from local producers at prices dictated by the Marcos government. Since the Revere-Marcos contract provided for 400,000 metric tons at $27 per picul while the international price was already at $54 per picul, this meant that Floirendo had already been assured profits of $150 million just as the contract was being signed.

Given all the institutional support, Revere experienced several years of profitable operations. For about four years, Revere had annual sales of about $250 million and its pre-tax profit totaled about $5 million a year.

The international nature of the transactions provided Floirendo yet another advantage. Since profits were being realized at the Revere end, this meant that a lot of the company earnings could be diverted to the Netherland Antilles companies which owned Revere and thereby hide the fact that they were going to Floirendo and Marcos. The shell corporations, moreover, not only hide ownership but they also have the advantage of lowering taxes. Since these front corporations are incorporated in the Netherlands Antilles where corporate taxes are non-existent or ridiculously low, shifting the majority of the ownership from Floirendo to the Netherland Antilles companies then had the added advantage of lowering the overall taxes paid by Revere.

The lucrative arrangements that Floirendo and Marcos had carved out for themselves attracted the attention of Imelda, who managed to elbow herself into the scheme by mid-1980. In 1983, for example, we find Imelda addressing the annual banquet of the Sugar Club of New York, an organization then headed by a Revere official. The event seems to have been arranged by Floirendo. Around this time also, the broker fees that had been previously paid to Floirendo were now assigned to a Hong Kong-based corporation, Thetaventure Limited. Gerald Walpin, a New York lawyer who had dealt with Floirendo, was quoted as saying, "it is our information that Thetaventure is owned by Floirendo (29). But there are indications that the real owner was Imelda Marcos herself and that Thetaventure was her way of playing a direct role in the lucrative sugar deals. The listed agent for Thetaventure was Vilma Bautista, a persona aide of Imelda Marcos who figured prominently in her New York real estate deals [30]. With the entry of Imelda as a broker of international sugar, it comes as no surprise that the broker fees increased. For example, according to sources, Revere Sugar paid $2.9 million to Thetaventure in the 1978-80.

While these fat broker's fees were being doled out to Floirendo and Imelda, Revere itself started to report financial difficulties. Antonio Lagdameo, Floirendo's son-in-law and a Revere vice-president, filed for bankruptcy in 1985. The law firm of Rosenman Colin Freund Lewis & Cohen, the group Floirendo used to buy the St. James Towers apartment, was retained during the bankruptcy proceedings. While the reasons cited for the difficulties were rising sugar costs and heavy competition from corn sweeteners, there were other factors at work which forced Revere to bankruptcy, the most obvious of which were the huge commissions received by Imelda and Floirendo and the expenses they incurred. Workers from Revere, for example, relate how Floirendo's entourage would include as many as three limousines when he visited the Charlestown, Massachusetts refinery [31].

Closer attention to Revere's 1985 Statement reveals yet another possible cause of Revere's collapse. At the time the company filed for bankruptcy, its total assets stood at $29,346,000, while its total liabilities were $12,462,000 in secured debt held by six parties and $15,532,000 in other forms of liabilities. If we keep in mind that the debtors and investors of Revere were also other Floirendo interests, that the liabilities of Revere were but assets of other Floirendo corporations, then it would become apparent that the bankruptcy move was merely a tactic to move money from one Floirendo concern, Revere, to other interests in the Netherlands Antilles. The implication is that Floirendo, through layers of front corporations, merely took money from one pocket and placed it in the other. This allowed Floirendo to hide behind the shroud of secrecy provided by his shell corporations.

The timing of the bankruptcy filing coincided with the growing instability and eventual downfall of the Marcos regime. Whether the timing was mere coincidence or by design, Revere's bankruptcy provided a convenient vehicle to move many Floirendo assets from one place to another. Within days of Marcos' exit, Revere started liquidating its assets and negotiating With a Boston developer, Francis Reilly, for the sale of the Massachusetts refinery [32].

It was thus at the hands of a Marcos crony that Sucrest, which started as a molasses business in 1869 and incorporated in New York in 1905 [33], met its demise. Four hundred American workers lost their jobs without sufficient warning. Ed Barkewicz, then resident of the Revere local union says, "All of a sudden the bottom of the barrel just dropped out. That's when the process of us gradually phasing out began" [34].

Apart from these displaced workers, hundreds of thousands of Philippine sugar workers also suffered. As Sucrest papers point out, its profits and Floirendo's commissions were dependent upon the difference between the price at which they sold refined sugar at the international market and the price at which they bought raw sugar from the Philippines. The Floirendo-engineered contract provided that a fall in the international price of refined sugar would be compensated for by an accompanying decrease in the price it paid for raw sugar to Philippine government trading agencies. The lower prices, however, were merely passed on by sugar centrals to the plantation owners and from them to sugar plantation workers in the form of lower wages. While Floirendo, Imelda, and Marcos were receiving their millions in profits and commissions, thousands of sugar workers broke their backs earning the equivalent of $0.55 a day [35]. Here we have another example of one of the themes we mentioned in the first chapter, of how wealth and poverty engender each other. Nowhere was the causal chain more obvious than in the case of Floirendo.

The glaring difference between the international price of sugar and the price at which Revere acquired it, together with the millions in broker's fees, led to intense criticism of these corrupt arrangements. Public pressure finally forced the government to end the give-away contracts. But when this contract was abrogated, it was done with a final parting gift to Floirendo: the Philippine government sugar agency, Nasutra, awarded Revere a "termination compensation" of $6 million.

After Marcos' downfall, Rodolfo del Rosario tried to defend Floirendo from criticism by saying "the only fault of Floirendo as far as I can make it was his closeness to the ex-President" [36]. As is hopefully clear in this short account of Floirendo's activities, it was through this "only fault" that all the other faults were possible.

Familiarity with Floirendo's story helps us appreciate the irony of the poster which graces the Olympic Towers condominium he held for Imelda. Surrounded by a panoramic View of Manhattan and its outlying boroughs, a pencil-sketch poster of Mr. Ford with models of his early cars hangs in Floirendo's dining room. Below the poster is a note from Ford which presumably this former Ford salesman from Davao has taken to be his own: "He who would really benefit mankind must reach them through his work."

Below is a partial list of corporations where Floirendo owned or had interests:

Company	Activity
United Motors & Equipment	Car & truck sales
Worldwide Mineral & Ind. Corp.	Mining
Cagayan de Oro Aggregates	Rocks & gravel
AOF Shipping Co. Inc.	Shipping
Panabo rucking & Services	Trucking
Pioneer Trading & Supply	Gen. Merchandise
San Vicente Terminal brokerage	Gen. Brokerage
Mining & Dev. Corp. of the Phil.	Mining
ANFLO Management & Investment	Business services
United Finance Corp.	Financial intermediary
Davao Agricultural Aviation	Agri-business
Rootcrop Philippines	Agri-busincss
Millennium Shipping Corp.	Shipping
Anflocars Inc.	Machinery & equipment
Cougar Security	Security guard business
September Trading & Industrial	General
National Stevedonng & Lighterage	Stevedoring

Endnotes

1. As quoted in *The Human Cost of Bananas*, p.8.
2. As we shall see in Chapter IV, Floirendo's links with United Fruit also provided him with a mechanism to move money out of the country.
3. Maria Hipon, "The Philippine Banana Export Industry," *Solidaridad*, Jan-Feb.1978 as quoted in *The Human Cost of Bananas*. See also David et al., "Transnational Corporations and the Philippine Banana in Industry," *Political Economy of Philippine Commodities* (Quezon City: Third World Studies Center, University of the Philippines, 1983), p.17.
4. "Transnational Corp. and the Banana Industry," p. 32.
5. Linda Blue F. Romero, "Floirendo banana deal peeled," *Philippine Daily Inquirer*, 29 March 1986.

6. ICL Research Team, *The Human Cost of Bananas*, p.8

7. "Alleged Marcos Stake in US Company Investigated by Philippine Commission," *Wall Street Journal,* 16 April 1986.

8. Linda Blue IF. Romero, "Floirendo banana deal peeled," *Philippine Daily Inquirer*, 29 March 1986.

9. *Human Cost*, p. 94

10. *Human Cost*, p. 8.

11. Please see the motion on Elizalde for a discussion of Panamin.

12. As quoted in Human Cost, pp.21-7.3.

13. *The Human Cost of Bananas*, p. 20. There is ample documentation on the role of banana and other agribusiness companies in uprooting communities from their land in Mindanao. We mention here a few of these studies: Fr. Pedro Salgado, OP, *The Rape of Mindanao-Sulo,*
(mimeographed); ICL Research Team, *The Human Cost of Bananas;* Third World Studies Program, *Political Economy of Philippine Commodities, (Quezon City: University of the Philippines, 1983).*

14. *Bulletin Today*, 7 July 1980.

15. *Human Cost of Bananas,* p. 129

16. As quoted in *Human Cost*, p. 45.

17. *Human Cost,* p. 52.

18. Discussed in Chapters I & IV

19. See section on Benedicto for the details.

20. Please see proceeding section on Benedicto for a fuller discussion of Philex.

21. "Did Fugitive Tycoon Operate As A Front Man in Pres. Marcos' Investments?," *Wall Street Journal*, 30 January 1986.

22. *Wall Street Journal*, 30 January 1986

23. NOTE M of the accounting report.

24. 30 July 1977.

25. 1983 Annual Franchise Tax Report, State of Delaware

26. Again, the reader is reminded of the comment earlier made concerning the perversity of the situation where the seller of sugar is the one paying the buyer. Neoclassical economies would explain this away as a case of a Giffen good, but tons of sugar traded in the international market certainly does not fall within this category.

27. Again, please see section on Benedicto for more details.

28. Speech delivered to the Rotary Club, Manila Hilton, 28 October 1980.

29. *Wall Street Journal*

30. See Chapter IV.

31. *Boston Globe*, 7 February 1986.

32. The way in which Revere assets were disposed have also raised questions. Reilly started negotiations for the property on April 1986, and after eight months of bargaining, he received a purchase and sale cement for property on 8 December 1986. But noon of the following day, Reilly was informed that the property was being sold to a company called Massport. Of the rather peculiar arrangement, Reilly was later quoted as saying, "I've never seen anything like it before."

33. Sucrest was originally known as American Molasses Company of New York.

34. *Boston Globe*, 7 February 1986.

35. See previous section on Benedicto.

36. *Philippine Daily Inquirer*, 26 May 1986.

JUAN PONCE ENRILE

Juan Ponce Enrile enjoyed a long and cozy relationship with Marcos and played important roles in his administration. Marcos amply rewarded Enrile's loyalty by showering him with choice government positions and by giving him control of the most lucrative areas of the economy.

Enrile first served Marcos during the latter's campaign for the presidency in 1965. He bagged the post of Commissioner of Customs soon after Marcos was elected, while Rafael Salas and Onofre D. Corpuz, two close colleagues of Enrile from Harvard, later received cabinet positions for their services.

The post of Commissioner of Customs was a coveted appointment. It was, and still is, one of the most sought-after positions since it exerted control over the goods imported into the country. Many aspired for the position because of the opportunity to engage in the illegal importation of goods and the potential bribes from importers who did not want to pay the full amount of taxes. Enrile's appointment clearly showed that Marcos regarded him as an important and favored asset.

There is no known evidence of impropriety on the part of Enrile during this time. It was later on, when Enrile was already Secretary of Defense, that we hear charges concerning his involvement in the smuggling of goods. Mijares cites an occasion where Enrile and other Marcos men were involved in the smuggling of rice. Recording the incident, Mijares recounts the story of Antonio Garcia, a former government official, concerning Enrile's activities:

> ...Garcia was seething with rage over another piece of evidence of the continuing corruption within the administration of President Marcos. He was looking at the time at a handwritten note of Marcos directing Garcia's friend and boss at the time, Rice and Corn General Manager Benny Villamor, to issue a permit for the landing in La Union of several shiploads of rice imported from abroad by Congressmen Jose Aspiras and Eduardo Cojuangco and Defense Secretary Enrile. Earlier, Supreme Court Justice Julio Villamor, father of the RCA chief warned his son that he could be sent to jail if he implemented the Marcos directive on the rice shipments which were illegal, since only the RCA was authorized to import cereals. Garcia recalls that the directive was in Marcos' own handwriting which he (Garcia) at that time thought should have been leaked to the press [1].

Enrile quickly rose the political ladder and was later appointed Secretary of Justice. It appears that this was a rather benign period in Enrile's career since it was a post held without any notable achievements, notwithstanding the law degree he held from Harvard Law School.

Enrile's loyalty earned him further rewards from Marcos. He was later named to the important post of Secretary of Defense [2]. Enrile, however, was not content with merely an appointive position. He later made a political gamble and resigned from the defense post to run in the 1971 senatorial elections. Enrile, together with the entire Marcos slate, suffered a humiliating loss during this election. In spite of this embarrassing loss, however, Marcos, foreseeing the role that Enrile could later have his own personal plans, chose to ignore the people's explicit rejection of Enrile as a public servant and reappointed him to his previous position as Secretary of National Defense, a post he has used to great advantage until the end of Marcos' rule.

Enrile controlled the biggest item in the national budget as head of the defense department. He also was the owner, a major investor, a director, or had some some of influence over numerous corporations in areas such as sugar, logging, shipping, coconut, banking, real estate, motorcycle manufacturing, and agri-business. He was named chairman of key government institutions such as the Philippine National Bank, National Investment & Development Corp., Philippine Coconut Authority, United Coconut Planters Bank, United Coconut Mills, apart from directorships in other government corporations. The rest of this section will focus on the part Enrile played in these economic institutions [3].

LAW PRACTICE

Enrile practiced corporate law as a senior partner with the law office of Ponce Enrile, Siguion Reyna, Montecillo & Belo prior to entering the government. He was later constrained to cut his formal ties with private law practice when he accepted positions in Marcos' government. But while he formally gave up private practice, Enrile continued to maintain strong yet informal ties with influential law firms. These links have led some people to believe that he was a silent partner in these firms or had a financial interest in them. These law firms are among the highest earners in the industry. One of these law firms is the Angara, Abello, Concepcion, Regala & Cruz law office (ACCRA), and another is the partnership of Cayetano Bautista Picazo eyes.

When the *Far Eastern Economic Review* mentioned Enrile in connection with the ACCRA [4], or the Angara Law Office as it was sometimes called, Enrile reacted vehemently. Using his powers as Secretary of Defense, he banned the publication from circulation in the Philippines and sued it for $865,000. The complaint said that as a result of the article Enrile had

suffered, and continue to suffer, moral damages by reason of mental anguish, serious anxiety. besmirched refutation, wounded feelings, moral shock, social humiliation, and similar injuries that they have cause him [5].

In further retaliation, the Marcos-controlled courts froze the furniture, electrical appliances, and other household goods belonging to Rodney Tasker, the Southeast Asia correspondent of the magazine.

The *mental anguish, etc* suffered by Enrile and his consequent reaction was both surprising and revealing. The whole article was about a corporate takeover of a bank by the Herdis group of companies (see section on Disini) and merely mentioned Enrile in one single line. A raw nerve must have been touched since most of the partners of the firm were close associates of Enrile and Marcos.

Edgardo Angara, a senior partner and former president of the firm, was a close friend of Enrile and a favored hand of Marcos [6]. He was the dictator's candidate for the presidency of the Integrated Bar of the Philippines, an endorsement which clinched the position for Angara. He was also named president of the University of the Philippines by the dictator [7]. Manuel Abello, another partner in the law of ICC, enjoyed close links with the Romualdez family (see section). The ACCRA was also involved in Enrile's takeover of the coconut industry, and it was again ACCRA which was retained when Enrile's associates in the coconut industry underwent investigation. Enrile's associates generously advanced $50,000 for the filing of nuisance suits against the post-Marcos administration.

While Enrile continually denied being a silent partner in ACCRA, these links make it understandable why the association was made in the mind of the public.

The Cayetano, Bautista, Picazo & Reyes partnership is another law firm associated with Enrile. It is said that Enrile has been a "patron and client" of this firm since September 1983 [8]. This 24-lawyer firm handles both Enrile's personal legal affairs and represents the corporations where he has interests. One of the partners of this firm admits that they receive a monthly retainer of $1,250 from Enrile for these services.

The association with a public figure like Enrile is invaluable to these firms. Enrile's referals to the Cayetano partnership reportedly accounted for 5% of the firm's business. Association with a person perceived to be politically well-placed is a major asset for any law firm operating in the Philippines. The companies and individuals who use the legal services of well-connected offices stand a better chance of being heard by those in power and are generally granted the concessions they seek. When political connections are given greater weight than legal expertise, it easy to mistake such lawyering for high-level influence peddling. Enrile's roles in both the Marcos and Aquino administrations have undoubtedly helped these firms. It was reported that 40% of Cayetano's new business stems from the moves of the post-Marcos administration to sequester properties believed to be stolen by the former regime. An article from the *American Lawyer* explained Enrile's value to the Cayetano law firm, describing it as

> *a firm that was powerful under Marcos and remains powerful under Aquino.... While Enrile is not formally a partner at the firm, the referrals he has made have cemented his public identification with it. With Enrile enjoying just as much clout in the Aquino administration as under the old regime, Cayetano Bautista is still perceived as having the inside track.*
> *....the perception that the firm has access to the Aquino government is immeasurable. In a country where political connections have historically been the ticket to business success, it's not surprising that some Filipinos envy the firm's easy transition from one government to another. And it is even less surprising that they view that transition in a cynical light [9].*

Given these extra-legal considerations, it is understandable why most Filipinos view the legal profession with skepticism. In the words of Eleazar Reyes, a partner in Cayetano, "the credibility of the profession itself is at stake" [10].

Enrile has since has come out of the closet and has been been less shy about admitting his connections with law firms. He has resumed private law practice with the law office of Ponce Enrile, Cayetano, Reyes & Manalastas.

LOGGING

The country enjoyed 12 million hectares of virgin forest as late as 50 years ago. This figure took a drastic dive to 6 million by 1970. By 1990, the virgin forest hectarage had already plummeted to an alarming 900,000 [11]. Viewed in another way, virgin forests, originally covering 60% of the country's land mass [12], presently cover only a meager 9% today [13]. At this rate, natural forests in the country will soon disappear [14].

During the last 6 years of the Marcos dictatorship (1979-1985), loggers stripped the land of one-seventh of her trees [15]. Living trees were logged for export to Korea, Taiwan, and Japan, becoming cardboard boxes to be thrown away after one use. In the period from 1978-1982, the Philippines exported a total of 8.163 million cubic meters of logs to Korea, Taiwan, and Japan. Almost half of the amount was estimated to be illegally exported, causing a drain of around $120.4 million a year in foreign exchange [16]. At the rate the Philippines cuts her forests and exports logs to other countries, she will not have enough trees for her own use by the year 2000 [17].

The rapid loss of trees results in soil erosion and landslides, floods and droughts, and irreparable damage to soil quality. The November 1991 deaths of 7,000 in Ormoc, Leyte from flash floods is a most appalling example of the effects of indiscriminate logging. One-fourth of the land has already been depleted by soil erosion. Apart from exhausting the country's natural resources, the practice of indiscriminate logging, whether illegal or sanctioned by the government, also deprives Philippine labor of potential work since minimally processed raw logs rather than finished goods are shipped to overseas markets.

Logging is a favored way of getting rich quickly. Relatively very little investment is needed, the key factor being the proper political connections to get into the limited list of logging concessionaires favored by the government. And since the granting of a logging concession is based on government patronage, the concessionaire inevitably looks at his operations with an eye to quick riches, long term ecological concerns sacrificed to short-sighted objectives. A journalist explains the system of patronage within the logging industry:

Almost since the Republic was founded, the right to cut huge chunks of forest has been part of the spoils of politics, to be handed out to those who serve the politicians well. Timber concessions were like party favors distributed amongst senators, congressmen, and governors or their relatives and supporters in exchange for their allegiance and support.
Later, when martial law made them more powerful, military officers and the persons close to them were wooed with timber licenses [18].

Marcos repeatedly denounced the get-rich-quick schemes of illegal loggers, warning of heavy penalties for offenders. Enrile also made public pronouncements against loggers and used the Philippine Constabulary on numerous occasions to arrest those suspected of such crimes. The pronouncements of Marcos and the arrests of Enrile, however laudable, stood in sharp contrast with the numerous concessions handed over to individuals close to the dictatorship. Among those close to the regime granted with loggng concessions were Juan Tuvera, presidential assistant, who owned Twi Peaks Corp.; a nephew of Isabela governor Faustino Dy, a close Marcos associate, who owned Pacific Timber and Liberty Logging Corp.; the family of Gen. Zosimo Paredes, former Ifugao governor, which owned Sanafe Timber [19].

Perhaps most notorious among these concessionaires was Alfonso Lirn, who has been described as "closely associated with deposed President Marcos and former defence minister Juan Ponce Enrile" [20]. Alfonso Lirn and his family enjoyed 7 logging concessions in Northern Luzon with a total area of 600,000 hectares. This grant was five times the constitutional limit of 100,000 hectares for logging concessions to any one family [21]. Taggat Industries alone, the flagship of Lim's logging companies, already operated a 111,545 hectare concession in northwestern Cagayan. Among Lim's logging and wood-based firms are

Taggat Industries
Acme Plywood
Oesco
Western Cagayan Lumber
Pamplona Redwood & Veneer Corp.
Acme Plywood & Veneer
Southern Plywood Corp. [22]

Apart from his own 10 in concessions, Lim also managed other wood-based companies base in Cagayan. When Eulogio Balao, the Marcos crony who served as chairman of the Reparations Commission, died, Lim was awarded the contract to manage three of Balao's lumber companies: Veterans Woodwork, Sierra Madre Wood Industries, Tropical Wood Industries [23]. A further indication of Lim's political influence was the impunity with which he has avoided the payment of license fees to the government. It was revealed in 1986 that Lim ad failed to pay the $123,000 in license fees for his concessions [24].

Such treatment sharply contrasted with the way the Dupaya family, the traditional political rivals of Enrile in Cagayan province, were treated. Tito Dupaya, a congressman from Cagayan, related his ordeal:

I had a big timber concession in Lallo, Gattaran, and Gonzaga (all in Cagayan)... I could easily make $1 million a year but whenever my logging operators went inside the concession, Philippine Constabulary soldiers stopped them...[25].

To this, Dupaya's wife, Teresa, governor of Cagayan, added:

The Enrile people threatened they would bum down our bulldozers if the concession operated... So we had to sell our house in Dasmarifias Village. We really suffered. My husband resorted to drinking because he could not stand the humiliation [26].

Alfonso Lim has further benefitted from the military support Enrile extended him. With the help of the military, Lim conducted his own private war against the guerillas who have been attempting to control the activities of illegal loggers. Lim's

Taggat Industries enlisted 150 soldiers and 50 security guards [27]. Further support came from ex-military draftees and trainees, who are categorized as part of the Civilian Home Defense Force. Training is provided by the military, while Lim took care of arming them and paying for their salaries. Taggat Industries therefore played a crucial role in the guerilla war in Enrile's home province of Cagayan:

> *[Taggat] company planes drop supplies when soldiers conduct military operations in north western Cagayan. The firm's airstrip is also used for counter-insurgency operations and its planes for reconnaissance and intelligence-gathering operations. The company also has its own armored-plating facilities which explain the armored-plated vehicles that guard the Taggat concession. It also gives allowances and supplies to soldiers guarding the concession and troops that conduct operations in the area.*
> *The military reciprocates in kind. The concession is kept secure by soldiers drawn from at least three infantry battalions. At one point last year, when there were continuous battles between rebels and soldiers in the area, the concession was kept under guard by helicopter gunships provided by the Amy [28].*

Enrile himself has his own economic enclave in the logging industry. He was also one of the few individuals favored by the Marcos government with logging concessions. For example, Ameco, an Enrile company operating in southern Philippines, was one of the few corporations owed by the government to cut and harvest rattan, a favorite raw material for handicrafts and export goods. Also, inspite of the much-touted total ban on log exports, Enrile was one of the few who was allowed by the government to export logs in the 1970's.

Among the logging and wood-based companies owned by or linked to Enrile are the followmg:

1. Ameco, a rattan and logging corporation in Bukidnon
2. Dolores Timber, in Samar
3. San Jose Timber, in northern Samar
4. Kasilagan Softwood Development Corp., in Butuan
5. Palawan-Apitong Corp., in Palawan
6. Eurasia Match, a match-making company operating in Cebu, and
7. Pan Oriental, a match-making company operating in Cebu and Butuan.
8. Royal Match
9. investments in a rubber plantation in Basilan.

Most of these firms are clear sources of big money. San Jose Timber was able to acquire a license for 95,770 hectares in Northern Samar in 1982, though its operations in the area had started much earlier [29]. Kasilagan Softwood Development Corp. received a 25-year lease in 1985 for 5,000 hectares of forest land to be used for a matchwood plantation. Enrile's match-making companies, Royal Match and Eurasia, together with Swedish-owned Phimco, enjoy a "stranglehold on the match industry" in the country [30). Most of these loggng corporations held office in Montepino Bldg., Gamboa St., Legaspi Village, Makati, but some of these companies have grown in size and earnings to enable them to later purchase their own buildings in Makati. Logs from these firms were shipped through Cresta Monte, a shipping company also linked to Enrile or his associates, thus providing an extra source of profits.

SHIPPING

When Enrile was named Secretary of National Defense in 1970, he concurrently took over the chair of PNB from Benedicto (discussed earlier). It was this important government bank that made possible the organization of Cresta Monte, a major shipping line which at one time boasted of 12 brand new international liners.

Loans for Cresta Monte were arranged through Rolando de la Cuesta, one of Enrile's most trusted aides. Dela Cuesta was a former Enrile colleague at the Customs Commission and served Enrile in different capacities – first in the PNB, then as Enrile's executive assistant at the Ministry of Defense, and later as Enrile's token administrator in the coconut industry.

Heading Cresta Monte was Ernesto Magboo, another colleague of Enrile from the Customs Commission. Sources in the shipping industry generally believed that Magboo, who had no known experience in the industry, was merely a nominal head of Cresta Monte and that the real power behind the company was Enrile himself.

While Cresta Monte was a new firm, having been formally organized and registered with the SEC in 1976, it was able to acquire substantial loans from the PNB and purchase new ships from Japan. De la Cuesta, who arranged the loans for the shipping firm, while stressing that Enrile is "definitely not involved" with Cresta Monte, also admits that it was "highly unusual for PNB to grant such guarantees for ship loans" [31].

The highly-placed connections of Cresta Monte have been helpful in acquiring shipping contracts. On December 1977, for example, Atlas Mining suddenly switched a contract from Maritime Trade Carriers (MTC) to Cresta Monte. The change was done in spite MTC'S recent purchase of a 16,000 DWT ore carrier specifically for the Atlas contract [32]. Enrile has at present substantial investments in the stocks of Atlas Consolidated Mining. Cresta Monte also later acquired a lucrative contract to carry freight for the government-owned National Power Corporation (NPC). Geronimo Velasco, the chairman of NPC, and Enrile are business partners and close friends. Enrile has substantial investments in at least two firms owned by Velasco, and a good indication of the friendship between the two is that Enrile provided Velasco a military escort when the latter fled the country after Marcos' downfall. These and similar contracts, as well as shipping logs to Japan, have made Cresta Monte a very profitable venture.

Other interests of Enrile in the shipping industry included the chair of the Luzon Stevedoring Corporation (Lusteveco).

JAKA AND OTHER INTERESTS

The interests of Enrile included directorships in many government corporations and the ownership, control, or investments in a number of private companies. After we outline these other interests, the rest of this section will concentrate on Enrile's economic empire in the coconut industry.

Among the government directorships Enrile enjoyed were those in the Philippine Veterans Bank (PVB) , the Philippine National Oil Co. (PNOC), and Petrophil. He was also chairman of Netracor. Enrile also at one time controlled over 19 radio stations which the military took over [33].

His private investments are managed through JAKA Investment Corp., a holding company named after his two children, Jackie and Katrina. A key person helping Enrile manage his many concerns is Norma Bitong, the overall manager o Jaka, which has recently bought its own building in Pasong Tamo, Makati.

Jaka was organized with paid-up capital of only $29,000 in 1974. By 1985, it had ballooned into a huge concern of more than a dozen subsidiaries and affiliates with $92.6 million in assets [34]. Jaka is now one of 200 biggest firms in country with investments in areas such as real estate, coconut, agribusiness, and manufacturing ventures. Apart from these investments, Jaka also generates income from the management fees it charges its affiliates, which amounted to $1.7 million in 1988 [35].

Enrile and his family formally own 73.3% of Jaka Investment [36]. Angara, the ACCRA lawyer, once served as director in the company. Enrile accounts for 35.6% ownership, while Cristina, Jaka's chairman, owns 37.3%. Jaka shareholder's equity in 1989 was reported at $19 million, a fact difficult to reconcile with Enrile's report to the Senate on April of the same year that his investments were worth only $837,000 [37]. Enrile claimed in his Senate report that his and his wife's net worth was on y $2.09 million, a figure which appears to be an understatement considering the magnitude of Jaka's interests [38].

The remaining 26.7% Jaka shares is owned by Enerprim International, apparently an overseas shell corporation. Enerprim's shareholders and directors are other overseas shell corporations, thus providing a further layer of secrecy for the real owners of these Jaka shares. Valday Co. S.A., a shell corporation behaved to be based in Panama, owns 99,998 of Enerprim's 100,000 shares, while Lire International, based in Macau, and Company Registration Services, based in Hong Kong, own 1 share each.

Enerprim has held the Jaka shares since 1977, but SEC records interestingly do not have any reference to investments made by Enerprim [39]. Apart from the secrecy concerning Enerprim's real owners, another intriguing move of this company has to do with its investment pattern:

The growth of Enerprim's holdings in Jaka Investments has been effected by converting accrued dividends payable into Jaka stock which for the period 1978~82 amounted to [$422,000]. Jaka investment's board -- on which Enerprim is not represented - apparently has been careful not to dilute Enerprim's stockholdings through the years. Every time Jaka increased capital, it applied the dividends due Enerprim to new stock subscriptions by the Hong Kong firm. [40].

Dividends due to Enerprim are continually reinvested in Jaka. Over time, this will have the effect of continually increasing Enerprim's ownership of Jaka. Whatever the real intentions of Enerprim's owners are for this move, it is an ingenious way of slowly transferring the ownership of Jaka overseas.

Among the other interests of Enrile are investments or directorships in the following areas:

* Real Estate
Enrile has been on a buying binge of prime buildings in the choicest areas of Makati. Sigma Investments, a real estate subsidiary of Jaka, is headed b Katrina, Enrile's daughter. Sigma was originally registered under the name of Angara, Enrile's associate. It bought two buildings in Ayala venue, which now house Enrile's match companies. The Elizalde Building was bought from Fred Elizalde on November 1989 for $3.3 million and was renamed Eurasia. Royal Match bought the 14-storey Cibeles Building from BenignoToda on August 1989 for $9.3 million. Sigma Investments also constructed Splendido Gardens, a luxury residential condominium in Salcedo Village, Makati [41]. Crismida Realty, Filiol Industrial Estates, and Eurasia Builders are other Enrile companies in the real estate business. Filiol and Crismida were organized on March and July 1974. SEC records also show that Enrile registered a $1.3 a million real estate company, the New Filipino Market Inc. in August 1979.

* Coconut
Enrile, apart from managing the coconut industry (discussed in the next pages), also had his own direct investments in coconut related activities. Cocoland Dev. Corp produces hybrid coconut seedlings. Lucena Dessicatcd Corp. manufactures desiccated coconut. It bought the plant of Red V Coconut Products for $4.6 million in December 1988. New Sunripe Coconut Products, a manufacturer of different coconut-based products and one of the companies which dominates industry, is also an Enrile company 42].

* Stock Investments
Enrile also has substantial investments in the stocks of well-known companies such as Sime Darby, Philippine Long Distance Telephone, Republic Glass Corp., Atlas Consolidated Mining & Dev. Corp:, Ayala Corp., Phil. Global Communications, Far East Bank
& Trust Co.
Republic Glass, the country's largest glass manufacturer, is a $140 million joint venture wit Asahi Glass Corp. of Japan [43). Enrile is the second largest stockholder in Republic Glass, owning 35%, while his friend, Velasco (see section), owns the majorityof the stocks. Dividends from these companies and Jaka affiliates amounted to around $2.14 million in 1987. Around $633,000 was generated in 1987 from the sale of securities [44].

* Telecommunications Firms
Enrile also served as board chairman of Philippine Communication Satellite (Philcomsat) and Philippine Overseas Telecommunications Corp. (POTC), two telecommunications companies where Marcos and other associates had substantial investments. Critics have charged these two companies as being involved in an attempt to create a telecommunications cartel.
Philcomsat was initially a government-controlled corporation, but the owners of the minority shares became the controlling interest, with Bongbong later serving as chairman The POTC had 15 subsidiaries and enjoyed an income which was conservatively estimated
at $3.67 million [46]. Marcos reportedly owned 40% of PTOC shares through Independent Realty and Mid-Pasig, shell companies organized by Jose Campos Yao and Rolando Gapud (see section). The dictator's interests in the POTC were equal to $19.6 million in 1986.

Other Marcos associates who had interests in these firms included Jose Campos Yao, Manuel and Jose Nieto, Jose Africa, Roberto Benedicto, Honorio Poblador, Potenciano Ilusorio, as well as Bongbong.

Critics have further charged of "dubious arrangements" with National Development Corp. (NDC), a government corporation, where the POTC purchased NDC's holdings in Philippine Communications Satellite Corp. (Philcomsat), another government firm under highly "unconscionable terms." There have also been charges that the POTC was involved in kickbacks in the purchase of equipment for Domestic Satellite Inc. (Domsat).

* Various Other Interests

Among the other interests of Enrile are Sigma Security Services, Lady 44 Corp., and Nobel Philippines. Sigma provides the security services for Enrile's many firms. Nobel is an explosives firm partly owned by Velasco.

Another company forming part of the Jaka conglomerate is RMI Marketing, RMI, together with many Enrile firms such as Royal Match, Splendido Gardens, and Jaka, occupies almost a whole city block in Makati.

Enrile also had interests in the PDCP and Central Azucarrera de Danao. A sugar mill, National Sugar Development Corp., registered with the SEC on September 1975 was another corporation.

A motorcycle manufacturing firm, the Motorcycle Development & Machineries, Co. Inc., was registered with the SEC with an authorized capitalization of $270,000 under Enrile's name in January 1979. This company was a joint venture with American capital.

Other corporations listed under Enrile's name were Phividec Railwa Inc., a transportation firm; Subic National Shipyard, a shipbuilding concern; National Warehousing Corp., a provider of warehousing services.

* Overseas Investments

Enrile and his wife, Cristina, have also been linked to several apartments and condominiums in San Francisco.

They bought a condominium in 2190 Broadway, San Francisco in 1979. It has been reported

that Enrile's family owned two condominiums in this location, one of which has been sold to Renatsac Inc. It is believed that Renatsac is also connected with Enrile interests since Enrile describes it as a company my wife used for business purposes." The term Renatsac is an anagram formed by reversing the order of the name of Enrile's wife, Castaner. Renatsac also bought a house at 2310 Broadway, San Francisco, for $1.8 million in 1982. When these overseas properties were exposed in the papers, Enrile claimed to have liquidated them, saying, "it was bought by a company and has been sold. We — my wife — was acting for someone. I won't tell you who it was. It's since been sold."

The investments of Enrile's other relatives are significant. His brother, Rafael, is a director of a savings bank. His brother-in-law, Leonardo Siquio-Reyna, is a director or has investments in important Philippine companies such as

Foremost Wood Products
Perafilms
RCBC
Philippine Refining Co.
Menzi Agriculture
Stanfilco (with Sycip & Yuchengco)
International Harvester
Ekman & Co.
Warner Barnes Phils.
Philippine Air Lines

Bank of America Finance
Richardson-Merril
Goodyear Tire & Rubber

COCONUT

Concurrently with his position as Minister of Defense, Enrile was Chairman of the Philippine Coconut Authority (PCA). The latter position, though innocuously named, was the key to Enrile's control over the country's most important economic activity, the coconut industry, a sector which provides the income for almost a third of the population and whose plantations cover almost a fourth of total croplands (47).

Enrile was able to control the coconut industry through numerous laws and presidential decrees mandating the complete cartelization of the industry at every level. This was achieved through an elaborate system of control over the financing, planting, milling, processing, local marketing, and international trading aspects of the industry. These decrees also imposed gigantic levies on the produce of the coconut farmer, resulting in extreme poverty for many small farmers but generating billions in revenue for the few individuals who lorded it over the industry.

The next pages analyze in detail how Marcos' presidential decrees, and the institutions these decrees created, allowed Enrile and Eduardo Cojuangco (see separate section) to reign over the coconut industry.

THE COCONUT LEVY [48]

The key to the control over the industry was the levy imposed on all the coconut or copra (dried coconut meat) produced. The coconut levy, the biggest taxation scheme imposed on the country, extracted billions from the produce of the coconut farmer and spawned a multimillion dollar international coconut conglomerate controlled by Enrile and Cojuangco. At the same time it worsened the poverty and hardship of the small coconut farmer.

The levy had its origins in Republic Act 6260. The law, promulgated in 1971, required that $.08 be collected for every 100 kilos of copra produced. The collections were to start in 1972 and would proceed for ten years or until $17.1 million was raised [49]. The levy was to be generated for three different coconut-based institutions:

1. a Coconut Investment Company,
2. an organization of coconut farmers called Cocofed;
3. the Philippine Coconut Authority (PCA).

The levy was created to fund a coconut investment company (sometimes referred to as cocofund) which would engage in different support activities within the industry. The coconut investment company was to be owned by the coconut farmer.

But the manner the levy was collected and the consequent ownership of the investment com any reveals a sharp contradiction between stated aims and actual results. The method of levy collection and the translation of these levies into actual ownership shares were so complicated that hardly any farmer was able to claim his part in the ownership of the investment company.

The levy was charged from the coconut farmer during first domestic copra sale but was collected by the PCA from the last domestic buyers in the marketing chain. The last domestic buyers were the copra end-users such as millers, desiccators, oil processors, exporters, and independent copra buyers. The last domestic buyers in turn pass on the levy costs to the farmer through the layers of middle men operating in the countryside and was reflected as lower prices paid to the farmer for his copra.

The effect of this scheme was that the levy was never directly felt by the farmer. All the coconut farmer encountered was the price of the copra that the middle man offered him. There was no way for the farmer to see that the levy was operating behind the buying price of copra the middle man was offering him. The coconut farmer took the price for granted and was not aware that the presence of the levy actually depressed the prices for his produce.

After the end-users of copra remitted the levy money to the PCA, they were given receipts for the payment. The receipts, issue in triplicate, were for the buyer's, producer's, registration copies. The end-user kept the buyer's copy, while the producer's and registration copies were supposed to go back to the farmer who paid for the levy.

The farmer, upon receiving the two sets of receipts, was to register them with the Cocofed, the organization which claimed to his interests. The Cocofed in turn was to return one set, the registration copy, and submit a conciliation report to the PCA.

The return of the receipts to the farmer and their consequent registration were the most important steps in the process since it was these receipts which established his ownership rights to the planned coconut investment company. The receipts established that the farmer paid the coconut levy and was therefore entitled to equity in the company.

The method was efficient in so far as the collection of the levy was concerned. It assured a 100% rate of levy collection for all the copra reported sold. By 1977, after five years of collecting the levy, almost half of the target amount had been collected [50]. But the return of the receipts to the farmer and their consequent registration with the Cocofed and the PCA was a different matter. According to David

> ...the coconut farmers register the receipts with the PCA through the kindness of the Cocofed, and the coconut farmers will have insured their ture right to become stockholders of history's first business corporation owned exclusive by by the lowly coconut farmers. It is not the entire story, however. Behind the process in paper is an operation which works to deprive the masses of coconut farmers of their vitality and to strengthen and enrich the landed few [51].

David discovered that only 28% of the receipts ever got registered and the ownership of the remaining 72% was "unknown" [52]. It was moreover found out that hardly any of the receipts went back to the coconut farmer. David's researches showed that the flow of the receipts to the farmer stopped at the very early stages and only 5% of them ever received receipts for the cocofund (53).

Since the receipts were in effect claims to ownership in the cocofund, unscrupulous individuals cornered them:

There are reports that some end-users and dealers sell to landlords the Cocofund Receipts allocated to them, or register these under their name if they happen to be coconut landowners. Others reportedly give the receipts as gifts to Cocofed officials and PCA ofiicials. This is credible in view of the understandably keen interest of some people to acquire Cocofund receipts -- each receipt has a corresponding equivalent in economic power [54].

But apart from not returning the receipts to the farmer, actual copra sales were understated or unreported to the PCA when possible [55]. This was to evade remitting the levy. This meant that while the farmer was being charged for the levy, the money was neither remitted nor reported to the PCA.

End-users remit the levy corresponding to whatever volume they report as their purchases. For whatever volume that is not reported, the levy is not remitted, therefore cheated [56].

To prove that there was underreporting of copra sales, David compared the volume of copra purchases with the amount of copra levied over two years. He found inconsistencies in them:

Year	Amount Purchased	Amount Levied
1973	2 million tons	1.6 million tons
1974	2 million tons	1.3 million tons

For David, these figures represent a

possible unremitted levy collections for 400,000 tons in 1973 and about 700,000 tons in 1974. At the rate of $0.80 per ton, a total of $1.04 million representing collections from 1.3 million tons of copra may not have been remitted to the PCA [57].

David further supported his thesis by studying the data on the production of copra. Since the levy took effect, there was a continuous decrease in the amount of copra purchased, possibly due to underreporting:

Volume of Registered Copra Purchases
1972 - 2.2 million metric tons
1973 - 2.0 million (when levy took effect)
1974 - 137 million

Studying the data for 1974, David found that the reported amount for that year was unreliable. Since coconut reduction is directly correlated with the amount of rainfall, David studied the rainfall during the period. He concluded that the proper amount for 1974 was two million metric tons, or an unreported volume of 630,000 metric tons [58].

Assuming an average levy rate of $10.30 per 100kilos in 1974, the missing or *unreported 630,000 metric tons is equivalent to about $65 million in unremitted levy collections. This figure is the least estimate of cheating in the process of levy collection for the year 1974 alone and does not include other years [59].*

David also discovered that the cost of administering the levy was 50% of the actual amount collected. Analyzing the expenses incurred as a percentage of the actual collection, pointed out that "to accumulate the projected $17 million Coconut Investment Fund, about $8.5 million shall be incurred as costs of collection" [60]. This is absurdly high.

Thus while the levy was instituted as a means for raising funds for a coconut investment company for the farmers, in reality it turned out to be a scheme where those who controlled the industry taxed the farmers and claimed the benefits for themselves. Calling the levy robbery, David concludes

...the Cocofund from its inception is a deception, and nothing but a scheme by shrewd and enterprising landlords to promote their selfish interests.
...A thorough review of all levy and subsidy transactions from the beginning will point to hundreds of millions of pesos lost by the government [61].

Cesar Climaco, former Mayor of Zamboanga who was later gunned down because of his outspoken criticism of the dictatorship, shared the view of David. In an open letter to Marcos, Climaco complained that the coconut levy

was primarily designed to protect and promote the selfish interests of a few who are obviously enriching themselves by exploiting their closeness to your administration [62].

THE PCA AND COCOFED

This was possible because the Cocofed, the organization which purported to represent the coconut farmer, and the PCA, the government body overseeing the process of levy collection, were controlled by a small group of individuals whose agenda was in opposition to the interests of the small farmer. The same is true of the coconut investment company which the levy funded.

It is important to analyze these three institutions since control over the billions raised from the levy, and control over the coconut industry itself, were premised on control over tese organizations. Whoever ran these institutions controlled the coconut industry. They were nothing more than different mechanisms to exploit the coconut farmer and steal the billions raised through the coconut levy. David contends that these institutions together were "like a Spartan spear threateningly poised against the poor coconut farmers" (63]. Since a thorough discussion of these three institutions are essential for understanding how the coconut industry was managed, we will again follow David's discussion of these institutions.

The Cocofed was ideally the private sector organization of all farmers in the coconut industry. It was through this organization that the coconut farmer would be represented in the planned investment company and would have a say in the future of the industry.

But surveys conducted by David exposed the true nature of Cocofed. David found that only 9% of coconut farmers were members of Cocofed [64] and that the leadership of the organization were composed not of real life coconut farmers but of big landowners, businessmen, professionals, and ex-politicians.

David presents these figures on the composition of the officers and directors of Cocofed:

Profile of Cocofed Offocials
National Officials
    Officers 100% landlord
    Directors 100% landlord
Provincial and Municipal
    Presidents 98% landlord
    1.5% owner-farmer [65]

Of the two "owner-farmers" comprising 1.5% of the total provincial and municipal presidents, one was an insurance underwriter and owner of a restaurant and movie theater; the other was a retired teacher. There was not a single genuine coconut farmer who served as an officer in this purported farmer's organization. David's survey clearly established that the Cocofed was not a genuine farmer's organization but an organization of elite interests in the industry. The problem was more pronounced when it came to the composition of the Cocofed board. It was composed of the biggest landlords in the coconut industry and highly-paid professionals who served their interests:

Eladio Chatlo
Jose Concepcion.
Jose Eleazar
Anastacio Emano
Doming Fspina
Sulplicio Granada
Maria Clara Lobregat
Jose Martinez
Bienvenido Marquez
Inaki Mendezona
Reynaldo Morente
Manuel del Rosario
Celestino Sabate [66]

Elite interests in the Cocofed were consolidated during the 1977 convention. Maria Clara Lobregat, a prominent landlord [67] and an Enrile associate, was elected president, while Rolando de la Cuesta, Enrile's buddy from the Customs Commission and Cresta Monte, was made chairman. Enrile was named "honorary chairman." Drawing money raised from the levy, all the expenses of the delegates to the convention were paid by Cocofed, topped with a generous $13 daily allowance [68].

The ostentation of the convention was in marked contrast with the life of the coconut farmer Cocofed purported to represent and from whose toil the levy was raised. The $135 daily allowance received by Cocofed delegates in the convention was the equivalent of the income of the typical coconut farmer for seven months.

Commenting on the composition of the Cocofed leadership, David observed that

...there are some people who call themselves "coconut famier" whose only contact with coconut, however, is their consumption of coconut products. The real coconut farmer has never even tasted or rarely consumes most of the finally-refined products that the nut he produces is made into [cooking oil, margarine, cosmetics, soap, cakes, biscuits, perfumes, etc], for want of sufficient purchasing power [69].

This organization was so unrepresentative of the industry that it had a difficult time raising organizational funds before Marcos and Enrile instituted the levy. But the moment the levy was decreed, Cocofed "struck a gold mine with allocation of levy funds." Cocofed no longer depended on voluntary contributions from its members but could count on its funds from the levy. The law stipulated that 10% of all the levies collected would go to the funding o Cocofed

for maintenance and operation of its principal office which shall be responsible for continuing liaison with the different sectors of the industry, the government and its own mass base.

This is the part of the levy which David calls "most vulgar" since farmers "subsidize the very organization anathema to their interests." According to David, the levy and the Cocofed therefore caused "the permanent immobilization of the coconut farmers" since Cocofed preempted their organization [70].

Cocofed was organized to legitimize the control of the industry. If an organization like Cocofed could claim to be composed of all the coconut farmers in the country, then the officers and other influential individuals in Cocofed could operate under the mantle of speaking for all the coconut farmers and the interests of the industry in general.

But the Cocofed leadership became so unpopular that there were continuous calls for its reorganization. In one occasion, 900,000 farmers from Bicol, a region were much coconut is grown, called for the resignation of Lobregat, charging that no real elections have been held since 1976 when Lobregat and her clique took over.

The PCA, the government body tasked to administer the industry and the levy, was also manned by the same people. Enrile assumed the chairmanship of the PCA in 1975. Opting for a less noticeable presence in the industry, he later relinquished the post to Rolando de la Cuesta in 1978. Eduardo Cojuangco served as one of the directors, and a military associate of Enrile, Col. Felix Duenas, later acted as PCA Administrator. Other members of the board were Hermenegildo Zayco and Jose Eleazar.

We again refer to David's study and quote at length his conclusions concerning the PCA:

...its operations are fertile areas for cheating and for graft and corruption, to which all type of unremoulded bad elements from the old society, both in the public and private sectors, are attracted.

...Behind the seemingly placid image in which the PCM has been projected to the public is a...mad scramble among old-society-type oligarchs, grafters and swindlers to grab the values that are the products of the coconut farmers' toil.

...Another factor that renders law enforcement work virtually useless is the association of the wrongdoers with some authorities inside and outside of the coconut industry. This is in fact the most serious barriers to the lawful public administration of the industry... This problem is but a reflection of the very basic problem of the coconut industry -- the control and dominance of the elite landlords through the combination of the Cocofed and the PCA in the administration of the industry [71].

The PCA and the Cocofed, the institutions which were supposed to collect and manage the levy funds, did not represent the interests of the majority of the coconut farmers but were merely the instruments of the individuals who wanted to manipulate the industry for their benefit. The infiltration and manipulation of these institutions by powerful individuals made the diversion of the billions in levy funds possible.

SOCIAL CONSEQUENCES

The coconut farmer earns $19 a month on the average [72]. This means that he can afford only 10% of what is considered the minimum requirement for food. The picture becomes more dismal when we bear in mind that the coconut farmer represents 25% of the country's population. This implies that at least one-fourth of the country's working popupation live a life of abject poverty. One writer described the life of the typical coconut farmer:

You have just arrived from the city, where many things can be had quickly at the wave of a hand, and here you stumble across conditions that are primitive, almost aboriginal. Here in the barrio you find the family established in a miserable shack, roosting as it were, with chickens and co-existing as best as they could with the rest of the livestock. The food ~ rice, salt and greens -- is the simplest you can find. The hut consists of one small room. You find neither privies nor privacy.... The small producer never gets enough from his crop to live comfortably on. He and his family live in a small hut and have little opportunity to raise their stage in life, owning a small battery-powered radio is a financial impossibility [73].

Yet despite the abject poverty of the coconut farmer, he is ironically also the most taxed in the country because of Enrile's and Cojuangco's levy.

From an initial $.08 for every 100 kilos of copra, the levy was continuously increased over the years, going up to $2.00 and peaking to $13.00. At other times it hovered around $8.00 and remained at $10.00 from 1977 through 1981 [74]. One estimate contended that the coconut farmer was underpaid for his copra by at least 25% compared to international price levels [75]. Since the farmer was not being paid the proper market value of his produce, it meant that he was being unduly taxed by the unscrupulous individuals who controlled the levy. Using an amount of $8.00 in his calculations, David contended that the levy actually ate up 33.8% of farm income [76]. This is a rate of taxation which only the rich in affluent countries like the US pay. "The levy makes the poor coconut farmers the heaviest taxed citizens of the whole country despite their poverty" [77].

The system was so structured that the onus of the levy would always be on the coconut farmer. PDs 276, 414, and 582, the laws authorizing the levy, clearly stipulated that the tax would be charged on the first sale of the farmer to the middle man [78]. This had the effect of automatically reducing the earnings of the farmer.

Even when Marcos made nominal changes in the way the levy was calculated and collected, the burden still remained on the back of the farmer.

When on 31 May 1980 Marcos shifted the levy from the farmer to the exporter, the change was merely nominal. The exporters and traders responded by shifting the charges back to the farmer in the form of lower prices. These nominal changes in the law merely masked the reality that it was the farmer who carried the burden of the levy. Coconut farmers from Davao complained in an open-letter to Marcos:

We feel that Cocofed and Unicom are causing a lot of problems and hardship to the coconut farmers. For one thing, their buying of copra is not based at prevailing price of the world's market. Cocofed and Unicom buy our copra at a very low price. They sell the finished product -- oil -- at a very high price. We understand that the selling price of oil all right here in Davao City is higher than that of the selling price of oil in the New York market. We understand that the $8.00 levy that was imposed by the PCA on every one hundred (100) kilos of copra sold is shifted to the exporters. Obviously, the exporters, whoever they are, will pass on the amount by lowering their buying price... Why change anything at all? We fear that this scheme is to the great disadvantage of the coconut farmer [79].

Marcos made further changes to the way the levy was calculated in January 1982, this time relating the amount of the levy to the international price of copra. The change made the situation worse for the farmer. The new formula calculated the levy before costs were deducted from the price of copra. This new method calculated the levy before insurance, brokers' fees, freight costs, millers' margins, real production costs, and inventory financing were subtracted from the price of copra. The government in effect was imposing a levy on an unrealistic, higher rice. In the concrete, this meant that while the new method calculated the levy at an estimated millgate price of $25.00 per 100 kilos of copra, the actual price aid to the farmer averaged only $18.00 when these costs were included [80]. The government was thus calculating the levy using a higher price than what the farmer was actually receiving. The new method therefore meant a greater burden for the already highly-taxed farmer.

The practice of passing the financial burden of the levy to the farmer reached the extreme situation where the price at which copra was bought from the farmer dipped so low that it was just enough to cover the levy. In the island of Samar, for example, the price dropped to as low as $8.00 per 100 kilos. This was just enough to pay for the levy. Nothing was left for the sustenance of the farmer and cover the costs of p anting [81]. And when the populace in Samar started to grumble because of their financial problems, Enrile sent in the military to suppress the dissent.

Such practices contrasted sharply with the way Unicom- and UCPB-connected oil mills purchased copra from local political bosses close to Cojuangco. The Enrile-Cojuangco coconut conglomerate purchased copra from the trading firms owned by these local political bosses at rates higher than market levels [82]. The ordinary coconut farmer was thus not only receiving much less than he deserved but he was also in effect subsidizing the better-paid copra traders who were politically well-connected.

The farmer was burdened by the levy throughout most of Marcos' regime. More presidential decrees were later assed increasing the coverage and amount of the levy, bringing greater hardship to the farmer while increasing the fund available to those in power.

The decline in the income of the coconut farmer would be easier to justify if the levy brought him some immediate benefit or the promise of a brighter future for his family. But while the levy caused extreme poverty for the farmer, the great wealth that it created was reserved for a powerful few. One estimate of the amount raised from the levy calculated it to reach more than $470 million. There has been no proper accounting of this fortune. But from what is known, most of it went to the rapacious thieves who controlled the coconut industry.

USES OF THE LEVY

The levy was supposed to provide funds for the development of the industry. The often-cited reasons were crop replanting and diversification, as well as the "vertical integration" of the industry. A lot of promises were made concerning "welfare programs" for coconut farmers.

But despite the rhetoric concerning the noble aims of the levy, the few individuals who controlled it refused to give any accounting and fiercely resisted any audit of the funds. "As controversial as the levy itself is the secrecy which has surrounded the accounts of the levy funds and a reluctance to report in detail to the farmers who are supposed to benefit from the levy which they pay" [83].

Maria Clara Lobregat, president of Cocofed, claimed that her organization was a "non-stock, non-profit private organization" and therefore exempt from government audit. She refused to accept the position that the public funds her organization received from the levy were subject to government audit. Lobregat later retained the ACCRA law office, advancing $50,000, and filed charges against those who wanted to audit her organization.

Officials of the post-Marcos administration estimated that a total of more than $475 million was raised from the levy. This may be a conservative count since those who controlled the industry resorted to many methods of underreporting. It known that $295 million had already been collected between 1973 and 1980 [84] and that the amount had increased to $392 million b 1981. David estimated the levy to average of $73 million a year. If David's figures are correct, then close to $585 million must have been raised from 1974 through 1982 . This astronomic amount merely represents the principal and does not include the interest which accrued over the years. This would therefore mean that the $475 million estimate of the Commission on Audit is $113 million or 19% short of the actual amount.

Commenting on the absence of audits, David, points out the contradiction that while the levy is really a government tax it is strangely exempt from government audit [85]:

There is reason for saying that all this money, more than being public grants, is private wealth as well. While these taxes are government funds, they are channeled to and used by the Cocofed, which is a private entry, without the benefit of government audit. The financial operations of the Cocofed as far as these funds are concerned have never been audited by the Commission on Audit because the latter is officially restrained, upon the objection the farmer, from performing an audit on the same [86].

During the post-Marcos era, some details finally emerged as to how the levy was used. Most of the expenditures had nothing to do with the stated aims of developing the industry and improving the lot of the farmer.

A plane, a Sugar King Air 200, was purchased for $1.4 million, while $1 million was spent or a twin-engine helicopter, presumably for the personal use of Cojuangco. Many Cojuangco companies were also beneficiaries of the levy, as we shall see in the section on Cojuangco.

Many Imelda projects got a slice of the levy as well. A Cocofed resolution [87] granted $2 million for the Coconut Palace (Coconut Center or Tahanang Maharlika), a structure made totally of coconut materials, constructed so that Imelda could use it to entertain personal friends such as Brooke Shields, Sean Connery, and Cristina Ford.

Other Imelda projects which received funding from the levy include the following:

Imelda Project	Amount
World Chess Championship	
Miss Universe Pageant	
"For integrated social services"	
Maligayang Pasko project	$90,000 (total of four)
Cultural Center	$1.3 million (unaccounted) [88]
Lungsod ng Kabataan Children's Hospital	$6.7 million [89]
Imelda Marcos Scholarship Program	$7.3 million (unaccounted)

Other disbursements from the levy fund included a $675,000 donation in 1977 to the Youth Health & Sports Center (PYHSC), an organization owned and controlled by Gilberto Duavit, a close Marcos assocrate. Jesus Hipolito, Marcos' public works minister, had an outstanding liability of $300,000 and owed a further $834,000 in damages for delays in construction work done. Marcos' last election campaign also received $8.3 million from levy funds [90].

Most of the funds, however, went to the PCA, the Cocofed, and other organizations Enrile and Cojuangco controlled.

The PCA got more than $137 million, or roughly 29% of levy. A sampling of how the PCA spent this money reveals very ambiguous if not outrightly questionable items:

$21.1 million	"research"
$105.32 million	"subsidy of coconut products"
$11.91 million	"0prating services"
31.1 million	"Cocofed chapters convention"
$37.2 million	"socioeconomic projects for coconut farmers" [91]

Another significant outstanding and unsettled item was for more than $22.3 million of accounts receivables, representing unpaid levy deficiencies and disallowed subsidy claims [92].

The bulk of the funds, a reported sum of $412 million [93], went to the Cocofed. The Commission on Audit later discovered many questionable investments and other unexplained expenses in the Cocofed accounts. Lobregat and de la Cuesta were discovered to have illegally received disbursements from the funds:

	Amount	**Cocofed Account**
Lobregat	$60,000	cash advances
	$245,000	discretionary fund
De la Cuesta	$62,000	cash advances
	$245,000	discretionary fund [94]

The Cocofed Marketing Corp. (Cocomark), a subsidiary of the Cocofed, also spent levy money in activities totally unrelated to the welfare of farmers.

It invested in urban real estate, sinking $4.7 million in two private companies, B.F. Homes Inc. (BFI) and Philippine Infrastructure Inc. (PII).

Cocomark also paid $12,500 for "travel expenses" of its directors, but there has been no proper accounting of this amount. Cash advances given to Cocomark officials amounting to $398,000 remained unliquidated. Some $30,000 was simply missing.

Corporate and management officers of Cocomark were granted "performance" bonuses amounting to $287,000 from 1980 through 1985. This was while the company was registering huge deficits.

Cocofed and Cocomark officials received from $2,700 to $27,000 each from 1983 through 1985 for undocumented "public information" expenses.

As if to add insult to injury, one item amounting to $745,000 was described as paying for expenses in administering above amounts for and in behalf of the "leaders of the coconut industry".

Functionaries of the post-Marcos administration studying Cocofed operations complained of the "serious deficiencies" in accounting procedures followed by Cocofed and Cocomark. They estimated that Cocofed officials got nearly $60 million from levy funds, and that these individuals have been living luxuriously: "Cocofed officials have been helping themselves freely as if these were private funds" [95]. Lobregat, president of both Cocofed and Cocomgrk, could not be reached for comment when these expenses were exposed.

By the time the Marcos government collapsed, the fund balance was a mere $7.9 million, but only $1.19 million in cash was in the bank [96].

EXPANSION OF COVERAGE

The levy became the object of much criticism. Emmanuel Pelaez, who served as Vice-President in the early 1960's and later as member of the Marcos parliament, called for a legislative hearing on the levy on 29 May 1980. He asked for a suspension of the levy, a full accounting of industry funds, and a review of the coconut industry rationalization program. Marcos responded by issuing a presidential decree two days later. The Marcos-controlled press carried the headlines "Marcos Suspends Coconut Levy To Aid Coco Farmer" [97]. The new decree, PD 1966, however, did not abolish the levy, but, as earlier discussed, it merely passed it on to the exporter. The new decree successfully deflected the criticisms of the levy and the requested investigation. Pelaez again called for a legislative investigation of the levy and filed a resolution with the National Assembly on November 1981. Marcos quashed all public debate a month later. Pelaez was later ambushed by gunmen who riddled his car with machine gun fire, seriously wounding him and killing his driver. The style with which the attack was carried out led many to believe that members of the military were responsible.

There were times that the criticisms of the levy became so intense that Marcos was forced to suspend it on 9 September 1981. Whether Marcos really meant to suspend the levy was highly uncertain because Unicom, a private organization controlled by Enrile and Cojuangco, fought back and "wielded its life-and-death powers in the industry" to get the levy back [98]. Unicorn, which controlled the coconut mills, refused to buy any more copra as long as the levy was suspended. On one occasion 200 trucks laden with produce had to return to Lucena City and other parts Quezon province after eight coconut-oil mills refused to take their cargo. Unicom also refused to sell any coconut oil. These moves effectively froze all activity within the industry and demonstrated the tight control exerted by a clique of a handful of individuals. It also showed the political acumen of Enrile and Cojuangco who realized early in the game that control over the marketing channels was paramount in controlling the industry. A rally of "farmers" was organized by Unicom and truckloads were carted from the provinces for a rally at the presidential palace to demand the return of the levy. Marcos readily agree to "give in" to the" demonstrators". The levy was promptly reinstated on 28 September 1981, a mere 22 days after it was suspended [99].

The suspension of the le was beneficial for the real coconut farmer since it relieved him of a eat inancial burden. It benefitted the millers and exporters since it meant t at their costs would decrease. The real opposition to the suspension really came from Enrile, Cojuangco, Lobregat, and those who profited immense y from the levy.

Paying no heed to the complaints, the expansion of the coverage of the levy continued.

Marcos and Enrile saw an excellent chance to increase the amount levied on the farmer when rice of copra increased in the world market in 1973. Presidential Decree 76 was issued, increasing the original $.08 to $2.00 per 100 kilos of copra sold, a considerably higher rate of taxation [100]. The pretext for the increase was that a fund was needed to subsidize the local prices of coconut-based products such as cooking oil, laundry soap, and animal feeds which had risen as a result of the increased demand in the international market. The ensuing collection was called the Coconut Consumers Stabilization Fund (CCSF).

While the ostensible reason for the CCSF was to protect consumer interests, the expanded scope of the levy presented greater opportunities for corruption. Local processors were to sell their products at "controlled" prices but would later receive subsidies equivalent to the difference between the controlled prices and whatever the government deemed to be the proper "market rice." The move had the effect of actually increasing or maintaining demand for the coconut products because of the subsidy. But it was again the already-suffering coconut farmer who shouldered the costs of the subsidy. Furthermore, such an arrangement left a lot of room for manipulating both the production prices and how the government defined the real "market" price in the presence of the subsidy. Production prices can be inflated, while the "market price could also be conveniently defined by the authorities at an arbitrarily high level, both moves resulting in greater subsidy payments. A description from a government publication at that time admitted that manufacturers could manipulate their costs of production so as to benefit from the expanded nature of the levy: "Losses incurred by manufacturers on the sale of these items at socialized prices are covered by subsidy payment." When a partial accounting was later made of these subsidy payments, it was calculated that the coconut farmer paid at least $105.32 million to subsidize Unicom and the other companies Enrile and Cojuangco controlled. David pointed out that, apart from the problems surrounding levy collections and receipt registration, another opportunity for graft and corruption and multi-million rackets on government funds was to be found in the CCSF subsidy payments [101].

The expanded levy was meant to be temporary and was to have ended on May 1974, but a month before this levy was to cease, Marcos issued a new presidential decree, PD 414, on 18 April 1974. Those who controlled the coconut industry realized that "a mechanism had been created which could raise large sums of money relatively painlessly" [102]. They therefore prevailed upon Marcos not only to continue with the levy but also to expand its coverage and make it more permanent. The new decree gave the PCA the power to determine the duration of the levy, periodically revise its amount, and to appropriate the funds for other uses.

Among the additional purposes of PD 414 were "investment in processing plants, research and development, and extension services" [103]. In the words of Eleazar, a prominent coconut landlord and associate of Enrile and Cojuangco, the fun would now be used to establish oil mills, soap and detergent factories, other coconut processing plants, transportation, banks, and marketing cooperatives for the industry. Not only would the levy subsidize the local prices of coconut products but now became a multipurpose fund for the industry.

The PCA board interestingly added funding for the Cocofed as another purpose for the levy: "an unexplained appropriation of $.30 out of the prevailmg rate for Cocofed" [104].

What was originally a temporary measure to meet a emergency became institutionalized and controlled by the PCA. This led the *Review* to comment that a multipurpose giant was created out of a cooking-oil crisis [105].

These two decrees added another nail to the coffin of the coconut farmer.

UNITED COCONUT PLANTERS BANK & UNICOM

The third institution organized and funded by the levy provided the remaining key to the control over the industry. The original intent of the law was to provide 10% of the levy funds to Cocofed and the PCA, while the bulk was to be used for the capitalization of an investment company [106]. As will be recalled, the idea was to accumulate $17.1 million and then organize the investment company to acquire banks, mills, and trading companies. It was this provision more than anything else that permitted Enrile and Cojuangco to totally integrate the industry vertically and complete their two-man monopoly. In practice, what was done was to create not one but two conglomerates within the coconut industry -- the United Coconut Planters Bank (UCPB), which concentrated on financing, and the United Coconut Mills (Unicom), which focused on manufacturing and trading. Most of the activities of Unicorn and its subsidiaries are discussed in this section, while detailed discussion of the UCPB is left until the section dealing with Cojuangco.

Using the "vertical integration" of the coconut industry as their pretext, Enrile and Cojuangco extended their control by organizing the United Coconut Mills (Umcom), a conglomerate of mills and trading companies which would cartelize both the milling and international trading of copra. The organization of Unicom in 1977 was next and final step in establishing monopoly control over the coconut industry.

Marcos gave complete support to the cartelization by LOI 956, calling for the "Rationalization of the Coconut Oil Milling Industry," in September 1979. The LOI authorized an initial capitalization of $136 million from the levy, the Coconut Industry Investment Fund (CIIF), to finance the purchase of mills and the marketing of copra.

The first mill to be bought, the Orcar Development Corp. in August 1977, was renamed Southern Luzon Coconut Oil Mills and formed the nucleus of the Unicorn conglomerate. A buying binge of coconut mills soon followed, resulting in the almost complete monopoly in the milling of copra.

Apart from the funding from the levy, Cojuangco's and Enrile's efforts to acquire mills were helped by the control they exerted over the UCPB and the Cocofed. Control over the supply of copra exercised by Cocofed, as well as control over the financing exerted through UCPB, were used to systematically coerce and buy up all of the coconut mills in the country.

The case of Legaspi Oil and its subsidiaries is illustrative. The biggest stockholder in Legaspi Oil, the privately-owned Bank of Philippine Islands (BPI), requested the government for tax privileges to set up its own processing plant and improve the capacity of Legaspi Oil. The request was refused, leaving the BPI no choice but to sell Legaspi Oil, its subsidiaries, and Cagayan de Oro Oil to the UCPB for $21.5 million.

Control of the copra supply was also crucial. Since the marketing of copra was handled by the Cocofed, millers who could not get enough copra could not fully utilize their milling capacity. The Granexport, for example, a subsidiary of the US-based multi-national Cargill, processed only 500 tons a day in 1979. This was half of its milling capacity, causing its net income to drop from $1.6 million in 1978 to $0.95 million in 1979 [107]. It was later bought by Unicorn. Most of the mills operated between 57% an 64% of total capacity [108]. Many of these mills soon became bankrupt. Cojuangco took advantage of the situation by buying these underutilized mills at giveaway prices. No less than $355 million from the levy was used to buy these mills. Some mills were not as lucky; there were instances where no money was ever offered but were merely "encouraged" to affiliate with Unicom in exchange for their holdings [109].

Among the more important mills and trading firms that Unicorn counted as part of its conglomerate Were:

Cagayan De Oro Oil
Davao Gulf Oil
Granexport Corp.
Granexport Manufacturing Corp.
Iligan Bay Express Co .
Iligan Bay Manufacturing
Iligan Coconut Industries Inc.
Iligan Bay Oil Mill
Legaspi Oil Mill
Legaspi Oils & subsidiaries
Legoil International
Mindanao Coconut Oil Mills
Mindophil, Medina, Misamis Oriental
Philagro Edible Oil Inc.
San Pablo Manufacturing Corp.
Southern Island Oil, Dipolog
Southern Luzon Oil Mills
Sulu Agro Industrial
United Cocoa Plantation

These companies were among the biggest in the industry. Legaspi Oil and its subsidiaries had assets estimated at $108 million. Granexport was valued at $98.1 million. San Pablo had a value of $49 million, while Cagayan de Oro Oil was $39.2 million. A grouping of 17 copra trading firms under Unicom had a combined value of another $108 million. One estimate of the value of the oil mill in the Unicorn group put it around $392.4 million [110].

Unicom bought out so many mills that it was estimated that the conglomerate controlled 93% of coconut milling and coconut-crushing trade during its peak [111]. Apart from the mills which formed part of the Unicom group, Enrile and his associates also had their privately owned mills. Two mills, International Copra and Lu Do & Lu Ym, were owned by Enrile associates but were described as "interlocked" and "managed by Unicom." These two were described as "independently-owned, but managed by Unicom" [112]. In his testimony to US authorities investigating the existence of cartels in the Philippine coconut industry, Douglas Lu Ym, a close associate of Enrile and Cojuangco, attested: "In obedience to the orders of the Philippine government, Lu Do & Lu Ym Corp. and Lu Do & Lu Ym of the Pacific were placed under the direct control of Unicom" [113]. Enrile himself was listed by the SEC as owning the Nido Oil Mills, registered with the SEC in January 1974 with a paid-up capitalization of $884,000 and an authorized capitalization of $17.7 million.

Some of the mills Unicom took over ended directly with Cojuangco and his relatives. The Indophil Oil Mills in Misamis Oriental, for example, ended up in the hands of Cojuangco's son, Mark. Three government-owned mills were leased at nominal cost to cronies. Two oil mills of the National Industrial Dev. Corp., a government corporation, one in Davao, another in Jimenez, were leased to Luy Kim Guan, a possible dummy, while Coco Chemical Atimonan was leased to Ramon M. Cordova who was associated with Unicom [114]. These three mills had financial assets of $392 million, a minimum of $91 million in fixed assets, and inventories amounting to $49 million. According to critics this deprived the government of $2.4 million in annual income [115].

Unicorn grew so fast that its sales within the first year of operations reached $430 million, making it one of the top five companies in sales. Such an impressive growth record was possible because of the backing the conglomerate received from the government. Marcos had already appropriated $13 million for Unicom merely within the first year of its copra buying operations [116].

UNICOM OWNERSHIP AND SUBSIDIARIES

While Unicom was quickly eating up all of the country's oil mills, its ownership was never openly known. There appeared to be a concerted effort to keep Unicom in a legal limbo and conceal its true ownership from the public. Even the question of whether it was a private or public corporation was never clarified.

The *Bulletin Today*, a Marcos-controlled newspaper, described Unicom as "owned by the country's coconut farmers" [117]. The *Daily Express*, similarly controlled by the regime, heralded the conglomerate as "a new holding firm owned by the country's coconut farmers" [118]. Public statements of Marcos regarding the corporate status of Unicom differed from those given by Cojuangco. The *Bulletin Today* quoted Marcos as saying that Unicorn was "a firm organized by the government to consolidate marketing and distribution of coconut products and stabilize prices." Cojuangco, on the other hand, stated in the same newspaper that Unicorn is "a private commercial entity which is majority owned by the coconut farmers."

Furthermore, the relationship between Unicom and the UCPB (see section on Cojuan co) was also unclear. Jaime Gandiaga, Unicorn Spokesman, claimed that Unicom while a subsidiary of UCPB is "not 100% directly owned" by the bank, further raising the question as to who actually owned the remaining shares.

Documents show that Unicom was incorporated in April 1977 not by coconut farmers but by five partners of Accra law firm who then served as Unicom's directors and officers. The firm was organized with an authorized capital of $13.5 million, a subscribed capital of $2.7 million, and paid-up capital of $675,000. The directors and officers of this corporation "owned by the coconut farmers" were Enrile, Cojuangco, and their cronies.

Among the directors were

Juan Ponce-Enrile, Chairman of the Board
Eduardo Cojuangco Jr.
Ma. Clara Lobregat
Jose R. Eleazar
Inaki Mendezona
Douglas Lu Ym
Jaime Gandioza
Emmanuel Almeda
Atty. Jose Concepcion
Atty. Teodoro Regala

Among the officers were

Eduardo Cojuangco, President
Jaime Gandiora, Executive vice-president for operations
Douglas Lu Ym, Executive vice-president for marketing
Jesus Pineda Jr., Treasurer
Amado Monruvia, Controller
Atty. Teodoro Regala, Secretary
Atty. Florentine Herrera III, Assistant corporate secretary.

Enrile and Cojuangco organized many Unicom subsidiaries in the industry, among them a cocochemical complex, an insurance company, a shipping fleet, and a management group. It appears that Enrile and Cojuangco agreed upon a modus vivende where Enrile would be chairman of Unicom and the other subsidiary companies, while Cojuangco would be president [119].

Marcos granted Enrile and Cojuangco a further control through Unichem (United Coconut Chemical Inca), a $108 million industrial-chemical complex designed to process coconut oil into fatty alcohol, acids, and glycerine for use in detergents, cosmetics, car tires, explosives and other pharmaceutical products. The chemical complex, based in Bauan, Batangas, had a capacity of processing 69,400 tons of coconut oil and receive technical support from Lurgi Umwelt und Chemotechnick, a unit of Metallgesellschaft of Germany [120]. Enrile was, again, chairman of Unichem, while Cojuangco was, again, president; the project was, again, funded through CIDF levy funds. Unichem received a total of $42.4 million from levy funds [121].

The Unichem project received complete support from the Marcos government. It was declared one of the government's 11 major industrial projects. The UCPB and its subsidiaries were ordered to invest in the activities of Unichem. Marcos went as far as ordering the replacement of the alkyl-benzene component in soap and other detergents so as to maximize the use of Unichem's products, thus providing a large captive market. The Board of Investments (BOI) granted pioneer-company status to companies which utilized the products om Unichem, qualifying them for tax breaks and other incentives. Unichem was granted tax exemptions on its infrastructure, materials, properties, and foreign technical assistance for 10 years. Presidential Decree 1863 furthermore granted a monopoly to Umchem in the importation of petrochemical materials which would compete with the products of the firm. A ban on the importation of competing products was finally imposed; with the proviso that should Unichem not be able to meet local demand, all of the importation would be done through this favored firm.

Among the companies which formed part of Enrile's and Cojuangco's empire in the coconut industry were

> United Coconut Planters Life Assurance Corp. (Cocolife)
> United Coconut Planters International
> United Cocoa Plantation Inc.
> United Coconut Planters Management Corp.
> United Coconut Chemical Inc.
> BBC-Luzon Intercoast Capra Trading Companies
> Davao Coconut Planters Trading Inc.
> Tagalo Coconut Planters Trading
> Biool Coconut Planters Trading Inc.
> Zamboanga Coconut Planters Trading Inc.
> Northern Mindanao Planters Trading Inc.
> Leyte Coconut Planters
> Visayas Coconut Planters Trading Inc.
> Agricultural Commodities Trading Companies [122]
> > Mt. Boribing Agricultural mmodities
> > Mt. Bulusan Aficultural Commodities
> > Lamitan Peak Agricultuial Commodities
> > Lamon Bay Agricultural Commodities
> > Mactan Agricultural Commodities
> > Maligayon Agricultural Commodities
> > Mandalangan Agricultural Inc.
> > Maopay Agricultural Commodities
> > Sharp Peak Agricultural Commodities
> > Mt. Tuayan Agricultural Commodities

Other areas of activity within the coconut industry did not escape the reach of Enrile and Cojuangco. Apart from the UCPB, some 13 rural banks were also part of the coconut conglomerate. An insurance company, United Coconut Planters Life Assurance Corp. (Cocolife), was organized supposedly to provide insurance for the coconut farmer. Levy money, one count giving it as $2.5 million, was again used to fund this project. The transportation of coconut products was also cornered, with the Luzon Intercoast Company Inc., a fleet of 21 vessels and barges, forming part of the conglomerate.

To help manage his vast empire, Enrile and Cojuangco organized another corporation, the United Coconut Planters Management Inc., registered with a paid-up capitalization of $1.3 million and an authorized capitalization of $5.4 million under Enrile's name in May 1980.

THE SHERMAN ACT

In a relatively short period of time, Enrile and Cojuangco succeeded in consolidating their hold over all aspects of the coconut industry. Through Unicom and UCPB, and with the help of presidential decrees, each of the different phases of the industry -- financing, planting, milling and processing, pricing policy, domestic and overseas trading, and even the technology of the industry itself — were drawn into the ambit of the overlapping empires of the two. Under the guise of the industry's "vertical and forward integration," a whole national industry came under the control of these individuals within a short time [123].

Since the Philippine coconut industry occupies a major role in the international market, the drive to cartelize the industry eventually led to the acquisition of overseas properties. Among the many foreign milling and trading firms Unicorn acquired were

* **Nouvelles Huilerles et Refineries Unipol**, France

* **Société Anonyme de Produit Excel**, France
Rather than provide employment for coconut workers and business for underutilized mills in the Philippines, Unicorn chose to invest $15 million in these two refineries in Marseille, France in 1980. Copra imported from the Philippines was processed into coconut oil through these two coconut-industrial complexes. In the words of a government publication, these were "investments into high-value end-product enterprises" [124]. The justification for Unicom's purchase of these French refineries was purportedly to escape the 7% and 25% tax imposed by Westem Europe on edible and technical grade use coconut oil imports. But the European tariffs were not that steep to require such a major investment. The benefits of employing Philippine labor and mills would have more than offset the tariffs imposed by Western Europe. This move is more intelligible if we view it as part of the over-all effort of Marcos cronies to move money overseas.

* **Pan Pacific Commodities, Los Angeles**, California
a wholly-owned subsidiary engaged in trading in the US commodity exchanges (according to

* **Crown Oil Corp., (US)**

* **Granexport Corp.,** 1301 Army St., San Francisco, California.
A former subsidiary of Cargill Industries USA bought by Unicom which refines coconut oil
 * **Coastal American Traders Inc.**
a trading firm partly owned by Helenita Borlano, Cojuangco's former personal secretary. The firm owns a $220,000 house in Santa Monica which Cojuangco uses.

* **Legaspi Oil International Ltd.,** Hong Kong
a wholly-owned subsidiary of Legaspi Oil

Encouraged b the irnpunit with which they monopolized the coconut industry in the Philippines, Enrile and Cojuangco attempted to cartelize the international market as well. They thought that an international trading cartel could be organized since the Philippines dominated the world coconut oil market (28% of the world's coconut hectarage, 60% of the world's coconut output, and 86.1 percent of total coconut products traded in world market). The market that was initially targeted for cartelization was the US since the Philippines supplied 95% of all coconut oil consumed there.

Most of what is known about these cartelization moves come from an anti-trust suit filed by the US Department of Justice against Enrile, Unicom, and its US subsidiaries. The suit, filed on 18 February 1981 in Los Angeles, charged that there was a conspiracy to fix prices of coconut oil sold in the US from October 1979 through March 1980 and various other violations of the Sherman Act. Among the defendants named were Unicorn subsidiaries based in the US:

Pan Pacific Commodities (main one used by Unicorn)
Legaspi Oil Co. (subsidiary
Cagayan de Oro Oil Co.)
Cargill Inc.
Granexport Mfg. Corp.
Crown Oil

It was alleged that Unicom's subsidiaries conspired to create an artificial shortage in the US market and drive up the price of coconut oil by hoarding more than 43,000 tons of the commodity. De la Cuesta, Enrile's crony in the PCA, himself acknowledged the conspiracy, conceding that Unicom had helped "slow down the fall in the price of coconut oil in the world market" and that higher prices of the commodity was due "the influence of Unicom by pooling the resources of the coconut industry" [125]. Marcos also put his foot in his mouth when he admitted that the "cohesive organization of the millers and farmers" allowed Unicorn to eliminate the underselling of coconut products in the world market [126]. When compelled to submit testimony in the case, Enrile himself had to admit that there was indeed a move to "systematize the flow of coconut products," declaring in his testimony to US courts that the Marcos government had

ordered the establishment of an organization that would systematize the flow of coconut products from source to end-users as a measure to cushion the effects of violent price fluctuations in the international market for fats and oils. The United Coconut Oil Mill, Inc. (Unicom) is the institution which the government ordered to pool and coordinate the resources of the coconut farmers and oil millers in the buying, milling, marketing of copra, coconut oil and their by-products [127].

The US government claimed $100 million in damages in the civil anti-trust suit. Rafael Fernando, who headed the marketing operations in the US as general manager of the Cojuangco-connected trading firm of Pan Pacific Commodities, refused to testify on the cartelization moves when subpoenaed by US courts [128]. Lobregat, who likewise refused to discuss the case, angrily responded when a similar investigation was requested in the Philippines:

What do they want to investigate?.... This is a private corporation. Why should we allow them to do that? We have our own auditors... If there are irregularities in the United States, the US government should investigate. Why investigate it here? [129]

In response, Marcos later stated that he did not think that the matter was "all that serious" [130].

The cartelization move backfired, however, due to the incompetence of the those who handled the US operations. While these managers were trying to create an OPEC-like cartel, which punsters called Cocopec, the failed to realize that coconut oil, unlike petroleum, had many substitutes. The move became a disaster when they failed to realize the Soviet grain embargo meant that soy beans would consequently saturate the US market and provide a cheap substitute to coconut oil. The *Washington Post* characterized the move as a "clumsy effort to comer US world market" [131]. Pelaez, whom we cited earlier, claimed that the Philippines had damaged her most important export industry and lost a big share of US coconut market.

In the end, buyers could not be found for the produce that had already accumulated in the warehouses. As interest rates rapidly rose at this time, costs of holding the inventories also increased, again due to gross miscalculation on the part of Cojuangco's marketing managers. In the end, Unicom had to sell the inventories at a loss of an estimated $10 million 132]. While attempts at cartelization are not unusual in commodity markets, it was commented that what was so unusual in this scheme was that it failed so completely [133].

The Reagan administration proposed to drop the suit since it could potentially prove to be quite embarrassing to Enrile and Cojuangco. If the case had proceeded, then two of the then-most powerful and influential men in the Philippines would have been compelled to give testimony in US courts. The US State Department thus intervened with the US Department of Justice and the suit was settled out of court. The defendants paid $11.3 million as settlement [134]. Given the tightly-integrated nature of the Philippine coconut industry, this settlement fine was surely passed on to the coconut farmer in the form of lower prices for his copra.

BIGGEST CASE OF GRAFT AND CORRUPTION

While the anti-trust suit was being heard in US courts, Enrile and Cojuangco engaged in a massive public relations campaign in the Philippines to refurbish their images. In a speech before the Marcos-controlled parliament on 4 February 1982, Enrile Justified the programs in the coconut industry and defended the "honor and integity of present industry leaders" (i.e., himself) against what he termed as "black propaganda."

Cojuangco, on the other hand, called for a news clamp on the topic. Saying that many of the criticisms are not "founded on solid grounds" and using "unity in the coconut industry" as his reason, Coluangco stated:

These destructive moves only serve to sow confusion and discontentment (sic) among the coconut farmers... The less said about the coconut industry, the better... the international market is quite sensitive to public discussions regarding the industry [135].

On another occasion, Enrile justified his involvement in the coconut industry by claiming it was in the interest of "national security." A lead article in the *Bulletin Today* entitled "Enrile Lashes Critics of the Coconut Industry," Enrile as legitirnizing his interests by saying:

> *The coconut farmers comprise one very important segment of the population whose allegiance to the government is altogether vital and decisive in the success of our campaign against dissidents, secessionists, and other forces who have persisted in undermining national stability and security [136].*

Marcos and Enrile ventured into the coconut industry with the claim of helping the coconut farmer. Marcos had declared it the policy of the state "to promote the accelerated growth and development of the coconut and palm oils industry so that the benefits of such growth shall accrue to the greatest number" [137]. Enrile justified his involvement in the organization of the UCPB and Unicom as an altruistic desire to help the farmers who approached him for fertilizer and farm equipment funds. Enrile said that he "suggested to them that we should not dissipate the fund. We should pool it and create a financial institution out of it" [138]. But our account of what has happened in the coconut industry belies these claims. We saw how presidential decrees were used to control a national industry and exploit a large part of the rural workforce. The policies Marcos, Enrile, an Cojuangco pursued shows concretely how poverty and wealth engender each other. The multimillion conglomerate of Enrile and Cojuangco was possible only because of the oppression of poor farmers.

While Enrile and Cojuangco were buying multimillion refineries in France and the US, workers in the local coconut mills were earning less than $1.00 a day. Wages in the milling sector of the industry re resented less than 1% of total production costs, an indication of both how the mill worker was underpaid as well as the profit margins enjoyed by those who controlled the industry. A study concluded that labor received $1.00 in wages for every $10.46 in profits generated. The study further cautioned that this ratio is a conservative one since "a large art of the real value of the desiccated coconut produced is possibly realized by the mother companies abroad through transfer pricing, which could not be reflected in the survey results" [139].

Added to the exploitation of both the coconut farmer and the worker in the mills was the complete ignorance and insensitivity to their plight by those who dominated the industry. Especially tragic are the views of officials of the Cocofed, the organization which purportedly represented the farmer. Eleazar went as far as describing the starving farmer as indolent [140]. Lobregat, referring to the poverty of the rural populace, has been quoted as saying, "We are teaching our people to eat more coconuts" [141]. And in spite of what Enrile says about dissidents and secessionists operating behind coconut trees, Eleazar finds the value of the coconut industry precisely in the docility of the easily-exploited coconut farmer:

> *Each and everyone of these land parcels is a virtual tropical white man's paradise. The people give no headache to the Republic -- no social unrest [142].*

While the Marcos has publicly raised the "magnanimity of the representatives of coconut industry" who selflessly considered "their moral responsibilities" to the coconut farmer, the reality is that the levy was the mechanism which caused great poverty and inequity. The schemes Marcos, Enrile, and Cojuangco engineered were, in the words of David, "biggest cases of graft and corruption in government" [143].

But there is yet another incident we should note which provides a commentary on Philippine institutions sadder than the ones we have already seen. When the post-Marcos administration organized the Presidential Commission for Good Government (PCGG) to recover the wealth stolen by Marcos and his cronies, Jovito Salonga, the head of the commission [144], refused to file charges against Enrile or even attempt to investigate him. Salonga, on the contrary, was one of the first to exonerate Enrile, possibly either out of fear or because the two belonged to the same fraternity at law school. Testifying before a committee of the Constitutional Commission attempting to draft a new constitution, Salonga, in a very carefully-worded testimony befitting a crafty lawyer, said that there was "no evidence" that "would warrant" the investigation of Enrile, that his name does not appear on any of the documents the PCGG had in its possession, and that there were no complaints against him. Salonga then proceeded to offer Enrile, then still the chairman of the United Coconut Planters Bank, five board seats in the multimillion bank as it was being reorganized.

Endnotes

1. Mijares, p52.
2. Among the other posts Enrile held under Marcos' administration were Acting Secretary of Finance, Acting Insurance Commrssioner, Acting Chairman of the Monetary Board of the Central Bank
3. The incidental role Enrile played in Marcos' downfall does not exonerate him from his activities during the dictatorship. Enrile, one of the key people behind the imposition of the dictatorship in 1972, never hesitated to use his position as Secretary of Defense and Chairman of the Executive Committee of the National Security Council to implement Marcos' mail-fisted policies on the country. While we are not aware that he personally engaged in torture, he still bears responsibility for the murders and tortures committed by the military which he headed. Torture and murder of political opponents was government policy rather than isolated acts of individual military men. Enrile also never hesitated to show his personal ambitions to power. As early as two months after the imposition of martial law, Enrile publicly declared on November 1972 that he would not hesitate to lead a military coup and take over governmental functions:
If the situation arises...that our civilian sector is unable or unwilling to carry on the job of pushing through the reform program of the President, the military will have no alternative but to take over the job, even if it would involve taking over purely Civilian functions.
The threat materialized on February 1986 when officers close to Enrile attempted to grab power from the teetering Marcos government. The plot, however, was discovered on n February, a few days before the peace demonstration which toppled the dictatorship. Enrile's motivations in seeking refuge in the military camp clearly was not to support the people's democratic aspirations. This former Minister of Defense and holder of a black belt in the Korean martial art of Taekwondo was desperately trying to escape arrest when the civilian populace and other military men came to his rescue in Camp Crame. He was not in any way leading a popular revolt against the dictatorship. The best discussion of these

events, including a scene depicting a desperate Enrile who thought that he was going to be overrun by Marcos forces, are best discussed in Bryan Johnson, *The Four Days of Courage* (New York: The Free Press).

4. *Far Eastern Economic Review*, 4 August 1978.

5. Quoted in *Far Eastem Economic Review*, 10 November 1978.

6. Among the firms where Angara had interests were

Company	Activity
Argonaut Mineral Exploration	Mining
Accra Investment Corp.	Investments
Sigma Investments	Investments
Coconut Rich Inc.	Coconut
Pansol Village Resort	Resorts
AK Wook Industries	Wood products
Company of Angels	Motion pictures
Phil. Cardonic Corp.	Chemicals
Avon Development Comp.	Real estate

7. Angara was later instrumental in granting Marcos' daughter, Imee, her controversial degree from the University of the Philippines. As has been mentioned in Chapter One, Imee was granted this degree even when there were strong doubts over her meeting the academic requirements of the university. During Marcos' 1982 State Visit to the US, Angara led an advance group of the presidential entourage. Arriving a few days before the dictator and Imelda, Angara held social gatherings in New York for loyal arcos supporters, while anti-Marcos activists protested outside, with Ninoy Aquino addressing in some of these rallies. When Angara returned to the US in 1985 to solicit funds for the govemment-funded University of the Philippines, school alumni sharply criticized him for his support of the dictatorship and pointed out that it was hypocritical for him to try to raise funds from school alumni while Marcos and his wife spent the people's money in frivolities. Angara also had investments with companies of other Marcos cronies. Sigma Investments was registered with the SEC jointly under the name of Angara and Ramon Siy, another Marcos associate. Given Angara's close association with the Marcos dictatorship, it was therefore surprising that Mrs. Aquino chose him to run in her senatorial slate and serve in her legislature.

8. Margot Cohen, "Reconciliation Or Revenge?," *American Lawyer*, October 1986, p.136.

9. Margot Cohen, "Reconciliation Or Revenge?," *American Lawyer*, October 1986, p.136.

10. Margot Cohen, "Reconciliation Or Revenge?," *American Lawyer*, October 1986, p.136.

11. Data from *Malabar Zoo - Garden, Aquarium, & Museum*, 1990.

12. Rizal once boasted of country's forests in a toast to his German hosts, saying that despite
Germany's beauty, nothing could compare to the rich vegetation of the Philippines.

13. Kazuhiro Kinoshita, "Deforestation Turns Philippine Mountains Into a Sterile Waste," *Asahi Evening News,* 3 October 1983.

14.*Asiaweek*, 13 July 1984.

15.*Asiaweek,* 13 July 1984.

16. The estimate is arrived at comparing the log imports of these countries from the Philippines with the log exports of the Philippines to these countries. The reported orts were exports only 4.397 million, almost half of the amount imported. *Manila Bulletin*, 23 March 1986.

17.*Asiaweek*, 13 July 1984.

18. Sheila Coronel, "The Politics of Logging," July 1987.

19. Sheila Coronel, 'The Politics of Logging," July 1987.

20. Sheila Coronel, "The Politics of Logging," July 1987.

21. *Philippine Daily Inquirer*, 22 March and 5 April 1986.

22. *Philippine Daily Inquirer*, 22 March and 5 April 1986.

23. Sheila Coronel, "The Politics of Logging," July 1987.

24. *Philippine Daily Inquirer,* 22 March and 5 April 1986.

25. Sheila Coronel, "The Politics of Logging," July 1987.
26. Sheila Coronel, "The Politics of Logging," July 1987.
27. Shiela Coronel, "The Forests as Battleground," July 1987.
28. Shiela Coronel, "The Forests as Battleground," July 1987.
29. There is therefore special significance in the extra-ordinary interest the military showed in suppressing dissent in Samar since 1979.
30. Rigoberto Tiglao, "Enrile's Conglomerate," *Far Eastern Economic Review*, 19 October 1939.
31. Bernard Wideman, "Filipino Shipping: Sailing Close to the Wind," *Insight*, April 1979, p.53.
32. Bernard Wideman, "Filipino Shipping: Sailing Close to the Wind," *Insight*, April,1979, p.53.
33. Doherty, p.180.
34. Rigoberto Tiglao, 'Enrile's Conglomerate," *FarEastem Economic Review*, 19 October 1989.
35. Rigoberto Tiglao, 'Enrile's Conglomerate," *Far Eastern Economic Review*, 19 October 1989.
36. Rigoberto Tiglao, "Enrile's Conglomerate," *Far Eastern Economic Review,* 19 October 1989.
37. Rigoberto Tiglao, "Enrile's Conglomerate," *Far Eastern Economic Review*, 19 October 1989.
38. Rigoberto Tiglao, "Enrile's Conglomerate," *Far Eastern Economic Review*, 19 October 1989.
39. Rigoberto Tiglao, "Enrile's Conglomerate," *Far Eastern Economic Review*, 19 October 1989.
40. Rigoberto Tiglao, 'Enrile's Conglomerate," *Far Eastern Economic Review*, 19 October 1989.
41. Rigoberto Tiglao, "Enrile's Conglomerate," *FarEastern Economic Review,* 19 October 1989.
42. Rigoberto Tiglao, "Enrile's Conglomerate," *Far Eastern Economic Review*, 19 October 1989.
43. Rigoberto Tiglao, "Enrile's Conglomerate," *Far Eastern Economic Review*, 19 October 1989.
44. Rigoberto Tiglao, "Enrile's Conglomerate," *Far Eastern Economic Review*, 19 October 1989.
45. *Business Day*, 12 March 1986.
46. *Manila Times*, 24 March 1986.
47. Virgilio David, The Barriers in the Development of the Philippine Coconut Industry, (Manila: Ateneo Graduate School of Business, 1977), p.2.
48. Our discussion of the operations of the coconut industry draws heavily on the pioneering work done by Virgilio M. David. David, a colonel with the Philippine Constabulary who served as the military administrator of the coconut industry, is a nationally recognized authority on the topic.   Drawing on his years of experience as military administrator in the coconut industry, David analyzed the operations of the industry, paying special attention to the loopholes in the law authorizing the coconut levy which we discuss in the next pages. The results of David's study were published as a masteral thesis, The Barriers in the Development of the Philippine Coconut Industry, presented to the Ateneo Graduate School of Business in 1977. Since we shall constantly refer to David's work in this section, we shall allow ourselves a short digression on the background of his work. David carried out his studies at great risk to his military career since among the principal culprits in the coconut industry were his direct superior, the Minister of Defense Juan Ponce Enrile, and the Commander-in-Chief of the Armed Forces, Marcos himself. Upon finishing his research and successfully defending his thesis, David resented copies to Marcos and Enrile, formally informing them of his findings. The conclusions were of course already well-known to both Marcos and Enrile, since they were

the architects of the various laws that placed the coconut industry under their control. Marcos ignored the two copies of the masteral thesis David sent him; Enrile, on the other hand, summoned David twice to his office and warned him to keep quiet. David continued his crusade. In an effort to inform the public of what was happening within the coconut industry, David funded a limited publication of his work. For his persistence in pursuing issues within the industry, he was stripped of his position as Military Administrator of the coconut industry and was consequently assigned a desk job. But David continued fighting for the rights of the coconut workers and later tried to organize the coconut farmers with the help of Luis Taruc, the leader of the agrarian rebellion which shook the government in the 1950's.

49. The figure is based on a projected total production of 20 million tons of copra over the 10 year period.

50. David, p.155-6.

51. David, pp.146-7.

52. David, p.157, 167.

53. David, p.159.

54. David, p.158.

55. For example, David reported that the department in the PCA charged with accounting for the levy collections did not engage in any physical inspection of the copra and merely left the measurements to the honesty of the person reporting the sale.

56. David, p.186.

57. David, p.156.

58. David, p.187.

59. David, pp.187-9.

60. David, p.166.

61. David, p.148,186.

62. Letter of 30 October 1981, quoted in William Branigin, "Philippines Slumps with Crop's Prices," *Washington Post*, 14 November 1981. Climaco was later assasinated.

63. David, p.130.

64. David, p.159.

65. David, p.106; pp.99-139.

66. as of 1986. *Malaya*, 11 July 1986.

67. Lobregat also owned Northern Samar Agri-business, a livestock company, and Zamboanga Hermosa Tours, a travel agency.

68. David, p.112.

69. David, p.39.

70. David, p.153-4.

71. David, p.184, 196, 200.

72. David, p.75.

73. Benjamin Salvosa, "Life in the Coconut Areas," *A Forward Look For the Coconut*, PHILCOA Special Magazine Publication, 20 November 1957, p.36, quoted in David.

74. On January 1982, Marcos announced that the levy amount would be tied to the international price of coconut oil.

75. *Malaya*, 10 March 1986.

76. David, p.180.

77. David, p.183.

78. David, p.175.

79. Quoted in Mar S. Soriano, "Group Seeks Dismantle of Unicom, Cocofed," *The Economic Monitor*, 1-7 September 1980.

80. *Far Eastern Economic Review*, 12 February 1982.

81. Shielah Ocampo, "Marcos Moves in on the Coconut Crisis," *Far Eastern Economic Review,* 6 June 1980.

82. *Far Eastern Economic Review*, 8 February 1990.

83. *Far Eastern Economic Review*, 8 January 1982.

84. *Far Eastern Economic Review*, 6 June 1980.
85. This was also claimed by Julie Amargo in an open letter to Marcos in *Ang Mamimili,* Vol. VII, No. 5.
86. David, p.118, p.169.
87. Cocofed Resolution No. 2-4-79, 31 August 1979. another source: Coconut Palace - P37m in 1980
88. But the records of the Cultural Center did not show any such donation. The actual recipient of the money remains a unknown. *Business Day*, 10 June 1986.
89. Cocofed Resolution No. 3-7-79 R, 7 July 1979. This hospital was placed in the capital, where it could cause much publicity, but it was totally inaccessible to coconut farmers.
90. "P170-M coco mess probed," *Malaya*, 6 August 1986.
91. David's work shows that hardly any of these so-called projects for coconut farmers were actually for their benefit.
92. *Philippine Daily Inquirer*, 10 June 1986.
93. *The Star*, 31 July 1986.
94. "Cocofed Set for Dismantling," *Tribune*, 2 July 1986.
95. *Manila Times*, 12 July 1986.
96. *Manila Times*, 12 July 1986.
97. *Bulletin Today*, 31 May 1980; *Times Journal*, 19 July 1981.
98. *Far Eastern Economic Review*, 16 October 1981
99. *Far Eastern Economic Review,* 16 October 1981.
100. *Far Eastern Economic Review*, 8 January 1982.
101. David, p.182.
102. *Far Eastern Economic Review*, 8 January 1982.
103. David, p.173.
104. *Far Eastern Economic Review*, 6 June 1980.
105. *Far Eastern Economic Review*, 8 January 1982.
106. But we earlier encountered data that tended to indicate that the bulk of the funds went to Cocofed.
107. *Far Eastern Economic Review*, 14 September 1979.
108. If exports were curbed, then the mills would be operating at 81.7% capacity. Prices in Europe were higher generally by 22% so those who controlled the supply and marketing of copra resorted to smuggling. While increases in the international price of oil brought windfall profits to copra and coconut oil exporters, it resulted in a crisis in the local consumers market, with the millers, and the lowly farmer.
109. Another fund was added to the levy in 1982, the Desiccated Coconut Rationalization Fund (DCRF), to acquire 7 ailing desiccated coconut mills, but some quarters claimed that about P39.5 million from this fund was used for Marcos' campaign and the private coffers of certain agency officers.
110. *Malaya*, 10 March 1986.
111. *Far Eastern Economic Review*, 6 June 1980.
112. *Far Eastern Economic Review*, 6 June 1980.
113. Affidavit of Douglas Lu Ym, 28 July 1981.
114. *Malaya*, 10 March 1986.
115. "Cojuangco Group Still Intact," *Malaya,* 10 March 1986
116. *Bulletin Today*, 10 June 1980.
117. *Bulletin Today*, 27 April 1980
118. *Daily Express*, 7 April 1980.
119. For example, Enrile was chairman of UCPB, Unicom, Unichem, while Cojuangco was of the three.
120. *Far Eastern Economic Review*, 29 January 1982.
121. *Philippine Daily Inquirer*, 26 June 1986.
122. The Unicorn monopoly was formally abolished by Marcos on 11 January 1985. But these 10 trading companies were organized right after to continue the monopoly.
123. *Far Eastern Economic Review*, 14 September 1979.

124. While Unicom's rationale was to escape the 7% and 25% tax for imposed on edible and technical grade use coconut oil Western Europe imposed, the tariffs were not that steep to require such a major investment. The benefits of employing Philippine labor and mills would have more than offset the tariffs imposed by Western Europe. This move is more intelligible if we view it as part of the pattern to move money overseas by the Marcos cronies.
125. *Daily Express,* 7 April 1980.
126. *Bulletin Today* 27 April 1980
127. Juan Ponce Enrile, Affidavit, US District Court, Northern District of California, 8 July 1981.
128. Fernando was later assigned to oversee the efforts to recover Marcos money in the US This appointment was extremely baffling considering Fernando's past record. Fernando had no other qualification for this position than being personally loyal to Jovito Salonga, head of the commission tasked to recover Marcos' wealth. Fernando belonged to Salonga's Liberal Party and organized to help Salonga gain the nomination for president. As we shall see in Chapter V, this appointment had disastrous consequences for the Philippine government's effort to recover money stolen by Marcos.
129. Quoted in William Branigin, "Philippines Slumps with Crop's Prices," *Washington Post,* 14 November 1981
130. Quoted in William Branigin, "Philippines Slumps with Crop's Prices," *Washington Post,* 14 November 1981
131. William Branigin, "Philippines Slumps with Crop's Prices," *Washington Post*, 14 November 1981
132. *Far Eastern Economic Review*, 8 January 1982.
133. *Far Eastern Economic Review*, 8 January 1982.
134. Rigoberto Tiglao, "Calling Up Old Debts," *Far Eastern Economic Review*, 8 February 1990.
135. *Bulletin Today*, 29 May 1980. The proper word is discontent. There is no such word as 'discontentment.'
136. *Bulletin Today*, 13 October 1979.
137. Presidential Decree 732, Section 1.
138. *Far Eastern Economic Review*, 8 January 1982.
139. *Ibon: Primer on the Philippine Coconut Industry*, p.33-5.
140. Eleazar, *The Coconut Story*, Phil. Coconut Producers Federation, mimeographed, p. 4, quoted in David, p39.
141. Quoted in William Branigin, "Philippines Slumps with Crop's Prices," *Washington Post,* 14 November 1981.
142. Quoted in David.
143. David, p.176.
144. The PCGG and Salonga are discussed fully in Chapter V.

COJUANGCO

LE FABLEUX DONA YSIDRA

The Cojuangco family traces its roots to two members of the Kho family from Hing-chiam, Fukien, China who came to the Philippines in the middle of the last century. The first arrival was Martin, later followed by his 13-year old son, Jose, who arrived in 1861 after living in Amoy (now Xiamen) (1). The original Chinese Kho Huang was hispanicized into Cojuangco, the suffix **co** denoting assimilation into the Chinese mestizo class [2].

Jose Cojuangco later married a woman named Antera Estrella, who bore him three children, Ysidra (1867), Melecio (1871), and Trinidad who died early [3].

While the Cojuangco family had already engaged in business at this time, such as dealing in junk and the milling and trading of rice [4], oral tradition amongst the old families in Central Luzon as well as contemporary historical studies trace the phenomenal wealth of this family to the turbulent times at the end of the last century.

One account of these events centers on the relationship between Ysidra, then a pretty 32-year old, and her lover, General Antonio Luna, the commander-in-chief of the Philippine army fighting the American occupation forces in 1899.

The nascent Philippine Republic at this time had just finished waging a revolution against Spain and was in the process of fighting the new American invaders. Lacking the proper logistics to counter the far-superior American military might, the young government authorized revolutionary leaders and other well-known personages to raise funds. The commission, given under very strict guidelines, required that the authorized person raising funds must be known in their localities, that contributions be solicited only in the places explicitly covered by an order, and that the proper receipts be issued [5]. One of the many individuals given this commission was General Manuel Tinio, who was then leading an army in the Ilocos region [6]. Tinio was tasked with raising funds in the northern provinces of Luzon, Cagayan, and Isabela [7]. On the other hand, General Luna, being the commander—in-chief of the Philippine forces, was tasked with providing the security for the convoys carrying the revolutionary funds from the provinces until they reached the constantly moving headquarters of the government.

In an article for the *Philippines Free Press*, historian Alfredo Saulo recounted the activities of his uncle, Eulalio Saulo y Gutierrez, who was one of the officers of General Manuel Tinio:

During the second phase of the revolution, Eulalio Saulo's house served as a transit station in the relay shipment of huge amounts of Spanish gold and silver coins seized from local treasuries in the Ilocos region by Katipuneros under General Manuel Tinio, a commander of General Aguinaldo's rear guard. The revolution had entered a new phase -- the war of resistance against the American invaders. Receiving money from special teams coming from the North, Saulo would pass it on to the next responsible Katipunan official along the relay route until it reached the seat of the revolutionary government, first at Malolos, Bulacan, then at San Fernando, Pampanga, and still later at San Isidro, Nueva Ecija. From there it was transferred to Tarlac, Tarlac, thence to Bayombong, Nueva Ecija, and finally to Bayambang, Pangasinan.
General Antonio Luna, the Belgian-trained commander-in-chief of the Filipino army in Luzon, saw to it that there was no hitch in the trans-shipment of the captured treasury chests to the revolution my capital, wherever it may be at the time, knowing the precarious financial position of the young Philippine republic in the uphill fight against the Americans.
Saulo's record in handling funds of the republic was spotlessly clean. His honesty was never in doubt. It was after passing the government's money to the next caretaker on the relay route that "accidents" happened. Sometimes the treasury convoy would be ambushed by bandits posing as insurrectos. Many such untoward incidents happened especially after General Luna's assassination in Cabanatuan, Nueva Ecija, on 5 June

1899. Several chests of gold money got "lost" when the seat of the national government was transferred to Bayombong, a few months after the tragedy at Cabanatuan [8].

What Saulo is probably referring to when he talks about "several chests of old" getting "lost" is the well-known story passed through generations in old families in Central Luzon concerning the Cojuangco family. Apparently part of the oral tradition of the region, the story recounts that General Luna and Ysidra Cojuangco were lovers, and that Luna had left revolutionary funds consisting of a cache of gold and jewels with Ysidra for safekeeping. But shortly thereafter, Luna was assassinated by the soldiers of General Aguinaldo who saw in Luna a threat to his leadership [9]. The money left with Dona Ysidra, the story goes, was then never returned.

Historian Agoncillo recounts in his Malolos: The Crisis of the Republic that Aguinaldo had ordered that all of the funds Luna had collected be turned over to the government, a fact that indicates Luna was indeed in possession of revolutionary collections at the time of his death:

On 13 June, Aguinaldo ordered the Secretary of War to ask Joaquin Luna, the late general's brother, to turn over all contributions he had collected to the Department of War. The following day, the Secretary of War wrote General José Alejandrino asking him to take an inventory of Luna's effects [10].

It is ironically from the Co'uangco family that one finds the Luna story repeated. Eduardo "Danding" Cojuangco, one of Ysidra's grandchildren and the principal personage in this section, is said to have commissioned Carlos Quirino, a well-known historian and former director of the National Library, to write a history of his family. But when the book was finished, Danding Cojuangco decided not to publish it. The Quirino book remains unpublished. Its contents, however, were summarized in the Philippine Daily Inquirer by the husband of Quirino's niece, columnist Hilarion Henares, and explains why Danding preferred to keep mum about his family history:

... General Antonio Luna, as chief of staff of the revolutionary army, had collected a sizeable sum from contributions with which to pay his soldiers. The person who collected for him was Tiburcio Hilario, Pampanga governor. Hilario's granddaughter, Ambassador Rafaelita Hilario Soriano, relates that her grandfather kept the gold and silver in sacks, including gold plates, chalices, and other church treasures taken from Bacolor, San Fernando, and Guagua.
After losing an encounter at Sto. Tomas, Pampanga, Luna ordered Hilario to bring the valuables to Tarlac, where the revolutionary government planned to establish its capital. General Luna, so the story goes, then turned over the treasure to Ysidra Cojuangco..., then an attractive 32-year-old woman, for safe-keeping. Then Luna proceeded to Cabanatuan to meet with Aguinaldo, there to be assassmated by the Caviteno's troopers. Why did the Ilocano general entrust Ysidra with the treasure? Rumors had it that she was his sweetheart and lover, and he trusted her to keep the treasure till he returned. Ysidra Cojuangco bore a child out of wedlock, and it was suspected that General Antonio Luna was the father. But the family insists that Ysidra fell in love with an unnamed Chinese mestizo who died before they could be married... [11].

Henares also related another source of the Cojuangco family's wealth. When General Arthur MacArthur was chasing General Aguinaldo northwards to Ilocos and Palanan, the American general stopped by the house of Ysidra's brother, Melecio, and asked for 10 lodging. Melecio then

> ... welcomed him as a guest and offered his capacious warehouses for the storing of US Army supplies.
> To reciprocate, General MacArthur gave orders that the Cojuangco family could use free of charge the train to bring their rice to Manila, since the train went back empty after bringing the Army supplies to Paniqui. With freight cost of P250 a sack saved, the Cojuangcos profited immensely by being nice to an enemy officer [12].

Another source reported that after the hostilities between Philippine and American forces had died down, the money left by Luna was later utilized by Dona Ysidra in money lending activities in Central Luzon. When Ysidra died in 1960, members of the family later found a "IOUs of laborers and the poor" totalling $1 million [13], then a huge amount. A member of the Cojuangco family once described this as "rural banking." Lands of peasants who could not pay her back were appropriated, allowing the Cojuangco family to acquire large agricultural holdings. It was reported that the Central Luzon lands of the Cojuangco family were so large that it permitted them to set the price of rice, the country's staple food, in island of Luzon [14].

> With the death of the father Don Jose, Ysidra the spinster became the head of the family. The Cojuangco family owned some 12,000 hectares, controlled the rice trade of the province and lent so much money to planters and businessmen of Tarlac, Pangasinan, and Nueva Ecija that Justice Antonio G. Lucero, the family lawyer, thought she practically owned Central Luzon [15].

Ysidra, upon the deaths of her father, Jose, and brother, Melecio, took charge of the family's businesses. She died at the age of 93 on 13 July 1960 [16]. Since she died, without having a direct heir [17] , the family fortune was divided equally between the four sons of Melecio:

Juan - of the four sons of Melecio, only Juan is a mystery. While many articles have come out discussing the achievements of the other children and grandchildren of Melecio, Juan is hardly mentioned.
Jose Jr. - the father of Congressman Jose 'Peping' Cojuangco and President Corazon Cojuangco Aquino.
Antonio - the father of Ramon Cojuangco of the Philippine long Distance Telephone (discussed later in this section).
Eduardo - the father of Eduardo 'Danding' Cojuangco Jr. (discussed later in this section).

The Cojuangco family later branched out into other areas such as sugar and commercial banking. Jose Jr. persuaded his Aunt Ysidra to invest in a new sugar mill, which later became the 6,443 hectare Hacienda Luisita, valued at $25 million in 1971. The Eduardo branch of the family had their own hacienda and sugar mill in Paniqui, Tarlac. The family also put up their own bank, the Philippine Bank of Commerce, with Jose Jr. as president. Jose Jr. later branched out on his own and set up the First United Bank (discussed later).

This section deals primarily with the Ramon "Monching" and Eduardo "Danding" branches of the Cojuangco family since they were the ones who enjoyed a close relationship with the Marcos regime. This section will attempt to document how the traditional wealth of the Danding and Monching branches of the family was expanded through the political and financial ties they maintained with the dictator.

But if the story about Ysidra and General Antonio Luna is true, then the wealth of the whole Cojuangco clan is open to challenge. Not only should the history and finances of the Danding and Monching branches of the family be questioned but the finances of all of the descendants of Dona Ysidra should be scrutinized as well, President Corazon Aquino herself included. If it can be shown that the account of Luna's revolutionary funds is essentially correct, then the question of restitution arises.

RAMON

Ramon C. Cojuangco's family had the exceptional luck to be close to both Marcos and Imelda. His family enjoyed warm personal ties with the Marcos couple since the early years of Marcos' first presidential term. Ramon's wife, Imelda Ongsiako, was one of the more prominent blue ladies of Imelda.

Ramon Cojuangco was chairman of the Domestic Satellite Phil. Inc., a company which deals with satellite communications facilities. The company was registered under Cojaungco's name with the SEC in 1975 with an authorized capitalization of $2.8 million. Included in the board of directors Domestic Satellite was Manuel Nieto Jr., another Marcos crony.

He also owned United Amherst Leasing & Finance, a large finance company, jointly with his brother-in-law, Luis Tirso Rivilla, a close friend of Imelda. United Amherst was registered with the SEC in 1977 under Rivilla's name with an authorized capitalization of $2.7 million. Other Rivilla investments included Biophil Inc., a joint venture with Japanese Kanegfuchi Takeda & Mitsui. Pedro Rivilla, the brother of Luis was connected with Banco de Oro, a large commercial bank. The Rivillas were also investors in Northern Cement, a company owned by Eduardo Cojuangco (discussed in the next pages). Among the other companies where Luis Tirso Rivilla had interests were

Company	Activity
Aggregate Mining Exponent	Mining
Wire Manufacturing Mktg.	Manufacturing
Tranex Brokerage Corp.	Customs brokers
Insurance Agencies Inc.	Insurance
Printing Exponenis Inc.	Printing
X-Ray & Electro Medical	Medical equipment

Ramon Cojuangco was also president of C&O Investment & Realty Corp. and was a director of the Philippine Commercial & Industrial Bank, a large bank controlled by other Marcos associates. Among the other companies where Ramon Cojuangco had interests were

Company	Activity
Metallurgicraft	Manufacturing
The Plaza Convenience	Canned goods
PLDT Agricultural Corp.	Agri-busmess

The next few pages will focus on Ramon Cojuangco's major interest, the Philippine Long Distance Telephone Company (PLDT), the country's telephone monopoly.

PLDT

The Philippine Lon Distance Telephone Co. (PLDT) was initially owned and controlled by the General Telephone & Electronics Corp. (GTE), an American telecommunications company. Ramon Cojuangco took over the monopoly in 1967 with the help of his brother-in-law, Luis Tirso Rivilla, financier Alfonso Yuchengco [18], and lawyer Antonio Meer. While some quarters trumpeted this move as a triumph of economic nationalism [19], closer analysis of the matter raises questions whether the move was indeed beneficial to the country.

Ten years after Cojuangco's group took over the PLDT, the US SEC revealed the details behind the takeover and charged Cojuangco, Rivilla, Yuchengco. and Meer with violating US federal securities law. The SEC charged that the deal involved secret commissions and kickbacks and cited Cojuangco and his associates for their failure to fully disclose their part in the transactions. The charges, filed with the US District Court in Washington on 12 January 1977, named the PLDT and two other corporations, the Philippine Telecommunications Investment Corp. (PTIC) and Stamford Trading Co. (STC), as defendants and also singled out the following for their involvement:

Ramon Cojuangco, president of PLDT
Alfonso Yuchengco. chairman of PLDT
Luis Tirso Rivilla, director and officer of PLDT
Antonio M. Meer, legal counsel of PLDT

In the papers filed with the court, the SEC charged that GTE had been prepared to sell its PLDT shares to another group of Filipino investors but that Philippine government officials at "the highest levels" had intervened in favor of Cojuangco's group:

...on orabout 1966, officials at the highest levels of the government of the Philippines urged GTE for political and purported security reasons not to sell its interest in PLDT [to a different group] and told GTE to deal with another group of Philippine nationals, referred to hereinafter as the "PTIC group" [20].

Cojuangco's group, however, did not have enough money to buy all the shares owned by GTE to complete the transaction. GTE, on the other hand, was under pressure to sell its 24% share in PLDT because the treaty which allowed American ownership of Filipino corporations was to expire soon. A scheme was therefore engineered permitting Cojuangco and his associates to acquire the PLDT under very favorable conditions.

The terms provided that the GTE shares in PLDT would be bought for $7 million in cash and $7 million in promissory notes. The purchaser was PTIC, a corporation which served as a holding company for the PLDT shares of Cojuangco, Yuchengco, Rivilla, and Meer.

What made the deal particularly beneficial to Cojuangco's group were the enticements GTE provided. Apart from the extremely liberal incentive of paying half the price of the shares with only promissory notes, there were direct payments as well. The money came in the form of "secret commissions, credits and uncollected loans" over a ten-year period [21]. The group netted $1 million in commissions and another $1 million in personal loans because of the deal [22]. GTE also agreed to pay an additional $2 million fee to Stamford Trading Co., "a Bahamian firm used as the conduit for the secret payments" [23]. It was later revealed that GTE had paid $484,000 in cash to Stamford between December 1967 and February 1976.

It would appear that Cojuangco, Yuchengco, Rivilla, and Meer received the following benefits from GTE:

* Personal Loans
A total of $1 million in personal loans were extended to the four.
Cojuangco $580,000
Rivilla $280,000
Yuchengco $100,000
Meer $40,000
GTE did not expect any payments for these loans and were later written off [24].

* Commissions
The four were granted 5-7% commissions on equipment the PLDT bought from GTE [25]. Since a $2.0 million contract was executed as soon as the four bought the GTE shares, this meant commissions worth another $1 million. It is known that the four were paid around $484,000 in commissions. The payments were rationalized as providing Cojuangco and his associates with "sufficient funds to pay back the loans" [26].

* Promissory Notes
Part of the payment for the GTE shares came in promissory notes worth $7 million. A significant part of these notes were never paid.
"GTE assigned the promissory notes to an independent escrow agent, with instructions to handle the notes 'in accordance' with the wishes of the people who signed the notes, the SEC said. This means that the notes can be cancelled without ever being paid" [27].
GTE credited $2.8 million on the promissory notes between December 1967 and February 1976. This move effectively meant that 52.8 million in principal and interest payments on the promissory notes were written off.

* Options
The four were also given options to buy 40% of the stock in GTE Industries Inc., a local subsidiary of the American firm that made telephone and related equipment. The four exercised their options three years later by giving GTE "a noninterest bearin romissory note for $486,45.40 payable at the rate of $1 per annum plus any dividends" [28]. It would be difficult to find better terms of repayment. This move in effect assured GTE of a local market for their products. GTE then gave back the $486,459 promissory note. Cojuangco's group in effect paid only $10 on the principal of the promissory note used to buy $486,459 worth of stocks.

These extremely generous terms were clear cases of payoffs since the four were never "expected to perform any services for GTE" [29]. The only thing expected from Cojuangco's group was that it would "make sure it bought the equipment from GTE" [30] once it controlled the PLDT. The loans, for example, were "made on the condition that PLDT promptly sign a $20 million equipment purchase agreement with GTE" [31]. The same was true of the commissions the four received: GTE agreed to pay the commissions only because PTIC "would cause" the PLDT "to buy from GTE" [32].

The costs of these payoffs were borne not by GTE but by the Filipino consumer who had to suffer higher prices and poorer phone services. The unpaid loans, commissions, and other payoffs were passed on as higher equipment prices, which in turn was reflected as higher telephone costs. This in fact, was very clear in the testimony of GTE officials to the SEC:

> GTE accutives have testified... that one of the factors in setting the price for equipment purchased by the PLDT was the amount of commissions GTE paid or credited through the Bahamas concern [Stamford Trading] [33].

The Cojuangco group also received many forms of aid from the Marcos government. One form of such help came in a controversial 1973 presidential order where Marcos required all those who received new telephone lines to acquire preferred shares in PLDT. The scheme, formally called the Subscriber Investment Plan (SIP), had the effect of dramatically increasing PLDT's capital through forced subscriptions. Other forms of government help came in the direct infusion of capital from government financial institutions, such as the purchase of $38.5 million worth of preferred shares of PLDT by the DBP, a move Cesar Virata, Marcos' Prime Minister, justified by appealing to the idea that foreign investors needed to be attracted [34].

The PLDT was theoretically a company owned by all subscribers to the telephone service, but in reality was controlled by Cojuangco's group. The majority of the phone company shares, approximately 91.37% of the total, were owned by individual subscribers to the telephone service, thanks to Marcos-imposed SIP subscriptions, but did not enjoy majority voting rights [35]. Since only 14.79% of PLDT issued stock had voting rights, the majority rights were spread over different US institutional investors who owned such stocks. This permitted the Cojuangco group which owned only 24.95% of PLDT common stock, or a mere 3.69% of total shares, to control all the 11 seats in the board. All members of the board were individuals close to Cojuangco, Yuchengco, or Marcos, as can be seen from the following list:

Alfonso Yuchengco - chairman and director
Oscar Africa - president and chief executive officer
Antonio Cojuangco - senior vice president & chief operating officer
Imelda Ongsiako Cojuangco
Manuel Montecillo
Oscar Ongsiako
Enrique Perez
John Quimson

Generoso Tanseco
Jose Yulo Jr.
Cesar Z. Zalamea [36]

Imelda Ongsiako is Ramon Cojuangco's wife. Antonio is their son. Oscar Ongsiako is Imelda's brother, while Manuel Montecillo was Oscar's friend [37].

Further inquiries revealed that the PTIC, the holding company used to buy the original GTE shares, was owned not only by Cojuangco, Yuchengco, and their associates, but also by Marcos through a dummy co oration organized by Gapud (see section). It turned out that Prime Holdings, a Marcos shell corporation, held 46% of PTIC [38]. The shares were secretly transferred to Prime Holdings on May 1978. Since PTIC owned 26.9% of PLDT, this meant that Marcos actually owned 2.4 million shares or 12.5% of PLDT [39]. These shares had a market value of $7.4 million in 1986 [40]. The full ownership of PTIC was as follows [41]:

Prime Holdings	46%
Cojuangco family	43%
Yuchengco	7%
Antonio Meer	4%

A further complication to the question of PLDT ownership was the question of interlocking directorates between the PLDT and its equipment suppliers and other companies with which it did business -- directors in these corporations were often found in the board of the PLDT and vice versa, leading to the possibility of patronage and cronyism. One instance of such a director interlock was that of Malayan Insurance; the company is controlled by Yuchengco family and was accused of benefitting from PLDT contracts [42]. Another case was that of Southeast Asia Dev. Corp., a holding company organized to manage PLDT's 12 affiliate companies, most of whom are equipment suppliers. Individuals previously associated with Southeast were eventually appointed to key positions in PLDT. The companies had the same directors, with the key positions rotated amongst themselves [43].

While this small group benefitted from the PLDT, the real owners of the telephone company, the subscribers and the daily users of the phone system, suffered in many ways. Most obvious was through poor service. By 1980, more than 13 years after Cojuangco and his associates took over the PLDT, there were still only 1.3 telephones per 100 people nationwide, and 90% of the phones were concentrated in urban areas [44]. There were equally many problems in transmission, a proliferation of party lines, and a lack of automatic exchanges. On the business side, the ordinary subscribers did not have an representation in the management of the company, while their shares did not appreciate, leading to the comment that the PLDT forcibly raised "cheap money from its subscribers while providing an insufficient return on investment" [45].

Despite these contradictions, the Marcos, government stood clearly behind the Cojuangco group's control over the telephone industry, as evidenced for example by public statements of Jose Dans Jr., Marcos' Transportation and Communications Minister, who went as far as to publicly state that *only the private sector can efficiently operate a telephone system... the government must stand ready to assist, guarantee and invest, if so required, in these large investments...[46].*

After Marcos' downfall, government investigators inquiring into the activities of the PLDT discovered other anomalies in PLDT operations. Among the questions raised were those concerning the non-repatriation of foreign exchange earnings, the purchase of overpriced equipment, and insider trading.

Foreign exchange earned from overseas correspondent telephone companies was not immediately remitted to the Philippines in many cases. This practice was in direct violation of a Central Bank ruling that required the remittance of foreign exchange earnings within 15 days. The earnings often were never reflected in PLDT local accounts and never audited. The accounts were kept exclusively under the control of Oscar T. Africa, PLDT president [47]. In some cases, the money was actually sold in the underground market for dollars. A common practice was to deposit monthly foreign exchange earnings with Citibank in New York for at least three months, allowing it to earn interest in time deposits, before remitting the money to the Philippines. According to Louie Sison, a representative of the PCGG [48] who studied the operations of the PLDT, the average monthly balance of these accounts was $10.2 million but the interest on them was never reported [49]. Consider, for example, the following cases:

* **$14 million** was placed in a time deposit account with Wells Fargo in Hong Kong in June 1984. Half of the amount was later sold to PCI Bank (Phil. Commercial International Bank) in October 1984, but $1 million in interest was diverted to a private account. Part of the Money was sold in the black market for dollars, while part was credited to Josefina Shipping, a Panamanian firm. According to Sison, Antonio Cojuangco later admitted that the funds were contributions to Marcos [50].
* **$7 million** was kept in time deposit for 22 months [51].
* **another $85** million in earnings kept abroad for between 36 months without being recorded in Philippine books [52].

Given a 12% interest rate in the US, these multimillion accounts could potentially earn a lot in a few months, but no interest earnings were ever registered in the documents studied. Furthermore, in some cases the figures reported proved to be wrong, as in the case of the dollar earnings from American Telegraph & Telephone Co. (ATT), where the amount of $63,672,408 was underreported at $53,838,336 [53]. A businessman who bought dollars from the PLDT claimed that he wrote out his check not to PLDT but to individual officials [54]. Sison, who wanted to publicize his report, was gagged by his superiors in the PCGG.

Another claim of Sison was that money was "being systematically siphoned off by management and that kickbacks on procurement decisions were legion" [55]. The case of Siemens was cited. Sison claimed that the German telecommunications giant won a $412.3 million contract to supply equipment "by entering into arrangements profitable to Marcos" [56]. Siemens was also accused of overpricing substandard equipment. Siemens, however, denied the charges. Another aspect of the Siemens deal which has caused concern were the terms of the two multimillion loans used to purchase the equipment. The first loan amounting to $105 million was to be paid at interest rates way above prevailing market rates -- 25% of entire loan package. Investigators think that almost half of the entire amount of first loan or equipment purchase was being diverted. Another questionable aspect of the Siemens deal was that the contract was signed even before the loan was approved [57]. Siemens got the contract after Marcos got angry with GTE because bribery schemes between PLDT and GTE were disclosed [58].

A day before the government was to sequester Marcos' shares in the PLDT, Alfonso Yuchengco unloaded a sizable amount of PLDT shares. The move led to charges of insider trading since it was expected that the sequestration of Marcos' shares would cause the PLDT stock to drop. Further fueling the charges of insider trading was that the PCGG commissioner who ordered the sequestration of Marcos' shares was a business associate of Yuchengco. The PCGG official and Yuchengco were respectively the vice-chairman and chairman of Malayan Zurich Insurance Corp., a company which owned and then sold PLDT stock right before the sequestration order. From 14 March through 20 March 1986, Yuchengo and his companies unloaded 198,552 shares worth $780,000 [59]. The clamor to investigate the charges of insider trading went unheeded. And neither was Yuchengo or the other associates of Cojuangco in the PLDT ever really investigated. Instead, Mrs. Aquino later named Yuchengco as Ambassador to China.

Many were of course baffled at the inaction of the Aquino government with regard to Cojuangco and his associates in the PLDT. The *Review*, attempting to explain the inaction related the account of a well-placed official close to the presidential palace:

> *...when all of PLDTwas briefly sequestered in 1986, [Antonio] Cojuangco 'pulled out the stops' to use family connections to convince Aquino that despite questions over his father's relationship with Marcos, current management was the only one capable of running PLDT [60].*

EDUARDO

The other Ysidra grand-nephew, Eduardo "Danding" Co'uangco, was described by the *Los Angeles Times* as "second only to Marcos in the systematic looting of t 6 Philippines" [61].

Cojuangco was one of Marcos' closest and most loyal cronies. Longtime friends, the two not only helped each other economically and politicaly but also had close family relationships. Cojuangco's wife, Soledad "Gretchen" Oppen, was a key figure in Marcos' 1965 bid for the presidency. Marcos and Cojuangco even developed interlocking godfatherships: Cojuangco is the godfather of Marcos' son and grandson, while Marcos was the godfather of Cojuangco's eldest son, appropriately named Marcos Cojuangco.

Marcos valued Cojuangco because of the latter's loyalty. Danding served Marcos as the representative from the province of Tarlac in the corrupt pre-martial law Congress, ensuring Marcos' interests in the Central Luzon provinces. When the time came for Marcos' reelection in 1969, Cojuangco helped deliver the votes, giving

Marcos 53,484 votes against the opposition's 12,415 in the first district of Tarlac, Cojuangco's political bailiwick. Cojuangco was later made chairman of Central Luzon chapter of the KBL party. Danding quickly became one of the key people in the Marcos dictatorship. He was one of the few and the only civilian without a government position who helped 1972 [62].

Cojuangco was amply rewarded for his services. One may recall Marcos' sanction of the illegal importation of rice which involved Enrile, Cojuangco, and Aspiras (discussed earlier in the section on Enrile). When Cojuangco faced the possibility of being summoned to testify in US courts in connection with charges of monopolizmg the trading of coconut, Marcos named him Ambassador-at-Large. The move granted Cojuangco instant diplomatic immunity and enabled him to accompany Marcos to Cancun, Mexico without any problems when passing through the US. Another example of the special treatment was a special executive order (11 April 1983) from Marcos which declared that the used aircraft Cojuangco was "donating" to the government be

> deductible in all for income-tax purposes and fully exempt from the donor's tax... All government fees and taxes including documentary taxes as may otherwise be required for effecting the registration [of the gift] shall be waived.

At the height of cronyism in the Philippines, Cojuangco controlled $1.5 billion in corporate assets [63], an amount estimated to equal 25% of the country's GNP [64]. He headed an agricultural and industrial conglomerate with interests in diverse areas as coconut, sugar, agri-business, banking, and a host of others. The *Wall Street Journal* observed that Cojuangco attempted to create "cartels in rice, sugar, flour, groceries, and soft drinks but ran out of time..." [65]. Referring to Cojuangco's tendency to create monopolies in the industries where he had investments, a journalist gave him the nickname Pacman [66], a reference to the computer game where the object is to eat as much as you can. Cojuangco's personal net worth was estimated at $500 million [67], making him among the country's richest men.

THE NETHERWORLD

Apart from his numerous companies, Danding's collection of guns, cars, and horses also provide a curious insight into his personality.

A man who distributes calendars with his photograph and BOSS printed across the top, Cojuangco appears to have an even more ominously darker side than being an ordinary grafter and favored Marcos crony. Not content with the rank of military reserve colonel Marcos bestowed upon him, Cojuangco has been long reported to maintain his own private army, estimated at more than 5,000 men at its peak. The army was reported to have been trained by Israeli mercenaries [68]. People close to Cojuangco do not deny the existence of this shadowy side. A friend interviewed by the *Christian Science Monitor* described Danding as "ruthless" [69]. Even Cojuangco's ever-faithful lawyer and spokesman, Gabriel Villareal, admitted to the *Wall Street Journal* that "Danding is capable to taking lives" [70]. Stephen Bosworth, the former US Ambassador to the Philippines, commenting on possible successors to Marcos' leadership, described Cojuangco in the following way:

"There's no way Danding could lead within a pluralistic system that held him accountable He operates best in the netherworld" [71].

This side of Cojuangco is what might have surfaced during a basketball game where Cojuangco and his oons were accused of roughing up rooters of the opposing camp. A basket all *aficionado*, he was accused in an open letter by three men, one of them a lawyer, of attacking high school kids after a basketball game between the teams of two rival schools. The open letter stated:

> *What is unforgivable is what Danding Cojuangco did when he brought several hundred goons with guns and lead pipes to beat up young Letran high school kids. A great La Sallite this Danding and what a way to go -- goons to beat up teenage high school kids [72].*

When he was appointed by Marcos as Project Director for Basketball [73] and later elected national committee chairman of the Basketball Association of the Philippines (BAP), the Association president, Gonzalo Puyat, hailed Danding's appointment with the following portentous words: "He is a dedicated sportsman who will not let anything stand in the way of his plans" [74].

After Marcos' downfall, government raiders found an assortment of high-powered firearms, explosives and ammunition when they raided one of Coiuangco's companies. Found in the premises of Cojuangco's Northern Cement factory in Sison, Pangasinan were the following:

1 Chinese submachinegun
1 .30 caliber machinegun
2 Thompson submachineguns
1 M-60 machine (used in helicopter gunships)
2 AK-47 rifles
1 armalite rifle
1 model 77 Ruger rifle
I Mark IV .380 caliber rifle
1 M-1 pistolized carbine
1 double-barrel rifle
1 .32 caliber survival rifle
1 .22 caliber Winchester rifle
1 .44 caliber magnum revolver
2 .45 caliber automatic pistols
1 .45 caliber Colt Commander automatic pistol
1 Walther PPK .22 caliber pistol
1 Browning .22 caliber target pistol
1 flare gun
200 flare cartridges
200 smoke grenades
50.000 rounds of M-16 bullets
1.000 rounds of 7.62 mm for M-60 machinegun
500 blasting caps

This assortment of sophisticated and expensive weaponry was only part of the collection Cojuangco had amassed in hiding places in the Visayas, Central Luzon, and Palawan [75]. Another cache, included 200 high-powered guns and a few hundred thousand rounds of bullets were earlier seized in other Danding hiding places in Northern and Central Luzon, Metro-Manila, Western Visayas, and Mindanao.

Cojuangco's love for firearms is what made the 1985 arrest of Douglas Lu Ym significant. Lu Ym, an associate of Cojuangco and Enrile, was arrested by US authorities for smuggling arms to the Philippines from the San Francisco International Airport [76]. Ingeniously packed in a golf bag checked-in with the Philippine Air Lines were components of a handgun, a military assault rifle, and a military-style laser scope. Lu Ym's travelling companion was John DeCamillis, a American employed as vice-president of the sports division of San Miguel Corp. Cojuangco was chairman of San Miguel. DeCamillis was later made a special assistant to the chairman.

CARS AND HORSES

Also found in Cojuangco's residence in New Manila was an expensive collection of sports cars and Vintage automobiles, including Ferraris and Rolls Royces [77]. Among those found in his motor pool were 21 of the 148 missing luxury cars which had been issued to officials of the Marcos government. Among the models of the cars in Cojuangco's possession were

* a fleet of Mercedes Benzes (including two 600cc models)
* 4 Ferraris
* a black 1971 Rolls Royce
* a Porsche 911f
* some BMWs
* a Bently Continental
* a Daimler sedan
* 2 Jaguars
* 2 Mustangs
* assorted Toyotas, Izusus, Fords, Dodges, Corvettes, Cortinas
* a rare De Lorean gull-winged sportscar [78]

Danding was also a horse aficionado and an ardent bettor in the San Lazaro Race Track from 1974 through 1977. Marcos, cognizant of Danding's penchant for horses, made him chairman of the Philippine Racing Commission (PRC), an institution directly under the office of the President supervising betting in racetracks. A notable achievement of Danding's stint with the PRC was to increase horse-racmg days to 3 times a week, thus significantly increasing the government's tax take from horse racing.

Cojuangco was also a collector of thoroughbreds, acquiring a stable of champion race horses locally and overseas. One acquisition which became news in the equestrian world was his 1980 purchase of a chestnut filly in an Australian auction. The horse was bought for a record $232,000 after Cojuangco won over all other international bidders [79]. Later, Cojuangco purchased his own horse farm in Australia, the Gooree Stud Farm, where he reeds dairy cows and race horses. The thoroughbred stud farm, valued at $25 million [80], is located at Mudgee, Northwestern New South Wales, some 260 miles from Sydney.

A favorite horse of Cojuangco was a horse named Manila, a grass runner champion which regularly competed in US races. Manila, an aspirant for the title of Horse of the Year (1987 [81], was a constant pick in US races, winning prizes such as the $150,000 United Nations Handicap at Atlantic City Race Course. Manila is a bay-colored colt whose pedigree was described by the *New York Times* as being the "son of Lyphard and the Le Fabuleux mare Dona Ysidra" [82]. Dona Ysidra was apparently a well-known mare who bred money-making race horses.

UCPB

The previous section on Enrile discussed the control he and Cojuangco exerted over the coconut industry. The next pages discuss how Cojuangco and Enrile used the coconut levy funds to organize the United Coconut Planters Bank (UCPB) as well as fund Danding's personal projects.

Changes in banking regulations in 1975 proved to be beneficial to many Marcos cronies who wanted to have their own banks. While banning the opening of new banks, the new Central Bank regulations increase the capitalization requirements for existing banks to P100 million. These requirements forced the owners of smaller banks to sell out or to merge with crony-owned which were then very liquid.

To avoid the clutches of Kokoy Romualdez (see section), who was eyeing the First United Bank (FUB), Jose Cojuangco Sr. (father of Corazon Aquino) gave his nephew Danding the first-purchase options to the bank [83]. This meant that Danding would have the first shot at buying the bank. Danding exercised this option and bought the FUB with the help of the funds from the coconut levy.

It appears that both sides of the Cojuangco family benefitted from the arrangement. Danding's purchase saved the FUB and the Jose Cojuangco-Aquino family from Kokoy Romualdez. Furthermore, it also appears that Danding did his uncle and cousins a favor in buying the bank: "Danding's lawyers claim it was a sale quite advantageous to the Aquino family as the purchase prices was 100% over the bank's par value" [84]. *The Far Eastern Economic Review* thus commented:

> *The sale of First United to Danding and the coconut monopoly is not merely a historical curiosity. If Jose Sr's family indeed had been granted a favor by Danding in buying the share at a good price, it could explain -- given the Filipino culture of* **utang na loob** *(debt of gratitude) -- why Corazon Aquino has not moved decisively against Danding in the past three years, despite reports that she believes he was involved in the conspiracy that led to the assassination of her husband [85].*

While such an observation on the part of the *Review* may border on the speculative, it certainly does belie the perception that serious rifts exist between the Jose Cojuangco-Aquino side of the family which fought the Marcos dictatorship and their cousin Danding, the chief beneficiary of Marcos' patronage. In fact, even when the Aquino family was in exile in Boston, Danding had helped his cousin Corazon Aquino by paying part of the cost of the Boston home where Ninoy and Mrs. Aquino stayed [86].

On the other hand, the purchase of the FUB was also to Danding's and Enrile's benefit since it gave them the bank they needed to systematize their control over the billions raised from the coconut levy. Cojuangco therefore exercised his first-purchase options to buy the EU but assigned them to Enrile, who was then administering the funds from the coconut levy [87]. The FUB was then purchased and reorganized into the United Coconut Planters Bank (UCPB) [88].

The purchase required the shares of the newly-organized UCPB be divided into Class A and Class B shares. The Class B shares, comprisuig 27.8% of the total, were to be retained by members of the Cojuangco family who previously owned the FUB. The remaining 72.2% were classified as Class A shares and were to be owned by the Philippine Coconut Authority (PCA) for "the benefit of the coconut farmers." According to the minutes of 30 June 1975 stockholder's meeting which formalized the new structure:

> *The shares acquired by the Philippine Coconut Authority for the benefit of the. coconut farmers of the Philippines, constituting 72.2% of the present outstanding capital stock of the bank, be considered Class A shares and the balance, constituting 27.8%, be considered Class B shares.*

The ACCRA law office (see section on Enrile) played a significant role in the organization of the UCPB. Eight of ACCRA's 12 senior members were stockholders of the bank at this time and were present during this crucial organizational meeting. And according to the minutes, two of these senior partners participated in the discussions. Moreover, corporate papers show that another partner of ACCRA, A.Q. Ongsioco, formaly received the SEC certificate of capital stock increase for the bank.

The arrangement had many subtle aspects which allowed Cojuangco and Enrile to control the newly-formed UCPB.

The division of the share into Class A and B and the definition of the rights of each group gave Cojuangco tremendous advantages. Holders of the Class B shares, that is to say, members of the Cojuangco family, were "absolutely entitled to preemptive rights" over the unissued portion of Class B shares. They also were permitted to subscribe to a proportionate increase in their shareholdings with any increase in Class A paid-up capital. These two conditions ensured that the family could easily increase their shares in the bank. Moreover, Class B shareholders had 5 years "from the call of the board of directors" to pay for their subscriptions. In contrast, the PCA, which held the 72.2% Class A shares of the bank's authorized capital "for the coconut farmers," did not have such advantages. The PCA was not entitled to the preemptive rights granted to Cojuangco. Furthermore, while Cojuangco had 5 years from an arbitrary date to be set by the board to pay, the PCA had to produce the $12 million in total subscriptions immediately [89].

While these were the formal arrangements made during the 30 June 1975 UCPB meeting, Cojuangco and Enrile shrewdly entered into other agreements with the PCA and the Cocofed (see the section on Enrile for a discussion of the PCA and Cocofed). These other schemes provided the final step in the control over the bank. Once these arrangements were made with the PCA and the Cocofed, control over the bank was assured.

A month before the crucial UCPB organizational meeting, Cojuangco entered into a contract with the PCA ensuring his power over the bank. The contract required the PCA "to cause" the bank's stockholders to a prove a management contract between the bank and Cojuangco. Since the PCA was the main stockholder, Cojuangco was readily granted the management contract during the organization of the UCPB. This was the first part of Cojuangco's fee for assigning his first-purchase options to the PCA.

A final resolution during a special June 1975 meeting authorized the directors of the bank to "negotiate and conclude a management contract...between the bank and such person as the reorganized board of directors may choose." The invitation to the shareholders to attend the meeting was more explicit: "To authorize the board of directors to negotiate and conclude a management contract by and between the bank and Eduardo M. Cojuangco Jr." The management contract, renewable every 5 years, stipulated that Cojuangco "shall be elected president" and could designate 3 of the 11 directors in the board. Thus, apart from the money Cojuangco would receive through his shares, the arrangement saw to it that he would get his management fees and handsome directors' salaries.

The second part to Cojuangco's fee was more significant. The arrangement also provided that Cojuangco would receive **10% of the coconut farmers' shares**. The contract between the PCA and Cojuangco provided that the stock certificates would be issued "one share in the name of the seller [Cojuangco] for every nine shares in the name of the buyer [the PCA]." Confirmation of this arrangement is seen in a 16 July 1975 memorandum presented to the chief securities examiner of the SEC, as well as public statements made by Enrile on 4 February 1982 when he admitted that Cojuangco was given "10% of the option shares" during the 1975 restructuring:

> As agreed by the stockholders, out of the 72.2% ownership of the PCA and its trustees, 10% had been transferred to a stockholder, therefore 10% of the P14.44 million worth of shares owned by PCA on the present issued an outstanding would amount to P1.44 million. (Emphasis ours).

This means that the PCA held only 64.97% of aid-in capital and not the 72.2% as resolved at the shareholders meeting. The outstanding 7.22% was transferred to Cojuangco. These shares were literally given to Cojuangco as a gift. They were directly paid out of levy funds, prompting an observer to comment that the UCPB was practically "handed to Cojuangco on a silver platter." The double-talk used to rationalize this theft was that PCA members doled out these shares to Cojuangco as "a voting trust" for the farmers.

The groundwork for this scandalous arrangement is to be found in a 12 January 1975 contract between Cojuangco and Lobregat of the Cocofed [90]. The contract gave Cojuangco blanket powers represent the "coconut farmers" in the UCPB [91]. The contract gave Cojuangco the total authority to

> exercise all such other powers and execute and deliver all such other documents and do all such acts and things as may be required or necessary in managing and

supervising UCPB'S affairs and operations [92].

As if this provision were not enough, another clause gave Cojuangco further implicit powers:

The foregoing powers shall not be construed to limit or restrict in any manner the general manager of UCPB, nor shall the expression of one thing be deemed to exclude another not expressed, if it be of like nature [93].

Another aspect of the agreement gave Cojuangco complete managerial control and a clear source of added income. It committed the UCPB to buy its supplies from contractors Cojuangco chose:

contracting for or purchase of, on behalf and in the name of UCPB, such labor, materials, equipment and supplies and properties such as lands and buildings as in the judgement of the manager may be necessary [94],

The contract between Cojuangco and Lobregat was highly anomalous on several points. The agreement provided that the shares and voting rights of the farmers were to be held in trust, with all decisions to be made by Enrile as chairman and Cojuangco as president. This was a clear betrayal of the interests of the farmer. The farmer supplied the money for the bank through his hard work, but he was completely shut off from the decisions to how his money was to be spent or how the "voting trust" would operate. There was no system of accountability as to how the levy money was going to be used. The farmer received no dividends and was not even able to sell his shares since they were frozen in the "voting trust" [95]. Furthermore, it was clearly shown in the previous section that Cocofed was never a legitimate representative of the coconut farmer. It was shown that the leadership of Cocofed was composed of landlords and professionals at the service of this elite. Lobregat herself was a landlord and a close associate of Cojuangco and Enrile. Lobregat and the Cocofed therefore had no right to speak for the coconut farmer, much less to hand over the rights of the farmer to Cojuangco. All arrangements arising from this "voting trust" contract should therefore be declared null and void *ab initio.*

The contracts between Cojuangco, the PCA, and the Cocofed ensured the total control over the bank. The source of the funds, the PCA, turned over its shares and the management of the bank to Cojuangco, while the Cocofed, the so-called representative of the coconut farmer, gave Cojuangco the right to speak for the farmers. These arrangements formalized the support rom government and private sectors and permitted the total control of the bank and its funds. So when the UCPB formally opened, the ownership of the shares, broken down as follows, were firmly in the hands of Enrile and Cojuangco:

Shares			
Class B	27.8%		Cojuangco family
Class A	72.2%		
		64.97%	PCA
		7.22%	Cojuangco

The government and those who controlled the industry tried their best to obscure the true ownership of the bank. When the UCPB was organized, a Cocofed resolution was passed lauding the bank as "a permanent solution to their perennial credit problems" of the farmers, implying that the bank was indeed owned by the coconut farmers. UCPB documents also perpetuated this myth by continually referring to the management of the UCPB as a "Voting trust" for the farmers.

But the UCPB board of directors and officers were in reality composed of Enrile, Cojuangco, and their associates. Not one of those who served the UCPB either as director or officer was a genuine coconut farmer:

Juan Poncé Enrile	chairman
Eduardo Cojuangco	president
Danilo Ursua	president
Andres Soriano III	vice chairman
Narciso 'Chitong" Pineda	close associate at Cojuangco
Jesus Pineda	Narciso's brother
Rolando de la Cuesta	Enrile's "gofer"
Accra Investment Corp.	connected with Accra law firm
Jaka Investments	company of Enrile and wife
Occur Santos PCA	chairman
Maria Clara Lobregat	Cocofed president
Jose Eleazar	Cocofed
Ilnaki Mendezona	Cocofed
Bienvenido Marquez	Cocofed
Hermenegildo Zayco	
Jose Cocepcion	ACCRA Investments Corp., ACCRA lawyer
Emmanuel Almeda	
Raul Roco	San Miguel corporate secretary, ACCRA lawyer
Carlos Soriano	
From Eizmendi	

Apart from the earlier management contract Cojuangco wangled from the PCA, a profit-sharing scheme was devised where the favored officers would divide amongst themselves *5% of the pre-tax profits* of the bank. The president (i.e., Cojuangco) was to receive 1% of the amount, while the rest would be apportioned amongst the senior officers. In addition, *another scheme* provided for the distribution of *5% of net earnings* to the board, with 1% going to chairman Enrile and the rest distributed among other board members. These were extremely generous terms, considering, for example, that the bank enjoyed a net income of $16 million in 1980, the largest reported in the banking industry at that time.

To cover his prominent role in the UCPB, Cojuangco nominally relinquished the presidency to Danilo S. Ursua. But it was well known that Cojuangco and Enrile remained the real powers behind the UCPB. Ursua also served as a "dummy" for Cojuangco's stocks in the bank. Ursua first claimed that the 5% holding in bank was his own, having purchased it after Cojuangco offered it to him in 1975. But he later admitted that he had endorsed these same bank stock certificates "in blank" and personally delivered them to Cojuangco to "secure a financial obligation" [9%]. It also was later discovered that Ursua endorsed and personally delivered the 5% of the pre-tax profits to Cojuangco. Ursua's shares in the bank showed dramatic increases, possibly reflecting the shares he held for Cojuangco and Marcos:

Shares

6,600,100.00	June 1978
13,200,000.00	December 1978 (doubled in 6 months)
22,221,024.00	May 1981

The best breakdown of the stock ownership of the UCPB available is the list as of May 1985, a few months before the downfall of Marcos:

Shares in millions

340	San Miguel
100	Legaspi Oil Co. Inc.
54.1	Eduardo M. Cojuangco Jr.
54.7	ECJ & Sons Agricultural Enterprises Inc.
14.7	ACCRA Investment Corp.
37.9	Jesus M. Pineda Jr.
37.5	Narciso M. Pineda
14.7	Balete Ranch Inc.
70	Pacific Warehouse Inc.
80	Packaging Products Co.
20	Lucena Oil Factory
20	PCY Oil Manufacturing Corp.
22.5	Metroplex Commodities Inc.
30	Granexport Mfg. Corp
20	San Pablo Manufacturing Co .
17.5	Southern Luzon Coconut Oil Mill
20	Iligan Coconut Industries Inc.

The list reflects the extent of Cojuangco's and Enrile's ownership of the UCPB. Some of the listed owners can be related directly to Enrile or Cojuangco, such as ECJ & Sons (Eduardo Cojuangco Jr. & Sons), while others are not as obvious. The Balete Ranch, for example, was held y Ursua and Pineda for Cojuangco, while Lucena Oil, PCY Oil, and Metroplex were coconut oil companies owned by Cojuangco. Christensen Plantation Inc., not in the list, was another company owned by Cojuangco which held shares in the bank. San Miguel was the industrial conglomerate Cojuangco took over using coconut industry funds, while the other companies were part of the Unicorn network of coconut mills which Cojuangco and Enrile controlled. One re report estimated that Cojuangco controlled more than 40%, possibly 60%, of the bank.

The Cocofed, instead of representing the interests of the coconut farmer, defrauded them. Its officials, led by Lobregat, connived with the PCA and the UCPB to convince the farmers to give up their levy receipts. It will be recalled that each receipt represented proof of ownership in the bank (see section on Enrile). Rather than inform the farmers of this fact, Cocofed ofiicials convince them that the receipts were worthless and should be sold. Complaining of Cooofed's tactics, farmers from Mindanao pointed to a Lobregat memorandum circulated on July 1982 setting guidelines for the purchase of these receipts. Lobregat's proposal was to purchase the levy receipts through the United Coconut Planters Life Assurance (Cocolife). The stated purpose was to "help alleviate the immediate financial needs of coconut farmers" by purchasing the receipts at "a fair price." The "fair price" at which Lobregat proposed to buy the receipts from the financially-strapped farmers was at the par value of $0.13 per share [97]. This price stood in sharp contrast with the $24.60 per share tag when PCA used the coconut farmers' money to purchase shares at the UCPB and hand them over to Cojuangco. Commenting on Lobregat's efforts to defraud them on behalf of UCPB officials, coconut farmers from Mindanao contended: "We are certain that an honest-to-goodness investigation into UCPB's ownership will reveal that a large number of those 1.3 million farmers have sold their shares to Mr. Cojuangco and his dummies" [98].

The ties Enrile and Cojuangco enjoyed with Marcos assured them of complete support from the dictator. A presidential decree was issued solely to authorize the use of the levy funds for the purchase of the UCPB. PD 755 was issued, authorizing the PCA to use the funds "to draw and utilize the collections under CCSF [levy] to pay for the financial commitments" connected with the purchase of UCPB. PD 755 merely legitimized what had already been done by Enrile and Cojuangco a month earlier. The levy money had already been spent in the purchase of the UCPB, but the presidential decree authorizing the use of the funds was issued only on 29 July 1975, a month after the bank's purchase. PD 755 further facilitated private control over the public funds by naming the Cocofed as the buyer of the UCPB rather than the PCA. The PCA was clearly subject to government audit, but the Cocofed, regardless of its use of public funds, would claim that it was a private organization and not subject to government audit. The initial PCA equity in the UCPB were therefore transferred to Cocofed which Lobregat nominally headed.

Further institutional help came with Central Bank authorization for the UCPB to become a universal bank, a financial institution allowed to invest directly into non-allied economic activities. While other banks had to meet stringent requirements before they were allowed to engage in universal banking, Jaime Laya, Marcos' Central Bank governor, interpreted banking regulations loosely and permitted the UCPB to become the first universal bank in the Philippines [9]. The UCPB was exempted from the requirement that at least 10% of the paid-up capital must be publicly owned and listed at the stock exchanges if the bank is to engage in expanded commercial banking. The Central Bank declared that owners of shares by Cocofed in UCPB constituted compliance with banking regulations [100] and allowed the UCPB to diversify from its hitherto coconut-oriented activities to other areas [101]. Its status as a universal bank allowed the UCPB "to invest funds collected from farmers in a private corporation which will pool and coordinate the resources of the farmers and the coconut oil millers in buying, milling and marketing copra and its by-products" [102]. This expansion of the UCPB permitte Enrile and Cojuangco to control the other areas of the coconut industry.

After a mere four years after its organization, the UCPB was already the third largest bank in terms of total net worth and the fifth biggest in terms of assets . It opened several dozen branches in different cities and constructed a multimillion eight-storey building in the country's financal district, moves highly incongruous with its claims to be the bank of the coconut farmers.

But UCPB's rapid growth had less to do with the banking acumen of Enrile and Cojuangco than with the support it received from the government and subsidy it enjoyed from the levy.

The billions collected from the levy were deposited with the UCPB, accompanied with lip-service proclamations that it was a bank collectively owned by the coconut farmers. A government publication at that time lauded the levy program, saying "the PCA has provided the incentive for the farmers to establish and own their own investment company, the Coconut Industry Investment Fund (CIIF)." But once the funds entered the coffers of the bank, their status and ultimate disposition became financially and legally problematic. After PD 755, two other presidential decrees concerning the UCPB were promulgated. Both tried to address, and obscure, the status of the levy money. A presidential decree issued on 8 November 1977 implicitly declared the funds as non-government and had the status of a special, judiciary fund; a later presidential decree, PD 1468, explicitly declare the money as private. The two decrees in effect declared the funds private to prevent any government audit.

But critics contended that the levy was a public fund. In raising the funds by upposmg a percentage on a product, a tax was in effect being charged, making the presidentially-decreed levy public in nature. The privatization of the funds for Cojuangco and Enrile through presidential decrees was therefore *illegal and unconstitutional* [103].

Apart from the legal aspects of the bank's operations, the financial management of the levy was cause for equal concern. The funds were deposited as demand deposits (i.e., a checking account) and were therefore *not entitled to interest* [104]. This in effect gave the UCPB a $17.8 million subsidy [105]. The farmer, already taxed of a significant part of his income, was in effect lending Cojuangco and Enrile billions without interest. Yet when the very same farmer approached the UCPB for a crop loan, he was charged a rate of 8-12% [106]. The contradiction, although difficult to comprehend, painfully existed: the starving farmer had to pay to borrow his own money, but lent this same money at no cost to millionaires like Cojuangco and Enrile. Considering that an estimated $80-120 million was raised every year from the levy [107], and also considering that interest rates in the country were extremely high, reaching as much as 20-25% at times because of continuing financial crises, there was great opportunity to earn hefty sums from the levy money just by investing in different financial and money markets.

Cojuangco acted as if the coconut levy money deposited with the UCPB were his own. For example, when demonstrations protesting the murder of Ninoy Aquino were at their height, Cojuangco assembled the employees of UCPB, thanked them for not joining the demonstrations, and gave each individual an envelope containing a $90.00 bonus [108]. As will be seen in the following pages, man Cojuangco firms also benefitted from the levy. For example, around 33% of the funds of UCPB Realty, a realty subsidiary of the bank, was invested in Cojuangco corporations [109].

BUGSUK ISLAND

Yet another presidential decree was issued authorizing greater levies on the produce of the coconut farmer. PD 582, issued on 14 November 1974, expanded the coverage of the levy and authorized another fund, the Coconut Industry Development Fund (CIDF). An initial $15 million was drawn from the original Coconut Consumers Stabilization Fund (CCSF) (see section on Enrile) to fund the CIDF, with additional provisions that a permanent share of $3.00 for every 100 kilos of copra be drawn from the original levy. The rationale put forward for extracting more of the farmer's income was to institute Coconut replanting program. The scheme proposed to create a coconut seed farm where special hybrid trees would be developed and later used in nationwide coconut replanting.

The project, however, suffered from a built-in loophole from the very beginning. Although the money for the replanting project came from the levy imposed on the farmers, it would benefit only selected landlords. The small farmer was automatically excluded because he owned no land to plant the new hybrid trees. From its very inception, the program was designed to widen the gap between the landed rich and the working poor in the coconut industry. David, the authority on the coconut industry, wrote:

> [$150 million] was provided by the poor coconut farmers to finance the production of super-hybrid seednuts that would be distributed free to selected landlords. The majority of the coconut farmers are disqualified from receiving these seednuts because they own no land, in the first place, to plant these on. But they are privileged to plant the seeds on the lands of their lords [110].

The primary beneficiary of the replanting program was Cojuangco, the biggest landlord in the coconut industry. Cojuangco, together with Enrile, engineered the Bugsuk seed garden, a project which milked the coconut levy program of millions. Enrile himself admitted his role in the planning of this program when he recounted the project as being pivotal in the organization of the UCPB:

> In one of our meetings while I was working out the Bugsuk seed garden project, which was handled by [Cojuangco] -- he mentioned to me about this. And so, I [as chairman of the PCA] brought the coconut farmers and [Cojuangco] together as joint venture in this bank [111].

The seed garden project consisted of two parts, both of which caused concern. The first, the acquisition of the land to be used, involved potential violations of the constitution and the law. The second, the financing of the replanting project itself, involved a questionable deal inimical to the interests of the government and coconut farmers.

To acquire the land for the coconut seed farm, Cojuangco entered into an arrangement with the Marcos government where lands Cojuangco owned would be swapped with those in the public domain. This allowed Cojuangco to exchange some of his lands in Central Luzon, then under the threat of land reform, w1th underdeveloped lands in Palawan. The agreed ratio was 10:1, where Cojuangco would get 10 hectares in exchange for each hectare of developed property he gave up. The deal was formalized on 5 January 1973 between Cojuangco, representing the heirs of Eduardo Cojuangco Sr. (his father) and Ernesto Oppen Jr. (his wife's father), and Arturo Tanco and Conrado Estrella, Marcos' Secretaries of Agriculture & Natural Resources and Agrarian Reform [112].

Danding chose four islands in Tablas Romblon, South Palawan as his prize: Bugsuk, Pandanan, Matanglue, Gabung.

Cojuangco got a total 14,673.73 hectares through the deal [113]. Bugsuk, the biggest island of the group, was 10,821.23 hectares. In the case of Bugsuk, only 6,980.73 hectares was covered by the original land swap agreement. The remaining 35% of the island or 3,852 hectares was granted through a separate "lease agreement" given to some 11 corporations Cojuangco owned [114].

The deal was roundly criticized when details of the deal filtered to the public. It was a patent violation of the constitutional provision which limited private corporations from holding more than 1,024 hectares. Another provision violated was the prohibition on corporations occupying and owning lands in the public domain [115].

Villareal, Cojuangco's loyal legal mouthpiece, countered that the lands were "malaria-infested" and that Cojuangco had developed the area and introduced infrastructure projects [116]. But Villareal's claims were belied by Rosalino Isler, a lawyer with the Bureau of Lands, who testified that a total of 85 families in Bugsuk had been displaced [117]. An earlier study, though, had given the much higher number of 7,000 minority families [118]. It was further reported that the owner occupants, most of whom were descendants of the original people who cleared the land [119], were forcibly evicted by armed men [120]). Another violation of the law appears to have taken place, since the government is prohibited from granting lands already occupied [121]. And since the place was already inhabited, another illegal move was the granting of the land without the required Quit Claims or Waiver of Rights of the occupants, whose families had been in the place for generations [122].

Cojuangco was supposed to hand over rice and sugar lands in the provinces of Tarlac, Nueva Ecija, Pangasinan, Occidental Mindoro but never fulfilled his part of the deal. Although Villareal claimed that 1,600 hectares were turned in, investigators from the Bureau of Lands and the Ministry of Natural Resources declared that "the Cojuangco group has yet to surrender to the government the certificates of titles covering an area of 1,320.6540 hectares" [123]. According to Isler of the Bureau of Lands, the only property turned over to the government was 282.57 hectares in Antique [124]. The chairman of the Ministry of Natural Resources team investigating the land grant, former Judge Alexander Castro, concurred that Cojuangco turned in only a token 300 hectares [125]. Officials also claimed that Cojuangco ignored later requests of the Ministry of Agrarian Reform to turn over the other titles [126].

The second aspect of the project involved the financing of the production and marketing of the hybrid seeds.

Cojuangco received an exclusive contract to supply hybrid seedlings to the coconut industry through the NIDC (National Investment & Dev. Corp], the government body initially assigned to administer the $170 million CIDF [127]. The contract, signed on 20 November 1974, was awarded to Agricultural Investors Inc. (AII), a Cojuangco firm. Cojuangco was both the chairman and president of the AII and was assisted by Antonio Carag and Amando Narciso in the firm's management. AII's assets were estimate at $40 million in 1990 [128]. Signing for the government was Agusto Orosa, senior Vice presrdent of NIDC.

The contract with the NIDC, covering a 40-year period from 1980 through 2020, assured Cojuangco reimbursement of all expenses related to the project, a captive market, and a guaranteed price for the tree seedlings coming from his farm.

Under the terms of the contract, the NIDC would pay for all the costs related to developing the project. Villareal admitted that under the arrangement, AII was

to be defrayed of its expenses and reimbursements (sic) for damages in the course of its implementation of the conditions for the coconut seed garden project, a major component of the government's' coconut subsidy program (sic) [129].

Cojuangco received an initial outlay of $58 million from the CIIF and the NIDC between 1974 and 1979 [130]. He was given another $59 million in 1982, representing "liquidated damages," bringing the total coconut levy money sunk into Cojuangco's seed garden to $117 million [131]. This means that 20% of the estimated $550 billion in levy funds went into Cojuangco's Bugsuk Island project. It was later revealed that the first outlay of $58 million, given in two batches of $6.5 million and a subsequent $350 million, were advanced to Cojuangco even before any replanting work had started in 1976 [1321]. Another estimate of the amount for the replanting project was given at $155 billion [133]. If this higher estimate is followed, then it means that at least 28% of the total levy funds was spent merely in the seed project.

Amado Narciso, general manager of A11, claimed in a press statement that there was nothing wrong with the arrangement [134], but officials of the Commission on Audit asserted that the contract so beneficial to AII was completely inimical to the interests of the coconut farmers [135].

The AII-NIDC contract assured Cojuangco of a market and a profitable price for his seedlings. It was initially promised that the seedlings would be "free," but these were later purchased by the PCA for distribution. Although the costs of farming and developing the seedlings were shouldered by the government, they had to be purchased from Cojuangco's farm by the PCA at $3.00 per seedling, including those which did not germinate [136)]. This was a multimillion subsidy: all the costs were covered, a market was assured, and a price was guaranteed. One reporter estimated that "well over [$350 million] has been spent for the replanting program" as of 1982 [137].

The trees that were introduced were the Mawa hybrids (Yellow Malayan Dwarf and West African tall varieties) from the Ivory Coast, Africa. It was claimed that these trees would take only four years to bear fruit and would yield 5 tons of copra per hectare, in contrast with the traditional varieties which produced only a ton. But the project turned out to be a disaster. Cojuangco's Mawa trees produced an average of only 1.6 tons per hectare, while crosses between local varieties produced as much as 4 tons per hectare [138]. Furthermore, the fruit from the new variety bore smaller nuts and less meat. They were also less weather resistant, the nuts easily blown off the trees by strong winds. Apart from the government outlays in infrastructure in Cojuangco's farm, wasted resources included the loss in income due to shifting from the old varieties to Cojuangco's Mawas, then back to the old varieties. Considering that it takes several years before coconut trees bear fruit, this represent a great loss of income over the non-productive years.

Capping the NIDC-Cojuangco contract was the provision that allowed All to pay the government a percentage of net operating income. By stipulating that Cojuangco should pay 25% of net income, rather than some fixed amount or a percentage of gross income, the contract assured that Cojuangco had the option of not paying at all. According to an official of the Commission on Audit, it was a situation of "no profit, no pay arrangement" 139]. It was a simple matter of adjusting the books so as to reflect no profits. Indeed, Cojuangco never remitted a single centavo to the government from 1979 through 1982, claiming that his farm fell short of its seed targets every year [140]:

Year	Production shortage
1979	60%
1980	38%
1981	38%
1982	47%

PEARLS

Since the hybrid seed project was a complete financial disaster, at least in so far as the coconut farmer and the government were concerned, it is natural to question the wisdom and motivation of Cojuangco in pursuing the project and choosing Bugsuk Island as his base of operations.

One might ask why Cojuangco was so eager to "barter" profitable rice and sugar lands in the provinces of Tarlac, Pangasinan, Nueva Ecija, Antique, and Occidental Mindoro for an undeveloped piece island far from the centers of commerce. Villareal, the Cojuangco apologist, admitted that Cojuangco had been advised against the Bugsuk project but that Danding insisted on pursuing it since "he wanted to continue what his ancestors ventured into, which was pioneering trailblazers in agricultural projects" [141], a possible reference to the entrepreneurial Dona Ysidra. Conveniently forgetting that the whole project was subsidized by the coconut levy, Villareal claimed that Cojuangco took a big risk in the project to develop malaria-infested lands, replacing the top soil and building infrastructure such as roads, a water system, irrigation, landing docks, and an airfield [142].

A study on soil conditions in the Philippines conducted over a 5-year period indicated that there were at least 10 provinces which were potential seed gardens, but that Bugsuk lacked the required nitrogen, sulfur, chlorine, potassium [143]. Cojuangco nevertheless proceeded with the Bugsuk project.

It appears that Cojuangco had made up his mind on Bugsuk from the very beginning and that the hybrid seedling project was an afterthought to provide the necessary funds and legitimacy or his occupation of Bugsuk and the three other islands. Henares, the journalist cited earlier in connection with Dona Ysidra, relates that Danding actually chose the place after Ramon Mitra, a former congressman who later helped Danding buy copra [144], showed the province of Palawan to Cojuangco on a plane trip:

... one day, Mitra got a phone call from Ninoy's cousin-in-law, Danding Cojuangco. Danding told Monching [Mitra] that his plane was waiting at the airport, that he wanted Monching to show him around Palawan.
As the plane circled all around Palawan, Danding pointed out an island at the southern tip of the province and said, "that is the one I want." The island he pointed to is called Bugsuk Island. For a longtime after that, we used to kid Monching Mirna for delivering the island to PACMAN, and Monching would grimace and say, 'Hell, I gave you guys first choice, did I not?" [145].

The reason for choosing the island was therefore not based on scientific considerations. There appear to be three other reasons why Cojuangco finally chose it.

The island, far from the centers of the country and isolated by the sea, was allegedly used by Cojuangco as a camp for his Israeli mercenaries to train his private army [146].

The islands were very near places where oil was known to exist and where other Marcos-connected firms had been exploring for oil. A foreign mining engineer who visited the islands claimed that the area was a reservoir of crude oil and other vital minerals [147].

The third reason, as explained by Henares, was that Danding was actually starting a pearl farm in Bugsuk islan [148]. Using the coconut seed replanting project as his guise and source of funds [149], Danding was actually farming pearls. Cojuangco registered Jewelmer International Corp. with the SEC on May 1980. The activities of this company were later expanded to include the marketing of pearls under the name "Pearl Island" [150]. Jewelmer has branches in San Francisco, Los Angeles, Texas, Australia, and the Manila Peninsula Hotel, the latter housing the South Island Pearl Museum. The holding company of Jewelmer is Bertex, a shell corporation which controls other Cojuangco interests in the US West Coast.
Henares also revealed that, while the pearls still continue to be farmed and exported, no public accounting of the pearls was ever made by the Aquino administration. It is a sad commentary on Philippine institutions that

it is bruited about in the business community that the pearl farm of Danding is now being rated under the auspices of three cabinet ministers [of the Aquino adminis-tration] who are also using Jewelmer as their marketing arm [51].

SAN MIGUEL

Money from the coconut levy gave Cojuangco the funds to invest in diverse activities such as agri-business, sugar, our, com, chemicals, soft drinks, and beer brewing. The transformation of the UCPB into a universal bank helped Danding's empire building tremendously since it legally permitted the bank to invest in other lines of business.

Cojuangco's most prized acquisition was San Miguel Corp. (SMC), the large beer, food, packaging, and livestock conglomerate. His entry into SMC meant not only control of one of the country's most profitable companies but also respectability that his previous activities had not been able to give him. SMC was an old company tracing its beginnings to the 1890's when the country was still under Spanish colonial rule, while Cojuangco's previous businesses had been relatively benign private ventures or grand government scams such as the UCPB and Unicom.

Danding's entry into SMC and his consequent election as its chairman also symbolically marked the complete politicalization of business in the Philippines. While other companies in the Philippines had been tainted much earlier with the blight of cronyism, SMC was one of the few which was relatively successful in remaining free from the clutches of Marcos and his pals. This changed when Cojuangco took over the leadership of the SMC. We find, for examppe, Cojuangco cancelling SMC's financial support for a symposium on Southeast Asia, held in Singapore on 1 October 1985, when it became known that his cousin Corazon Aquino was to be one of the speakers [152]. SMC had been a traditional financier of the yearly symposium. SM also began to pick up favors from the Marcos government. When taxes on liquor and cigarettes were raised on January 1986, the excise taxes (sales and specific taxes) on beer went down. Beer is one of the main products of SMC. The tax cut meant a savings of $40 million for SMC that year [153]. Thus, while Cojuangco's main aim in entering SMC was to acquire respectability in the corporate world, the company ironically became tainted by his very presence.

Feuds between the traditional managers of SMC permitted Cojuangco to enter and wrest control of the company. The 1982-83 board room fights between cousins Enrique Zobel and Andres Soriano Jr. sapped the energies and finances of both camps and left the field open for Danding.

He entered SMC in early 1983 when he bought most of the 20 million shares Enrique Zobel owned in the company. The shares, worth $49 million, represented 20% of SMC [154]. A stock brokerage firm connected to UCPB, Venture Securities, figured prominently in the purchase [155].

Cojuangco acquired the Soriano stocks later that year through a series of complicated and secret agreements. Danding did not have to rely on overt political pressure to acquire the Soriano shares. Andres Soriano Jr., terminally ill with cancer, was already predisposed to sell the family shares to pay the heavy debts his family incurred in the war with Zobel. Armed with the money from the coconut levy, Cojuangco was able to easily enter the select SMC card with the "apparent cooperation of the Sorianos" [156].

Cojuangco purchased 33 million shares of SMC through the following 14 holding companies:

Holding Company	Shares owned (in millions)
Old Owners	
ASC Investors Inc. (Eduardo Soriano)	7.5
Soriano Shares Inc. (Eduardo Soriano)	1.25
ARC Investors Inc. (Antonio Roxas)	4.4
Antonio Roxas Shares Inc.	2.2
Benigno Toda Holdings	3.4

San Miguel Officers Corp. (Ernest Kahn)	2.4
Antonio Prieto Holdings	1.6
Jose P. Fernandez Holdings	.8

Teodoro Regala

Te Deum Resources	2.7
Anglo Ventures Co.	1
First Meridian Dev, Inc.	1

Raul Roco

Rock Steel Resources Inc	2.4
Valhalla Properties Ltd. Inc.	1.3
Randy Allied Ventures Inc.	1

Total	**32.95**

The holding companies Cojuangco used to buy the shares may be divided into two groups. Belonging to one group were the 6 companies organized by ACCRA lawyers Teodoro Regala an Raul Roco. Apart from Roco and Regala, these companies had as their incorporators other ACCRA personalities such as Frranklin Drilon, Avelino Cruz, R. Vinluan, and Victor Lazatin.

Ilt appears that the second grou was composed of companies previously owned old holders of SMC stoc but later bought by Cojuangco. They were ho din companies of families which had been traditional owners of SMC stocks ut were later reorganized on August 1983 prior to Cojuangco's purchase of the SMC shares. Again, ACCRA had a major hand in the reorganization of these com anies, with the followin lawyers serving as incorporators: Francis Jardelgza, Luis Vera Cruz Jr., oel Bodegon, Lorna Patajo-Ka unan, and Raul Roco. Other incorporators were SMC officers Eduardo gbriano, Ernest Kahn, Jose Antonio Garcia, Francisco Eizmendi, Jose Gabriel Olives, and Benigno Toda [157]

These co orations permitted Cojuangco to control more than 60% of SMC shares (3.58]. Enrile and ACCRA also had interests in SMC. A breakdown of the shares where Cojuangco, Enrile, and ACCRA controlled:

% of SMC	Owner
Cojuangco	
31.3%	coconut levy money
18%	companies linked to Cojuangco
5.2%	government
5.2%	SMC employee retirement fund
Enrile E: ACCRA	
1.8%	Enrile
1.8%	Jaka Investment Corp.
1.8%	ACCRA Investment Corp.

A key feature of the Cojuangco-Soriano deal was a "voting trust agreement" that stipulated that Andres Jr. or his heirs would proxy over the votes of the shares owned by Soriano and Cojuangco. The "voting trust agreement" covered around 30% of the outstanding shares of SMC and would last for 5 years. This arrangement would enable the Sorianos to retain management control of SMC, a traditional source of lucrative fees for the family, for the same period. Furthermore, in exchange for an SMC investment of $45 million in non-voting preferred shares in UCPB, Soriano would serve as the vice-chairman of the bank of coconut farmers. The deal was sufficiently acceptable to the Sorianos. On the other hand, Cojuangco, in return for investing funds from the coconut levy, was named vice-chairman of SMC. The board of SMC was also expanded from 11 to 15, with Cojuangco having the privilege to appoint the nominees to the new seats.

While coconut levy funds were used to buy the Soriano shares, Cojuangco did not name coconut farmers but key members of the ACCRA law firm to serve in the expanded SMC board:

* Raul Roco - ACCRA senior partner
* Edgardo Angara - ACCRA senior partner (see section on Enrile)
* Jose Concepcion -ACCRA senior partner, director of UCPB, Unicom, and a number
    of coconut milling companies. Concepcion was made SMC corporate secretary. Concepcion was described as behind many of Cojuangco's maneuvers and "in on every deal" [159]. "Concepcion is an important if, like everything else connected with Cojuangco, shadowy figure" [160].
* Danilo Ursua - described as Cojuangco's 'main financial henchmen at UCPB" [161]. He was tasked with the day-to-day running of SMC.

This move led to the accusation that Cojuangco was merely using the lawyers as dummies to deprive the coconut farmers of their representation as stockholders of the SMC [162]. Co]uangco's moves also caused concern because ACCRA lawyers were also active in many takeovers of coconut mills.

The lawyers are also identified as belonging to the Cojuangco group because the law firm is known to have used its partners as nominees in eflective takeovers of many of the coconut mills that were to become the United Coconut Oil Mills and have worked with UCPB since its inception [163].

It appears that the Cojuangco-Soriano deal contained agreements intended to be kept secret from the public. One such document came to light only five years after it was concluded. The document, "Principles and Framework of Mutual Cooperation and Assistance," governed the rules for the conduct of management of SMC and the disposition of the shares Cojuangco bought. Cojuangco and Soriano signed the document on 19 February 1983 in the presence of three ACCRA lawyers: Edgardo T. Angara, Teodoro D. Regala, and Jose C. Concepcion.

What was not mentioned in these transactions was that the money used to buy the SMC shares came from the coconut levy. This was never referred to in the incorporation papers of the holding companies, nor in any of the papers documenting the sale, nor the newspaper articles of that period. The truth was that these 14 companies were funded by institutions which depended upon the coconut levy such as the UCPB, Unicom, United Coconut Planters Life Assurance Corp. (Cocolife) (see section on Enrile). Cojuangco and his ACCRA lawyers used the funds from 6 large coconut oil mills and 10 copra trading companies to borrow money from the UCPB and purchase these holding companies and SMC stocks. Danding used $150 million from the coconut levy, broken down as follows:

Amount (in millions)	Source	Purpose
$22.26	Oil mills	equity in holding companies
$65.6	Oil mills	loan to holding companies
$61.2	UCPB	loan to holding companies [164]

The entire amount therefore came from the coconut levy, some passing through the Unicorn oil mills, some directly from the UCPB. is means that the levy money funded the biggest single block of shares in SMC. Behind these corporate transactions was a socral revolution in potentia – coconut farmers, one of the poorest segments of Philippine society, were actually buying enough shares to capture the management of the most prestigious corporation, traditionally the monopoly of the cacique (ruling) class. But since Co uangco was usurping the interests of the coconut farmer with the help of highly- aid ACCRA lawyers, the moves served not to create a social revolution ut merely to bury the farmer in the abyss of reaction.

Cojuangco controlled SMC from 1983 until Marcos was deposed in 1986 [165].

PEPSI

The conservative Soriano interests had consistently and vehemently fought off entrants into the SMC board who could threaten the lucrative management contracts they enjoyed from the firm. Since SMC was a large firm and was in many major lines of business, it was easy for the Soriano interests to claim that an unwanted entrant represented the interests of a competing firm and use this as the reason for rejecting a board aspirant. This was the tactic adopted to keep John Gokongwei, a Filipino-Chinese businessman, from the SMC board? The Soriano family also used the same tactic when they fought off their relative Enrique Zobel. Cojuangco and the Soriano interests continued this practice and tightened their control by formally banning unwanted individuals from the SMC board. Cojuangco and the Soriano family agreed prevent "intra-corporate disputes brought about by persons and/or their nominees seeking control of the management."

The selective manner in which this prohibition was practiced proved that it was meant really to protect the management contract the Soriano family enjoyed rather than the interests of SMC. If one is to be consistent, Cojuangco should also have been banned from the SMC board since he was the main person behind Pepsi Cola, one of the biggest competitors of Coca Cola which SMC produced locally. But since Cojuangco initially did not appear to be a threat to the Soriano family, Cojuangco was permitted to enter the SMC board, notwithstanding the conflict-of-interest issue.

As in the case of most of the companies Cojuangco set up, the corporations connected with Pepsi were organized using money from the coconut levy. Ernesto

O. Escaler, a close family friend of Cajuangco, served as Danding's trustee in these firms [166].

Cojuangco and Escaler organized three multi-million corporations Within a span of two weeks in ear y 1985. The incredible speed in organizing and registering these corporations was again made possible through "milking the coconut levy [167]. The three Cojuangco Pepsi companies were the folowing:

* **ECI Challenge Corp.** was the holding company for all of Cojuangco's Pepsi Cola operations. The company was nominally owned by Ernesto O. Escaler, who owned 99% of the firm as a "trustee" 168. Other stockholders were Ernest Escaler, Augusto Barcelon, Georginna Susan, and Franklin Drilon who each held a share [169]. Drilon was one of the ACCRA lawyers who helped Cojuangco in his takeover of SMC. The firm bought Pepsi Cola Bottling Co. of the Philippines in 1985.

* **Pepsi Cola Bottling Group (PCBG)**, the bottling arm of Pepsi, had 13 plants and assets conservatively estimated at $80.6 million [170]. The major subscriber of PCBG stock was ECI Challenge which owned $10.743 million of $10.748 million of the paid-up capital.

These two companies were organized within two days of each other. ECI was organized on 7 March 1985. The $1.3 million fully-subscribed and paid-up capital was paid through funds from the coconut levy drawn on a check from the UCPB. The PCBG was organized the following day, 8 March, with the $10.748 million paid-up capital again using coconut levy funds drawn from a UCPB check [171]. The funds from UCPB, amounting to a total of $13.7 million, were released on the very day that these companies were registered with the SEC [172].

* **Pepsi Cola Distributors (PCD),** the distributing arm, was the third company in the group. It was organized on 15 March 1985, a mere week after its parent companies, ECI and PCBG were organized. The major stockholder of PDC was PCBG, which held $1.611 million of the firm's $1.612 million paid-up capital [173]. PCD had an authorized stock of $6.4 million at the time of its organization [174]. The PCD had an infusion of at least $4 million in levy funds in 1986.

SUGAR AND FLOUR

After establishing a presence in the local soft drinks industry through SMC and Pepsi, Cojuangco attempted to duplicate his monopoly on coconuts in the sugar industry. The move was a shrewd one since Cojuangco already controlled a big share of the domestic demand for sugar. SMC's products, which include an assortment of soft drinks, fruit juices, ice cream, already accounted for 30% of local industrial demand [17].

Danding thus twice attempted to control the marketing of sugar in 1985. He offered to fund the Philippine Sugar Marketing Corp., the organization being organized to replace the National Sugar Trading Corp. (see section on Benedicto). Cojuangco dangled $13.5 million to the cash-strapped sugar planters and millers organizing the new marketing group. In exchange, Cojaungco wanted 50% ownership and control of the marketing firm. Furthermore, he demanded a monopoly on sales to domestic and export markets [176]. These conditions, together with the strong presence Cojuangco already exerted on local industrial sugar demand, would have seriously affected local sugar consumption patterns [177]. Cojuangco would most probably have ultimately succeeded in monopohzing the marketing of sugar had Marcos not been deposed the following year.

Around the same time Cojuangco was foraying into sugar, he was also scheming to grab control of the $160 million flour industry.

Danding tried to dislodge the millers from their monopoly of wheat importation through a presidential decree [178]. Marcos opted the less controversial but equally effective method of splitting the monopoly of imports between the wheat millers who traditionally controlled the trade and the association of local bakers who wanted a piece of the cake. Importation privileges were therefore split between the Philippine Association of Flour millers (Pafmil), the organization of millers, and the Federation of Philippine Bakers Association.

Cojuangco then invested $1.3 million in Philbake Inc., the marketing and importing arm of the Bakers Association [179]. He owned 29,992 shares and provided half of the firm's capital. Philbake was immediately able to import wheat worth $2.7 million. The wheat, which came in two shipments of 12,500 and 6,000 metric tons, was obtained through a commodity loan of the Commercial Credit Corp. of America [180]. Cojuangco without doubt would have created another monopoly in the wheat and flour industry had political events not overtaken him. By mid-1985, he had already organized 6 wheat importing groups using money from UCPB and the coconut levy [181]. By the time Marcos was deposed and only a few months after he started his activities in the wheat and flour industry, Cojuangco had already registered not less than 20 companies to import wheat [182]. The companies were valued at $300,000 million to $1.5 million. Among the bigger of these companies were

* Oriental Winds - incorporators: Francisco Leonor, Mane Lascano, Virgilio Lascano, Gerardo Bongco, Gabriel Villareal
* Northern Negros Industries - incorporators: Henry Salgado, Danilo Gamboa, Aurelio Lacson, Rafael Abello, Eduardo Villarama
* Aggregate Trading — incorporators: Rodolfo Tmsay, Far Alba, Antonio Corral, Norman Campos, Rizalino Mendoza
* Produce Market Dev. - incorporators: Gabriel Valdes, Raymond Moreno, Eusebio Tanco, Salvador Hocson, Dakila Castro
* Commerce Innovators & Developers - incorporators: Alejo Arrellano, Reynaldo Moriclla, Elmer Gorospe, Adgardo Ayaquil, Rolando Jao
* Coastline Tradin Corp. - incorporators: Ramon Esguerra, Vicente Gutierrez, Ramon Cordova Jr., Martin Diaz Jr., Jaime Carmat
* Foodcraft Trading Inc. - incorporators: Rafael Guiriba, Renato de Leon, Antonio Jesus Moya, Celso de la Cruz, Rogelio de Guzman
* Bahaghari Dev. Corp.
* Bulalakaw Enterprises Inc.
* Gintong Uhay International Trading
* Riverside Commodities Trading Inc.
* Mainland Commodities Corp.

LAND AND OTHER AGRI-BUSINESSES

Cojuangco also exerted a strong presence in the sugar industry through the haciendas he owned. Of the estimated 35,530 sugar cane farmers in country, 23,000 or 65% owned less than 5 hectares each. Cojuangco belonged to the select group of 530, representing less than 1.5% of all sugar land owners, who each owned 100 or more hectares [183]. Cojuangco was probably the biggest owner of sugar cane plantations in this select group [184].

Taking advantage of the slump in the sugar industry and the increasing bankruptcies amongst sugar planters in the 1980's, Cojuangco went on a buying spree of sugar plantations and other agricultural lands. He even went as far as offering to buy any hacienda between La Carlota and Bacolod, key cities in the island of Negros [185]. The offer was not to help the bankrupt plantation owners but to amass as much land as possible. Revealing of Cojuangco's tactics were his moves when sugar planters in southern Negros, facing a slump in the international market for sugar, shifted to planting corn. Cojuangco was allowed to import huge quantities of corn, consequently driving the prices down in 1984-85. This allowed Cojuangco's SMC, the biggest consumer of high protein hybrid corn, to furnish feeds for its livestock farms inexpensively [186]. The move also had the effect of further depressing prices of the farms lands Cojuangco wanted to buy.

Amon the plantations, other lands, agri-businesses Cojuangco owned were the following [187]:

* 700 hectare Hacienda Bonifacia, Bago City
* Hacienda Nieva in Himalayan, Negros Occidental
* 4 haciendas totalling 2,400 hectares in La Carlota City. One of these, Hacienda Fe, was estimated to be worth P15 million in 1982 [188].
* 4 haciendas totalling 1,085 hectares in Pontevedra town
* 4 farms in La Castellana town, totalling 2,570 hectares
* 300 hectare property in Mansilingan, Bacolod City
* Inampulogan Island, Guimaras, Panay
* 18,245,841 square meters, covered by 27 land titles. under the name of Eduardo Cojuangco & Sons Agricultural Enterprises [189].
* the Palale Fish Pond, covering several hundred hectares in Sta. Margarita, Samar, estimated at $500,000 in 1986.
* cacao and coconut plantation in Guihing, Davao del Sur run by Cocoa Investors Inc.
* two plantations in Malita, Davao del Sur, where San Miguel Farms grows coconuts, and United Cocoa Planters produced cacao
* prawn farm in Malita run by All
* cocoa, coconut, and palm oil plantations in Agusan del Norte and Davao
* other agri-husiness interests include fish and prawn farms, as well as coconut, sugar, and cocoa plantations in Pampanga, Tarlac, Bataan, Negros Occidental, Davao provinces, Bohol, Palawan. and Agusan. Some of these interests are the name of Northeastern Agro-Industrial Development Co ., a Cojuangco holding company organized on 22 Febnrary 1983. Incorporators were Rodolfo Tinsay, Rafae Abello, Francisco Leonor, Marte Lascano, Victor Gross.
* Aquacultural Investors, another agri—business firm. was 0 nized on 20 March 1983. Incorporators were Marcos Cojuangco, Margarita Barrera, mon Ang, Carmen Cojuangco, Miguel Barrera, Prudencio Teodoro
* Danding and his wife Gretchen own at least 22 residential lots in Metro-Manila, Tarlac, La Union, while their son, Enrique, owns land In Quezon City.

Some of these acquisition have been controversial. One instance is that of lands in Prosperidad, Agusan del Sur where 5,210.9642 hectares of public domain was granted to Cojuangco in 1983 through the Prosperidad Agricultural Corp. PD 1768 ha declared 7,601.671 hectares of land in Prosperidad as agro-forestry reservation on 12 June 1981. Cojuangco appropriated 69% of this reserve [190].

Another source of controversy was the case of two haciendas in Ilagan, Isabela covering a total of 13,085 hectares, Hacienda Santa Isabel (11,000 hectares) and Hacienda San Antonio (2,085 hectares) were acquired by the Spanish firm of *Compania General de Tabacos de Filipinas* (Tabacalera) through a royal grant 1882. Different generations of tenants and theirs had been been working in these haciendas and paying taxes on these properties for many decades under extremely oppressive working conditions:

Each farmer is required to produce a minimum of 250 kilos of tobacco per hectare before he is allowed to plant side crops like corn, rice or peanuts. Tabacalera is the sole buyer of tobacco produced, and has the sole right to grade it. The farmers complain that most of their produce is given the lowest C grade, worth only $0.82 per kilo. They say 2,000 cigarettes can be made from each kilo.
... [A sharecropping arrangement prevails where] the landlord gets only 30% of the crop, but which sees the tenant shouldering all production costs. But in many cases, tenants surrender as much as 50% of their produce to compensate for the money borrowed from their landlords at interest mm of 30-50% on loans repayable within six months. In some cases, if repayments are late, the interest during the succeeding harvest is doubled.
The latest government figures on income distribution are for1975, when Isabela peasants had an average annual family income of only [675]... [191]

The only thing that mitigated these despotic conditions was Tabacalera's promise that the lands would be turned over to them at the centenary celebration of the land grant (1982). But the 30,000 tillers who had been waiting for this occasion were surprised to learn that the lands were suddenly transferred two years before the centenary to firm named ANCA between April and May 1980 [192].

There were strong indications that the Marcos government had intervened on behalf of ANCA. The company was owned and named after Antonio Carag, the associate Cojuangco used in Bugsuk island [193]. It was even reported that Carag was merely "acting on behalf" of Cojuangco [194]. Faustino Dy, the provincial governor and a faithful Marcos follower, said Marcos gave permission for the transaction [195]. The project director for the transfer was Tomas Diaz, one of Marcos' favored generals [196].

When the tenants pressed for their titles, ANCA responded by giving them two choices, both of which were difficult terms for the tenants who rightly believed that they were robbed of their rights to own land:

1. sell their land rights at P2000 per hectare then leave the place, or
2. receive half of land, title free of charge, et financial aid, on condition that they cooperate with ANCA agricultural plantation scheme [197].

The tenants were given the carrot-and-stick approach. Some leaders of the affected communities were treated to "merrymaking, massage, wine, women at the Manila Peninsula Hotel," while the local military camp was reinforced with soliders who staged "military operations" [198]. The community leaders were brought to Manila on 24 May and 30 May 1980 to meet Cojuangco. It was reported that Cojuangco favored the second alternative and that the farmers "were made to agree under duress" [199].

The tenants who were coerced into accepting the second proposal later complained that they "did so under duress and got less than half the true value of the property" [200]. In a letter to Marcos, the tenants complained:

We are also faced with the problem of harassment. Not only has the owner threatened to make us leave the hacienda and receive a payment of $250 per hecatre, but he has also insinuated the slitting of our necks if we do not give in to his demands [201].

The tenants summarized their plight in a November 1980 manifesto entitled *This is Our Plight, This is Our Struggle:*

We have lived and worked under difficult conditions set by Tabacalera, but we never imagined that one day we would actually be victims of land grabbing, land size reduction, demolition, ejection, and transfer from the place of our birth and our ancestors' graves. This is what the recent Tabacalera-Cojuangco transaction means for us [202].

The leaders of the communities from the two haciendas later voiced fears for their lives if they continued to oppose Coiuangco's de51gns.

Referring to the ANCA land transfer, the Ministry of Agrarian Reform claimed that the project was "a novel way of implementing land reform by private business without using government funds and without burden to the farmers" [203].

OTHER COJUANGCO ENTERESTS

Among the other interests of Cojuangco were in the areas of shipping, media, manufacturing, retail stores, lumber and woodworks.

One of the companies of Cojuangco in the shipping industry is Filsov Shipping Co., a joint venture with the Soviets. Filsov has assets of 3 million, 40% is owned by the Soviets, with Cojuangco owning most of the remaining 60%. The Rivilla family, the in-laws of the Cojuangcos, are also reported have interests in Filsov. There were reports that a Filsov ship was used in transporting gold and other valuables out of the country right after Marcos' overthrow (see Chapter 4). Cojuangco also had interests in First United Transport. He was also connected with Luzon Intercoast, a shipping company owned by Unicom, which shipped copra and coconut oil overseas.

Cojuangco also commanded a chain of radio stations in Visayas and Mindanao, an ideal political tool for shaping public opinion. At least two corporations were linked to these radio stations, Radio Audience Developers Integrated

Organization Inc. and Philippine Radio Corp., the latter owning 10 radio stations [204].

Another useful political tool was United Sari Sari & Livelihood Corp., started by Danding in 1984. The idea was to organize small neighborhood stores and provide them with financing, but to exercise marketing control. Cojuangco supplied the credit and the goods to these stores. They were required to sell only Cojuangco products [205]. The move was useful politically since it provided access to communities in different provincial areas.

Danding also ventured into the textile industry, organizing Diversified Holdings, a firm which bought textile mills [206].

Apart from the livestock business of SMC, Cojuangco also entered the meat mdustry, organizing Beef & Associated Corporate Business on September l984. Incoporators were Narciso Pineda, Macario Brillantes, Veronica Carino, Robert Eduardo, and Gabriel Villareal.

Another Cojuangco corporation was Cojuangco Resources Corp., organized on August1984, with the following relatives and close associates serving as incorporators: Cojuangco Jr., Soledad Cojuangco, Danilo Ursua, Amado Mamuric, Jose Concepcion, and Marcos COJuangco.

A list of some of the other firms where Cojuangco had interests [207]:

Agro-Investment & Trading
Apo-Resources & Dev. Corp.
Amalgamated Systems & Business Equipment
Amalgamated Travel Center
Balete Ranch inc.
Commercial Motors Corp.
Cristensen Plantation Inc.
Dutch Boy Philippines
E.M. Cojuangco & Sons Agriculture Enterprises
Eastern Pacific Drydock Corp.
EC Development & Management Corp.
ECJ & Sons Agricultural Enterprises
Filsov Shipping Inc.
Fiscal Managers Inc.
G&E Tradin Co.
G.D. Realty Investor
Golden Times Trading
Gooree Stud Farm (Mudgee, Australia)
Indo Phils Oil Mills
Integrated Agro-Industrial Management
J&E Realty Corp.
JMC Development Corp.
JMC Mining Exploration Corp.
Lucena Oil Factory Inc.
Maximum Trading Co.
Metroplex Commodities
Northern Cement Corp.

Odel Marketing Enterprises
Pamplona Redwood Veneer Co.
Panique Knitting Industries
Panique Sugar Corp.
Paniqui Producers Marketing
PCY Oil Manufacturing Corp.
R&E Agricultural
Sierra Madre Wood Industrial Corp.
Southern Islands Textile Mills
Universal Motors Corp.
Veteran Woodworks

It is necessary to emphasize that these companies are not the ordinary Mom and Dad stores found at the neighborhood corner but multi-million ventures, most of which were created from the money of the coconut levy. For example, Cojuangco's Dutch Boy Philippines, was estimated to have assets of $20 million in 1990. UCPB Realty, a realty firm funded by the levy, had a 33% in the firm, while Cojuangco Traders Holdings owned 37%.

Villareal, the ever-faithful defender of Danding, said that Cojuangco's wealth gained through "hard work" and "honest dealings" [208].

Endnotes

1. Hilarion Henares, "From Doha Ysidra Came the Cojuangco Fortune," *Philippine Daily Inquirer*, 1 December 1987.
2. Sandra Burton, *Impossible Dream*, (New York: Warner Books, 1989), p. 54.
3. Hilarion Henares. "Dona Ysidra," *Philippine Daily Inquirer*, 1 December 1987.
4. Sandra Burton. *Impossible Dream*, (New York: Warner Books, 1989), p. 54.
5. Teodoro Agoncillo, *Malolos: The Crisis of the Republic*, (Quezon City. University of the Philippines, 1960), p. 477-8.
6. Orlino Ochosa, The Tinio Brigade: *Anti-American Resistance in the Ilocos Provinces, 1899-1901,* (Quezon City: New Day Publishers, 1989).
7. Teodoro Agoncillo, *Malolos: The Crisis of the Republic,* (Quezon City: University of the Philippines, 1960), p. 477-8.
8. Alfredo Saulo, *"Pride of Santa Rosa: Eulalio Saulo y Gutierrez,"* *Philippines Free Press*, 1 July 1972.
9. The circumstances behind Luna's murder and probable involvement of Aguinaldo is discussed in Vivencio R. Jose, The Rise and Fall of Antonio Luna, (Metro-Manila: Solar Publishing Corp., 1972).
10. Teodoro Agoncillo, *Malolos: The Crisis of the Republic,* (Quezon City: University of the Philippines, 1960), p. 537.
11. Hilarion Henares, "Doha Ysidra," *Philippine Daily Inquirer*, 1 December 1987.
12. Hilarion Henares, "Doha Ysidra," *Philippine Daily Inquirer*, 1 December 1987.
13. Hilarion Henares, "Dor'ra Ysidra," *Philippine Daily Inquirer*, 1 December 1987.
14. Sandra Burton, *Impossible Dream*, (New York: Warner Books, 1989), p. 54.
15. Hilarion Henares, "Doha Ysidra,*" Philippine Daily Inquirer*, 1 December 1987.
16. Hilarion Henares, "Doha Ysidra," *Philippine Daily Inquirer*, 1 December 1987 .
17. This then raises the question as to what happened to the child she bore which some say was General Luna's
18. Yuchengco, together with Geronimo Velasco, worked with Harry Stonehill, the American millionaire who corrupted all major post-war Filipino politicians. It is beyond the scope of this book to render an account of the activities of the so-called "Stonehill Gang," the term referring to individuals who managed Stonehill's vast properties. Most of the

members of this group later became Marcos cronies, e.g., Velasco. Among Yuchengco's interests are a large commercial bank, a major investment house, and a string of insurance companies.

19. *Far Easrern Economic Review*, 6 October 1988.
20. United States District Court, District of Columbia, SEC vs. PLDT, Civil Action No. 77-0067, 12 January 19T7, paragraph 12
21. "SEC Charges GTE Made Payments in Philippines," *New York Times*, 13 January 1977.
22. "GTE Accused of Giving Big Loans for Pact," *Los Angeles Times*, 13 January 1977.
23. "GTE Accused of Giving Big Loans for Pact," *Los Angeles Times*, 13 January 1977.
24. "New Details on GTE Philippine Payments Disclosed in SEC Suit Against 3 Concerns," *Wall Street Journal*, 13 January 1977.
25. "GTE Accused of Giving Big Loans for Pact," *Los Angeles Times*, 13 January 1977.
26. "New Details on GTE Philippine Payments Disclosed in SEC Suit Against 3 Concerns," *Wall Street Journal*, 13 January 1977.
27. "GTE Accused of Giving Big Loans for Pact," *Los Angeles Times*, 13 January 1977.
28. "New Details on GTE Philippine Payments Disclosed in SEC Suit Against 3 Concerns," *Wall Street Journal*, 13 January 1977
29. "New Details on GTE Phiilppine Payments Disclosed in SEC Suit Against 3 Concerns," *Wall Street Journal*, 13 January 1977.
30. "GTE Accused of Giving Big Loans for Pact," *Los Angeles Times,* 13 January 1977.
31. "New Details on GTE Philippine Payments Disclosed in SEC Suit Against 3 Concerns," *Wall Street Journal*, 13 January 1977. Also in "GTE Accused of Giving Big Loans for Pact," *Los Angeles Times*, 13 January 1977.
32. "New Details on GTE Philippine Payments Disclosed in SEC Suit Against 3 Concerns," *Wall Street Journal*, 13 January 1977.
33. "New Details on GTE Philippine Payments Disclosed in SEC Suit Against 3 Concerns," *Wall Street Journal,* 13 January 1977.
34. *Far Eastern Economic Review*, 9 April 1982.
35. *Far Eastern Economic Review*, 6 October 1988.
36. These were the members as of 1985. Africa took over the presidency when Ramon Cojuangco died. Africa was later replaced by Cojuangco's son, Antonio.
37. *Philippine Daily Inquirer*, 16 June 1986. Tanseco, Yulo, and Zalamea are discussed in other parts of this book.
38. *Far Eastern Economic Review*, 6 October 1988.
39. Another telecommunications corporation where Marcos interests was the POTC. Please see preceeding section on Enrile.
40. Ellen Tordesillas, "PLDT Kept $85 Million in US Bank," *Malaya*, 19 July 1986.
41. *Far Eastern Economic Review*, 6 October 1988.
42. *Far Eastern Economic Review*, 6 October 1988.
43. *Philippine Daily Inquirer*, 16 June 1986.
44. *Far Eastern Economic Review*, 12 December 1980.
45. *Far Eastern Economic Review*, 6 October 1988.
46. *Bulletin Today,* June 30, 1980.
47. Geselle Militante, "PLDT in Technical Dollar Salting," *Business Day*, 22 April 1986.
48. Please see Chapter V for a discussion of the PCGG.
49. Geselle Militante, "PLDT in Technical Dollar Salting," *Business Day*, 22 April 1986.
50. Geselle Militante, "PLDT in Technical Dollar Salting," *Business Day*, 22 April 1986.
51. Ellen Tordwillas, "PLDT Kept $85 Million in US Bank," *Malaya,* 19 July 1986.
52. Ellen Tordesillas, "PLDT Kept $85 Million in US Bank," *Malaya,* 19 July 1986.
53. Geselle Militante, "PLDT in Technical Dollar Salting," *Business Day*, 22 April 1986.
54. Ellen Tordesillas, "PLDT Kept $85 Million in US Bank," *Malaya*, 19 July 1986.
55. Far Eastern *Economic Review*, 6 October 1988.
56. Far Eastern *Economic Review*, 6 October 1988.
57. Winnie Velasquez, "PLDT Loan Terms Found Irregular," *Malaya*, 3 July 1986.

58. *Business Day*, 12 March 1986.
59. Geselle Militante, "Yuchengco Group Sold PLDT Shares a Day Before Sequestration," *Business Day,* 16 April 1986.
60. *Far Eastern Economic Review*, 6 October 1988.
61. *Los Angeles Times*, 30 December 1990.
62. Enrile was the only other civilian in this group. He was then Minister of Defense.
63.*Los Angeles Times*, 30 December 1990.
64. *Far Eastern Economic Review*, 8 February 1990.
65. *Wall Street Journal*, 2 April 1990
66. Hilarion Henares, 'Danding's Pearl of the Orient Seas," *Philippine Daily Inquirer*, 5 July 1986.
67. *Far Eastern Economic Review*, 8 February 1990.
68. *Christian Science Monitor*, 5 December 1983; *Los Angeles Times*, 30 December 1990.
69. *Christian Science Monitor*, 5 December 1983.
70. *Wall Street Journal*, 2 April 1990
71. *Wall Street Journal,* 2 April 1990
72. Atty. Nestor Zapata, Jun Gutierrez, Guillermo Chua, "Arriba Letran," *Mr. & Ms,* 18-24 July 1986
73. *People's Journal*, 6 July 1980.
74. *People's Journal,* 6 July 1980.
75. *Philippine Daily Inquirer,* 15 July 1986; *Daily Express*, 15 July 1986; *The Tribune,* 15 July 1986.
76. Case docketed as No. 3—85—796—FW.
77. *Business Day*, 30 April 1986.
78. *Manila Bulletin*, 30 April 1986.
79. *Bulletin Today*, 10 April 1980.
80. *Newsweek*, 17 March 1986.
81. *New York Times,* 16 July 1987.
82. *New York Times*, 16 July 1987.
83. Rigoberto Tiglao, "Calling Up Old Debts," *Far Eastern Economic Review*, 8 February 1990.
84. Rigoberto Tiglao, "Calling Up Old Debts," *Far Eastern Economic Review*, 8 February 1990.
85. *Far Eastern Economic Review*, 8 February 1990.
86. *Wall Street Journal*, 2 April 1990.
87. Rigoberto Tiglao, "Calling Up Old Debts," *Far Eastem Economic Review*, 8 February 1990.
88. Initially named First United Coconut Bank, it was changed to its present name after a month.
89. *Far Eastem Economic Review*, 8 January 1982
90. *Manila Bulletin*, 26 June 1986.
91. Jun Velasco, "Cocofed-Cojuangco Contract Questioned," *Bulletin Today*, 26 June 1986
92. "Broad Power Given To Cojuangco," *Manila Times*, 27 June 1986; *Manila Bulletin*, 26 June 1986.
93. *Manila Bulletin*, 26 June 1986.
94. *Manila Bulletin*, 26 June 1986.
95. *Far Eastern Economic Review,* 7 June 1984.
96. *Philippine Daily Inquirer*, 23 May 1986; *Manila Bulletin*, 24 May 1986.
97. *Manila Bulletin*, 22 June 1986.
98. "Ouster of Cocofed Leaders Sought," *Manila Times,* 23 June 1986; *Manila Bulletin*, 22 June 1986.
99. *Bulletin Today*, 1 March 1981
100. MB Resolution No. 243, 6 February 1981.
101. *Bulletin Today*, 1 March 1981.
102. *Far Eastem Economic Review*, 14 September 1979

103. The law clearly prohibits the use of public funds to benefit private persons.

104. *Far Eastem Economic Review*, 6 June 1980

105. It was pointed out that despite receiving on interest-free deposits "the UCPB could not match the growth of other banks without such advantages." Rigoberto Tiglao, "Calling Up Old Debts," *Far Eastem Economic Review*, 8 February 1990.

106. *Philippine Financial Institutions*, p. 27.

107. The divergence in the dollar amount is due to the changes of the exchange rate over the years.

108. *Far Eastern Economic Review*, 7 June 1984.

109. *Far Eastern Economic Review*, 8 February 1990.

110. David, *Barriers*, p. 179.

111. *Far Eastern Economic Review*, 8 January 1982

112. *Manila Times*, 73 April 1986.

113. *Manila Times,* 23 April 1986.

114. *Manila Times,* 23 April 1986.

115. Article XIV, Section 11.

116. *Manila Bulletin*, 6 April 1986; *Business Day*, 16 April 1986.

117. *Manila Times*, 3 April 1986.

118. Doherty, p37.

119. *Manila Times,* 23 April 1986.

120. *Manila Bulletin,* 4 May 1986.

121. *Manila Bulletin,* 4 May 1986.

122. *Manila Times*, 23 April 1986.

123. *Manila Times,* 23 April 1986.

124. *Manila Times,* 23 April 1986.

125. "Cojuangco [and Swap Deal Voided," *Philippine Daily Inquirer*, 27 June 1986. Another report counts only 160 instead of 300 hectares.

126. *Manila Times*, 23 April 1986.

127. But at least half of the $170 million was actually deposited with the UCPB rather than administered by the NIDC.

128. *Far Eastern Economic Review*, 8 February 1990.

129. Quoted in The Tribune, 10 June 1986. Apparently English is not one of the strong points of this Cojuangco spokesman.

130. *Manila Times*, 9 June 1986; *Business Day,* 10 June 1986.

131. *Philippine Daily Inquirer*, 7 June 1986; *Business Day,* 10 June 1986; *Manila Chronicle*, 14 June 1 ; *Malaya*, 10 June 1986.

132. *Malaya*, 2 May 1986.

133. *Malaya,* 2 May 1986; *Manila Bulletin*, 2 April 1986.

134. *Manila Chronicle*, 14 June 1986.

135. *Business Day,* 10 June 1986.

136. *Business Day*, 9 June 1986; *Manila Chronicle,* 14 June 1986.

137. Guy Sacerdoti, "Cracks in the Coconut Shell," *Far Eastem Economic Review*, 8 January 1982

138. *Malaya*, 2 May 1986.

139. *Philippine Daily Inquirer*, 7 June 1986

140. *Philippine Daily Inquirer*, 7 June 1986; *Business Day*, 9 June 1986; *Manila Times,* 9 June 1986.

141. *Manila Bulletin*, 16 April 1986.

142. *Manila Bulletin*, 6 April 1986; *Business Day*, 16 April 1986; *Manila Times*, 23 April 1986.

143. *The Tribune*, 10 June 1986.

144. Ninoy Aquino remarked in 1980 that Mitra had forfeited all claims to national leadership
because of his association with Cojuangco.

145. Hilarion Henares, 'Danding's Pearl," *Philippine Daily Inquirer*, 5 July 1986.

146. *The Manila Times,* 2 April 1986.
147. *Manila Bulletin,* 4 May 1986.
148. Hilarion Henares, 'Danding's Pearl," *Philippine Daily Inquirer*, 5 July 1986.
149. Hilarion Henares, "Danding's Pearl," *Philippine Daily Inquirer*, 5 July 1986.
150. Hilarion Henares, "Danding's Pearl," *Philippine Daily Inquirer*, 5 July 1986.
151. Hilarion Henares, "Danding's Pearl," *Philippine Daily Inquirer*, 5 July 1986.
152. *Far Eastern Economic Review*, 5 September 1985.
153. *Asiaweek*, 25 May 1986. Despite the cuts, SMC maintained its retail price for beer. *Business Day*, 21 March 1986.
154. *Far Eastern Economic Review*, 19 May 1983.
155. *Far Eastern Economic Review*, 19 May 1983.
156. *Far Eastern Economic Review*, 15 May 1986.
157. Noel de Luna, "The Reality of the Cojuangco Empire," *Business Day*, 18 April 1986.
158. *Asiaweek*, 25 May 1986.
159. *Far Eastern Economic Review*, 7 June 1984.
160. *Far Eastern Economic Review*, 7 June 1984.
161. *Far Eastern Economic Review*, 7 June 1984.
162. "Minus the Sweeteners," *Ibon,* 31 March 1984.
163. *Far Eastern Economic Review*, 5 January 1984.
164. *Bulletin Today,* 16 June 1986.
165. Serious questions of propriety and law have been raised by the way the Soriano family tried to recover its shares in the SMC after Marcos' downfall. A discussion of this is unfortunately beyond the scope of the present book.
166. *Manila Bulletin,* 1 October 1986.
167. *Daily Express*, 26 September 1986.
168. *Daily Express*, 26 September 1986.
169. *Daily Express*, 26 September 1986.
170. *Manila Bulletin*, 1 October 1986.
171. *Business Day*, 26 September 1986.
172. *Manila Bulletin*, 1 October 1986; Business Day, 10 October 1986.
173. *Manila Bulletin*, 1 October 1986.
174. *Daily Express*, 26 September 1986.
175. *Far Eastern Economic Review,* 19 December 1985.
176. *Far Eastern Economic Review*, 19 December 1985.
177. *Far Eastern Economic Review*, 19 December 1985.
178. *Far Eastern Economic Review*, 19 December 1985.
179. *Philippine Daily Inquirer*, 24 April 1986; *Malaya*, 2 May 1986.
180. *Philippine Daily Inquirer*, 24 April 1986; *Malaya*, 2 May 1986.
181. *Far Eastern Economic Review*, 19 December 1985.
182. Noel de Luna, The Reality of the Cojuangco Empire," *Business Day*, 18 April 1986.
183. *Business Day*, 15 April 1986.
184. *Business Day*, 15 April 1986.
185. *We Forum,* 4-6 August 1982.
186. *Far Eastern Economic Review*, 31 October 1985.
187. *Business Day*, 9 June 1986.
188. *We Forum*, 4—6 August 1982.
189. *Manila Times*, 10 June 1986.
190. *Business Day*, 16 April 1986.
191. Sheilah Ocampo, "Spur for a peasant's revolt," *Far Eastem Economic Review*, 21 November 1980
192. *Malaya*, 8 June 1986.
193. *Times Journal,* 13 November 1980; *We Forum*, 4—6 August 1982.
194. Sheilah Ocampo, "Spur for a peasant's revolt," *Far Eastern Economic Review*, 21 November 1980.
195.*Ibon,* 15 January 1981.

196._Ibon_, 15 January 1981.
197._Ibon,_ 15 January 1981.
198._Ibon_, 15 January 1981.
199. Sheilah Ocampo, "Spur for a peasant's revolt," _Far Eastern Economic Review_, 21 November 1980
200. Sheilah Ocampo, "Spur for a peasant's revolt," _Far Eastem Economic Review_, 21 November 1980
201. Quoted in Sheilah Ocampo, "Spur for a peasant's revolt," _Far Eastern Economic Review_, 21 November 1980.
202. Quoted in _Ibon,_ 15 January 1981.
203. _Bulletin Today_, 17 November 1980.
204. _Manila Bulletin_, 19 October 1986.
205. Noel de Luna, "The Reality of the Cojuangco Empire," _Business Day_, 18 April 1986.
206. Noel de Luna, "The Reality of the Cojuangco Empire," _Business Day_, 18 April 1986.
207. _Far Easlern Economic Review_, 8 February 1990; Ellen Tordcsillas, "Sandigan will try Marcos," _Malaya,_ 9 May 1986. List is also drawn directly from SEC records.
208. _Philippine Daily Inquirer_, 10 June 1986. Did Villareal use the word "dealings" when he really meant "deals"?

ELIZALDE

Manuel Elizalde Jr. and Fred Elizalde, grandchildren of the Spaniard Don Jose Joaquin M. Elizalde, are members of the old elite who have maintained and entrenched their economic power through the Marcos regime. The Elizalde brothers are engaged in diverse activities covering the fields of mining, abaca farming, sugar centrals, tin plate manufacturing, paints, foods, distillery, shipping, life-insurance, real estate, rural banking, agri-business, the exploitation sugar workers, and the oppression of cultural minorities.

Fred J. Elizalde was a trusted ally of Marcos. He was one of those handpicked by Marcos to run in the Metro-Manila KBL slate during the bogus legislative elections of 1978. When Marcos needed a closer and a more efficient coordination between the state and private business, the two largest business groups, the Phil. Chamber of Industries and the Chamber of Commerce of the Phil, were merged at Marcos' order, forming the Philippine Chamber of Commerce & Industry (PCCI). Showing the importance that he attached to this new organization, Marcos dubbed it as the "Baranggay of Business," implying that it would form the basic social matrix of businesses. With Fred Elizalde as president, Marcos had hoped that there would be closer cooperation between the private sector and the government. In his capacity as president of the PCCI, Fred Elizalde always took positions contrary to the interests of the general populace, like vehemently opposing all demands for wage increases during tripartite conferences between labor, capital, and the state, in spite of skyrocketing prices of basic commodities.

SUGAR

Fred Elizalde's adamant opposition to any kind of wage increase during his stint as PCCI president was fairly consistent with how workers were treated at Central Azucarrera de la Carlota. La Carlota, the fifth largest sugar mill in the country, is owned by Fred Elizalde.

After several months of reasoning, pleading, and waiting for Elizalde to implement the l3-month bonus required by law, workers at the La Carlota sugar mill called a strike on January 1982. They wanted Elizalde to implement PD 851 which provided that workers be given an annual bonus equal to a month's salary. The workers merely asked for the law be implemented to supplement their meager income. Wages of the workers in La Carlota at this time were at starvation levels: $2-3 dollars a day for mill workers and $l-2 for the field hands.

Apart from PD 851 to back up their demands, the workers were also armed with a 30 November 1981 agreement between the Central Azucarrera de la Carlota and the National Federation of Sugar Workers (NFSW), the union representing the workers at the mill. The agreement, signed by both parties, stipulated that the 13-month bonus would be paid. Moreover, while La Carlota had engaged in legal maneuvers to avoid payment, the workers had won their cases in court and their demands had also been sustained by the Supreme Court on 15 December 1981.

But Elizalde adamantly refused to pay. When the workers demanded implementation, the management handed them a telegram from Blas Ople, Marcos' Minister of Labor, exempting Elizalde from paying the 13-month bonus. The Ministry of Labor order said that the 13—month pay did not apply to Central Azucarrera de La Carlota. The Ministry of Labor furthermore declared strike illegal. Though the work stoppage was orderly and the workers were disciplined, Carlota retaliated by terminating 215 of the striking workers in January 1982.

Elizalde had problems not only with his workers but also with other sugar planters. The National Federation of Sugarcane Planters claimed that he had malversed public funds amounting to more than $2.9 million in a suit filed before the Tanodbayan [1].

Marcos cronies had centralized the trading of sugar (see section on Benedicto), and Fred Elizalde, a director of the Nasutra, the government sugar trading arm, had made use of two of his sugar mills to store the sugar of other planters. The normal procedure for with drawing the sugar deposited in these warehouses was to present and surrender the quedans or warehouse receipts representing the sugar; this method, when followed properly, assures that the physical inventory of sugar would always tally with the quedans circulating. But the sugar planters who deposited their sugar with the two Elizalde mills, the Central Azucarrera de la Carlota and the Central Azucarrera del Pilar, charged that Elizalde withdrew sugar worth $2.92 million from his warehouses without the proper quedan receipts.

The discrepancy was discovered when an inventory was conducted after Marcos fled the country. The planters claimed that export quality sugar they had deosited between 1983 and 1985 could not be accounted for. Sugar worth 2 million or 202,492.61 piculs were no longer in the La Carlota warehouses, while $1.2 million or 121,842.52 piculs were missing from the del Pilar warehouses. Held culpable for the losses were Elizalde, Joaquin Teves, and Paul Belita, the latter two being the Elizalde's resident managers at La Carlota and del Pilar.

Notwithstanding his record, Fred Elizalde was named by Mrs. Aquino to important government positions dealing with the sugar industry. He was designated as Chairman of Sugar Industry Advisory Council and as officer-in-charge of Philsucom, the sugar trading arm of 1the government formerly headed by Benedicto. He also became the chairman of Philsuma (Philippine Sugar Marketing Corp) under the new government, but his record here has been controversial as well: one of his first moves was to use the ships of another Marcos crony, Benedicto, to transport sugar to overseas markets, a move which was roundly criticized [2].

STEEL

Fred's brother, Manuel Elizalde, was Marcos' cabinet minister in charge of Filipino ethnic groups which have been usually referred to as "cultural minorities." Manuel or Manda also owned large firms which benefitted from Marcos' help.

Manda's steel companies were favored with much assistance from the government in the form of funding and regulations which ensured it of lucrative markets.

Elizalde was allowed to organize his own integrated steel mill despite government promises that no integrated steel mill would be allowed to operate until the previously organized one, named IISMI, had become viable. Owners of the IISMI had been promised that, since the steel industry was still in a stage of infancy, no further mills would be allowed until a sufficiently developed market could assure profitability in the industry. But, since the owners of this mill were not identified with the Marcoses, Elizalde became a favored exception to the rule and was allowed to organize the Elizalde Rolling Mills (Elirol) in the 1970's. And, furthermore, since the owners of the initial steel mill had been accused of contributing to the political campaigns of Marcos' opponents, Elizalde was further allowed to import products in competition with ISMI in a move to put it out of business.

The Elizalde Steel Consolidated Industries Inc. (Eliscon), another company which Elizalde heads, is the exclusive producer of tin plates in the country. This monopoly enabled Elizalde to raise the prices of tin plates at will and browbeat the market with price increases. For example, Elizalde unilaterally raised the price of tin plates by 17% in March 1980 and threatened a further increase of 7.5% if the government did not allow tax-free importation of raw materials [3]. Yet with the advantageous position it already enjoyed, Eliscon also got financial assistance from the government on several occasions, like a $90 million loan from the $500 million Industrial Fund administered by the Central Bank.

Another Elizalde interest is the First Philippine Can Corporation, a multimillion peso corporation organized in May 1980 as a joint-venture with American Can Corp. [4]. The organization of this company has allowed Elizalde to use the tin he produces to manufacture cans, consequently profiting immensely from a vertically integrated industry.

The increasing prices of tin and tin cans have caused great hardship for the public. While other countries have fairly efficient distribution and marketing systems for food, many basic commodities in the Philippines have to be canned before they reach the consumer. An inadequate distribution system which depends on canning food rather than on fresh produce not only has nutritional consequences but it also has the inevitable effect of increasing prices because of the fluctuating prices of tin cans. The case of milk is most notable here. In contrast with other countries where fresh milk is readily available in the grocery, milk in the Philippines is distributed as canned evaporated milk, with the cost of the can representing a great part of the retail price. Thus, with the continuous increase in the price of tin, food processors merely passed on the costs to the consumers, and many poor families could no longer afford to purchase milk for their infants.

Other Elizalde companies forming linkages within the steel industry also got government help. Ramitex benefitted from military contracts. Elizco, a hand-tool company, received major financing from the government, but these debts were later assumed by other government firms (the National Steel Corp. and the National Development Corp) when this Elizalde firm began to lose money and had to be rescued by the government.

The case of Elitool Corp., another Elizalde enterprise, is indicative of how Elizalde received favors from Marcos.

Elitool manufactured armaments under license from Colt Industries and supplied part of the armament needs of the Philippine military. This provided a ready and captive market. Not content with this, Marcos also tried to procure overseas markets for this Elizalde company. When Colt refused Elizalde's request to be able to export firearms from tile Philippines, Marcos brought the matter up with the Pentagon. The Pentagon likewise turned it down. Marcos then retaliated by cancelling the contract to buy Colt armaments through Elitool but resumed buying when Elizalde became the licensee of another arms manufacturer.

Another Elitool controversy involved what was dubbed as the M16A1 Rifle Project [5]. Elitool entered into a contract with the Armed Forces of the Philippines (AFP) on 16 October 1978 to manufacture 150,000 M16A1 rifles and spare parts equivalent to 22,500 rifles. Elizalde later re nested to "borrow" 20,000 M16A1 rifles under the guise of exporting them to Thailand. Marcos approved Elizalde's proposal to borrow from AFP stocks on 11 April 1981. But the rifles were not exported to Thailand as originally requested but were sold back to the Philippine Constabulary-INP, the police arm of the AFP, for $7.3 million or $340 per rifle, a move which was sanctioned by Minister of Defense Enrile on 12 August 1983. The money was supposed to have been used by Elitool to manufacture an equivalent number of replacement rifles. An agreement between AFP and Elitool dated 12 September 1983 stipulated that the rifles would be replaced within two years. The PC-INP had fully paid Elitool the $7.3 million by 9 August 1984, but no replacement rifles were forthcoming. Elitool asked, and got, a year's extension on the deadline. But by the end of the new deadline, there still no rifles. By the end of Marcos' regime, Elizalde had not given back a single rifle.

Elizalde also had interests in real estate. He acquired 206 hectares of virgin forest land in Buyayao, Roxas, in Occidental Mindoro. This acquisition, done through a 1974 timber lease agreement with the government, was more than the limit of 144 hectares for forest lands per company set by law. Managed by Greenland Realty

Dev. Corp., the area was converted from a public domain to a private resort, complete with rest houses, a heliport, pelota courts, and concrete roads along the coast. The resort was built using funds borrowed from the PNB, with a balance of $300,000 still outstanding [6].

PANAMIN

Elizalde astounded the world on 7 June 1971 by announcing that a Stone Age tribe, hitherto without contact with other cultures, had been discovered inside the jungles of South Cotobato, 1,200 kilometers south of Manila. Elizalde called his discovery of the Tasaday, as the tribe was called, the "most important discovery in anthropology in this century." *National Geographic* devoted two issues to the topic and called Elizalde "a visionary idealist" who cared more about "the hard-pressed national minorities than about his family fortune." *Encyclopedia Britannica* included an article concerning the tribe, while John Nance, a journalist from the Associated Press, wrote an idyllic book entitled *The Gentle Tasaday.*

All of these aforementioned studies, however, were done under the strictly controlled guidance of Panamin (Presidential Assistance on National Minorities), headed by Elizalde himself. The Panamin was charged with ensuring "justice and protection" of Philippine cultural minorities and reported directly to the Office of the President [7].

While *Encyclopedia Britannica* published a short article and the *National Geographic* printed some colored photographs, *there was never any scholarly paper published on the Tasaday.* There was never any definitive corroboration from independent scientists concerning the veracity of Elizalde's claims. PD 1017 prohibited unauthorized persons from entering the Tasaday Reservation Area. And while Charles Lindbergh and actress Gina Lolobrigida were able to visit the place, independent anthropologists could not.

It was only after Marcos fell from power that independent researchers were able to enter the area. On March 1986, a month after the Marcos downfall, a Swiss journalist, Oswald Iten, entered the area and saw the members of this so-called Stone Age tribe wearing T-shirts and living in huts. He later concluded that the Tasaday had been previously rehearsed by Elizalde to look like cave dwellers. Anthropologists from the University of the Philippines raised questions regarding Elizalde's claim. Jerom Bailen, an anthropologist, decried the Elizalde claims as "elaborate hoax" in an international social science symposium. Another social scientist, Zeus Salazar, an ethnologist who holds a doctorate from the Sorbonne, concluded that the Tasaday were assembled from other backward tribes "to stage this drama of the prehistoric people" [8].

Whatever doubts there may be concerning the actual anthropological status of the Tasaday [9], what is certain is that the hype produced by his announcements concerning them had allowed Elizalde to transform the Panamin into a successful money-generating project.

Marcos, capitalizing on the "anthropological find of the century," bestowed the rank of cabinet minister upon Elizalde in 1975 and expanded the functions of the Panamin. At the same time, Elizalde carried on many other projects with different

Philippine cultural minorities and successfully raised funds from a variety of private and government sources. Let us review the record in some of these cases [10].

Government money intended for the use of minorities was misspent by Panamin on non-existent projects or directly lined Elizalde's pocket. A telling case is in a revelation made by the president of the Panamin Employees Ass. (Panamea), Franco Cortez. He revealed that a ranking executive of the Elizalde group of companies housed five Panamin employees in a Manila downtown hotel and ordered them to falsify records to cover some $1.6 cash advances made to Elizalde during the fourth quarter of 1983 and the first and second quarters of 1984. This was done as a desperate effort to cover some disbursements for Elizalde due to an impending audit by the COA. According to Cortez, the cash advances were made "in blatant violation of existing accounting and auditing procedures." Cortez testified that since "not a single centavo was spent for the cultural minorities, the only way to justify the disbursements was through forgery" [11].

When the Panamin was finally audited after the downfall of Marcos, at least $17 million of government money earmarked for cultural minorities was missmg.

While Elizalde made his last personal trip to the Tasadays in 1974, and Panamin ended its Tasaday expeditions in 1979, Elizalde was able to capitalize on. the popularity of the Tasadays for a long time and raised funds from private sources.

Elizalde organized a private foundation, the Panamin Foundation Inc, to act as the counterpart of the government agency. The foundation raised funds from a variety of sources, including international agencies and foreign governments. Since the Panamin Foundation was a private organization receiving contributions from non-governmental sources, its funds were not subject to audits by the COA.

But questions were also raised concerning the finances of this foundation. In one case, some $880,000 was paid in 1982 to a company for services which were never rendered. It contracted the Agro-Industrial Development Foundation of the Phil. (also known as Philaids) to initiate projects for minorities such as goat dispersal, rattan manufacturing, training an recruitment programs, but the whole agreement was replete with anomalies. The contract, made in December 1980 with a supplemental agreement signed on 16 January 1981, provided for the payment 0 $610,000 for feasibility studies, a huge figure considering that the amount was only for the preliminary studies. Moreover, it was discovered that more than $922,000 had been advanced to the officials of the firm even before the feasibility studies had been completed [12]. The money was doled out to favored officials under the pretext of "technical and confidential allowances." Cash advances had been meted out as early as 1979, but they remain unliquidated up to the present. Whatever vouchers were presented were forgeries. The following table lists the amounts disbursed:

Year	Amount in Pesos
1979	$1.01 million
1980	$119,000
1981	$738,000
1982	$89,000
Total	$1,956,000

Not a single centavo of this money was liquidated or accounted for. Colonel Jose Guerrero, vice-president and a director of the Panamin Foundation, cancelled his interview appointments with newspapers when he learned that they were going to question him about the foundation's finances. Guerrero is now an executlve of Elizalde & Co.

Panamin was also used by Elizalde to further his mining interests. Among the Elizalde companies engaged in mining are North Davao Mining, Samar Mining, Marcopper Mining. Allegations that Elizalde is using Panamin as a cover and a ruse for its mining interests surfaced as early as the first term of Marcos when Elizalde's operations were exposed by then Congressman Chiongbian. The modus operandi of Elizalde was to claim that certain cultural minorities were in need of Panamin assistance whenever a mining possibility was identified. Panamin then entered the area concerned, cordoned it off with goons, and mining operations were started. The inhabitants were moved from their original dwellings and herded into "reservations" from which they had limited mobility. There have also been reports that members of these communities have to render forced labor in the mines. This was how Elizalde ran his mining interests.

An example of this was Northern Davao Mining, a mining concern in Davao the Elizaldes shared with the Ayala family. Northern Davao Mining is a 250 hectare open-pit copper mine which processes $400,000 worth of copper ore daily. It also processes gold and silver by-products. Two hundred sixty-five families, eighty of which were occupying and tilling 350 hectares of flat land, had to be uprooted.

> For Northern Davao Mining, four dams are projected. One whole baranggay will be removed to create a dumping site for the waste from the mine. The corporation, represented by Panamin Foundation, offered to handle the relocation of Bananggay New Leyte residents. One of the Elizaldes is head of Panamin, whose avowed aim is assistance to the cultural communities. However, all of their forays into cultural communities include prospecting for minerals on the site. In Davao, this has undoubtedly paid off [13].

Lands of cultural minorities extending from the hinterlands of northern Philippines to the remotest areas in the south have been so usurped by Panamin. This is despite PD 410 (1975) which declared that lands occupied by cultural minorities were "inalienable and indisposable." These activities openly benefitted Elizalde and other Marcos cronies such as Disini and Floirendo (see these sections for a fuller account).

An example of the methods of land grabbing and terrorism is in how Panamin coerced and manipulated the Kalinga an Bontoc tribes in an effort to neutralize their opposition to the construction of the World Bank-financed Chico River Basin project. We quote an account of an incident which personally involved Elizalde:

> Panamin's method of dealing with the Kalinga and Bontoc was quite similar to its method of dealing with the cultural communities in Mindanao and in other areas of the country. Through bribery, deception and force, Secretary Elizalde, the head of Panamin, inveigled peace pact holders to sign letters and petitions endorsing Panamin as the exclusive authority to deal with their problems including the problem of Chico

IV [the proposed dam which was to ultimately flood their anceslral lands]. Signatories often signed blank sheets to be filled in later by Panamin staff. To the sheets were attached envelopes with money inside... Aside from these so-called resolutions of the people, baranggay oflicials were coerced into signing a letter to President Marcos unanimously and unqualifiedly endorsing the construction of the dam. 0f 68 who signed this letter 52 came from areas not affected by the dam.... Later the Kalingas told what happened. They were brought to Manila and kept at the home of Secretary Elizalde for five days. During that time they were subjected to threats, cajolery, promises and more threats. The issue was whether to sign blank sheets with their names already typed on them. To do so would violate the decision taken in Kalinga not to sign anything. They were told if they did not sign they could not return home [14].

The real record of Elizalde and Panamin with the Kalinga and Bontocs in the north, the Tinggian of Abra, and other minorities in Bukidnon, South Cotobato, Davao, Misamis Oriental has been a record of deceit, opportunism, and forms of high-handedness. A fairly accurate evaluation of Panamin is found in the following:

Panamin's avowed aims stated above are contradicted by its tactics. It has undermined traditional leadership patterns, set natives against natives, treated cultural communities as wards, exploited their traditional trust, herded them on to reservations to better control them as logging companies, construction projects and agri-business take over their traditional lands. In arming them for its own purposes, it has aggravated the peace and order situation in Mindanao. What is worse, even natives on the reservations will know no security. On most of the reservations there are known or at least suspected minerals. Once the government or private enterprise is ready to exploit these minerals, the natives now on the reservations will either be uprooted again or forced into a form of slave labor in the mine. The fact that the reservations are all on government land, and that, the government, in spite of a PD making native lands inalienable and indisposable, has been unwilling to release these lands to the natives, should give some indication of the extent to which the government will protect the cultural communities against future efforts to displace them. When the President states that Panamin has been solving the most pressing problem of the tribal groups which is land by restoring 810,000hectares to their rightful owners, he is being evasive to say the least. The 810,000 hectares are the government lands on which Panamin imprisons the people after evicting them from their ancestral lands desired by agri-business. The 372 centers referred to by the President are basically to manipulate the tribal groups and divide them [15].

Once the reservations were established, no outsiders were allowed in them. Even when the people in these reservations requested for churches or religious ministers none were permitted to come in.

Panamin also had a para-military function. Members of cultural minorities who came under the Panamin were armed and trained to suppress members of other cultural minorities who objected to Panamin influence. This is what happened in Bukidinon in 1975 after members of tribal communities rose up in arms when their lands were expropriated by Bukidnon Sugar Co. (Busco), a firm owned by Benedicto (see section). Datu Gawilan, one of the leaders of the revolt, was coopted and given amnesty, put in a reservation, and later armed and trained to fight against his fellow natives. The pattern was repeated in South Cotobato where members of the *T'boli* tribe were armed and set up as a unit of the Civilian Home Defense Force (CHDF), the civilian group which Marcos organized into a fighting force to counter rebellion in the countryside. Some of the directors of Panamin were retired military officers who worked with the hill tribes in Vietnam during the war. The training and arming of native inhabitants had the further function of helping in the over-all effort to contain guerilla warfare since the new recruits were familiar with the ways of the mountain and countryside.

> The main reason behind this seems to be the establishment of a para-military force with access to the mountains and forests to facilitate the work of military in protecting agri-business and mining interests against armed dissidents. These forces are also used against other natives to prevent them from giving expression to their legitimate grievances [16].

Elizalde tried to depict himself as a Philanthrophist, a ground-breaking anthropologist, and a humanitarian totally committed to the welfare of the cultural minorities. He went through great lengths to publicize that his expensive house at the White Plains subdivision is home to those he has adopted from cultural minorities. Brimming with paternalism, he has delighted in being called "Great Uncle Tasaday Spirit of Good Fortune" by the "Tasadays."

Yet behind this facade was hypocrisy, deceit, and tyranny. While the stated goal of Panamin was the protection of cultural minorities, the actual record of Panamin was the exact opposite. Panamin was a bloody record of oppression of cultural minorities. Our discussion of Panamin's activities strongly suggest that Panamin activities revolved around four distinct yet relate functions:

1. a front for land grabbing for Marcos corporations;
2. as a front for the mining activities of the Elizaldes;
3. as conduit for siphoning government money for the Elizaldes;
4. as organizer of para-military groups in the drive against armed rebellion.

> The designation of tribal groups as minorities has been used by many up to the present time as a license to confiscate land for timber concessions, for agri-business purposes or far homesites using the argument of the rights of the majority versus those of the minority, of primitiveness or underdevelopment versus development. In the Philippines there is not one cultural group at present that can be defined as a majority over all others. The Philippines is made up of distinct cultural groups and all of these groups together have to respected in their unique identity in any overall framework of motivation and development. To do otherwise is to accept a very crude interpretation of the democratic process by which a so-called majority is asked to vote on the sacrifice on an entire way of life of a people they term either for convenience sake or to soothe their consciences "a minority" [17].

Elizalde fled the Philippines at height of demonstrations in 1983 after the killing of Benigno Aqumo. He lived in Costa Rica and built a tourist complex there. But the heavily guarded complex, rare in Costa Rica, as well as the "presence of numbers of young girls at his home aroused questions and complaints" and Elizalde was eventually expelled [18].

Below is a partial list of the companies the Elizaldes own:

Company	Activity
Metropolitan Automotive Repairs	Manufacturing
White Flower Foods	Food

Zebra Investments	Real Estate
Elimin Trading	Mahineries
Meja Management Group	Management Consultants
Detroit Diesel Power Corp.	Manufacturing
Elizalde Consolidated Steel	Manufacturing
Rural Bank of Balasan	Banking
Alngon Diversified Industries	Trading
Northern Capiz Agro—Industrial	Agri-Business
Sugrains Agricultural Dev.	Agri-Business
Phil. International Corp.	Trading
Asian Diesel Industries	Manufacturing
Asian Business Corp. Gen.	Merchandise
Security Manufacturing Corp.	Manufacturing
Metro Taisho Insurance	Insurance
Diversified Growth Corp.	Services
Coral Islands Resorts	Hotels
Continuum Structures	Construction
Elca Management Corp,	Services
Central Azucarera de la Carlota	Sugar
General Diesel Power	Manufacturing
Tanduay Distillery Inc.	Wines & Liquor
Metropolitan Insurance	Insurance
Elizalde Paint & Oil	Manufacturing

Endnotes

1. The *Tanodbayan* is the Filipino term for ombudsman. The suit was filed on 26 June 1986 by Fermin Caram for the federation of sugar cane planters.
2. The vessels of Benedicto that were used were La Carlota, Dona Carmen, Don Salvador, and DoNa Paz. Elizalde's spokesman, Elpi Cuna, justified this by claiming that foreign buyers, Philipp Bros. and Farr, Man & Co., chose the ships. "Philsuma sugar shipments use Benedicto-owned ships," *Business Day*, 24 April 1986.
3. *Evening Post*, 9 May 1980.
4. *Bulletin Today,* 29 May 1980.
5. Material on this rifle project is based on an open letter by Brig. Gen. Antonio Lukban to the *Philippine Daily Inquirer,* 17 July 1991.
6. According to the Director of the Bureau of Lands. *Tribune*, 26 July 1986.
7. The original office was the Commission on National Integration (CNI). PD 919 issued in 1975 changed the name to Panamin and elevated Elizalde to cabinet status.
There are 44 tribal groups comprising 16% of the population which may be categorized as part of the cultural minority. But the appropriateness of the category "cultural minority" has been questioned by William Henry Scott who rightly points out that it is not so much a cultural term as a political category: the term really refers to the indigenous Filipinos who have resisted integration into dominant political culture, whether it be the Spanish, American, or mainstream urban Filipino. William Henry Scott, *The Creation of a Cultural Minority*, Third World Series, No. 4, University of the Phil. It is not our purpose here to join this debate and we merely note that we fully concur with the issues raised by Scott.
8. June Kronholz, "Saga of 'Lost' Tribe In Philippines Shows Marcos Era's Dark Side,"*Wall Street Journal*, 15 September 1986.
9. These questions concerning the Tasaday hurt the pride of some Filipino politicians. Some members of Mrs. Aquino's Congress considered the attacks on the Tasaday as attacks on the Philippine Republic. They promptly passed a resolution proclaiming the Tasadays to be genuine. It is a sign of the absolute stupidity of the present Philippine Congress to try to legislate the veracity or untruth of an anthropological assertion. One is

reminded of the Inquisition forcing Galileo to admit the earth does not move. And yet it moves. If the Philippine Congress continues along this track, they might well consider repealing the law of supply and demand, or changing some natural laws through legislation.

10. Since there are other studies on cultural minorities and the activities of Panamin, we shall limit ourselves to citing specific cases so as to provide the reader an insight into the background of Manda Elizalde. We encourage the reader to look up these specialized studies up since they can present the case for Philippine cultural minorities much more competently than we can do here: William Henry Scott, *The Creation of a Cultural Minority*, (University of the Philippines: Third World Series, No. 4), mimeo.; *Report on the Tribal Filipinos in Mindanao* (Manila: ICL Research, 1979); Fr. Pedro Salgado, O.P., *The Rape of Mindanao*, mimeo.; Felix Casalmo, *The Vision of a New Society*, (Manila: 1980); "*Isneg and the Abulug Dams*," *IBON*, 15 October 1979.

11. Desiree Carlos, 'Panamin's P18 M mess a mystery," *Malaya* August 1984.

12. *We Forum,* 21-23 July 1982.

13. Doherty, p.232.

14. Felix Casalmo, *The Vision of A New Society*, pp.44-5.

15. Casalrno, *Ibid.* pp.58—59.

16. Casalmo, *Ibid.* p.55.

17. Casalmo, *Ibid.*, p. 338-9.

18. "Costa Rica's Image as Haven Fading," *New York Times,* 11 September 1986.

RICARDO C. SILVERIO

The Ricardo Silverio story is the best example of how a person of extremely modest origins came to own a conglomerate of several dozen companies and become part of the set of millionaires called the Marcos *nouveau riche.*

Silverio confesses that he is the 9th of 10 children from what he himself describes as "a peasant family." His father, Ricardo St., was a small textile merchant with relatively modest means until he developed ties with Marcos, the first of which concerned Central Bank foreign exchange allocations and the consequent black marketing of dollars. The Silverio family has since become close to the Marcoses and at one time there was talk of marriage between the children of the two families.

At the height of their empire, the Silverio family owned a spectrum of some 50 companies, amuse themselves with heavy betting in big-time cockfights, developed real estate interests in California, and took over a whole island to use as their private get-away.

The Silverio empire was built with generous government assistance in the form of helpful legislation, loans from government financial institutions, and prized benefits from Japanese War Reparations payments.

THE SPINNER: DELTA MOTOR CORPORATION

Members of this family embarked on their road to prominence when Ricardo St., the head of the clan, established the Delta Motor Corp. DMC) in 1961 and received the exclusive right to assemble and distribute Toyota cars and trucks. Silverio's Delta Motors expanded rapidly with the help of cheap government-backed loans, Japanese war reparations money, and a captive market in the form of government demand for Toyota vehicles.

There is evidence of Delta Motor's privileged access to government markets dating to as early as 1968, when Marcos was running for presidential reelection. Mijares, citing former overnment officials from the Social Security System (SSS), relates that 50 brand new Toyota jeeps supplied by Delta Motors to the SSS were used for Marcos' reelection bid [1].

Uneven application of government regulations also considerably helped Silverio interests. The review committee of the Progressive Car Manufacturing Program, a government scheme designed to rationalize the car industry in the Philippines, imposed regulations on the applications of Ford Motor Corp. but waived these very same requirements for Delta. While Ford was required to phase out the production of a current model in order to produce the Mazda, Delta was not given any such requirement when it applied to produce the Toyota Starlet in April 1980 [2]. There were other glaring examples of such double standards. There was a rule that cars assembled and sold in Philippines must contain a substantial amount of locally made parts, but exceptions to this rule would be made if car companies would make components that can be exported from the Philippines. Seeking to avail of this exception, Ford set up a $36 million plant in Bataan to make body panels, while GM invested $17 million in a plant that would make transmissions. As soon as these investments were made, the government reneged on their promise and changed the rules: exports of components would be allowed to compensate for only 15% of local content requirement. Silverio's company was again exempted from all of these requirements [3].

Additional help came from the Board of Investments, with the Silverio group privileged to be among the only twelve firms to receive incentives to put up overseas trading offices. Delta was then able to open markets which no other ASEAN nation had ever reached and made shipments of its Mini-Cruiser, a military vehicle, to Italy, and its Tamaraw, a general purpose van, to Egypt.

Silverio repaid the generous support from the government by giving kickbacks to the dictator. Silverio admitted to giving bribes to Marcos in the form of endorsing cash dividends and shares of Delta Motor in blank to Marcos.

JAPANESE CONNECTIONS

Silverio's Toyota also received considerable help from the Japanese mother company in the form of "special consultants" in financing, manufacturing, and marketing. These Japanese "consultants" were in reality important supervisors in the managerial staff of DMC, a provision recognizing that the Japanese giant had considerable interests to protect: "parts for the assembly of DMC cars are from

Toyota, and the firm itself is heavily tied up with Toyota through technical and financial loan agreements" [4].

The initial financial success of DMC spun-off joint ventures with Japanese industrial giants.

Toyota of Japan also became a co-investor in the Delta International Corp.. This company consistently ranked high in the lists of marketing firms selling vehicles [5].

Sumitomo formed a partnership with Silverio's Delta Electric Motor Manufacturing Corp. to assemble electric motors made by the Japanese firm Maidensha Electric Manufacturing Co. Inc.

Among the other Silverio firms which had Japanese tie-ups were:

* Daikin (Phils.) Inc. - assembled Daikin brand air-conditioning and refrigeration units after acquiring the national franchise
* Nippondenso Phils. - assembled Nippondenso air-conditioners for automobiles
* Mariwasa Manufacturing - a joint-venture in ceramics with Noritake Co.
* Sigma-Mariwasa
* Mariwasa-Honda

THE REST OF THE BROOD

Silverio also owned the Delta Motor Sales Corp. and enjoyed the privilege of being the sole distributor of Komatsu construction equipment and German MAN trucks.
Other interests that Silverio either owned or had an exclusive distributorship were with Frigidaire and White Consolidated refrigerators, Japanese Sharp TV's, integrated circuits with Sprague Electronics.

He also engaged in air and water transport activities. Silverio's air transport firms were Astro Air Services, Air Manila Int., and Delta Air Corp. Silver Lmes Inc. was his water transport company.

Silverio also had a gold mining company, a loggin company (C&M Timber Corp), and a livestock farm (Silver Acres Inc.). Ilis chemlca firm, the Edge Fertilizer and Chemical Corp, of which Edmundo "Dante" Silverio was president, specialized in farm products and at one time introduced a soil conditioner called "agrispon."

The Silverio conglomerate also owned the Celebrity Plaza, a $17 million sports club in Quezon City [6]. The real estate development arm of the Silverio group, Land Project Manager Affiliates, had at one time started putting up two subdivisions in Metro Manila which were called, appropriately enough, Deltaville and Silvertown.

A lot of these corporations reached the yearly lists of the top 1,000 local companies.

FINANCING COMPANIES AND TROUBLE

To manage and finance this diversified empire, Silverio organized his own management firm, Silverio Management Corp., and owned or controlled a number of banks and underwriting firms. He was the chairman of Filipinas Manufacturers Bank (Filman Bank) and the director of companies such as Sterling Life Assurance and Manufacturers Bank & Trust Co. (Phil). For its financing needs, the group had the Philippine Finance Securities Corp. and the Pilipinas Development & Finance Corp. [7]. A counterpart in the insurance field was also organized, Philippine Underwriters Finance Corp.

The pattern of government patronage was again evident in the treatment of Silverio's financial firms. Philfinance, one of the main financing arms of Silverio, ignored or broke many banking regulations.

Since Philfinance was a financial intermediary without a quasi-banking license, it was allowed to have no more than 19 money market placers in 1978 (investors or lenders) if government regulations were to be strictly followed. This firm, however, enjoyed some 1,895 money market placers during this period [8]. At this time, Philfinance floated $5.5 million worth of promissory notes, overshooting its authorized limit of $340,000 million [9]. Some of these promissory notes later turned out to be bogus, with the companies in whose names the notes were issued disowning them. It was charged that Philfinance was guilty of

> not just outright violation of Central Bank regulations governing the operations of investment houses, but that some of the paper it passed around was bogus. [10].

The same company also incurred huge debts, shooting over its credit limits. While Philfinance was authorized to borrow only up to $22 million, it had outstanding debts of $115 million at one time [11]. The need for cash drove Silverio's Philfinance to borrow not only from the more traditional sources of government and private credit but also from the Human Settlements Corp. and the National Home Mortgage Financing Corp. [12]. When the Silverio conglomerate collapsed and Philfinance was finally liquidated, it owed its creditors around $76 million.

BAIL OUT AND GOVERNMENT HELP AGAIN

But even when Philfinance breached many regulations, the government still helped Silverio's companies when they start having difficulties.

The government was quick to bail out Silverio's Filipinas Manufacturers Bank (Filman Bank) when it started to write in red ink. While the government usually let non-crony banks fail, it readily rescued this bank. The Central Bank appointed the PNB as a receiver and set up a relief fund. Though this measure made the PNB part-owner of Filman Bank, Silverio retained controlling interest. The move had the effect of infusing new capital to this crony-owned bank.

This move was necessary because the Silverio group was finding it difficult to obtain commercial loans. A reputation had developed in financial circles that many of Silverio's projects were not viable in the long-term and that they have been initiated have with little or no experience. Sources in the banking and shipping industries point to Silver lines as an example of this lack and as the type of project with no long-term viability. These sources suggest that Silverio may have been organizing these companies not so much because they would be viable ventures but for other more suspect reasons.

These reservations proved correct in the long run. Apart from the $76 million owed by Philfinance to its creditors, there was a maze of debts left behind by other Silverio companies.

Even Silverio's flagship com any, Delta Motors Corp., fell into difficulties. After operating successfully for several years, Delta suffered losses of $2.5 million in 1980 and an estimated $8 in 1981. By 1982, Delta owed the PNB $117.09 million, half of it in short-term maturities. Delta also owed Toyota Motor of Japan $36 million, representing trade credits and royalties due to the Japanese company [13]. And to top everything off, it was discovered that Delta Motor Corp. defrauded government in penalties and charges of customs levy and was one of highest in the list of tax delinquent corporations [14].

How and why could such a fate have befallen Silverio's empire? Silverio later claimed that he was a victim of Marcos and that credit was refused to him when differences between him and the dictator arose. But as has been seen in our brief discussion, more credit and government assistance had been provided to Silverio than any other mortal could hope for. Silverio's defence is therefore not factually accurate.

We have to keep in mind that Silverio himself was quoted as saying that his entire conglomerate could not cover the $76 million to rescue Philfinance and that he would invest it elsewhere if he had the money. Where, then, did Philfinance's funds go? Most of it was used to fund Silverio corporations. Loans to other Silverio companies represented the major part of Philfinance's investments. When Silverio closed shop, the Silverio conglomerate owed Philfinance some $25.3 million [15].

What did these other Silverio companies do with the funds -- funds from government and private loans, Japanese reparations money, and money raised from their profitable years of busmess?

He brought most of these funds to California where he has been busy buying real estate and organizing shopping malls. Ricardo Silverio, the 9th of 10 children from a peasant family, is a successful California real estate magnate. AmoTransportng his properties are houses and condominiums in California, purchased using Silcor, one of corporations of the Silverio conglomerate. Silverio also made several major land purchases for a shopping mall and residential complex. These overseas properties, as well as the other overseas investments of other cronies, will be discussed in the next chapter.

A partial list of companies in the Philippines where the Silverio family had interests:

Company	Activity

Air Manila	Transport
BGS Realty	Real Estate
Celebrity Sports Plaza	Sports complex
Ceraglaze Manufacturing	Manufacturing
Corona Motor Center	Vehicle repair
Corona Motor Sales	Machinery
Daikin Phil. Engineering	Appliances
Daikin Phil.	Airconditioners
Dante Marketing Corp.	Marketing
Delta Air	Transport
Delta Audio Systems	Appliances
Delta Electric Motor	Manufacturing
Delta Electronics Corp.	Appliances
Delta Export & Import	Trading
Delta Express Tours	Travel
Delta Hi-Steel	Steel
Delta Int. Corp.	Transport
Delta Mining & Ind. Dev.	Mining
Delta Motor Sales	Sales
Delta Motors	Transport
Delta Heavy Machineries	Machineries
Deltron Automation	Macinery
Edge Fertilizer & Chemical	Fertilizers
Filman Bank	Banking
Golden Ventures Merc.	Trading
Komatsu Inds. Phil.	Machinery
Land Project Manager	Real estate
Maani Agro—Dev. Co .	Agri-business
Manufacturers Bank 2 Trust	Banking
Mariwasa International	Chinaware
Nippondenso Phil.	Airconditioners
Phil. Eel Development	Fishing
Phil. Underwriters Finance	Finance
Philfinance Securities	Finance
RCSI Industrial Security	Services
Refrigeration Industries	Air conditioners
Reliable Security	Security services
Service Factors	Business services
Seryna Chain Corp.	Restaurants
Siltra Trading	Sugar
Silver Acres	Livestock
Silver Line	Transport
Silverio Management Corp.	Managament
SST Machincnes	Machinery
Sterling Life Assurance	Insurance
Tower Avionics	Machinery

Endnotes

1. Mijares, p.53.
2. *Bulletin Today*, 14 April 1980.
3. *Fortune*, 27 July 1981.
4. *Bulletin Today*, 2 December 1975.

5. According to the 1976 list of Business Day.
6. *Bulletin Today*, 21 June 1981.
7. *Daily Express*, 28 July 1981.
8. *Business Day*, 23 July 1981.
9. *Business Day*, 23 July 1981.
10. *Far Eastern Economic Review*, 14 May 1982.
11. *Bulletin Today*, 21 June 1981.
12. *Far Eastern Economic Review,* 14 May 1982.
13. Emilia Tagaza, 'Marcos deploys secret force to fight crime," *Christian Science Monitor*, 22 June 1984.
14. Ellen Gallardo, "Nasutra owes P22 billion," *Philippine Daily Inquirer,* 11 March 1986.
15. *Bulletin Today*, 22 July 1981.

RODOLFO CUENCA

The Rodolfo Cuenca story is the classic tale of how a Marcos golfing crony was able to become a business tycoon in a relatively short time.

Cuenca dropped out of college at the age of 19 and became a small-time road contractor with the help of his father who had been a high official of the Department of Highways [1]. The Cuenca Construction Company did not perform well. Cuenca's wife admitted that her husband's desperation to gain contracts led him to continually bid lowest. This naturally resulted in heavy losses and made him bankrupt in three years.

He was able to save a truck from his creditors and hauled construction materials for a time. Cuenca's luck changed with Marcos' election as president. Within a few years, Cuenca was able to transform his fledgling trucking company into the biggest construction firm in Asia, with two McGraw-Hill research publications ranking it 48 in a list of 168 international contractors. At the height of his success, Cuenca's construction firm had some 30 subsidiaries and affiliates and was the sixth biggest Philippine company in terms of assets.

This former college dropout once became chairman of the Philippine branch of the International Chamber of Commerce.

Cuenca always tried to depict himself as a hard-working entrepreneur and claimed that he worked 18 hours a day. To underscore these claims, Cuenca had his construction company publish a children's book for the 1979 International Year of the Child depicting an archetypal child named Ompong who became a financial success due to perseverance. When interviewed about the book, Cuenca emphasized the importance of work and entrepreneurship and pointed to his construction conglomerate as a model. Cuenca firmly denied that his success was due to his association with Marcos and also dismissed accusations that the strongman had a financial interest in his companies. But Cuenca's history suggests that he could not have built his empire were it not for his close personal friendship with the dictator.

Cuenca campaigned and raised funds for Marcos during the 1965 presidential elections. He became one of the favorite golfing partners of the dictator, who bestowed upon Cuenca the title Project Director for Golf. Cuenca's favorite photograph shows himself and Marcos in white shorts holding golf clubs. The picture, prominently displayed in Cuenca's office, bore Marcos' personal dedication saying, "To Rudi, Good golfing always, F.E. Marcos".

GOVERNMENT HELP

Cuenca formed the Construction & Development Corporation of the Philippines (CDCP) in 1966. He claims that this was in response to the Private Financing Act of 1963 which encouraged the private sector to build infrastructure. But evidence suggests that the CDCP was organized mainly to take advantage of the rewards that came from backing the right presidential horse.

CDCP got off the ground in 1967 when it was awarded the contracts for two main highways in the Philippines. While the CDCP had capital of only $650,000, it won government contracts for the Manila North Expressway for $7.4 million and the Manila South Expressway for $8.7 million.

These were soon followed by other major government projects, and CDCP quickly became the major public highway builder under the Marcos administration.

From the time the CDCP started business in 1967 to 1978, the conglomerate's revenue increased at an annual rate of 83%. The group of some 30-odd companies grossed $541 million from 1970 through 1979, of which $277 million was raised in 1979 alone. By 1980, the CDCP had a revenue of $288.6 million.

The following table illustrates how well the CDCP did over the years compared to the top 1,000 companies in terms of sales:

Year	Rank
1975	34
1976	23
1977	19
1978	13

From the time the CDCP started business in 1967 through 1978, the company's profits rose by an average of 92% [2]. Profits from 1970 through 1979 was estimated at $41 million. Profits for 1980 stood at $15.5 million.

Within a relatively short period of time, Cuenca's company had zoomed a long way from the fledgling and continually bankrupt transportation firm. The CDCP quickly became the biggest civil engineering firm in the country in terms of assets and the size of contracts. By 1978, the CDCP had accounted for 26.97% of the industry's total revenues. It ultimately became the biggest construction firm in Southeast Asia.

CDCP's astronomical rise came primarily through the construction contracts Cuenca received from the government. The construction group alone posted $230.4 million in gross revenues in 1979, accounting for 82% of the CDCP conglomerate's total revenues for that year [3].

The CDCP enjoyed a most favored status with the dictatorship which permitted it to acquire lucrative government contracts. According to sources m the construction industry, Cuenca had openly bragged that no major government contracts were bidded unless they were previously cleared with him. A legitimizing procedure was concocted where the CDCP chose its bidding "competitors" who submitted bids higher than those of the CDCP. After Cuenca clinched the contracts, he would then pass 5% to the bidders who "lost" as their fee for participating in the scam.

Pedro O. Valdez, an uncle of the dictator and the president of a big construction company bearing his name, once served as chairman of CDCP. A notable incorporator of CDCP was Marcos' Secretary of Public Works, Baltazar Aquino, who has since admitted to being a front for Marcos. Aquino had awarded public works contracts worth many millions to the CDCP.

An example of government help received by CDCP was in the awarding of the contracts to construct the new Manila International Airport and corollary facilities. It was an international agency, the Asian Development Bank (ADB), which conducted the bidding since they were financing a third of the project with $30 million, but the CDCP was also helped by the Marcos government. The construction work was divided into three arts and contracts: civil works, buildings, and electro-mechanical work. CDCP won the first two but lost the third to Taisei of Japan, whose bid was 25% below that of CDCP. The government then requested the ADB to reconsider the contract, arguing that the yen revaluation would make the Japanese bid higher than that of the CDCP. The ADB did not agree and insisted that the contract be fulfilled by Taisei. The government retaliated by refusing Taisei permission to start work. After a year of waiting the Japanese firm went home, whereupon CDCP lowered its bid to match Taisei's and was awarded the contract.

HIGHWAY ROBBERY

Another example of government patronage is seen in the ease with which the CDCP was able to raise the toll fees in the North Diversion Road and South Expressways, the country's two mam highways.

Its highway construction contract with the government allowed the CDCP to operate the northern Manila-Tabang and the southern Manila-Alabang highways as franchises. Thecontract authorized the CDCP to collect toll fees from the expressways for 10 years starting from 1968 or until it accumulated $6.1 mxfiion, whichever came first. But with help from the Marcos administration, Cuenca was able not only to extend the franchise beyond its original limits but also at a lucrative captive market from the users of the highway through presidential decree.

When, for example, bus companies boycotted CDCP-built roads in favor of public service roads to protect unwarranted increases in toll fees in 1975, Marcos issued a presidential decree which banned buses on the service roads, leaving them no alternative but to pay the CDCP-imposed toll.

The toll charges and increases were legitimized through agreements between the Toll Regulatory Board (TRB) and the CDCP. The Toll Operation Agreement signed 18 October 1977 and PDs 1112 and 1113 authorized the CDCP to seek adjustment of toll rates. The CDCP took full advantage of these presidential decrees to impose toll hikes. Within a little over a year starting mid-1979, toll increases ranged from 53% for cars and jeepneys, 94% for passenger buses, and 250% for heavy vehicles. The Office of the Solicitor General, instead of protecting the interests of the public and opposing these bikes, not only legitimized them by signing the agreements between the government and the CDCP but also showed its partiality to CDCP by actually recommending the toll increases.

In one of the many instances of toll increases, the CDCP claimed that its operating costs were increasing. The CDCP stated that it had already spent $108.4 million and needed $176.2 million more to finance related highways projects. The position of this crony company was that its 1977 franchise (i.e., monopoly control) over the two main highways of the country obliged it not only to maintain the highways but also to improve and "expand" them. Part of the argument was that its government franchise was on a "total basis." The clause meant that costs for the expansion of the highways would be computed as part of the costs of maintaining the existing part. In plain language, this meant that the CDCP could charge the costs of adding new roads to the toll fees that it collected from the public.

There was an enormous public outcry. The Federation of Paranaque Homeowners Association, representing 77 subdivisions and more than 15,000 affected families, contend that the CDCP's insistence on contemplating the expressways contract on a "total basis" was irregular, immoral, if not illegal. The federation further pointed out that CDCP'S reasoning would result in no portion of the expressways ever getting paid since any contemplated future road could be charged to the costs of existing ones. Another affected group, the Haulers Association of the Philippines, argued that the toll-paying public would in effect be subsidizing future road constructions of CDCP and should therefore become stockholders of that company.

The homeowners complained that Cuenca's franchise had victimized the travelling public. They presented a resolution to Marcos requesting the lifting of the franchise. The federation further argued in a June 1980 court brief that the CDCP had been overpaid in the form of toll fees already. The federation cited a TRB report that the CDCP had collected more than $25.6 million in toll fees from 1976 to 1977, as against the original contract price of $6.1 million. It was furthermore pointed out that the CDCP had been collecting the fees for more than the allowed ten years.

The critics suggested that CDCP should have used its own capital for construction and only charged toll fees when the roads were already fully usable. But inspite of these objections, the Office of the Solicitor-General recommended an increase of 17%. The TRB, however, outdid the Solicitor-General and granted the full 50% increase the CDCP had requested. This 1 July 1980 hike increased the average daily take from the tolls of the CDCP tolls from $32,000 to $47,000. Furthermore, the duration of the franchise was increased to 30 years.

SUPERFLUOUS PROJECTS

The Marcos government engaged the CDCP to construct many multi-million projects which were unnecessary.

At Imelda's behest, the CDCP constructed the longest bridge in the Philippines in 1974, the San Juanico bridge, linking the two relatively undeveloped islands of Leyte and Samar. The project was severely criticized as superfluous since the traffic between the two islands was not large enough to warrant its construction. Apart from satisfying Imelda's whim to provide a bridge between her native province and its neighbor, the only other purpose of the bridge was to give the people from the two islands an opportunity to promenade.

Again at Imelda's behest, the CDCP embarked on reclaiming land from Manila Bay to create a 240-hectare white beach right behind Imelda's Cultural Center. The rationale for the beach was Imelda's wish to impress the visitors to the Manila Film Festival [4]. Imelda believed that providing a white beach to the visitors would help recreate the atmosphere at Cannes. In an archipelago of 7,100 islands where beaches are plentiful, white sand was quarried from the outlying cities of Mariveles and Cavite to create a beach in the middle of a city.

Yet again at Imelda's behest, the CDCP and other construction companies worked feverishly to construct a huge complex of native-style pavilions for the delegates of the May 1979 UNCTAD Conference in Manila. Simply because Imelda wanted the delegates to view samples of Philippine goods, workers labored day and night to finish the complex within 12 days, just enough time for Imelda to inaugurate the project before the delegates left Manila. The complex has since become a virtual ghost town.

Another CDCP project whose importance has been questioned is the Light Rail Transport (LRT), an elevated commuter railway linking parts of Metro-Manila. The project was partly financed by a $40 million loan from the Belgian government, with the CDCP acting as the Philippine counterpart of the consortium of Belgian companies building the project. The CDCP was appointed by the Marcos government for this task and Cuenca's company was to provide the civil engineering for the 15 kilometer project extending from Pasay to Caloocan City.

But many questions have been raised concerning the appropriateness of the project. 1977 World Bank study contended that Manila did not require such a system but instead proposed a street-level transport system. According to this study the street-level system would have cost only $8.1 million, in contrast to the light rail system which was initially estimated at $216 million but ultimately ballooned to $278 million. *Business Day*, a respected business publication, further contended that the LRT would incur a net deficit of $30 million during its first year of operation and would require continuous government subsidies until 1993 to stay running. Despite the questions, the Marcos government gave Cuenca the go signal to start construction on October 1981 [5].

LAND RECLAMATION

The largest CDCP project was the $1 billion Manila Bay reclamation project. The gargantuan project which was started in 1974 aimed to reclaim land from Manila Bay and create a 10-kilometer southern highway to Cavite. The project, alternately called "New City" or the Manila-Cavite Coastal Road and Reclamation Project (MCCRRP), was to initially add 1,160 hectares to the city, but the coverage was later increased, first to 2,700, then to 3,000 hectares. In Cuenca's words, the project would "irreversibly commit some 10% of Manila Bay's present shoreline."

One of the reasons CDCP cited for the project was the claim that it would alleviate the perennial problem of traffic jams and parking.

As the area coverage changed, so did the timetable. Deadlines were continually redrawn, with the CDCP first quoting a date of 1990, but later stretching it to 2,004.

Thin did not augur well for CDCP. After examining the reclamation project, a US planning and management expert pointed out that the physical plans had "technical defects." The defects had to be later corrected later by another sub-contracted package, thereby increasing the costs of the project.

The company had planned to finance the project by selling the land as it was being reclaimed, a strategy similar to the one use in the construction of the expressways. It had hoped to retain half the reclaimed land for speculative real estate deals, while selling the other half to finance the entire project.

At one time, it was hoped that $427 million could be raised from the advanced sales of the property. CDCP had planned to lure multinational companies based in Hong Kong and Singapore to invest in the reclaimed land. But when these companies did not show interest, the CDCP got the Marcos government to appeal for funds from the World Bank, which refused to get involved in the project.

Since multinational companies and international funding agencies could not be drawn into Cuenca's grand project, the CDCP had to depend on traditional government patronage. The DBP and PNB, for example, funded 70% of the work. Other government agencies were persuaded to put up their new offices there and buy land which still was in the process of reclamation.

Citing what it called the "heavy outflow of funds," the CDCP was also able to secure government approval on October 1979 to sell 222 hectares of reclaimed land to the public. Two CDCP subsidiaries, Manila Land Corporation and Marina Properties Corporation, handled the marketing of the properties. The first company concentrated on financing and marketing 13 hectares of prime commercial land to businesses, while the latter concentrated on selling residential properties. Marina Properties was headed Cuenca's son, Bobby. Another CDCP subsidiary, the Dasmarinas Estate Development Co ., developed land south of the reclamation project together with the NDC. The aim was to develop an industrial estate on 772 hectares land in Dasmarinas, Cavite [6].

Cuenca saw the reclamation project as a source of quick money. Hoping to acquire huge profits, he dragged public funds into this personal venture. This was a patently criminal act on the part of Cuenca and his associates. There was absolutely no need to have started this reclamation project. Unlike land-scarce Japan or Hong Kong, the Philippines had a lot of unused and undeveloped properties. National resources and efforts could have been used for more productive and pressing needs. The only rationale for this reclamation project was speculation. Through the artificial creation of what was hoped to be prime waterfront land, Cuenca believed he could reap great profits. The actual effect was to mire government resources into his personal venture and replace the famed breathtaking view of sunset in historic Manila Bay with that of the sun falling behind a broad expanse of mud.

JOINT VENTURES AND GOVERNMENT CONTRACTS

Because of its size and the clout it enjoyed with the government, the CDCP was a favorite local partner for many transnational corporations.

The company teamed up with Kawasaki Steel to construct two main sections of a pipeline system which would move 400,000 cubic meters of water daily for Manila. The contract, awarded by the Metropolitan Waterworks & Sewerage System, cost $27 million. Kawasaki provided the engineering and management, while CDCP undertook the work.

Iit was sub-contracted by Marubeni of Japan for a $42 million project to prepare the foundation of the plant of the Philippine Associated Smelting & Refining Corp. (Pasar). CDCP task was to excavate and cement the foundation, fabricate and erect the steel structure, and install and test the machinery.

A CDCP subsidiary, the Negros Cement Corp., won another a $150 million contract over five competitors to construct a gigantic cement plant in Basay, Negros Oriental. The project again receive support from the government and transnational corporations. Roberto Ongpin, Marcos' Minister of Trade & Industry, planned to incorporate the million-ton-a-year cement plant as part of the government's ill-fated attempts to create 11 major industrial projects. The American firm of Philip Bros. and a Hong Kong-based construction company planned to invest a total of 30% equity and buy 70% of the plant's production.

The CDCP Mining Co. and Atlantic Richfield Co. of Los Angeles were awarded a geophysical survey contract for oil exploration by the Ministry of Energy. The two companies had the option to turn these contracts into service contracts to drill 11 wells in offshore areas on the west coast of Zambales, Bataan, and Batangas.

LOGGING AND THE REST OF THE FAMILY

There were many other grand CDCP projects supported by the Marcos government.

The Pantabangan Dam and the Candaba viaduct projects, two herculean water projects, were built by CDCP and Hydro Resources Contractors, another consortium of contractors with close ties to Marcos.

Hydro's president, Honrado Lopez, was a known Marcos associate. Among Lopez' interests in the construction industry were the following firms:

H.R. Lopez Co Inc.	President
Associated General Builders	owner
Filipinas Cement	substantial investments
Lakeview Industrial	substantial investments

Many of Lopez's firms grew at phenomenal rates due to the contracts it received from the government. Hydro Resources, for example, exhibited a 400% increase in revenues in 1978, partly because of the construction of the Magat River multipurpose dam estimated to cost $231 million.

CDCP diversified in areas as agri-business, logging and wood processing, land transportation, mining, banking, and a host of others concerns.

A top earner for the Cuenca conglomerate was the CDCP Farms. Citing Marcos' General Order 47, which required corporations to develop one hectare of land for every seven employees, the CDCP Farms Corporation entered the lucrative business of capitalist agri-business. Setting its main operations in Bukidnon, it expanded to 10 provinces in a relatively short period of time, covering areas such as Bulacan, Pampanga, Bataan, Nueva Ecija, Tarlac, and Isabela in Luzon; Iloilo and Capiz in the Visayas; and Cotabato in Mindanao. Its farming operations in Don Carlos, Bukidnon covered 100 hectares for sorghum, 400 for corn, and 1,000 for sugar. Its livestock operations boasted of a modern steel slaughterhouse and some 2,000 heads of cattle. The multimillion slaughterhouse, however, never got to kill a single steer or pig.

While General Order 47 was designed to increase food production, and while it had also created profits for companies like the CDCP, it also had the effect of reducing former independent owner-farmers to hired wage-labor in their farms. The big firms provided the inputs, technology, marketing, and management, while the former peasants provided their labor. While some might say that employment was being provided for the workers, others point out that agri-business created dependence on the part of formerly self- sufficient farmers, if not more unemployment for the population as a whole. There is no question, however, that agri-business had been profitable for Cuenca himself.

Tierra Factors, another CDCP subsidiary, was one of the top manufacturers of earth-moving equipment. It too has benefitted from the government through many incentives provided by the BOI.

Cuenca was also one of the few favored cronies to have received logging licenses, operating Sta. Ines Plywood and Sta. Ines Melale Forest Products. Sta. Ines Melale Forest Products realized profits of $626,794 in 30 June 1980, placing it at the top of the eight wood firms that made any money at all during that year.

Cuenca also tried to cash in on the tourism promotion program of the government. Through the Resort Hotels, the CDCP owned or had interests in hotels and tourist spots such as the Pines Hotel (Baguio City, Northern Luzon), Taal Vista

Lodge, the Mindanao Hotel, and the Hyatt Regency. He also owned a transportation service specifically for tourists, the Resort Tourist Transport Buses.

SHIPPING

Cuenca soon organized Galleon Shipping to complement his logging operations. Galleon was organized in 1977 a joint venture between two other Cuenca firms, Sta. Ines and the CDCP, and had another close Marcos associate, General Romeo Espino, Marcos' former Chief-of-Staff, as an incorporator. Manuel Tinio, Cuenca's son-in-law, managed both Galleon Shipping and Sta. Ines.

Galleon Shipping started by acquiring five of the seven ships of the United Philippine Lines, a shipping line which had gone bankrupt. Sources in the shipping industry claim that the transfer was made on presidential orders and did not involve any payments. This move gave Cuenca an instant fleet.

Cuenca then expanded his fleet by going on a shopping spree for new ships using a $100 million foreign loan fully backed by the Central Bank. The wisdom of these purchases were questioned by those who pointed out that the shipping services market was already saturated at this time. Industry sources indicated that the real purpose for these purchases were the commissions involved, which were estimated to be around 20% of the purchase price:

> the company invested heavily in new liners when there was no well-defined market base. It can readily surmised that the vessels were bought to enable the collection of kickbacks.

Kickbacks from overseas purchases such as these are difficult to establish since they can be easily hidden in foreign bank accounts. But the charge was later confirmed when Cuenca and Trans-Asia Marine Corp., Galleon's US subsidiary, were sued in New York by a former president of the company. The suit, which asked for $5.5 million in damages, alleged that Cuenca had pocketed $41.8 million in kickbacks. The government DBP was also a source of funds for the purchase of these ships.

Since a market was lacking for his new ships, Cuenca ate into the business of his competitors. Presidential intervention assured that government shipping would use Cuenca's company. Galleon then came to dominate the lucrative liner service between the Philippines and the US. Galleon Shipping became number 257 in the top 1000 corporations within two years. Many of Galleon's competitors soon went out of business [7].

The golfing crony expanded his reach by entering the stevedoring business. Cuenca acquired the Luzon Stevedoring Co. (Lusteveco) and its affiliates from the government on August 1979. The move was considered a significant one by industry sources since Lusteveco and its affiliates, Consolidated Terminal and Transcon Transport Contractors, were the leading stevedoring concern in the country.

The purchase of Lusteveco gave Cuenca a stronghold over the stevedoring business in the Philippines since it possessed big cranes and vital handling equipment that were in short supply at Manila's ports.

It also gave him access to additional government resources.

Cuenca's acquisition and management of the stevedoring concern is again illustrative of how government money was poured into Cuenca corporations. The $38 million required to purchase the company from the Philippine National Oil Co. (PNOC) was acquired through a government loan. This by itself already represented an anomalous situation since government money was being used to purchase a government-owned company.

Cuenca then embarked on an ambitious $40 million expansion and modernization program. Industry sources claimed that most of the cargo-handling equipment Cuenca purchased using government funds, such as an order for 37 new forklifts, were bought at an overprice, a clear indication of kickbacks.

Lusteveco resources were also used to invest in a 39% equity in Galleon Shipping, thus giving Cuenca's shipping company further resources.

Cuenca returned Lusteveco to the government two years later after milking it dry. Lusteveco was declared bankrupt by the government. But even the classification of the company as "distressed" was an occasion for further benefits for Cuenca. It meant that Cuenca was absolved from paying the $25.3 million which represented the unpaid art of original purchase price of $38 million [8]. Marcos made this write-of explicit by issuing a presidential LOI which directed the government-run NDC to assume Cuenca's debts with the PNOC, the original owner of Lusteveco. This move was tantamount to giving Cuenca a $13.1 million doleout. Furthermore, Marcos directed the DBP and the NDC to purchase whatever assets still remained with Lusteveco and reimburse CDCP for them.

These moves meant that Cuenca was able to "purchase" a company without paying for it, suck it dry until it became bankrupt, and still be compensated with government funds for whatever money was still left in the company after it was declared a "distressed" company. All of these moves were legitimized by the magic of presidential decree.

OVERSEAS

The former college dropout was equally ubiquitous in the international scene. CDCP won half of all of the overseas contracts of Filipino construction firms, an indication of the government favor Cuenca received.

A clear case of government patronage involved the construction of a 140-kilometer highway project in Iraq. The CDCP was granted an advance payment of $28.5 million by the PNB on Marcos' orders. Instead of having to wait for the completion of the project, the Marcos government paid the CDCP for work in a foreign country which had not yet been completed. The advance gave Cuenca tremendous advantages in interest alone. The advance furthermore had the effect of assuring payment to the CDCP irrespective of the outcome of the project.

Other overseas projects of the CDCP included multimillion dollar contracts in countries such as Malaysia, Indonesia, Hong Kong, the People's Republic of China, the Marianas, Saudi Arabia, and Gahon. Tierra Factors, the CDCP heavy equipment subsidiary, had successful projects in Malaysia and Singapore. Mindanao Air, a small airline of the CDCP, operated routes to Taiwan and southern Philippines such as Zamboanga, Kota Kinabalu, and Sandakan. CDCP was also in construction projects in Sabah, a territory under dispute between the Philippines and Malaysia. CDCP also acquired many important Middle East contracts and became a major employer of Philippine labor in the area. Among the Middle East projects were a 279 million 106-km highway in Saudi Arabia, a $180 million storm drainage project in Mecca, and the earlier-mentioned major road building program in Iraq worth $285 million.

To better manage its overseas operations, CDCP organized the International Construction Operations and the Pacific Operations Group. The former undertook operations in the Middle East, Africa, West Asia, and the Asean countries, while the latter concentrated on Hong Kong, China, and the Marianas.

The growth of its overseas projects was phenomenal. Starting from scratch in 1976, CDCP overseas construction projects amounted to $34 million in 1978 and an estimated $964 million in 1979. Company officials confided that CDCP had hoped to shift the base of their operations from the Philippines to overseas, With the intention that overseas business would account ultimately for 75% of total earnings.

The efforts to internationalize CDCP's operations were interpreted by some analysts as an integral part of Cuenca's business strategy. These moves were viewed as "making hay while the sun shone," of preparing for the time that Marcos and Cuenca would be leaving the Philippine scene.

Already, the CDCP had organized a Hong Kong subsidiary, CDCP International. It allowed CDCP to circumvent foreign loan limitations imposed on local companies by the IMF and the Central Bank. This also had the advantage of being able to circumvent Central Bank restrictions on holding foreign currencies abroad. The foreign subsidiary was not required to repatriate profits from overseas operations to the Philippines, thereby amassing a comfortable nest egg abroad. With these obvious advantages in shifting its cash to different countries, CDCP planned to shift its financial
base to Hong Kong where it had won a few large contracts.

This may explain why Cuenca had been acquiring many overseas properties while his local companies were allowed to go bankrupt.

While the CDCP was organizing overseas companies, Cuenca himself was busy buying US real estate for his personal use. Among these were an expensive coop apartment in New York and several properties in California (please see Chapter IV).

RISING DEBT AND CUENCA'S STRATEGY

While the CDCP experienced phenomenal growth, its sudden collapse was equally dramatic. Certain traits common to all of Cuenca's companies provide us with clues to their astronomical rise and equally dramatic demise. Among these are

1. large size and grandiose design;
2. dependence on government and foreign loans for funds;
3. captive markets provided by the government;
4. heavy equipment purchases, even when not necessary;
5. sudden growth followed by sudden collapse;
6. high debt to equity ratio.

The growth of Cuenca's firms was propelled by great amounts of debt and prodded by a dependence on the Marcos government for markets.

Cuenca claimed that the CDCP experienced great difficulties and faced "cash flow problems" towards the end of the 1970's. The conglomerate had to restructure many of its loans with foreign banks and issue bonds [9]. The significant thing in CDCP's bond issues was that most of the buyers of the bonds were government agencies. The GSIS, for example, bought $26.3 million worth of subordinated debenture bonds in April 1980. There were very few buyers of the bonds from the private sector. In fact, Bancom, a respected private investment bank, withdrew from underwriting the CDCP bonds since the project was not deemed feasible and no one could be found to co-underwrite the venture. The bond issues were therefore another way through which increase its debts with the government.

By the end of 1978, total debt of CDCP was at $158 million, composed mostly of government loans or those guaranteed by the government. This amount rose to $650 million by 1980.

The problem got worse by the early 1980's. Galleon Shipping reported a net loss of $3.5 million for the first half of 1980, in contrast to a net profit of $254,000 in same period the previous year. Profits of the conglomerate fell by 82% in 1981 and suffered a further 25% decline in 1982.

Underscoring the problems of CDCP were the chronic delays of the salaries of the 30,000 employees of the conglomerate. Even the traditional Christmas bonus was canceled in 1980.

This seeming contradiction of phenomenal growth and financial collapse is best understood by analyzing the strategy Cuenca adopted to make money. He encouraged CDCP to expand, incurred multimillion debts, procured legions of equipment, and took on many government projects because these methods allowed him to milk these companies and profit personally. Cuenca was not interested in professionally managing his companies as legitimate centers of profit but was interested in using them to extract gigantic commissions which he split between Marcos an himself.

A member of Cuenca's inner circle outlined the methods used by this Marcos crony to get kickbacks:

1. contracts and bids awarded to him by Marcos;
2. the procurement of equipment;
3. the buying up of whole companies.

Cuenca won government contracts at bloated prices, and the difference was split as a commission between Marcos and Cuenca. The bigger the project, the bigger the overprice and the greater the commission. Secretary of Highways Baltazar Aquino's presence in CDCP was to ensure this profitable arrangement.

Cuenca bought unneeded heavy equipment and acquired new companies and subsidiaries use of the kickbacks from these transactions. It is significant to note that while the construction group of the CDCP conglomerate acquired contracts worth $1 billion in 1981, its profits sharply fell from $15 million to $2.5, indicating huge expenses. One might question what fraction of the expenses were legitimate business costs, and what part was diverted for Cuenca's pocket.

Another example related to us by construction industry sources are instances where CDCP bought some heavy machinery abroad in the late 1970's. After the purchases were made and Cuenca collected his commissions from the overseas suppliers, the equipment were left idle and unused in the pier.

While Cuenca defended himself by saying, "my trouble is overenthusiasm, not mismanagement or stealing money," he continually refused to heed several signs of impending trouble and continued to pile up debts. When the Marcos government first came to his rescue in 1981, Cuenca accepted the $266 million that came with the program but refused to implement the proposals which called for a balanced mix of capital expansion and restructuring. The plan included refinancing of short-term loans into longer maturities. By the mid-1981, CDCP had a record debt-equity ratio of 5:1 [10].

GOVERNMENT BAILOUT

The Marcos government diverted massive public resources over a three-year period into the CDCP. Special presidential decrees were promulgated to legitimize the unprecedented government bailout. One example was already seen in the Lusteveco case.

The pattern was repeated with other Cuenca companies. In the case of the Resort Hotels, the government-run NDC and DBP took over the hotels connected with the chain, such as the Taal Vista Lodge and Hotel Mindanao, in April 1981. Marcos further directed that $5.06 million of the $163 million the Resort Hotels owed to DBP be converted into shares, a cosmetic maneuver to hide Cuenca's rising debts.

Yet Cuenca had the gall to blame the government for his troubles. He claimed in mid-1980 that his "cash flow" problems arose because the government was late in paying him $19.7 million in collectibles [11]. Cuenca ad conveniently overlooked that by that time the CDCP already owed $685 million to its creditors.

While many small private contractors had approved but uncollected claims of more than $101.2 million from the government in 1981, Cuenca continued to be favored with aid. By June of that year, the CDCP had received $70 million in government bailout funds [12].

Inspite of all these problems, Marcos sent a memo to top officials of government offices to extend help to the CDCP. The offices involved were the ministries of Public Highways and Public Works, the Central Bank, NDC, DBP, PNB, GSIS, NPC, National Irrigation Administration, Metropolitan Waterworks & Sewerage System [13].

This was followed by LOIs 1295 and 1296 directing the PNB and other state financial institutions to take over CDCP. In this case it meant taking over the debts. The CDCP by this time had incurred a total of $450 million in debts with the government. Following the pattern set with Lusteveco and Resort Hotels, the government loans were converted into equity.

Government money kept pouring into Cuenca's companies either through new loans or the conversion of old debts into government equity. A total of $202.5 million of new government funds had been injected into CDCP by the end of 1981. The money came from government financial institutions. Part of the money came in the form of a loan of $40 million drawn from the Industrial Rescue Fund which had been set up by the government to rescue failing crony companies. Another $31.6 million came in the form the purchase of equity, giving the NDC a 30% share in the firm. Later, the Marcos government started converting the loans into equity. For example, the government cancelled $140.5 milion of CDCP's obligations on February 1982 in exchange for the worthless Manila Bay reclamation project. By 1983, CDCP debts totalling $351 million had been converted into equity by the government.

When the takeover was finally completed in 1983, the government had put in a total of $460 million in CDCP, representing 90% of company's equity. The total state investment of $460 million was divided amongst the following government institutions:

PNB	40%
NDC	19%
DBP	13%
GSIS	10%
Philguarantee	7%
Land Bank	0.14%
Total	**89.14% [14]**

This amount was equal to 20% of the M1 measure of country's money supply (i.e., the total cash in circulation and the funds in checking accounts). Putting the amount in perspective, Jaime Ongpm, a well-known busmessman, pointed out

Just how large a sum is $460 million? It happens to be 20% of Philip ine money supply ($2.3 billion), 10% of the entire government expendituree for 1982 ($4.73 billion), 25% of all taxes collected by the BIR in 1981 ($1.8 billion), and 20% of Philippine foreign exchange reserves ($2.5 billion). In other words, the $460 million equity investment in CDCP is a frighteningly large number [15].

Some quarters naively suggested that the "take-over" of Minister of Industry Roberto Ongpin of the chairmanship of CDCP was an effort on the part of the government to clean up its act with regard to crony companies. The evidence, however, pointed otherwise. The conditions under which the billions were poured into CDCP are highly suspect.

The takeover was in direct violation of the country's existing banking laws which limited a bank's equity investment in a single enterprise to 15% of the bank's own equity. By 1981, the PNB had already invested $228 million in CDCP, representing 70% of bank's equity of that year. In the following year, PNB investments in CDCP was 60% of the banks total equity.

Between $400 million [16] and $700 million [17] worth of debts had been converted into equity by the first quarter of 1983. Since the CDCP was a losing company, this meant that the government was throwing away the money. The amount of $700 million was roughly equal to one-third of the government's total revenue in first six months of 1983. To help give us perspective of the magnitude of the amount being written off, the *Wall Street Journal* pointed out, "put in terms of the US budget, that would be about $100 billion" [18]. Jaime Ongpin described the bailout as "the most obscene, brazen and disgraceful misallocation of taxpayer's money in the history of the Philippines" [19].

This conversion of debts into equity was an implicit admission on the part of the government that Cuenca could not or would not pay the debts and that the only way to balance the accounting ledgers was to throw good public money after a bad Cuenca investment. The cases of Lusteveco and Resort Hotels were clear examples of this. The effect of these conversions was to decrease CDCP's debts insofar as the accounting books were concerned. But the real effect was to enable Cuenca to acquire further loans because the debt-equity conversion technically meant the old debts had been paid.

Business Day further pointed out if the state bank swaps its debt for equity, it would forego the interest on these loans. PNB was also in effect cancelling other amounts due to it in the form of uncollected interest. "The bank's $228 million locked in CDCP will be earning nothing even as PNB bears the entire burden of the interest charges" [20].

Another questionable aspect of the takeover was the obvious double standard applied to what have been termed as "distressed" companies. Some were more favored than others. While other companies were required to put up substantial amounts of counterpart equity from existing shareholders before government assistance was made available, the CDCP was conveniently exempted from this requirement. Of the $650 million Industrial Rescue Fund for "distressed" companies, $125 million went to CDCP.

The chair of CDCP was assumed by Roberto Ongpin, a Marcos cabinet minister and a long-time supporter of many of Cuenca s projects, but Cuenca remained president, allowing him to continue his role as a Marcos money collector. Cuenca was also owed to retain 7% ownership of the firm.

The so-called takeover of the CDCP, described by Time magazine as "a Chrysler-size package put through without any debate or publicity," [21] was a thinly-veiled ruse to extend more government money to the conglomerate which was used as a milking cow. After bilking the government through overpriced contracts, incurring giant foreign and government debts, collecting kickbacks from equipment purchases, and doing everything to bankrupt the companies, the people were then burdened with the final indignity of bailing Cuenca out of his self-created mess for $460 million.

A partial list of companies which formed part of Cuenca's conglomerate:

Galleon Shipping
Luzon Stevedoring
Galleon Shipping Corp.
Luzon Stevedoring Corp.
CDCP Farms Inc.
Tierra Factors Corp.
CDCP Mining Corp.
Philkasan Industries Corp.
Builders Insurance Corp.
Land Project Manager Affiliates Corp.
TUBO Agricultural and Dev. Corp.
BBC Nomelex Corp.
Filmanbank
Busco
CDCP International in Hong Kong
Galleon Shipping - Phil. shipping line
Trans-Asia Marine Corp.

Endnotes

1. One source says he was Secretary, another says he was a Commissioner.
2. Though still highly profitable, profits slowed down to 72% in 1969, but it significantly rose to 93% after martial rule was imposed in 1972.
3. This was a 49% increase over the previous year.
4. Please see Chapter I.
5. Sheilah Ocampo, "Manila's High-flyer," *Far Eastern Economic Review*, 13 January 1983.
6. The aim was to develop industrial plants for electric motors, equipment, asbestos products,
PVC products, and wire rope.
7. In the process of researching for this book, we encountered documents from executives of the Maritime Company of the Philppines pleading for government assistance. The firm was on the verge of bankruptcy. US creditors had initiated proceedings to seize one of its ocean liners as soon as it docked In the US. The Marcos cabinet official concerned turned a deaf ear. The company, an old established shipping firm, went out of business. Cuenco's principal competitor fort e lucrative US-Philippines route was thus eliminated.
8. *Far Eastern Economic Review*, 1 May 1981.

9. By 1979, foreign loans totaling $31.946 million were refinanced through a syndicate of banks lead by Asia Pacific Capital Corporation. Wells Fargo Bank also restructured its $16 million loan due July 1981 into a 7-year loan with a 2-year grace period and a 1/2% reduction spread.
10. *Fortune*, 27 July 1981.
11. This is despite the fact that CDCP grossed $670 million in 1980, largely due to government contracts.
12. *Bulletin Today*, 5 June 1981.
13. *Business Day*, 21 July 1981.
14. *Business Day*, 24 February 1983.
15. Mimeographed article, circa March 1983.
16. *The Economist*, 5 March 1983.
17. *Wall Street Journal*, 4 November 1983.
18. *Wall Street Journal*, 4 November 1983.
19. *The Economist,* 5 March 1983.
20. *Business Day*, 1 June 1983.
21. "Friends in Need," *Time*, 24 August 1981.

GERONIMO VELASCO

Marcos' energy minister, Geronimo Velasco, was the richest member of the cabinet. Government investigators probing cases of corruption committed during Marcos' regime estimated the net worth of Velasco to be around $50 million by the dictatorship's fall in 1986 [1]. Among the assets linked to Velasco are real estate properties in expensive areas in Manila and California, as well as a number of private corporations in the Philippines.

Among the real estate properties linked to Velasco are [2]:

* a $15 million amnion in Woodside, California;
* a $675,000 condominium in Century Hill, Los Angeles;
* a $400,000 condominium in a luxury building in Russian Hill, San Francisco;
* two houses in the subdivision of Bel-Air, Makati, Metro-Manila;
* one house in the subdivision of Magallanes, Makati, Metro-Manila;
* one home in the expensive area of Greenhills, Metro-Manila;
* two houses in the subdivision of Dasmarinas, Makati, Metro-Manila, one of which was reportedly renovated to contain parts of an "old ancestral home";
* a 7-storey building in Salcedo Village, Makati, financed by Benedicto's Traders Royal Bank, where Gervel, Velasco's holding corporation, occupies one floor,
* a reported resort house on the Bataan peninsula situated on the side of a cliff overlooking the South China Sea so isolated from the public that it can be reached only by helicopter or boat.

Apart from these real estate interests and his position in Marcos' cabinet, Velasco also served as chairman or director of many government and private corporations. A partial list of these corporations are:

Company	Activity/Extent of Interest
ACI Fiberglass Phil. Inc.	Manufacturing
Bataan Refining Corp.	Petroleum
Cello Realty Corp.	owns 35%. Real estate
Dolel Philippines	president. Agri-business
Ledtok Inc.	owns 22%
Malangas Coal Corp.	Coal mining
Manila Memorial Park	owns 10%. Funeral homes
National Power Corp.	chairman, Power utility
Nobel Phil.	Owns 22%
Orient Overseas Phil.	
Phil. Aerospace Dev. Corp.	
Phil. Air Lines Corp.	director
Phil. Dockyard Corp.	Transportation
Phil. Global Comm. Inc.	5% interest, Communications
Phil. National Bank	director
Phil. Petroleum	Petroleum
Phil. Tuna Ventures	owns 50%
Phil. National Oil Co. (PNOC)	president, Petroleum
PNOC Alcohol Corp.	Manufacturing
PNOC Energy Dev. Corp.	Mineral exploration
PNOC Exploration	Mineral exploration
PNOC Petroleum Tanker	Transportation
PNOC Shipping & Transport Corp.	Transportation
PNOC Shipyard Corp.	Transportation
PNOC Tankers Corp.	Shipplng
Petron TBA Corp.	Petroleum
Petrophil	Petroleum
Petrophil Tankers Corp.	Shipping
Planters Products	Ago-business, together with the crony Benedicto
Regublic Glass Corp.	has 51% interest, Manufacturing
RGC Investment Corp.	
Stanfilco	Agri-business
Telin Dev. Corp.	owns 85%
Yulo King Ranch	Cattle/Agri-business

Velasco was understandably the loudest to react when the Marcos regime came under intense criticism for corruption. He claimed that reports of his wealth were nothing more than "a rehash of old gossip designed for obvious political ends." Velasco then offered to resign from his cabinet position, telling the dictator that "my usefulness to your government and to our people has been adversely eroded, the truth and clear conscience not-withstanding." But the criticism continued despite Velasco's display of indignation.

He then tried to parry the mounting criticism by saying that people often forgot that he held a very lucrative positron in a major multinational company and had a net worth of more than $1 million before joining the Marcos administration. Velasco added:

> Part of my compensation was in US Dollars and in stock options in the Castle & Cooke chain consistent with the company's benefit plans for its executives. It is a matter of record in the Bureau of Internal Revenue that I paid on the peso value of my foreign

income.

Velasco carefully orchestrated his public defense by trying to depict himself as a manager who operated on a purely professional basis both in his private and public positions [3]. But a careful analysis of the man's activities reveal that most of his public statements were misleading, inconsistent, and often factually incorrect.

Velasco claimed that his network of corporations had never profited from or had any dealings with the government. He made this claim to government probers investigating his finances as well as in a letter to Marcos. In a 5 June 1984 letter, written after he was facing criticism of his wealth, Velasco wrote to Marcos

neither I personally nor my related interests have had any dealings whatsoever with any government financial institution and we are free of even a single centavo of government loan or guarantees [4].

While Velasco had consistently implied that his wealth has nothing to do with his connections with the Marcos dictatorship, the actual facts suggest otherwise. Velasco claimed to have a net worth of $5.4 million [5] before he joined the government in 1973, but investigators estimated his wealth to be around $50 million in 1986 [6], a phenomenal growth of 825% in 13 years.

Most of the private companies connected with Velasco were organized after he joined the Marcos government. Of the 11 companies associated with Velasco, seven were organized after he joined the government in 1973 [7].

Despite his claims that neither he nor his associates "have had any dealings whatsoever" with the government, there is definite proof that Velasoo's corporations were the recipients of government contracts. Republic Glass, a large manufacturing concern where Velasco and David Sycip have substantial interests, was a major government supplier. Velasco himself stated this in a 3 August 1981 letter:

Republic Glass is the only company in the Philippines manufacturing plane and sheet glass. The government has no other recourse but to purchase its requirements of plate and sheet glass, either directly or indirectly through Republic Glass Corp. 's independent dealers.

Another firm, Nobel Phil, was also a government supplier. Velasco admitted that some "government corporations engaged in exploration and mining purchase their requirements from this company." While he claimed that the transactions of these companies with the government were "not a significant portion of the total busmess of such corporations," he preferred not to provide exact figures on how much Republic Glass and Noble Philippines sold to the government. Velasco had a 51% interest in Republic Glass.

Other Velasco firms have also had their share of government deals. Gervel, Velasco's holding company, controls "the ownership of a building which is presently under lease by the Ministry of Trade" through an affiliate. Philippine Global Communications Inc. had a telecommunications franchise from the government. Philippine Tuna Ventures enjoyed a fishing permit from the government. Velasco claims that the contracts of the last two companies were granted before he joined the government. In the case of Tuna Ventures, Velasco sanctimoniously contended that the contract was aimed "before my appointment as Cabinet Minister of the Fourth Republic." What Velasco has consistently failed to mention was that he enjoyed a close relationship with Marcos even before he served as Marcos' cabinet minister. Velasco was an original trustee and incorporator of the Marcos Foundation when in was organized in 1969. This post was privileged position which Marcos reserved only for his closest associates.

A very clear example of government patronage was the support given to the Yulo-King Ranch, a large cattle ranch in Busuanga, Palawan. Velasco disavows any connection with the ranch, alleging

> As far as know, I had only a nominal share in the company to qualify me as a director... I do not recall having attended any board meeting of this company, much less was I involved in any of its operations, for I have never seen the ranch.

But records from the SEC show Velasco is a co-chairman of this venture together with Luis Yulo, a close personal friend of Marcos. The Yulo family, a clan which had great interests in the sugar industry, was very close to the Marcoses, the dictator and his wife making occasional visits to their large Canlubang Sugar Estate.

The Yulo-King Ranch was organized in 1975 as a 4,047 hectare venture to supply meat to a captive government market. Government-owned or controlled institutions such as the Philippine Integrated Meat Corp., the Armed Forces of the Philippines, and the luxury hotels in Metro-Manila acquired their meat from this ranch. Resources of the Armed Forces of the Philippines, such as security from the Philippine Constabulary and the transportation of cattle and other materials by Air Force planes, were used while the ranch was being organized.

Two later presidential decrees gave the Yulo King Ranch further benefits. PD 1297, issued 30 January 1978, expanded the ranch to 40,000 hectares and declared it as a government "experimental ranch" [8]. This decree gave the ranch a yearly appropriation of $2.7 million. A second decree, PD 1593, issued later in the year, declared the ranch as the sole unloading and discharging point for imported cattle. All cattle brought into the country, irrespective of whether they were for breeding or slaughter, had to go through the Yulo King Ranch. The Palawan ranch therefore formed a crucial part in the efforts to create a "meat cartel" in the country, discussed earlier in this chapter in the section on Benedicto. The cartel was merely one of the many joint projects between Benedicto and Velasco. The Yulo King Ranch had an estimated value of almost $6 million in 1979.

OIL PRICES

Controversy in Velasco's career, however, centered on his management of the oil industry. Serious questions have been raised concerning his multimillion purchases of crude oil and shipping vessels as Marcos' Minister of Energy. There have been charges that the incentives and rebates the Marcos government gave to the multinational oil companies actually ended as further rebate? and commissions to Marcos, Velasco, and the firms under their control.

Most controversial among the energy policies of Velasco was the manner through which the retail price of gasoline was set and the corresponding taxes the dictatorship imposed on its sale. Researches conducted by *Business Day* and other groups revealed that a great percentage of the retail price of gasoline was due to the taxes and levies imposed by the government. A typical breakdown of the cost components of gasoline is shown in the following table:

Cost Component	Price of Gasoline per Liter [9]	
	Premium	Regular
Share of Oil Companies	2.50	2.279
Dealer/Hauler Margin	0.177	0.169
Share of Government		
Consumer Price Equalization Fund (CPEF)	1.036	1.099
Energy Development Tax	0.483	0.438
Special Tax	1.10	1.060
Unaccounted Cost	0.004	0.005
Total Retail Cost of One Liter	**5.30**	**5.05**

The preceeding table reveals that more than 50% of the retail cost of gasoline went to the Marcos government in the form of taxes. Other studies computed higher percentages of the costs, averaging between 50-65% of the retail price of gasoline, as going to the government [10].

The most controversial of these government taxes was the Crude Oil Equalization Fund (COEF) [11]. On average, around 20% of the retail cost of gasoline went to this fund, a sizeable sum considering the huge demand for gasoline.

Velasco and the dictatorship continually justified the COEF. Among the official reasons given by Velasco were that it is a fund to serve as a cushion for future price increases of the international price of oil, as a safeguard against the continual depreciation of the peso, as a means to prevent oil shortages, etc.

A closer analysis of these justifications, however, show that these reasons offered to the public were totally misleading.

The COEF was established in March 1979 when OPEC abandoned cartelized pricing and started selling crude oil at different prices. Velasco maintained that such a fund would be needed to subsidize purchases of the oil companies which bought crude oil at prices higher than Arabian light oil, the benchmark used for the price of crude oil. It was claimed that the purpose of the fund was to equalize the cost of crude oil the companies were buying, supposedly to prevent the oil companies who were paying higher prices for crude oil from passing these higher costs to the consumer.

The reasoning suffers from both logical and historical inconsistencies. Firstly, if the COEF was intended to prevent oil companies from passing the higher costs to the consumer, then it made absolutely no sense to charge the consumer a levy to subsidize the oil companies which buy crude oil prices higher than the benchmark. This is a total contradiction. Secondly, the reasoning is also historically inaccurate. When the cartelized pricing of OPEC broke down in 1979, there was not a shortage of oil but a glut in the market and prices or crude oil were plummeting. It was a buyer's market, with the oil producing nations undercutting each other with lower prices. There was therefore no danger of shortage since the world market had a relative oversupply of oil at prices cheaper than the previous period of cartelized pricing. Velasco himself recognized the existence of this glut and the consequent decreases in the price of oil:"...the price of crude imported into the Philippines has gone down by $1.80 for every barrel from the level in March 1981..." [12]. Given the relative glut and continually falling prices of crude oil since 1981, the probability of impending oil shortages similar to those of the early 70's were virtually nil. Furthermore, when OPEC restored its cartelized pricing strategy on October 1981, the original basis for the fund no longer existed, leading one to hope that the extra charge would be abolished, but Velasco and the dictatorship still continued to charge the COEF. The reasoning is specious both on logical and historical grounds.

The subsidies awarded to multinational oil companies which bought at inefficient -- i.e., higher -- prices stood in sharp contrast with the high praises sung concerning the virtues of laissez-faire capitalism. Velasco's policies appeared to reward the inefficient buyers at the expense of the consumer. The logic of capitalism would appear to dictate that the inefficient firms should be allowed to give way to the more efficient firms through competition.

Velasco thus had to introduce other reasons for the existence of the Fund.

He maintained that without this mechanism there would be an "imbalance in oil supplies, since oil companies may be tempted to cut purchases as crude oil prices soar, thereby creating a domestic oil shortage" [13]. The Board of Energy justified the COEF by saying that the

> oil companies have been incurring additional costs in bringing the various kinds and grades of crude oil into the Philippines.... The oil companies must be assured the capability to import crude oil, otherwise we may reach a point in time when it would already be too late even for making a choice between the pain of a price increase and the crisis of petroleum shortage.

Again. the reasoning is faulty and misleading. One study revealed that oil companies profited at every step of the marketing chain from the time the crude oil is purchased to the time it is sold as gasoline in the gas station. Assuming a crude oil of $30 per barrel and a retail price of 5.30 pesos for every liter, oil companies on average reaped a profit of 33%, covering a total of five cost categories:

Category	Profit per liter	% a retail price in pesos
Crude oil	1.41	
Shipping	0.01	
Refining	0.01	
Marketing	0.01	
Other Charges	0.02	
Total	1.783	33%

All available data show a very high profit rate for the oil companies. The fund therefore cannot be justified by saying that the oil companies will go out of business if they are not subsidized.

The claim that the fund was needed to ensure a steady supply of imported oil was really a convenient mechanism to assure profits for the oil companies. The COEF was in reality an incentive and a legal cover for these companies to overprice the crude oil they buy from their mother companies. The government would reimburse the oil companies if they chose to buy crude only at higher prices. The Board of Energy, under Velasco's control, defined the COEF reimbursement scheme in the following manner:

Actual FOB of crude oil paid by oil company
minus
Benchmark price set by BOB
= Reimbursement to oil company [14].

The higher the price at which it purchased crude oil, the greater the reimbursement the oil company received from the government. A publication from the Ministry of Energy explained that the COEF was collected and held by the government to pay "oil companies in case they purchase crude at prices higher than the posted prices of Arabian Light crude". This therefore acted as an incentive for the oil companies to buy crude oil at higher rather than lower prices. The mechanism permitted the oil companies to realize profits at several levels in the international pricing chain. Not only was the importing oil company assured of reaping profits but the parent oil company which supplied the overpriced crude oil benefitted as well [15]. The scheme allowed oil companies recovery of all their costs plus profits. Instead of controlling the purchasing decisions of the oil companies, Velasco and the Marcos dictatorship were actually providing incentives for the oil companies to buy at higher prices. What the COEF did in effect was to subsidize and insure the profits those who were inefficient (or corrupt) at the expense of the ordinary consumer of gasoline.

The anomalous arrangement was brought to light when one company revealed that it had bought at prices lower than the benchmark set by the Board of Energy. While the major oil companies continued to buy at prices higher than the benchmark, Filipinas Shell confessed that it had bought crude oil lower than the benchmark and was therefore being over-remitted. The admission showed that the major international oil companies were profiting not only through the reimbursements provided by Velasco but also by buying crude oil at the international market at substantially inflated prices. Only after Filipinas Shell publicly called the attention of the Board of Energy was it embarrassed into issuing BOE Resolution No. 82-02, ordering the oil companies to turn over all over-recovered amounts to the CPEF. It had to be Filipinas Shell, a private oil company, that had to call the attention of the government that it was being overpaid. Neither the Board of Energy, nor the Ministry of Energy, nor Petrophil, the state oil company, nor any of the agencies which Velasco controlled called attention to this anomaly.

The absurdity of Velasco-engineered subsidies become more obvious when one considers that oil companies do not lose but rather profit greatly from oil price increases. They make money with OPEC price increases through at least two ways: 1) price increases provide a justification for the oil companies to increase their prices, consequently increasing their profits as well, and 2) the oil companies acquire windfall profits on their old stock. Under no circumstances are there decreases in the profits or profit margins.

For example, there were 12 price hikes between January 1973 and 3 August 1980, representing an aggregate increase of 1,432% over eight years, while OPEC prices increased only by an average of 517% during the same period. This clearly shows that oil companies gain rather than lose with continual price increases. Furthermore, oil companies also gain because old stocks are immediately sold at new prices. Since the oil stocks are generally equivalent to the supply of several months, windfall profits from such pricing gimmicks were considerable. In 1981, for example, oil companies made $303.8 million in 13 months, representing a monthly average of $23.4 million. The government then passed PD 1709 of 13 August 80 and Revenue Regulation No.7-8 in an attempt to give the appearance of regulating the windfall profits of the oil companies. But the law strangely provided that the windfall profit taxes be deducted not from the actual profits of the oil companies but from the CPOF [16]. This proved to be a non-tax tax since the entity charged was not the oil companies but the consuming public who paid for the CPOF.

Another boon to the oil companies was the government's policy on exchange rates. When OPEC members succeeded in restoring cartelized pricing on October 1981, the original basis for the CPEF ceased to exist, but Velasco refused to end it, cooking up other reasons for its existence. This time the dictatorship resorted to the problem of international exchange rates to justify the fund. The Board of Energy passed a resolution assuring the oil companies a *fixed* peso-dollar exchange rate of 7.65 pesos to the dollar. Board of Energy Resolution No. 81-10, issued on 1 July 1981, provided reimbursement to the oil companies for "..increases in the peso cost of crude oil... due to the adjustment in the peso-dollar exchange rate beyond P7.65 to US$1.00. [17]. In Velasco's words, the fund "...became a convenient mechanism to use in responding to the new problem of foreign exchange fluctuation" [18]. The differences in the actual exchange rate and the subsidized *rate* of 7.65 s to the dollar assured the oil companies an additional source of funds. The continuous depreciation of the peso further meant that the subsidy of the oil companies grew as the foreign exchange crisis worsened [19]. This was a privilege which has never been extended to Philippine industries which continually need dollars to import badly-needed machinery.

The CPEF ballooned into a gigantic sum in a little over three years after it was established. The Ministry of Energy reported that the total collection had reached $948.5 million as of 30 June 1982, with $714.3 million, representing 75.3% of the amount, already disbursed to the oil companies. The windfall to the oil companies was more than the $586 million the government had put aside to rescue ailing firms for that year. The practice of charging levies such as the CPEF on top of regular taxes continued throughout the years of Marcos' rule.

While the funds were collected through government fiat, they were inexplicably controlled by the oil companies. The ideal institution to administer the funds was the National Treasury, since the CPEF was in reality a tax which the 'government imposed on the consuming public. But Velasco permitted the oil companies to directly hold on to the funds instead of turning them over to the government. The Ministry of Energy gave the oil companies one month to apply for certificates authorizing them to hold on to the CPEF collections, leaving huge financial resources at the immediate disposal of these companies.

The fund was divided amongst five companies, with the following average monthly shares:

Oil Company	Relative Share
Petrophil	40%
Caltex	27%
Shell	17%
Mobil	15%
Getty	3% [20]

Petrophil, the firm which consistently cornered the lion's share of the fund, was marketing subsidiary of state-run Philippine National Oil Company (PNOC). Both entities were chaired by Velasco. Getty's shares of the fund were later absorbed by BASIC-Landoil Energy, a Marcos oil conglomerate run by Jose de Venecia, a pal of Marcos from the old Congress, and Alejandro Melchor, Marcos' executive secretary, getting a 4% share of the funds.

The figures seriously call into question the wisdom of Velasco's policies and the sincerity of the Marcos government. The PNOC had bragged that it "handled virtually all of the country's crude imports using its own fleet, supplemented by time-charters." The Velasco-controlled firm imported 48% of the country's oil requirements in 1978, 53% in 1979, ultimately accounting for 60% in later years. The oil would later be sold at a profit to Bataan Refining Corp where Velasco was chairman. The Bataan Refining would refine the crude oil and later sell it again at a profit to Petrophil where Velasco was again chairman. Petrophil in turn sold the gasoline to consumers at a profit. One may question the rationale for the state to continually burden its citizens with onerous taxes while maintaining a highly profitable network for its government corporations.

These government corporations were staffed by other favored men who drew large salaries and fees. The PNOC, the country's largest corporation [21], had Velasco as chairman and president, while its directors were Marcos' favorite ministers such as Cesar Virata (Finance), Vicente Paterno (Industry), Estelito Mendoza (Solicitor General), Juan Ponce Enrile (Defense), Jaime iaya (Central Bank) [22], despite a May 1978 government order forbidding positions in companies if their cabinet duties are not related to the functions of the corporations.

An equally fundamental question is why Petrophil, a state corporation, also had to avail of the CPEF. Why need a government corporation, ideally an entity at the service of the people, burden its citizens with additional monetary impositions because it chose to buy crude oil higher than the benchmark?

The interests of Velasco and Marcos were so wedded to the oil industry that there were times that when the overnment even urged the oil firms to petition the BOE for price hikes [23].

Because of all of the privileges the oil companies enjoyed through the policies of the Marcos state, the fund was called the "milking cow" of the oil companies [24]. Given the large share of the booty enjoyed y the Velasco-controlled state corporations, one might more accurately say that the fund was the "milking cow" of Marcos and Velasco. If Velasco was really sincere in his resignation offer when it was learned that he had a mansion abroad, he should at least explain the absurd energy policies he pursued and revealing how much he earned from all of the government corporations where he serve as chairman or director.

The continual increases in the prices of petroleum products, as well as the taxes and other state-imposed costs such as the CPEF, drastically cut into the living wage of the Pilipmo. The ordinary consumer suffered in several ways to pay or the burdens imposed upon him by the Marcos government and Velasco's oil companies. Direct payment came through increased fuel rices, the CPEF, and other forms of taxes. Indirect payments came through increased prices in fares, rice and other staples, milk, sugar, cooking oil, soap, school supplies, and many other commodities which made up the consumer basket of the ordinary person. So dire was the effect of fuel price increases that Marcos himself had to admit the role that this had in the inflation rate during his 1979 State of the Nation Address:

The increase of oil prices and related developments have exceeded our original inflation assumption of 7% as contained in the plan. Nonetheless, the government will intensify efforts to contain inflation at around 15% [25].

Velasco's policies caused great hardship. Direct costs in the form of taxes alone was already enormous. Taxes from oil and petroleum made up 7% of total revenues of government in 1972, but by 1981 the amount had leaped to 37%. Over the period from 1972 to 1981, the dictatorship had exacted a total of $5.85 billion in taxes from oil. One study revealed that the oil tax burden per capita was already $27.38 in 1979, meaning that each Filipino on the average had paid the government that amount in the form of taxes on oil. This is catastrophic, considering that the Annual Report of the Ministry of Social Services & Development (MSSD) for this year, 1979, had reported that 30% of the opulation, representing the poorest segment, was earning
only $34 a month.

These figures are from just direct taxes. They do not include money extracted from consumers through the CPEF and other schemes within the oil industry. The overnment, for example, had allocated the equivalent of 7% of the national budget for the CPEF. The true extent of Velasco's policies can be exposed only when we consider the other forms of direct taxation such as the CPEF and the indirect factors such as the consequent rise in the price of basic commodities. Only then can we appreciate how the populace suffered because of the policies of a few in power.

Attempting to justify his taxation schemes, Marcos was quoted by Enerconews, the publication of the Ministry of Energy, as saying "we must be ruthless with ourselves" [26].

But while "we are already ruthless with ourselves," or better yet, while they had been ruthless with us, high government officials were exempt from paying these taxes. Presidential LOI 835, issued 26 March 79, exempted Batasan [Legislature] members and other overnment officials" from paying taxes on 400 liters of gasoline every month. Velasco, who presumably also enjoyed the privilege, justified the figure of 400 liters, saying "the per capita consumption of gasoline is based on an average car spending 40 liters a week or 160 liters a month." Critics pointed out that the monthly allowance granted to government officials was good for three to four cars a month [27].

Thus, while the officials were enjoying such privileges, self-employed drivers who eked out a living by plying long hours suffered losses in their income, while the riding public was forced to pay higher fares to be able to continue their daily scourge of pushing and shoving to get a ride in a crowded jeepney. Instead of extending some form of amelioration to the very people they taxed, Velasco and other government officials continued to take the meat away from their tables.

THE QUESTTON OF KICKBACKS

The foregoing discussion covered only one of the costs making up the price of premium gasoline, the CPEF. The other cost categories must also he scrutinized, and the exercise must be extended to cover other petroleum products such as regular gasoline, diesel, bunker fuel, aviation fuel, industrial oils and lubricants, asphalt etc to fully appreciate the burden Marcos and Velasco inflicted upon the consuming public.

Another monetary imposition the gang cooked up, for example, was the Energy Development Fund. Organize with the pretext of developing local sources of energy, this account was financed through a Special Fund Tax. Some $533.3 million had been collected by 1980 for this fund. While Velasco pompously claimed to the press that this was "...the only special fund of the government whose disbursements were regularly reported to the public [28], he never gave an accounting of it. It was later discovered that the prirnary beneficiaries of this tax were companies Marcos and his cronies controlled, such as Balabac Oil, Landoil, PNOC, Mapocor, and Meralco [29].

Other researches have uncovered another interesting discrepancy in the retail pricing of gasoline. They detected that there was an unaccounted .004 to .005 centavo per liter of gasoline sold [30]. While the amount is merely a thousandth of a peso, it ultimately represented a huge sum since the estimated national annual consumption was 12.72 billion liters at this time. This discrepancy would mean between $658,000 to $790,000 a year in 1980.

The legal status of these funds was never made clear. The government spent enormous sums in newspaper advertisements to explain that it was not a tax. Velasco himself admitted that this fund was "not a tax because it goes back to the oil companies in the form of rebates" [31]. But while the dictatorship was very clear as to what it was not, they were murky as to what it was. When Jaime Laya, Marcos' budget minister and a director of the PNOC, was questioned in public regarding the legal basis of this fund, he was evasive and did not answer, saying only that "the fund collected is actually a trust fund, and under the law creating trust funds, this is automatically appropriated so that it would not be diverted for other purposes" [32].

It was very convenient for Velasco and Marcos to maintain the legal ambiguity concerning the fund. if the fund was a government tax, then the responsibility of collecting, accounting, and auditing the fund lay in the government. The money would then automatically turned over to the national treasury, and it would then be subject to the auditing regulations of the COA. But if, the money was a private fund of the oil comanies, then it would be beyond the jurisdiction of the COA. The fund would then simply be a private account of the oil companies. But a contradiction then arises. If the money is private fund of the oil companies, then why did the Marcos government require the consumers to pay for it? It had all the appearances of a tax since it was a government-imposed fee on a commodity which everyone had to pay upon purchase. But it was more convenient not to order an audit of the money that had been raised, hence the legal ambiguity surrounding the account.

Velasco tried his best to avoid audits of the government corporations he controlled and the different funds collected from the sales of petroleum.

Velasco, for example, adamantly denied that the COA had jurisdiction of the PNOC. Velasco served as president and chairman of PNOC, one of the largest corporations in the country. It was extremely profitable, increasing its net profit from $39.88 million in 1983 to $55.77 million in 1984. Velasco claimed that the PNOC charter prohibited external audits of the PNOC and its subsidiaries, and that a special presidential decree, PD 334, also exempted PNOC from such audits. But wiiile Velasco vehemently fought off these external audits, a revealing incident occurred. The resident auditor issued a disclaimer concerning the accuracy and fairness of the PNOC's financial statements. This made the PNOC the only government on corporation where the resident auditor had raised such major objections and publicized his reservations. The auditor claimed that the PNOC had failed to submit data on payroll disbursements and other major financial documents for examination.

Velasco fought off government audits of the different special funds. He claimed that the Oil Industry Special Fund was regularly audited by a respectable private accounting firm, a tactic Velasco frequently employed in his public statements. What Velasco habitually failed to mention was that the accounting firm he constantly referred to was SGV, a firm which enjoyed a cozy relationship with many Marcos- and crony-owned corporations [33]. One of founding partners of this accounting firm was Alfredo Velayo, the uncle of two Marcos cabinet members and a close associate of Disini (see section). Velasco is also known to have used the address of a Hong Kong branch of the SGV, SGV Byrne, in organizing shell corporations to hide his real estate investments in the US (please see Chapter IV). The audits of SGV are therefore automatically suspect.

When the Marcos dictatorship fell, investigations on Velasco's corporations were attempted, but these efforts were fruitless. Velasco quickly fled the country, with is safe passage assured by Minister of Defense Enrile assigning him a military escort. Velasco then asked Antonio V. del Rosario, Velasoo's second in command at the PNOC, to immediately resign from his post to avoid being questioned. Had del Rosario, the Executive Director and Senior Vice President of PNOC and a trusted aide of Velasco, been questioned, he would have been able to shed a lot of light on Velasco's finances. But investigators working for the government of Mrs. Aquino never seriously pursued an investigation of Velasco. The Wall Street Journal later explained why a thorough investigation into Velasco's financial dealings became almost impossible:

Both the securities commission and the Bureau of Internal Revenue, long staffed by Marcos appointees, said computer problems destroyed some of their records right after the 1986 revolution. So investigators are digging through warehouses for paper copies of tax returns erased by the computer. Similarly, Aquino-appointed managers of the state oil company found that about 75% of the concem's records had been destroyed [34].

Other accusations went beyond the lack of audits and the destruction of records and were of a more serious nature. The New York Times cited reports coming from presidential palace circles that Velasco was getting "a commission for every barrel of imported crude" [35].

Velasco quickly denied these allegations. In letters to Marcos later made public, Velasco defended himself by saying that transactions between governments were not susceptible to what he termed "wrongdoing." In one letter, Velasco claimed that

the very nature of our crude contracts as govemment-to-govemment transaction (sic) precludes any possibility of wrongdoing. It would betray lack of diplomatic finesse and would indeed be downright insulting even to hint that governments... could participate in undehanded methods to sell their crude to a small country like ours whose importations could hardly have any significant impact on their crude sales volumes.

Even when there was a supply glut in January 1983 and it was relatively easy to buy oil in the international market, Velasco still persisted on what he called G-to-G transactions. While clearly admitting that there were advantages in spot market transactions, Velasco still insisted on carrying out the purchases through the government:

we found it desirable to review our oil sourcing policy since price-wise there appeared *to some advantages in shifting from govemment-to-govemment (G-to-G) contracts to spot market supply arrangementss. If it were true that irregularities were being committed in the crude tmportations, this could have presented a golden opportunity for me to discard existing G-to-G commitments where under-the-table commissions are impossible and make some "deals" with spot market suppliers. ....the records will bear out that I strongly recommended maintenance of exisring G-to-G arrangements in view of over-all politico-economic considerations...*

Velasco continued his policy even as international prices dropped in August 1985 and even when there was in his own words a "dramatic softening of crude oil prices" in September 1985.

Velasco's arguments are suspect.

On the grounds of consistency alone, he may be faulted. It is not true that Velasco always "strongly recommended maintenance of existing G-to-G arrangements in view of over-all politico-economic considerations." When there was a move to separate functions of chairman and president of the PNOC, Velasco resisted the move by arguing that he should keep both positions since transactions in international oil market were conducted on "a purely personal basis."

He also claimed that the purchasing arrangements he engineered were necessary to maintain the "good will of Middle East suppliers" and ensure job opportunities for overseas Filipinos and stability in Mindanao. The implication was that the success of certain aspects of Philippine foreign policy were totally dependent on him being the sole purchaser of crude oil for the country.

Furthermore, the premise that governments are not capable of wrong-doing is absurd. There are many instances of how governments acted against the interests of its citizens. The generous favors Marcos and Velasco extended to the oil companies are clear examples. Velasco's policies and decisions as Minister of Energy were so scandalously in favor of the oil industry that one wonders whether Velasco was a government official or an employee of the oil companies. If therefore Velasco and Marcos showered the oil companies with many financial incentives, then one may reasonably ask, what would prevent these oil companies from reciprocatmg with equal generosity in the form of other "rebates" or "commissions" to Marcos and Velasco?

This was precisely the charge made by a *New York Times* investigative article. The *Times* reported that elasco had received undeclared rebates on purchases of crude oil [36]. The charge is completely plausible since there were many times in the early 1980's that prices dipped so low that it was a buyer's market and oil companies would have been quite willing to provide incentives to their buyers. More damaging was the charge of a bank official that the National Commercial Bank of Saudi Arabia, an institution which dealt closely with the PNOC and an important Philippine creditor, had "balked" at the Marcos government's request to restructure its debt in 1983 "because of information that Mr. Velasco was pocketing some oil company funds intended for oil purchases" [37]. Teofisto Guingona of the COA also charged:

> He took a staggering amount... We really don't know how much it was, or how much went to Marcos, because for all these years PNOC was never audited.

The charges against Velasco extended to questions oonceming the purchase of oil tankers, overpriced freight charges, and improper insurance costs.

Velasco's letters and memoranda to Marcos reveal that the purchase and construction of new oil tankers and ships for the PNOC were one with the help of close Marcos cronies. Most of the tankers were purchased throu Roberto Benedicto, while the new vessels were constructed through the Romualdez-owned Baseco (see sections on Benedicto and Romualdez).

In a letter to Marcos dated 5 August 1974, Velasco wrote concerning the purchase of three oil tankers with an estimated cost of $81 million, adding that "Ambassador R.S. Benedicto has been requested to handle the negotiation for the purchase and financing of the project" [38]. A second letter written on 14 August updated Marcos on the progress of the negotiations for the new tankers and again mentions Benedicto's involvement. Two months later, he again wrote to Marcos informing him that Northern Lines, Benedicto's shipping line, would be used to inspect the tankers, while Reyes & Lim Co. woul conduct further tests. One of the tankers would be bought from an Israeli shipping company for $28 million, with the negotiations to be concluded in Tokyo on November 1974 with Benedicto's presence: "Ambassador Benedicto conducted the negotiations for the purchase of the tankers, I have requested his presence during the closing and he has agreed to attend." Other letters similarly reveal that the two worked closely in the purchase of other tankers. Guingona, working for the Commission on Audit, later charged that three oil tankers bought between 1974-5 from Japan, priced between $16.8 million to $28.5 million each, appear to have been overpriced by more than 10% [39]. Money for the tankers, like the urchase of a Lear jet for Velasco's use, came horn the Oil Industry Special Fund, a $400 million discretionary fund which was controlled solely by Velasco and Marcos.

Other documents show Velasco arranging the construction of ships through Baseco. A 5 August 1974 letter shows Velasco contracting Baseco to construct three shallow draft vessels for $24 million. He also interceded with the government to allow Baseco to import the materials and equipment for the construction of these ships tax-free.

Despite the purchases and construction of new ships, Velasco still chartered private vessels to transport around 25% of the PNOC's shipments. The *New York Times* reported that "...Mr. Velasco negotiated to pay an extra 5% commission whenever the national oil company chartered tankers to carry crude oil to the Philipines" [40]. The *Bulletin Today* reported that government auditors had calculated this extra 5% amounted to an overpayment of more than $3.76 million durin the 11-year period (1974 throu 1985) that Velasco controlled the oil industry [41]. There were a total of 254 charter contracts during the period, costing the PNOC $75.2 million. No less than 57 of these contracts involved excessively high brokerage commissions, reaching as high as 8.75%, in contrast with the usual commission rates of 1.25% to 2.5% [42]. The majp/rity of the contracts were through three brokerage firms: Philipp Brothers, Warren Philippines, Reyes & Lim Co.

The *Bulletin Today* reported that "...automatic arrangements with brokers wherein the commissions went to a person or an unnamed account outside of the country as soon as the shipment was lifted" [43]. These commissions do not yet include the "questionable" amounts involved in freight fees and demurrage charges and other expenses [44]. The *New York Times* reported the head of a major ship chartering service in Manila as saying that the extra commissions were kicked back and paid through the treasurer of Gervel, Carmencita Clavecilla, a relative of Velasco, an were deposited in bank accounts in Hong Kong and the US.

Insurance for the PNOC shipments was another matter raised against Velasco. The insurance was handled by Integral Factors, a company owned by Benedicto. The PNOC was reported to have paid more than 1% of value of crude oil being transported per voyage, while the premium other oil companies paid was only .0625%. it was estimated that at these rates the PNOC would be aying more than $200,000 per tanker voyage. Velasco defended himself saying that

> ...PNOC had to throu h Integral Factors Corp. (IFC) as it was the GSIS general agent through which GSIS directed PNOC to secure insurance. There is also an insinuation that the rates were high. My recollection was that crude insurance was about 085% and not the more than one percent stated in a news article.

Velasco unfortunately did not provide the appropriate documentation to back up his "recollection" on the msurance rates. In any case, the PNOC should have been paying lower, instead of higher, premiums since it could avail of fleet discounts. The reference to the GSIS moreover was a patent attempt to pass the blame to the government insurance system, also run by another crony. The more important question was why Integral Factors was named the general agent of the GSIS in the first place.

Given these allegations against Velasco, it becomes understandable why an American diplomat who knows Velasco was quoted by the New York Times as having said: "It goes without saying Velasco will have a very comfortable retirement" [45].

FRONT CORPORATIONS

It appears that Velasco's preparation for a comfortable retirement started as early as 1964 when he organized Gervel, a corporation designed as a holding com any for Velasco's many interests. The name is an acronym formed from the first three letters of Velasco's first and last names. The Times reported that Gervel's articles of incorporation are missing from the SEC, a serious violation of law, that the company was not listed in the telephone directory, and that the secretary assigned to answer phone calls claimed she did not know how to contact the company's officers [46].

A source with access to Gervel's articles of incorporation claims that Velasco directly owns 25% of the company, while his three sons and two daughters hold 52%. Gervel's president is Alfredo R. de Borja, a relative of Velasco. The Times also reported that Bienvenido Tan Jr., a Manila businessman, had acknowledge that he had

> served as a nominee for many of Mr. Velasco's shares in Gervel... Moreover, Mr. Tan is chairman of Republic Glass and holds 40 pereent of the shares of The Manila Times on Mr. Velasco's behalf; so Mr. Velasco's investment would not be public knowledge... [47].

Another person associated with Velasco companies was Tomas Alcantara, a college friend of Alfredo de Borja. Alcantara served as a director or stockholder in Velasco-controlled companies such as Gervel and Cello Realty Corp. Alcantara was asked to be a front for Velasco's children, later turning their shares to them. The Aquino government later appointed Alcantara as Deputy Minister for Industry and Investment, while Bienvenido Tan Jr. was given the coveted post of commissioner of Bureau of Internal Revenue [48].

Velasco defended himself by claiming that

Gervel as well as its subsidiaries never took advantage of my Government (sic) position to receive any special treatment by way of highly advantageous contracts with the Government (sic). In fact, there was no contract of any significance entered into by Gervel or its subsidiaries with any Government (sic) entity [49].

Velasco never provided a list of government contracts his companies received so that the public could verify his claim that they were insignificant. Whether or not his corporations received government support, Velasco's fortunes soared. In the statement of assets and liabilities he filed in 1973 before he became Marcos' Minister, he confessed that he had a net worth of only $1.09 million and investments of $740,000. By 1981, however, Gervel was reporting total assets worth $20.2 million and a net worth of $13.9 million "as adjusted on the basis of the then estimated market values of its assets". Given the strong interests Velasco has in Gervel, it would therefore be interesting to investigate the exact relationship between the finances of the company and Velasco's increase in his person net worth during this period.

If some investigators are to be believed, the key to understanding the profitable operations of Gervel lies in Velasco's control of the oil industry. According to them

the shadowy company, Gervel, may have been used by Geronimo Z. Velasco, the former Energy Minister and chairman of the government-owned Philippine National Oil Company, as a conduit to siphon off millions of dollars in illegal kickbacks and rebates from the company.

Another company linked to Velasco is Decision Research Management. Ltd., a front corporation registered in Hong Kong. Velasco initially claimed that he did not "know anything about Decision Research" and that he had "never heard of the company." But when it was revealed that his sons were shareholders of the company and that Alfredo de Borja was a director, Velasco changed his story, providing a long account about the company and the real estate properties in the US linked to it:

To my knowledge, DR is controlled by a group of foreign investors organized by a friend and business associate whose identity I cannot disclose withouthis permission, although I must point out that this person has no dealings whatsoever with MOE or PNOC. He is a European-based investor with a solid reputation in international financial circles. This friend was instrumental in arranging the financing on the acquisition by DR of the houses in Woodside, CA and Century City LA which were mentioned as belonging to me. Due to legal requirements imposed by the counsel for the financiers, title to the properties is reserved by DR but I have a right to use the premises and also the option to purchase the same.

Of the 10,000 shares of Decision Research, 9,998 are controlled Wellwyn Investment Corp., a front corporation based in Panama, while the two remaining token shares are owned by Velasco's sons. The shareholders and directors of the company:

Shareholders	*Directors*
Welwyn Investment	Patrick de Borja
Urbano Velasco	Alfredo de Borja
Gemonimo Jr.	Francis de Borja
	Cipher Ltd.
	Directorate Ltd.

The only known address for Decision Research is the office of SGV-Byrne, an accounting firm based Hong Kong which has connections with SGV in Manila. The only known address for Wellwyn Investment is Johnson, Stokes, & Master, British law firm in Hong Kong which specializes in handling dummy companies. Cipher Ltd. and Directorate Ltd. are both listed at SGV Byrne's address at the Hopewell Centre in Hong Kong. Cipher, "identified as vehicle for high-level capital flight," has been linked with Amworld, a shady company implicated with the misappropriation of US aid funds.

It is believed that Alfredo de Borja manages all of Velasco's offshore funds, a View disclaimed by Velasco: "Alfredo e Bor'a is my nephew, but I don't know anything about his managing my supposed overseas properties." De Borja is also the founder and president of the Overland Trading Co., a US-based company which does the purchasing for the Ministry of Energy.

With the help of Enrile, Velasco left the Philippines on the day of Marcos' downfall, flying to Singapore on the PNOC Lear jet. He spent three weeks in his mansron in Woodside, California, then proceeded to Geneva and met with Sheik Ahmed Zaki Yamani, the Oil Minister of Saudi Arabia and close friend.

Endnotes

1. Jessica Densing, "Velasco's Net Worth: P1 billion, say probers," *Philippine Daily Inquirer*, 5 July 1986
2. Velasco's real estate holdings are discussed in more detail in Chapter 4, the dealing with the overseas properties.
3. Whenever Velasco talks about his career before he joined the Marcos government, he constantly refers to his training as a mechanical engineer and that he was the president of Dole Pineapple Philippines, the local subsidiary of Castle & Cooke. He conveniently fails to mention his association with Harry Stonehill, the American businessman who claimed to control over all postwar Filipino politicians by the pockets. Velasco was one of key people in the so-called Stonehill Gang," the term used to refer to the close associates of Stonehill. Republic Glass, where Velasco has substantial interests, was originally a Stonehill company. Velasco headed this company after Stonehill was deported from the country. Knowing how Stonehill's former associates such as Velasco and Alfonso Yuchengco

became close to the Marcos regime will shed much light on what actually happened to the vast properties of Stonehill after he was deported from the country.

4. Letter of 5 June 1984 to Marcos.

5. P110 million

6. Jessica Densing, "Velasco's Net Worth: P1 billion, say probers," *Philippine Daily Inquirer*, 5 July 1986.

7. Jessica Densing, "Velasco's Net Worth: P1 billion, say probers," *Philippine Daily Inquirer*, 5 July 1986.

8. Business Day, 29 April 1986.

9. Business Day, 23 March 1981. While the retail prices of gasoline and other petroleum products continually changed during Marcos' regime, the following breakdown of the price components is typical of how the costs were apportioned between the oil companies and the Marcos government. Figures are given in Philippine pesos.

10. See for example *Ibon, Primer on Oil Industry,* p. 13, 1981 and the government publication **Enerconews** published in 1980.

11. This fund has undergone several changes of name. Crude Equalization Fund, Consumer Price Equalization Fund (CPEF), etc. have been used.

12. Velasco, "Petroleum Product Prices: Why They Are Moving," December 1982, quoted *Ibon,* 15 January 1983.

13. *Far Eastern Economic Review*, 15 August 1980.

14. "Unmasking the Oil Cover-up," *Ibon,* 15 January 1983. The Board of Energy defined different benchmarks for each type of crude oil.

15. The hearings conducted by Senator Jose W. Diokno in the Senate in the early 1970's on the pricing strategies of the oil companies clearly showed that the oil companies engaged in transfer pricing: different subsidiaries of the same company bought crude oil from their mother companies at substantial profits to the mother company. Given the special pricing arrangements oil companies have with their mother companies, the cost which the oil companies quote as their purchasing price should therefore be subjected to carefully scrutiny.

Current research shows that while international oil companies were selling crude oil between $20-30 a barrel, the FOB price at which they acquired the crude oil from Saudi Arabia was an average $6 a barrel.

16. The 1980 Equalization Fund amounted to $700 million. [*Business Day*, 5 August 1980], but the windfall profits tax was a meager $63.2 million [*Business Day*, 9 October 1980], leaving a substantial amount for the oil companies.

17. Board of Energy, Resolution No.81-80, 1 July 1981.

18. G.Z. Velasco, "Petroleum Product Prices: Why They Are Moving," Dec. 82 press release.

19. *Ibon* constructed a very useful exercise showing how depreciation in the peso beyond P7.65 to the dollar actually benefited the oil companies through the CPEF. *Ibon,* 5 January 1983.

20. These are rounded figures. Sheilah Ocampo, "Fighting the Philippines' costly energy crunch," *Far Eastern Economic Review,* 15 August 1980.

21. The PNOC was organized in 1973. Within 5 years made it to Fortune' top 500 industrial corporations (1978), the only Philippine firm to reach the list. It then had total sales of $1.023 billion, assets of $676.423 million, and net income of $32.646 million.

22. *Bulletin Today*, 4 October 78

23. *Business Day* 30 Dec. 1982.

24. *Bulletin Today*, 11 August 80.

25. "Report to the Nation," 26 July 1979. While Marcos was saying that he wanted to control inflation at 15%, other government sources were already saying that it had already reached 20.4%.

26. Enerconews, February 80

27. *Ibon,* 15 August 1980.

28. *Bulletin Today*, 26 July 1980

29. *Bulletin Today,* 26 July 1980
30. Villegas, p.103
31. *Times Journal,* 26 July 80,
32. *Bulletin Today,* 11 August 80
33. Belinda Olivares Cunanan, "Marcos, the Cronies and the SGV," *Philippine Daily Inquirer,* 21 April 1986; Julie A. Amargo, *Malaya,* 3 June 1986.
34. June Kronholz, "Much Marcos Wealth, Still Carefully Hidden, Eludes Investigators," *Wall Street Journal,* February 11, 1987
35. Fox Butterfield, "Marcos Crony Returning Despite Fraud Evidence," *New York Times,* 24 March 1986.
36. Fox Butterfield, "Marcos Crony Returning Despite Fraud Evidence," *New York Times,* 24 March 1986.
37. Velasco arplained his side by alleging that "...the opposition of National Commercial Bank of Saudi Arabia (NCB) was basically its esire to maintain PNOC as its debtor and preclude the powbility of its restructures exposures from being used the Central Bank to finance some other activity." Fox Butterfield, Marcos Crony Returning espite Fraud Evidence," *New York Times,* 24 March 1986.
38. Letter of 5 August 1974.
39. Fox Butterfield, "Marcos Crony Returning Despite Fraud Evidence," *New York Times,* 24 March 1986.
40. Fort Butterfield, "Marcos Crony Returning Despite Fraud Evidence," *New York Times,* 24 March 1986.
41. Ellen P. Samaniego, "Gov't Probes Velasco Deals," *Bulletin,* July 3 1986.
42. The estimated $3.76 overpayment represents the execs over the normal 2.5% paid by PNOC.
43. Ellen P. Samanjego, "Gov't Probes Velasco Deals," *Bulletin,* July 3 1986.
44. Ellen P. Samaniego, 'Gov't Probes Velasco Deals," *Bulletin,* July 3 1986.
45. Fox Butterfield, "Marcos Crony Returning Despite Fraud Evidence," *New York Times,* 24 March 1986.
46. Fox Butterfield, "Marcos Crony Returning Despite Fraud Evidence," *New York Times,* 24 March 1986.
47. Fox Butterfield, "Marcos Crony Returning Despite Fraud Evidence," *New York Times,* 24 March 1986. Strangely, the government of Corazon Aquino later assigned Tan first as commissioner of internal revenue then as Ambassador to Austria.
48. The wisdom of these appointments are therefore clearly dubious.
49. Letter of 16 April 1986.

HERMINIO DISINI

The magnitude of Herminio Disini's empire and the speed with which it was built is nothing short of astonishing.

Disini started his operations with a rented one-room office manned by only a secretary and a messenger in 1969. The company, called Herdis [1] Management & Investment Corp., was capitalized with a small bank loan of $3,500. Within a little over half a decade, Disini came to head a vast conglomerate of more than 50 companies covering diverse areas as tobacco filters, logging and pulp processing, petroleum and petrochemicals, cellophane, fabrics and yarn, nuclear power, real estate, airlines, computer services, insurance and banking. Within six years of starting operations, Disini's empire enjoyed $140 million in total consolidated assets and ranked 15th among the country's top 1000 corporations in 1976 [2]. The conglomerate had an estimated total assets of over $200 million by 1978 [3]. 6 capital accumulation continued until the Disini empire reached its peak with total assets of $1 billion.

What made Disini's rise more surprising is that he led a rather ordinary career before he amassed the several dozen companies which comprised his conglomerate. He worked as a certified public accountant for Peat, Marwick, Mitchell and Co. in California for ten years after he acquired his Master's in Business Administration from Sta. Clara University, California. He then served as a financial officer and director of F.E. Zuellig Inc. in Manila. His superiors in these firms noted Disini as a hardworking, though not extraordinary, employee who moonlighted to supplement his income.

Disini's remarkable success at becoming an entrepreneur extraordinaire lies less in his business acumen as it does with his personal links with the Marcos couple. Disini is married to Dra. Inday Escolin, Imelda's first cousin who served as Mrs. Marcos' personal physician and a governess of the Marcos children. Disini himself hails from Narvacan, Ilocos Sur, and was a golfing artner of Marcos. The benefits Disini derived from presidential help clearly illustrate how "one of several close friends and relatives of the Marcoses have prospered as the President acquired power to issue governmental contracts and rewrite tax rovisions by decree" [4]. An Amencan banker who knows Disini describedp him as "right up to his armpits" in presidential favors [5].

After being involved in many controversial projects in the Philippines, Disini fled the country. He applied and got Austrian citizenship in 1982 and is now living in a luxur1ous villa in the outskirts of Vienna, in Maria Anzabach, Piesting [6]. The villa, held under the name of Liechtenstein Co., is completely secure from intruders, with extra security provided by two Great Danes which Disini pampers with meat bought from the butcher shops of Vienna. *Trend*, an Austrian monthly, quotes the remarks of utter amazement at the opulence of Disini's new dwelling by a worker doing renovation work on the villa: "Selbst das Klo ist so schon, dab du dich gar nicht draufsetzen traust" [7].

Disini acquired Austrian citizenship through the promise of heavy investments and cultivating close ties with Austrian politicians. He promised to manufacture the inputs for semiconductors, but had not yet established the factory four years after he received his new citizenship. Disini befriended Dr. Walther Konrad, a former assistant of the Austrian Federal Chamber of Commerce who has had ties with other Marcos cronies, and Walter Zimper, the mayor of Piesting, where Disini's villa is located [8]. Helping Dismi with his application was a certain Dr. Helm, a lawyer who has also worked with the citizenship applications of other Marcos associates.

Burgermeister Zimper recommended Disini's citizenship application to the government of Lower Austria because of the "auBerordentlichen Leistungen auf wirtschaftlichem Gebiet im Interesse der Republik Osterreich" [9]. And when the authorities from Lower Austria finally recommended the application to the federal government, it was claimed that it was because of

> *Die personlichen Vomussetzungen des Staatsburgers und sein in seiner Stellung im Rahmen der Herdis-Gruppe begrundeter organisatorischer and finanzieller Ruckhalt geben AnlaB, seine Aktivitaten auf wirtschaftlichem Gebeitals auBerordentliche Leistungen zu bezeichnen [10].*

Because of these strong recommendations from Austrian politicians, who referred to his business history as the reasons for approving his application, Disini was quickly granted Austrian citizenship. Disini has since been involved in some scandals in Austria and is also believed to be engaged in the nefarious business of selling arms. Given the high esteem Austrian authorities bestowed upon Disini, it is therefore important to review his activities in the Philippines.

THE BIG BREAK

Disini's first major venture was marked with controversy from the very beginning.

He organized the Philippine Tobacco Filters Corp. (PTFC) in 1970 with his meager capital, supplemented by a 30% investment in the shares by Baumgartner Papiers of Switzerland. The venture would have remained an insignificant one, but Disini got his big break when a controversial presidential decree forced his competitors out of business.

Marcos issued PD 750 on 21 July 1975 ordering an increase in the tariffs on the raw materials imported by Disini's main competitor, Filtrona Phil. Inc. The decree slapped a 100% duty on the acetate tow and other raw materials the American and British-owned company imported for use in manufacturing cigarette filters. PD 750 claimed that its aim was to ensure "fair competition in the local cigarette industry as well as to stimulate the development and growth of the local manufacturers of cigarette filter rods." While the decree raised the tariff of Filtrona's imports from 10% to 100%, it exempted Disini's company from the increase [11]. The decree forced Filtrona out of business.

The *New York Times* quoted a former executive of Filtrona as saying that the decree was issued only when Filtrona had rejected an offer from Disini to buy it out. When US Ambassador William Sullivan protested the moves, Marcos is said to have blackmailed Filtrona by suggesting it go into a $40 million joint venture with Disini to manufacture cellulose for filters.

The maneuver gave Disini control over 75% of the market for the manufacture and distribution of tobacco filters.

Disini then quickly moved to establish a presence in the tobacco industry. He contracted with Lucio Tan, the Marcos crony who dominated the cigarette industry (see section), to supply Tan's Fortune Tobacco with its raw materials. The move assured Disini's company a steady market for its products since Fortune Tobacco was the largest local cigarette manufacturer.

Disini then organized another company, Technosphere Manufacturers & Recyclers Inc., to produce homogenized or reconstituted tobacco for reuse as cigarette filters, pipe mixture, and cigar binders. Another cigarette filter manufacturing company was also organized in Thailand, Cigfil Ltd., as a joint venture with a leading Thai company.

After Disini had consolidated his grip over the manufacture of cigarette filters, Marcos issued another presidential decree on 14 January 19 3, PD 1858, lowering the import duties on the acetate tow Disini imported from 20% to 10%.

CRC AND THE PILLAGE OF HILL TRIBES [12]

The Herdis Management & investment Corp. entered into other ventures within the first few years of its operations.

Disini's next major project was timber and pulpwood operations in the timber-rich provinces of Abra and Kalinga-Apayao in Northern Luzon. His logging activities in these two northern mountain provinces are a good example of how the rights of the poor and the defenseless were trampled upon for the benefit of the few individuals who were favored by the Marcos dictatorship. Military force, stealth, the finances of well-funded companies, and the weight of the Marcos bureaucracy were all marshalled to evict hundreds of amilies from their ancestral lands for the benefit of the logging companies of this favored relative and golfing partner. Many presidential decrees were promulgated to help Dismi's logging operations. In some occasions, laws were blatantly broken to facilitate his activities.

Loggng activities started in September 1972 when Disini's men conducted secret surveys of the logging potential of the province of Abra. As soon as the initial studies were completed, the Cellophil Resources Corp. (CRC) was incorporated on 4 May 1973. Within a few months of CRC's organization, the Marcos government, acting through Minister Arturo Tanco of the Ministry of Agricultural and Natural esouroes, granted the company logging concessions in the timber-rich provinces of Abra and Kahnga-Apayao. The Timber and Pulpwood License Agreement (TPLA 261), signed on 15 October 1973, gave CRC authority to exploit 99,565 hectares of choice pine forests in the two northern provinces.

Disini's plan was to first engage in pulp mill and forestry operations and then organize a rayon staple fiber plant to use the by-products of pulp mill. Contracts for these ventures were secured with European firms in Switzerland in 1974. Experts from the French firm Spie Batignolles constructed the mill in lowland Abra, which, in the company's own words, was designed to be "one of the most modern and sophisticated" long fibre pulp mills in the world.

Another Herdis company, the Cellulose Processing Corp. CPC), was incorporated on 11 January 1974. The new company was grante additional logging concessions within three months after its incorporation. The new concessions, sanctioned by TPLA 268 issued on 11 March, gave 99,230 hectares of timber land adjacent to the original concessions of CRC in Abra and other northern provinces.

These two logging concessions effectively awarded some 200,000 hectares of choice forest land to the companies of Disini.

The fact that these two corporations belonged to the same mother company and engaged in basically the same type of operations have lead many to conclude that the CPC was merely a dummy corporation organized to circumvent the constitutional limit of 1,024 hectares a private corporation may own.

Other aspects of the logging concessions were also in violation of the constitution and other forestry laws and regulations. Articles II (10) and XV (11) of the 1973 Constitution specifically provided that the State shall respect the customs and traditions of cultural minorities and ensure their development as self-reliant communities. Forestry Administrative Order No. 11, issued in 1970, also required that any license granted must respect the rights of cultural minorities residing in the area. The logging grants were awarded to Disini in clear disregard for these constitutional and legal provisions since they directly encroached upon the rights of the Tinggian tribe and other cultural minorities residing in the two provinces.

That Marcos and Disini would not hesitate to break the law or bend it for their purposes became very clear with the presidential decrees and orders Marcos issued on behalf of Disini's logging companies.

One presidential order banned all logging operations in the Illocos region and directed the Department of Natural Resources to cancel all existing licenses. But this move merely eliminated all of Disini's competitors in the area since the order excluded Cellophil, even though its concession lay astride the main drainage divide of Northern Luzon where trees were especially necessary.

Another example was PD 410. The decree dealing with cultural minorities was issued on 11 March 1974, the very day CPC was granted its concession. While PD 410 declared that ancestral areas occupied and cultivated by national cultural minorities are "inalienable and indisposable" and are to be set aside for their exclusive use, the province of Abra where Disini operated and the Tinggians [13] who lived in the area were conveniently excluded. The omission raised fears for the future of the northern tribes and created the suspicion that "the Tinggians were not accorded 'ancestral land' status because their ancestral lands were to be given to Cellophil for its logging operations" [14]. When the Tinggians petitioned Marcos for inclusion in the decree, their letters and pleas were left unanswered.

The circumstances under which the logging concessions were granted were a further cause of concern. TPLA 261 and 268 were granted to Disini in 1973 and 1974 in secrecy despite the existence of forestry regulations which specifically required that "concession bids be publicly announced in the province and municipalities concerned. Consequently, its physical entry into its concession areas came as something of a surprise to residents, and in one case, even provincial officials" [15]. Members of the Tinggian tribe living in the area were surprised to suddenly encounter "swarms of roving jeeps marked *Cellophil* and *Herdis* which were accompanied by what they claimed to be Malacanan Palace guards."

While it was initially claimed that the company's license agreement carried adequate safeguards for the local populace, Disini's companies continually victimized the inhabitants of the areas where they operated.

Forestry regulations explicitly required that the rights of cultural minorities be identified "prior to the granting of any license" and stipulated that areas occupied by cultural minorities "shall be deemed excluded from the concession of licensed area." But Disini's logging concessions usurped the ancestral lands, rice fields, pasture lands, and communal forests of the cultural minorities in the two provinces. The life and culture of the 54,154 Tinggans who lived in Abra were undermined by the concessions of Disini. Members of other neighboring mountain tribes, the Kalingas and the Bontocs, were also affected. Some 11 upland and 7 lowland communities were dislocated by Disini's operations. The Balbalasang watershed, a national park and a forest reserve area, was incorporated into Disini's concession in 1974. These and other sites were acquired at the cost of displacing the original inhabitants, as for example when the CRC constructed their logging mills in 1975.

To construct a road from its timber concessions to its projected mill, the CRC forcibly grabbed 55 hectares of agricultural land. When farmers insisted on holding on to their properties, CRC fenced off the surrounding lots and forced them to sell their lands. But the CRC later realized that another area would be a more economical site for their mill. The new location in Gaddani, Tayum, where all of Abra's main rivers converge, was deemed a more suitable location since it would enable the CRC to simply float the logs down the rivers to the new 66,000 long-ton fibre kraft pulp mill site. But an additional 60 hectares was needed for this project. Force was again used to acquire the new lands. Those who refused to sell their lands had their crops bulldozed or earth piled around their lots, cutting off their water supply. The residents were later told that the company would get a presidential decree to confiscate their lands should they continue to refuse CRC's overtures. The people were thus forced to sell their lands at the prices dictated by the CRC, but even these already-low prices were not honored by the company when payment time came. Disini received a further boost for this project when the Bureau of Forest Development, acting on behalf of CRC, obtained World Bank financing for a 33,000 hectare pine tree plantation close the Gaddani mill site. The new concession was given to CRC so that it could cut its transportation costs and initial expenditures while the new mill was being constructed. Another 5,000 Tinggians were evicted from their pasture lands in this area.

An anthropological study conducted in Abra in 1977 documented the effects of Disini's logging operations [16]. The study concluded that traditional grazing lands had been declared off-limits to animals, pasture lands were to be converted into CRC tree nurseries, and that people had been prohibited from cutting trees for lumber and firewood and from collectin rattan. The study also asserted that CRC operations endangered the traditional Tinggian vision of communal ownership of land and property. In effect, CRC logging and milling operations in the area were thoroughly in conflict with the traditional means of livelihood and culturally threatened the Tinggian community as a people. In place of the CRC promises of regular and gainful employment for the local populace and the general development of the area, CRC only brought prohibitive social costs upon the Tinggians. Beer gardens, gambling dens and red houses mushroomed around the CRC field offices. A Tinggian summarized the feelings of his people:

In exchange for this rotten kind of [seasonal] employment [offered by CRC], we shall be giving up an economy based on agicultuml production, river-brook water supply, forest products and pasture lands. As added interest; we gain floods, landslides, pollution and drought.

The CRC tried to appease the hill tribes by saying that their rights were protected by the agreement with the Bureau of Forestry, but the people were never furnished a copy of this agreement. When the Tinggians requested for more firm guarantees that CRC would respect their rights, the company passed off these requests lightly. The Tinggians were "curtly informed that Cellophil had not come to make any deals, or get any agreements, but rather merely to inform them of the company's programs" [17].

The Tinggians were therefore forced to organize themselves and fight for their rights and endangered traditional way of life. They resolved "not to permit the operation of any company within their area and never to accept any condition offered."

Disini's companies responded by using all the resources at their disposal. Marcos "retired" the incumbent governor of Abra on September 1977 and appointed Arturo Barbero to the post. Arturo Barbero was an executive of the Herdis conglomerate prior to this appointment and the son of Marcos' Defense Undersecretary Carmelo Barbero. Within days of his appointment, Governor Barbero was quoted by Cellophil's magazine, *Rangtay*, as saying "I would like my administration to be in very close liaison with Cellophil" [18]. The Herdis-employee-turned-governor also spoke of a "new promise" and a "season of grace" during his governorship. The "season of grace" turned to be the complete militarization of the areas where there was Tinggian opposition to Disini's companies. Captain Alfredo Cuyupan of the Philippine Constabulary in Abra, for example, imposed his own version of martial law on the Tinggian community in Tineg, Abra. He banned all community meetings, declared opposition to CRC operations as "anti-government" and "subversive," and made people work for free on "baranggay" (community) roads and bridges, even during harvest time, with Dismi's companies immensely benefitting from the improved roads built through the force labor of the people. Governor Barbero later appointed military officers as mayors in "troublesome" Tinggian towns. The Philippine Constabulary then conducted military operations to neutralize all opposition in the area.

When the affected tribes scheduled a tribal peace pact on 25 January 1979 to plan a common strategy, the CRC and its collaborators tried to preempt the meeting by having the governor call a separate one two days earlier. Attempts were made to bribe the Tinggians by offering $63.4 million to build roads (which were of course to be used by CRC). In an apparent reference to the priests who took up the cause of the Tinggians, Deputy Minister of Defence Carmelo Barbero warned the people against bein influenced by "outsiders" and "white foreigners" during the meeting and branded the priests as "subversive" and "anti-govemment." The peace pact pushed through, however, and was widely attended. Twenty of the twenty-one delegations present voted on outright opposition to CRC while one delegation remained neutral. They drafted a resolution to Marcos deploring the moves of CRC and the Bureau of Forest Development which had made any dialogue virtually impossible. They also protested the military harassment and the accusation that they were allowing themselves to be influenced by outsiders and other "self-serving groups".

The Tinggian resolution did not receive any reply. All the peace pact participants were instead forced to attend another meeting on March 1979 called by Governor Barbero. The government attacked the resolutions reached at the January peace pact as illegal, null, and instigated by "subversives' and "interfering oreigners." The peace act articipants were ultimately coerced into withdrawing the original and legitimate community decisions and were forced to sign under duress a document lifting the prohibition against working for CRC. A dummy organization, the Association of Peace Pact Holders and Elders of Abra, was then organized to speak for the mountain tribes. Members of the new association included Governor Barbero, the Philippine Constabulary Provincial Commander for Abra, and some Tinggian mayors who had succumbed to coercion and bribery.

The CRC tried to counter dissent in Abra by engaging in a propaganda campaign to improve its image. It tried to depict itself as a social change agent that would bring economic upliftment to the communities they affected. Th company newsletter, *Rangtay*, was published by the CRC partly to discredit the peace pact organizers who opposed CRC operations and partly to try to convince people that the Herdis conglomerate was there for their benefit. Inspite of -- or because of -- the great adverse publicity surrounding CRC operations, *Rangtay* tried to portray CRC as a "responsible change agent" and a "novel and humane company" which has made great efforts to foster economic development in the hinterlands and has tried to affect "the hearts and minds" of people. Public relations efforts of Herdis also got a boost from the Marcos media when *Focus* magazine carried a special supplement on CRC and described it as "an industrial firm with a civic conscience" and a "responsible change agent" which safeguarded the environment [19]. The Marcos-controlled magazine further asserted that the "anti-Cellophil moves" were "manipulated by outsiders." Disini described his relationship with Marcos and how this relationship relates to the salvific nature of his company operations:

> We went into pioneering industries because we wanted to do our share in the economic development of the country. It is an admitted fact that the President and myself are very close friends, and this personal relationship has made us aware of our responsibility in helping government speed up the industrialization and development of the economy in God-forsaken places [20].

THE NUCLEAR POWER PLANT

The most controversial project Disini engineered for Marcos was the nuclear power plant in Bataan province. The project, the most costly single venture in Philippine history, involved a high-powered nuclear power plant constructed by Westinghouse. After more than ten years of work on the project and continually escalating costs, the plant had not yet functioned by the time Marcos was ousted from power. The magnitude of the costs, the secrecy and haste with which the contract was awarded, the personalities and institutions involved, all point to the inescapable conclusion of corruption of the highest order. The project has been described as "gigantic swindle" where Disini and Marcos received multimillions in commissions from Westinghouse.

The plan to build the Bataan nuclear power plant lay in corruption within the Marcos government as well as the peculiar condition of the nuclear power market in the US during the 1970's. The US nuclear power industry at this time faced the problem of a fast contracting market for its products and technology. Westinghouse and General Electric, two of the leading American firms in file nuclear power industry, began to feel the crunch of a steadily reduced sales in both the US and international markets. Among the factors contributing to decreased sales of US nuclear technology were the general decrease in the world demand for electricity and energy due to rising oil prices, newly emergent competition from German and French companies, and also, among others, the militant opposition of various groups around the world to nuclear power due to the safety hazards involved. Westinghouse, together with its competitor General Electric, generated 10% of its revenues from the sale of nuclear equipment and therefore had to develop new markets for their technology.

The market for US nuclear technology came when the Marcos government awarded a multimillion contract to Westinghouse under very questionable circumstances. General Electric had originally submitted a "thoroughly documented proposal" with detailed costings and specifications for two 600 megawatt reactors amountin to a total of $700 million. Westinghouse, on the other hand, submitted nothing more than its standard advertising brochures, quoting a price of $500 million for two reactors of the same megawatt. it then seemed that GE would receive the contract, since the Philippine National Power Corp. had already signed a contract with GE's local consulting firm [21]. Marcos, however, "unexpectedly intervened and surprised a number of advisers by ordering that the profitable contract be awarded to Westinghouse" [22].

The contract was widely criticized the moment news of it reached the public. One critic commented that "Westinghouse bided with a brochure, and the brochure won." Marcos countered by saying that the Westinhouse proposal was "technically and scientifically better than that of GE" but did not provide any details of the Westinghouse proposal [23].

When Westinghouse submitted its formal proposal on June 1974, the price had been increased to $1.2 billion for the two reactors. The price shot in again when a second quotation was submitted on November 1975 – this time to $1.1 billion for one 620 megawatt reactor and $1.6 billion for two reactors, making the Westinhouse bid considerably more expensive than the original GE proposal. By March 1981, the costs associated with the plant rose to $1.9 billion [24], making the Bataan nuclear power plant the costliest in the world. The increased prices led to further criticism. A government official complained in a memorandum that the government was being offered "one reactor for the price of two." The Phil. National Computer Center compared the costs with similar Westinghouse plants built in Yugoslavia, Sout Korea, and Taiwan, and concluded that the plant was overpriced by at least $75 million. Inspite of the opposition to the project, the Westinghouse price prevailed and the contract was quickly approved y Marcos who "wanted the nuclear power project to go ahead quickly and without hitches."

Westinghouse grabbed the contract from the jaws of GE because of Disini's connections with Marcos. Len Sabol, the Westinghouse district manager in the Philippines, approached Jesus Vergara, Disini's close associate, in a desperate effort to land the project, hoping that Disini's connections could make the difference. Disini was not interested in the project at first, but quickly changed his mind the moment he learned that commissions could run into the millions [25]. Shortly after, Westinghouse officials were presenting their case directly to Marcos.

A Westinghouse representative, Monroe Walcher, was quoted as saying that a substantial commission was paid to a Filipino businessman for facilitating the deal between his company and the Philippine government. An official of the National Power Corp., the government body officially buying the plant, admitted at one point that the decision to choose Westinghouse was a "political decision" [26] made within Malacañan. Jesus Vergara, president of Asia Industries Inc. (AII), the Disini company which holds the Philippine franchise of Westinghouse, was quoted as asting "to leave it to Hermi [Disini] to deal with Marcos. That's his job" 27]. Another Westinghouse official stated that the influence of Disini and Vergara "was essential" [28].

Westinghouse finally admitted in a statement that commissions totaling $17 million over 10 years [29] were paid "for assistance in obtaining and implementing the contract" [30] for the Philippine nuclear power plant. But Westinghouse officials refuse to disclose the exact circumstances behind the commissions or detail the services Disini erformed, claiming that these were "proprietary information for commercial and competitive reasons" [31]. Westinghouse strongly denied any wrongdoing. Gordon C. Hurlbert, president of Westinghouse Electric Power Systems Co., claimed that the commissions were in accordance with "established practices." The US Justice Department was drawn into the fray and investigated possible violations of US federal law. After the 1977 Justice Department investigation, Westinghouse proudly quoted the carefully worded statement of the investigators that they found "no evidence that any commissions paid by Westinghouse were passed on to any Philippine Government official, their affiliates or families." The statement was technically correct -- the phrasing was so carefully circumscribed that it excluded many other possibilities of commission payments. It carefully said that "no evidence was found" that payments were made to "government officials," their affiliates, or families. Behind the legalese was the possibility that commissions were actually paid to individuals such as Disini or private corporations such as AII.

It appears that Westinghouse carefully planned the payment of the commissrons to circumvent US laws. There are strict financtal disclosure re uirements and limits to the amount of commissions that can be granted to individuals under US federal law. As a first step, Westinghouse helped Disini acquire its local representative AII, a local firm which istributes and services industrial equipment and machinery, from its American owners in 1975. While US laws limit the amount of commissions that can be legally paid to an individual, payments from one corporation to another, especially when the transaction is disguised as a payment for undefined "services," are easier to justify legally. AII was therefore used as the conduit for the commissions [3], as we as other Disini firms which won subcontracts for the project. Marcos awarded the contract to Westinghouse in early 1976 soon after Disini acquired AII [33]. Westinghouse then organized a subsidiary in Switzerland, Westinghouse Electric SA, to deal with Disini and pay the commissions to special accounts set up in different European banks. This move was done precisely to allow the payment of large commissions and avoid reporting the transactions to US authorities [34]. It is clear that the Swiss branch was organized specifically for the payment of the commissions since it merely passed the contract to Westinghouse International Projects Co., which in turn assed it on to Westinghouse Electric Co., the parent company in Pittsburgh [35]. In this way, Westinghouse attempted to avoid charges of bribery or violating financral disclosure requirements. The ploy seems to have had some legal merit since the US Justice Department and Securities & Exchange Commissions, two US federal bodies which investigated the deal in 1978, decided not to file charges against Disini.

After Marcos was deposed, later US federal investigators were more inclined to finger Marcos, Disini, Westinghouse, and Burns & Roe Enterprises Inc., a company based in Oracle , NJ. which got the consulting, architectural, engineering subcontracts for the nuclear plant, and accuse them of violating US Federal law. In preliminary hearings on a suit against Westinghouse, US District Judge Dickinson Debevoise, a federal judge in New Jersey, issued a 22 September 1991 ruling which in part said:

> There is ample evidence that Bums & Roe and Westinghouse retained Disini for the purpose of obtaining President Marcos' favorable attention and that both companies expected payments to Disini would, in whole or in part, be passed on to or for the benefit of the Presuient.

While Westinghouse only admits to paying commissions of $17 million, an accounting note on another Herdis document listed two further payments described as "W commissions" totaling $19.5 million. Documents Marcos carried into exile in Hawaii showed notes indicating "commissions received from Westinghouse 1976-82" totalled $11,210,433 [36]. Disini himself was reported to have bragged that he received a 7% commission for the deal [37]. This amounts to more than $43 million in commissions for "assistance in obtaining the contract and for implementation services." Vergara is known to have admitted in private that the actual amount Disini received in com-missions was close to $50 million [38]. An investigative article from the New York Times later reported the amount as $80 million [39]. Vergara also said that Marcos ot $30 million, while he, Disini, and Rodolfo Jacob, the Herdis president, split the rest [40]. Vergara, when later interviewed by Fortune, denied what that he, Disini, or Jacob ever pocketed money. According to Vergara, "the Westinghouse deal was the cleanest Marcos deal" [41].

Marcos and Disini were in such a hurry to collect their commissions that there were no sufficient studies on the economic and safety aspects of the plant before Westinghouse was awarded the contract.

Officials of the US Exim Bank, the institution which financed the deal, were later forced to admit before a US congressional hearing in 1978 that they had not made any comparative costings of other ener sources before they funded the project. A study of the economics of the plant showed that it would have been cheaper to have considered other methods of energy production:

Method of Emery Generation	Cost per kilowatt
nuclear energy	$1,500
hydro-electric	$1,000
coal	$800
geothermal	$900

Marcos' Energy Minister, Geronimo Velasco, claiming that the government "panicked" during the 1973 oil crisis and impulsively ecided to build the plant, admitted that "perhaps with the knowledge of today, we would not have built the plant. There are now cheaper sources of energy" [42].

It is clear that very little studies were made concerning the safety of the plant before Marcos gave the contract to Westinghouse. While the US Nuclear Regulatory Commission (NCR) normall took a period of "six man-years" to study the safety of a nuclear plant, it had sent only one expert to the Philippines for two weeks [43]. Later studies by the Union of Concerned Scientists (Philippines) discovered that the reactor was plagued with more than 200 design defects. Robert Pollard of Union of Concerned Scientists (Washington) visited the plant and concluded that the plant could not be licensed in the US, prompting him to write to Marcos, warning him that the "design defects and omissions render the plant too dangerous to begin operation" [44]. Individuals from the White House Council on Environmental Quality and NCR also privately raised questions on the safety of the plant [45].

The location was also ill-chosen. Within a 100 mile radius of the reactor are five volcanos, four of them active, with the nearest one merely ten miles away. It was also within 25 miles of three geologic faults [46]. In US congressional hearings, Clarence D. Long, chairman of House Appropriations Subcommittee on Foreign Operations, blasted John L. Moore J r., president of the Exim Bank for not carefully lookin into the safety aspects of the project: "Is it no problem to you that this plant is being built near five volcanos.... Don't you care if the plant is safe?" [47]. Moore admitted that he had not been fully informed of the safety aspects, but countered that additional safeguards were "built into the plant to withstand an eruptions of those volcanos" [48], an indirect admission of the poor choice of site. James Woeber, plant manager for Westinghouse, was more candid about the bad location of the plant, admitting that they had to "literally move a mountain" to build the plant:

We have excavated more than 5. 4 million cubic meters of earth, a quantity that is enough to fill a hole the size of Rizal Park nine and half meters deep... We have placed over 15,000 cubic meters of concrete out of an estimated 255,000 cubic meters to complete the plant's requirements. The quantity of cement poured into the project is enough to built; a two-lane highway 124 kilometers long. We have installed over 16,000 metric tons of reinforced steel bars needed for the plant complex. This is enough to manufacture 22,089 cars [49].

These expenses resulted in cost overruns. Velasco himself admitted in 1984 that $100 million had already spent merely to install additional safety devices [50].

It appears that safety was never a major concern of Westinghouse or US, regulatory authorities. Westinghouse had sunk $200 million in the plant before adequate safety tests had been conducted on the site [51]. Such a major investment irreversibly committed Westinghouse to the site even when safety concerns later surfaced. When technical problems were uncovered by independent experts, Westinghouse attempted to hide the problems by rewriting the requirements or destroying the evidence. Paul van Gemst, a Swedis engineer working with the International Atomic Energy Agency, recounts stories of how Westinghouse solved faulty base plates for the plant's pipe support brackets:

> Westinghouse tried to recalculate the hangers and base plates to prove that they did meet specifications... When they failed to meet the specifications, Westinghouse modified the [requirements] [52].

In another case, Sabol, the Westinghouse executive who approached Vergara, destroyed six volumes of documents relating to the project. Sabol has since retired from Westinghouse, and the company has refuse to divulge his whereabouts [53].

Despite these problems, the Marcos regime hurried the implementation of the project. Minister Velasco privately urged Librado Ibe, head of the Philippine Atomic Energy Commission studying the adequacy of the site, to approve the project. Marcos was also known to have been anxious about an early start to the project [54].

Westinghouse, eager to operate the plant, attempted to hasten the licensing process by filing suits in US courts when it felt that the NRC and the US State Department were unduly holding up permits due to safety concerns. The Westinghouse suit charged that the NRC and the State De artment were guilty of "arbitrary and capricious conduct in excess of their authority under the Atomic Energy Act" when they considered health and safety aspects [55]. The NRC later permitted the export of the plant on 6 May 1980, ruling that risks other than the damage to the "global commons" -- the atmosphere and the oceans -- do not come under its jurisdiction [56]. In other words, the potential harm that the plant could inflict on Filipinos was of no concern to the NCR. Many American and Filipino government institutions wash their hands of the responsibility in the event that a nuclear accident were to occur. The US Energy Research and Development Agency bluntly stated that the sale of the nuclear reactor was nothing more than a "commercial transaction" and that the US warranted neither suitability nor completeness.

Apart from the commissions he received, Disini also profited from the nuclear power plant through his other corporations which were able to acquire subcontracts for the project. Herdis by this time had either acquired or set up the necessary subsidiaries to take advantage of the component contracts of the first and only nuclear plant in the country. The contracts were awarded by Marcos without any public bidding. Westingouse Power Systems Co. designated AII as its local representative and subcontractor for the project the moment it was awarded the contract. AII entered into a joint-venture with Westinghouse, Westinghouse Asia Controls Corp., to manufacture circuit breakers and control equipment for the plant. AII also became the agent for ITT and subcontracted with the transnational to install the communications facilities at the project site. Other Herdis subsidiaries clinched the various other contracts in the deal, raising serious questions of law, policy, and propriety. Power Contractors Inc., a Herdis company barely a year old, was selected to be the chief sub-contractor of civil works. Although the firm had incorporated itself only on 30 January 1975, a year before the public announcement of the deal [57], it was deemed "competent and capable" or this crucial project. Vergara and Rodolfo J. Jacob, another key Disini associate, are members of board of Power Contractors. Technosphere Consultants Group Inc., another Herdis company, received the contract for engineering and construction management. Summa Insurance Corp., a previously small-time insurance company of the Herdis group, wrote largest single policy ever written in the Philippines for the plant, a $668 million insurance policy involving a premium of $10 million. Since the amount was too large for Summa, the Government Service Insurance System (GSIS) had to be brought in should liabilities actually occur, thus further raising the question why Summa was chosen in the first place.

The controversy surrounding the nuclear power plant led the US Exim Bank to try to distance itself from the project. William Casey, then chairman of Exim Bank and later CIA head [58], considered it a transaction purely between Westinghouse and the Philippines and was quoted as saying,

> If they [Westinghouse] charge too much, the Philippines has to pay for it. It's their government; they have to protect themselves from being fleeced. We cannot nor would we do it for them.

Moore supported this position by stating that matters of conflicts of interest were not the concern of the Bank [59].

But entire picture is more complex than this. The Exim Bank, far from being an ordinary financing institution, has the function of locating overseas markets [60] for US companies and providing the funding for the projects, a role which has sometimes led the Exim Bank to be associated with third world dictatorships. Critics pointed out several peculiar aspects with the Exim Bank's funding of the project which indicates unusual interest on the part of the bank [61]:

* High cost of project
The Bank could not have failed to notice the huge discrepancies in costs between the Philippine reactor and another which they approved for Spain on the very same day. The Bank approved contracts for two reactors on 18 December 1975, a 620 megawatt reactor for the Philippines for $1.1 billion, another for a much larger 930 megawatt plant which cost Spain only $687 million.

* Prior warning
A study was reportedly made by the US Embassy in Manila and forwarded to Washington which questioned many aspects of the project, such as inflated prices, reported payoffs, and the inability of the project to pay for itself [62]. Despite this report, Casey still approved the project after visiting Manila. A spokesman for the Bank claimed there was nothing improper with Casey's move [61]. Another Bank spokesman, J. Ross Boner, also defended Casey by saying that William H. Sullivan, then the US

Ambassador to the Phili pines, strongly supported the loans and that they were not aware of any critical report: "If there was a report from anyone at the embassy questioning it, we never saw it" [64].

* Beyond borrowing limit
The Exim Bank already stopped guaranteeing applications for loans to the Philippines in 1976 because the World Bank loan limits had already been reached [65]. The nuclear power plant was made an exception.

* The of loan approval
Westinghouse submitted its proposal on November 1975. The Bank approved the contract on 18 December 1975.

* The size of the loan
It was the biggest financial package put together by the Bank, allotting an initial $644 million, $277.2 million in direct loans and $67.2 in financial guarantees. This was "the largest deal the agency had backed anywhere in the world" [66]. The Bank's exposure jumped to $900 million by 1986 [67].

* Bond guarantees
The Bank went out of its way to guarantee the sale of bonds by a foreign public corporation (the Phil. National Power Corp.) to US investors in order to cover part of the reactor costs which commercial banks were unwilling to cover. This is the first time the Bank ever made such a guarantee.

* Liberal payment schedule
The Bank provided a very liberal repayment schedule. Payments were to start only on June 1992, six years beyond the usual grace period of eleven years.

MORE SCAMS

Disini carried out many other scams which were instigated or abetted by Marcos.

Disini entered the textile business and organized the Herdis Textile Corp. (Herditex), a fully-integrated textile mill that produced a variety of fashionable and expensive fabrics from filament yarns, such as the "double- knit" fabric in vogue at that time. Since it claimed that its products were for solely for the export market and located itself in the Bataan Export Processing Zone, Herditex enjoyed a lot of advantages such as tax exemptions from the government and cheap labor. But desplte these advantages, the company fared miserably, reportedly losing $1.5 million annually in the ten years that it operated. Herditex's fabrics plant in Bataan had outstanding loans of $19 million by the time it folded up [68]. To help Herditex, Marcos directed the Philippine Armed Forces to buy its clothing materials from Disini's firm, leading to the imponderable situation of soldiers wearing Herditex-produced luxury double-knit clothing as they went into combat against communist guerillas.

Like many Disini companies, Herditex appears to have been organized merely as a way of getting government loans and moving money to secret Swiss accounts. The *Washington Post* quoted a Herditex source as claiming that the company used "inflated invoices" purchasing foreign equipment to accumulate substantial sums in European banks [69].

The acquisition of USIPHIL, the local distributor of Caterpillar Tractors, is another clear case of Marcos patronage. Disini was able to acquire a $25 million loan to buy the firm in 1977, with the loan guaranteed y the Philippine National Bank. When objections were raised within government circles concerning the wisdom of the loan, Marcos ignored them and said that the government guarantees of the loan should proceed because of "national security" considerations. Marcos claimed that the heavy-equipment tractor parts could be used in military tanks in emergencies [70].

Another involved a planned $800 million petrochemical complex where Disini was again named the government agent for the project through the Asian Petrochemical Dev. Corp, another subsidiary belonging to the Herdis conglomerate. When a senior executive of a major US petrochemical company expressed interest in investing in the complex, he was told that his company would have to pay Disini a commission of 2-3% of its investment as an agent's fee. The fee, which could have amounted to over $10 million, was characterized by the executive as "the most blatant, rotten thing I've heard in all my life."

A more notorious incident was when Disini and Marcos connived to take over an oil prospecting firm and manipulate the stock market in 1976.

The Seafront Petroleum & Mineral Resources was an oil prospecting firm whose directors were closely connected with the Marcos government. The chairman, Gregorio Floro, was connected with the Romualdez family through his investments in Philtrust and FPHC (see section on Romualdez). The president, Alfredo Velayo, was a key figure in the Herdis conglomerate. The other directors of Seafront were Bienvenido Tantoco (see section) and Ramon Orosa, who was connected to both Disini and Kokoy Romualdez. Alfonso Yuchengco, earlier discussed in the section on Cojuangco, was also a director of the company.

Disini and Marcos hatched a (plan to make quick money by playing with Seafront's stocks. Disini first prodded Yuchengco to turn over the options for 1.5 billion shares worth $3 million. Yuchengco handed these options over to Disini on 5 April 1976. Yuchengco had acqurred these shares a few months earlier when Seafront started a drilling partnership with Amoco of the US and Salen of Sweden.

The options were assigned to Mid-Pasig Land Development Corp. for $0.15. Salen's options to buy 1.278 billion shares were also transferred to Independent Realty Corp. for "some ridiculous amount." Both the Mid-Pasig Land Development and Independent Realty were dummy corporations organized by Jose Campos Yao (see section) on behalf of Marcos. Disini soon followed suit and called Yuchengco, informing him that he wanted all the 1.8 billion shares of unissued stock in Seafront be transferred to a company named Relcom. Yuchengco was informed that Disini "wanted a reply wrthin 24 hlpurs or else." The shares were transferred, but Disini made no payments at all [71].

As soon as the stocks were transferred, Marcos appeared on national television to announce a major oil strike and that oil was flowing from the Seafront well. The oil well was dry, except for a small quantity of gas, but the effect of the announcement was to cause a stampede for Seafront's stocks in the local stock market. Disini then promptly unloaded his 1.8 billion shares at a profit of $9.5 million. The sudden sale of such a large block of shares caused Seafront's stocks to drop 65% over the succeeding days. Marcos then again went on television to announce an investigation why the stocks dropped despite his earlier announcement and determine who profited. Yuchengco termed Marcos' calls for an investigation "the biggest hipocrisy of all time." The SEC claimed it found no evidence of wrongdoing [72].

The real victim in the scam was not Yuchengco. The benefits he derived from his connections could compensate for his losses. The real victim was the ordinary investor who lost $9.5 million to Disini within a few days. Some of these investors were low-income people who invested their modest and hard-earned savings in the hope of supplementing their income.

DISINI ASSOCIATES AND OTHER INTERESTS

Disini enjoyed the help of many individuals who assisted him to manage the Herdis conglomerate. Among the more trusted Disini associates and their corporate interests were

Alfredo Velayo
One of the most important partners of Disini, Velayo joined the Herdis conglomerate in 1976 as vice-president of HMIC. Velayo is the uncle of two of Marcos' cabinet members, Roberto and Jaime Ongpin, and is a founding partner of Sycip, Gorres, & Velayo (SGV), the giant auditing firm which handled the accounts of many Marcos corporations. Velayo was also a director of HMC Marketing, a Herdis subsidiary. Together with Jose Bengson, Velayo was also a director in Food Industries, another Herdis company. Among the firms where Velayo had interest were

Company	Activity
Conrad Mark Manuf.	Synthetic fibers
Amvel Investment	General investment
Kamrich Investment	General investments
Semirara Coal	Business services
Far East Bank & Trust Co.	Banking
Filipinas Synthetic Fiber Corp.	Synthetic fibers
NCR	Services
Manila Cordage	Manufacturing
Lepanto Consolidated	Mining
Phil. Tobacco Filters	Tobacco
Atlantic, Gulf, & Pacific Co.	Consruction
Filmag (Phil.)	Services
Bancom	Finance

Rodolfo Jacob
Jacob, vice-chairman and chief operations officer of the Herdis Management and Investment Corp., is very unassuming but is considered by some to be the brains behind many Herdis operations. Disini, Velayo, and Jacob form the management

"troika' in the Herdis conglomerate.

Jesus Vergara
As president of Asian Industries, the Disini-owned local contractor for the
Westinghouse nuclear plant, Vergara was the key person in the construction of the
plant and had intimate knowledge of the commissions Marcos and Disini received.
Apart from All, Vergara is known to have interests in USIPHIL and Koppel, two other
Disini firms, and Traders Royal Bank.

Sixto and Ramon Orosa
The father and son team ofSixto and Ramon Orosa closely worked with Disini in
financial operations. The son, Ramon, served as a special consultant to Disini who
personally invited Orosa to assist him "in the reassessment and re-
conceptualization of the goals, objectives and directions of the Herdis group." Prior
to joining the Herdis conglomerate, the Orosas were accused of mishandling millions
of schoolteachers' investment funds. The acted as consultants and investors for the
Philippine Public School Teachers Association (PPSTA). The PPSTA, composed of
poorly paid public school teachers, later complained that they could neither
determine the status of their investments nor trace its whereabouts. Ramon Orosa
was also connected with the Romualdez family through First Philippine Holdings
Corp. Among the interests of the Orosas were investments in the following
corporations:

Company	Activity
Poseidon Mining & Exp.	Mining
Pentland Management	Consultancy
Sterling Phil.	Air transport
Trinidad Resorts	Tourism
Dolphin Resort Dev.	Real estate
Orola Gold	Mining
Metro Gallery	Art suplies
Ital-Phil. Dev.	Construction
Tri-Union Ind. Dev.	Textiles
Triple A Food	Restaurants
ICB	Banking
Taggat Industries	Logging
Investment & Underwriting Corp.	Finance
U-Bix	Services
Asia Pacific Finance	Finance
Binalbagan Isabela	Sugar
Victorias	Sugar
Bancom	Finance

The Herdis conglomerate extended into areas such as heavy machinery, shipping,
airlines, financial institutions, and a host of other concerns. Vulcan Industrial & Mineral
Exploration and Sulu Seas Oil Development were two Herdis mining companies which,
together with Seafront, engaged in coal mining in Semirara Island, off the northwest coast of
Antique. The group also has engaged in joint ventures with foreign corporations, such as its
project to manufacture ferrochrome with the Austrian firm of Voest Alpine for the export
market starting August 1980. Among the other companies belonging to the conglomerate
were

Company	Activity
HMC Marketing	Services
Food Industries	Food services

Asia Industries	Construction
Koppel	Machinery
Farm Machinery Corp.	Machinery
Tambuli Telecommunications	Telecommunications
Beta Electrical	Construction
Westinghouse-Asia Controls Corp.	Construction
Summit Phil. Airways	Transport
Luneta Park Hotel Corp.	Hotels
Phil. Cellophane Film	Cellophane
Cellophil Resources	Logging
Technosphere	Engineering consultants
Cellulose Processing Corp.	Timber products
Sterling Phil.	Air transport
Sportslandia	Trading
Sterling International Brokerage	Services

OVERSEAS

The foreign operations of Disini's corporations also received government assistance. The Herdis International Trading Corp. (HITC) was one of the few firms chosen to participate in the government's export drive and received a subsidy of as much as $100,000 every year for every overseas trading office (OTO) it established. The annual subsidy came from the Central Bank. The Herdis group planned at least 8 of these offices, the initial four to be established in Tokyo, Hong Kong, Singapore, and San Francisco. To be exported were the products of Herdis corporations such as chrome concentrates, garments, refractory bricks, prawns and seafoods, cigarette filters and homogenized tobacco, electrical components, coal, ferrochrome, cement, including services such as airlines, computer encoding and programming, engineering and construction.

Apart from the cigarette filter company in Thailand, the Herdis conglomerate, through the help of the administration, was able to land three major industrial projects in China in July 1980: the manufacture of photocopiers, the establishment of an integrated food processing and canning complex, and the construction of a 500-room resort hotel. Atrium Capital Corp., the principal financial arm of the Herdis conglomerate, also had close links with Tetra Finance (HK) Ltd., a deposit-taking company operating in Hong Kong.

Among the documents Marcos brought with him into exile in Hawaii were some that gave an insight into the magnitude of Disini's foreign operations. A summary of the international operations the Herdis Management and Investment Corporation revealed that the overseas investments of HMIC and other Herdis companies totaled $31.7 million by the end of 1981. The notes indicated that part of this amount was a $1.3 million on deposit at the United Orient Bank in New York.

Disini also invested in US real estate and owned a $348,340 condominium in the expensive Nob Hill section in San Francisco. Two other condominiums in the same 1177 California St. address, listed as belonging to Asia Resources Int., a California Corp., are believed to be in fact owned by Disini. The condominium under Disini's name gives the Menlo Park address of Asia Resources Int.

FINANCING INSTITUTIONS AND BOGUS PENALTIES

The brazen manner with which Disini pushed the construction of the nuclear power plant and the other crude methods he employed to profit with his relationship with Marcos led to much criticism.

To deflect mounting accusations that he was using his political power to hand out special favors, Marcos pandered to public opinion and promised to conduct a broad investigation of Disini's holdings and acquisitions. When criticism of the nuclear power project continued to escalate, Marcos tried to further distance himself from Dismi, saying,

> *Westinghouse has some things to explain to our government. If there has been anything illegal committed by Westinghouse, our lawyers are considering cancelling the contract with Westinghouse and giving it to somebody else [73].*

Marcos announced that this particular crony would be divested of some of his more important corporations. A presidential letter of instruction, LOI 658, was issued directing the divestment of Disini's corporations. Marcos ordered that the following three companies from the Herdis conglomerate be taken from Disini:

Cellophil Resources Corp. (CRC)
Herdis Textile Corp. (Herditex)
Philippine Cellophane Film Corp.

Disini claimed that he was the victim of a conspiracy from "foreign interests." He further complained that these three firms were major manufacturing concerns and were intended to be the group's profit centers within the next five years. But sources knowledgeable of his operations maintained that these three companies were the least viable of the several dozen corporations belonging to Disini's conglomerate and that these three firms had in fact incurred losses of $32 million. The Cellophil Resources Corp. (CRC), for example, was taken over by the government National Development Co. in April 1981, but the CRC had already ceased operating since February of that year.

What was propagandized by Marcos as a "divestment" was actually convenient method for Disini to get rid of unprofitable corporations without paying the debts he incurred in acquiring them. Disini would first acquire firms with loans from foreign, government, and local private sources. He would then milk these firms and dissipate its assets. After bleeding the firms to the point of bankruptcy, he would turn these firms over to the government, which was then left holding an empty bag.

This business strategy is seen most clearly in the manner Disini acquired financing institutions and took out government-guaranteed loans for his corporations.

Although Disini prided himself as a "deer" and attributed the growth of his conglomerate to his business skills, the record shows that his companies grew because of heavy borrowing from foreign banks which were guaranteed by the Philippine overnment. The rapid pace of acquisitions and investments were possible on y through the loans that Disini got. Bankers in Manila say that Disini often "put little or no security of its own" and needed only "political approval to win government guarantees." By 1978, eight ears after Disini's entry into business, his foreign loans, all guaranteed by Philippine government banks, had already accumulated to $200 million [74]. When Disini folded operations in 1981, it was estimated that the government had pumped in at least $400 million in these Disini companies.

Crucial in his business strategy of milking his corporations was the acquisition of a battery of financial institutions.

Disini first acquired the Investment & Underwriting Corp. of the Phil. (IUCP), an underwriting and financing firm where the Orosa family had a controlling interest [75]. This firm was later merged with a large brokerage company, the Anselmo Trinidad & Co. Inc. (ATCO), consequently forming the Atrium Capital Corp. Within a few years, Atrium had become the foremost investment house with total assets of $210 million.

Disini also took control of the International Corporate Bank (ICB), another highly profitable institution with the help of Ramon Orosa [76]. Orosa, chairman and president of the ICB, bought 32% of the bank, raising his holdings to around 60% of the bank's equity. But Orosa clearly appears to have been acting for Disini [77], since he had made arrangements to transfer these shares to the Herdis while he was acquiring them from their owners. What is particularly interesting in this deal is that the shares Disini acquired were the ones which were owned by Philip Ang, Dewey Dee, Ramon Siy, and Willy Co. These individuals were members of a banking group which were also connected with Marcos (see section Yao and Gapud, and Lucio Tan). The acquisition of the equity of these individuals appear crucial since it appears that this was a strategic step in Marcos' efforts to bring money out of the country. ICB later became the major creditor of Dewey Dee (see Chapter IV), who later absconded with millions in a major loan scam.

Alfredo Velayo later succeeded Orosa in managing ICB for Disini. Antonio Gatmaitan, a well—known Manila banker, headed Atrium Capital Corp. and was chairman of another Herdis bank, the Commercial Bank of Manila. Anselmo Trinidad, another well known Manila financier, joined Disini's group after his brokerage firm was acquired by Herdis.

The Overseas Bank of Manila was likewise connected with the Disini conglomerate through Orosa. The Herdis group also ventured into rural banking and organized the Summa Savings Bank. Summa savings then promptly acquired three other rural banks [78].

With his financial network in place, Disini went into the last phase of his operations. He continued to borrow heavily and pushed his corporations to their debt limits. All of these loans, whether they came from foreign or local sources, were guaranteed by the government. The assets of these firms were then systematically dissipated and ultimately found their way into Disini's foreign bank accounts. Because Disini's loans were completely guaranteed, the overnment had to assume the debts he incurred when his companies went bankrupt. The government took over these firms in the name of "divestment" or bailouts. Since the assets of these firms were completely dissipated, the only alternative for the government was to convert the Disini debts into equity in the failing corporations. While this move balances the accounting sheet, it really meant a complete doleout to Disini because the government guaranteed debts became equity in totally worthless companies. It was a convenient way for Disini to liquidate his conglomerate and move the cash out of the country.

The debts incurred by Interbank were settled in this way. Interbank held $152 million in liabilities representing the interest and emergency loans drawn from the Central Bank. These were funds used to bail out two insolvent finance companies of the Herdis conglomerate, Asia Pacific Capital (Apcor) and Atrium Capital. Disini gave up stock in 12 subsidiaries and transferred them to the NDC on 16 April 1982 to cancel this $152 million debt [79].

The same procedure was followed with Asia Industries, the local contractor for the nuclear power plant. Claiming cash flow problems due to the acquisition of various affiliates [80], $5.06 million in loans were transformed into 30% equity in Asia Industries in 1981. In place of the $25 million used to purchase the tractor-that-could-become-a-tank firm, Usiphil, the Philippine National Bank was left holding 30% equity and three board seats in companies that were not worth anything.

The financial firms were especially susceptible to Disini's machinations. His corporations lent heavily to Dewey Dee (see section) and ignored all accepted lending procedures. Money far in excess of the value of the firms use as collateral was lent out. Dewey Dee later absconded with around $80 million in 1981, precipitating a banking crisis. To meet the rush of investor withdrawals and premature pullouts of money market fund placements, Disini issued commercial papers using promissory notes of big reputable companies as collateral [81]. The notes later turned out to be fabricated, further aggravating financial uncertainty in the country. The government again stepped in to "bail out" Disini. Atrium alone received at least $63.2 million from the DBP [82]. It further supplemented this amount by borrowing over $127 million from the Central Bank as lender of last resort [83].

Marcos organized an Industrial Fund specifically to help such "ailing" companies of the cronies. An estimated $28 million of government money was used to help Disini's conglomerate [84].

And while it was claimed that these bailouts were a wholesale transfer of equity and management, Herdis still maintained management control of these "divested" firms, leaving open the possibility of a further dissipation of assets. Thus, for example, while the Development Bank of the Philippines sunk millions into Dismi's companies, Herdis still maintained management control inspite of the majority equity of the government bank [85]. Jacob claims that holding over the Herdis management was necessary to "help train the new owners acquire expertise in the operations before turn-over is made. This is to assure smooth transition from us to the new owners." But no time limit was ever given for the "training" or the actual transfer of the firms.

Commenting on the massive "bailout" of his corporations, Disini, before leaving the country and retiring in his mansion in Austria with the millions he stole, had the gall to joke, "I could write a book entitled 10,000 ways not to do things" [86].

Endnotes

1. An acronym formed from Disini's name.
2. *Business Day*, 17 Jan. 1978.
3. Tales From Disiniland," *Time,* 23 January 1978, p. 56.
4. *New York Times,* 14 Jan. 1978.
5. *Fortune,* 27 July 1981.
6. To be precise, Lower Austria, 5, am Kleinen Weinberg, Maria Anzbach.
7. 'The toilet is so pretty that you would not even dare sit on it." Our translation. Quoted in "Stationen eines Gliidrsritters, *Trend,* May 1986, p. 45.
8. Please also see Chapter IV.
9. "outstanding leadership in the business field in the interest of the Republic of Austria." Our translation. Quoted in an, Tan, Tan, und Chuaunsu: Der Burgermeister von Piesting hat groBtes Interesse an neuen osterreichischen Staatsburgen," *Profil*, Nr. 16 / 14, p.58, 14 April 1986.
10. "The personal background of the citizen and his position in the Herdis Group as organizing entrepreneur, financial supporter, and his activities in the business field are the qualifying reasons. Our translation. *Ibid.*
11. *New York Times,* 14 January 1978.
12. The most detailed study to have come our way is a report by the Anthropological Association of the Philippines entitled, *The Tinggians of Abra and Cellophil,* (Baguio City: Anthropological Association of the Philippines, mimeographed with several appendices, April 1979). Articles in *WHO* magazine, 13 January 1979 and 15 September 1979, and *Panorama,* 25 March 1979 also discuss the effects of Disini's operations in the mountain provinces.
13. The Tinggians are a distinct cultural community with their own language, traditions, and political system; they comprise 36.9% of Abra's population, giving them the distinction of being the majority ethnic group in the province.
14. *WHO*, 15 September 1979.
15. Francisco Suling, 'The Cellophil Story: Is A Giant Stomping Out The Hill-Tribes?," *WHO,* 15 Sept. 1979.
16. Anthropological Association of the Philippines entitled, The Tinggians of Abra and Cellophil, (Baguio City. Anthroplogical Association of the Philippines, mimeographed with several appendices, April 1979.
17. *WHO*
18. *Rangtay*, September 1977.
19. 30 June 1979.
20. *Business Day*, 20 January 1978.
21. 'Tales From Disiniland," *Ibid.,* p. 61.
22. "Tales From Disiniland," *Ibid.*
23. "Tales From Disiniland," *Ibid.*
24. *Bulletin Today*, 7 March 1981. As early as 1981, this article had already reported that the price may even go as high as $2 billion.
25. *Fortune*, 1 September 1986.
26. *Washington Post*, 19 December 1977.
27. 'Tales From Disiniland," p. 61.
28. *Washington Post,* 19 December 1977.
29. *Time,* 31 March 1986.
30. *New York Times*, 7 March 1986.

31. *New York Times*, 7 March 1986.
32. *New York Times*, 7 March 1986.
33. *Washington Post*, 19 December 1977.
34. *New York Times*, 7 March 1986.
35. *New York Times*, 7 March 1986.
36. *Wall Street Journal*, 21 March 1986.
37. 'Tales From Disiniland," p. 61.
38. This was admitted by Vergara to one of his golfin partners. This represents a little less than 5% of the project. This is also the figure quoted in *Fortune*, 1 September 1986.
39. *New York Times*, 7 March 1986.
40. From these figures it appears that Disini pocketed a bigger portion of the commissions that he turned over the Marcos. No honor among thieves.
41. *Fortune*, 1 September 1986.
42. *New York Times,* 22 October 1986.
43. *Washington Post*, 9 February 1978.
44. *Christian Science Monitor*, 30 November 1984.
45. *Washington Post*, 8 February 1978.
46. *Fortune,* 1 September 1986.
47. *Washington Post*, 9 February 1978.
48. *Washington Post*, 9 February 1978.
49. *Times Journal*, 2 March 1981.
50. *Christian Science Monitor,* 30 November 1984.
51. *Fortune*, 1 September 1986.
52. *Fortune,* 1 September 1986.
53. *Fortune*, 1 September 1986.
54. *Fortune,* 1 September 1986.
55. *Washington Post*, 31 August 1979.
56. *Washington Post*, 7 May 1980.
57. *Washington Post,* 19 December 1977.
58. Also served in President Ford's foreign intelligence advisory board.
59. *Washington Post*, 9 February 1978.
60. Thus the name, Export-Import Bank.
61. *500-Mile Island: The Philippine Nuclear Reactor Deal,* Pacific Research, Vol. X no. 1, p. 9.
62. *New York Times*, 7 March 1986.
63. *New Yak Times*, 7 March 1986.
64. *New York Times*, 7 March 1986.
65. *New York Times*, 7 March 1986.
66. *New York Times*, 7 March 1986.
67. *New York Times*, 7 March 1986.
68. *Washington Post*, 18 January 1978.
69. Washington Post, 18 January 1978.
70. *Wall Street Journal*, 4 November 1983.
71. An ear account of this deal reports that Disini paid $675,000 for the shares (14 January 1978 New ork Times). But a later article from the Times reported an account by Yuchengo that no payments were ever made.
72. *New York Times*, 14 January 1978.
73. "Tales From Disiniland," p. 56. It is possible that Marcos came out with this statement partly to improve his image, and partly to exert pressure on Westinghouse and extract more commissions
74. *New York Times*, 14 January 1978.
75. The 40% equity of the Orosas was acquired by Disini.
76. The total earnings rose 64%, from P83 million in 1978 to P129 million in 1979.
77. *Times Journal*, 19 July 1980.
78. *Times Journal,* 30 August 1980.

79. Among the firms involved in the transfer were: Acoje Mining, Asia Industries Energy Corp., Multinational Resources Refractories Corp., San Jose Oil, Seafront Petroleum, Semirara Coal, Summa Insurance, Usiphil, Vulcan Industrial & Mining, Asia Pacific Finance Corp. (Apcor), International Corporate Bank (Interbank) (where Disini held 22%). The Phil. Tobacco ilters was taken over by government in 1983.
80. Namely, Usiphil, Koppel, and Equipment Credit from US Industries of the US.
81. *Bulletin Today*, 21 June 1981.
82. *Business Day,* 21 July 1981.
83. *Far Eastem Economic Review*, 31 July 1981.
84. *Evening Post*, 30 July 1981. Government had some $400 million in Herdis companies by this time.
85. *Evening Post,* 30 July 1981.
86. *Far Eastern Economic Review,* 14 May 1982.

LUCIO TAN

Lucio Tan, an immigrant from Fujian, China, started as a janitor, worked his way to become a chemist and later a trader, and ultimately became "one of the Philippine's richest men, with multi-billion peso business holdings" [1].

Tan describes his prosperity as due to "hard work." Defending himself against criticism that his success was due to his connections with Marcos, Tan wrote in an open letter to Mrs. Aquino

We can proudly say that we have never defended on dole-outs, government assistance or monopoly protection throughout our history. The basic ingredients of our growth have been self-reliance and hard work [2].

Many would disagree with this View. A prominent member of the local business and bankin circle described Tan as "a dubious character" who profited immensely from the Marcos regime through the non-payment of taxes and other favors from the government. Critics

...attribute Tan's success mainly to a steady disregard for regulatory and tax laws, coupled with a knack for winning patrons in the top echelons of government... [3]
...Tan really did not achieve prominence until after Marcos declared martial law in 1972. It was during martial law that Tan apparently developed his extensive patronage relationship with the former president, winning extensive tax, financing, and regulatory concessions in exchange for direct cash payments and political contributions to KBL and its candidates [4].

Although for the moment there is no direct way to quantify the benefits Tan received, one estimate claims that he was able to evade as much as $50 million a year in taxes through government concessions [5]. Apart from liberal tax breaks, Tan was also granted exemptions from government limits on overseas remittances of dollars and the amount of foreign exchange that could be used to import machinery.

In return, Tan gave Marcos regular cash payments and contributed heavily to the dictator's coffers. It was calculated that Tan made cash contribut1ons of at least $2.7 million a year to Marcos' secret accounts in Security Bank [6]. Another source claimed that Tan paid $25 million for "preferential treatment" between 1980-1986 [7]. When asked whether a reported $11 million was an accurate figure for total payoffs, Tan replied, "add one zero, maybe two" [8]. Apart from cash payments, Tan also gave Marcos in 1985 60% of Shareholdings Inc., Tan's holding company for his vast empire. Other favors Tan did for Marcos included illegally importing 30 trucks and mini-vans to help in Marcos' 1986 election campaign. As vice president of the Federation of Filipino-Chinese Chambers of Commerce & Industry, Tan also served as Marcos' liaison with the economically influential Chinese business community.

It is difficult to assess the extent of Tan's empire since he has consistently refused to submit the required corporate papers to the SEC. Tan controls at least 48 companies [9], many of them important firms in the packaging, chemicals, textile, real estate, hotels, farming, construction, manufacturing, banking and finance, brewing and beverages, and tobacco industries.

He also holds substantial investments overseas. He owns a bakery chain and shopping center in Guam, tobacco and steel companies in New Guinea, and banks in California and British Columbia. He is also one of Canada's largest carpet manufacturers [10].

While Tan flew to Switzerland in 1989 for possible surgery "to remove a chicken bone stuck in his throat" [11], it also might have been to look after investments he had made earlier in Europe. Following the lead of Disini, Tan applied for Austrian citizenship shortly after he arrived there in January 1984. Joming Tan in his application were his brother Harry Hua Tan and a business associate, Jesus Dyliaco Chuaunsu. These three Filipinos were described by *Profil*, a well-known Austrian magazine, as "Finanzileuten" (money men or financiers) [12] because, as in the case of Disini, they attempted to acquire their citizenship through their money. Tan contributed $750,000 (15 million shillings) to a publishing house owned by a political group to facilitate their application. The publisign firm of Kremser Faber-Verlag was on the brink of bankruptcy and was only too happy to accept the investment from Tan who became its "stille Faber-Teflhaber" (silent business partner) [13]. The investments were made between October 1984 and July 1985. In his application Tan gave his address as Dreistetten 91 /7 Piesting, Lower Austria. Helping Tan in his application was Dr. Helm, the lawyer of Disini, and Walter Zimper, the mayor of Piesting who is also connected with the Kremser publishing house. This led *Profil* to sarcastically subtitle its article on Tan "Der Burgermeister von Piesting hat groBtes Interesse an neuen oisterreichischen Staatsbiirgen" [14]. The Federal State of Lower Austria consequently requested the Austrian Federal Government to grant citizenship to the three in February 1985, but it appears that this application may have run into difficulties because of the controversial background of the applicants.

TOBACCO

The principal pillar of Tan's empire is Fortune Tobacco Corp., the country's largest cigar and cigarette maker. Fortune and its affiliates dominate the tobacco and cigarette industry through the six local and three international brands they manufacture [15]. One source estimated that Tan controls 60% of the annual P62 billion local cigarette market [16], while another estimate says that he controls as much as 77% if all his interests in the industry are combined [17].

Tan also had interests in two Disini companies, Cellophil Resources Corp. and Philippine Cellophane Film Corp., allowing him a say in the manufacture of Cigarette filters.

Critics have claimed that a large part of the profits from the tobacco and cigarette industry ended up with the dictator. Mijares identified Tan and Conrado Diaz, Marcos' Deputy Commissioner of Internal Revenue, as the dictator's fronts in the lucrative tobacco industry [18].

These connections have been very useful for Fortune Tobacco. It has been alleged that Fortune Tobacco did not pay the right taxes to the government, an accusation which continues to the present. The cigarette tax law operant during Marcos' time was reportedly designed to suit Tan's interests. It was penned by Fortune Tobacco executives who presented the document to Marcos for signature [19]. Furthermore, despite the already favorable tax law, critics charge that Tan still attempted to cheat the government by smuggling cigarettes and printing fake internal revenue stamps for use on his cigarette packs. Fortune Tobacco

avoided paying billions of pesos in taxes over the past decade, using schemes ranging from the printing of fake tax seals to the illegal expart and reimport of cigarettes [20].

The Review summarized the benefits Tan received from the government:

Between 1972 and 1980, Tan's Fortune Tobacco rocketed to the top of the market as one consideration after another was granted by Malacarian Palace. By Marcos' 1986 departure, Tan, along with Marcos golfing partner Herminio Disini, had a hammerlock over the importation of materials needed to make cigarettes and had a tax regime in place that avored Fortune's brands over all others [21].

Fortune is reported to have an annual turnover of $30-35 million 22 , but the real size of its operations is difficult to assess since records for Tan's companies are not available. The latest records for Fortune with the SEC are from 1984. Records for the years before that are also spotty. Fortune has kept a tight lid on its financial operations and since 1973 has repeatedly failed to submit the required financial reports, causing the SEC to first warn and later penalize the company [23]. But Tan, continuing to thumb his nose at the authorities, preferred to pay a modest daily fine rather than disclose his operations to the SEC [24].

Fortune continued to expand and has now started to export its Hope and Champion brands to China. The turnover of money within Fortune was so fast that Tan and other associates seriously considered organizing their own tobacco bank [25].

ALLIED BANK

Instead putting up a bank for the tobacco industry, Lucio Tan concentrated on strengthening his Allied Banking Corp.

Allied Banking started on 1 June 1977 when Tan and the other Chinese cronies of Marcos acquired the ailing General Bank & Trust (Genbank). Genbank ran into difficulties in 1976 when it was deserted by its British partner, National & Grindley's Bank Ltd. of London. A bank run ensued. The Yujuico family, then majority owners, turned to the government for help. The Central Bank extended emergency loans, while the Land Bank helped in the form of temporary equity participation [26]. The Yujuico family consequently gave way to Tan and his associates, and the bank was renamed as Allied Banking Corp.

Among the principal shareholders of the newly-constituted bank were Lucio Tan, Ignacio Gimenez, Willy Co, Ramon C. Lee, Ching Poe Kee, Mariano Khoo, Domingo Chua, Tan Eng Lian, Florencio Santos, Mariano Ordonez, and Sixto Orosa. Ignacio Gimenez, former chairman of Manila Stock Exchange, is the husban of Fe Roa-Gimenez, Imelda's social secretary. It is believed that the shares he held in the bank were for Marcos [27]. Mariano Ordonez, the former chief of the Metrocom, Marcos' special para-military and police unit, also held shares in the bank, while also serving as president of Fortune Tobacco. Ramon Siy was also used by Marcos in the take-over of Security Bank (discussed earlier). Other members included the Co brothers, again individuals extensively used by Marcos in his financial dealings. Sixto Orosa was a business partner of Koko Romualdez and Disini (see sections). Romeo Co, a close friend of Gregorio Licaros, Marcos' Central Bank governor, was named president of the bank, while his brother, Willy, became vice-chairman. Lucio Tan was named chairman [28].

The government cited the change in ownership as "a model for similarly-afflicted banks, and... as an argument for broadening ownership and professionalizing management of banking institutions..." [29]. Minority owners, however, cried foul and claimed that Tan and his group had "arbitrarily and fraudulently" wrested control of the bank [30].

The consequent growth of the bank was phenomenal. Starting from the bankrupt state of Genbank, Allied was able to expand its deposits by 317% to $103 million, increase its assets by 221% from $80 million to $255 million, and expand its loans and investments (earning assets) by 228% to $215 million in during the first seven months of operations rom May to December of 1976. In a little more than half a year, Allied realized a net income of $2.6 million, boosting the bank's net worth to $30 million [31]. From the insolvent Gen-bank, Allied skyrocketed to 11th place among the 26 privately owned commercial banks in terms of assets during its operations during the latter part of 1976. It continued its growth and jumped to third place by mid-1979.

Allied continued its vigorous growth until it became the largest private domestic commercial bank by 1980 [32], with its total assets reaching $956 million [33].

The miraculous recovery for this once-troubled bank reflects the heavy traffic of money from Marcos corporations. The bank was used both as repository of funds as well as a way station for the transit of money overseas.

Allied continued its expansion and branched out to overseas operations with the blessings of the Central Bank. Allied got a further boost when the Board of Investments named it as one of 12 companies favored with cash and tax incentives to put up trading offices abroad. It organized Allied International Export-Import Corp. as its international trading arm.

Allied's expansion program included setting up of a bank, to be initially capitalized at $4 million, in San Francisco, with the aim of facilitating "trade financing between local businesses and American parties" [34]. Other international branches of the Allied syndicate included the Allied Capital Resources Ltd. in Hong Kong and the Allied London Representative Office in England. Allied also operated in the Middle East, converting its Bahrain office into an off-shore ank, the Bahrain Offshore Bank, to make use of excess Arab petro-dollars and take advantage of the construction boom in the Middle East, making it the first Filipino bank in the Middle East [35]. By early 1981 Allied had accumulated enough capital and had gained international respectability to become the first domestic bank to jom a consortium of international financial institutions that granted a $200M loan to the Central Bank [36].

BEER

Another case where Marcos intervened for Tan was in the organization of a new beer company to compete with the established brand sold by San Miguel Corp. San Miguel Beer previously had enjoyed the status of an "overcrowded industry," but this classification was misleading since it was the only brand manufactured in the country. This government classification laced great barriers to entrants in the industry and in effect granted San Miguel the status of a government-sponsored monopoly.

Tan lobbied to have beer "delisted" as an "overcrowded" industry. This permitted him to overcome the first obstacles. Had beer continue to be classified as "overcrowded," Tan would have had to contend with strict government regulations concerning foreign exchange, government loans, and taxes. His companies would have had to face strict scrutiny of its imports, denied government peso and foreign currency loans, and lose tax incentives. Sources say that Marcos had taken a keen interest in the issue and personally directed the National Economic Development Authority to delist beer.

Lucio Tan then organized the Asia Brewery in 1978 and Pan Philippine Industries Inc. (PPII) in 1979 to engage in beer making. The Pan-Philippine Industries Inc. was listed as having a paid-up capitalization of $14 million and an authorized capitalization of $136 million, while Asia Brewery was capitalized $190 million. The period these corporations were organized is significant since both of them were set up long before there was an official recommendation from the government inter-agency committee tasked to review the proposals to delist beer. Asia Brewery was organized in 1978, while PPII started in April 1979. The official government recommendation to delist beer came only on August 1979, five months after the PPII was organized. This indicates that Lucio Tan already had advanced knowledge of how the government would decide regarding this issue of delisting beer. Asia Brewery started full operations in 1981.

Tan thus entered the market under favorable terms. The government directive on beer delisting had further stipulated that only one other corporation would be allowed to enter the profitable beer making industry. This corporation was, of course, Asia Brewery, chaired by Lucio Tan.

One of the biggest and most modern fully-integrated breweries in Asia was therefore put up in a 320-hectare complex in Cabuyao, Laguna, 45 kilometers southeast of Manila. The brewery, organized with the help of Carlsberg Beer of Denmark, has a capacity of four million hectoliters of beer. Apart from the brewery, the complex mcludes bottling facilities, a glass container manufacturing plant, a plastic crate/case manufacturing plant, a water treatment plant, water tanks, warehouses, and an electric power plant. A complementary "mass-making operation was also organized in Tabangao, Batangas, with half of its output earmarked for beer bottles. Critics pointed out that the plant facilities were "imported with preferential credit terms at a time the economy was facing a serious foreign-exchange shortage" [37].

Asia Brewery uses the distribution network of Fortune Tobacco to market the five beer brands it manufactures [38].

OTHER INTERESTS

Other Tan interests include Himmel, a chemical manufacturing and tradin com any. Tan also has interests in the Century Park Sheraton Hotel, held t rou Shareholdings Inc., the holding company for many of his corporations.

He also owns the country's largest livestock farm, Foremost Farms, described as "one of the most advanced farms in Asia" [39]. Its piggery operations are the biggest source of meat in the country. But critics have also questioned the operations of Foremost, accusing it of tax evasion, since the pigs are sold for cash, leaving a lot of elbow room for avoiding taxes [40].

Below is a partial list of the companies where Lucio Tan owns or controls:

Green Acres Farms
Allied Banking Corp.
Grandspan Dev. Corp.
Dominium Realty & Construction
Pan-Philippine Industries
Pan-Asian Securities Corp.
Small & Medium Scale Industries Dev. Corp.

Endnotes

1. *Far Eastem Economic Review*, 15 December 1988
2. *Far Eastem Economic Review*, 15 December 1988

3. *Far Eastern Economic Review*, 15 December 1988
4. *Far Eastern Economic Review*, 15 December 1988
5. *Business Day*, 10 December 1986.
6. Rigoberto Tiglao, "Smoking Out Tan," *Far Eastem Economic Review*, 24 August 1989.
7. *Far Eastern Economic Review*, 15 December 1988.
8. *Business Day,* 10 December 1986.
9. *Far Eastern Economic Review,* 15 December 1988
10. *Far Eastern Economic Review,* 15 December 1988
11. Rigoberto Tiglao, "Smoking Out Tan," *Far Eastem Economic Review*, 24 August 1989.
12. "Tan, Tan, und Chuaunsu: Der Burgemeister von Piesting hat groBtes Interesse an neuen deterreichischen Staatsburgen," *Profil*, Nr. 16 / 14, p.58, 14 April 1986.
13. "Tan, Tan, und Chuaunsu: Der Burgermeister von Piesting hat groBtes Interesse an neuen fisterreichischen Staatburgen," *Profil,* r. 16/ 14, p.58, 14 April 1986.
14. "The Mayor of Piesting has a great interest in new Austrian citizens." Our translation.
15. Among them Camel, Champion, Hope, K001, Pall Mall, More, Winston.
16. *Far Eastern Economic Review*, 15 December 1988
17. *Bulletin Today*, 24 June 1980
18. Mijares, p205
19. *Far Eastern Economic Review*, 15 December 1988
20. *Far Eastern Economic Review,* 15 December 1988
21. *Far Eastern Economic Review*, 15 December 1988
22. *Far Eastern Economic Review*, 15 December 1988
23. *Times Journal*, 15 July 1980
24. *Far Eastern Economic Review*, 15 December 1988.
25. *Bulletin Today*, 24 June 1980.
26. *Far Eastem Economic Review,* 14 Jan 77
27. *Manila Bulletin,* 24 June 1986.
28. *Times Journal*, 26 June 1980; *IBON* 15 June 1983
29. *Far Eastern Economic Review*, 3 March 1978.
30. *Far Eastern Economic Review*, 15 December 1988
31. *Far Eastem Economic Review*, 3 March 1978
32. *Times Journal,* 29 July 1980
33. *Daily Express*, 3 March 1981.
34. *Times Journal and Daily Express,* 26 June 1980.
35. *Times Journal*, 3 Sept. 1980
36. *Daily Express*, 3 March 1981
37. *Far Eastem Economic Review*, 15 December 1988.
38. Among them, Carlsberg, Beer Pale Pilsen, Beer Hansen, Max Beer.
39. *Far Eastern Economic Review*, 15 December 1988
40. *Far Eastem Economic Review,* 15 December 1988

CAMPOS YAO AND ROLANDO GAPUD

Jose Campos Yao was one of the more trusted cronies of the dictator. Tracing a relationship starting in the mid-1950's, Yao served Marcos as a close financial advisor, a dependable front man, and a loyal business partner until the very end. The relationship started when Marcos was first elected congressman. Yao later became one of Marcos' financiers during the 1965 election. One of Yao's first fronting roles was as Mr. Z in the stock scam of the late 1960's called the Benguet-

Bahamas Deal, each of Marcos' fronts acquiring the code names of Mr. X, Y, and Z.

In exchange for his loyalty, Marcos showered government support upon Yao's companies. United boratories, Yao's drug company, grew to be one of Asia's largest pharmaceutical firms largely throu this help. Yao ultimately became a very rich man, building a multimillion dollar real estate empire in Hawaii, Texas, Seattle, and Canada.

UNILAB

United Laboratories (Unilab) was organized with a capitalization of $500,000 in 1953. At a time when access to scarce foreign exchange spelled the difference between success or failure in business, the new company wisely enlisted Marcos' help in acquiring much-needed dollars to import medicines and chemicals. Marcos was then a powerful member of Congress who controlled the allocation of foreign exchange.

Another charge levelled against Unilab was that drugs donated by international agencies and other governments have at times been found relabeled as Unilab products. Mijares, testifying before an investigative committee of the US Congress, alleged that medicines purchased by the Philippine Department of Health through US aid money ended up with Yao's drug company:

> In the purchase of medicines by the Department of Health, part of which is funded with US aid, the later bulk of the purchase order, about 60%, goes to the United Drug, the biggest pharmaceutical firm in the country which is owned by the front man of the President in the drug business, a Mr. Joselito Campos [1].

Access to the government market was a major factor in the phenomenal growth of Unilab. It enjoyed a virtual monopoly as distributor of drugs to the Ministry of Health and all its public hospitals and clinics. Unilab accounted for at least 80% of government medicine purchases. When the government embarked on a campaign to provide medicine for rural areas - the so-called **MARCOS Medicine** - it was Unilab which acted as the government's supplier.

But at the same time there also existed a conscious attempt on the part of Unilab to conceal its profitable relationship with the overnment. A confidential report on Unilab alleged that Ernesto S. Abalos, Unilab's Vice-President for Finance and a Yao associate for more than 30 years, would know all of Campos financial and accounting manipulations. Referring to government purchases, the reported claimed that Abalos

> does not enter it as part of United Laboratories commercial sales, and yet, all the raw materials, direct labor, and overhead costs were all charged as part of the total cost of commercial business. In effect, all income from government sales would have been an addition to net profit.

The ploy increased costs and lowered sales in the accounting books. This had the effect of not only lowering the tax liability of Unilab but it also permitted the drug company to circumvent the profit sharing plan it had with its employees. Unilab employees enjoyed a profit-sharing plan of 10% of net profit. Sales to the government amounted to around $11.7 million in 1982. This would mean that Unilab employees should have gotten around $1.17 million under the profit-sharing plan. But due to the accounting manipulations, profits reported were much less.

A private auditing firm was supposed to oversee the books, but the so-called independent "private" auditIng firm was no other than one which Abalos himself headed, Ernesto Abalos & Associates.

> *Actually and in fact, all of the personnel were paid United Labomtories employees Under Abalos holding office right at the United Laboratories Accounting Office. ...later, in order to disguise this blatant operation, Abalos designated another employee of United Lab -- Benny Barsabal -- one of his "directors" working with him in his supposedly independent auditing firm which was renamed Barsabal & Associates.*

The auditing firm was then transferred outside of Unilab to another Campos commercial building in Mandaluyong. The ploy facilitated "the hiding of the real business transactions" of Unilab. The report concluded that

> *considering the number of years that Marcos [was] in power, the total amount that they were able to hide and kept for themselves from their "independent auditors " could have reached a billion mark.*

Yao, however, has admitted paying very little taxes on his properties with the rationalization that "Imelda will just squander [the taxes] anyway".

Unilab remained the exclusive property of the original 1953 incorporators. It appears that Marcos never held any seat in the board of the drug chain but was content with merely asking and in turn giving favors to his close business partner who had since become a close personal friend and godfather to his son Bongbong. The stockholders of Unilab:

* **Jose Campos Yao** - chairman and majority owner
* **Mariano K. Tan (Tan Ma Chick)** - Unilab comptroller and close Yao associate. Also involved with Yao's overseas real estate investments.
* **Howard Dee** - brother-in-law of Yao and former vice-chairman of the board. Now a permanent resident of Vancouver. Canada
* **Arsenic Ong** and **Ting Lang** (wife of Ong)

Among the key personnel of the United Drug chain upon whom Yao has depended are

* **Francisco G. de Guzman** – lawyer,. corporate legal officer, and vice president. He has been described as the "person who knows everything" about the real ownership of all of Yao's assets, taking care of all legal matters pertaining to corporate ownership whenever Yao purchased or organized a new venture. He originally wanted to resign to concentrate on his law practice but was prevailed upon to stay because he was so valuable to Yao, holding "the key" to all Marcos~Yao joint-ventures and Yao's overseas corporations, including the pharmaceutical companies in Indonesia and Thailand. Guzman, together with Abalos and Mariano K. Tan, can also shed much light on the operations of Greenfield Dev. Corp., a key Yao company.

* **Guillermo 'Mike' C. Gastrock** - president for 10 years and was later promoted to vice-chairman of board after the departure of Dee. He has been described as a faithful follower of Yao and Mariano Tan.

* **Angel A. Florentin** - Yao's family doctor, godfather of Yao's eldest son, Butch, a senior vice-president of Unilab, president of Unilab's antibiotic company at the Canlubang sugar estate. Florentin was one of the few executives of Unilab which Campos used as incorporators his many other companies.

Other key Yao people:

Jesus R. Salomon, Senior VP
Alfredo Mombay, VP, Manufacturing
Rodolfo Ibanez, Executive VP
Dr. Manny Samson, VP
Tan Wan Lian, Sr VP, marketing
Cesar Orosa, VP sales
Jose Laurente, VP sales
Ed Raceles, VP sales
Pete Diaz, VP

Among the subsidiaries and pharmaceutical other companies forming part of United Laboratories drug chain are

Adenphar Pharmaceuticals Inc.
Atlas Veterinary Products
Biomedis, Inc.
Consumer Products Inc.
General Drug & Chemicals Inc.
International Research Corp.
Krieger Confectionery Corp.
Medichem Pharmaceuticals Inc.
Medway Pharmaceuticals Inc.
Myra Pharmaceuticals Inc.
Pediatrics, Inc.
Phil. Health Food Center Inc.
Phil. Health Food Manufacturing Inc.
Therpharma Ltd.
Unipharma, Inc.
United American Pharmaceuticals Inc.
United Drug Co. Inc.
Univet Agricultural Products, Inc.
Westmont Pharmaceuticals Inc.

OTHER YAO INTERESTS

Unilab grew rapidly, dominating the Philippine pharmaceutical industry and growing even to include pharmaceutical firms in Thailand and Indonesra engaged in the manufacture and export of drugs. Dr. Delfin "Sonny" Samson, who became Unilab president after Gastrock, was in charge of operations in Southeast Asia. The confidential report on Unilab earlier cited also claimed that these Thai and Indonesian firms have been instrumental in manipulating "the dollar operations in the Southeast Asian markets."

A drug firm known to have been jointly owned by Marcos and Yao was Chemfields. Marcos owned 60% of the firm through companies, each with 20% equity, while the remaining 40% was held by Unilab.

SEC records list Yao as the owner of San Mariano Mining Corp., registered with the SEC on June 1974 with an authorized capitalization of $590,000, but Yao later admitted that he was fronting for Marcos in this company.

Yao also has investments in Union Glass & Container Corp. and First Philippine Holdings Corp., another Marcos company.

Among the other Philippine companies that Yao owns are

Benedict Investment & Realty Corp.
Clinton Investment & Realty Corp.
Dynavision Dev. Investment Corp.
Dao Investment & Mgt. Corp.
Express Traders Corp.
Fidelity Investment Corp.
Fortune Securities Inc.
Greenfield Dev. Corp.
Heritage Properties Inc.
Imperial, DeGuzman & Abalos & Co. Inc.
JDC Investment Corp.
Jaycem Investment Corp.
Dolmar Realty Estate Corp.
Par Investment Corp.
Rainbow Real Estate Dev. Corp.
Shaw Blvd. Shopping Terminal Corp.

GAPUD AND FRONT CORPORATIONS

A person who collaborated closely with Yao was Rolando Gapud, a financial consultant who had worked with the respected investment banking firm of Bancom Development Corp. from 1965 through 1980. Apart from providing financial consultancy services to Bancom's regular clients, Gapud also worked for Yao on a part-time basis starting in the late 60's, assisting the pharmaceutical magnate with Unilab's corporate financial planning and strategy for operations. Gapud worked closely with Yao and met Umlab's officers and managers weekly. By the mid-1970's, Gapud had already sufficiently wormed his way to Yao's confidence to merit description as "one of his trusted people" who could be counted upon to perform "professional services" when he was introduced to Marcos.

When Yao suffered a heart attack in 1979, Marcos took the opportunity to reorganize the corporate holdings held under Yao's name. An attempt was made to consolidate the Marcos empire. The Marcos children were especially concerned with conducting a thorough audit of all of the holdings of their father, whose health was equally becoming frail. Yao was asked to relieve himself of some of the businesses Marcos entrusted him, and the administration and supervision of these assets were transferred to Rolando Gapud.

Gapud was asked to perform a financial and management audit of specific companies which were headed by known Marcos fronts and associates. Among these companies were those "under the supervision and ownership of Pablo Roman, Roberto Sabido, Frankie Teodoro, Luis Yulo, Trinidad Enriquez, Eulogio Balao." Gapud claimed that his work for Marcos was done on a "purely rofessional basis," but it will be seen that Gapud's role went far beyon the "evaluation of proposals, insuring proper documentation, audit of operations" and other routine tasks. He ultimately became the top financial adviser to Marcos and his son Bongbong. He, together with Yao, formed a huge network of front corporations to hide and facilitate the movement of Marcos assets. Gapud was also named head of the Marcos Foundation and other key financial concerns.

Yao and Gapud both played a key role in organizing a formidable collection of front corporations and trusts for Marcos and members of his immediate family. These interests included choice real estate properties, mining companies, banks, as well as shell corporations based in Hong Kong, Panama, and the Netherlands Antilles [2]. Yao himself has admitted that he, his wife, and children served as Marcos' fronts in many corporations, executing blank deeds of trust and assignment in favor of unnamed beneficiaries. The originals of these deeds and assignments were later delivered to Marcos.

Among the corporations that Yao admitted organizing for Marcos in the Philippines were [3]:

Performance Investment Corp.
Mid-Pasi Land Development Corp.
Anchor Estate, Inc.
Independent Realty Corp.
Novo Properties Inc.
Oesco Timber Inc.
Earthcore Holdings Corp.
Trans Oriental Holdings Corp.
Universal Holdings Inc.
Universal Silk Corp.
Universal Comtrade Inc.
San Mariano Mining Corp.
Fairmont Real Estate
Solid Strand Properties
Multi Assets Corp.
Gainful Holdin Corp.
Master Assets Corp.
Security Bank & Trust
Tri-Island Corporate Holdings Corp.
Country Land Corp.
Prime Holdings Corp.
Land Value Inc.
Renown Group Corp.
Century Wealth Group
Hyper-Growth Equity Inc.
Centrum Wealth Group Inc.
Hubbard Agri-Venture Corp.

Yao also admitted that other key individuals within the Unilab group helped in organizing and maintaining the corporations for Marcos. When Gapud took over most of Yao's responsibilities, he contrnued to utilize basically the same set of officers and employees Yao used to administer these companies:

Ernesto S. Abalos
Joselito D. Campos Jr.
Elizabeth S. Campos
Rodolfo Dimaano
Manuel Engwa
Angel A. Florentin
Lourdes F. Florentino
Guillermo C. Gastrock
Gervasio T. Gaviola
Francisco G. de Guzman
Rafael de Guzman
Renato E. Lirio
Dante C. Llapitan
Luciano E. Salazar
Daniel O. Tan
Mariano K. Tan

REAL ESTATE [4]

Among the areas Marcos, Yao, and Gapud entered into were heavy investments in real estate in the Philippines and overseas [5]. Choice land in Metro-Manila, Rizal, Laguna, Cavite, Bataan, and Baguio were part of this real estate empire. The plots, totalling an approximate 2.2 million square meters, were covered by some 238 land titles [6]. These properties were choice holdings, as the followrng sampling reveals:

* an expensive residence in Dasmarinas Village for the Marcos children [7]
* choice lots in Baguio City
* 184,891 square meters of prime land at Valle Verde-Ortigas, near the Meralco compound worth more than $9.07 million, covered by two titles
* 120 hectares of seafront property in Mariveles, Bataan including a huge vacation mansion [8]
* land in Laguna, extendi from South Superhighway to Calamba and highway to Puerto Azul, amounting to a to area of 17,186,787 square meters, covered by 192 titles

The properties in Laguna were acquired very cheaply because they were bought before highways and main roads were constructe by the overnment. But the lands appreciated rapidly after the highways an roads were constructed, delivering a huge windfall for the conspirators.

Among the firms Yao and Gapud regularly used for their real estate transactions were the following:

* Greenfield Dev. Corp. - reported to be a key company used in the acquisition of land in Laguna. Gapud was the president of this company, while Renato Lirio, a loyal Yao associate, was vice-president. Lirio was reported to be familiar

with all the real estate acquisitions in Laguna. Lirio, a trusted vice-president at Unilab, was described as "the action man" of Campos in all corporate activities outside Unilab.

* Fairmont Real Estate Inc. - organized on July 1968 with the following directors: Campos, de Guzman, Dimaano, Marcos, Balatbat, and Edmundo Buenaventura. External auditor was Barsabal's firm, Barsabal, Salvador, Santos & Co. Fairmont held titles to land in Binan and Sta. Rosa, Laguna.

* Anchor Estate Corp. - organized on 8 May 1968 with the following directors: Campos, Ricardo Silverio, Francisco de Guzman, Guillermo Gastrock, Rodolfo Dimaano. Originally named Maharlika Estate Corp.

* Mid-Pasig Land Development - organized on 5 August 1971 with the following directors: Campos, de Guzman, Dimaano, Mariano Tan, Gervasio Gaviola. This firm held the titles to expensive land Ortigas Ave, Pasig. Two titles alone held by Mid-Pasig already covered 184,891 square meters worth more than $5.4 million.

* Independent Realty Corp. (IRC) - SEC papers date the incorporation of this company as 16 February 1981, but it appears that it was organized as early as 23 August 1967. Directors: Campos, Gapud, Gastrock, Gaviola, Dimaano. Independent Realty held at least 173 land titles covering 15.8 million square meters of land along South Superhighway in Laguna and Cavite, extending up to Puerto Azul, with an estimated worth of $38.8 million. This company grew to be a huge conglomerate composed of 23 subsidiaries in diverse areas. IRC had stakes in the mining industry: it organized San Mariano Mining Corp. and enjoyed the ownership of 14.15% of the stocks of Marcopper Mining, It also had investments in Oriental Petroleum. It enjoyed substantial holdings in Phil. Integrated Meat Corp. estimated to be more than $6.6 million. It had investments in Phil-Asia Food Industries worth more than $39.2 million. Independent was also reported to be the largest single stockholder in Phil. Overseas Satellite Communications Corp.

Just three of these real estate firms by themselves -- Independent Realty Corp., Mid-Pasig Land Develoment, Fairmont Real Estate -- were already estimated to be worth $45.2 million. Another real estate firm connected with Yao and Gapud was Mapalad Realty Co.

OTHER INTERESTS

Yao and Gapud also had many investments in many other areas.

There were ma'or investments in the etroleum and mining industries. Shares to Seafront etroleum & Mineral esources were endorsed or held on Marcos' behalf. Shares to Oriental Petroleum were also held b Indeplendent Realty, Performance Investment, Mid-Pasig Land, Fabian er, and incent Recto [9]. Marcos, through Campos, also owned 48.95% of Marcoppler Mining Corp., a large mining firm with a book value of more than $9.3 m' 'on. The equrty in Marco per were held through

Performance Investment (28.2%), Independent 14.15%), Mid-Pasig Land (76%), and Fairmont Realty (0.874%).

Marcos also held 71,442 common and 33,349 personal shares in the PLDT through three corporations -- J DC Investment & Realty Enterprises, Clinton Investment, and Realty Enterprises. The incorporators in these front corporations were Gapud, Gervasio . Gaviola, Rodolfo Dimaano, Renato Lino, and FG. de Guzman. This same group is also believed to have held shares for Marcos with Philcomsat. This group also the 815,531 shares in Benedict Investment & Realty Corp. for the three children of Campos. Benedict investment held office at 66 United, a known Campos.

Among the other firms forming part of Marcos, Yao, and Gapud conglomerate are the following companies which have an almost identical set of incorporators:

* Universal Comtrade Phil. - organized 31 January 1977 but papers are missing from the SEC. Directors: Lutgardo Panganiban, Rogelio Mendoza, Editha Moran, Orencio Terayo, Arturo Canicosa Jr.

* OescoTimber Inc. - organized 31 August 1977.1ncorporators: Agusto Barcelon, Gapud, Renato Lirio, Raymundo Feliciano, de Guzman.

* Universal Holdings - organized 5 October 1977. Incorporators: Gastrock, Lirio, Dimaano, Gaviola, Gapud.

* Prime Holdins - also organized in 1977. Incorporators: Gapud, Jose Campos Jr., Ernesto Abalos Jr., Lirio, Gaviola.

* Novo Properties Corp - organized in 1978 but financial statements not submitted to SEC until 1984. Incorporators: Gapud, Campos Jr., Lirio, Gaviola, Abalos.

* Country Land Corp. - organized in 1978 but financial statements not submitted to SEC until 1984 (same pattem as Novo Properties). Incorporators: Gapud, Gaviola, de Guzman, Campos Jr, Lirio.

* Tri-Islands Corporate Holdings Inc. - organized formed in 1978, but external auditor claimed that it has not operated. Incorporators: Gastmck, Lirio, Dimaano, Gaviola, Gapud. No profit and loss statement.

* Earthcore Holdings Corp. – 0rganized1978.

* Multi-Assets Corp. - organized 9 August 1979, but external auditor claimed that it has not operated. Incorporators: Gapud, Gaviola, Abalos, Gastrock, Campos Jr. No profit and loss statement.

* Master Assets - organized 16 August 1979, but external auditor claimed that it has not operated. Incorporators: Gapud, Campos Jr., Abalos, Lirio, Gaviola. No profit and loss made.

* Gainful Holdings Corp. - organized 20 August 1979. Incorporators: Gapud, de Guzman, Lirio, Campos Jr., Gaviola.

* Solid Strand Properties Corp. - organized 20 August 1979. Incorporators: Gapud, Gastrock, de Guzman, Lirio, Gaviola. External auditor claims that the company has no income generating operations and therefore no profit and loss statements.

* Universal Silk - organized 26 May 1980. Incorporators: Gapud, Lirio, Crisanto Gualberto ll, Campos Jr., de Guzman, Manuel Engwa.

* Trans Oriental Woodworks Inc - organized 23 September 1980. Incorporators: Gapud, Campos Jr., Gaviola, Feliciano, Lirio.

* Land Value Inc. - organized 15 April 1983. Incorporators: Gapud, Dimaano, Gastrock, Lirio, Gaviola.

* Hyper Growth Equity - organized 12 April 1983. Same incorporators and capital structure as Land Value.

* Century Wealth Group Inc. - organized 12 April 1983. Same incorporators and capital structure as land Value.

* Renown Group Corp. - organized 12 April 19%. Same incorporators and capital structure as [and Value.

* Centrum Land Corp. - organized 18 April 1983. Same incorporators and capital structure as Land Value.

* In-House Management Services - organized 8 August 1983. Formerly called International Mercantile Ass.. Inc. incorporators: Campos Jr., de Guzman, Gastrock, Abalos.

* Hubbard Agri-Ventures Corp. - organized 11 November 1983.

HANS MENZI AND THE BULLETIN

Marcos used Gapud to take over the publishing empire of Hans Menzi. Menzi, a close friend and faithful senior military aide-de-camp of Marcos, had died intestate, leaving behind a substantial agro-industrial and publishing empire. Marcos took the opportunity of Menzi's failing health and eventual death to take over his publishing interests.

Menzi was the publisher of the *Bulletin Today*, the largest and most profitable English daily during Marcos' regime. Its advertising revenues accounted for almost half of the total advertisements of the top seven dailies. While most of the other newspapers were largely losing financial ventures, it was only the *Bulletin Today* which has been making any money [10], the Bulletin blishing Corp. reporting a net income of $898,000 in 1982, increasing to $1.8 million in 1983. Forming part of Menzi's publishing empire were *Panorama,* the Sunday magazine of the *Bulletin,* the daily *Tempo, Balita*, *WHO, Liwayway, Bum, Banawag, and Song Cavalcade* magazines.

Menzi was also the executive vice president and general manager of the Menzi Dev. Corp., a high-quality pulp and paper mill which supplied the paper needs of the newspaper industry by producing pulp and paper from manila hemp. Menzi's companies also produced the *Senorita* brand pad papers widely used throughout the school system.

Menzi was also chairman of the Menzi Group of Companies, Holland Milk Products, National Zipper, and Basic Foods Corp. He was the president and general manager of Menzi & Co. Inc.; Menzi Industries Inc.; M&M Consolidated Inc.; Menzi Agricultural Corp. Part of the Menzi agro-industrial empire is a vast mango plantation in Davao, reported to be the biggest mango hacienda in the country.

Menzi also had interests in the following corporations as member of the board: Paper Industries Corp. of the Phil, Goodyear Tire & Rubber Co. of the Phil, Delgado Bros. Hotel Corp., Manila Hilton Hotel, Council for Economic Development, Philippine Airlines.

The following is a partial list of the corporations where Menzi had interests:

Company	*Activity*
The Bulletin Today	Newspaper publishing
Menzi & Co.	Services
Menzi Agricultural Corp.	Agri-business
Menzi Industries Inc.	Manufacturing
M&M Consolidated Inc.	Services
Menzi Development Corp.	Pulp & paper mills

The takeover of Menzi's interests were accomplished in three stages:

1. purchase of shares through nominees after the imposition of martial law;
2. transfer of Menzi's interests through HM Holdings & Management in 1983, engineered by Gapud; and
3. acquisition of bulk of Menzi's estate through an anomalous purchase in 1985 by Marcos agents [11].

Through these tactics, Marcos ended owning 75 % of Bulletin Publishing Corp. and 92% of Liwayway Publishing Corp., a sister company.

After newspapers had been shut down when martial law was imposed, the *Manila Daily Bulletin,* later renamed *Bulletin Today,* was permitted to resume publication two months later on the condition that Menzi reduce his ownership in the newspaper. Marcos invoked a presidential decree which limited the ownership of newspapers by individuals to 20%, forcing Menzi to sell all his shares above the 20% limit to a group of "special people" composed of Campos, Cesar Zalamea, Ramon Cojuangco. Ramon later made way for his cousin Eduardo Cojuangco.

These Marcos nominees later transferred $1.2 million shares to HM Holdings & Management Inc., a front company organized by a certain lawyer named Manuel Montecillo, with Rolando Gapud signing for HM as Vice-resident and treasurer. Menzi himself transferred s ares worth more than §26 million to HM from his different companies such as Liwayway Publishing, Menzi & Co., Menzi Development Corp, M&M Consolidate , and Menzi Agricultural Corp.

Mariano Quimson, the vice chairman and president of Bulletin Publishing who had worked 27 years for the company, later recalled in a sworn statement that Menzi had said at the time of the stock transfer that "He [Marcos] knows I [Menzi] am sickly, and the [Marcos] children now want a piece of the action." Quirnson was later instructed by Menzi on orders of "the Pesident" "to make monthly reports to Gapud on operations of Bulletin Publishing and Liwayway and deliver all dividend checks to Gapud."

After a lingering illness, Menzi died on 27 June 1984. Through means which are still unclear, Montecillo, who then was the secretary of HM Holdings & Management, became the administrator and executor of the Menzi Estate.

Montecillo "surprised" other trustees of the Menzi Trust Fund by presenting a "motion for confirmation of sale of shares of stock." According to Montecillo's motion, Menzi, who by that time was already dead, had executed a stock option agr ement with Emilio T. Yap and a certain company named US Automotive Co. to sell the shares in Bulletin Publishing. It was claimed that Menzi had sold 154,472 shares to US Automotive for about $1.3 million. But Montecillo could not provide any documentation to support his claims of a sale, and Quimson, the ong-tirne associate of Menzi, said that he was not aware of any such plan on Menzi's part.

To support his claim, Montecillo called upon a former classmate, Judge Alfredo Cruz of the Manila regional trial court, who then legally pronounced that there was indeed a sale even when no deed of sale had ever been produced. The issue was finally put to rest when Montecillo told the members of the Menzi Trust Fund that Marcos was involved in the transaction. According to Quirnson,

> At this point, Atty. Montecillo strongly and persistently persuaded the trustees of the Fund to withdraw their objections to the sale of shares to US Automotive, bluntly stating that President Marcos was the real buyer of the shares [12].

The Menzi Trust Fund was then forced to sell 20% of the remaining 22% in Bulletin Publishing still held by the Menzi Estate to "one of the stockholders of the company". The shares were sold in 1985 at their 1983 bookvalue.

Emilio T. Yap, earlier mentioned in connection with the sale of Menzi's shares, became the chairman of the Menzi Foundation and chairman and publisher of the Bulletin Publishing Corp. Yap also owns Philippine President Lines and has substantial interests in Phil Trust Bank [13]. He also was a director of Baseco, the shipping firm owned by Bejo Romualdez [14].

MOVEMENT 0F ASSETS AND SECURTTY BANK
A closer analysis of many of the firms Yao and Gapud organized for Marcos shows that a great number of them were used to hide and move assets. Consider for instance these figures from Mid-Pasig Land:

	Assets	Liabilities	Loans & Advances Payable:
1981	114.49	201.58	
1982	102.87	218.06	172.38
1983	102.22	225.93	177.82
1984	116.62	254.56	201.44 [15]

The figures are typical of many of the companies Yao and Gapud organized. Many liabilities and loans were incurred, very often in amounts far exceeding the value of the company. Universal Holdings was a clear example: by 1984, after onl two years of operation, it had already accumulated liabilities of $13.14 milion on assets worth $5.58 million. In some cases, large liabilities were piling up even when the company was not yet in operation, as in the case of Master Assets, where liabilities worth $7.27 million had already been incurred by 1983 on assets worth $7.3 million even as its external auditor claimed that it was not yet operating.

The figures also show that while the assets were increasing liabilities, especially loans and advances payables, were increasing faster. This means that these corporations were merely shells or front corporations, or organized simply to act as conduits in the passage of money. The category "advances payables" occurred frequently in many of these companies, leading a writer to comment:

> *Financial profile of these companies showed substantial deficits... Although the companies... have verifiable assets, the liabilities are peculiar in the sense that "advances payable" occurs frequently. This feature raises curious questions: Does the item "advances payable" represent an outward remittance of money? Were the companies simply conduits deliberately designed to lose financtally to cover up the outward remittances that could have been amassed by their beneficial owner deposed President Marcos?*

Marcos, Yao, and Gapud also acquired a major bank, the Security Bank & Trust Company (SBTC), to help them hide their money and facilitate outward remittances [16].

Gapud engineered the take-over of the SBTC with the help of other trusted Marcos men such as Ramon Siy, Willy Co, Philip Ang, Dewey Dee, and Manuel Zamora Jr., the latter a brother of Ronnie Zamora, another Marcos crony [17]. The owners of the bank, brothers Jesus and Nicanor Jacinto, were bitter about selling the bank their family founded, but they were hardly given any choice. During the negotiations, the exact identity of the buyers were kept a secret, but the dailies kept on taking about the involvement of a "secret investor" [18]. The new owners held 90% equity in the bank.

Gapud then transferred at least 53% of the shares to either to front corporations he and Yao organized (Gainful Assets 20.0% and Master Assets 20.0%), or to close Marcos associates he requested to act as nominees (R. Cojuangco 7.3%, de Guzman 4.5%, Africa 1.0%), forming a total of 53.7% The usual blank deeds of trust and assignment were executed. The bank shares were transferred on the condition that Gapud would be retained as chairman, president, and chief operating officer of the bank, a clear indication of the central role Gapud came to occupy in Marcos' financial dealings. He formally resigned from his post with the investment banking firm of Bancom on luly 1980 and assumed his positions with the SBTC the following month.

Gapud then organized numbered accounts and trusts within the SBTC for Marcos and members of his family. The accounts, opened between 1981-82, were both dollar and peso accounts and were aimed at facilitating Marcos' local banking needs as well as transporting money overseas. Some of the accounts were also opened for Marcos and Imelda around 1980 through the Chartered Bank Hong Kong Trustee Ltd. upon instructions from Yao. Some of these accounts were savings accounts, while others -- "SBTC Trust Account No. 7700" and "SBTC Trust Account No. 7710" -- were dollar accounts. instructions on the disbursements were always given verbally by Marcos and were conducted with utmost secrecy. No one else apart from Gapud knew who owned the accounts or where the disbursements ultimately went. Gapud himself admitted the trust accounts were "run on a very confidential basis" and that except for him "no one in the bank knows to whom they belong or where the disbursements go or in whose favor they were made." Among the accounts Gapud organized or Marcos in the SBTC were

Accounts	TrustAccaunts
S/A 272685	7700
S/A 274240	7710
S/A 275050	7720
	7740
	7760
	7770
	7780
	2021
	2022
	2023
	6100

Gapud confessed that Security Bank received "wire transfers from many sources and that these were credited to the "trust accounts and savings accounts of Mr. Marcos". The owners of these accounts never borrowed money nor went into overdraft, limiting themselves to mere deposit, withdrawal, and placement transactions, an indication that the owners were extremely liquid and that the accounts were merely passage points in the transit of money. The accounts started with low balances but later grew to sizable amounts. Gapud admitted that among the sources of the funds for these accounts were the following:

* 60% equity in Fortune Tobacco, Asia Brewery, Allied Bank, and Foremost Farms granted to Marcos by Lucio Tan.
* $3.3 - 5.4 million regular payment by Tan "in exchange for privileges and concessions Mr. Marcos had been giving him."
* dividends from Bulletin Today (around $4.3 million in 1985).
* payments from businesrnan Ralph Nubla
* money from Philcomsat, Oriental Petroleum, Balabac Oil & Exploration Co.

Gapud also admitted that large amounts from the Security Bank number "77" trust accounts were later transmitted to the United States and other places "for investment and other purposes".

As will be seen in the next chapter when we discuss the overseas empire of Marcos and his cronies, Yao and Gapud have also played a major role in the acquisition of overseas properties and in the transfer of money. Gapud played a major role in the Redwood Bank of California, while Yao had substantial real estate investments in the US and Canada. But as will be seen in the last chapter, none of these properties were ever recovered, and neither have Yao nor Gapud been effectively investigated or prosecuted.

Endnotes

1. Mijares, p.371.
2. See Chapter IV.
3. According to a sworn statement Yao gave on 23 March 1986.
4. Noel de Luna, "Marcos Firms Formed by Campos Detailed," *Business Day*, 8 April 1986.
5. See Chapter IV for the overseas investments.
6. *Manila Times*, 10 June 1986.
7. Held under the name of Novo Properties.
8. Held under the name of the following four real estate companies: Mid-Pasig Land, Fairmont Real Estate, Independent Realty, Anchor Estate.
9. *Manila Bulletin*, 12 April 1986.
10. Alan Robles, "Special Report on the Publishing Industry," *Business Day*, 18 June 1981.
11. *Philippine Daily Inquirer*, 6 August 1986; *Malaya* 5 August 1985.
12. *Business Day*, 14 October 1986.
13. *Ibon,* 15 August 1984.
14. Given Yap's background, it is therefore surprising that Mrs. Aquino gave him a presidential award for socially responsflile journalism in 1991.
15. The figures are in millions and are denominated in pesos.
16. Please see Chapter IV.
17. *Daily Express*, 26 June 1980.
18. *Times Journal,* 18 June 1980.

ROMAN CRUZ

Roman A. Cruz Jr. enjoyed the choicest positions in the Marcos government and served as one o the most faithful lackeys of Imelda.

Cruz first served the regime as Marcos' Undersecretary of Finance between 1968 and 1970, but in the course of the years, he became more identified as an Imelda toady. He managed the Philippine Air Lines which bankrolled Imelda's numerous trips, headed the GSIS which financed many of Imelda's projects, and was a director of banks which served as conduits for Imelda's insatiable need for cash.

Roman is the brother of J.V. Cruz, a former newspaper columnist and apologist for Marcos who was later appointed Ambassadorship to Egypt for his services.

PAL

Cruz took complete control of the Philippine Air Lines (PAL) after the former owner of the airline was forced out through a presidential order.

The former owner of PAL, Benigno Toda, had received control of the national flagship airline as political largesse from Marcos' predecessor, President Macapagal [1]. When administrations changed, Toda cultivated ties with the new rulers and successfully maintained warm links with the Marcoses for a time.

But Toda's relationship with his new masters soured when a steadily rising PAL debt forced him to bill Imelda for the flight expenses she had been accumulating. The national airline began to incur huge losses and debts because of Imelda's junkets abroad. At that time Toda presented his bill, Imelda had alread accumulated a reported total of $6 million in expenses, but Toda mustered enough courage to charge $3 million, giving Imelda a 50% discount.

Toda quickly fell out of grace because of this move. On October 1977, Marcos ordered the implementation of a 1966 PAL board decision to increase the capitalization from $3.5 million to $14 million, a move that Toda could not meet. This presidential order to enforce an 11-year old board decision effectively sealed Toda's fate. Toda was sacked. Money from the GSIS, the government insurance system Cruz headed, was then poured into PAL at Marcos' order. Cruz was named chairman and president of the airline two weeks later. It is said that Cruz was personally handpicked by Imelda to take Toda's place to ensure that misunderstandings regarding the billing of Imelda's flights would no longer occur.

One of Cruz's first moves as chairman was to threaten Newsweek with court action for writing an account regarding the sacking of Toda. This empty threat was followed by a lot of bold announcements regarding drastic changes within PAL.

Not having had any experience in the airline industry, Cruz immediately encountered problems in managing PAL and consequently had to eat his bold words. A journalist who interviewed him during this period described Cruz and his first few months at the PAL:

...he came on almost immediate with loud promises of drastic changes. By the beginning of this year [1978], the armer undersecretary of finance stated that on-time reliability of domestic operations would be raised to 95 % byMarch and that PAL would be the region's top international carrier by the end of 1980. He later admitted to this correspondent that he had spoken prematurely and was unaware of just how complex the problems were [2].

Cruz loved to boast about the academic degrees and awards he has received, such as an economics undergraduate degree from Cornell, a graduate degree in public administration from Harvard, TOYM (Ten Outstanding Youn Men) award for economics, etc, ad nauseam. But these titles do not seem to have been of much help to Cruz in managing PAL. Throughout his stewardship, the airline was a poorly managed organization and a steadily losing venture. From 1979 through 1980, operating expenses rose 56%, from $290 million to $448 million, while finance charges rose 132%, from $14 million to $32.3 million. Below is the record of losses of PAL throughout the years Cruz headed PAL:

Year	PAL Losses (in millions)
1979	$33 (3)

1980	$52 (4)
1981	$75 (5)
1982	$27 (6)
1983	$63 (7)

Losses for 1979 would have been greater were they not offset by the sale of equipment.

In an effort to minimize the red ink, Cruz resorted to asking for help from Malacanan. Local competitors were first swallowed up. And when this proved inadequate, PAL requested further government assistance. GSIS interests in PAL were supplemented with money from another government corporation, the National Development Corp. where industry minister Roberto Ongpin was chairman. The capitalization of PAL was increased from $127 million to $380 million, and $63 million of NDC money went to PAL. This secured Ongpin a directorship in PAL and opened the way for Eduardo Romualdez to become the new PAL chairman [8].

Yet despite this further infusion of overnment money, the losses continued. Desperation then led Cruz to ask the government let PAL monopolize the flights of all Filipino contract workers leaving for overseas assignments [9]. A more desperate move came a month later when Cruz went as far as proposing a system of "standard ticketing" that would give PAL control of the cash and markets of other airlines. Under this proposal, PAL alone would issue tickets for all contract workers leaving the country. This would effectively mean that PAL would have control of the cash flow of other airlines and have access to their markets. This proposal has been strongly criticized by the international airlines community. An airline executive commented on the proposed "standard ticketing":

> ...by centralizing the ticketing, PAL can get hold of and utilize the cash flow of other carriers flying the contract workers out o the Philippines... Furthermore, through detailed documentations handed in for ticketing, PAL will soon get at the sources of the labor market and can easily monopolize the labor traffic at the expense of other international carriers who will stand to lose such business [10].

Apart from financial difficulties and desperate attempts to corner markets, there were also other issues related to the basic management of PAL. Many questions were raised concerning the safety of PAL planes. An irate PAL passenger wrote to Cruz:

> You never answered my first open letter; that is understandable since it only dealt with normal and mundane matters as incompetents, dishonest vice-presidents and billion peso losses at PAL. But this time you must answer because something slightly more important, the safety of human lives, is involved. . .. Is it true that the management headed by Mr. Robert Jorgensen, your executive vice-president for Technical Group, a powerful position which includes Passenger service, Maintenance and Operations, insists that PAL pilots fly planes with defects, maintaining that these are merely "go" defects, not "no go"? (Mr. Jorgensen is a former minor employee fiom Hughes Air West, a minor U.S. airline)... Is it true that three pilots who refused to fly on airbus because of a dangerous defect (no reverse thrust on engines) were placed off-schedule as a result of their refusal to fly the airbus? Is it true that a few days ago, on a Hong Kong flight, the same airbus without engine reverse thrust had to fly below the glide path, at several miles below required speed, in violation of Hong Kong approach procedure, because

the replacement PAL pilot who took over had to fly that way so he would not run out of the runway? And that the wheels and tires were so overheated that cold water had to be poured on the landing gear to enable the plane to take off on schedule, again without engine reverse thrust? ...PAL purchased so many new and now unutilized 747's and airbuses, with spare parts for half a decade, yet paradoxically it compels pilots to fly defective airbuses....[11]

The letter went on and covered other aspects of PAL management such as the overpricing of domestic fares, the dominant management positions foreigners enjoyed within the national airline, the political use of advertisements to camouflage the reality behind PAL operations.

PAL would not have been such a big management flop and a financial nightmare if it were managed properly. A big drain on PAL 3 resources were Imelda's indiscriminate international junkets. Cruz himself misspent PAL money by using it to buy real estate properties in California, expenses which have absolutely no relation to the operations of a government airline.

If people were sure that they would be getting proper airline service, that they could be reasonably certain that PAL planes are not flying coffins, then Cruz would not have had to force Filipino overseas contract workers to ride PAL or terrorize other international airlines into handing over their markets.

But airline service did not seem to be the primary goal of Cruz and the other directors of PAL. PAL was seen and used as a propaganda tool. PAL was viewed not as an airline but as an advertising firm for the repressive regime. Commenting on the financial difficulties of PAL, Cesar Virata, Marcos' Prime Minister and himself a director of the airline, admitted that there were considerations apart from financial ones in evaluating PAL. Virata said that PAL operations are "not purely commercial but also a national service" [12]. Financial losses were not important as long as the propaganda function was met. Cruz was more explicit in this regard. In a luncheon speech given in mid-1985, Cruz ignored all the financial and management problems of PAL and just spoke of PAL as "marketing" the Marcos regime:

The country needs the airline as a marketing arm.. Linking the Philippines to the world is not on our mandate but our lifeblood. Serving the Republic is both our business and our duty.... We are its ambassador to the world. And today we are its most dedicated saleman...[13]

GSIS

Cruz's other enclave, the Government Service and Insurance System (GSIS), where he was both president and general manager, was managed just like PAL.

The GSIS, formally a financial institution for low-salaried government employees, was used as a source of funds, a national milking cow, or different crony companies and projects of Imelda.

The GSIS received a total of $1.3 billion in premium income from 1971 through 1980. Most of this amount came from the compulsory deductions from the meager salaries of lowly government employees. But most of this money did not go back these employees in the form of retirement benefits or services provided. Most of it went to finance Imelda's caprices and the failing companies which Marcos cronies had abused.

The majority of investments and loans of the GSIS in 1971 were policy, salary, and housing loans to GSIS members. These loans represented 82% of GSIS investments. These loans to members, however, had declined dramatically by 1980. Housing loans for members, for example, were phased out. But during the same period, loans and investments of the GSIS in Marcos-connected companies and Imelda-inspired projects rose to $843 million or 65% of the $1.3 billion the GSIS earned as income by the end of 1980. This is a 220% increase over the corresponding figure for 1971 for GSIS investments in stocks and bonds of both private and government institutions [14].

To impress delegates to the IMF-World Bank conference held in Manila in 1976, Imelda went into a spate of luxury hotel-building using GSIS money. The GSIS poured a total of $202 million into four hotels connected with Marcos cronies: Kanlaon Towers, Philippine Village Hotel (Sulo sa Nayon), Phil. Plaza, and the Manila Hotel. Most of these construction projects were totally unnecessary) and exceedingly extravagant, a strong indication of the possibility of kickbacks. In one project for example, government auditors found out that the of $133 million the GSIS spent on an unfinished building on reclaimed land, $83.4 million or 63% was superfluous. Contractors and consultants for the project were overpaid by at least $3 million. While similar office buildings were constructed at $390 per square meter, the GSIS had spent $1,050, representing a price difference of 167% [15].

Since most of the hotels were built with GSIS money, Cruz became a director in these crony-owned establishments, consequently deriving handsome director fees. Cruz, for example, became the chairman and president of the Manila Hotel Corp. simply because GSIS savings of poor government employees were used to reconstruct the historic edifice.

Cruz also heavily invested GSIS money with the companies of the more favored cronies such as Cuenca and Disini (see appropriate sections). The CDCP conglomerate of Cuenca was a constant recipient of GSIS money, from the start of the construction boom until the time that this conglomerate collapsed. The GSIS also invested in Disini's Commercial Bank of Manila, another crony firm which was in financial trouble. Cruz again became chairman of this bank.

Because Imelda's brother, Benjamin, was appointed Ambassador to China, GSIS money was used as tool in international diplomacy. Using GSIS funds, Cruz organized in 1980 the Phil-China Friendship Hotels Corp. (PCFHC), a corporation with $26 million authorized capitalization, the purpose of which was to construct and manage two 500-room first class hotels in China, one in Canton, another in Peking [16]. Cruz was both chairman of the board and president of the PCFHC. Other interests in this corporation included Cuenca's CDCP.

Other GSIS investments of Cruz include real estate in San Francisco and political contributions to San Francisco city government officials (see Chapter IV).

When the GSIS was audited after Marcos' downfall, it was found that $285,000 in cash advances to around 20 GSIS officials from 1984-86 remained unliquidated, a clear violation of government regulations that require liquidation of accounts within 10 days of completion of project.

Another report revealed that directors of GSIS had chalked up $46,000 with the Manila Hotel and Hyatt Regency for food and services in 1985. Some of the expenses were incurred by relatives of GSIS directors. The bills were all shouldered by the GSIS. Unspecified expenses worth $97,000 were charged to the GSIS discretionary fund in 1985. Documents detailing the expenses were allegedly sent to Francisco Tantuico, Marcos' Commission on Audit Chairman and a close Imelda associate, but no formal audit or accounting was ever made. Another $403,000 was claimed as "representation and miscellaneous expenses" for 1985, but only $14,000 was actually spent on "public relations." Such "miscellaneous expenses" had actually peaked to $1.04 million l 1984, promoting ordinary GSIS employees to criticize Cruz and their other bosses [17].

These are flagrant examples of improper uses of the GSIS funds. Money saved by low-salaried and retired government employees through the GSIS did not return to them in the form of housing or other basic services but went to build Imelda's tourism infrastructure, support failing crony firms, build hotels in China, and pamper GSIS officials. Investments in PAL alone covered 96.4% of the capital of the airline. While the GSIS was spending on projects totally unrelated to its original functions, it was also abolishing housing loans for its members. Fr. Doherty rightly observes: "Again GSIS money, not available for housing for almost two-thirds of the population of the Philippines, is being used to build hotels in China" [18].

The inevitable effect of all of these expenses was that the GSIS could no longer meet the pension and other claims of government employees by 1980. Despite record revenues from its members, the GSIS began to suffer liquidity problems and could no longer meet its obligations to retired government employees.

OTHER INTERESTS

Apart from the interests already mentioned, Cruz headed or was connected with a long list of other Marcos corporations.

He was chairman of the board of Puerto Azul Beach and Country Club, a position which suggested close relations with the Marcoses who built and own the resort through the Enriquez-Panlilio family (see section). Cruz also had interests in the Hotel Enterprises of the Phil. (Hyatt Regency). When the Manila Hyatt defaulted on GSIS loans, the GSIS also took over this hotel. These interests gave Cruz a lot of clout within the tourism and travel industry.

He also had interests with the San Miguel Corp., controlled by another Marcos man, Danding Cojuangco; the PLDT, a public utility privately also owned by the Cojuangco clan; Menzi Dev. Corp., of the Menzi conglomerate which was taken over by other Marcos cronies; Batangas Sugar Central, a sugar mill where the GSIS had interests.

In the banking sector, Cruz had interests in the Amanah Bank and was chairman of the National Reinsurance Corp. of the Phil. Cruz was also in the board of the Phil. Bank of California, a San Francisco-based bank of Marcos and other pro- Marcos Filipino-Americans. Cruz with flew re larly to California to represent Marcos in the board meetings of this bank. He was also the chairman of the Century Bank in Los Angeles, a branch of PNB.

Cruz was also busy buying expensive properties in California. Among Cruz's real estate investments were

* four lots in Brooktrails Vacation Village, a vacation resort in Willits, Mendocino County, estimated a taxable value of $66,014 in 1985.
* a condominium, Unit #602, at 840 Powell Street in San Francisco, bought under the name of Cruz on 9 June 1979 but transferred to Middlesborough N.V., a Netherlands Antilles shell corporation, a month later on 17 August 1979. This unit was later sold for $650,000 in 1984.
* six units, Units #52-57, at the Cypress Point condominium complex in Daly City, were purchased on 10 April 1980 for $900,000 using money from the Philippine Air Lines. Other Marcos cronies, such as Nemesio Yabut, are known to have condominiums in this complex.

Below is a partial list of corporations where Roman Cruz has interests either as chairman, director, president, manager, or Marcos functionary:

Company	Activity
GSIS	Insurance
PAL	Airline
Manila Hotel Corp.	Hotel
Hotel Enterprises of the Phil.	Hotel
Phil-China Friendship Hotels	Hotel
National Reinsurance Corp.	Insurance
Puerto Azul Beach & Country Club	Resorts
PLDT	Communications
Phil. Bank of California	Banking
San Miguel Corp.	Manufacturing
Phil. Amanah Bank	Banking
CDCP	Construction
Phil. Aerospace Dev. Corp.	Transportation
United Lab. Drug	
Phil.Tobaoco Flue-Curing & Redrying	Manufacturing
The Medical City	Hospital
Liquid Gas Corp.	Manufacturing
Polymedic Hospital	Hospital
National Steel Corp.	Manufacturing
Pasig Steel Corp.	Manufacturing

Endnotes

1. One could characterize Toda as a Macapagal crony, though the term was not in vogue at that time. Toda's administration of the airline has been characterized as incompetent by some critics and as corrupt by others.
2. Mat Miller, "How will the public like relying on one airline?," *Far Eastem Economic Review*, 17 November 1978.

3. *Far Eastern Economic Review*, 6 February 1981.

4. *FarEastem Economic Review*, 1 May 1981.

5. *FarEastcm Economic Review*, 9 June 1983.

6. *FarEastem Economic Review*, 9 June 1983.

7. *Far Eastern Economic Review*, 16 February 1984.

8. This saved the way for Imelda to become the PAL as Chairwoman at a later date. Eduardo Romualdez, Imelda's uncle, was made chairman of the airline in 1983. But when Romualdez was assigned as Ambassador to US, Imelda took over as PAL Chairwoman. Other directors of the PAL were favorite Marcos cabinet ministers such as Cesar Virata, Finance Minister, and Roberto Ongpin, chairman of the National Development Corp. *Far Eastern Economic Review,* 1 May 1981 & 9 June 1983.

9. *FarEastem Economic Review* 29 Jan. 82

10. AFP news report date lined Hong Kong, 1 Feb 1982

11. "PAL Planes Defective?," *We*, 30 June 1982.

12. *Far Eastem Economic Review*, 1 May 1981.

13. Speech before the Phil. Marketing Association at the Hyatt Regency.

14. *The Philippine Financial System*: A Primer, (Manila: Ibon Databank, 1983), p.28-29

15. *Manila Chronicle*, 24 September 1986.

16. *Business Day*, 7 January 1980.

17. Chay Florentino, "Marcos Cronies owe GSIS P5.3M," *Philippine Daily Inquirer*, 3 May 1986.

18. Doherty, p. 2A7.

ENRIQUEZ & PANLILIO

The Enriquez and Panlilio families were among the closest of Imelda's followers. The loyalty of these two families to Imelda lasted long after the Marcoses were deposed. The show of loyalty of these two families reached its extreme form when Rebecco and Erlinda Panlilio participated in the attempted coup on December 1989 where many innocent people were wounded and killed.

Such loyalty was amply rewarded by the Marcos regime. The hotel and restaurant industry interests of the Enriquez and Panlilio families were the recipients of many government contracts and favors.

Starting from the modest D&E (Diaz-Enriquez) restaurant in Quezon City, the Enriquezes substantially expanded their catering interests to include the 60-room Sulo Hotel, the 515-room Philippine V' age Hotel, and the 565-room Silahis International Hotel.

This family was able to carry out this spectacular expansion program largely because of their connections w1th Imelda and other Imelda associates like Roman Cruz (see section).

Trinidad Diaz Enriquez, who comes from the province of Leyte, capitalized on her relationship with Imelda to acquire government loans and contracts. The Enriquez family hotels were the recipients of generous funding from overnment institutions like the Development Bank of the Philippines. Trinidad's son, Leonardo, operated a construction corporation which received favored government contracts. When the Playboy Club of Manila opened in the Silahis Hotel, it was personally inaugurated by Imelda, who was present because the club was owned by Trinidad's son-in-law, Rebecco Panlilio.

The relationship of the Enriquezes with Roman Cruz was also of help. They enjoyed the privilege of supplying the catering needs of the government institutions Cruz headed, such as the Philippine Air Lines. After Marcos was deposed, investigators discovered that Enriquez-connected restaurants topped the list of food caterers for Imelda's gatherings in 1985, the Sulo Restaurant accounting for $172,000, while the Philippine Village Hotel claimed $154,000.

The greatest venture of the Enriquezes was to build the multimillion peso Puerto Azul resort complex in Ternate, Cavite and manage it through their Fantasia Resorts Inc. This resort complex, one of the favorite recreation spots of Marcos, covers 3,000 hectares and was dubbed as "the biggest and most ambitious piece of tourism infrastructure yet conceived in the hilippine provinces" [1].

As in the case of many projects carried out during the Marcos regime, Puerto Azul was constructed at the cost of disrupting the lives of many poor families. Land for the resort complex was expropriated from the residents who had been living in that lace since their ancestors came from Moluccas in 1633 [2]. The dislocated families described their plight in an open-letter they wrote to Marcos in vain in 1978:

> *...Fantasia Resorts (owned by millionaire families Panlilio and Enriquez) put up their Puerto Azul Resort, on exclusive recreation center for the rich. They occupied a wide area of our town which was facing Manila Bay and the China Sea. They fenced the areas that were allegedly their "private property" with barbed wire and even put sentry points to accost people and vehicles along the new public road where a great deal of the money of the taxpayers of this nation was passed. Are the public roads also owned by the Panlilios and Enriquezes? The fishing boats of the Ternatenos can no longer land on the shores of Puerto Azul. Is it not that, according to law, nobody can own the shorelines? We cannot even fish in the surrounding waters of Puerto Azul because its guards shoot at any fishing out in sight. Is the area owned by the millionaire class? [3].*

The SEC lists the following corporations as belonging to the Enriquez and Panlilio families:

Company	Activity
Rizal Park Hotel	Hotel
Swedish Services Inc.	Turkish baths
Enriquez Management Corp.	Management services
Sportsline Corp.	Sporting goods
Samar-Leyte Shipping Lines	Shipping
Development & Constmction Ctr.	Construction
Remma Resources Inc.	Finance
Cannonball Merchandising	Wholesale trade
Mac Agricultural Dev. Corp.	Real estate
Panvil Realty Dev. Corp.	Real estate
B&P Realty Inc.	Real estate
L&R Development Inc.	Real estate

Endnotes

1. *Insight,* August 77.
2. *We Forum,* April 1980.
3. Quoted in *Ibon,* 31 August 1980.

TANTOCO

The husband and wife team of Bienvenido and Gliceria "Glecy" Tantoco were Imelda's fronts and associates in the large chain of Rustan corporations, mining concerns, and multimillion overseas real estate investments.

The Tantocos have been Imelda's partners as early as the 1960's during Marcos' first presidential term. The have been among the closest and most loyal of the cronies. As a reward for their loyalty and service, they were named to choice positions and were showered with different forms of government assistance and Imelda's generous patronage. Bienvenido was granted the choice position of Ambassador to the Vatican and named president of Metropolitan Museum of Manila Foundation. Glecy served as Imelda's personal confidant, managing many overseas bank accounts and multimillion dollar transactions in art and New York real estate. Glecy was also made a member of the board of trustees of the Metropolitan Museum foundation.

OVERSEAS PROPERTIES

Even after the fall of the Marcos regime, the Tantocos continued to serve the Marcoses. Bienvenido used his Villa in Via Appia Antica, Rome to stockpile an armscache of 10 handguns, Israeli Uzi rapid-fire rifles, electrified truncheons, bullet-proof vests, walkie-talkies, which Italian newspapers suggested was for Marcos supporters in the Philippines. Bienvenido was arrested by Italian authorities and sentenced to three years in prison, but his incarceration was later suspended due to the intervention of some friends Tantoco made while he was Ambassador to the Vatican.

It was in the Tantoco residence in 2338 Makiki Heights Drive, Honolulu where the Marcoses stayed. The house, just across the home of crony Floirendo, was bought for $717,000 on 14 July 1977 under the name of Bienvenido and Gliceria. The Tantocos also have an 11,000 square foot lot in same neighborhood, purchased through an exchange of some 2.5 acres of land in Clark County, Mo. To protect their ownership, the Tantocos have transferred the titles of these properties to a Panamanian company, the New York Financial Inc. [1].

RUSTAN CHAIN

Many of the goods Imelda bought were acquired through Glecy's chain of stores.

The art works and antiques discussed in the first chapter were acquired with the help of Glecy Tantoco who almost always accompanied Imelda in her shopping trips. Glecy's Galerie Bleue, an art and poster shop, was used in the purchase of the art works, with money for the art acquisitions passing through Banque Paribas in Geneva under the name of the shop. Glecy's price was a 5% commission on art deals [2].

Goods for Imelda were also purchased through the Rustan chain of stores, the name being an acronym of her maiden and married names, Rustia and Tantoco. The Rustan's Flower Shop, for example, was among the top suppliers for the First Couple, representing a bill of P5.8 million for purchases in a single year. Most of these flowers were used in Imelda's disco pad at the Maiacafian presidential palace. The Rustan's Supermarkets supplied the imported steaks served at the residential palace. Rustan's Commercial Corp. supplied the expensive Philippine handicrafts such as jusi and pina cloth, mother-of-pearl picture frames, flower arrangements, jewelry boxes, and Philippine shells which Imelda presented as either gifts to guests and visiting foreign dignitaries or presents taken along her trips abroad. Rustan's Commercial Corp., of which Glecy is president, supplied nearly $360,000 worth of goods in 1984 and $430,000 in 1985 to Imelda and her pet projects.

Most of these expenses were incurred without following the normal government procedures governing purchases. The purchases of flowers, for example, were carried out either through ordinary phone calls or simple order slips.

Assistance to the Rustan chain was not limited to providing markets for its products. The Marcos bureaucracy was also used to help Rustan against its competitors. In April 1978, for example, Rustan Marketing and Holiday Cosmetics were able to get the Court of Appeals to intervene and restrain the business activities of a competitor, Beautifont and Aura Laboratories, arguing that the activities of these two Avon-owned companies would be detrimental to the Tantoco corporations. Only a threat of a demonstration by an irate 600 Beautifont and Aura employees and some 24,000 independent dealers prevented the implementation of this court decision [3].

The Rustan's International Marketing, which also belongs to the Rustan conglomerate, was amon the 12 favored with generous incentives by the government to set up trade houses abroad [4].

The Tantocos also owned Sanmar Export Corp., a trading company based in New York which served as Rustan's purchasing agent in the US. Sanmar was one of those mentioned in the indictment for mail and bank fraud handed down against Tantoco and Imelda. Glecy is the chief operating officer of Sanmar.

TOURIST DUTY FREE SHOPS

A 1974 presidential decree gave the Tantoco family a lucrative franchise to operate tourist duty-free shops at international airports, hotels, and choice commercial centers. The decree permitted the Tantoco famlilly to import luxury goods without paying the duties and taxes on imports. The franchise boasted of 11 shops in Makati, the international airport, and other choice places in Metro-Manila, as well as outlets in the provinces such as Cebu.

The Rustan Duty-Free Shops Inc. was incorporated with the SEC on March 1974, conveniently around the same time the presidential decree took effect. The incorporators were relatively unknown individuals, but it was well accepted that these individuals were merely fronts of the Tantoco family. Two daughters of Bienvenido and Gliceria, Maria Lourdes T. Pineda and Carmencita T. Lopez, managed the day-to-day operations of the franchise, while Dominador Santiago acted as their dummy in his capacity as chairman of Tourist Duty Free Shops (TDFS), the name the franchise later assumed.

There is evidence indicating that members of the Tantoco family asked favors from government officials for the duty-free shops. Gliceria, for example, wrote letters to Jaime Laya, Marcos' Central Bank governor, on behalf of the company.

More telling is the letter of Maria Lourdes Tantoco-Pineda addressed to Imelda asking that the government issue a presidential decree which would exempt the company from all taxes. Attached to the letter was the draft of the presidential decree, ready for the signature of Marcos. The request was granted. PD 1193 issued in 1974 gave the Tantocos special privileges. It granted the TDFS a 25-year franchise starting 6 September 1977 and exempted it from all business and income taxes. A separate presidential letter of instruction made this franchise exclusive.

While the official purpose of the duty-free shops was to supply imported tax-free goods for tourists, the shops were used for other Tantoco-related purposes. Since the franchise allowed the company to import luxury items tax-free, it was used by the Tantocos to supply their Rustan chain of stores with the tax-free luxury items imported through the duty-free franchise. This was done through manipulatin the inventories of the chain. The duty-free shops imported highly-taxable luxury items into the country without paying taxes but only a small portion of this inventory were sold through the duty-free shops. The bulk of these goods, which included brand-name items like Christian Dior, Cartier, Chanel, Nina Ricci, Oleg Cassini, ended up being sold through the regular outlets of Rustan Commercial Corp. at considerable profit. The latter company of the Tantocos enjoyed an exclusive right to market these brand-name luxuries in the domestic market.

This explains why the Tantocos consistently imported amounts in excess of what was allowed y Central Bank regulations, a scheme done with the with knowledge and participation of Dominador Santiago, the token chairman of the TDFS. At times, Glecy would also marshall the services of Imelda who would also shop for the Rustan chain whenever she went on her sprees abroad. The goods would then enter the country without passing through customs.

This system of smuggling was so well known to the public that the Tantocos had to make statements denying their guilt. Zenaida Tantoco Huang, Executive Vice-President and General Manager of Rustan Commercial Corp., was quoted by the papers as saying that, although there were no direct references to the Tantocos in the criticisms, it was clear that they were the ones targeted:

...although there is no definite mention of Rustan as the store in question, indications are clear that the 27-year-old shop is being pin-pointed since Christian Dior, Carrier and Chanel, the brands specifically mentioned to be present in both the local and duty-flee shops and Rustan, are exclusively carried by Rustan in the domestic market, and in quantities that cannot be matched by neighboring shops. If only our critics will check on the facts, records will show that Rustan, 23 years before the duty-free shops came into existence, has been carrying prestige brands like Christian Dior, Nina Ricci, and Oleg Cassini [5]

But when critics did try to check on the facts later, the Tantocos adamantly refused to turn over company documents to government investigators and retained the influential ACCRA law firm (see sections on Enrile and Cojuangco) as the legal counsel of the TDFS.

Apart from this method of inventory manipulation, the Tantocos illegally sold products to non-tourists, a patent violation of the stated purposes of the TDFS. These methods allowed the Tantocos to realize big profits. While the company started with a paid-up capital of $37,000, it was estimated that it generated an income of $100,000 a day from all outlets, with its annual sales reached $25 million at one point. Gliceria herself wrote letters to Imelda reporting that profits of the company far exceeded their best projections.

The only thing required of the TDFS was a minimal franchise tax of 7% of their income. But the Tantocos also found a way to circumvent even this minimal tax. Whatever franchise taxes were paid, the proceeds went not to the government but back to the Tantocos themselves or to the projects of Imelda. Marcos declared that of the 7%, 2% would go to the national government, while 5%, representing the bulk of taxes would go to Imelda's *"Nutrition Center and other projects determined by the President"* (italics ours). Bienvenido Tantoco Jr. received $3 million from 1981 through March 1986 from these funds. Many of the organizations which funded Imelda's caprices discussed in previous sections also received part of the booty. The Nutrition Center received $6 million from January 1980 through March 1986. Other Imelda projects such as the Manila Seedling Bank and Mt. Samat Reforestation also received largesse in the millions [6]. Despite their official sounding names, the Nutrition Center, the Manila Seedling Bank, and the Mt. Samat Reforestation were private Imelda foundations.

MINING

The Tantocos were also active in gold, copper, and precious ore mining ventures. They were helped by the Bureau of Mines which located the sources of rich ore deposits and awarded the exclusive mining rights to the Tantoco corporations. One may cite the case of Surigao Consolidated Co. and Azure Mining Corp. Azure Mining, a subsidiary of the Rustan conglomerate and managed by Rustan Investment & Management Co. (RIMCO), was a relatively new corporation when it purchased the ore mill of Surigao Consolidated for the rather inexpensive price of $300,000 on December 1979 [73]. Azure Mining had been registered with the SEC with a capitalization of $1.8 million under the name of Bienvenido Tantoco on March 1979. Barely a month after the purchase, the *Bulletin Today* [8] announced that the Bureau of Mines confirmed that there were rich ore deposits in the Barbo-Siana old mines of Surigao Consolidated, a strong indication that the Tantocos had known about the deposits before they made the purchase.

This pattern was repeated in the old mines of Paracale in the Bicol province. These mines were abandoned during the war, but in 1980 the Bureau of Mines confirmed that there were rich gold deposits in this area [9]. A few months later, Bienvenido Tantoco announced that Metals Exploration Asia Inc., a mining corporation where he was president, had already started drilling and mining operations with an Australian company [10]. Tantoco revealed that the proven gold ore reserve in Paracale was 1.5 million metric tons with grades in excess of 0.5 ounce per ton. He further announced that it was expected that full production would be attained soon and that the mill was expected to operate at a capacity of 500 metric tons daily.

Another Tantoco mining interest was Eagle Mining Corp. It was later discovered that more than half of the endowment of $595,000 0 Metropolitan Museum of Manila Foundation was "loaned" to Eagle Mines [11].

Amon the other interests of the Tantocos were investments in the RCBC, FUJI Xerox, Hi Mktg, PICOP, and other big corporations. Rustan Investment & Management Corp. was also in agri-business. The Tantocos were one of the big buyers of raw abaca which is used in the Rustan Pulp & Paper Mills. Most if not all of the corporations listed by SEC under the name of the Tantocos were heavily capitalized.

A partial list of the Tantoco companies:

Company	Activity
L&J Agriultural Inc.	Agri-business
Rustan Wood Corp.	Construction materials
Rustan Duty Free Shops	General merchandise
Rustan Clay Craft	Ceramics
Rustan International Trading	Import-export (antiques)
Malayan Income Fund	Investments
RIMCO Int. Trading	Machineries
Phil. Int. Products & Service	General merchandise
A&I. Tantoco Commodity Corp.	Real estate
B&G Management & Dev. Corp.	Finance
Phil. Eagle Trading Corp.	Wholesale trade
Azure Mining Corp.	Gold mining
Phil. Sericulture Ind.	Textiles
Heritan Dev. Corp.	Real estate
Rustan Supermarkets	Supermarket chain
Rustan Commercial Corp.	Services
Rustan Manufacturing Corp.	Manufacturing
Rustan Pulp & Paper	Pulp processing
Industrial Finance Corp.	Finance
Rustan's Int. Marketing	Services
Eagle Mining Corp.	Mining
Rustans Investment & Management	Services
Galerie Bleue	Art gallery

Endnotes

1. Please see Chapter IV for a fuller discussion of the overseas properties.
2. William Sherman, "The Marcos Collection,"*ARTnews,* October 1990.
3. *Far Eastern Economic Review*, 4 May 1978
4. *Daily Express*, 4 March 1981.
5. *Bulletin Today* 2 July 1980
6. *Business Day,* 24 April 1986.
7. *Bulletin Today*, 27 December 1979.
8. *Bulletin Today*, 21 January 1980.
9. *Bulletin Today,* 21 January 1980.
10. *Times Journal*, 26 July 1980.
11. William Sherman, "The Marcos Collection,"*ARTnews*, October 1990.

THE ROMUALDEZ FAMILY

Imelda was one of eleven children fathered by Vicente Romualdez. Vicente's first marriage brought him the first set of five children, while Imelda belonged to the second set through a second marriage. Imelda's early childhood was marked by tragedy and privation. Both of Vicente's wives had died early, with the death of Imelda's mother, Remedios, being particularly painful because she died in a garage in Manila amidst poverty and family squabbles. Thus, while some members of the Romualdez family from the province of Leyte had acquired earlier prominence through the political ofiices they had previously held, the achievements of these relatives only served to underscore the bitter poverty Imelda experienced in her childhood. She had to serve and live with her more prosperous relatives after her mother's death. Imelda at one time describe how her mouth watered when she realized that the neighbors' bread had margarine on them [1].

The fortune of Imelda and her relatives, particularly her brothers and sisters from her father's second marriage, drastically changed with her marriage to Marcos. At the zenith of Marcos' power, Imelda could claim to be one of the richest women of the world, with her two brothers, Benjamin and Alfredo, owning powerful business conglomerates in the country.

KOKOY

Benjamin, better known as Kokoy, was the most favored of Imelda's brothers. Kokoy had faithfully performed many favors for Marcos, such as helping rig the results of the l971 Constitutional Convention and the 1973 January plebiscite [2], and was in turn given control over the national power utility, a number of the country's newspapers, banks and other interests, apart being assigned ambassador to Peking and Washington. Because of Kokoy's close relationship with the dictator, he was often said to be Marcos' favorite brother-in-law.

Kokoy led a very simple life and had no accomplishrnent to speak of before Marcos came into power. Although he had somehow managed to finish law school, he was too intimidated by the idea of taking the bar exams and could not practice the profession. A businessman who knew him during this period described him as a generally unemployed "bum" who at times worked as a messenger and performed other menial jobs to make ends meet.

But Kokoy's fortunes soon changed with the imposition of the dictatorship. He received several choice political assignments such as Ambassador to Peking when diplomatic relations were opened after Nixon's historic visit, Ambassador to Washinton from May 1982 to 1986, and concurrently Governor of Leyte, the home province of the Romualdez family. The two latter appointments were patently illegal since Marcos' own constitution prohibited the appointment of elective officials [3]. But Kokoy's designation as ambassador to the US was much criticized not only because it was illegal but more so because he was known to have a difficult time with the English language and could potentially cause great embarrassment for the country. But Imelda firmly supported her brother, saying that the choice would be "good for the United States." Kokoy thus kept the position, except for a brief interlude when another Imelda relative, Eduardo Romualdez, held the post.

Kokoy was also a big spender almost equalling Imelda's extravagance. Once when his guests at the Stork Club in New York offered to pay part of the costs of the evening's dinner, Kokoy, reportedly said, "You don't pay, the Filipino people pay for my expenses anywhere!" [4]. Kokoy, who had a weakness for women, was apparently trying to impress one of his guests, a Filipina who came from a wealthy family in the Philippines [5]. Kokoy, however, was not content with raiding the national coffers for his expenses and was also active in generating funds for himself and Marcos, generally through the coercion of privately-owned companies for a part of their assets or profits. Described as "ambitious, rapacious, and insatiable" [6], Koko reportedly required new companies to surrender a considerable part of their equity to him:

> Every new company [must cough up] from 10% to 25% of their euity holdings to Kokoy. He alwalgs stresses, of course, that he holds such shares in the name of President Marcos. In smaller areas of operation, Kokoy holds the shares in his own name. Established businesses in the Philippines, whether owned by Filipinos or Americans, have been approached by Kokoy direct or through emissaries and told that they would get better business from, or establish better relations with the biggest business establishment in the Philippines -- the government -- if they should make it appear or make known that the honorable governor from Leyte is a major stockholder of theirs. The gratuitous equity usually demanded is 25% to 40% from domestic firms, and from 10% to 25% of foreign-owned companies [7].

The most brazen example of Koko 's arm twisting methods involved his takeover of the empire of the Lopez amily, the richest famil in the Philippines before Marcos imposed martial law. The Lopez family ad extensive interests in sugar, electric utilities, and the media. Eu enio Lopez Sr., the head of the clan, was considered as the "king-maker" of the country since it was his financial support which largel influenced the outcome of presidential races. it was money from Eugenio pez which permitted Marcos to grab the nomination for president during the Nacionalista Party convention, with Alfredo Montelibano, a trusted associate of Lopez, bringing suitcases of cash to the convention to buy the votes of the delegates. But Marcos ultimately turned against his former benefactor and allowed Kokoy and other members of the Romualdez family to gobble up the Lopez empire when martial law was declared in 1972.

Kokoy used the dictatorship's shut-down of newspapers to publish his own. Not only did the paper support the government but it was also a golden opportunity for him to make money because of the absence of competitors. Presidential Letter of Authority No. 3, issued on October 1972, barely a month after the other newspapers had been closed, granted Kokoy permission to publish the Times Journal. A front, the Philippine Journalists Inc. (PJI), was organized to mask Kokoy's involvement with the paper. Rosario Olivarez served as president of PJI, while Manuel B. Salak worked as assistant publisher. Among the publications of the Kokoy's PJI were *Times Journal, People's Journal, People's Tonight, Taliba,* and the *Women's Journal.*

The original arrangement was to publish the *Times Journal* by contracting the facilities of another newspaper on a daily basis. But Kokoy soon realized that his profitability could be increased if he were not burdened by this arrangement. He then summarily took over the facilities of the Manila Chronicle, owned by the Lopez family. The grab was legitimized by a "leasing" arrangement Kokoy dictated on the Lopezes who had no choice but to agree since they knew they were not going to be allowed to publish under martial law. Thus, the editorial offices, typesetting equipment, and printing facilities of the *Manila Chronicle*, then the most modern in Asia, were turned over to Kokoy, leaving an estimated 900 staff writers from the Manila Chronicle unemployed. But the terms of the "lease" were not honored by Kokoy, who paid only half of the amount [8].

Other obligations were also incurred by the PJI with the government. By the end of Marcos' regime, PJ I owed the government close to $13 million.

Kokoy then moved in on other Lopez interests. The Manila Electric Company (Meralco), the lucrative national power monopoly controlled by the Lopez family, was next to be acquired. The acquisition of Meralco, however, prove to be more complicated than the seizure of the *Manila Chronicle* because it was owned by a public company, the Meralco Securities Co . (MSC). The Lopez family controlled the MSC through the ownership of 33% of its shares, the largest block of stocks in the company. These shares were either owned directly by the Lopezes or through Benpres Corp., a family corporation named after Eugenio Lopez's children. But the rest of the MS shares were owned by the public. This public ownership thus posed an initial complication to Kokoy's plans.

Kokoy gained control over Meralco by coercing Eugenio Lopez to transfer the Lopez and Benpres shares to the Meralco Foundation, a newly formed corporation Kokoy controlled. To force Lopez to give up his shares, the Marcos government started by reducing a previously authorized utility rate increase from 36.5% to 20.9%, a move which would force Meralco to incur losses. Kokoy also directly told Lopez Sr. that his son, Eugenio Lopez Jr., who had been incarcerated on charges of attempting to assassinate Marcos, would be released from prison if he agreed to Kokoy's terms. The old man then capitulated and agreed to turn over the family's shares to Kokoy. Eager for the release of his son, the elder Lopez then signed a document he had seen for the first time during a 29 November 1973 Honolulu meeting. The document, the "Stock Purchase Agreement" between the Lopez-owned Benpres and the Meralco Foundation Kokoy controlled, effectively turned over all the Lopez shares to Kokoy. While Kokoy was present in this meeting, one of his associates, Senen Gabaldon, president and chairman of the newly-formed Meralco Foundation, signed the agreement, with two other Koko associates, Antonio Ayala and Delia Tantuico, acting as witnesses. Also heavily involved in the negotiations was Emilio Abello who had served the Lopez family as chairman and president of Meralco but later changed his allegiance.

The agreement provided for the payment of $1,500 as an initial down payment, a ridiculously low amount or the purchase of a national power utility. While the arrangement provided for the payment of $6 million over a stipulated number of years, additional payments were never made because of a loophole Kokoy built into the Stock Purchase Agreement:

> The principal installments and interest on each Series B Note [the notes to Benpres] shall be payable... **only to the extent that the cash flow of the Foundation** (as determined by the independent external auditors of the Foundation) **permits payment** of interest and principal installments as these fall due... [emphasis supplied].
> [Benpres and the Lopez family] shall give due consideration to a request to renegotiate the terms of payment...in case the Foundation is unable to make payment ...in accordance with their tenor due to acts of God or an extraordinary rise in the price of fuel oil which materially and adversely affects MECO'S (Meralco's) normal cash flow as projected [emphasis supplied].

Since these clauses provided for possible "acts of God" and required payments only when the "cash flow" permitted it, these provisions absolved Kokoy from any legal obligation to make further ayments to Lopez. They permitted Meralco Foundation to delay or completely withhold other payments to Benpres and the Lopez family. Kokoy and other members of the Romualdez family bled Meralco, thereby reducing its cash flow, with the result that no further payments were ever made beyond the initial $1,500. Expenses for Imelda's 2 July 1974 birthday party, for example, were shouldered by Meralco: the catering personnel of the Meralco restaurant and cafeteria, including the expensive silverware, china, and glassware of the company, were marshalled and flown from Manila to Leyte using company planes to serve Imelda's guests. The following year, a new private 9-seater jet costing more than a million dollars was ordered using company funds. Such expenses were ultimately shouldered by the poor Filipino consumer who has to endure the increasing rates imposed by Meralco. Lopez further explained the scheme in a later interview:

> The agreement is only a document which enables the Foundation to take over our family's holdings of MSC. According to the terms of the agreement, the Foundation is not really obligated to pay me anything, except the down payment of Pesos 10,000 ($1,500). The agreement states that the net principal amount of $5,700,000 plus interest is payable overa ten-year period with the first payment due 30 months after the "closing." However, the terms of the agreement provide that the payments to Benpres shall be made only if the "cash flow" of the Foundation permits. This simply means that payments will be made to me if the Foundation has excess funds after all other obligations, expenses, etc., are met. Since the income of the Foundation is controlled by the Foundation itself and by the Philippine government through its control on the electric rates of MECO, it is very simple to regulate the "cash flow" so that there will never be any excess funds to pay Benpres. I do not apect to ever receive anything out of the sale of Benpres [9].

As soon as Kokoy acquired Meralco, the electric rates, controlled by the government when the Lopezes were in charge, were increased by 100%, with the rates continually increasing throughout the whole time Kokoy assumed control. A new pricing scheme was then introduced in the form of a rate adjustment clause which permitted Meralco to increase rates if the price of crude oil increased or if dollar exchange rates became unfavorable. Thus, merely a year after Kokoy's takeover, Meralco grossed the biggest sales in the country, and outdid San Miguel, the country's biggest corporation.

The Romualdez camp justified their takeover in different ways. Imelda, for example, claimed that Lopez "wrote, called, and came begging on my birthday" for the Marcos government to relieve him of the company because it had become a loosing venture. Spokesmen of Kokoy, on the other hand, claimed that the move was done for the good of the consuming public. Senen Gabaldon and Emilio Abello, Kokoy's top men at the Meralco Foundation and at the MSC, claimed that

> The significance of the Meralco Foundation ultimately derives from its being one of the first realized stirrings of a Philippine society determine to live an authentic democracy. The Meralco Foundation constitutes the vehicle by which the stock ownership base of the Meralco Securities Corporation, and thereby of the utility company, has been broadened to include all the customers of Meralco. Non-stock in structure, with no profit inuring to any single private person or group of individuals, the Meralco Foundation has been designed solely for public-purpose activities, for the greater good of it's more than 600,000 customers [10].

As part of the claimed "broadening" of the "ownership base" of the firm, a Stock Warrants Distribution Program was instituted in 1975 where

> ...594,705 customers (or 89% of the total number of Meralco customers) will each be given a stock warrant or one common share in the Memlco Securities Corporation, which owns Meralco. In effect, by becoming a stockholder of the MSC, one would also become a co-owner of Meralco and thus participate in the dividends from this public utility [11].

If this stock plan had been implemented, it would have meant that the public would have benefitted from a more diffused ownership of the power monopoly. It is not desirable that a single family should control the most essential utility upon which the industries in the nation's capital depends. Moreover, another strong reason for broadenin the ownership base of the bank was that the state-owned Philippine National Bank had been a guarantor in the sale. But after Kokoy's Meralco Foundation had taken over the interests of the Lopez family, all talk about diffusing the ownership of Meralco was shelved. Kokoy's men instead started talking about the opposite, of how difficult it would be to sell Meralco's stocks to the public:
> ...because the sale of all the shares of MSC, and not merely those held by BENPRES, would have been difficult to carry out within a reasonable period of time and would certainly have further depressed the price of the shares in the stock market which was already several times below book value [12].

It is not clear that Meralco shares in the stock market would have dropped had they been offered to the public. As noted earlier, utility rates were increased drastically right after the take-over and thus appreciably increased the earnings of Meralco. It seems clear that Kokoy and his men merely used the stock dispersal plan as a ruse to take over the interests of the Lopez family and replace the control over the strategic and lucrative company from one powerful family to another [13].

Kokoy then assigned trusted individuals to the Meralco board [14]:

Antonio Ozaeta	chairman
Placido Mapa	board vice-president [15]
Delia S. Tantuico	corporate secretary
Danilo M. Celestial	
Jovencio Cinco	
Florentino P. Feliciano	
Senen J. Gabaldon	
Francisco V. Gatmaitan	
Ramon R. Ravanzo	
Wilfredo C. Tecson	
Rolando Sosa	

The takeover permitted Kokoy to form his own empire. He acquired control not only of Meralco but also the 15 other corporations which formed the Meralco Securities Corp. (MSC) conglomerate.

As soon as Kokoy was firmly entrenched, he reorganized the MSC and renamed it as the First Philippine Holdings Corp. (FPHC). Furthermore, a major modification was made with original takeover agreements. Kokoy's Meralco Foundation had originally agreed to pay the creditors of Benpres, but after the reorganization, payments from Kokoy's Meralco Foundation were made not to the creditors but to Kokoy's First Philippine Holdings Corp. It was a case of one Kokoy company paying another.

Indicative of the close relationship between the Meralco Foundation and the First Philippine Holdings Corp. was the fact that they had many company officers in common. All are men beholden to Kokoy. Meralco chairman and president Emilio Abello was made chairman of the board of FPHC. Mario Camacho, who also served as Meralco's president, was a director of FPHC. Senen Gabaldon, formerly a vice-president of Meralco, also served in a company under the FPHC group, the Meralco Securities Industrial Corp. Allt the key men in both corporations were known to be close associates of Kokoy, such as Emilio Abello, Cesar Zalamea, Antonio Ozaeta, Alfredo Montelibano, Mario Camacho, and Eduardo Regala.

Such a closely-knit management on was desirable in view of Kokoy's plans to milk Meralco. As soon as the MSC was transformed into the FPHC, Meralco, composed of the power plant and the transmission and distribution facilities (T&D), was quickly sold in its entirety to Kokoy's Meralco Foundation. The Meralco Foundation in turn sold the power plant to the government-run National Power Corporation (NPC) but retained the transmission and distribution facilities. Kokoy's Meralco Foundation received $217.2 million from the government in 1978 in exchange for the power plant, an amount many felt was a substantial overprice since it was meant to be merely a down payment, with further payments expected.

Meralco sold the power plant because Kokoy did not want to bother about the production of power but merely concentrated on its distribution, the most lucrative part of the whole operation. Power would be generated by the government, while Meralco would merely distribute it, charging the consumer a fat mark-up.

Corporations under the wing of the FPHC conglomerate have also been the recipients of government help. When the local operations of the EEI, an electrical engineerin firm which was part of the FPHC, started to sag, it branched out into Middle East operations with the help of the government in 1976, a move which made its net income soar to 155% the following year. Apart from maintaining a large work-force in Saudi Arabia, among the other overseas projects of the EEI was a joint venture for a liquefied natural gas plant in Sarawak, Malaysia. Another firm, Ecco-Asia was the building contractor for the highly overpriced nuclear plant in Bataan (see section on Disini). The participation Ecco-Asia in the construction of the plant was criticized for many anomalies, such as the "mismanagement of cost of work funds; unreasonable delay in the payment of vendors and suppliers of materials and equipment; inefficiency in purchasing material and equipment" [16]. Cesar Zalamea and Emilio Abello, two key associates of Kokoy, served as key figures in the EEI and Ecco-Asia.

Among the companies Kokoy had interests in are

Shell (Philippines)
Filipinas Shell Petroleum Corp.
Philippine Petroleum Corporation
Shell Corporation
Engineering & Construction Corporation of Asia (Ecco-Asia)
Philippine Electric Corporation (PECO)
Philippine Engineering Co.
Philippine Commercial & Industrial Bank (PCIB)
Philippine Trust Company
Universal Broadcasting Corp.
The *Times Journal*
Olympic Mines & Development Corp. (through FPHC)
Pasol Mining Corp. (through FPHC) [17].

Kokoy also owned Benguet Corp., a large mining concern listed in the New York Stock Exchange. Fronting in the ownership of Benguet were two other Kokoy realty firms, Palm Avenue Realty and Palm Avenue Holdings which held 16,237,339 in Benguet common shares.

Kokoy also has extensive interests in real estate. He is the owner of a $1.5 million estate in Southampton, Long Island, New York. His wife, Juliet is also known to hold real estate properties in Mabalacat, in the Central Luzon province of Pampanga. He also had substantial real estate interests in expensive villages in Makati, the prime residential area in Metro-Manila. Among the houses and lots Kokoy owns in the area are real estate properties totalling more than $2 million:

* house and lot in Palm Ave. Forbes Park, area of 4,979 square meters, valued at approximately $981,000
* house and lot in Paraiso St., Dasmarinas Village, area of 721 square meters, valued

at $196,000
* house and lot on Tamarind Road, Dasmarinas Village, area of 2,844 square meters, valued at $491,000
* house and lot at 5390 Amorsolo St. Dasmarinas Village, valued at $343,400, held under the name of Jose Manuel Romualdez, Imelda's nephew.

BEJO

The case of Alfredo or "Bejo" Romualdez, another Imelda brother, provides another example of how state power was used to enrich the members of the Romualdez family.

When Marcos was preparing to run for his reelection in 1969, agricultural and industrial enterprises were encouraged to take out loans from government financing institutions. The businesses were enticed into borrowing by overvaluing the collateral offered and consequently promising loans which were considerably larger than what the collateral would normally allow. The catch was that the borrowers would have to "cough up" between 7% to 33% of the value of the loans for the 1969 election campaign of Marcos [18]. Many cash-strapped businesses fell for the offer. While those who qualified for the loans were nominally entitled to receive 50% of amount in the initial release, they had to immediately make the full 30% contribution to Marcos' campaign, leaving them with merely 20% of the loan to start their projects. The result was massive overspending. A conservative estimate of Marcos' expenses in 1969 was estimated at $250 million [19], an astronomical amount given the size of the official money supply at that time. An unprecedented inflation resulted and the Philippine peso was consequently devalued at the insistence of the International Monetary Fund. To further contain the inflation, Marcos also ordered that the remaining 50% of the loans be withheld by the funding mstitutions.

Many businesses went bankrupt because of the credit squeeze. Hundreds of agricultural and industrial projects, primarily investments in rice mills, fishponds, pasture lands, and ranches, were abandoned. But soon after Marcos declared martial law in 1972, he issued Presidential Decree No. 385 providing for the automatic foreclosure of all the mortgaged properties [20]. The decree, issued in early 1973, also provided that its implementation could not be challenged by any restraining order, temporary or permanent injunction that courts might issue [21]. The result was that hundreds of businesses were foreclosed by government financing institutions such as the DBP, PNB, SSS, GSIS. The foreclosed mortgages proved to be an instant boon for Bejo Romualdez, as well as other cronies such as Benedicto, who immediately used their political connections to restructure the loans and takeover the properties. Bejo, who already controlled some rural banks at this time, organized a rice warehousing operation, Kamalig Phil. Inc., and concentrated on acquiring the properties of indebted rice millers through the help of the very same financial institutions which had pulled the rug from under the feet of the indebted businesses [22].

After his participation in this caper, Bejo was further favored by Marcos being given exclusive control over several lucrative areas in the economy. The shipbuilding and repair, stevedoring, and gambling activities were specifically chosen for Bejo because this brother-in-law, a former officer of the Philippine navy upon whom Marcos had later bestowed the rank of reserve commodore, could presumably use his experience profitably in these activities.

The control of two major corporations permitted Bejo to dominate the ship building and ship repair industries. Mijares wrote that Bejo received the first of these corporations as a reward for facilitating a sexual liaison for Marcos [23]. Because of the favor, Marcos then granted his brother-in-law control over the Bataan Shipyard and Engineering Co. (Baseco). The firm controlled the country's major dockyard and specialized in ship repair. A second corporation, the Philippine Dockyard Corp. (PDC), was granted to Bejo in 1978. The PDC controlled the largest shipyard in the country and specialized in ship building. Directors and officers of the two corporations were close associates of Bejo and Marcos, like Generoso Tanseco, a retired army colonel.

Bejo's ventures received strong support from the Marcos government. A 1975 decree permitted the tax-free importation of ship building equipment, boosting the profitability of these firms. Baseco, which took over the facilities of another firm which had been disbanded [24], was the recipient of liberal funding from the government-owned NIDC, a subsidiary of the PNB. Baseco also received a grant of 300-hectares in the Mariveles Free Trade Zone through a secret presidential decree, while small farmers who had been living in the area were disallowed from claiming land within the zone. The organization of the second firm, PDC, is also revealing of the support Bejo got from the government. The PDC received heavy funding from tiie government when it was being organized. Loans which Baseco could not pay to the NIDC were converted into equity in the new PDC. This was in effect a $13.6 million doleout from the government financing firm. Another company, Luzon Stevedoring, a light cargo company which at that time was owned by the government, threw in another $4.4 million. An industry source estimated in 1980 that the overnment had sunk in around $50 million in ship-building equipment in Bejo's two firms, with the figure rising to $120 million if other assets given the two firms were included.

Despite the financial help the PDC received from the government, it had difficulty building ships. The heavily-funded facility was capable in principle of building 65,000 DWT vessels, but the PDC was able to build only a 6,000 DWT ship after much difficulty. One foreign advisor noted that the ship cost 60% more than if it had been built in Western Europe. The ship went directly to the use of Maritime Trade Carriers (MTC) Inc., a new shipping line controlled by Bejo, and was paid for by a loan from the government-run NIDC. The ship was launched by no less than Marcos and Imelda, indicating the support of the couple.

Bejo was assigned to control the ship building industry not only because of his naval back ound but also because the shipping industry in the Philippines presented the possibility of quick money. The acquisrtion of ships using government money or loan guarantees, for example, was a prime source of kick backs. A government source estimated that the overpricing on contracts ran in the neighborhood of 20% per vessel, with the purchases done abroad, making the kickbacks easier to deposit in foreign bank accounts [25]. It was also for this reason that Marcos assigned Generoso Tanseco, one of Bejo's directors in Baseco, to head the Maritime Industry Authority (Marina), a government institution which oversaw the acquisition and building of ships. Tanseco also headed the PNL Leasing Company the financing arm of Marina, a position which made arrangements between the purchaser, the creditor, and the supplier easy to establish. The purchasing and financing policies of Marina and Tanseco were clearly in favor of persons close to the dictatorship. The purchase of ships by Bejo, as well as other Marcos cronies such as Benedicto and Cuenca, for example, were clearly overpriced but were still allowed by Tanseco. In one case, Marina permitted a newly-organized firm to purchase 6 big bulk-container ships, ostensibly to ply between Europe and the Philippines, but the liner service was soon discontinued, with the vessels being chartered out to other firms by the inexperienced management. It was generally accepted in shipping and banking circles that all the company was organized not to engage in legitimate business but merely as a conduit for kickbacks .

Not content with control over the ship building and repair industries, Bejo also attempted to impose a monopoly on the stevedoring services at the Manila South Harbor, the country's premier port of entry for maritime cargo. Bejo, working through the Philippine Ports Authority (PPA), the government agency in charge of the country's ports, acquired an exclusive franchise to run the lucrative stevedoring services in the Manila harbor. The monopoly was granted to the Overseas Terminal Services Inc. (OTSI), a firm which Bejo controlled, and the subsidiaries it later organized, Metro-Port Services Inc. (MPSI) and Manila International Container Port Terminals Inc. (MIPTI).

Bejo also organized two other freight handling companies, Asiatic integrated Merchandising Corp. on November 1975 and Fleet Cargo Forwarders & Brokerage on April 1979.

The PPA General Manager, Eustaquio Baclig, a colonel in the military, claimed that the move would result in a more systematic and efficient handling of cargo, decrease smuggling and pilferage, and a better deal for the stevedores [26]. Baclig said that the policy of integration would eliminate kickbacks and "useless" competition and would also "stop the exploitation of the poor stevedores whose earnings are just enough to make th ends meet" [27]. Baclig further claimed that the choice was made after a comprehensive "point system" rating the different stevedoring companies in terms of existing equipment and management capability had determined that OTSI was the best contractor [28].

The move created a big stir. The award was granted on 27 June 1980 and was to take effect on 27 August 1980, giving the other stevedoring firms merely three months to plan for their dissolution. Thirteen other firms, which employed a labor force of about 12,000 [29] and had combined assets of $2.6 million, were affected. The stevedores claimed that the move was tantamount to a "death penalty" [30] for them. The Philippine Association of Stevedoring Operators & Contractors (Pasco) claimed in an open letter to Marcos that the slated dislocation of these 12,000 men had created a "virtual powder keg" in the harbor area.

Baclig's moves were not so much an effort to promote efficiency in the stevedoring industry as it was an attempt to impose a monopoly on the country's cargo handling. While Baclig was publicly talking about the systematization of the country's stevedoring services, Bejo was equally busy working on monopolizing it. Bejo, for example, approachq1ed an owner of one of the stevedoring companies threatened with dislocation and shamelessly blackmailed the guy, saying "if you give me 60% of the shares, perhaps we can keep you there" [31].

A group of cargo-handling firms challenged Baclig's assertion that OTSI was the best choice by pointing out that the PPA itself had chosen another firm as the "Most Outstandin Stevedoring Operator" in South Harbor earlier and that OTSI had never been considered outstanding. The group also exposed another inconsistency with the PPA's choice, pointing out that PPA's own records on the volume of cargo handled indicated that Bejo's company 'as not "very active." The group concluded that "a mystery shrouds the granting of a franchise to OTSI" [32], insinuating that extremely influential persons were known to be behind the move. The executive vice-president of Pasco, Jose Tatco Jr., pointed out that the move would not result in the integration or rationalization of stevedoring services but "a selection of a small firm whose competence and capability has yet to be tested" [33].

Other groups joined the fray. The local manager of Hapag-Lloyd, the German line considered to be one of the world's biggest, pointed out that most ports in developed maritime nations employ several stevedoring operators, and that shipping lines should be free to choose their operators [34]. The Far East Freight Conference (FEFC), one of the world's biggest shipping groups, complained that shipping lines already had made substantial investments in special types of cargo-handling equipment in order to save on stevedoring costs. The Conference further expressed fears that a stevedoring monopoly would lead to inefficiency and increased cost to shippers, vesse operators, and the recipients of the cargo [35]. The Pasco summarized the complaints about the planned monopoly, saying that the contract between PPA and OTSI was

* illegal and criminal since it created a monopoly in restraint of trade and therefore violated Article 186 of the Revised Penal Code;

* violative of the Anti-Graft & Corrupt Practices Act because the PPA gave OTSI unwarranted advantage and preference;

* violative of due (process because it was done in secrecy and extreme haste and was to be implemented even before any other stevedoring firm had heard about it;

* arbitrary and against public interest because there were no objective criteria to determine the competence and worthiness of OTSI;

* clearly inconsistent with the announced policy of the PPA for integration, ideally the merging of the different firms rather that the irrational exclusivity of one [36].

Yet, despite the complaints from the different affected sectors, the PPA was determined to push through with its decision. The Manila City Court of First Instance lifted a restraining order on 3 September 1980 which had temporarily prohibited the plan. Three days later, PPA's Baclig told ship operators and agents that they would not be allowed to berth if they did not avail of the servrces of OTSI. OTSI promptly started its services on 13 September without any formal contracts with the shipping lines or announcements concerning its rates.

When martial law was declared, gambling was labeled a "disease of the old society" and all casinos were declared illegal and ordered closed. Imelda in particular publicly denounced gambling on many occasions and singled out casinos as the breeding ground for vice.

But after the rhetoric had died down, gambling activities surfaced again, but this time it was done through a private monopoly officially sanctioned by the government. The Games and Amusement Board, the government body charged with administering gamblingactivities, granted an exclusive franchise to the Philippine Amusement & Gaming Corp. (Pagcor), a private corporation controlled by Bejo Romualdez, to control all the gambling activities in the country.

Bejo started by acquiring the lucrative franchise for the game of jai alai. The fast ball game, introduced into the country by Spanish Basques, is a popular sport which regularly draws huge crowds. Bejo acquired the jai alai franchise in 1975 from its previous owners and took over the popular *fronton* (jai alai walls) in Taft Avenue which was always frequented by large crowd eager to gamble. Bejo organized the Jai Alai Amusement Corp. to avail of the franchise and named Enrique Razon, an old friend, as head of the new corporation, while Razon's brother-in-law was appointed manager. The exclusive concession meant that Bejo could easily raise large amounts through the popular game. But not content with the revenues from this already profitable operation, Bejo, with the acquiescence of the government, expanded the restricted betting on the *fronton* and opened off-fronton betting stations all over Manila, thus expanding the gambling market and what Imelda had earlier referred to as "breeding grounds of vice."

Bejo's next project was the organization of floating casinos where ships devoted soley to gambling activities were berthed in the harbors of the cities of Manila and Cebu. A separate Bejo corporation, the Manila Bay Enterprises (MBE), handled the franchises for these floating casinos which offered games such as baccarat, blackjack, chemin de fer, and roulette. Reportedly involved with these floating casinos was Stanley Ho, known as Asia's Gambling Czar, whose gambling syndicates controlled the casinos in Macau [37]. Also involved with the floating casinos was Roberto Benedicto (see section). Fronting for Bejo and Benedicto in the casinos was Edward Marcelo, an associate who also worked in the Baseco shipyard and specialized in the building of pleasure craft and patrol boats [38]. Marcos and Imelda personally inaugurated the first floating casino in Manila Bay in 1976 [39], despite their earlier protestations concerning the evils of gambling.

The floating casinos were enormously profitable and were reported to have earned $200 million a year. The money gained from the gambling activities were supposed to go to the government's flood control program and to Imelda's "community development" projects which took up a minimum of $13 million yearly. But the actual disposition of these funds have been difficult to ascertain. One source said that 10% of the earnings went to the government, 50% was paid to the winnings of customers, but that the remaining 40% went to the managers. It impossible to verify these assertions because the funds were exempt from government audit. An official of the Securities & Exchange Commission says that MBE has never filed a financial statement, as required by law [40]. Further complicating the matter was that the funds were deposited with the Traders Royal Bank, owned by Benedicto, which never made an accounting of the funds. A few days after Marcos fled the country, $3.25 million in cas believed to be from the casino was found in a van in Bejo's house.

The arrangements concerning the ships used as floating casinos was another source of funds for Bejo. The first floating casino, called the *Philippine Tourist*, was purchased in 1975 by the Peninsula Tourist & Shipping Co., a front corporation managed by Marcelo. The company then leased the vessel to the government, which in turn leased it back to Bejo's Manila Bay Enterprises. The arrangement was rather odd since Marcelo headed both companies. The double leasing arrangement appears to be nothing more than a way of making extra money. Bejo also derived extra income from the ships by insuring them through Country Bankers Insurance, a company controlled by the Rural Bankers Association. Although Bejo's name does not appear on the corporate documents of either company, he is the real power in the Association and maintains an office in their Manila headquarters [41].

The first floating casino later mysteriously burned down, but Bejo had the operations later moved to the Philippine Village Hotel, a venture ran by persons close to the Romualdez family. Seven other casinos, floating as well as stationary, were later organized in the Pines Hotel in Baguio, Insular Hotel in Davao, Zamboanga Plaza Hotel, Zamboanga City, and other cities such as Angeles, Olongapo, Iloilo, and Cebu. And to ensure that this brother-in-law would not encounter competition, Marcos "commissioned a special task force against gambling, headed by the President's private secretary, Sirnplicio Taguiam" [42].

Bejo was also charged with involvement in the illegal transfer of a overnment-owned 50-hectare lot to a private corporation. The lot, owned fiy the National Shipyard and Steel Corp. (NSSC), was valued at $46,000 but was sold to the Philippine Smelters Corp. or only $4,600. The company was owned by Jose T. Marcelo Jr., person believed to be close to Bejo. Another individual implicated in the case was Arturo Pacificador, a loyal Marcos supporter in the legislative assembly.

Bejo is also known to have owned at least three ships: Legazpi II, Seacraft MV Marina, and Seacraft MV Legazpi.

Among the other properties that Bejo Romualdez owned were several realty firms and choice pieces of real estate in Tacloban City, the Romualdez family enclave. Among these properties were

* a towering eye referral center building, corner of Romualdez and del Pilar, Tacloban.
* the Green House, a two-story residential building, comer of Padre Burgos and Juan Luna, Tacloban
* Roms Realty Corp., Port Area, Tacloban.
* Aviles Realty Corp. [43].

Other companies owned by Bejo were two finance companies, Island Development Bank, a thrift bank organized on July 1979 and based in Tacloban City, and Rural Banks Liquidity Guaranty Fund, a finance company which shared offices with Baseco, organized on August 1976 . Other companies were Conspec Marketing, a general merchandise company organized on February 1975, and Leyte Tourist Services, a handicrafts dealer, organized on April 1977.

OTHER ROMUALDEZ RELATIVES AND ASSOCIATES

The Martel Family

Another set of relatives who have directly benefited from the Marcos regime was the Martel family. Alita Martel is Imelda's younger sister and is married to Rodolfo "Rudy" Martel. This family, which became exceedingly affluent in a short time, as substantial interests in the steel industry, agricultural machinery, hotels, and other investments which received help from Japanese companies which needed connections with the Marcos government.

A clear case of the use of political clout concerns the case of Eduardo Figueras, a former business associate of the Martel family. The family and Figueras were among those lucky enough to acquire a ship, the S.S. Don Jose Figueras, through the war reparations agreement with the Japanese. When the ship sank, Figueras collected the insurance under his name, angering members of the Martel family. When martial law was declared, the Martels exacted revenge and had Figueras arrested on charges of attempting to assassinate Marcos. Figueras was reported to have been consequently tortured by the military:

> *I personally know that [Eduardo Figueras] has been tortured by the interrogators of General Ver-Crisologo, the commander of the Presidential Security Command. The torture had been sanctioned not only by General Ver-Crisologo himself, but by both President and Mrs. Marcos -- on the personal plea of Mrs. Alita Romualdez-Martel, sister of Mrs. Marcos. Even the incarceration of Eddie Figueras was instigated by the Martels, Rodolfo Martel, husband of Alita, and Antonio Martel, elder brother of Rodolfo [44].*

The Martels were also associated with the Century Park Sheraton Hotel, a plush five-star hotel which boasts of a one-acre lobby, complete with indoor waterfall and lagoon, where a harpist performs on an artificial island. The Martel family was believed to own 60% of the hotel through Maranaw Hotels Dev. Corp., headed by brother-in-law Antonio Martel. The Century Park is located in the Harrison Plaza, a shopping center which occupies a several large city blocks which were combine to form a huge complex. The place, located in the heart of Manila, was previously home to a large number of poor families. The families were cleared from the area under the guise of expanding the adjacent city zoo. But after it was cleared, the property was awarded to the Martels in secret negotiations with Antonio Villegas, the Mayor of Manila, who gave a long-term lease to the property with nominal fees.

The family was also a major force in the steel industry. Antonio Martel is listed by the SEC as the principal owner of Marsteel Consolidated Inc, a giant steel company registered with the SEC in April 1976. Another brother-in-law, Jose Martel, helps Antonio in the operations of Marsteel and another related company, Armco-Marsteel Alloy, another steel corporation. Through Marsteel, the Martel family has also expanded into related activities such as the manufacture of machinery and oil drilling, largely in cooperation with Japanese companies. Among these large-scale joint ventures with Japanese capital are Okura-Marsteel Crane Co., a crane manufacturing firm organized in January 1976, and Kubota- Marsteel Machinery Co., Inc, an agricultural equipment company organized in February 1977. The latter firm supplies the Department of Agriculture with farming equipment:

> *Within the Central Bank of the Philippines and the Department of Agriculture, the "franchise holder" is Alita Martel, a younger sister of Imelda. Alita's husband, Rodolfo, and brother-in-law, Antonio Martel, are in charge a supplying the agriculture department with Kubota farming materials and supplies. This is one reason Marcos has not been able to fire Secretary of Agriculture Arturo R. Tanco. Alita protects him [45].*

Among the other interests of Antonio Martel are a big pulp and paper company, Scott Paper Mills, and investments in First National City Bank. A partial list of the owned by the Martel family:

Company	Activity
LIMAR Dev. Corp.	Real estate
Pioneer Bay Forest Industries	Forest products
FACOM Computers Phil	Computers
Okura-Marsteel Crane	Steel cranes
Marsteel Consolidated	Steel manufacturing
IB Plaza Inn Co.	Restaurants
Eastern Davao Oil Mills	Oil mills
Aegis Insurance Broker	Insurance agency
Manibay Sugar Milling	Sugar mills
Varangao Food Services	Restaurant
Yaohan Marketing Corp.	General merchandising
M Systems Trade Corp.	General merchandising
Kubo-Marsteel Machinery	Machinery
TOWA International Phi .	Appliances
LPM Enterprises.	Restaurants
Food Systems Inc.	Restaurants
Marine Ventures Phil	Agriculture
Ago-Industrial Machinery Trading	Wholesale trade
Filipina Micro-Circuits	Electrical machinery
Sucro Chemicals	Chemical products

Yap

Conchita R. Yap is another sister of Imelda. Her husband, Edon Yap, rose from the rank of colonel to Brigadier General during Marcos' rule and served as Imelda's military aide-de-camp. Edon was also designated Commanding General, Army Reserve Command of the Philippine Army.

Armando Romualdez

Armando "Mandong" Romualdez is the relatively obscure brother of Imelda. In the early 70's he acquired GCFI (Golden Country Farms Inc.) with heavy funding from government institutions. He received more than $23 million in loans from the DBP and NIDC, while the NFA extended generous credits for commodity loans, leading to a marked increase in gross sales, reaching $29.24 million in 1983. He also held a timber concession, Consumers Export Co., registered with the SEC on October 1974. Armando was also the owner and president of Highway Builders Inc., a construction company which received government contracts. Armando also owns properties in California [46].

Eduardo Romualdez

Eduardo Romualdez was Imelda's uncle who became Ambassador to the US. His family has extensive real estate interests in the US (see Chapter IV). Among the corporations registered under his name in the Philippmes are the following:

Company	Activity
Arobo Mining	Mining
Dyker Fertilizer	Fertilizers
Central Atok Consolidated	Mining
La Suerte Grains	Agri-business
Phil. Projects Dev. Corp.	Real estate
Bolbok Dev. Corp.	Agri-business
Romact Marketing	General Merchandise
Chawiteg Exploration	Mining
Mindanao Builders	Construction
Lemarco Agri-business	Poultry
Marvelle Business Conglomerate	Business services
Industrial Alliance Inc.	Finance
RCD & Comp.	Finance
Var Mineral Dev. Corp.	Mining
Scientific Systems	Machinery
Carabao Carrier	Transport
Prime Ventures	Real estate
Romdy Wood Dev.	Logging

Another relative, Vincent, had the followtng corporations:

Company	Activity
Leyte Geothermal Paper	Paper products
V.R. Development Corp.	Hotels
Atlas Arrastre & Stevedoring	Stevedoring
VRJ Corporate Security	Security agency
Asian Technologists	Technology
Hanil-Gonzales Const.	Construction
Nissan Overseas Const.	Construction
Interzone Resources	Construction
Fabrica Lumber	Logging
Pacific Geothermal	Power plant
V.R. Corporate Management	Business services
Virom Agro-Industrial	Warehouses
Romualdez Enterprises	Trading
Tolosa Dev. Corp.	Real estate
VRJ Marketing	Construction
Gamma Dev. & Construction	Construction
Cinematic Operations	Photography
Vasser Construction	Construction

Other Romualdez Associates

Cesar Zalamea, a close associate of Romualdez, served as Governor of the Central Bank and director of numerous corporations linked to the Romualdez family such as the FPHC, EEI, Ecco-Asia, the latter firm a construction company involved with the controversial Westinghouse nuclear power plant deal. Zalamea was also a director at Philamlife together with other Marcos cronies such as Emilio Abello and A. Sycip. Zalamea also served as a consultant to Ministry of Transportation, where Jose Dans, a Zalamea associate [47], served as Minister. (Dans was also president & chairman of Erectors Inc, a large construction firm, and chairman of the board of Mantrade, a transportation firm which was the subject of a Kokoy takeover.) Among the companies where Zalamea had interests were

> Republic Glass
> Bacnotan Consolidated
> Phil. Petroleum
> Allied Thread
> Phil. Electric Corp.
> Philmagen, insurance
> Philamlife

Emilio Abello, chairman of the board of First Philippine Holdings, also served the Marcos regime in many other ways. He was chairman of Enercon and was also an assemblyman in the Marcos-controlled Interim Batasang Pambansa, using the latter position to push for constitutional amendments that would allow Marcos to perpetuate himself in power.

Among the other interests of Abello were the chairmanship of Philippine Commercial & Industrial Bank and directorships in corporations such as Phil. Petroleum and Phil. Electric Corp. Abello's son, Jose, was a director of PAIC, while another son, Manuel, was a director in corporations such as Philtrust, Phil. Vinyl Consortium, International Pipe Industries. A partial list of companies where the Abellos had interests:

Company	*Activity*
Mermaid Marketing	General merchandise
Rio Camel Agricultural	Agri-business
Econotech Inc.	Business services
Citadel Capital Management	Business services
Cocoa Investors Inc.	Agri-business
March International Trading	Trading

Mario Camacho, as earlier noted, served Kokoy in different capacities after the Meralco takeover. Amon the firms where Camacho had interests were U-Bix, Shell Chem., Bank of the Philippine Islands, Ault & Wiborg, Globe Mackay.

Antonio Ozaeta of FPHC also served as president of Phil. Commercial and Industrial Bank (PCIB), one of the larger commercial banks. Ramon Ozaeta was a director of companies such as Manphil Investment Corp., ICB, Lakeview Industrial Corp. Ramon, together with Jose Ozaeta and Albino Sycip, had investments in Alfa Integrated Textiles. Among the companies where the Ozaetas had an interest were

Company	Activity
Computer Information Systems	Data processing
Tamanli Dev. Corp.	Real estate
Ancel Dev. Corp.	Real estate
Phil. Comm. & Industrial Finance	Finance
First Phil. Leasing	Credit
FPCC Brokerage	Commercial brokerage
First Phil. Trading	Machinery
Mayamot Dev. Corp.	Real estate
Victoria Manufacturing	Manufacturing
People's Car	Transportation
Phil. Petroleum.	Services

Sixto Orosa Sr. and Ramon Orosa are among the other known business partners of Kokoy are (see sectlon on Dlsini).

Generoso Tanseco, a trusted and close associate of Bejo Romualdez, hadsubstantlal mterests in the Shlpping, banking, agri-business, and transportation industries.

Tanseco's interests in the shipping industry started when he headed the United Philippine Lines, a company operated by retired military officers. UPL got a blg break when it was able to acquire 7 surplus American ships used in the invasion of the Philippines during WWII. A further boost came when new liners were bought by the government under the Japanese war reparations program. Although UPL closed down in 1974, Tanseco's influence within the shipping industry expanded during the Marcos regime.

Tanseco was named head of the Maritime Industry Authority (Marina) and with his son, Renato, was given directorships in choice crony companies such as Philseco Shipyard and Philippine Ship Building Co., a joint venture between the government and Kawasaki Heavy industrles of Japan. Renato also headed the Bataan Shipyard & Engineering Co. (Baseco), the largest shipyard in the country. He also ran another shipping company, Ekman Shipping Inc.

Other Tanseco interests include a trucking firm which transported sugar from the sugar mills to different centers and ports for Philsucom. It is believed that this crony won this contract even when he charged higher rates than other trucking firms. He also sat as a director in two sugar centrals and also had interests with Phil. Pigment & Resins. Generoso was also a director of the PNB, while Renato was in Filmanbank. Among the corporations connected to the Tansecos were

Company	Activity
PNL Leasing Co.	Finance
Ekman Welding	Manufacturing
Ekman Shipping	Transport
Ekman Minlng	Mining
Ekman Construction	Construction
Ekman Forestry	Logging
Union Cargo	Transport
Ekman Farms	Sugar

OTHER ROMUALDEZES

Among the properties owned by members of the Romualdez family in the province of Leyte are:

* a stud farm in Busali, Naval, Biliran subprovince ($1.96 million)
* People's Center building, Real St., Tacloban City ($98,000)
* a resthouse in Olot, Tolosa, Leyte ($41,000)
* nipa hut (govemor's mansion), Jones St., Tacloban City, registered under the name of Zenaida Ocampo ($147,101)
* Price Mansion (govemor's guest house), corner of Justice Romualdez and Sto. Nino Sts., Tacloban Clty ($669,000)
* a television station, University Broadcasting Corp., (value undetermined)
* radio Station DYMM, including land and building, Universal Broadcasting Corp., Old Road, Sagkaan, Tacloban
* radio stations DYBRAM and DYDRFM, including land and building, East Visayan Broadcasting, Old Road, Sagkaan, Tacloban
* Tabuan Hand Bungto commercial building, land and building, Marasbaras. Tacloban
* establishments located within Tabuan Hand Bungto compound: Rural Bank of Tacloban (building), Island Development Bank (building), Fixit MotorShop
* Deo Island resort
* Baluarte Beach Resort, San Jose, Tacloban
* Bilat farm, Bilat, San Roque, Tolosa

Endnotes

1-The definitive biography of Imelda is Carmen Pedrosa's *The Untold Story of Imelda Romualdez Marcos*
2. Mijares, p. 34
3. The pertinent part of Marcos' constitution read: "unless otherwise provided by law, no elective official shall be eliglble for appointment to any office or position during his tenure except as member of the Cabinet."
4. Mijares, p. 222.
5. Mijares claims that Kokoy would not have hesitated to add the Filipina to what he referred to as Kokoy's "harem." Mijares, p. 222. Because of Kokoy's many affairs with many married women in the Philippines, Mijares mischievously described Kokoy as the "husband-in-law" of many men in the Philippines.
6. Mijares, p. 12.
7. Mijares, p. 206
8. Mijares, p. 198.
9. Quoted in Mijares, p. 200.
10. Summary of the Joint Statement of Mr. Emilio Abello, President and Chairman, Meralco Securities Corporation and Manila Electric Company and Mr. Senen Gabaldon, President and Chairman, Meralco Foundation Inc. on the Benpres-Meralco Foundation transaction.
11. Joint Statement of Abello and Gabaldon.
12. Joint Statement of Abello and Gabaldon.
13. Given the brazen manner Kokoy used state power to victimize the ordinary consumers of electricity after he took over the interests of the Lopez family in Meralco, the description of Kokoy offered by a correspondent of the Washington Post seems to be off the mark:"...Romualdez has had a relatively benign influence on the Philippine economy....he has tried to build up lasting institutions, brought in professional managers and refrained from interfering in their operations... He's probably a little bit more sophisticated in his

outlook." William Branigin, "Crony Capitalism Blamed for Economic Crisis," *Washington Post*, 16 August 1984.

14. These were the board members when Marcos was deposed in 1986.

15. Mapa was also president of the government-owned Philippine National Bank. He was active in many other Marcos corporations.

16. Doherty, p.104; "Ecco—Asia Loses N-Plant Job," *Business Day*, 18 October 1979.

17. Doherty, p.248

18. Mijares, p. 193, p. 207-8.

19. Mijares, p. 208.

20. Mijares, p. 208.

21. Mijares, p. 208.

22. Mijares, p. 208.

23. Mijares wrote: "... an important political prisoner in the concentration camp operated near the Malamfian golf course suddenly enjoyed visiting privileges from his socialite sister. It turned out that the privilege was accorded him through the court of Alfredo "Bejo" Romualdez... [Bejo had scarred the woman] for his commander-in-chief... Bejo was amply rewarded later on with an award of the Baseco to his private outfit." Mijares, p. 319.

24. NASSCO (National Shipyards and Engineering Co.).

25. Bernard Wideman, "Filipino Shipping: Sailing Close to the Wind," *Insight,* April 1979

26. "Baclig defends OTSI rates," *Times Journal*, 2 August 1980.

27. "Rebates out soon with integration," *Times Journal,* 25 August 1980.

28. "Integration scheme at Manila South Harbor to begin," *Evening Post,* 22 August 1980.

29. Excluding dependents.

30. "Stevedores to strike," *People's Journal,* 9 September 1980.

31. *New York Times,* 27 April 1990.

32. "Row on stevedoring franchise turns South Harbor into powderkeg" *Times Journal,* July 15, 1980.

33. "PPA to insist on 10% share in port earnings," *Daily Eapress,* 8 August 1980.

34. "Conference hits monopoly}; *Times Journal,* 2 August 1980.

35. "Conference hits monopoly," *Times Journal,* 2 August 1980.

36. "Open Letter to the President-Franc Minister" July 25, 1980

37. "Floating away a fortune," *Far Eastern Economic Review*, 17 February 1978.

38. Bernard Wideman, "Winning Ways of the Marcos Cabal," *Insight*, September 1978.

39. Doherty, p.248

40. Bernard Wideman, "Winning Ways of the Marcos Cabal," *Insight*, September 1978.

41. Bernard Wideman, "Whining Ways of the Marcos Cabal," *Insight*, September 1978.

42. Doherty, P248

43. Ellen Tordesillas, "Sandigan will try Marcos," *Malaya,* 9 May 1986.

44. Mijares, p.

45. Mijares, 206

46. See Chapter IV.

47. Doherty, p.104.

THE MARCOS FAMILY

THE BROTHER

Dr. Pacifico Marcos, the younger brother of Ferdinand, has the distinction of personally accumulating one of the longest lists of corporations among the presidential relatives.

Pacifico's official position in the government bureaucracy was Chairman of the Medical Care Commission, the agency in charge of the much-criticized health program of the government. When the program was instituted shortly before martial law was imposed and a compulsory contribution from every wage-earner was required, man labor groups demonstrated in the streets and criticized the moves as another form of undue taxation. Denouncing the scheme as yet another way to extract from them their hard-eamed money, worker groups argued that the scheme would not bring them any real health benefits and would only dig more deeply into their already hurting pockets. In the years that the medical program was inplace, no worker received, either in terms of actual health or material benefits, the amount which had been deducted from his salary. This however was only one side of the story. Doctors also complained that they were not being paid their proper professional dues [1].

While Pacifico Marcos has not been too successful either as a professional doctor or as Chairman of the Medical Commission, he outdid irnself in the business world. Pacifico was chairman of several companies and ventured into almost every conceivable area of business activity: insurance, mining, real estate, management consultancy, sugar, car, hotels, tours, banking, agri-business, publishing, and general management. He was the principal owner of Monarch Estates Dev., the corporation that owns the Tradewinds Hotel. He was a director of Benedicto's bank, the RPB. It was the usual practice of corporations seeking favors from the regime to invite Pacifico into their board either as director or as chairman. Deals were generally made through a military colonel close to Pacifico who usually asked for no less than 20% of the business.

Pacifico Marcos is married to Lloyd "Lydia" Velez Marcos who also has her own set of corporations. LVM Timber, a logging company where Pacifico was chairman, was named after her.

Mariano "Nonong" Marcos II, the only son of Pacifico and Lydia and the namesake of the father of Ferdinand, was also deep into business, utilizing a core of young professional managers to handle the family corporations. Nonong left the Philippines after his uncle's downfall and is presently stayin in California where he owns real estate. He is known to have acquired real estate properties in California as early as 1980 when he bought a condominium in San Francisco, #1602 Ten Miller Place Condo, on 18 November.

An example of the business operations of Pacifico and Nonong Marcos can be found in their acquisition of Insular Sugar Refining Corp. in August 1980. At a time when the international price of sugar was high, the Victorias Sugar Milling Co., one of the world's largest sugar mills, sold its majority control in Insular Sugar Refining Corporation, a large refinery which processed 1.7 million 50-kilo bags of sugar a year. The buyer was Sucro Managers Inc., a corporation where Pacifico was chairman. The sale caused quite a stir in the sugar industry because it did not make economic sense since demand for sugar was high and rising in both the local and international markets at that time. When sought out for an interview by the *Times Journal*, Pacifico was unavailable for comment, and Carlos Luzurriaga, an Insular Sugar executive and son of the former company President Eduardo, "decline to divulge the reasons for the sell-out" [2]. Nonong Marcos, president of Sucro Managers Inc., became the new president of Insular Sugar Refining. Funding for the buyout was arranged by Nonong with a loan of $3.3 million from the UCPB [3].

Among the other properties of Nonong in the sugar industry were estates totalling 4,000 hectares in the province of Negros spread throughout the Bacolod area, E.B. Magalona town, and Cadiz City. An individual named Eduardo Lopingco was used as a front in acquiring these properties [4].

Among the other interests of Pacifico Marcos in sugar were the Central Azucarrera de Baez and the Central Azucarrera Refmeria de Bataan, Inc. (Carebi) in Botolan, Zambales. Aside from Pacifico Marcos, other members of the Board of Directors of Carebi were are Brig. General Prospero Olivas; the former law classmate of Ferdinand Marcos, Jose Unson of Philsucom; and Jose Osias, the son-in-law of Pacifico [5]. Jose "'Tito" Osias is the husband of Pinky Marcos, the daughter of Pacifico. He was also deep into the family business. Osias headed the Bliss Marketing Corp. of Imelda's Ministry of Human Settlements and also served as one of the ministry's regional directors. Osias was fingered as the "tactician" who handled the rigged elections of January 1980 in Tagaytay City [6]. Tito Osias ensured that the KBL bet, Noel Benitez, would win the post of Vice-Mayor. Noel Benitez is the brother of Jose Conrado "Jolly" Benitez, former Deputy Minister of the MHS and errand boy of Imelda.

A partial list of corporations where Pacifico and Lydia had interests:

Company	*Activity*
Fortune Insurance	Insurance
Intemcontinental Wood Processing	Lumber
Malayan Integrated Industries	Manufacturing
Philippine Iron & Steel Corp.	Manufacturing
Far East Bank & Trust Co.	Banking
Philippine Comm. & Ind. Bank	Banking
Eternal Gardens Memorial Park	Memorial Park
Orchids Fishing	Fishponds
Worldwide Construction	General contracting
LVM Timber	Logging
Luz Travel & Tours	Tourism
Dama Trading	Import/export
Unlad Ago-Industrial	Agribusiness
Bayanihan Mineral Dev. Corp.	Mining
Sanwa Phil. Realty	Real estate
Philippine Multi-Agency	General merchandise

Marvel Investment	General investment
Malaya Publishing	Publishing
Dinagat Mineral	Mineral exploration
Dahlia Hotel Corp.	Hotels
Montevideo Realty	Real estate
Noroil Mills	Agri-business
Rainbow Service Center	Janitorial services
Kahirup Publications	Printing press
Pacil Management Corp.	General management
Jade Petrochemicals	Petrochemicals
Cor Tech Phil.	Panel boards
Jade Garments Industries	Garments manufacturing
Teracos International Corp.	Navigational apparatus
Inter Communication Publishers	Publishing
La Familia Construction Co.	Construction
Magkaibigan Trading	Minerals trading
Philippine Cruising Ventures	Transport services
Consolidated Sugar Corp.	Foods
Phil-Asiatic Dev. Corp.	Wholesale trade
Artistic Resources & Tech.	Advertising
Majelly Integrated & Dev. Corp.	Fishing
Southward Fishing	Fishing
New Love Cinema & Shopping	Motion pictures
Negros Cassava Mills	Agri-business

A partial list of corporations where their son Nonong had an interest were

Company	Activity
Diwata Realty	Real estate
Milaneta Acres Realty	Real estate
Hi-Grade Concrete & Steel Prods.	Construction materials
Rara Avis Promotions	General promotions
Southern Games & Amusement Dev. Corp	Amusement services
Masagana Agro. & Ind. Resources	Agri-business
Multiconstruction Services	Construction
Avamotor Corp.	Transport equipment
Karma Maintenance Systems	Janitorial services
Sarilikha Rattan Manufacturing	Furniture
Struan & Co.	Wholesale trade
Amcor Management Systems	Business services
GCCBI Trucking Services	Transport services
Four Seasons Films	Motion pictures

THE MOTHER AND THE SISTERS

Josefa Edralin Marcos is the mother of Ferdinand. Inspite of her age, she was quite active in business corporations and in other money-making ventures which capitalized on her special relationship with her powerful son.

Dona Josefa headed the Doha Josefa Edralin Marcos Foundation, which was the financial holding group of the more than a dozen companies where she was chairman of the board. SEC records reveal that she was involved many areas such as sugar, logging, shipping, and foods. Dona Josefa was helped by a core of close relatives who did the spade-work for her. By making contributions to her foundation, businessmen were able to ask her to intercede with various government officials for favors. All she had to do was to lend her name to corporations so that their business deals would be facilitated.

It has been claimed, for example, that she lent her name to a resort development concern that sold shares in a planned golf and country club on choice suburban land [7]. It turned out that the offer was fraudulent and that the company never owned the land in the first place, leaving investors holding on to pieces of worthless paper.

Among the logging concessions Dona Josefa held under her name were:

Bicol Loggers
Serarose Igevelowent Corp.
Intercontinental Wood Processing Dev. Corp.

The mother also had investments in agricultural schools through the Dona Josefa Edralin Marcos Foundation. Among these were four multi-million agricultural schools in Davao City, Davao del Sur, Davao Oriental:

Agro Far East Foundation
Agro-Industrial Foundation College of the Philippines
Davao Institute of Agriculture Foundation
Assemblyman Mariano Marcos Memorial Foundation

Among the members of the board managing these schools were her daughter Fortuna Barba, Rogelio Barba, Mal'COS crony Antonio Florrendo, and Rodolfo del Rosario, Florrendo's assoc1ate. Dor'ra Josefa also owned or had interests in the following corporations:

East Negros Millin	Sugar milling
Asean Integrated Marine Carriers	Shipping
Coral Phil. Corp.	Foods & beverages
Phividec	Services
Olympia Int.	

Another example of the mother's entrepreneurship was given by Mi'ares who documented some of the activities of Dona Josefa and Fortuna "Baby" Marcos-Barba, Ferdinand's youngest sister. Mijares claims that Dona Josefa and Fortuna engaged in the "virtual blackmarketing" of rice when the country was facing a shortage of this staple food. Mijares also related that mother and sister team pressured the General Manager of the Rice and Corn Administration (RCA), Benny Villamor, to grant retail licenses to their friends so that they could engage in the profitable business of selling rice to the public during this time.

mother and daughter Marcos engaged in virtual "black-marketing" of rice while there was a severe shortage of supply of the cereal throughout the country. Doria Josefa has been making demands on Villamor that certain parties be given RCA retailer's license "because they are supporters of Doria Josefa Marcos Foundation." Fortuna was also badgering Villamor for similar concessions. At one time Villamor refused to receive Fortuna as she kept circling the block on G. Tuason, Quezon City, where the Villamor residence was located. An angry Fortuna was heard by Villamor's guard shouting, "The

President will hear about this!" [8].

Villamor was romptly fired from his job by Marcos upon the imposition of martial law on the charges of "corruption."

From her initial experience in the above-mentioned scam, Fortuna progressed to own a whole slew of corporations in different fields. Fortuna and her husband, Colonel Marcelino Barba, have made a fortune from government logging concessions. Some of these concessions were accused of illegal activities in Aurora province where logging was banned in some areas [9]. Among the logging corporations of the areas were:

Philwoods Integrated Timber Ind.
Filipinas Loggers
Federated imber & Dev. Corp.
Philippine Intergrated Timber Inc.

Fortuna also acquired mining concessions and owned several mining companies:

Omico Mining
Asbestos Multi-mining & Industrial Corporation
Bayanihan Mineral Dev. Corp.
Liberty Mines
Polar ines
Multimining and Industrial Dev.

Colonel Barba was chairman of Custom Integrated Stevedoring & Arrastre Co. He was also chairman of Phil. International Shipping Corp. (PISC), a company where the wife was a director. PISC was able to purchase new container ships through government help, permitting the couple to run a lucrative container service to Europe. Other members of the board of this corporation included other Marcos men such as former Minister of Trade Troadio Quiazon and Maritime Industry Authority presrdent Generoso Tanseco. Colonel Barba was also involved in Marcos' illegal shipment of gold (please see Chapter IV). The son Avelino Marcos Barba, was also involved in business but is best known for his role in the Buendia murder, where he shot an unarmed man after losing a volleyball game.

Fortuna has also made several real estate investments in California (see Chapter IV)

A partial list of other companies where Fortuna, Marcelino, or their son had interests:

Company	Activity
Fortune Realty Dev. Corp.	Real estate
Ocean-World Shipping	Shipping
Hasmin Tours & Travels	Tourism
Forward Manufacturing	Industrial chemicals
Equitorial Manner Mechanical	Construction
Focal Point Inc.	Wholesale trade
Standard Imports & Trading	Machinery

L&B Logging Co.	Logging
P&B Marketing Co.	Broker/dealer
Trans-Philippines Port Services	Stevedoring
Fortune Realty Dev. Corp.	Real estate
Forward Manufacturing Corp.	Industrial chemicals
Koyophil Inc.	General merchandising
Custom Integrated Stevedoring	Stevedoring
Barba Press Co.	Publishing

Elizabeth Marcos Keon Roca, another sister of Ferdinand, was the long-standing governor of Ilocos. Elizabeth was married twice, in both cases to Australians. Her second marriage was the subject of much talk in Manila since the second husband was her junior in years and she had just recently separated from her first one. Elizabeth's new mate, Mr. Roca, was the owner and head of an agricultural company which cornered a lot of contracts to supply agricultural equipment, especially in the Ilocos region where there were a lot of agri-business projects. Mr. Roca was later reported to have absconded with part of Elizabeth's money when she became terminally ill.

Her son by her previous Australian mate, Michael Keon, was appointed Project Director of Gintong Alay, the generously-funded sports program of Marcos. It at one time enjoyed a $400,000 grant. Michael tried to centralize his personal control over the country's sports program through his position. An example of Keon's controversial style was is high-handed suspension of Lydia de Vega, the 15 year-old track star who ranked as one of Asia's best and dubbed as the "wonder girl of Philippine athletics," due to personality conflicts with Lydia's father. As a result of this suspension, Lydia de Vega was banned from participating for any track event in the count , Michael Keon citing presidential LOI 955 as giving him the authority to order the ban [10]. Michael was also designated by Marcos as president of Amateur Boxing Associationof the Philippines (ABAP), head of Phil. Amateur Track and Field Ass. (Patafa), and president of Phil. Olympic Committee (POC).

Among the corporations where Elizabeth Keon had interests were

Company	*Activity*
Elmar Integrated	Restaurants
Sagittarius Integrated Resources	Agri-business
Integrated Aviation & Dev. Corp.	Aircarafts
Timber & Industrial Dev.	Logging
Marla Marketing Corp.	Industrial chemicals

THE UNCLES

Judge Pio Marcos, an uncle, gained notoriety due to his involvement in the Golden Buddha scandal, where Ferdinand and Pio stole a olden Buddha filled with precious jewels inside from its owners on April 1971. Both Josefa reportedly wanted to buy the 28-inch statue but was refused by the owners. Judge Pio Marcos ordered the golden statue to be confiscated, but the figure was never turned over to the authorities. When the courts ordered the buddha to be returned, a fake one made of brass was turned in. A subsequent 310-page report by a Senate investigative committee concluded that the owner's rights had been "wantonly violated by Judge Pio Marcos."

Pio Marcos has also used his position to appropriate huge tracts of choice land in Baguio, the summer capital of the Philippines. Among the corporations listed by the SEC as belonging to Pio were firms in areas such as real estate, construction, lumber, mining, shipping, memorial parks, agri-business, sugar, and tourism:

Company	Activity
San Fernando Realty & Dev.	Real estate
Baguio Homes Corp.	Construction
Ilocos Sur Dev. & Housing Corp.	Real estate
Blackgold Consolidated Mines	Mining
New Era Lumber Enterprises	Logging
Phil-Asia Laboratories	Pharmaceuticals
Marcomen Shipping	Shipping
Neso Dev. Corp.	Mining exploration
Everlasting Memorial Park	Memorial parks
Lamar Agro-Industrial	Industrial equipment
Negros Occ. Agro-Industrial	Agri-business
Masagana Sugar Mills	Sugar refinery
Kennon Resorts	Resort services
Triple Harvest Fertilizers	Mining
PJA Trading & International	Agricultural sales
Solid Rock Mining	Mining
Mapeya Trucking	Transport
Pacific Basin Resources	Consulting services
St. Martha Manufacturing	Manufacturing
Columbus Shipping	Transport
Mindanao Integrated Terminal	Passenger services

Judge Pio Marcos worked closely with Simeon Marcos Valdez, another uncle of Ferdinand who built a financial conglomerate from construction contracts awarded him by the overnment. Apart from his interests in the construction industry, Simeon also had interests in corporations where other Marcos associates had investments. He was a board member in two corporations associated with the military: Veterans Electronic Communications and Phividec. He was also involved in Olympia international with Dona Josefa. He also had interests in FEBTC and PCIB, two banks where Pacifico also had interests. Pio was also a member of the board of another bank, RCBC, owned by the Sycip-Yuchengco interests.

Company	Activity
Olympia Financing Corp.	Finance
Zamboanga Wood Products	Logging
Dumlao & Valdez Realty	Real estate
Crosswood Inc.	Furniture
Maharlika Resources	Oil exploration
Special Construction Products	Construction products
CIA Machinery Inc.	Industrial equipment
Valdez-Alcanzare Trading	Industrial equipment
Veteran Tours & Travel	Travel agency
Lykes Lines Co.	Passenger transport
Veleca Mining Exploration Co.	Mineral exploration

Luzon Erglort-Import Corp.	Machinery
Phividec Eectronics	Appliances
Creative Tex-wood Corp.	General merchandising
Asian Management & Dev. Group	Business services
General Handicrafts Supply	Handicrafts

Another uncle, Pedro O. Valdez, was active in the construction business and headed a construction company bearing his name. Among his other companies were

Company	Activity
Varied Ventures Marketing	General merchandise
Econde Construction	Construction
Phil. International Tours	Tourism
POV Enterprises	Metal products
SNC Enterprises	Iron & steel products

Juan L. Manuel is another uncle of Ferdinand Marcos. He married the youngest sister of Dona Josefa. Manuel was the phlegmatic Secretary of Eucation who, inspite of his old age, had overstayed in that position. His record as Secretary of Education was quite scandalous. For example, there were cases where textbooks intended to be distributed free found their way into bookstores during his term. However, the greatest scandal where Juan Manuel has been involved was the November 1978 Baguio City Teachers Camp anomaly which defrauded the government of ahnost $2 million. Close to 1,000 checks amountin to $1.8 million were cashed with the National Treasury for supposed Ministry of Education projects. The checks were significantly of series 1977, but were found to be ante-dated 1975. Further investigation showed that these withdrawals were certified by Secretary Juan Manuel. When the anomaly was later uncovered and brought out in the Manila papers, innocent minor government officials from the Ministry of Education were made scapegoats. One of them received a record 573 years conviction in a decision penned by Malacanan for the Sandiganbayan, the government prosecutorial body.

Juan Manuel also engaged in other fraudulent business practices. The Cityland Dev. Corp. which he chaired was the object of investigations for violations of the Philippine Securities Act. The SEC had planned to issue a cease-and-desist order to Cityland to stop it from engaging in the outlawed "pyramid" marketing, a fraudulent method of raising funds from ignorant investors [11]. Another company owned by Manuel was City Farms Corp., an agri-business company registered with the SEC in March 1980. Other companies where Manuel had interests were Insurance Corp. of the Phil., Corrimercial Credit Corp, Steniel Paper, Autoworld, and Super Industrial Steel.

THE SECOND GENERATION 0F BLOODSUCKERS

The Marcos children were also active in business. The eldest daughter, Imee, took control of television networks and was involved in the garment industry, while Greggy Araneta, the husband of Marcos' younger daughter, Irene, was involved in different undertakings.

Imee Marcos-Manotoc organized two garment firms, De Soleil Apparel Manufacturing and American Inter-Fashion, and took over the export quotas of another firm, the Glorious Sun Fashion Garments Manufacturing. Jose Rono and Roberto Ongpin, two influential Marcos cabinet members, helped Imee execute this caper. Rono, the cabinet minister in charge of local governments, helped Imee organize the firms in 1984, while On in, the trade minister, han led marketing. Ongpin "maneuvered to strip Glorious Sun of its quota" [12] and pass it on to the two firms owned by Imee [13]. The assignment of export quotas is extremely critical to garment firms since that assures them of ready overseas markets.

Imee also took over the following television networks: BBC (Channel 2), RPN (Channel 9), and IBC (Channel 13). She also controlled DWNW, a 10-kilowatt radio station which was part of t e Banahaw Broadcasting Corp. [14].

A newspaper article described Gregorio "Greggy" Araneta, the husband of the younger daughter, as "greedy," as having "a penchant for larceny," and as having gone on a rampage of acquisitions" as soon as he married Irene Marcos. The article, entitled "Second Generation of Bloodsuckers," further stated that Greggy acquired "the Disini banks," enjoyed a "monopoly of car parts importation" and competed with Glecy Tantoco in the "importation of luxury items" [15].

One of the man acquisitions of Araneta was the Pantranco North Express. When the NIDC, a subsidiary of the PNB, announced in 1984 its intention to sell Pantranco, the second biggest bus firm in Luzon, Fernando Balatbat, an associate of Araneta, signified Araneta's interest in the firm. Since the PNB and the NIDC announced that they preferred an entity with "a good business record in the transportation industry," Araneta approached Dolores A. Potenciano, executive vice- resident and general manager of Batangas-Laguna-Tayabas Bus Co. (BLTB), in February 1985 and proposed to use her company as the vehicle to purchase Pantranco. The intention was to buy Pantranco through the BLTB, with Dolores acting as president and boar chairman of the acquired firm. This arrangement would then meet the directive of the PNB to sell the firm to an established transportation company.

But after Potenciano informed the PNB on 4 March 1985 of her intent to purchase, Balatbat maneuvered with PNB officials to produce an arrangement which not only served to give Araneta total control over the firm but also allowed him to profit.

The memorandum of agreement, signed in September 1985, stipulated that the Pantranco, its bus fleet and terminals, was to be sold for $40.6 million. A downpayment of $3 million was required, with the balance to be paid over a 12 year period. Behind these form conditions were other arrangements. It turned out that it would not be Potenciano's BLTB that woul acquire Pantranco but a new organization, North Express Transport Inc. (NETI), a paper corporation owned by Araneta. Araneta required Potenciano to sign a deed of trust and assignment of stocks in favor of an unnamed beneficiary. The deed of trust and assignment of stocks, signed for Potenciano by her associate Max Joseph, was turned over to the treasurer of NETI. Araneta also required Potenciano to sign on behalf of NETI an undated $1.6 million promissory note in favor of Security Bank, a bank controlled by the Marcoses (see section on Yao and Gapud). The Security Bank, in turn, gave a $1.3 million loan to Imexco (Irene Marcos Export Co.) which Araneta ran.

These machinations not only transferred the ownership of Pantranco to Araneta's NETI but it also allowed Araneta to borrow money from the Security Bank on the strength of the $1.6 million promissory note from the bus company. Critics of the deal pointed out that the corporate assets of Pantranco were being raided to line the pockets of Araneta.

There are other questionable as ects to the deal. It is doubtful that the required down ayment was ever 1pai at all: NETI only had $269,000 paid up capital as of arch 1985, far be ow the required $3 million downpayment. This aspect of the deal is quite suspicious because, while there are records of the preliminary arrangements between the PNB and NETI, a deed of sale has yet to be produced.

Inspite of these highly irregular arrangements, Araneta was allowed to operate the Pantranco franchise two months before the Purchase Agreement was finalized and executed. This "premature" transfer allowed Araneta to derive an income from the revenues of Pantranco even before he actually owned it. Between the time Araneta actually took over the assets of Pantranco and the time the Purchase Agreement was finalized, a total of $4.6 million was generated by the transportation company. Thus, even if it is granted that Araneta did pay the downpayment of $3 million, this was amply covered by the income of the bus company he was buying, with a profit of $1.6 million. This is a highly anomalous situation where a person is paid to buy something [16].

Apart from Balatbat, the government officials who helped Araneta in this deal were:

Placido Mapa Jr.	PNB president & economic planning minister
Fernando Manama	PNB senior executive vice president
J. Lorenzo S. Vergara	PNB executive vice president
Ramon F. Aviado Jr.	PNB assistant chief legal counsel
Dominador H. Lopez Jr.	assistant vice president
Jose C. Crisanto Jr.	general manager of PNBowned PNEI

Araneta also bilked others apart from government institutions. As resident of HE. Heacock, a garment manufacturing firm, Araneta borrowed $225,000 from the Associated Bank between 6 December 1985 to 11 February 1986, purportedly to serve as "working capital" for the production of export goods. But the money was never used or this purpose, and it was never paid.

Araneta was also the president of Asialand, a real estate company.

Critics further charged that Araneta illegally imported fancy cars, mostly from the United States and Italy, without paying the stipulated 300% duty. These purchases were done through dummy corporations and resulted in $13.4 million in lost government revenues. Apart from cars, Araneta also enjoyed a monopoly of the importation of car parts.

* * *

El hijo de tigre nace rayado
(The tiger's son 18 born with stripes).

- a Spanish proverb

Endnotes

1. *Times Journal,* 22 July 1980.
2. *Times Journal,* 30 August 1980.
3. *Times Journal,* 31 August 1980.
4. *Business Day,* 9 June 1986.
5. *Bulletin Today,* 16 October 1980.
6. *Bulletin Today,* 27 January 1980.
7. *New York Times,* 30 March 1986.
8. Mijares, pp; 52-53.
9. Sheila Coronel, "The Politics of Logging," July 1987.
10. *Daily Express* and *Bulletin Today,* 8 July 1980.
11. *Ecmomic Monitor,* 4-10 February 1980.
12. *Business Day,* 27 January 1987.
13. *Manila Bulletin*, 2 October 1986.
14. *Manila Bulletin*, 19 October 1986.
15. Hilarion MHenares Jr, "Second generation of bloodsuckers," *Philippine Daily Inquirer*, 13 June 1986.
16. Neoclassical economists might want to point out that goods with a disutility precisely are such goods, that we pay sanitation men to acquire our garbage. A profitable transportation firm clearly does not fall under this category of goods.

Chapter IV

THE OVERSEAS EMPIRE

*Se llevaba una fortuna consigo, grandes cantidades depositadas en los Bancos de
Europa le esperaban, tenia hoteles, pero habla lastimado a muchos...*
            — *Jose Rizal, El Filibusterismo, 1891* *

*("He took a fortune with him. Great amounts deposited in European banks awaited him. He had hotels.
But he had caused injury to many..." Our translation. Jose Rizal, El Filibusterismo, p.257.)

*Si vous voyez un banquier suisse sauter d'une fenetre, sautez derriére lui. IL y a
surement de l'argent a gagner.*   — *Voltaire [1]*

The previous chapters documented the history and methods of crony
capitalism in the Philippines. This chapter discusses how Marcos and his associates
organized an elaborate network of money laundering and international investment
havens to create an overseas empire spanning places as diverse as New York,
California, Washington, Texas, London, Vienna, Rome, Marseille, Switzerland,
Liechtenstein, the Netherlands Antilles, Australia, Hong Kong, Singapore.

The overseas properties belonging to Marcos and his associates spanned
almost eveery conceivable area. Multimillion investments in New York real estate,
California banks, and Swiss bank accounts are the better known of these properties.
Lesser known are those in other areas such as estates and villas in Austria, London,
and Rome, a tuna fishing fleet in Seattle, Washington, first class hotels in Singapore
and Puerto Rico, a lucrative oil trading firm in Austria, gold and diamond investments
in South Africa, banks and hotels in Israel. The Marcos cronies discussed in the
precedin chapter successfully drained the resources of their corporations and
diverted the loans they drew from foreign banks and Philippine government financial
institutions only to redirect these to their private overseas investments. A crony who
enriched himself through construction contracts built what has been described as "a
castle" in Glendale, California and bought a fleet of expensive cars for his family.
Five of the cars were Mercedes Benzes which the family used, while two were
BMWs reserved for his son. When his only daughter graduated from the University
of Southern California, she wore an expensive backless silk dress and a ruby and
diamond tiara during the graduation party and was treated to a tour of Europe
through the Orient Express as her graduation gift. Marcos' only nephew, Mariano II,
is now investing the money he made from his corporations in the Philippines in new
business ventures in California where he has settled. A sugar commodities trader
who worked for Benedicto, one of Marcos' most loyal cronies, is reported to have
stashed millions in investments in the Basque region of Spain. Roberto Ongin, the
Marcos cabinet minister who managed the black market for foreign exchange, is
now living comfortably in London, driving a two-toned Rolls Royce, totally

unconcerned with the damage he caused. Disini, the crook who received $50 million in commissions to build a non-functioning nuclear power plant, is now living in a luxurious villa in the outskirts of Vienna and is the holder of a televrsion network franchise there. When the Marcos government collapsed in 1986, a Disini associate, a well-known corporate lawyer in Manila, terrified that his finances would be scrutinized, tried to dispose of 12 first-rate condominium apartments in New York. The lawyer's wife was reportedly on the verge of a nervous breakdown as she frantically tried to transfer the ownership of these condominiums, the cheapest of which was priced at $570,000.

THE TRANSFER OF CAPITAL AND DIRTY MONEY

There is nothing intrinsically wrong with international capital transfers. Billions cross national boundaries every hour as part of the normal pattern of international trade. Money is regularly exchanged as payment for goods and services. The classic statement of this problem is to be found in a 'ttle- known essay by David Hume, *Of the Balance of Trade,* written in 1752 [2]. Financial transfers also occur in response to changes in interest rates in the major world monetary centers and capital gravitates towards what Adam Smith and the tradition of classical political economy called a "centre of repose and continuance" [3].

International capital transfers have become so common that total foreign investments in the United States alone is now nearing a record $1 trillion. The most visible of these are Japanese investments in American companies and real estate. Less visible but no less significant are those investments which represent capital from the underdeveloped countries of the third world seeking financial refuge in the US and ot er countries which are perceived to be more politically stable.

While there are many ways of describing international capital movements, the most convenient method of categorizing the types of capital transfers would be to analyze the purpose for which the transfers are made. This approach will help us better understand the nature of the Marcos overseas empire and the phenomenon of *dirty money.*

There is an immediate temptation to equate the term *dirty money* withthe illegal or immoral means through which the money may have been generated. Images conjured in the mind are those of the Mafia and international drug dealers transporting suitcases stuffed with money from their nefarious activities. When dirty money is perceived in this way, relating it to an actual commission of a crime, it is easy for many to claim that their international capital transfers do not fall under the rubric of dirty money.

Marcos apologists adopted precisely this approach in their defense of the overseas investments of Marcos and his cronies. Estelito Mendoza, Marcos' Solicitor General, adopted a legalistic defense concerning Philippine capital flight. In response to questions concerning the foreign properties of Marcos and his cronies, Mendoza defended them through trite legalisms: "..I must emphasize that under our laws, the ownership of assets abroad is not per se an offense or a crime" [4]. Another former Marcos government official, Adrian Cristobal Cruz, chairman the Social Security System during the Marcos regime, similarly believed that his investment in a San Francisco condominium was legitimate because it all "depends on how [the purchase was] done."

Another form of legitimation looks at dirty money as a means of self-preservation for third world elites from the hyperinflation and political instability plaguing the underdeveloped world. Some money exchangers see their job as a moral task to help move money to places where its value can be preserved from financial erosion and political revolutions.

The most extreme form of justifying dirty money is to completely deny its existence. This position holds that there is no such thing as dirty money and that all foreign exchange transactions are totally legitimate. Global monetarism is the most extreme theoretical statement of this ideological position. The Law of One Price [5], a central tenet of global monetarism, precisely assumes the totally free movement of capital across national boundaries, a position which recalls Frédéric Bastiat's *Sophismes Economiques* and the pleas for free trade he delivered to the French Chamber of Deputies in 1845 through his famous *Petition of the Candlemakers.*

While we saw in the previous chapters how Marcos and his cronies subverted many laws to aaquire their fortunes, our approach to the phenomenon of dirty money will prescind from the legal issues. Neither shall we engage in a theoretical debate with the ideology oiglobal monetarism or any of its variants since this is not the place for the arcana of international finance. We shall go for the jugular and concentrate on what we consider to be the core problem concerning capital flight and dirty money.

Jean Ziegler, who has written much about the faults of the Swiss banking system as an academic and has crusaded for laws regulating it as a member of the Swiss parliament, provides an extremely useful insight mto the problem. He defines dirty money as "... capital whose transfer does not relate to any repayment of debt or trading transaction" [6}. Such a definition is particularly useful since it completely strips all legal and moral judgements from the term and allows us to use it as a purely technical concept in our analysis of Marcos wealth.

This definition excludes monetary transfers which are legitimately related to the payments of the importation of goods and services and the payment of international debt but allows us to focus on the speculative aspects of monetary transfers as dirty money seeks political and financial refuge in international investment havens. Dirty money is the movement of wealth across national boundaries whose purpose is not the payment of goods, services, or debt but the escape from the uncertainties of one country to the perceived financial and political security of another. Value moves merely in one direction without any equal compensatory movement in the other.

Ziegler's definition, then, provides the focus of this chapter. Whereas the previous chapters discuss how wealth was extracted by causing great poverty, this chapter analyzes how this wealth was transferred to the various overseas investment havens which form the Marcos overseas empire.

HISTORICAL CONTEXT

While Marcos and his associates regularly smuggled money out of the country throughout the years they were in power, it was in the early 1980's that the practice reached an unprecedented pace and involved incredible amounts.

The hegira of capital in the early 1980's was precipitated by a succession of political and economic events which forced Marcos and his cronies to seek refuge for their capital in places they considered to be more stable than the Phihppines. The propaganda actions carried out by Gerardo Esguerra, Rolando Montiel, an other members of the clandestme April 6 Liberation Movement and the *Kasapi* during the later part of 1980, Marcos' uncertain health, Benigno Aquino's assassmation, the deep recession and hyperinflation engulfing the country, the continual devaluations of the Philippine peso all contributed to the nervousness that Marcos and his cronies felt for the safety of the capital they had accumulated in their years in power. Insurance had to be secured. Stolen pesos were therefore converted into flying dollars.

All known estimates of Philippine capital flight during this period are unanimous in their assessment that capital was hemorrhaging out of the country at an alarming rate. The *Review* calculated that capital flowed out at the rate of about $2 million every day at the height of the recession in 1983 [7]. A Philippine newspaper gave a higher estimate of $3 million daily. A government commission appointed by Marcos to study capital flight concluded that $1 billion left the country in 1983, with another $2 billion leaving in 1984. The estimate is probably as accurate as it can get since the person Marcos chose to head the commission, Roberto Ongpin, was also one of the key persons associated with the so-called Binondo Central Bank, an elaborate yet underground syndicate of local exchangers who specialized in monetary transmissions to secret overseas accounts [8].

Marcos and his cronies availed of all imaginable means to transfer such huge amounts out of the country. Both the formal mechanisms of the international financial system, as well as the informal and often times illegal methods of international money launderers, were employed by Marcos and his cronies. In some instances, new methods of monetary transfers were ingeniously devised to suit the special needs of Marcos and his associates.

The use of couriers to personally transport cash was expanded by Marcos and his cronies from the typical transaction which involved a single trip to a regular method by which millions were smuggled out of the country. In 1981, for example, a woman from Hong Kong was arrested at the Manila International Airport during an attempt to transport cash stuffed in two suitcases. It turned out upon investigation that this shipment, amounting to $1 million, was merely one of the 33 trips she had made between the Philippines and Hong Kong during a period of` 18 months and that an official of the Philippine Air Lines, the national flagship airline controlled by Imelda, had been facilitating her trips. The pattern continued up to the last days of the Marcos regime. Even as their government was collapsing, Marcos and Imelda were reported to still have been able to convert some of their financial holdings into $4 million worth of bearer notes and certificates of deposits which could be easily cashed [9]. Their eldest daughter, Imee, perhaps in an attempt to elicit public sympathy, was photographed carrying *Pamper* diaper boxes for the Marcos infants as they were boarding their US Air Force plane out of the country. But when US Customs officials inspected the giant diaper boxes, they turned out to be full of precious jewels. A few days later, the equivalent of $5 million in newly printed Philippine currency was intercepted in a van belonging to Imelda's brother, Bejo Romualdez, on its way to the Manila International Airport.

DEWEY DEE

A most dramatic use of a personal courier to move money out of the country occurred in early 1981 when a wealthy Marcos crony fled Manila and absconded with millions of dollars.

Dewey Dee, a rich Marcos associate of Filipino-Chinese ancestry, defrauded his private and overnment creditors of millions when he fled the Philippines on 9 January 1 81. The getaway was a successful attempt on the part of Marcos and his cronies to move a huge amount of money immediately and effectively at a time when local political conditions were quickly becoming tenuous. Dee embezzled and fled with an amount initially estimated at $70 million [10], but later estimates revised the figure to $100 million [11].

Dee was a crony who, apart from diddling an occasional game of golf with the dictator at the Wack Wack Golf & Country Club, played an active part in fronting for Marcos' interests in the banking industry. Gerald G. Goldstein, Dee's lawyer in Vancouver, Canada, where Dee has sought refuge, does not deny his client's connections with the dictator. Goldstein admits that Dee "was a nominee of the president" [12].

Dee served as one of Marcos' fronts in Security Bank & Trust, an important local bank, and the Redwood Bank, a San Francisco bank controlled by Marcos associates. Dee was part of the coup led by Ramon Siy, another rich Filipino-Chinese Marcos crony, which took over the Security Bank and held interests in the Redwood Bank on behalf of Marcos [13]. Dee's links with Marcos and Ramon Siy extended to the textile industry as well, where Dee had interests in Solid Mills, an important textile company where Siy was president and where Luis Villafuerte, Marcos' Minister of Trade, had substantial interests.

Dewey Dee was so wealthy that he was described as playing "the commodities markets the way some lesser men play craps" [14]. His interests extended to Hong Kong, where he had investments in the finance and the garment industries. He had a joint-venture in a Hong Kong garment firm with the Japanese giant Mitsubishi. Dee also engaged in gol trading and owned Prime Securities, a Hong Kong stock brokerage firm.

Dee's wealth and acceptance within local and international financial circles made him suitably qualified for one of the grandest embezzlement schemes ever to be devised.

Using two of his local firms as collateral, Dee went on a borrowing binge and drew loans from almost every major financial firm in the Philippines. Loans were drawn from a total of 16 commercial banks, 12 investment houses, and 17 financial institutions and other creditors.

Dee accumulated million-dollar loans from his government and private creditors by borrowing on the strength of two of his companies, Continental Manufacturing and Redson Textile Manufacturing. The two corporations had an aggregate worth of $10 million. Continent Manufacturing, a joint-venture with three Japanese transnationals (Mitsubishi, Marubeni, and Mitsubishi Rayon), had a net worth of $8.8 million. The second firm, Redson Textile, was a joint-venture with Toshin Shohi of Japan and had a net worth of $1.2 million.

Dee was able to borrow loans which far exceeded the value of these two firms. Such loans were in direct and clear contravention of existing regulations which limited the size of the debt that could be incurred. Philippine Central Bank rules stipulated that "bank lending to any single corporate borrower must not exceed 15 % of the borrowing company's assets" [15]. Redson Textile, however, was allowed to draw approximately $36 million in loans while it was valued only at $1.2 million. The other firm, Continental Manufacturing, was authorized to borrow only up to $12.7 million as of December 1979, according to Philippine Securities & Exchange Commission regulations, but these regulations were not honored. Loans of up to at least $64 million were drawn on this firm [16].

Dee engineered the caper by issuing corporate commercial papers with unregistered numbers to his creditors or commercial papers with identical numbers to different lenders [17]. This method, the corporate eguivalent of taking several mortgages on the same house with different lending institutions, allowed him to borrow loans several times the worth of his firms. The by-laws of the two corporations were amended to allow Dee to duplicate the functions of the board of directors, giving Dee blanket powers to deal for the firms. The scheme thus permitted Dee to borrow an amount in the neighborhood of $100 million by using two companies with a net worth of only 10 million.

Dec absconded the moment he got the loans and settled comfortably in Vancouver, Canada, where many other rich Marcos cronies have chosen to set up residence.

The acquisition and transportation of an amount of money as big as Dee's debts was possible only through the approval and complicity of the highest offices in the country. Drawmg a small loan from banks in Manila requires undergoing a gamut of red tape and the payment of many bribes. Drawing loans of any significant amount required Marcos' scrutiny and the payment of a commission between 15-20% before they got approved by any of the banks. Gregorio Licaros, then Central Bank Governor, must surely have been aware of Dee's moves because of the extraordinary amount of the loans. Pirating the money out of the country in a relatively short period of time also required the knowledge if not the actual cooperation of the Philippine Central Bank. The loans that Dee incurred and the pretenses he used to acquire the money clearly reguired the knowledge and complicity of many overnment officials who would have acted only at the orders of Marcos. It is therefore very reasonable to conclude that Marcos had a direct hand in the whole thing. As we saw in the previous chapters, all economic transactions of any significance had to first pass Marcos' scrutiny, and Dewey Dee's loans would certainly have not been an exception.

There is also evidence to suggest that some Marcos cronies had fore-knowledge, or at least should have had an inkling, that something was afoot and that Dee was in the process of making important changes in his business strategy. Dee had applied for citizenship in Canada while he was accumulating his huge debts. He also liquidated his interests in both the Redwood Bank and the Security Bank shortly before he fled, the interests in the latter bank on 31 December 1980, a mere week before he disappeared. The directors in these banks were all known Marcos associates such as Rolando Gapud, who was Marcos' financial advisor, and Siy, who was president of Security Bank. And, as a final nugget, it was Siy's travel company which arranged Dee's departure by securing his tickets to Hong Kong.

What Dewey Dee himself says in this context is extremely enlightening. Dee has commented little publicly on the embezzlement, but what he has said already explains the relative impunity that the has enjoyed. In sworn court documents presented to Canadian authorities, Dee avers:

The government and president of the Philippines would want that I be placed under their jurisdiction... to be sure that I be placed incommunicado in order to ensure my silence and to prevent me from making a complete explanation or give evidence as to the circumstances with regard to my leaving the Philippines. My business transactions, and my relationships with very high government officials will prove to be an embarrassment to the government of the Philippines [18].

The *San Francisco Chronicle*, after describing Dee as a possible "run-amok front man for some of the biggest crooks in the Ph ppines" [19], concluded:

*The mystery in the story of Dewey Dee is how — given the stringent bank controls in the Philippines and the government handcuffs on capital leaving the country - one man could manage to borrow so much money in so short a time and get ourt of the country with it. Various answers to this mystery is suggested, and most of them are in the category of Sheriock Holmes' remark to Watson in **The Hound of the Baskervilles** – "the significant thing was that the dog did not bark at night" [20].*

The effects on the economy were disastrous. It brought the country to the brink of economic collapse. Panic ensued. Depositors withdrew their savings. Investors tried to cash their money market placements. Many of Dee's creditors suffered runs on their accounts and soon went out of business. Confidence in the country's financial institutions crumbled. Credit, already difficult, was further tightened. An already faltering economy plummeted into a deep recession. Unemployment exacerbated.

Officials of the Marcos administration treated lightly the event which had plunged the country into its deepest financial crisis. Cesar Virata, Marcos' Finance Minister at the time, suggested in a statement typical of his mentality that the swindle would have good effects: "Banks will be more collateral-minded" [21]. Jaime Laya, who later replaced Licaros as Central Bank Governor, nonchalantly stated, "Some banks run away with money. Some banks get held up. Some banks get flooded out. These things happen" [22].

INTERNATIONAL PRIVATE BANKS AND CAPITAL FLIGHT

The use of personal couriers and the Dewey Dee caper formed merely a small and relatively innocuous part of the overall strategy to move money out of the country. To move bigger amounts with greater efficiency and secrecy, Marcos and his cronies employed the more sophisticated techniques of international money laundering.

Money laundering was a term coined by the Mafia to describe the process where money is cleansed or "washed" of any connection from its source [23]. The whole idea is to hide the source of the money and provide complete anonymity for the owners. Cash from drug sales or other illegal activities would be sent to Swiss banks to hide its origins and then later reinvested in legal businesses. The mone can then be used freely without any fear of discovery from authorities. While the term had its origins with the Mafia, the practice as since been adopted by large corporations and wealthy individuals who have resorted to such means to avoid paying high taxes on their income and other assets. The practice, now more politely referred to with the euphemism of international private banking, was greatly availed of by Marcos and his cronies to secretly move their assets out of the Philippines and establish their overseas empire.

Deak & Co., for example, handled $11 million worth of capital fleeing the Philipines in the latter part of the 1970's. The money, stuffed in envelopes and declared as "documents," was mailed from the Philippines by two businessmen, George Lai Man and Arthur F. Gimenez, and was a dressed to individual employees in the San Francisco office of Deak & Co. The packages, which had Gimenez's office in Manila as a return address, was discovered in December 1975 by a US Customs inspector in Honolulu in a routine inspection of overseas mail. According to the testimony of the inspector:

The money was put together in stacks... Then individual stacks were interlaced and overlapped and staple together... Some were like brick work… stapled together so from the outside it had the feel and appearance ofa thick package of papers [24].

The package, which contained more than $16,000, was merely a small part of the $11 million which Deak & Co. had handled for Gimenez over two years. Deak & Co. was later convicted in a US federal court for failing to report the cash transaction to US federal authorities.

Crocker National Bank in San Francisco, rather than face the prospect of a court case and a possible conviction, settled with the US Treasury Department and paid $2.25 million in fines. The fine was imposed because Crocker failed to comply with US banking regulations which required banks to disclose significant cash transactions. Crocker did not report $4 billion in cash deposits from 1980 through 1984 from six Hong Kong-based banks. Hong Kong, one of the world's most important banking centers, was a favorite of Filipino money launderers because the absence of foreign exchange controls in Hong Kong made it impossible to determine the origin of the money. Crocker, which maintains an office in the Philippines, claimed that the money was from "various Asian countries."

Juan Frivaldo, a former governor of Sorsogon province who later went into exile in the US, singles out Solomon Brothers as havin "handled huge accounts" for the "instant Filipino nabobs" who have started investing flight capital in the US.

The many instances where financial institutions have broken the law or appear to have acted improperly raises the question whether money laundering is an integral part of international private banking. Highly respected institutions have been severely penalized or are facing investigation for money laundering. A report noted that 21 institutions had been penalized for not complying with US federal disclosure requirements covering cash transactions over $10,000. The reprtn also mentioned that another 41 had been under investigation for the "pizza connection" where the Mafia used pizza parlors and financial institutions to launder their profits. Well-known firms were mentioned as having been involved in the Mafia transactions, including Merrill Lynch, Pierce, Fenner & Smith which handled $4.9 million, and E.F. Hutton which handled $15.6 million.

Among the US banks most active in international private banking are Bank of America, Chase Manhattan, Morgan Guaranty, Citibank.

They all have very active calling programs designed to recruit new clients. They all play an active role in hehping wealthy [clients] get their money out of the country. They all help such customers design sophisticated offshore trusts and investment companies to shelter income from taxes and political exposure. They all try very hard to keep the identity of their customers a secret. They are all more or less actively involved in lobbying US authorities to preserve policies toward taxation, bank regulation, and bank secrecy that are favorable to their clients.

Citibank is considered to be the most aggressive in the field of international private banking. It has over 1,500 peop;e around the world dedicated solely to the activity and handles over $26 billion in assets from their international private banking clients. While cultivating the appearance of having a large exposure in third world loans, Citibank fosters capital flight from the very debt-ridden countries which owe them these loans. Special offices in Latin American countries such as Argentina, Chile, Mexico, Panama, Venezuela help the elite from these countries move their money abroad. Citibank, for example, while appearing to suffer from $4 billion in loan exposures to Brazil, actively promotes Brazilian capital flight from an office in Montevideo to take advantage of Uruguay's strict bank secrecy laws.

The activities of Citibank in the Philippines follow the same pattem. After extending multimillion dollar loans to Marcos corporations, Citibank then provided its "international private banking" services to Marcos and his cronies to bring money out of tile country. When, for example, US federal authorities investigated the accounts of Gliceria Tantoco, Imelda's associate in the purchase of New York real estate, the records subpoenaed from Citibank showed that Tantoco maintained 58 accounts under her name in Citibank alone.

Vilma Bautista, Ilmelda's personal secretary in New York, maintained several bank accounts which were used for Imelda's expenses and real estate purchases. Two known accounts in Bankers Trust and the Irving Trust had combined deposits amounting to several million dollars from 1983 through March 1986. Fe Roa

Gimenez, Imelda's social secretary, had another account at Bankers Trust which at one time held $40 million.

Among the many accounts Imelda held was one in Lloyds Bank in Los Angeles. It held $675,000 in US Treasury bills and $112,000 in cash. Another account was in a New Jersey bank held for Marcos' eldest daughter, Imee. The account was under the custody of Theresa Fernandez, a first cousin of Tommy Manotoc, Imee Marcos' husband. A resident of North Bergen, New Jersey, Fernandez admitted to being the custodian of $320,980.83 in a checking account with the United Jersey Bank in Englewood Cliffs, New Jersey.

The cronies discussed in the previous chapter had their own overseas accounts as well. There is reason to believe that Disini, for example, at one time had a $1.3 million on deposit at the United Orient Bank in ew York [25]. Benedicto at one time held $3 million in the California Overseas Bank.

DIRTY MONEY AND MARCOS TRANSNATIONAL COMPANIES

One way through which international private banking was able to move Marcos money out of the country was by arranging "back-to-back" loans for the corporations Marcos and his cronies owned. A back-to-back loan is an arrangement where a bank loans the client his own money. The purpose of this type of loan is either the lowering of the client's taxes, or secrecy in moving money from one place to another. An example can be seen in an arrangement where Antonio Floirendo, the crony who controlled the banana industry in the Philippines, arranged a variation of the typical back-to-back loan with Chase Manhattan, Manufacturers Hanover Trust, and a bank branch in the Bahamas.

Using Tadeco, the giant banana company subsidized by the government, Floirendo acquired two multimillion loans from Manufacturers Hanover Trust. The first of the loans, amounting to $5.42 million, was granted to Floirendo on 28 April 1980, with a second loan, amounting to $4 million, following on 1 May 1981.

The loans were granted through several overlapping agreements involving Floirendo, Manufacturers Hanover Trust, and Chase Manhattan:

I. Retention Account Agreement
This agreement stipulated that proceeds from Tadeco's banana exports would be turned
over to Manufacturers Hanover [26]. The specific arrangement required that proceeds from the Box and Fruit Purchase Agreement between Chiquita Int. Traders Corp. (Citco), a subsidiary of United Fruit, and Tadeco would be assigned to Manufacturers Hanover a payment for the loans granted to Floirendo. The effect of this arrangement was two-fold. It meant that Floirendo got an advance of more than $9 million from Manufacturers Hanover based the future earnings of Tadeco. It also meant that while the loans were being personally granted to Floirendo, it would be the government-subsidized Tadeco which would be paying in return. This arrange ment is far more convenient than if Floirendo had directly pocketed the money from Tadeco because it meant that Floirendo got the money in a lump sum rather than having to wait for it over several years. The arrangement, moreover, had a semblance of legality since the arrangements between all parties did not appear to violate any law [27].

2. Special Far East Account

Part of the arrangement required that Tadeco maintain a special account, Special Far East Account (#544-0-56803), with Manufacturers Hanover and authorize the bank to collect charges for interest and other expenses from the account. This account allows Manufacturers to cover whatever expenses it may incur in their loan to Floirendo.

3. Personal Guarantee Account

A further account, called a personal guarantee account, was established with Chase Manhattan.

4. Nassau (Cash) Collateral Account

Out of the preceeding Personal Guarantee Acoount with Chase Manhattan, Manufacturers was authorized to draw letters of credit in favor of a branch in Nassau, Bahamas. The Bahamas branch would then invest the money in the euro-dollar market at the prevailing rate. This account, together with the preceeding one, not only assured Manufacturers that they could hold on to a guarantee for the repayment of the loans they extended to Floirendo but it also meant that these loan guarantees could be safely and anonymously invested in the euro-dollar market for a profit without revealing that the money was Floirendo's. At an average rate of 12% per year, $9 million in the euro-dollar market would bring an additional income of more than a million dollars a year for Floirendo. Since the investments were made in Bahamas, this would further mean that this amount would be free from taxes.

The scheme was rationalized by Philippine government authorities as a way of raising dollars. What was referred to as the Euro-dollar Loan agreement was approved in two resolutions by the Philippine Central Bank Monetary Board, No. 42 dated 4 January 1980 and No. 2063 dated 30 October 1980. Permission for the loan was granted to Floirendo under the condition that "dollars obtained should be inwardly remitted for sale to domestic banks." But a report on the loan agreements showed that dollars were not being remitted to the Philippines but were bein retained in overseas accounts [28]. The 1984 financial statement of Tadeco, for example, disclosed that a balance of $8 million remained in overseas accounts, clearly indicating that "the dollar loans have not been remitted to the domestic market as required by the Central bank." The report further asserted that there were other special Tadeco accounts similar to the one described and that the dollars retained overseas had amounted to over $20 million by the time the Marcos regime collapsed in 1986. If this amount were invested in the euro-dollar and euro-bond markets at the rate of 12%, this would mean a further $2.4 million in yearly tax-free income.

It further appears that the loan agreements with the Central Bank served more to legitimrze the retention of dollars overseas rather than generate foreign exchange for the Philippines. Floirendo started hoarding dollars under the scheme as early as January 1978, but the euro-dollar arrangement was sanctioned by Central Bank authorities only in 1980. It definitely leaves the impression that it was a "scheme, if not an afterthought, to cover-up or justify the hoarding or salting of US dollars" [29].

It was an excellent way of transferring money overseas -- dollars owed to Philippine corporations were merely prevented from reaching the country. Back-to-back loans were arranged using these assets, deposited in overseas accounts, and were later reinvested in the euro-dollar market and other ventures. In this way, Marcos cronies did not have to worry about smuggling the money out of the country

-- they just made sure that it never reached its destination. The layers of bank accounts ending in the Bahamas provided the further advantage of anonymity.

The Floirendo back-to-back loan arrangements was merely one of the methods through which Marcos cronies were able to stash money overseas through their corporations. Their ownership of large transnational corporations permitted them to avail of a host of other methods not easily available to individuals.

We are certain that a thorough audit of the multimillion overseas corporations of Marcos and his cronies will reveal similar scams. We can do no more at this point than make a partial listing the many sizable overseas firms Marcos and cronies owned:

Firm	Location	Principal/Crony
Czarnikov-Rionda Inc.	120 Wall St., NY	Benedicto/Leandro Vasquez
Revere Sugar Corp.	Boston, Chicago, NY	Floirendo
Granex Corp.	San Francisco	Enrile/Cojuangco
Pan Pacific Commodities	Los Angeles	Enrile/Cojuangco
Crown Oil Corp.	Los Angeles	Enrile/Cojuangco
Coastal American Traders	Los Angeles	Helenita Boriano/Cojuangco
Nouvelles Huileries et Refineries Unipol	Marseille	Enrile/Cojuangco
SA. de Produit Excel	Marseille	Enrile/Cojuangco
Legaspi Oil Int. Ltd.	Hong Kong	Enrile/Coguangco

Czarnikov-Rionda, a large sugar trading firm based in New York, is estimated at $68 million, while Revere Sugar Corp., the sugar trading firm and its three refineries, was valued at $11.8 million (see separate sections on Benedicto and Floirendo). The two coconut refineries in France were worth 15 million.

Ownership of large corporations such as these allowed Marcos and his cronies to use these companies to generate money abroad and hoard it in secret bank accounts and investment havens.

There were reports, for example that Marcos had deposited $300 million in three Hong Kong banks from 1980 through 1984 using five Mindanao-based firms run by cronies [30]. The companies were identified as agri-business companies associated wrth Floirendo and Bejo Romualdez, Marcos' brother-in-law: Lianga Bay Logging (Surigao del Sur), Tagum Agricultural Dev. Corp. (Davao), Nestfarm (Davao), Davao Agricultural Ventures (Davao), Bukidnon Sugar Milling (Davao).

Control over the country's major export industries led to the organization or overseas trading firms which became convenient mechanisms for retaining money in overseas accounts. The crony-owned conglomerates discussed in the previous chapter were encouraged by the Marcos government to open "overseas trading offices" and were given not only tax breaks but also cash subsidies under the guise of promoting the country's exports. Disini's Herdis conglomerate, for example, was authorized by the Board of investments to receive a government cash-subsidy of $100,000 every year for every overseas trading office (OTO) it established [31]. The sections on Benedicto and Floirendo detailed how their overseas trading firms were able to generate millions in New York through their control of the sugar industry. In one instance, the shipment of 500,000 metric tons of raw sugar from the government led to a $5 million payment to a "Philippine Veterans Special Account" in a Paris bank [32]. The sections on Enrile and Cojuangco showed how their control over the coconut industry was continually expanded until they established overseas refineries and attempted to establish a cartel in the US market. The discussion in the previous chapter of the activities of the cronies demonstrated that one simple pattern was followed in all the areas of the economy where an industry had a potential to earn foreign exchange: control the industry with the help of the government, maintain overseas branches, and then retain the dollars generated in overseas accounts.

It is for this reason that accurate figures on Philippine exports and balance of payments statistics have been a closely guarded secret. But the data that have become public reveals great discrepancies that leads one to conclude that a large part of the export earnings of the country never reached the Philippines but were retained in overseas accounts.

Business Day, a respected Philippine business publication, reported inconsistencies in 1984 figures of Philippine exports to Japan and Japanese imports from the Philippines. Japanese imports from the Philippines and Philippine exports to Japan should ideally equal each other since they are merely two different ways of looking at the same transaction, but figures revealed a discrepancy of $355 million in 1984. The Japanese reported more imports than what Philippine businesses claimed they exported. Figures from Philippine exporters were undervalued by as much as 50%.

A 1985 World Bank study [33] noted the same problem of underreporting or undervaluation of Philippine exports. While the World Bank wanted to keep the report secret, its contents were exposed by opposition members of the Marcos-controlled legislature during the deliberations for the 1985 budget. It reported that substantial export earnings, together with foreign loans, were missing. While the data was spotty and covered different periods for different categories, the missing amount totalled $13 billion since 1965, the year Marcos assumed the presidency:

Amount	Item	Period
$3.6 billion	merchandise exports to Japan	1965-82
$240.8 million	hardwood exports to Japan	1977-80
$11.05 billion	merchandise exports to US	1972-83
$5.3 billion	remittances of overseas workers	1977-84
$3.1 billion	foreign loans which did not reach country 1978-82 [34]	

These amounts are too large to overlook and cannot be explained away as merely the products of statistical or computational errors. Such magnitudes can only be the result of consistent and systematic efforts to undervalue foreign exchange receipts. The incontrovertibly show that Philippine exporters systematically undervalued their exports and deposited the difference in bank accounts abroad. The scheme perrnitted the Philippine exporter to lower the taxes he had to pay the government, while at the same time keeping his money in an overseas account.

The obverse of export undervaluation, the overvaluation of imports, was also a method used to transfer money abroad. Whenever corporations imported machinery or raw materials, over-billing would occur, and the overprice would being kept in overseas accounts. This explains why cronies such as Cuenca continually sought loans and bought equipment even when they were not needed by his companies. Instances of such purchases were seen in the previous chapter, but Cuenca also continued such purchasing practices in the US. A former resident of Trans-Asia Marine, the US subsidiary of Cuenca's Galleon Shipping Lines, alleged in a suit filed in New York that Cuenca pocketed $41.8 million for purchases of overpriced ships. The overpriced ships were paid from loans extended by the government-owned Development Bank of the Philippines. The suit sued Cuenca for $5.5 million in damages. The previous chapter also discussed how Benedicto and Velasco bought highly overpriced ships from Japan. The commissions received from these transactions would then be deposited in secret overseas accounts or invested in assets abroad. A related practice would be to acquire foreign exchange for fictitious imports, or as we earlier saw, draw loans from foreign sources, and merely stash the money in personal accounts without ever making the purchase.

After the fall of the Marcos regime, the Ministry of Natural Resources (MNR) revealed data on Philippme log exports which showed another method through which money was stashed abroad by Marcos and his cronies. The MNR report estimated that Marcos and his cronies could have made as much as $12.6 million in kickbacks from favored loggers who were secretly granted export quotas in between November and December 1985. Seventy selected logging firms were permitted to export logs, but only half of these firms really qualified for export quotas since not all had their own wood processing plants, the principal requirement for the granting of export allocations. But these firms were nevertheless granted such quotas, and despite its disastrous effects on Philippine forests, these favored logging firms exported 1.264 million cubic meters, a third beyond the 800,000 log export ceiling for the previous year. The MNR estimated that, based on $10 "grease-money" for every cubic meter of logs exported, Marcos and his cronies could have raised as much as $12.6 million, depositing the kickbacks in foreign bank accounts since payments for the log exports were made abroad.

Marcos or crony ownership of large overseas companies permitted the use of all the sophisticated financial and accounting techniques used by transnational coporations to escape high taxes and move money secretly. Among these methods was transfer pricing, a technique where subsrdiaries or phony intermediaries would form part of the marketing and purchasing chain so that prices could be adjusted anywhere in the chain to avail of lower taxes in a particular place, or increase or lower invoice prices whenever convenient. An example of this practice was seen in the previous chapter which discussed the international trading of sugar.

As further example of how the use of foreign loans helped Marcos and his associates accumulate assets abroad can be seen in the operations of Asian Reliability Corp. Inc. (ARCI), a California firm specializing in high-technology firms in Silicon Valley. Using a $25 million Philippine government-guaranteed loan, the ACRI bought three Silicon Valley companies worth $14 million:

Interlek Inc.   San Jose

Test International Inc.   San Jose
Tool & Die Master   Santa Clara

Marcos had a direct interest in these firms. They were run by Vicente Chuidian, a businessman who personally knew Marcos, with the help of Dr. Alfred Tong, a computer scientist who was employed with Ministry of Human Settlements, the super-ministry headed by Imelda. Apart from the loans, funds for these firms also came from the Ministry of Human Settlements. It should be noted that these multimillion investments in high-technology firms in Silicon Valley were quite removed from the avowed aim of the Ministry of Human Settlements of meeting the "basic needs" of the Filipino. But they certainl provided a convenient way of moving assets overseas – borrow money rom overseas sources, invest the loan in overseas assets, and pay for the loan from local sources. This is a perfectly "legal" way of moving assets across national boundaries.

CAPTIVE BANKS AND LOAN FRAUD

Closely related to the foregoing practice of drawing loans from foreign banks while paying for the debt from Philippine sources was the method of foreign exchange swaps. National currengy in one place would be exchanged for other currencies in another nation location. A dollar account in a California bank, for example, would be credited, while a corresponding debit would be made in a Philippine peso account in Manila. While this method may appear to merely be a sirnple matter of balancing debits and credits for a bank, it has the effect of transferring money across national boundaries.

Marcos and his cronies were not content to use the traditional international private banking channels offered by the big international banks. To maximize their use of the highly intricate techniques of international money laundering and efficiently transport huge sums out of the country, Marcos and his associates acquired several "captive" overseas banks.

They also resorted to organizing "captive" banks because of the many benefits it would bring in hiding and movmg their money. A captive bank is one organized solely for the benefit of an individual or a group. While a captive bank appears to operate just as any normal bank, it in reality exists solely to serve the interests of its organizers and owners. California was a favorite of Marcos and his cronies. Several captive banks were organized in California. Among the banks were:

Bank	Location	Principal/Crony
Redwood Bank	San Francisco	Gapud/Marcos
Oceanic Bank	San Franciso	Lucio Tan
Phil. Bank of California	San Francisco	Roman Cruz
Century Bank	Los Angeles	Roman Cruz
Phil.Comm.& Ind.Bank	LosAngeles	Cesar Zalamea
California Overseas Bank	Los Angeles	Benedicto

These banks are classic examples of captive banks. The Redwood Bank was organized Rolando Gapud the financial adviser to Marcos and his son Bongbong. Dee described Gapud as "the key negotiator, the key decision-maker, the leader of the group behind the Redwood Bank. The Oceanic Bank is held by

Allied Bank, a Philippine company headed by close Marcos associates such as Lucio Tan, Romeo and Willy Co, Philipp Ang. Roman Cruz, a Marcos cabinet minister and an Imelda errand boy, was a member of the board of the Philippine Bank of California. He travelled between Manila and San Francisco every month to represent Marcos in the board meeting of this bank. Cruz was also the chairman of the Century Bank, a branch of the Philippine National Bank. The Philippine Commercial & Industrial Bank (PCIB) has an office in Los Angeles. The chairman of the PCIB was Cesar Zalamea, a close Marcos associate who served as a founding member of the Marcos Foundation.

The manner in which these banks were managed only added to the suspicion that they were primarily organized not to engage in legitimate banking activities but to serve as captive banks for a select group of Filipinos. Some of the business decisions made in connection with the purchase and management of the bank were indeed highly unusual.

The Century Bank, for example, was purchased from the Financial Corp. of America for 14.75 million. The money for the purchase came from five Philippine government agencies, with the Philippine National Bank taking the lead. While one may question why Philippine government agencies would want to purchase a California bank, the more surprising aspect of the purchase was that the price was estimated to be "two-and-a-half times" of what it was worth at the time of purchase. The bank was then headed by Gilberto Teodoro, a close Marcos presidential aide. The bank suffered a $755,000 loss in 1982 and was forced to merge with the Philippine Bank of California in 1983, with a combined net loss of $490,000.

The case of the Redwood Bank in San Francisco is equally instructive. It was purchased by Rolando Gapud, Romeo and Willy Co, Dewey Dee, and Ramon Siy. Dewey Dee was a major stockholder in this bank, owning as much as 20% of the bank's stocks before he absconded. Bought in 1980 for about $18 million, it immediately lost $25 million from 1982 through 1984 because of the loans that it extended. The comment of a source familiar with the operations of the Redwood Bank is very instructive as to how these Marcos captive banks were managed:

> You got to work at losing money like that... I am not in aposition to make a statement about why they lost the money, but you don't lose $18 million in operations. You lose it by giving it away to bum loans, or having it taken away from you in some way.

It would be a highly lucrative venture to purchase the controlling interest in a bank, lend money to yourself or your nominees, and then default on the loans. While it may ultimately mean the captive bank's ruin, it has the effect of raising large amounts of cash. While this was a common practice with the Marcos cronies while they were in the Philippines, their attempts to replicate their shenanrignans in the US ultimately attracted the attention of US monetary authorities. The management and loan practices of the Redwood Bank was the subject of an investigation by the Federal Deposit Insurance Corp (FDIC). The FDIC also noted the case of one Philippine bank operating in the US which extended large loans to Filipinos. The dollar loans were granted using peso accounts in banks in Manila as collateral, but the dollar loans and the interest on them were paid only when bank examiners noticed them. This was again a convenient way of transferring and raising cash overseas.

Other instances of bank-related fraud the Marcos cronies committed in the US involved the California Overseas Bank (COB). Rodolfo Arambulo organized the COB in 1976 under direction of Benedicto as a conduit for money. Benedicto, who at one time owned 100% of the referred stock and 88% of the common stock of the COB, was the bank's chairman, while Arambulo served as president and board member. Benedicto also had a personal account with the bank amounting to a $3 million deposit. The bank ad total assets $133 million. Apart from Benedicto, the following were the directors of the COB, most of whom were close Marcos associates: Rodolfo T. Arambulo, Miguel V. Gonzalez, James J. McNally, Dominador R. Pangilinan, Pag-asa San Agustin.

The C0B was indicted by a federal grand jury sitting in the US District Court for the Southern District of New York on 21 October 1988. The indictment was for mail fraud and violation of the Racketeer Influenced & Corrupt Organizations Act (RICO). The indictment charged that the COB attempted to defraud the FDIC by presenting "false and audulent" state- ments to the FDIC in an attempt to obtain and secure the benefits of FDIC insurance." The indictment detailed the instances of mail fraud where the COB violated the US postal code. Benedicto and Arambulo were also personally indicted for their roles. The indictment also revealed that the California Overseas bank maintained accounts or interests in the following other 50 US banks:

American Savings	Guardian Savings & Loan
Bank of America	Highland Federal Savings & Loan
Bank of California	Irving Trust Company
Beverly Hills Savings	Lloyds Bank
Brookside Saving & Loan	Manhattan Beach Saving
Cal American Savings	Manufacturers Hanover Trust
Carver Savings	Merit Savings & Loan
Chase Manhattan Bank	Mitsubishi Bank
City National Bank	Mitsui Manufacturers Bank
Coast Bank	National Bank of California
Columbia Savings & loan	Pacific Savings & Loan
County Savings	Republic Bank
Crocker National Bank	Santa Barbara Savings
Downey Savings & loan	Security Pacific National Bank
East-West Savings & Loan	Southern California Savings
Far West Savings & Loan	Southwest Savings
Fidelity Federal Savings & Loan	State Savings & flan
First Central Bank	Tokai Bank
First Federal Savings Bank of Ca.	Traders Royal Bank
First Interstate Bank	Union Bank
First National City Bank of NY	United Savings & Loan
First Network Savings Bank	Wells Fargo Bank
Founders Savings & Loan	Western Financial Savings Bank
Glendale Savings & Loan	Western State Bank
Guaranty Bank of California	Westlake Thrift

In attempting to build their overseas empire, Marcos and his cronies also resorted to loan fraud. Gliceria and Bienvenido Tantoco, the two Imelda associates discussed in the previous chapter, were also included in the US Federal indictment for loan fraud. The indictment charged that the Tantocos attempted to engage in a "fraudulent scheme" to defraud Citibank of more than $35 million around July 1983. The Tantocos, it charged, attempted to obtain the amount in connection with the purchase of New York real estate properties. (The purchases of real estate is discussed later in this chapter.)

The Tantocos were also charged with another instance of loan fraud in the indictment. It involved a second "fraudulent scheme" to draw more than $100 million in loans from the Security Pacific Bank and the Security Pacific Mortgage Corporation. The loans were again for the refinancing of New York real estate which Imelda and Tantoco purchased.

The theft of foreign aid and loans from foreign and local banks was also a common practice among the Marcos cronies. US military aid was pocketed by Marcos' Chief of Sta , General Fabian Ver through front corporations dealing with the Philippine military. Loans from the World Bank were placed in an interest bearing account, and the interest was diverted to Imelda's projects. Benedicto cornered Japanese war reparations money.

Japanese loans and war reparations money were diverted with the complicity of Japanese corporations whose services were contracted using loan and reparation funds. Andres Genito, a Quezon City councilor, acted as the "bagman" for the 15-10% commissions received from Japanese companies such as Sumitomo, Marubeni, Toyo, Sakai Heavy Equipment, Nisho-Iwai, Mitsui, C. Itoh. The kickbacks, given in exchange for construction contracts in the Philippines, totalled $53 million from July 1965 through February 1986. Genito passed the money to Eugenio Balao, head of Reparations Commission, who in turn arranged for it to be deposited into secret Marcos overseas accounts [35].

Figures from the World Bank earlier cited indicated that $3.1 billion in foreign loans did not reach the country from 1978 through 1982. While this amount covers only 4 out of the 20 years Marcos was in power, it gives us a floor figure from which we can gauge the amount of foreign loans which never reached the country. The Marcos cronies, so used to the abuse of privilege in the Philippines, attempted to apply the same methods of raising cash in the US by organizing captive banks and engaging in loan fraud.

Apart from organizing captive banks, the Marcos cronies also used the overseas branches of Philippine government banks are if they were their own personal banks [36]. The New York branch of the Philippine National Bank (PNB) was described as Imelda's "piggy bank" from w ere she would draw cash whenever she needed money for her shopping sprees in New York. Oscar Carino, who was later rewarded with the post of Philippine Consul General to Toronto for his services to Imelda [37], admitted to delivering $100,000 in suitcases to Imelda's suite at the Waldorf-Astoria whenever Imelda was in New York. The money came directly from the accounts of the New York branch of the PNB. Benjamin "Kokoy" Romualdez, Imelda's brother and Philippine Ambassador to the US from 1982 through 1986, also treated the PNB as his personal piggy bank and withdrew hundreds of thousands of dollars from the same York branch. Rebecca Presti, a vice-president with the PNB in New York, was the co-signatory of many checks from PNB accounts drawn in favor of Oscar Carino, Antonio Floirendo, Fe Roa Gimenez, and Vilma Bautista. The latter two are Imelda's personal secretaries and were closely connected with Imelda's purchase of US real estate. The abuse of the PNB became so blatant that US Federal and state banking authorities threatened to revoke its license.

THE GOLDEN FLEECE

Philippine government banks served not only as personal "piggy banks" for Imelda's shopping trips. They also served as a major source of funds for Marcos' secret overseas bank accounts and as a fool-proof mechanism for the large-scale transport and laundering these funds out of the country.

The gold and silver reserves of the national treasury were methodically looted over several years from the vaults of the Philippine Central Bank and the national mint. The quantity of precious metals stolen from the national coffers was so great that it has to be measured not by the ounce or the pound but by the ton. The amount of gold and silver bars pilfered over this period was so great that an investigative journalist described the scheme as the "biggest bank heist in history [38].

The gold and silver bars were later moved out of the country and transferred to Marcos' secret bank accounts in Switzerland through the help of a network of professional money launderers and select international private banks, as well as the active participation of Central Bank authorities.

This theft from the national treasury involved colossal proportions that many incredulous people could hardly believe that such an operation could be possible. Marcos cunningly encouraged this disbelief by engaging in a disinformation campaign that spawned unbelievable yarns about the source and the quantity of the gold deals. Marcos' favorite hoax was that the source of the gold was the treasure hoard the Japanese General Tomoyuki Yamashita had looted from different Asian countries and had buried in northern Philippines during his retreat at the close of World War II. But beyond Marcos' claim that he had discovered Yamashita's loot, there has been absolutely no evidence that Marcos had indeed discovered the booty nor is there even any indication that such a hoard had ever existed. Another disinformation tactic was to exaggerate the gold amounts involved into ridiculous proportions. One amount quoted concerning the value of the precious metals Marcos had in his possessron was the incredible figure of $240 billion [39].

These yarns served Marcos well. He concocted wild tales about the source and the quantity of the gold, floated the stories, and encouraged their dissemination. Since the stories were so unreal, they would be dismissed by everyone, except the most gullible [40]. This would have the effect that when bits of information concerning the real gold and precious metals transactions surfaced, the public would equally discount them as part of the large yarns earlier floated. This tactic, typical of the subterfuge Marcos continually practiced while in power, provided an effective cover for his actual gold and precious metals transactions [41].

Inspite of the incredible stories, there is no doubt that a gold cache does exist, even if it is not Yamashita's treasure. The existence of the hoard is confirmed through the different overseas shipments which have come to light, through analysis of Central Bank data, and through the testimony of individuals who have actually seen the hoard. The evidence further indicates that the real source of the gold and silver are the Philippine gold mines Marcos and his cronies controlled and the vaults of the Philippine Central Bank and the national mint.

Most of the gold bars believed to belong to Marcos and offered in the international mariet were of unconventional size. While they were 24-karat bars with a purity of 999.95 per 1,000 parts, conforming to internationally accepted standards of gold purity, they were 75-kilogram bars measurin 18 x 4 x 4 inches, an unusual size for the international gold market. Some of the bars bore strange marks, believed to be either Japanese or Chinese characters, and also had markings such as *Sumatra* and *AAA*, according to some of those who have actually seen the bars.

The strange markings were an attempt to disguise the hoard by passin it off as Yamashita treasure. General Fabian Ver, Marcos' chief of staff and personal body guard, had earlier consulted with Robert Curtis, a gold refining expert from Nevada, and inquired as to how his purported Yamashita gold could be secretly sold in the international market. Curtis recalls Ver as saying:

> *The laundering facility must become operational as soon as possible because retrieval of additional gold could create a serious problem of safe storage and security unless it could be laundered and sold as it was retrieved [42].*

The advice was to smelt what was presented as Yamashita treasure into bars which could be passed off as gold from the Phili pine Central Bank. But what Marcos did was to use the advice in reverse. Since the gold was really from the coffers of the Central Bank, it was resmelted into odd-shaped bars with strange markings, made to look like pre-World War II vintage, and passed off as Yamashita treasure. In this way, Marcos hoped to conceal the purloined nature of the gold. To add credibility to the scam, Marcos "secretly" organized a group of retlred military officers to hunt for the elusive Yamashita treasure and explore possible contacts with different gold dealers in Hong Kong to unload the non-existent war booty. The treasure search and the trips to Hong Kong of course led nowhere except a wild-goose chase where the retired officers spent a substantial amount of their personal savings.

A senior official of the Philippine Associated Smelting & Refining Corporation, the govemment-run smelting plant, later admitted to investigators that standard-size gold bars from the Central Bank had been resmelted into larger bars of unconventional size [43]. The resmelting of the bars was clearly an attempt on the part of Marcos to conceal the origin of the gold by packaging it as Yamashita treasure [44].

We also have Marcos' own testimony that the gold directly came from the Central Bank. Richard Hirschfeld, an investment lawyer from Virginia, secretly taped his conversations with Marcos while the former dictator was plotting to return to the Philippines from his exile in Hawaii. Hirschfeld's tapes, parts of which were later played during US congressional hearings, show, among many other things, Marcos' admission of the source of the gold. Hirschfeld attests:

I didn't even know how to pronounce Yamashita. That's why I got the distinct impression, when we first started talking about 'reminting,' that it wasn't the treasure at all, that it was money that had been diverted from the Cenaal Bank He was very specific that it came from the Central Bank - he made no bones about it. That's on the tapes. He said that was gold from the Central Bank, but it was my gold, and he had separate marking on it.
It seemed to me that he had disseminated the story about having found the treasure in order to substantiate the existence of the bars that he had apparently stolen from the Central Bank. He deviated in his story. At one point he said it was the treasure, and then at another point he came right out and said, 'Look, I got it from the Central Bank ' I could certainly testify under oath that the man had made it clear to me that he took the gold from the Central Bank to a large extent, had it reminted, converted into bars that appeared to be treasure bars, then sold in the black market or otherwise. The money ended up in the Swiss accounts. Very clear, very concise, very specific [45].

Discrepancies in Central Bank data have added to the suspicion that the national coffer was the real source of the gold. Marcos had given the Central Bank the sole authority to refine and sell all the gold mined in the Philippines through a 1978 presidential decree. But the Central Bank gold accounts were later discovered to have major inconsistencies. It was reported that while the Bureau of Mines had sent 62 tons from 1978 through 1984 to the Central Bank to be refined, the bank could only account for 55 tons in its annual reports. Juanito Fernandez, then the director of the Bureau of Mines, was quoted as saying that the amount of gold sent by the Bureau of Mines should equal the amount of gold refined by the Central Bank: "Those two figures should be the same. That big a difference can only mean one thing: the gold has somehow been diverte from the treasury" [46].

Several people have claimed to have seen the cache or part of the cache. Ron Lusk, an American soldier of fortune who was requested by General Ver to arrange some gold shipments to Zurich, attested to seeing 50 tons of gold in an underground tunnel near Marcos' house in Mariveles, north of Manila. The gold was stacked in copper cases. Lusk, whose testimony has been characterized by US officials as "impeccable," claims that he inspected each of the cases [47]. Another who saw the hoard in Mariveles was Curtis, who stated that he saw the gold bars "stacked from floor to ceiling" [48]. Colonei Marcelino Barba, Marcos' brother-in-law, guarded the cache in Mariveles.

There were many reported attempts to secretly ship the gold out of the country. Several inquiries were made in 1983 with different people in Hong Kong concerning the sales of sizable amounts of gold. One Chinese gold dealer who was approached claimed that more than 50 tons, amounting to around a billion dollars, was being sold. Another source, a British lawyer based in Hon Kong, reported that 80 75-kilogram bars were offered during this time, half of which were already in Hong Kong, while the rest were still in the Philippines [49]. A retired colonel, working at the behest of Marcos and General Ver, met with different potential brokers in Hong Kong, one of whom was Brian Lendrum, who then headed the private banking services of American Express in Hong Kong. Lendrum claimed that the retired colonel wrote that "the highest person in the land" was involved in moving the gold out of the Philippmes [50]. The names of Jaime Laya, Marcos' Central Bank governor at that time, and other prominent officials of Marcos' government were also mentioned as being involved in the deal. Another Hong Kong gold dealer reports of similar inquiries during this period, and an intriguing set of documents obtained in 1986 by the London team of a major US television network seems to indicate that indeed a serious attempt was made to unload a substantial amount of gold in Hong Kong around this time. The documents, dating from September 1982 through April 1983, were secret letters and code communications discussing the sale of gold and appears to have involved much the same set of Marcos functionaries involve with the other inquiries made in Hong Kong at this time.

Marcos and General Ver made special use of the expertise of international professionals-for-hire in their schemes to launder gold. Ver recruited Lusk into the gold operations and requested him to organize two Boeing 747s to fly the gold from Manila to Bankers Trust AG Zurich. Norman Kirst, an American from Wisconsin, was another person involved. Kirst was tasked with selling the resmelted gold in Zurich and London. We shall see in the last chapter that there is strong indication that certain groups within the American intelligence community, as well as some shady figures in the international arms market, were also involved in the operations.

A clear case of an attempt to secretly move gold out of the Philippines came in September 1983, when a Korean Airlines Boeing 747 commercial jet was unable to take-off and sped off the runway [51]. The pilot later admitted to investigators that the plane, which was leaving from Manila to Zurich with a stopover in Bahrain, could not take-off because of "the weight of the gold" in its cargo [52]. The incident happened two weeks after the killing of Benigno Aquino. It is believed that a high-ranking member of Marcos' cabinet was accompanying this flight.

There have been reports of other attempts to smuggle gold out of the country. One such report names a certain individual named Andrew Tan, who is believed to be close to Marcos' son. Tan was reported to have offered a substantial amount for sale through a Singaporean company on 27 September 1985. Another report involved attempts to unload 37 metric tons in 27 May 1983, which was then approximated to be $500 million. During the last days of Marcos' regime, Quantas Airlines was requested on 5 February 1986 to fly 10 tons of gold to Australia. The plan was to remint the hoard in Australia, offers having been made in the meantime to pay for the services of the state government mint in Perth, West Australia, and later reintroduce it 'to the intemational market. Quantas Airlines wisely refused to fly the cargo. It is believed that another carrier was found and that the cache finally found its way to Europe [53].

It is very difficult to determine the exact number of these secret flights because of the *sub rosa* nature of the arrangements. While details of an unconsummated deal or a bungled flight may filter to the public, it is in the interest of the parties concerned -- Marcos as well as the international bankers and mercenaries he utilized - to keep mum concerning a successfully concluded caper. But some details of one of these *sub rosa* flights became known. Another Boeing

707 passenger jet was chartered on October 1983. The flight's purported purpose was to ship flowers from Manila to Zurich. The plane actually carried gold bullion. Marcos' son, Bongbong [54], was reported to have strap the gold bars onto the passenger seats to distribute the weight more evenly in the plane and avert a repetition of the Korean Airlines fiasco a month earlier [55]. The cargo was later discovered to have been shipped with a "diplomatic" airway bill, thus avoiding the need for customs inspection.

Paul Erdman, a former president of a Swiss Bank and the author of several popular books on finance, also attests to similar shipment which happened a year earlier. In a 1986 TV interview, Erdman recounted:

> Well, it's - well, he did it, at least in one case, in a very clever way, I think the only way to do it. He just, in 1982, he put five tons of gold onto an airplane and flew it to Zurich and stashed it in a Swiss bank. Now, that's the smart way to do it, because you can't leave - there's no paper record, right? You just onload the gold, offload it in Zurich [56].

An estimated 14 to 17.5 tons of gold, worth between $168 million and $213 million, were flown to London and Zurich in three flights between late 1983 and early 1984 [57]. There is no accurate count of all of the secret flights transporting bullion available, neither is an approximate of the value of precious metals transported in these flights.

Another shipment, this time using a ship owned by Danding Cojuangco, was alleged to have been made soon after the downfall of the dictatorship. Tons of gold, as well as silver, currency, art and antiques, were reported to have been misdeclared as coins and shipped to Europe via Hong Kong. A Central Bank governor was supposed to have engineered the scheme, using M/V Gulovano, a vessel of the Filsov shipping line, a joint-venture between crony Cojuangco and the Soviets [58].

Marcos had at his disposal another method of transporting gold which entailed less risk and was far more efficient than making such clandestine trips. Since he was the head of state and also controlled banking officials in the country, Marcos simply had most of the gold shipped overseas as "official" transactions of the Philippine Central Bank. His private overseas accounts in Switzerland were then credited after the gold left the country.

The Central Bank had to admit later, albeit grudgingly, that it regularly shipped gold and silver out of the country during a four-year period. The shipments, done from 1981 through 1985, were sent to private brokers, most of whom were based in New York:

Date	Destination	Number of Bars
21 December 1981	Brinks Inc.	
	1981	**254**
4 January 1982	Mocatta Metals Corp.	
3 February 1982	Brinks Inc.	
4 March 1982	Republic National Bank of New York	
6 April 1982	Brinks Inc. & J. Aron Co. Inc.	
29 April 1982	Sun Hun Kai Bullion Co., Hong Kong	

9 July 1982	Philipps Bros. Inc.	
11 October 1982	Marc Rich & Co., Int. Ltd.	
1 December 1982	Merill Lynch	
	1982	**1,888 (gold & silver)**
24 March 1983	Philipps Bros	
13 April 1983	J. Aron Co. Inc.	
9 September 1983	Morgan Guaranty Trust Co.	
28 October 1983	J. Aron Co. Inc.	
10 November 1983	J. Aron Co. Inc.	
	1983	**1,186**
19 January 1984	Drexel Bumham Lambert	
19 January 1984	Drexel Burnham Lambert (second shipment on same day)	
20 January 1984	J. Aron Co. Inc.	
26 January 1984	Dorel Metals, Hong Kong	
12 December 1984	N.M. Rothschild	
	1984	**869**
7 shipments in 1985	J. Aron Co. Inc.	
	1985	**971** (gold & silver)

[59]

A total of 59,522 kilos of gold and silver bars, having an estimated value of $373 million, were brought out of the country in 27 separate shipments during this period [60].

The shipments were shrouded first with secrecy, then with controversy. The Centr Bank considered the gold transfers a "top-level management secret" [61]. Documents show that all of these transactions were handled by the same set of four Central Bank officials: Caridad Valdehueza, Mario Zipagang, Eugene Ty, and Angel Corpuzd[62]. While the initial shipments were monitored by the Commission on Au 1t (COA), the auditors were later prevented from examinin the rest of the transfers [63]. When news of the shipments later reached t e public, the Central Bank was forced to admit that it had indeed made the transfers but tried to obscure the issues in technical language, describing the shipments as "location swaps" or as part of the "gold-leasmg program" authorized by Central Bank Monetary Board Resolutions No. 2135 (2 November 1981) and No. 1180 (25 June 1982). The Central Bank refused to divulge the details of the transfers, such as the amounts involved and the parties which received the gold, citing reasons of "professional ethics" [64].

But the little that is known about these transfers is enough to raise important questions.

If these transfers were legitimate sales of gold on the part of the Central Bank, then the sales should be reflected as an increase in the country's dollar reserves. If the gold was being sold in the international market, then there should be a corresponding addition to the foreign exchange reserves because of the sales. But the exact opposite happened. There was an unexplained decrease in the country's foreign exchange.

According to data from the International Monetary Fund (IMF), Philippine gold reserves decreased from 65 tons in 1982 to about 10 tons in 1983. The decrease represented the sale of 55 tons of gold which was supposedly sold for

$600 million. The gold is believed to have ended in London, Zurich, New York, and Hong Kong. It was possible to liquidate such a large percentage of the country's gold reserves because Jaime Laya, Marcos' Central Bank Governor, had abrogated an earlier standby credit arrangement with the IMF where the Fund would monitor the country's gold reserves. The sale should have bolstered the country's foreign reserves by the corresponding amount of $600 million. But the accounting ledgers of the Central Bank showed no such increase. Instead, Laya attempted to mask the discrepancy by inflating the bank's books, a move which was unfortunately discovered by the IMF auditors, resulting in great embarrassment for the Marcos regime.

The discrepancy was never adequately explained. Marcos later claimed that he had "borrowed" from the gold buyers with authorization from the Central Bank. But there was no official explanation of where the $600 million went.

While there has been neither an adequate official explanation for these transfers nor an accounting of the gold and foreign exchange reserves, aspects of some of the transactions have filtered back to the public.

The shipment of gold to the London branch of Morgan Guaranty Trust in September 1983 occurred under highly questionable circumstances. The 247 gold bars in this shipment, bundled in 62 packages and weighing more than 3 tons, was carried on board Flight 864 of KLM Royal Dutch Airlines which flew from Manila to London via Amsterdam. But the KLM airway bill declared the $39.158 million cargo as having "no commercial value." Morgan Guaranty, which was listed as both the sender and receiver of the cargo, has not explained the circumstances behind the misdeclaration [65].

The Central Bank tried to explain the transaction but only succeeded to mire itself in contradictions. Three years after the gold transfer, the Central Bank claimed that the shipment was an "official transaction" and that credits were given for the shipment in the New York branches of Morgan Guaranty ($14.479 million) and Citibank ($24.679 million) [66]. The Central Ban further claimed that the transaction was done "to beef up liquidity at a time when the Central Bank was having difficulty meeting its foreign exchange payments" [67], but as has been pointed out earlier, these credits were not reflected in an increase in the foreign exchange reserves of the bank. Neither do these assertions explain why there was a misdeclaration.

*The Central Bank eventually attempted to explain the matter in CB Review, its official publication. An article called **Clearing the Doubts** however, achieved eractly the opposite. It reported that the 247 gold bars had been 'sold' to Morgan Guaranty for cash, but two pages later the same transaction was listed as a location swap, an entirely different animal that wouldn't have required the wiring of $39 million to New York [68].*

The inconsistencies were never really adequately resolved. An official statement of the Central bank called the shipments part of "yield optimization and fund generation needs" but nowhere define what they meant by the jargon. Central Bank spokesman Mike Avancena added "security" as another reason why the transfers were made, saying that the gold reserves were shipped out because "we do not have the sophisticated security measures to keep them here." There were thus several different reasons given for the transfer, some of which logically excluded the others: "gold leasing," "location swap," "yield optimization," "beef-up liquidity," "security."

None of these stated reasons explained why the precious metals were kept with the private brokers for several months after they left the country. If the gold and silver were indeed meant to be sold for foreign exchange, it was extremely odd that the precious metals should stay with the brokers for an extended period of time rather than immediately turn them over to the Bank of London and the Federal Reserve of New York and thereby receive foreign exchange credits for the Philippine Central Bank. The Central Bank claimed that brokers paid a "safekeeping" deposit fee for the gold [69]. This "explanation" again merely added to the confusion since it does not really explain why the brokers would want to keep the gold and pay a premium for hoarding it. Moreover, there is no evidence that the brokers ever paid the premiums to the Central Bank. The only logical explanation was that the brokers were instructed by the Central Bank itself to hold on to the hoard, possibly because Marcos wanted to speculate on gold prices in the international market while arrangements were being made to launder the cache.

Most of the shipments were done through established financial and brokerage institutions in New York such as Morgan Guaranty Trust, Merill Lynch, Marc Rich, and Drexel Burnham Lambert. All of the seven shipments in 1985 were sent through J. Aron Co. Inc., a division of Goldman Sachs, another respected Wall Street firm. But the fact that the Philippine Central Bank dealt with highly-respected financial firms does not guarantee that the Marcos-controlled bank acted properly. A secret US intelligence report which discusses one of the many Central Bank shipments in 1985 reveals how Marcos used the shipments for his private ends.

The Central Bank made three secret shipments of gold and silver bars during the later art of 1985. These shipments are interestintgly not included in the list of official Central Bank shipments cited earlier. US Navy Intelligence operating in Manila caught wind of these shipments and provided details of the last of the three batches of gold and silver shipments. Working from information provided by a trusted Filipino source, US Navy intelligence agents conveyed the following information to Washington on October 1985:

> *Source reported that the Central Bank of the Philippines has made three suspicious shipments of gold and silver to the US... The precious metals, which according to source were physically transported from the Central Bank to an American President Lines [ship], were escorted by Presidential Security Command personnel. Source stated that those involved with the shipment have speculated that the shipments are being made by members of the family of President Marcos, who are illegally diverting the precious metals to Switzerland, where the metals are held in personal accounts [70].*

Another secret report prepared by the US Treasury, later circulated with other US Federal agencies such as the FBI and the Bureau of Firearms, Alcohol & Tobacco, confirmed the Navy report and provided more details of the shipments. The three shipments carried 8.4 tons of gold with an approximate worth of $90 million and 8.2 tons of silver bullion with an approximate worth of $2.6 million. The

244 silver bars which comprised the third batch were transported on 11 October 1985 using the *President Kennedy* liner of the American Presidents Line, with the bill of lading provided by United Transport Inc. The bill of lading listed only 224 silver bars, while the US Navy source counted 244 bars. Security was provided by the Philippine Presidential Guard, which was under the direct supervision of General Ver. The cargo arrived in Los Angeles and was transported to New York by Alba Forwarding Co. Inc., which maintains offices at One World Trade Center, New York. Drexel Burnham Lambert, an established Wall Street brokerage firm, handled the sale of the precious metals and credited the accounts of the Philippine Central Bank at the US Federal Reserve Bank in New York. The Central Bank then wired the money to Marcos' accounts in Switzerland and Luxembourg.

Drexel Burnham Lambert later confirmed the sale of the precious metals to authorities. The brokerage firm apparently did not break any laws since it was formally trading for the Philippine Central Bank and had met US financial disclosure requirements. It was only when the Philippine Central Bank transferred the funds to Marcos' secret accounts in Europe that any formal charge of wrong-doing could be levelled.

These shipments provide the key to understanding the *modus operandi* with the gold and silver bars the Philippine Central Bank transported over the years. The trick was to ship the precious metals as official transactions of the bank, sell them in the international market as Philippine Central Bank gold, and then later credit Marcos' personal accounts from the money raised in the sales. This move had obvious advantages. While large sales of gold by an individual would be a cause of major news in the international precious metals market, the sale of a few tons of gold at a time by a foreign government is likely to attract less attention. The practice also had the advantage of allowing the gold and silver to be officially shipped as part of the national reserves of the Central Bank. The risk of shipping the bullion and the costs of transportation and insurance would therefore borne by the bank. The sale would be made under the name of the Philippine Central Bank, making it look like an official transaction, and only when the sale has been consummated would the funds be transferred to Marcos' secret private accounts. The genius of Marcos was to distinguish the actual physical transfer of the gold and silver with the transfer of ownership of the assets. Only after the bullion had been transferred out of the country and transformed into cash under the auspices of the Central Bank did Marcos finally claim it as his personal possession.

Towards the end of 1985, as it was becoming clear that Marcos' hold on power was progressively eroding, the Central Bank shipped gold at an unprecedented pace. The Central Bank transferred almost $94 million from its US Federal Reserve accounts through 20 wire transfers to Marcos' secret accounts in Switzerland and Luxembourg during the last two and a half months of Marcos' rule [71].

THE SACRAMENT OF SECRECY AND SHELL CORPORATIONS

Marcos and his cronies chose to launder their money through the Swiss banking system first because the Swiss are the traditional masters in the art of providing anonimity for banking clients. While other countries and other international banking centers have tried to emulate the Swiss model of banking secrecy, Marcos and his associates correctly understood that transporting and hoarding their dirty millions required the expertise of the Zurich and Geneva bankers who had successfully transformed the practice of money laundering into a precise science.

The Swiss enjoy unparalleled expertise in money laundering because of the central role they bestow upon secrecy. The Swiss banking system is built around the provision not only of financial services but more importantly secrecy in the provision of these services. Banking secrecy is not only enshrined in the Swiss constitution and codified in the country's banking laws, but it is also a cultural more with dee historical roots central to the Swiss character. Ziegler's remarks on the historical and sociological origins of banking secrecy in his homeland are insightful:

> In Switzerland, the handling of money has a quasi-sacramental character. Holding money, accepting it, counting it, hoarding it, speculating and receiving, are all activities which, since the first influx of protestant refugees to Geneva in the 16th century, have been invested with an almost metaphysic majesty. No words must intervene to sully such lofty activities: everything is done in contemplative silence. Anyone who commits the sin of talking too much desecrates the sanctuary: such sacrilege is punishable by law.
> In the Calvinist theory of hoarding as holy work, this silence and contemplation have a corollary. The banker in Geneva (or Basle orZurich or in the Swiss bank in Panama) accepts his function as a staunch guardian of morality.- in a world of sinners and unbelievers, his silence keeps virtue secure [72].

The strict rules on banking secrecy are necessary because the Swiss economy is highly dependent on its banking system. The five banking empires of the Swiss Bank Corporation, Crédit Suisse, Union Bank of Switzerland, Banque Populaire, and Banque Leu enjoy earnings paralleling the size of Switzerland's GNP [73]. The provision of anonymity is therefore a most valued national ideal. It is so central to the Swiss banking system that any attempt to break the silence is equated with treason, or, as Ziegler points out, sacrilege.

Marcos and his cronies initially availed of the services of the Swiss to transport and hoard their dirty money. After learning the techniques of international money laundering at the feet of the Swiss, they later branched out and used other money laundering centers in places such as Liechtenstein, Hong Kong, Panama, and the Netherlands Antilles.

These countries also proved to be convenient alternatives for Marcos and his cronies since these places, equally hungry for dirty money, have tried to copy, then outdo, the Swiss in providing anonymity for their clients. Austria, where Disini, Lucio Tan, and other important Marcos associates have heavily invested and applied for citizenship, also has its own tradition of banking secrecy which dates to the Austro-Hungarian empire. The Austrian tradition of secrecy, though not as old, is equally if not more strict than that of the Swiss. A 1979 law allows accounts to be opened without the client ever revealing his name, a feature not available even in Switzerland, permitting depositors to remain unknown as long as they wish. Marcos and his cronies also utilized locations such as Hong Kong, Panama, and the Netherland Antilles because these places have developed their own traditions of banking secrecy. Hong Kong was convenient because, apart from its proximity to the Philippines, it has highly developed facilities for the transport of money and the ready availability of a whole cabal of British lawyers who are ready to organize front or "she " corporations for a fee. Panama, a favorite of launderers of drug money, was utilized because of its corrupt politicians and its convenience as a transit point to the US. Marcos and his cronies also utilized the Netherland Antilles, the home of more than 35,000 front or "shell" cor- porations, to organize many such "shells" and invest anonymously in US real estate and the overseas financial markets. The Netherland Antilles became a favorite of Marcos and his cronies because investing in the lucrative multi-billion euro-bond and euro-dollar markets was relatively easy to accomplish from this archipelago of five small Caribbean islands.

Marcos and his cronies utilized Switzerland and these other international investment havens for the followmg three related purposes:

1. move the money from its source to a more secure location;
2. hide the origin or ownership of the money;
3. hoard, store, or reinvest the money.

The earlier sections discussed the methods Marcos used to move money out of the country. The use of personal couriers, the flight of Dewey Dee, and all the techniques of money laundering used by certain international private banks presupposed the existence of these international investment havens. These havens served as a place of refuge where dirty money could find financial asylum, a "center of repose and continuance" to borrow Adam Smith's expression, before they are recycled as "clean" money and reintroduced to the international financial system. These investment havens provided not only a physical location for the stolen assets, but also a base which provided a legal cloak, first to hide the ownership of the dirty money, then to reinvest it in other ventures. These investment havens function, in the judgement of Ziegler, as a "fence" for the safeguarding and the profitable reinvestment of "accumulated plunder" [74].

Such havens were useful partly because they provided the technology necessary for the movement of dirty money, such as banking facilities, money exchanges, telecommunications, transportation facilities. But, more importantly, these investment shelters were indispensable to the Marcoses and his cromes because they provided the service of secrecy, the necessary condition for dirty money, by furnishing the legal basis for the organization of "shell" or paper corporations. The use of shell corporations, clearly analogous to the use of fronts and nominees in the Philippine corporations documented in the previous chapters, assured that the ownership of assets of questionable origins would remain unknown. Offshore, front, dummy or "shell" corporations render required reporting forms totally useless since the name that appears in the forms would be a surrogate name, a "shell" shielding the identity of the real owner. These corporations were organized not to conduct regular business but solely for the purpose of moving and hiding the true ownership of assets.

It was relatively easy for Marcos and his cronies to organize these shell corporations. The laws and regulations covering investment, taxation, foreign exchange remittances, and the incorporation of paper companies in these investment havens were extremely liberal and were specially designed to accommodate the client's need for anonymity. Incorporation in the Netherlands

Antilles, where the Marcos gang organize many shells, can be accomplished by mail, paying a relatively small fee of $1,500 to a local notary, who will then handle the whole rocess. There have been occasions where the procedure took only a few days to accomplish. Only one director need be listed, and this person can be a resident of the Netherlands Antilles who functions as a nominee who has lent his name to the true owners. An example of such absentee directorships and management by long-distance can be found in the arrangement between Ancor Holdings NV and Curacao International Trust Co. (Citco). In 1980 Ancor Holdings, the Netherlands Antilles shell company Imelda and Floirendo used to purchase New York real estate, contracted Citco, a well-established offshore management company, to be its local representative in the Netherlands Antilles. These local nominees function without ever knowing for whom the work or the true purpose of the shell corporation, their curiosity satisfied by the annual administration fee paid by the foreign lawyer who occasionally gives them instructions. Opening an account in Switzerland is equally easy. One merely needs an identity document and an address. The identity provided can be fictitious because it is never officially checked, and the address can be a post-office box number in the Bahamas [75].

Helping Marcos and his cronies organize shell corporations and acquire overseas properties was a whole slew of highly-paid lawyers, accountants, investment consultants, and portfolio managers. Some of the other professionals Marcos and his cronies utilized in the organization and management of their overseas properties were the following law offices and investment consultants:

* Commence Consultants, Hong Kong [76]
Several Hong Kong investment consulting firms specializing in the organization of shell corporations were used by Marcos and his cronies. Among them was Commence Consultants. One of the investment advisors of Commence Consultants was Anthony Golamco, a Filipino-Chinese partner of SGV, the Manila-based accounting firm extensively used by Marcos crony companies.

* Golden Assets Ltd., Hong Kong [77]
This company, formerly known as GTK Associates, is closely associated with Commence Consultants and uses its address.
Amworld, a dealer of military equipment linked to General Ver and associate Raymond Moreno incorporated in California, is wholly-owncd by Golden Assets. Amworld, awarded the major part of a controversial 1982 $35 million contract to provide communications equipment to the Philippine military, was probed by the US Justice Department on the belief that at least $6 million of the funds were diverted to General Ver and Moreno. Subscribers and shareholders to Golden Assets are other nominee companies, providing another layer of secrecy. The exclusive shareholders are listed as Chaparral Ltd. and Myrete Ltd. Subscribers are Cipher Ltd. and Directorate Ltd. Cipher and Directorate are also listed as directors of Decision Research Management, the shell company Velasco, Marcos' Minister of Energy, used to purchase California real estate.
Cipher has been "indentified as vehicle for high-level capital flight" from the Philippines.

* SGV Byrne, Hong Kong [78]
Another Hong Kong company is SGV Byme, an accounting firm connected with the Manila-based firm. It serves as either the secretary or auditor for 10 Hong Kong deposit-taking companies which have extensive dealings with the Philippines.
Velasco's Decision Research uses SGV Byme office in the 41st Floor of the Hopewell Centre as its address, as does Cipher and Directorate.

When asked if the company's clients could possibly be in violation of Philippine law, an SGV Byme spokesman, Gabriel Azedo, refused to commit himself, saying "It's not appropriate for us to talk about our clients."

* Johnson, Stokes, & Master, Hong Kong
The firm of Johnson, Stokes, & Master is a British law firm in Hong Kong which Specializes in organizing dummy companies. It was used by Wellwyn Investment, a shell corporation associated with Velasco as a drop for its mail.

* Graham & James, 1 Maritime Plaza, San Francisco
The law firm of Graham & James was used in the purchase of real estate properties in the San Francisco Bay Area. Among their clientswere Juan Ponce-Enrile, Marcos' Defense Minister, and Rodolfb Cuenca, the golfing crony who controlled the construction industry. Roger MacKenzie, an attorney with Graham & ames, served as president of TRA Equities Inc., a corporation based in Delaware believed to be a Cuenca corporation. Properties which were initially under Cuenca's name were later transfered to TRA Equities.
Mackenzie claims he does not know if Cuenca is involved with TRA Equities [79]. Alexander "Sandy" Calhoun Jr., another lawyer with this firm, provided legal help in the purchases of the Redwood Bank, Oceanic Bank, and the California Overseas Bank.

* Rosenman, Colin, Freund, Lewis & Cohen, 575 Madison Ave, New York
It was this firm which helped Imelda Marcos purchase the apartments in Olympic Towers in New York (discussed later). Irwin Jay Robinson, a senior partner of the firm, was an officer of Philippine-American Chamber of Commerce and represented Imelda and Floirendo in New York in the transactions for Olympic Towers. He also represented Floirendo in the apartments in St. James (see section). Robinson was also a director In the Redwood Bank in San Francisco and was a source of legal advice for the bank. The Redwood Bank paid $1.8 million in legal fees in 1983, 74% of which went to Robinson's law firm.

* Bernstein, Carter, & Deyo, 29 West 57th St., New York
The Bernstein, Carter, & Deyo law office was one which was heavily used by Marcos and his cronies in their shell corporations and real estate investments in New York. Joseph E. Bernstein, a senior partner of the firm, specialized in offshore tax havens in the graduate tax law program at New York University and once worked with Irwin Jay Robinson as an associate in Rosenman, Colin, Freund, Lewis & Cohen. Joseph's brother, Ralph, also worked with the Bernstein law office and was also active in foreign investments. The Bernstein brothers actively helped Imelda organize shell companies based in the Netherland Antilles, acquire New York real estate, and manage these properties through New York Land Co., the real estate company which the two brothers owned (discussed later). The Bernstein law office represented Imelda in practically all her major real estate purchases. It also represented Floirendo, the Marcos crony earlier discussed, in his purchases. William Deyo, another partner of the firm, was also involved with other Marcos-related shell corporations and was likewise active in the real estate transactions of Imelda and Floirendo.

The lawyers who organized the shell corporations also arranged fiduciary agreements to further obscure the real ownership of the properties. A fiduciary agreement is one where one person holds the property for the benefit of some other party. Marcos and his cronies selected trusted individuals to serve as their nominees where they would manage and front for them in their shell corporations under fiduciary arrangements. Joseph Bernstein, for example, signed two declarations of trust stating that he would act as a trustee for Marcos. The first declaration, dated 4

April 1982, was prepared by Rolando Gapud while Bernstein was in Manila and was legally binding under the laws of New York. The handwritten declaration of trust stipulated that Bernstein would act solely on the instructions of Marcos when matters pertained to Lasutra, a paper corporation based in the Netherland Antilles used to acquire New York real estate. The document read "by this instrument the undersigned [Bernstein] hereby acknowledges that he shall act as a trustee for the benefit of President Ferdinand E. Marcos with respect to all matters relating to Lasutra NV, a Netherlands Antilles corporation" [80]. Gapud changed the arrangement the following day and redrafted a practically identical declaration substituting Marcos for Beneficio Investment, Inc., a shell corporation based in Panama, thus providing another layer in the scheme to hide the ownership of assets. Most of the overseas properties of Marcos and his cronies had similar arrangements.

What Adrian Cristobal Cruz, the Marcos government official earlier quoted, says about the ownership of his condominium in San Francisco is revealing of such absentee ownerships:

> It belongs to me in the sense that I am paying for it.... This is an arrangement between myself and a relative who's a resident of the US. The money used to buy it was his money, and it was not made in the Philippines. I have 30 years to pay. It's a very loose arrangement. If I can pay for it, it's mine. If not, I can just use it. I have a son studying at Berkeley, and he uses it now. It's my relative's money. No money left the Philippines.

Shares in these shell companies were usually issued in bearer form. This means that ownership of the shell company belonged to whomever held the certificates of ownership. These certificates were usually transferable without endorsement so that ownership of these paper corporations were easily transferred from the nominees or fronts to the real owners through the simple act of transferring the possession of the certificates. As a further precaution, different paper corporations were organized, sometimes involving different countries with varying investment and secrecy laws, forming a multi-layered shield of corporations where the owner of one corporation in one far-flung Caribbean island was yet another corporation on the other side of the globe.

These legal tricks assured that a formidable cloak would conceal the extent of Marcos' overseas empire. They made it almost impossible to verify the real ownership of the paper corporations Marcos and his cronies organized. These legal devices made it difficult even for the officials from these international investment havens to know where the paper trail lead. The anonymity of the actors and the secrecy of their operations was thus assured. A lawyer who worked for the rich Filipinos investing in the San Francisco Bay Area declared:

> You'll never find out who the principals are. Every time I've ever dealt with these guys, I've never dealt with a document signed by a principal. Ninety-nine percent of the time they just tell me what to do, and I do it [81].

Marcos and his cronies were therefore able to organize a multitude of shell corporations and provide the much-needed cover for their overseas investments. A partial list of the different off-shore corporations Marcos and his cronies organized:

Dummy	Principal/Crony
Hong Kong	
Independent Foreign Holdings Ltd.	Jose Campos Yao/Ferdinand Marcos
Foreign Securities Co. Ltd.	Jose Campos Yao/Ferdinand Marcos
Thetaventure Ltd.	Vilma Bautista/Imelda Marcos
Commence Consultants	
SGV Byrne	
Decision Research Management	Velsaco
Cipher Ltd.	
Directorate Ltd.	
Golden Assets Ltd.	
Chaparral Ltd.	
Myrete Ltd.	
Kinship Capital Ltd	
Waitomo Lid.	
Nethertand Antilles	
Unique Investment N.V.	Jose Campos Yao/Ferdinand Marcos
Goodland Investment N.V.	Jose Campos Yao/Ferdinand Marcos
Lyra Corporation, N.V.	Gliceria Tantoco
Ancor Holdings N.V.	
Edgewood Investments	Sylvia Lichauco
Stanway N.V.	Sylvia Lichauco
Albany Enterprises Ltd.	Jose Campos Yao & Associates
Bowen Investment Corp. N.V.	Jose Campos Yao & Associates
Breton Property Corp. N.V.	Jose Campos Yao & Associates
Chilliwack Investment Corp. N.V.	Jose Campos Yao & Associates
Cordillera Investment Corp.	Jose Campos Yao & Associates
Denman Investment Corp. N.V.	Jose Campos Yao & Associates
Devon Investment Coro. N.V.	Jose Campos Yao & Associates
Ellesmere Investment Corp. N.V.	Jose Campos Yao & Associates
Galiano Investment Corp. N.V.	Jose Campos Yao& Associates
Greenfield Estates Ltd.	Jose Campos Yao & Associates
Haney Investment Corp.	Jose Campos Yao & Associates
Haney Texas Corp. N.V.	Jose Campos Yao & Associates
Hornby Investment Corp.	Jose Campos Yao & Associates
Kamloops Investment Corp. N.V.	Jose Campos Yao & Associates
Kelowna Investment Corp. N.V.	Jose Campos Yao & Associates
Langley Investment Corp. N.V.	Jose Campos Yao & Associates
Melville Investment Coro. N.V.	Jose Campos Yao & Associates
Pemberton Investment Corp. N.V.	Jose Campos Yao & Associates
Pender Investment Corp. N.V.	Jose Campos Yao & Associates
Penticton Investment Corp. N.V.	Jose Campos Yao & Associates
Point Grey Investment Corp. N.V.	Jose Campos Yao & Associates
Revelstoke Investment Corp. N.V.	Jose Campos Yao & Associates
Silkstone Investment Corp. N.V.	Jose Campos Yao & Associates
Teslin Investment Corp. N.V.	Jose Campos Yao & Associates
Transconti Investment Corp. N.V.	Jose Campos Yao & Associates
Unam International Corp. N.V.	Jose Campos Yao & Associates
Unam Investment Corp.	Jose Campos Yao & Associates
Vernon Investment Corp. N.V.	Jose Campos Yao & Associates
Panama	
Beneficio Investments	Rolando Gapud/Marcos
Premium Holdings Corp.	Jose Campos Yao

Tropical Resources Corp.	Jose Campos Yao
Paradela Holding Corporation	Roberto Benedicto
Isaac Peral de Panama, S-A.	Roberto Benedicto
Agricola Y Mercantil de Pontevedra, S.A.	Roberto Benedicto
Phil. Engineering Service Corp.	Roberto Benedicto
Techno Philippines Services Co.	Roberto Benedicto
El Parabien, S A.	Roberto Benedicto
El P.SA. - (El Porvenir)	Roberto Benedicto
Sebastian El Cano, SA.	Roberto Benedicto
Commercio Insular, SA.	Roberto Benedicto
Rio Pucura, SA.	Roberto Benedicto
Rio Topalisa, SA.	Roberto Benedicto

All of the Panamanian corporations associated with Benedicto had P.O. Box 8342, Panama 7 as its mailing address. Some of his Panamanian corporations, such as Sebastian El Cano and Commercio Insular, also had P.O. Box 3803 Beverly Hills, CA 90212-0803 as a secondary address.

Other Shell	**Location**	**Principal/Crony**
Renford Company	New York	Gliceria Tantoco
Hanover Trading Corp.		Gliceria Tantoco
Kashgar	New York	Gliceria Tantoco/New York Land
Lei Invest. Ltd.	Channel Islands, England	Gliceria Tantoco
Sanmar Export Corp.	New York	Gliceria Tantoco
Sigma International		Adnan Khasoggi
Sigma - X International		Adnan Khasoggi
Triad		Adnan Khasoggi
Triad Asia		Adnan Khasoggi
Triad International		Adnan Khasoggi
Greenfield Inv. Corp.	Vancouver, BC	Jose Campos Yao
1460 Westwood Blvd. Corp.	Bevely Hills, CA	Roberto Benedicto
Azucarera La Yaguara	Curacao, Venezuela	Roberto Benedicto
Palmira Overseas Inc.	Madrid, Spain	Roberto Benedicto
Tradewinds Int. Bank	St. Vincent, West Indies	Roberto Benedicto
Services Ltd.	St. Vincent, West Indies	Roberto Benedicto
Oscarmen Holdings Ltd.	New York	Oscar Carino

Once these shell corporations were organized, Marcos and his cronies then proceeded to use them to launder dirty money out of the Philippines and invest overseas. The organization of these dummy companies assured that Marcos and his cronies would be able to effectively address their dirty money concerns with regard to the triangle of uncertainty, secrecy, and profits [82]. Moving their money out of the Philippines allowed them to escape the country's political uncertainty. Secrecy was bought by employing the services of unscrupulous lawyers, accountants, investment consultants, money launderers, and Swiss bankers who functioned as Marcos' high-class smurfs. In the world of money laundering, a smurf is a courier who regularly runs to the bank teller's window and deposits dirty money in small amounts so as not to arouse suspicion. In the case of Marcos, it was these high-powered professional money managers who functioned as his smurfs. The yield of these assets were maximized by reinvesting them in different areas overseas. Thes are the three sides of the Marcos dirty money triangle.

We have already described aspects of this triangle when we discussed the methods of money laundering, the sacrament of secrecy, the organization of captive banks, and investments in overseas companies. The next sections discuss in more detail the assets hidden in Swiss accounts and the investments in overseas real estate properties. These are two areas where Marcos and his cronies had substantial investments.

THE GNOMES OF ZURICH

Marcos started opening accounts in overseas banks soon after assuming the presidency in 1965. Because he was still relatively inexperienced with the methods of dirty money, Marcos ill-advisedly deposited $215,000 under his name in Chase Manhattan Bank on July 1967. This deposit attracted attention, not merely because it was a personal account of a head of state, but also because the amount was more than what he could have possibly been earning with his regular salary as president.

After this bank account was exposed, Marcos turned to the Swiss for more professional advice in laundermg dirty money. He examined around 20 international banks to find out which among them would be most ideal for his purposes. Six Japanese banks were vetoed from the list of potential money launderers even after these banks had already paid him bribes for investment opportunities in the Philippines. Marcos finally zeroed in on the Chartered Bank in Hong Kong and Credit Suisse in Zurich as his initial collaborators [83].

It was not by coincidence that Marcos would heavily favor these banks. Apart from being among the biggest banks in Switzerland, the Swiss Bank Corp. and Credit Suisse also are among the most notorious of the Swiss banks for their money laundering operations on behalf of drug barons and other international crooks. The Swiss Bank Corp. and Credit Suisse, together with the Bank of Boston, were among nine European banks which handled more than $1.6 billion for German money launderers attempting to hide proceeds from the heroin trade in Turkey [84]. Credit Suisse has been particularly arrant. In the 1970's, the bank handled dirty money from Italian companies trying to evade taxes. When these companies later went bankrupt, Credit Suisse refused to give the money back, but the companies could not   find   relief in court since it would mean admitting that they had been laundering money [85].

The documentary evidence that exists shows that it was Credit Suisse that helped Marcos start his secret Swiss accounts and played the biggest role in his money laundering capers. Credit Suisse offices in Manila, Hong Kong, and Zurich were mobilized to serve these accounts. Walter Fessler, Ernest Scheiler, and Charles Souviron attended the dictator from Zurich, while Rolf Klein served as the contact in Hong Kong. Fessler is known to have personally visited the dictator in 1968. Credit Suisse specified that one of their men would be stationed in Hong Kong so that Marcos could be easily attended to within a few hours notice.

Credit Suisse soon reaped the benefits of the financial advice it extended to Marcos. It received the bulk of Marcos' initial investments in the Swiss accounts. Within a few months, Marcos and Imelda had already opened four accounts in the Hong Kong branch of Credit Suisse. Three accounts were current accounts, while one was a securities account. The first deposit in these accounts was for $950,000 in 1968.

The couple used pseudonyms for these accounts and a set of code words when communicating with the bank. Marcos used William Saunders as his pseudonym, while Imelda used Jane Ryan. William Saunders was the name Marcos found on the dogtag he had stolen from a dead American GI during the war. In a recovered contract, Imelda signed herself as Jane Ryan, and then re-signed below as Imelda R. Marcos. Regina Marquez and Mrs. Santos were other names Imelda used in her Swiss accounts. It was agreed that all correspondence between Credit Suisse and Marcos would have the words "for GEP on the first page, and code words such as Sugar, Copra, Lumber, would be used to designate the month. Withdrawals would Dear "Happy Birthday" as a code. These code words would be supplemented by code numbers as a further security measure. All the communications would be in two envelopes. The outer would have the proper code words and designated PO Box address, while the inner envelope would be free from writing. Mail from Switzerland was sometimes sent to Marcos through a fictitious name and a post office box address: Antonio Martinez, PO Box 4539, Manila.

Available records show that among the earliest deposits into these accounts were transmittals from Security First National Bank in Beverly Hills. The account under the name of William Saunders (Credit Suisse Acct. No. 417571) was credited with $200,000, while the account under the name of Mrs. Jane Ryan (Credit Suisse Acct. No. 415059) was credited an amount of $100,000. Both transmittals occurred on 27 March 1968.

When the Saunders account grew, Credit Suisse provided another layer of precaution by transferring some of the funds to newly-opened accounts in Liechtenstein. Around a million dollars was transferred in 1970 from the Saunders to Xandy, a foundation organized by Credit Suisse in Vaduz, the capital of Liechtenstein. At least 15 accounts are known to have been established in Liechtenstein.

Other recovered records clearly show the deep involvement of Credit Suisse with Marcos in the late 1960's and early 70's. One Credit Suisse document dated 17 December 1969 showed a balance of $69,605.56 for Account #362050, named "[not clear! Investment." The document also showed that the account held shares in the Marinduque Mining & Industrial Corp., a large Philippine mining concern, as of the prior week (10 December 1969). Another bank statement dated 31 December 1969 showed a balance of $99,998.10 for another Credit Suisse account, #362049/07.   Another
statement from the same period revealed yet another account from Credit Suisse as receiving a credit of $17,189.43 on 12 January 1970, representing interest earned on a fiduciary account of $330,000.

Another early Swiss account organized by Marcos was Foundation Rosalys, a Marcos family foundation organized in September 1971 with an initial deposit of $1.198 million. Close Marcos associates such as Benedicto, Jose Campos Yao, and Baltazar Aquino helped organize this foundation [86]. Money for the foundation came from "deed of gift" handwritten by Mateos.

Different associates have admitted their knowledge of Marcos' money laundering schemes involving Swiss banks. Baltazar Aquino, a former cabinet member, admitted laundering between $400,000-$600,000 every two weeks. The money represented kickbacks from Japanese corporations doing business in the Philippines. Aquino changed the payoffs which were denominated in yen to dollars through money changers in Hong Kong, and then wired the funds to Fribourg, Switzerland [87]. Another cabinet member, Jaime Laya, the former Central Bank Governor and Minister of Finance, also admitted to the close links Marcos enjoyed with the Swiss. Laya claims that during the financial crisis in 1983, the dictator directed his Swiss bankers to use his accounts to purchase a substantial amount of treasury notes [88].

Marcos then later branched out and utilized other banks, both in Switzerland as well as other places, for his dirty money transactions. When his bedroom safe was studied after he fled Malacanan, among the documents that surfaced were papers establishing that Marcos had also been working through Bankers Trust AG Zurich for years. Another item discovered was a fiduciary account with a balance of $350,000 as of 23 December 1969 with the Bank of Montreal, Canada.

A special trust account was also established for the Marcos children. The account, numbered C7711, was to be shared amongst the three children when Marcos and Imelda died. The account was worth more than $20 million in 1982.

Throughout his years in power, Marcos established many accounts under fictitious names and under the names of the many "foundations" to hide the ownership of the assets in these secret accounts. He regularly deposited his loot in these accounts. We believe we are not exaggerating when we say that Marcos and his cronies can qualify as one of the best customers the Swiss banking system ever had.

Other documents dealing with the Swiss accounts that were retrieved from Marcos' files show how Marcos utilized nominees to manage and front for his Swiss accounts. The papers show Marcos opening fiduciary accounts through a financial management firm, Corraterie Gestion Coges S.A., and later delegating the equivalent of a Power-of-Attorney to Stephane Cattaui, a private banker from the Geneva-based Banque Paribas [89], to act on his behalf.

Among the documents recovered was a letter to Corraterie Gestion Coges directing the firm to open a fiduciary account on Marcos' behalf. The letter authorized the Corraterie Gestion Coges to use the firm's name and invest in short-term accounts for Marcos' accounts. The letter, written in French and personally signed by Marcos, stated:

> *Je vous autorise par la presente d proceder, selon votre libre appreciation, au placement partiel de mes liquidites et notamment a effectuer en votre nom, mais a titre fiduciare pour mon compte et a mes risques et perils, des depots a court terme, portant interets, aupres de banques de votre choix, aux meilleures conditions du marche.*
> *Pour ces depots, je vous serais oblige de crediter un compte fiduciare a mon nom du ou des montants des depots que vous aurez effectues aupres de banques pour mon*

compte [90],

Another document, again personally signed by Marcos, gave Stephane Cattaui blanket powers to manage and dispose of some of Marcos' assets. The document endowed Cattaui with

> *Une PROCURATION GENERALE comprenant les pouvoirs les plus intendus de representation, de gestion, d'administration et de desposition; cas echeant, ces pouvoirs*
> *s'entendent au contu de tous coffres dipendant du compte precise ci-apres.*

It appears that Cattaui was one of the Swiss bankers Marcos trusted most. Cattaui had served as the personal banker of Marcos and Imelda since 1981 and was given great discretion over the Swiss assets of the Marcos family. In a 17 May 1984 letter to Banque Paribas, Marcos instructed that all his assets in several accounts, Account #036521N, 036517J, 037973R, 038150L, and 038489Z, be transferred to Lombard Odier & Cie in Geneva, later to be credited to COGES 00777, a special account with Credit Suisse. Marcos gave Cattaui full powers over these accounts. In a declaration of trust executed in Geneva, Marcos wrote that Cattaui was

> *empowered to act in full faith on my behalf, and to take all decisions he will see fit to the best of my interests.*
> *Furthermore, Mr. Cattaui is to remain a Director of all the companies and/or foun-dations on which he is presently acting on my behalf, until notice to the contrary is given in writing by me or my attorneys, [original in English]*

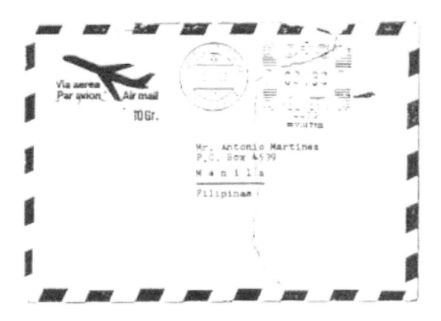

Photocopy of an airmail envelope addressed to Antonio Martinez from Switzerland. *Antonio Martinez* was one of the names Marcos used for his Swiss correspondence.

Photocopy of bank document personally signed by Marcos giving Stephane Cattaui Power-of-Attorney for some of his Swiss accounts.

At least $83 million was sent into the Cattaui-managed account from 1982 through 1986. Some of the funds came from the Security Bank in Manila.

Apart from managing their accounts, Cattaui was also the account officer who handled the initial $34 million loan for the acquisition of the building now known as the Crown Building in New York (discussed in the section on real estate). The loan from Banque Paribas was extended to Lastura Corp. NV, the front corporation used by Imelda for her real estate deals. Cattaui is now employed by Corraterie Gestion Coges S.A., an affiliate of Lombard Odier & Cie. Marcos also has accounts in both Lombard Odier and Corraterie Gestion.

Anticipating his eventual downfall, Marcos tried to destroy all evidence relating to nis Swiss accounts. Six heavy-duty paper shredders were put to work. After two weeks of continuous use, four of the paper shredders conked out due to sheer exhaustion, while two continued to function even as the mob came rushing into the Malacanan presidential palace as Marcos fled. Inspite of the continuous work of the paper shredders and the indiscriminate damage caused by the unruly mobs, important papers relating to the Swiss accounts were still recovered. The documents, several inches thick, were account statements from Swiss banks such as the Swiss Bank Corp. and Credit Suisse. A partial listing of these Marcos accounts, including a partial listing of the known accounts of some of his cronies in bank accounts in Switzerland and other places:

Account	Number	Bank	Account Holder
Aurora Marcos			
Avertina Foundatkm	211924	Credit Suisse	Marcos
Azio Foundation	212174	Credit Suisse	Marcos
Charis Foundation	248619	Credit Suisse	Marcos
Eulogio Balao	51244	Credit Suisse	Marcos
Ferdinand Marcos	362-049	Credit Suisse	Marcos
Ferdinand Marcos	362-050	Credit Suisse	Marcos
Ferdinand Marcos	40940	Credit Suisse	Marcos
Jane Ryan	51960	Credit Suisse	Marcos
Jane Ryan	52616.4	Credit Suisse	Marcos
Jane Ryan	93667	Credit Suisse	Marcos
Jane Ryan	94687	Credit Suisse	Marcos
Jane Ryan	98929	Credit Suisse	Marcos
Jane Ryan	415059	Credit Suisse	Marcos
Maler Foundation	134240	Credit Suisse	Marcos
Palmy Foundation	391528	Credit Suisse	Marcos
Spinus Foundation	444434	Credit Suisse	Marcos
Valamo Foundation	467429	Credit Suisse	Marcos
Verso Foundation	469393	Credit Suisse	Marcos
Vibur Foundation	469857	Credit Suisse	Marcos
William Saunders	417571	Credit Suisse	Marcos
Wintrop Foundation	487324	Credit Suisse	Marcos
Xandy Foundation	491972	Credit Suisse	Marcos
Etablissement Mabari		Lombard, Odier & Cie	Marcos
Etablissement Gladiator	00777	Corraterie Gestion Coges	Marcos
Angenit Inv. Corp.	01-001-8850-9	Wing Lung Bank Ltd.	Marcos
Bullseye –		Banque Paribas –	Marcos
Cesar –		Banque Paribas –	Marcos

Account	Number	Bank	Owner
Establissement Gladiator –		Banque Paribas –	Marcos
Establissement Mabari –		Banque Paribas –	Marcos
Pretorian –		Banque Paribas –	Marcos
	018-9-8064-58 –	Hong Kong Shanghai –	Tantoco
Pyrenean Inv. Co. -	-	Chemical Bank (Suisse) –	Tantoco
- 5759 -	Banca Nazionale Del Lavorro – Tantoco		
Sanmar Export Corp -	-	Citibank –	Tantoco
Rustan Comm. Corp –	43169 –	Citibank –	Tantoco
Sanmar Export Corp. –	544-0-78500 –	Manufacturers Hanover –	Tantoco
Sanmar Export Corp. –	1224247601 –	Standard Chartered Bank –	Tantoco
Paradela Holding –	100104140-28 –	Banco Pedroso NA –	Benedicto
Tradewinds Int. Bank & Trust -		Banco Pedroso NA –	Benedicto
Rio Picura -		Banco Pedroso NA –	Benedicto
Rio Topalisa -		Banco Pedroso NA –	Benedicto
El Parabien -		Banco Pedroso NA –	Benedicto
Julia Benedicto -		Banco Pedroso NA –	Benedicto
Benedicto -		Banco Pedroso NA –	Benedicto
Francisca B. Paulino -		Banco Pedroso NA –	Benedicto
- 10010410828 -	Banco Pedroso NA –	Benedicto	
- 10010411628 -	Banco Pedroso NA –	Benedicto	

Account	Number	Bank	Owner
Benedicto		California Overseas	Benedicto
Tradewinds Int. Bank & Trust		California Overseas	Benedicto
Errol E.C. Layne	792-003437	California Overseas	Benedicto
Benedicto		Standard Chartered	Benedicto
Azucarera-La Yaguara	06 13216-C	Banco Prov. NV	Benedicto
Azucarera-La Yaguara	66205242	Banco Prov. NV	Benedicto
Paradela Hold. Corp.		Banco Prov. NV	Benedicto
Paradela Hold. Corp.	910-1-636142	Chase Manhattan NY	Benedicto
Paradela Hold. Corp.	8900112	Banco Consolidado CA	Benedicto
Paradela Hold. Corp.	8900295	Banco Consolidado CA	Benedicto
Paradela Hold. Corp.	8900230	Banco Consolidado CA	Benedicto
White & Case Trust	018-410191	South East Bank	Benedicto
First Vancouver	94000-004-0902	Toronto Dominion Bank	Benedicto
First Vancouver	482084	Toronto Dominion Bank	Benedicto
Palmiro Invst. Ltd.	320/631684	Societe Generate Alsacienne	Benedicto
Etablissement Mabari		Lombard Odier & Cie	Adnan Khashoggi
Etablissement Gladiator	00777	Corraterie Gestion Coges	Adnan Khashoggi
Rodolfo Arambuloo	616-101406-126	Belgian Bank	R. Arambulo
Rodolfo Arambulo	216121358	Security Pacific National	R. Arambulo

This is merely a partial listing of the accounts. We are sure that there are many more accounts which have not yet been uncovered. But from the data already in our possession, it is possible not only get an idea of the magnitude of the amounts involved but also concretely show how dirty money is recycled.

To understand how the Swiss banking system recycles dirty money it is necessary to take a detailed look at some of the documents recovered from Marcos' files. While the documents that escaped Marcos' paper shredders cover different time periods and are therefore somewhat uneven and spotty in their coverage, our present discussion will be the most detailed expos6 of the workings of the Swiss banking system that has hitherto been made. Our discussion of a few selected accounts will draw on the official bank statements that Credit Suisse issued for the different foundations Marcos used to shelter his assets:

AVERTINA

The Avertina Foundation had two accounts with Credit Suisse totalling $115.5 million [91]. Account No. 211924 had investments in oil, office and computer equipment, real estate, financial holding companies, and non-ferrous metals in USA, Canada, Aruba-Curacao, Luxembourg, Norway, Federal Republic of Germany, Netherlands, Sweden, Switzerland, and the Philippines, It also held US Treasury Bills through Swiss American Securities Inc. (SASI) in New York.

Account No. 211925 had investments in steel and coal, aluminum, non-ferrous metals, oil, chemicals, aircraft and aerospace, electrical equipment and electronics, office equipment and supplies, industrial equipment, food and soft drinks, drugs and cosmetics, containers, financial holding companies, public utilities (electricity, gas, water), service industries and unclassified securities in the Philippines, Great Britain, USA, Canada, Aruba-Curacao, Luxembourg, Australia Bahamas, Japan, Panama, and others.

The second Avertina account has gold bars kept with the Bank of Delaware, Wilmington, Delaware, USA as part of its precious metals investments. The gold bars are described as *"Fein"/"Fein Oder Besser"* (i.e., Auf Englisch, of fine or high-grade quality or better). These deposits are interesting to note in light of our previous discussions concerning the gold reserves of the Philippine treasury.

AVERTINA FOUNDATION: Crddit Suisse Account No. 211924
Mosey Market Investments:
USA Treasury Bills with SASI New York
Bonds and Similar Investments:
AB Volvo
Ciba-Geigy Int. Nederland with Deutsche Bank Ag, Frankfurt
Citicorp Overseas Finance Corp. NV - Notes
Communaute Europeenne Du Charbon e de L'Acier Ceca, Luxembourg, SASI – Notes
Communaute Europeenne Du V. Charbon e de L'Acier, CECA, Luxembourg
GMAC Overseas Finance Corp. - Notes
IBM World Trade Corp. - Notes
Mafina BV
Norsk Hydro
Province of Quebec
Province of Saskatchewan
Schuldsch. Bundes-Republik Deutschland with Credit Suisse Luxembourg
Shares and Similar Investments:
Atlantic Richfield Co. with SASI
International Business Machines Corp. Swiss Certificates
Marinduque Mining & Industrial Corp. with SASI
Vetropack Holding, SA, Saint-Prex
Investment Trusts:
Anteile Interswiss Schweiz.Liegenschaften-Anlagefonds

Total Market Value:$4,013,217.00
DM CURRENT ACCT. -3467($1,300.00)
US$ CURRENT ACCT. -865($865.00)

TOTAL$4,011,052.00

AVERTINA FOUNDATION: Credit Suisse Account No. 211925 [92]
Money Market Investments:
Barclays, London Fiduz.Festgeldanlage

CS London Fiduz.Festgeldanlage 089179315
CS London Fiduz.Festgeldanlage 989177494
Hypo, Luxembourg, Fiduz-Festgeldkonto
Bonds and Similar Investments:
AB Volvo
Air Canada with Deutsche Bank Ag, Frankfurt
Australia with Deutsche Bank Ag, Frankfurt
Best Electric Co. Ltd. - Notes
BHP Finance Ltd.
Broken Hill Proprietary Co. Ltd. Private Placement
Credit Suisse (Bahamas) Ltd. 1982
Credit Suisse (Bahamas) Ltd. 1983
Desterreichische Kontrollbank Ag Okb Wen with Dresdner Bank, Ag Frankfurt
Electricite de France with Bayerische Hypotheken-Wechselbank, Miinchen
Intl. Bank for Reconstruction & Development World Bank Swiss-Franc Linked Bonds
Int. Bank for Recon. & Dev. (World Bank)
Int. Bank for Recon. & Dev. (World Bank) - Notes
Mafina BV
Norsk Hydro
Notes Oesterreich with WestDeutsche Landesbank, Duesseldorf
Ontario-Hydro 1981
Ontario-Hydro 1982
Province of Quebec, with Commerzbank Ag, Frankfurt
Renault Acceptance, Amsterdam with Deutsche Bank Ag, Frankfurt
Ricoh Co. Ltd. Tokyo with Commerzbank Ag, Frankfurt
Ropex Corp. (Del.) with SASI
Sanyo Electric Co. Ltd. Osaka
Schuldsch.Bundes-Republik Deutschland with Credit Suisse Luxembourg
Schuldsch.Bundes-Republik Deutschland with Credit Suisse Luxembourg
Schweden with Deutsche Bank, Ag Frankfurt
Schweden with Deutsche Bank, Ag Frankfurt
Teotlisuuden Voima DV-Industrins Kraft An with Westdeutscfae Landesbank, Dusseldorf
Texaco Capital NV – Notes
Shares and Similar Investments:
American Hospital Supply Corp. with SASI USA
Atlantic Richfield Co. with SASI USA
Boeing Co. with SASI USA
Broken Hill Proprietary Co. Ltd. with ANZ Nominees, Ltd. Melbourne
  AUSTRALIA
Centex Corp. with SASI USA
Cetus Corp. with SASI USA
Credit Suisse, Zurich, SWITZERLAND
Digital Equipment Corp. with SASI USA
F. Hoffman-La Roche & Co., Ag Basel SWITZERLAND
Fortune Systems Corp. with SASI USA
Fujitsu Ltd. with Daiwa Securities Ltd. Tokyo JAPAN
General Dynamics Corp. with SASI USA
General Electric Co. Swiss Cert. USA

General Instrument Corp. with SASI USA
Getty Oil Co. with SASI USA
Hewlett-Packard Co. with SASI USA
IFI Int., LUXEMBOURG
Intl. Business Machines Corp. IBM Swiss Certificates USA
Intl. Business Machines Corp. IBM with SASI USA
Johnson & Johnson with SASI USA
Marinduque Mining & Industrial Corp. with SASI PHILIPPINES
Mitchell Energy & Development Corp. with SASI USA
Namen-AkL Gba-Geigy Ag, Basel, SWITZERLAND
NEC Corp., with Daiwa Securities Ltd. Tokyo JAPAN
Noble Affiliates Inc. with SASI USA
Northern Telecom Ltd. with SASI CANADA
Oakbridge ltd. with Anz Nominees Ltd. Melbourne AUSTRALIA
Peko Wallsend Ltd. with Anz Nominees Ltd. Melbourne AUSTRALIA
Pennzoil Co. Swiss Cert. USA
Raytheon Co. with SASI USA
Ropex Corp. (Del.) with SASI RESTRICTED USA
Ropex Corp. (Del.) with SASI RESTRICTED USA
Sandoz, Basle, SWITZERLAND
Schlumberger Ltd. Curacao with SASI ARUBA-CURACAO
SCI/Tech SA with Kredietbank, SA, LUXEMBOURG
Shell Oil Co. with SASI USA
Standard Oil Co. Indiana Swiss Cert. USA
Sntex Corp. with SASI PANAMA
nited Energy Resources Inc. with SASI USA
United States Surgical Corp. with SASI USA
Weeks Petroleum Ltd. Bermuda with ANZ Nominees Ltd. Melbourne BERMUDA
Woodside Petroleum Ltd. with Anz Nominees Ltd. Melbourne AUST RALIA
Zurich Vereicherungs-Gesellschaft, Zurich, SWITZERLAND

Investment Trusts:
Anteile Interswiss Scbweiz-liegenschaften-Anlagefonds
Precious Metals
Goldbarren 1 Kilo Fein with SASI/Bank of Delaware, Wilmington
Goldbarren Standard Fein Oder Besser with SASI/Bank of Delaware, Wilmington
Goldbarren Standard Fein with SASI/Bank of Delaware, Wilmington

                                    Total Market Value$108,088,446.00
                         * * *

PALMY FOUNDATION: Credit Suisse Account No. 391526 [93]
The Palmy Foundation had investments in buildings, oil, chemicals, electrical equipment and electronics, office equipment and supplies, food and soft drinks, tobacco and alcoholic beverages, drugs and cosmetics, containers, retail trade, banking and finance, and insurance in Switzerland, Belgium/Luxembourg, Germany, Netherlands, Canada, USA and other countries.
Investments in the following
Aetna Life and Casualty Co. with SASI
American Telephone and Telegraph Overseas Finance

Bayer Ag
Bek Electric Co. Ltd.
Ciba-Geigy Ltd. Basle
Citicorp with SASI
Colgate Palmolive Company with SASI
Credit Suisse (Bahamas) Ltd.
Crown Cork and Seal Co. Inc. with SASI
Dow Chemical Co. Swiss Certificates
Hi Lilly & Co. with SASI
F. Hoffman-La Roche and Co. Ltd. Basle
Gersy (?) Pacific Fund Ltd. Bermuda with Bank of Bermuda Hamilton
Halliburton Co. with SASI
Heineken NV Amsterdam with Bank Morgan Labouchere Nv A Dan
Hilton Int. Co.
IBM World Trade Corporation Notes
International BusinessMachines Corp. IBM Swiss Certificates
Interswiss Swiss Mutual Fund for Real Estate
Int. Bank for Recon. & Dev. (World Bank) with Bk F. Gemeinwirtschaft
Frankfurt
Intl. Standard Electric Coro.
K-Mart Corporation with SASI
Norton-Simon Inc. with SASI
Petrofina SA Bruxelles with Boue Bruxelles Lambert
Philip Morris Inc. Swiss Certificates
Phillips Petroleum Co. Swiss Certificates
Revco D.S. Inc. with SASI
Revlon Inc. with SASI
Royal Bank of Canada with Credit Suisse Canada Toronto
Royal Dutch Petroleum Co.
Siemens Ag
Swissmobil Neue Serie Schweiz.Immobiliar-anlagen
Texas Oil and Gas Corp. with SASI
Transocean Gulf Oil Co. - New Gulf Oil Corp.
USA Treasury Bills with SASI
Weyerhaeuser Co. with SASI

Total Market Value: $4,205,871.01
Credit Balance on US$ Account$4,644.71
Credit Balance on DM-Account$430.88
Credit Balance on Gold Account $394,400.00
Fiduciary Account at CS. London$189,211.68
Fiduciary Account at GS. London$605,000.00
TOTAL$5,399,558.28

* * *

SCOLARI FOUNDATION: Credit Suisse Account No. 435070 [94]
The Scolari Foundation had several million dollars in fiduciary accounts with Credit Suisse accounts in London. The account also included investments in oil, chemicals, office equipment and supplies, food and soft drinks, drugs and cosmetics, photo and optical products, and retail trade in Switzerland, Netherlands, other European countries, USA, Canada, and others.
Investments in the following

Avon Products Inc. with SASI
Colgate Palmolive Co. with SASI
Credit Suisse
Dow Chemical Co. with SASI
Eastman Kodak Co. with SASI
Eli Lilly & Co. with SASI
Halliburton Co. with SASI
International Business Machines Corp. w/ SASI New York
Instituto Per Le Opere Di Religjone Citta Del Vaticano Notes
Minnesota Mining and Manufacturing Co. Swiss Certificates
Norton Simon Inc. with SASI
Phillips Petroleum Cp. with SASI
Royal Dutch Co.
S.S. Kresge Co. with SASI
Transocean Gulf Oil Co.
Union Oil Int. Finance Corp.

Total Market VateeSI,672,864.00
Balance on FRS Account$15,814.13
Balance on DM Account$l,206.25
Balance on US$ Account$49,118.01
Fiduciary Accounts:
US$ - Credit Suisse London$l,570,000.00
US$ - Credit Suisse LondonSl,040,000.00
US$ - Credit Suisse London$l,570,000.00
US$ - Credit Suisse London$l,570,000.00
USS - Crddit Suisse LondonSl,050,000.00
US$ - Credit Suisse London$800,000.00
USS - Credit Suisse London$1,200,000.00
US$ - Credit Suisse London$350,000.00
USS - Crddit Suisse London$3,000,000.00
USS - Credit Suisse London$1,280,000.00
USS - Credit Suisse London$11,525,000.00
TOTAL$26,694,002.39

* * *

SPINOS FOUNDATION: Crddit Suisse Account No. 444434 [95]
The Spince Foundation had investments in government and corporate bonds and company stocks, as well as several fiduciary accounts. The total investments amounted to $77,616,043.44. This statement is curious in that it did not contain a summary description of the industries, and there were discrepancies between the total amount in the statement and the actual amount as we calculated it in our spreadsheet [96].
Investments in the following
Australia Notes
Austria Notes with Westdeuts. Landesbk. Dusseldorf
Baker Int. Corp. Swiss Certificates
Bank of Japan Finance Notes
BBC Brown Boveri Finance - Curacao NV
Best Denki Notes
Boeing Co. with SASI
Broken Hill Proprietary Co. Ltd. ANZ Nominees Ltd. Melbourne
Cetus Corp with SASI
EG A G Inc. with SASI
Eurofima Ste. Europ. Pour Le Finance de Material Ferroviaire Notes with SASI
F. Hoffman-La Roche and Co. Ltd. Basle
Fujitsu Ltd. - Daiwa Sec. Co. Ltd. Tokyo
Galaxy Oil Int. NV

General Dynamics Corp. with SASI
Getty Oil Co. with SASI
Heizer Group with SASI
Helmerich & Payne Inc. with SASI
IFI Int. SA
International Business Machines Corp. with SASI
Int. Bank for Recon. & Dev. (World Bank) Notes Second Issue
Int. Bank for Recon. & Dev. (World Bank)
Mitchell Energy & Development Corp. with SASI
Nippon Electnc Co. Ltd. Daiwa Sec. Co. Ltd. Tokyo
Noble Affiliates Inc with SASI
Oakbridge Ltd. ANZ Nominees Ltd. Melbourne
Oesterreichische Kontrollbank - Dresdner Bank Ag Frankfurt
Peko Walbend Ltd. ANZ Nominees Ltd. Melbourne
Ricoh Co. Ltd. Tokyo with Commerzbank Ag Frankfort
Sandoz ltd. Basle
Schlumberger Ltd., Curacao with SASI
Schuldscheine Badische Kommunale Landesbank-Girozentrale with Credit Suisse-
Luxem.Luxembourg
Shell Oil Co. with SASI
Standard oil Co. Indiana. Swiss Certificates
Swiss Aluminum Ltd. Alusuisse Chippis
Tauemautobahn Ag Salzburg with Westdeuts. Landesbk. Diisseldorf
Texaco, Inc. Swiss Certificates
United Energy Resources Inc. with SASI
United States Surgical Corp. with SASI
Varco Intl. Finance NV
Veba Ag - Schuloscheindarlehen
Weeks Petroleum Ltd. ANZ Nominees Ltd. Melbourne
Woodside Petroleum Ltd. ANZ Nominees Ltd. Melbourne

Total Market Value:$7,788,894.00
Credit Balance on SFR Acct.:$50,258.90
Debit Balance on DM Acct.:$2,229.15
Debit Balance on USS Acct.:S3,464.91
Subtotal: $7,883,458.84
Fiduciary Accounts
Barclays Bank Int., London$lO,000,000.00
Barclays Bank Int., London$2,674,964.40
Barclays Bank, London$6,000,000.00
Barclays Bank, London$6,000,000.00
Barclays Bank, Luxembourg$610,000.00
BOA Wien$2,780,000.00
Deutsche Bank, Luxembourg$340,000.00
Deutsche Bank, Luxembourg$5,140,000.00
Deutsche Bank, Luxembourg$6,000,000.00
Deutsche Bank, Luxembourg$6,000,000.00
Deutsche Bank, Luxembourg$2,949,148.25
Dresdner Bank, Luxembourg$6,000,000.00
Dresdner Bank, Luxembpurg$2,563,507.55
Dresdner Bank, Luxembourg$2,674,964.40
Lloyds Bank Int. LondonSlO,000,000.00
TOTAL$77,616,843.44

* * *

TRINIDAD FOUNDATION: Credit Suisse Account No. 463498 [97]
The Trinidad Foundation had investments in non-ferrous metals, buildings, oil, chemicals,

electrical equipment and electronics, office equipment and supplies, passenger cars and trucks, tire and rubber, food and soft drinks, tobacco and alcoholic beverages, drugs and cosmetics, containers, retail trade, banking and finance, insurance and service industries in Switzerland, Belgium/Luxembourg, Germany, Netherlands, USA, Canada and others.

Investments in the following:
Adam Opel Ag Ruesselsheim
Allg. Elcktr.-GesAeg-Telefunken Berlin-Frankfurt
American Brands Overseas NV
Bayer Ag Leverkusen
Borden Overseas Capital Corp.
Cargill Inc. Notes with SASI
Chevron Overseas Finance Co. with SASI
Ciba-Geigy Ltd. Basle
General Shopping SA
Heineken Nv Amsterdam w/ F. Van Lanschot Hertogenbo6ch
Hilton Int. Co.
Hoffman-La Roche U. Co. Ltd. Basle
Int. Nickel Co. of Canada Ltd. Swiss Certificates
Intl. Standard Electric Coip. New York with SASI
K-Mart Australia Properties Finance Ltd.
Petrofina Sa Bruxelles with Generale Brussels
Royal Bank of Canada w/ Credit Suisse Canada Ltd. Montreal
Royal Dutch Co.
Siemens Ag
Swissimmobil New Series
Transocean Gulf Oil Co.
Transocean Gulf Oil Co. Notes
Uniroyal Inc. Swiss Certificates
Weyerhaeuser Co. with SASI

Total Market Valued,$2,246,207.00

Balance on S.Frs. Account$33,774.09
Balance on DM Account$l,409.45
Balance on Dollar Account$27,089.26
Balance on Fiduciary Account$184,426.00

TOTAL:$2,492,905.80

* * *

VALAMO FOUNDATION: Credit Suisse Account No. 467429 [98]
The Valamo Foundation had investments in aluminum, oil, aircraft and aerospace, electrical equipment and electronics, office equipment and supplies, industrial equipment, drugs and cosmetics, financial holding companies, public utilities, electricity, gas, water in Switzerland, Belgium/Luxembourg, Germany, other European countries, USA, and other countries.
Investments in the following:
Australia Notes
Austria Notes with Westdeuts. Landesbk. Diisseldorf
Baker Int. Corp. Swiss Certificates
BBC Brown Boveri Finance Curacao
Best Denki conve.
Boeing Co. with SASI
Eg & G Inc. with SASI
Eurofima Ste Europ. Pour le Finance de Materiel Ferroviare Notes with SASI
General Dynamics Corp. with SASI
Getty Oil Co. with SASI

Helmerich and Payne Inc. with SASI
IFI Int. SA
Int. Bank for Reconstruction and Development 77-84
Int. Bank for Reconstruction and Development Notes 76-83
International Business Machines Corp. with SASI
Long Term Credit Bank of Japan Finance Notes
Mitchell Energy and Development Corp. with SASI
Noble Affiliates Inc. with SASI
Oesterreich Kontrollbank Notes with Dresdner Bank Ag Frankfort
Pennzoil Co. Swiss Certificates
Ricoh Co. Ltd. Tokyo with Commerzbank ag Frankfort
Sandoz Ltd. Basle
Schlumberger Ltd. Curacao with SASI
Schuldscheine Badische Kommunale Landesbank-Girozentrale with Credit Suisse Luxembourg
Schuldscheine Deutsche Bank with Deutsche Bank ag Diisseldorf
Swiss Aluminum Ltd. Alusuisse Chippis
Tauemautobahn Ag Salzburg with Westdeuts.Landesbk. Diisseldorf
United Energy Resources Inc. with SASI
Veba Ag Schuldscheinedarlehen

Total Market Value:$7,513,629.00
Credit Balance on DM Acct.$ll,874.35
Credit Balance on SFR Acct.$12,271.66
Credit Balance on USS Acct.$8,492*9

Fiduciary Accounts
DM w/Nederi. Credietbank NV, Amsterdam$5,181*47.15
DM with Credit Suisse, London$l,709,844*6
DM with N. Creditbank, Amsterdam$l,968,911.92
DM with Nederl. Credietbank, Amsterdam$2.331,606.22
US$455,000.00
US$2,300,000.00
USS w/ Can.Imp.Bank of Commerce Toronto$5,870,000.00
USS with Amro, Rotterdam$3,700,000.00
USS with Crddit Suisse, London$5,000,000.00
USS with Credit Suisse, London$5,500,000.00
USS with de Bary, Amsterdam$2,650,000.00
USS with Hypo, Luxembourg$5,000,000.00
USS with Rabo, Amsterdam$8,200,000.00
USS with Toronto Dominion, Toronto$8,100,000.00

TOTAL$65,512,977.45

* * *

WINTROP FOUNDATION: Credit Suisse Account No. 487324 [99]
The Wintrop Foundation had two accounts with **Credit Suisse.**
Account No. 487324 had investments in aluminum, non-ferrous metals, oil, chemicals, electrical equipment and electronics, office equipment and supplies, food and soft drinks, drugs and cosmetics, and containers in Switzerland, Germany, Netherlands, other European countries, Canada, USA, and others.
Account No. 487325 had investments non-ferrous metals, oil, office equipment and supplies, food and soft drinks, containers in Switzerland, Belguim/Luxembourg, Germany, France, Netherlands, other European countries, Canada, USA, and others.

Investments in the following;
Akzo NV Arnhem

Akzo Nv Arnhem Conv.
Allied Chemical Corp. with SASI
Alusuisse Capital Ltd. Conv.
American Home Products Corp. with SASI
Atlantic Richfield Co. with SASI
Australia Notes
Best Denki Conv.
Broken Hill Proprietary Co. Ltd.
Canada Notes with Deutsche Bank Ag Frankfort
Ciba-Geigy Ltd. Basle
Fiat Finance Corp. Notes
General Electric Co. Swiss Certificates
Halliburton Co. Swiss Certificates
International Business Machines Corp. Swiss Certificates
Interswiss Schweiz.Liegenschaftenanlagefonds Zurich
Mafina BV
Marinduque Mining and Industrial Corp. Phil, with SASI
Min.Industrial Bank of Japan Finance Co. Notes
New Zealand with Commerzbank Ag Frankfort
Norton Simon Inc. with SASI
Norway Notes
Province of Ontario with Warburg-Brinckm.Wirtz Hamburg
Sanyo Electric Co. Ltd.
Schering-Plough Corp. with SASI
Schuldsch.Bayerische Landesanstalt Fuer Aufbaufinanzierung
Schuldscheine Deutsche Bank with Deutsche Bank Ag Diisseldorf
Schuldscheine Westdeutsche Landesbank Girozentrale with Westdeuts.Landesbk.
Diisseldorf
Shell International Finance Notes 1977-87
Shell International Finance Notes 1978-90
Sumitomo Forestry Co. Ltd. Notes
Swiss Aluminum Ltd. Alusuisse Chippis
Tauemkraftwerke AgSalzburg
Teollisuuden VoimaDy Industrins Kraft
Vetropack Holding SA St-Prcx
Volvo Goeteborg
Warner-Lambert Co. Swiss Certificates

Total Market Value:
$12,397,192.00
Fiduciary Accounts:
DM Credit Suisse London$2,642,487.04
DM Credit Suisse London$2,176,165.80
DM Deutsche Bank Luxembourg$176,165.80
US$600,000.00
USS Credit Suisse London$l,620,000.00
USS Toronto Dominion Bank Montreal$2,200,000.00

Subtotal$21,812,010.64
Balance on DM Acct.$2,888.31

Debit Balance on USS Acct.($6,844.62)
TOTAL$21,808,054.33

* * *

WINTROP FOUNDATION: Credit Suisse Account No. 487325 [100]

Investments in the following:
    AB Volvo Goetebrog
    Atlantic Richfield Co. with SASI
    Australia Notes
    Bank of Tokyo Ltd. Notes
    Banque Francaise Du Commerce Exterieur Notes
    Citicorp Overseas Finance Corp. Ltd. Notes
    Eurofima Ste Europ. Pour le Finance de Materiel Ferroviaire Basle
    European Investment Bank Notes
    High Authority of the Europ. Coal & Steel Community Notes with SASI
    High Authority of the Europ. Coal and Steel Community
    International Business Machines Corp. Swiss Certificates
    Interswiss Schweiz.Liegenschaften-An!agefonds Zurich
    Mafina BV
    Marinduque Mining & Industrial Corp. Phil, with SASI
    Norsk Hydro As
    Norton Simon Inc. with SASI
    Norway Notes
    Norway Notes with SASI
    Province of Ontario with Warburg-Brinckm.Wirtz Hamburg
    Province of Quebec Notes
    Province of Saskatchewan
    Schuldscheine Landesbank Schleswig-Holstein Girozentrale with Credit Suisse-
    Luxemb. Luxembourg
    Tauemkraftwerke Ag Salzburg
    Vetropack Holding SA

                                        Total Market Vahie:$3,074,144.00

                                                Fiduciary Accounts:
                    USS The Credit Suisse Luxembourg SA$820,000.00
                                                    US$$160,000.00
                                    Balance on USS Acct.$20,839.80
                                            TOTAL$4,074,983.80

                                        * * *

XANDY FOUNDATION: Credit Suisse Account No. 491972 [191]
The Xandy Foundation had two accounts with **Credit Suisse**.
Account No. 491972 had investments non-ferrous metals, oil, office equipment and supplies, food and soft drinks and containers in Switzerland, Belgium/Luxembourg, Germany, France, Great Britain, Netherlands, other European countries, USA, Canada, and other countries. Account No. 491973 had investments in aluminum, non-ferrous metals, oil, chemicals, electrical equipment and electronics, office equipment and supplies, food and soft drinks, drugs and cosmetics, and containers in Switzerland, Germany, Great Britain, Netherlands, other European countries, USA, Canada, and other countries.

Investments in the following;
    Atlantic Richfield Co. with SASI
    Australia Notes
    Bank of Tokyo Ltd. Notes
    Banque Francaise Du Commerce Exterieur Notes
    Bayerische Landesbank Girozentrale Serie - Globalzert.Quellensteuerfrei with
    Dresdner Bank Ag Frankfurt
    British Petroleum Co. Ltd.
    Credit Commercial de France Notes
    Eurofima Ste Europ. Pour le Finance de Materiel Ferroviaire Basle

European Investment Bank 1975-80
European Investment Bank Notes 1975-82
High Authority of the Europ. Coal and Steel Community 1976-84 Notes
High Authority of the Europ. Coal and Steel Community 1976-86
International Business Machines Corp. Swiss Certificates
Interswiss Schweiz.Liegenschaftenanlagefond Zurich
Mafina BV
Marinduque Mining and Industrial Corp. Phil, with SASI
Norges Kommunalbank with Westdeutsche Landesbk Diisseldorf
Norsk Hydro Ag
Norton Simon Inc. with SASI
Norway Notes 1976-81
Norway Notes 1976-81 with SASI
Philips Gloeilampenfabrieken NV Notes 1972-79
Philips Gloeilampenfabrieken NV Notes 1975-80
Province of Ontario with Warburg-BrinkmWirtz Hamburg
Province of Quebec Notes
Province of Saskatchewan
Sanwa Bank Ltd. with Credit Suisse While Weld Ltd. London
Tauemkraftwerke Ag Salzburg
Vetropack Holding
Volvo Goeteborg

Total Market Value:$3,602,860.00

Fiduciary Account:
USS Canadian Imperial Bank Toronto$l10,000.00
Balance on USS Acct. $34,861.86
TOTAU$3,747,721.86

* * *

XANDY FOUNDATION: Credit Suisse Account No. 491973 [102]
Investments in the following:
Akzo NV Arnhem
Allied Chemical Corp. with SASI
Alusuisse Int. Willemstad Conv.
American Home Products Corp. with SASI
Atlantic Richfield Co. with SASI
Australia Notes
British Petroleum Co. Ltd. Notes
Broken Hill Proprietary Co. Ltd. Private Placement
Canada Notes with Deutsche Bank Ag Frankfort
Ciba-Geigy Ltd. Basle
Fiat Finance Corp. Notes
General Electric Co. Swiss Certificates
Halliburton Co. Swiss Certificates
Industrial Bank of Japan Finance Co. Notes
International Business Machines Corp. Swiss Certificates
Interswiss Schweiz.Liegenschaftenanlagefond Zurich
Mafina
Marinduque Mining and Industrial Corp. Phil, with SASI
New Zealand with Commerzbank Ag Frankfort
Norges Kommunalbank with Westdeutsche Landesbk Diisseldorf
Norton Simon Inc. with SASI
Norway
Philips Gloeilampenfabrieken NV Notes 1972-79
Philips Gloeilampenfabrieken NV Notes 1975-80

Province of Ontario with Warburg-Brinckm.Wirtz Hamburg
Schering-Plough Corp. with SASI
Schuldsch.Bayerische Landesanstalt Fuer Aufbaufinanzierung Westdeutsche Landesbk Diisseldorf
Shell Int. Finance NV Notes 1977-87
Shell Int. Finance NV Notes 1978-90
Swiss Aluminum Ltd.
Tauemkraftwerke Ag Salzburg
Teollisuuden Voima Oy Industrins Kraft with Westdeutsche Landesbk Diisseldorf
Vetropack Holding SA St-Prex
Volvo Goeteborg
Warner-Lambert Co. Swiss Certificates

Total Market Valu«$12,267,501.00
Balance on DM Acct.$8,521.45
Balance on US$ Acct.$63,084.95

Fiduciary Accounts:
USS Canadian Imperial BantToronto$I,250,000.00
USS Canadian Imperial Bank Toronto$500,000.00
USS Canadian Imperial Bank Toronto$2,100,000.00
US$ Canadian Imperial Bank Toronto$200,000.00
US$ Credit Suisse London$I,100,000.00
USS Toronto Dominion Bank Montreal$I,250,000.00
TOTAL$18,739,107.40

* * *

These bank statements represent only a small part of total number of the Swiss accounts Marcos owned. They are merely sample statements from eight accounts in one Swiss bank, Credit Suisse. Our sample list does not include the other accounts and foundations that Marcos held with Credit Suisse and other banks in Switzerland, Liechtenstein, Luxembourg, and Austria. Marcos is known to have at least 15 accounts under names of foundations in Liechtenstein. At least one of these accounts was reported to have $800 million [103]. We are also convinced that many accounts belonging to Marcos and his cronies remain unknown.

Another limitation with the data is that they are summary statements of the accounts at a particular point in time. They do not give an indication of how the accounts grew over time through interest and investment earnings, and the injection of new funds.

But inspite of the inherent limitations of our data, much is still revealed by these bank statements. They show in a very concrete way how Marcos dirty money was recycled and reintroduced to the international monetary system as "clean money." The statements from Credit Suisse show that the money Marcos deposited in his Swiss accounts were later reinvested in different forms of financial assets such as stocks, corporate and government bonds, treasury notes from different countries, fiduciary accounts in other banks, money market placements, investment trusts, and investments in precious metals. The companies where Marcos dirty money was reinvested cover a variety of investment areas and are among the most stable and respected of the world's firms.

It appears that the recycling of dirty pesos into clean, crisp dollars started early in Marcos' career. Records indicate that Credit Suisse reinvested money from the

Saunders and Ryan accounts in different financial markets as early as 1970. Recovered papers show that Credit Suisse, working from Zurich, bought $35,000 worth of shares from Mellon National Bank & Trust, London through the Stock Exchange of London on 6 February 1970. The purchase was for Marcos under the William Saunders account. Imelda had ner share as well. Records also show that Credit Suisse bought OTC (over-the-counter) securities worth $15,907.56 for the Mrs. Jane Ryan, account on 23 January 1970.

These early transactions with the Saunders and Ryan accounts defined the pattern for recycling Marcos dirty money which was later used for the other accounts. Money stolen from Philippine corporations and the national treasury were transported through different methods, deposited in accounts under fictitious names and private foundations, and later reinvested in real assets such as real estate purchases and overseas corporations, or financial assets such as those earlier enumerated.

A closer examination of these accounts also reveals the precise method of how Credit Suisse recycled the bulk of Marcos money. The records clearly show that Marcos investments in company shares and in US Treasury bills were done through SASI (Swiss American Securities Inc.). SASI, a subsidiary of Credit Suisse, is a stockbrokerage firm operating in New York and trades with the most important US stock exchanges sucn as the New York Stock Exchange [104]. Such investments allow money of questionable origins to be reintroduced to the international financial system and thus complete the cycle of Marcos dirty money.

Such a flow of hiding and transporting stolen pesos and later reintro- ducing them into the international monetary system as legitimate dollars can be presented in a model diagram:

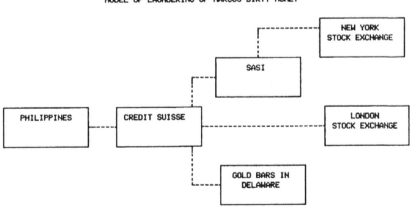

MODEL OF LAUNDERING OF MARCOS DIRTY MONEY

It is to be emphasized that this graph is presented as a model to understand the general process of how Marcos dirty money was laundered. A detailed accounting of how each stolen peso was transformed into overseas investments is not possible within the scope of the present book and the present state of knowledge concerning the overseas properties of Marcos and his cronies. But the preceeding discussion should be able to give a good idea of how the Marcos gang was able to launder money and invest m all kinds of financial assets. In the next section we shall take a look at one form of investment which became a favorite of Marcos and his cronies.

DIRTY MONEY AND REAL ESTATE INVESTMENTS

Real estate investments in the US was another way through which Marcos and his cronies employed their extra cash [105]. They splurged millions and bought properties in the most expensive areas. The US East and West coasts were favorites for acquisition, but there were also important investments in Texas and Washington state.

Kokoy Romualdez [106], Imelda's brother, is believed to have purchased an expensive estate in Long Island, New York using a front corporation, White Fence Inc. The corporation was organized by the Wall street law firm of Davis, Polk & Wardweil on July 1980, the time the purchase of the estate was made. Allan Flynn, a partner of the law firm, said that all his firm did was to forward bills to the owners, whom he declined to identify. Daniel Romualdez, Imelda's nephew, and Lydia Nicasio, the niece of Kokoy's wife, are believed to also have been involved in the purchase. The estate, located in First Neck Lane, Southampton, was purchased for $425,000   in   cash   in   July 1980 and is known to have undergone an extensive $600,000 renovation. The place is also believed to have been used to temporarily hide the expensive art works and antiques which were housed in the East 66th Townhouse [107].

Other members of the Romualdez family were also busy buying properties at other places.

Tolosa Resources, named after the town in Leyte where the Romualdezes originated, was organized in California on 6 June 1983 to acquire properties in the US West Coast. Incorporators were members of the family of Eduardo Romualdez Sr., Imelda's uncle and former ambassador to the US:

* Concepcion V. Romualdez - wife of Eduardo Romualdez
* Eduardo V. Romualdez, Jr. - son of Eduardo Sr.
* Antonio V. Romualdez - son of Eduardo
* Norma Romualdez Nierras - daughter of Eduardo
* Jose V. Romualdez - a son of Dr. Alberto Romualdez, the brother of Eduardo Sr.

Among the purchases of this group were

* house at 23411 Armita Street, Canoga Park, I os Angeles for $218,900 in 7 March 1983.
The bouse was initially bought under the name of Concepcion but the title was later transferred toTokxa Resources on 28 March 1984. The value of the property was estimated at $350,000 in 1985.
* house at 3778 Callan Boulevard, South San Francisco, purchased by Eduardo Jr. and his wife, Buena T. Romualdez on 13 December 1984 for $120,000.
* a residence at 1580 Forest Villa Lane, McLean, Virginia owned by Antonio. This 4-bedroom, 3-bath, 2-fireplace, fully air-conditioned home was originally purchased at $191,345 but was estimated at $500,000 in 1985.

Another member of the Romualdez family busy purchasing US real estate was Margarita Romualdez, one of Imelda's favorite nieces and wife of Abelardo Licaros Jr., the son of Marcos' Central Bank governor. Among the purchases of Margarita were expensive residences and condominiums in California:

• a million-dollar estate at 2940 Privet Drive, Hillsborough, California which Margarita uses as a residence
• a half-million dollar condominium, Unit #70, at Stem Grove Condominium complex, located at comer of 19th Avenue and Sloath Boulevard in San Francisco
        • a second half-million dollar condominium Unit #77 at the Stem Grove complex
• a condominium unit at 1970 Scott Drive, San Francisco, purchased in July 1978 for a reported $200,000.
• a residence at 281 Lake Drive, San Bruno, California, purchased in July 1983 for a reported $200,000.

Imelda's youngest brother, Armando, and his wife, Vilma, were also busy buying properties in Sacramento, California. They bought a $197,000 2,500-sauare-foot house on 1 June 1982 in Rancho Murieta, Sacramento. Armando followed this purchase by buying five vacant lots in the area, two vacant lots next to his house, at the corner of Pera Drive and Piano Court, followed by purchases of three other vacant lots worth $225,000 [108].

Armando was reported to be so much in a hurry to occupy the house that he did not mind tnat it was without furnishings. He solved the problem by immediately going to Brauners, a local department store, and bought furniture worth $30,000 in an afternoon. A store employee, describing how Armando paid for the furniture, said that the money was m $20 bills and were in $2,000 bundles: "When it came time to pay, he went out to the car and came back with a paper sack full of cash" [109]. Armando also bought a new car within the week of his stay in Sacramento. A Sacramento   developer describes Armando's habits:

He was always dropping money. And he only carried $100's and $50's. He hated anything smaller than a $20 bill and sometimes just threw his small change into a paper bag [110].

Armando and his family occupied the house for only a short period and then left it vacant for years.

Other individuals and groups connected with the Marcos regime were also busy making real estate purchases throughout the US.

Fortuna Marcos Barba, the dictator's sister, purchased real estate in California, among which were

* a lot in Lancaster County for $150,000 on 3 December 1980
* a three bedroom house, 511 North Oxford Ave., Los Angeles, California
* another three bedroom house, 2352 Lynn Court, West Covina, California, on 5 October 1981

Ricardo Silverio, after acquiring multimillion loans from foreign banks and government institutions, milked his companies and became a big-time investor in California. An odd collection of eight properties in the southern San Francisco area, including two Shell gasoline stations and a 7-11 Super-market, was estimated at $10 million in 1985. Aside from these, Silverio also used Astroair, Silcor, and other shell corporations to purchase many expensive real estate properties. One investment was 105 acres of land for a condominium and shopping mall in Lancaster, Los Angeles. When his real estate offices were opened in Daly City, south of San Francisco, it was reported that Cristina, Enrile's wife, was present in the inaugural ceremonies. A partial list of Silverio's real estate properties:

* two parcels of land in Lancaster, Los Angeles, on December 1984 for $6 million, intended for a planned housing and shopping center, purchased through three shell corporations: Silcor (Nevada), Lancaster Properties of Oregon, and Oregon Co-Partnership.
* residence at Hillsborough, the "millionaires row" in the San Francisco Bay Area, purchased for $850,000 in 1981
* house, 1115 Lakeview Drive, also in Hillsborough, bought through a shell corporation based in Nevada, Astroair Services, (sold in April 1985)
* condominium in Harbor View Villas complex, bought through Astroair on September 1981
* condominium, #10, Lot 30, Hillsdale, San Mateo, (sold in 1979)
* condominium, #10, Lot 31, Hillsdale, San Mateo, purchased on August 1978 through Astroair Services
* condominium, Golden Gateway Commons, San Francisco, purchased in 1980 through Astroair Services, estimated at $400,000 in 1985
* ten parcels of land, Pointe Pacific Estates, Daly City, California, purchased through Silcor.

Danding Coiuangco [111] and his wife, Soledad "Gretchen" Oppen, started their purchases as early as 13 October 1977, purchasing an apartment, Apt. #1508, at 10535 Wilshire Blvd, Los Angeles. This was followed by a condominium, #1024, at 1177 California St., San Francisco, purchased for $750,000 in 1981 through Bertex Estates Ltd., a shell corporation based in Hong Kong. Signatory for Bertex was Isabel Cojuangco Suntay. Bertex is also the registered owner of Jewelmer, a jewelry store in Beverly Hills, one of the most exclusive residential areas in tne US. Cojuangco owns another jewelry store of the same name in Manila which specializes in pearls. Soleaad also purchased two other apartment units (#109 and #110) at Park Westwood Towers, Los Angeles, on 28 June 1984. The units were later transferred to Ferman N.V., a shell corporation based in the Netherlands Antilles, presumably to hide ownership. Apart from concealing ownership, the transfer was also possibly an attempt to evade taxes. The units were purchased for $555,005 m 1981 but were sold for $550,005 in 1984, a period when land values in the area had considerably appreciated. Selling it at a "loss" to the shell corporation exempted them from capital gains taxes.

The murder of Benigno Aquino precipitated a rash of further real estate purchases. Edna Guiyab Camcam, described by a US State Department official as the "long-time mistress" of General Ver, went on a "condo-buving spree" seven weeks after Aquino's assassination [112]. She bought three Manhattan condominiums at 80 Park Ave. for $441,500 in October 1983. Camcam also owns a lavish waterfront home in Islip, Long Island. The 8,600-square-foot brick and stucco house boasts of 13-rooms and 4 baths and its own private road. The house was bought for $495,000 on January 1982 but is now estimated to be worth more than $1 million. The house is reported to have specially-built closets which conveniently partition Camcam's wardrobe into the different seasons of the year. Her son is known to drive around New York in expensive sports cars.

A sampling of other known purchases gives an idea of the extent of Marcos and crony investments in US real estate:

* an expensive coop apartment in 700 Park Ave., New York, owned by Rodolfo Cuenca
* a 13-story hotel, the Webster, on West 45th St., between 5th and 6th Aves., New York. This hotel was purchased on 23 June 1980 for $1,577,000 by Consolidated Equities, a limited partnership owned by Agusto Camacho and Pablo Figueroa, individuals who were Imelda's partners in the purchase of other real estate properties (discussed later). Other partners mcluded Thelma Figueroa, wife of Pablo; Bernadette Reyes, the daughter of Eduardo Reyes, a trusted Marcos government official; Avelino Aventura, the director of Imelda's Philippine Heart Center. Other investors included Romeo Gatan, brought into the deal by Figueroa, who invested $169,000 into the hotel. A former military officer, Jose Fronda, testified before the US congressional Committee on Foreign Affairs on February 1985 that Gatan was one of those who paid him to "execute or liquidate certain persons whom the military establishment wants to be executed or liquidated for various reasons." The testimony admitted to the murders of at least 50 Marcos opponents. The hotel was later sold for $5.5 million in April 1985.
• a 403-acre subdivision outside of Spokane, Washington owned through a Netherland Antilles shell corporation connected to the Marcoses was reported by the Seattle Post-Intelligencer [113].
• The Oregonian, a newspaper also based in Washington, reported another purchase in the state, involving 14 acres in the Camas area, just on Northwest Sierra Lane, providing a grand view of the Columbia river. According to an investigative article by Holley Gilbert, a writer for the paper, Mariano D. Bondoc and Manuel D. Martinez, two Filipinos   formerly connected with the Ministry of Human Settlements, Imelda's super-ministry, signed a $205,000 contract in 1982 representing half-interest in the choice Camas property [114].
* a 14-story 456-room hotel in San Juan, Puerto Rico was among the properties of one of the architects Imelda used as fronts and partners in real estate investments [115]. The brother of this architect had other real estate properties in New Orleans.
* The Granville Hotel, a deluxe 40-unit hotel in an exclusive area of Los Angeles, was also owned by men close to the Marco6 regime. The hotel was purchased by Voltaire Investments in August 1983. The president of this company is a Filipino named Efrenilo M. Cayanga, but it is widely believed that the key people behind this $5 million hotel are General Ver and Michael de Guzman, a financier close to Ver and Marcos, who operate through several Hong Kong shell corporations, one of which is Sorgain Co. Ltd. De Guzman was also connected with an Austrian bank believed to have links to Marcos (discussed later in this section).

The major real estate investments in the US were Imelda's purchases of real estate in New York, Yao's investments in Texas and Seattle, and crony purchases in California. The more important of these investments and the use of shell corporations to hide the ownership of these properties will now be discussed in detail.

To facilitate her purchases of prime real estate properties in Manhattan, Imelda organized many shell corporations based in Hong Kong, Panama, and the Netherland Antilles and enlisted the help of the following key individuals [116].

* **Gliceria Tantoco** was one of the closest friends and business associates of Imelda [117]. Tantoco assisted Imelda in the purchase of precious art and antiques for the East 66th Townhouse, as well as multimillion dollar buildings in Manhattan, such as the Crown Building, the Herald Center, 40 Wall Street, and 200 Madison Avenue (discussed in more detail later), using front corporations. Tantoco sent coded cable messages to Imelda in Manila to report on tne status of the buildings, using names such as Midtown Cement for 200 Madison Ave., Farragamo for the Crown Building, Bridgetown for 40 Wall Street, and Lafayette for the Herald Center. Esquire was used hide the identity of Joseph Bernstein, another key participant in the Manhattan real estate purchases.
Many documents later recovered show Tantoco's deep involvement in the purchases, such as a hand-written letter to Imelda and a three-page memorandum addressed to The Beneficial Owners of Canadian, Voloby, NY Land, and Glockhurst analyzing use of $37.5 million loan from Citibank for NYLand, a company used in the purchases. A handwritten 1984 report by one of Imelda's personal aides shows Tantoco receiving a payment of $5.5 million in connection with the buildings. Also closely involved in these purchases was her son, Rico, who held certificates of Voloby Ltd., another front corporation. Tantoco arranged for loans for the Manhattan properties but was later discovered to have diverted $7.5 million from a Citibank loan to pay for a "personal indebtedness" to the bank. A US federal grand jury sitting in New York later indicted Tantoco for wire fraud and the making of false statements in connection with the bank loans, the purchase of 200 Madison Avenue, and the refinancing of the Herald Center and the Crown Building. Tantoco never appeared before the grand jury to answer these charges and was later declared to be a fugitive from justice.
* **Antonio Floirendo** was instrumental in Imelda's involvement in the lucrative sugar trading business in New York as well as the use of Hong Kong front corporations to purchase the Olympic Towers (discussed in Chapter III and in the next pages).

* **Rolando Gapud,** one of Marcos' financial advisers [118], replaced Tantoco in February 1985 as the Marcos' representative in New York real estate deals. Gapud was deeply involved in dollar remittances to the US using the Security Bank, partly to finance the purchase of New York commercial properties. He was also key in developing the shell corporations in Hong Kong, Panama, and Netherlands Antilles used to acquire these properties. Closely helping Gapud in these deals was Rolando Zamora, Marcos' assistant for legal affairs. Gapud ctoeely worked with lawyer Irwin Robinson and the Bernstein brothers in connection with the Manhattan properties. Gapud was also used by Marcos with some California firms, such as ACRI/Dynetics.

* **Fe Bea Gimenez and Vilma H. Bautista**, personal assistants of Imelda, also played important roles in the purchase of Manhattan real estate. Gimenez was Imelda's executive secretary and personal aide, while Bautista served as personal secretary whenever Imelda was in New York. Bautista, who worked in the Philippine Consulate in New York and in the Philippine Mission to the United Nations as part of her cover, coordinated with Gimenez in renovating some of the properties for Imelda, such as the Lindenmere and the Townhouse. Bautista, reporting to Gimenez, also disbursed funds from Thetaventures, one of their front corporations, as evidenced by March 1984 report which mentions a payment of $6 million to Floirendo.

* **Joseph and Ralph Bernstein** played key roles in helping the Marcoses purchase and conceal ownership of their Manhattan properties. The two brothers are not well liked by New York real estate insiders who wonder how they were able to accumulate capital rapidly. While relatively inexperienced, they were able to use their New York Land Co. (NYLand) to engineer multimillion deals with the help of Marcos financing.

The purchase of the Crown Building was the first project of the Bernsteins involving significant Manhattan real estate.

NYLand bought 40 Wall St., renovated Crown Building, developed Herald Center. Ralph managed the Townhouse and the other New York commercial properties for Imelda.

Joseph Bernstein was called to testify on the real estate holdings of the Marcoses by a US congressional committee and was cited for contempt when he refused to testify. His moves to invoke attorney-client privilege when he refused to disclose his dealings with Imelda were not considered by the US Congress.

Among the other properties associated with NYLand and the Bernstein brothers are 30 Wall St., a historic building, reportedly purchased by NYLand on September 1982; the New York Realty Building (29 West 5vth St.) purchased through the office of Bernstein, Carter & Deyo and Shalimar Ltd., a shell corporation based in the British Virgin Islands, for $9.4 million on March 1982; the 55-story Americas Tower on the Avenue of the Americas, between 45th and 46th Sts., a joint-venture with Kumagai Gumi, a Japanese construction company which did business in the Philippines with Disini, a favored Marcos crony. Construction costs for the latter project was estimated at $150 million in 1985, but costs may have gone up during the last few years of the building's construction [119].

The next pages outline how shell corporations were used in the purchase in some of the major real estate properties in the US.

* * *

SEATTLE

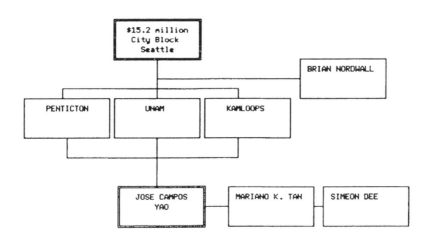

SEATTLE

Jose Campos Yao, the trusted Marcos ally and crony we discussed in the previous chapter, together with his associates, purchased a whole city block in Seattle, Washington in 1983.

Using Unam Investment Corp., a shell corporation based in the Netherlands Antilles, Yao and his associates purchased Seattle real estate worth $9,178,215 on

13 May 1983. The acquisition included the following properties:

600 Pike St.
614 Pike St.
1506 Sixth Ave.
1520 Sixth Ave.
1515 Seventh Ave.
1521 Seventh Ave.
1575 Seventh Ave. [120]

The original plan for the block was to raze the Payne apartments, displacing the low-income families, and build a convention center. The purchase proved to be a bargain for Yao since the previous owner had asked for $19.6 million when the properties were put up for sale a year earlier.

Two other shell corporations connected with Yao made other real estate purchases in Seattle. Kamloops Investment Coro, acquired the defunct Central Hotel on 1520 Fifth Ave., which was valued by King County assessor at $3.4 million. Penticton Investment Corp. bought two other properties on 19 December 1983, 525 Cherry St. and 516 James St., paying a total of $3.1 million for both. These purchases, together with the previous Unam acquisitions, brought the value of all the Seattle holdings known to be connected with Yao to a total of $15.2 million.

Jose Campos Yao is the president of Unam Investment Corp. and is the vice-president of Kamloops and Penticton, while Mariano K. Tan, a close Yao associate, is the president of the latter firms. Simeon Dee, Yao's uncle who is based in Vancouver, British Columbia is also associated with these firms. Unam has offices in offices in Manila, Hong Kong, and Vancouver, and, together with Kamloops, has links with Curacao Corp. Co., another Netherlands Antilles corporation.

Apart from using shell corporations for the purchase, Yao and his associates also hid their identities from the Seattle attorney who represented them and worked through Simeon Dee until the final negotiations.

The common origin of these three shell corporations was noted by Seattle Deputy Assessor Bernie Ryan who pointed out that all three companies paid their taxes using identical checks. Further evidence of the close connection between these firms is that Brian Nordwall, a Seattle attorney, is the registered agent for all three firms.

TEXAS

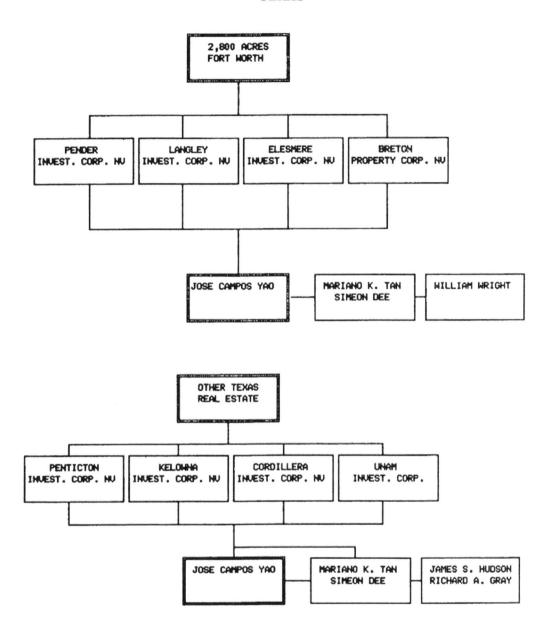

TEXAS

Yao also bought as much as 5,000 acres of prime Texas land in the late 1970's and early 1980's. The land was primarily in Tarrant County, Dallas, but the acquisitions also included land in San Antonio and Corpus Cristi. These land holdings, consisting of primarily choice rural acreage, were valued at $51 million [121].

A total of 2,773 acres near Fort Worth and Dallas were bought in 1977 and 1978. The land came in five large tracts ranging from 13.5 to 948 acres in size. The tracts were along

US 287 and Interstate 35-W north of Fort Worth;
Boat Club Road near Lake Country Estates northwest of Fort Worth;
along 1-35 W south of Fort Worth.

The properties were assessed at $13,165,630 in 1984. The land was acquired using the following Netherland Antilles shell corporations:

Pender Investment Corp NV
Langley Investment Corp. NV
Elesmere Investment Corp NV
Breton Property Corp NV.

Richard Gray Jr., a Dallas broker who handled most of these transactions for Yao, initially denied any connection with Yao or Marcos, saying that these purchases were done by "..just a businessman from the Philippines." But Yao has since admitted to owning these shell corporations and properties.

Other land Yao and his associates owned in Texas, however, has already been liquidated. Unam, for example, sold a 297-acre tract along Eagle Mountain Lake to the Texas Parks and Wildlife Dept, in July 1980 [122]. Other Yao-owned Netherland Antilles corporations such as Cordillera Inv. Corp., Kelowna Inv. Corp., and Penticton Inv. Corp. and individuals close to Yao were also busy buying and selling land in Texas. An example of the purchase and sale of land m Texas using shell corporations from the Netherlands Antilles was documented by the *Fort Worth Star-Telegram*. The following sequence of events is a good example of the attempt to conceal the identities of the principals:

* 15 April 1979 - James S. Hudson, a business partner of Richard A. Gray, buys two parcels totalling 624 acres from the Tarrant Savings Association
* 9 July 1979 - Hudson sells the 624 acres to Penticton & Kelowna
* 17 October 1980 - Cordillera buys a 13.5 acre tract from Routen Realty Co.
* 6 December 1982 - Cordillera files Power of Attorney for Addison Wilson III and Richard A. Gray. The Power-of-Attomey is signed by Simeon Dee, Cordillera's treasurer
* 7 February 1983 - Cordillera sells the land to Addison Wilson III, who sells the land the same day to 3 Houston men

The layers of shell corporations and individuals serving as nominees were convenient measures that concealed the ownership of the properties. Cordillera Inv. Corp. N.V has the following officers:

Jose Y. Campos - President
Mariano K. Tan - Vice-president
Simeon Dee - Treasurer
William J. Wright - Secretary

Wright is the Vancouver-based attorney of Campos. He also is connected with Unam. Kelowna and Penticton have an identical set of officers:

Mariano K. Tan - President
Jose Campos Yao - Vice-president
Secretary and Treasurer - Simeon Dee

CALIFORNIA: VELASCO

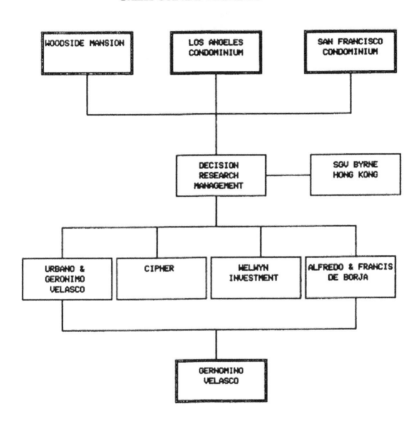

CALIFORNIA: VELASCO

Geronimo Velasco, Marcos' Minister of Energy, was connected with several expensive properties in California:

- mansion, 140 Farm Road, Woodside, CA, $15 million (price as of 1986)
- condominium, 2185 Century Hill, LA., $675,000 (price as of 3 June 1982)
- luxury condominium, #1104,999 Green St., Russian Hill, San Francisco, $400,000 (price as of 1984)

The properties were acquired through either Decision Research Management, a shell company based in Hong Kong, or through Velasco's nephew, Alfredo de Borja.

On one occasion, Velasco swore that he "never heard" of Decision Research Management. On another occasion he claimed that "I don't know anything about

Decision Research M. Ltd." On yet another occasion, Velasco exhibited detailed knowledge of Decision Research while continuing to disclaim any connections with it:

> To my knowledge, DR is controlled by a group of foreign investors organized by a friend and business associate whose identity I cannot disclose without his permission, although
> I must point out that this person has no dealings whatsoever with MOE or PNOC. He is a European-based investor with a solid reputation in international financial circles.
> This friend was instrumental in arranging the financing on the acquisition by DR of the houses in Woodside, CA and Century City LA which were mentioned as belonging to me. Due to legal requirements imposed by the counsel for the financiers, title to the properties is reserved by DR but I have a right to use the premises and also the option to purchase the same.

While Velasco disclaims any interest in these properties, records show that the Hong Kong-based shell company has Velasco's children, Urbano and Geronimo Jr., as shareholders, and that three of Velasco's nephews are directors. Listed as directors of Decision Research are:

Patrick De Boija
Alfredo De Boija
Francis De Boija
Cipher Ltd.
Directorate Ltd.

We had the opportunity to note earlier that Cipher Ltd. and Directorate Ltd. were two Hong Kong-based shell companies linked to SGV Byrne and were involved in the transit of dirty money from the Philippines.

Velasco's sons own two of the 10,000 shares of Decision Research, while Wellwyn Investment Corp., another shell corporation based in Panama, controlled the remaining 9,998. Wellwyn lists its address with Johnson, Stokes, & Master, a Hong Kong-based British law firm which specializes in shell companies. Decision Research, on the other hand, lists its address with the office of SGV-Byme.

Alfredo de Borja, Velasco's nephew, reportedly manages most of Velasco's overseas properties. De Boqa served as the agent purchasing the Woodside house, signing a $675,000 promissory note on the property in 1979 [123].

While Velasco has tried to again disclaim his connection with the Woodside mansion [124], Patrick, Alfredo's brother, resides in it. Patrick de Boija describes the house, which boasts of an elaborate security system, as a "family home" where Velasco stays. After the fall of the Marcos government, Velasco used this mansion as his base of operations while making trips to Singapore and Geneva.

Alfred de Boija is the founder and president of the Overland Trading Co. The firm is the company which handles the US purchases of the Ministry of Energy, the government department headed by Velasco.

CALIFORNIA: CUENCA

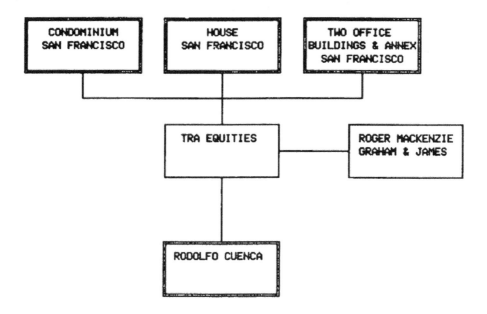

CALIFORNIA: CUENCA

Rodolfo Cuenca, discussed in the previous chapter as the crony who dominated the Philippine construction industry, was connected with several real estate purchases in San Francisco through TRA Equities Inc., a shell corporation registered in the state of Delaware [125]. A list of the San Francisco properties connected with either Cuenca or TRA Equities Inc.:

* condominium, 1177 California St., San Francisco
* home in 2741 Bershire Dr., San Bruno (half-interest)
* home, 131 Devonshire, San Francisco
* 2 office buildings, 625 Market St., San Francisco
* annex, 25 New Montgomery, San Francisco

The condominium on California St. was listed originally under Cuenca's name, but the papers were later transferred to TRA Equities, Inc. And while formal ownership of the house in Devonshire St. also has been transferred to TRA Equities, but it continues to be occupied by Cuenca's daughter, Marianne. Cuenca's lawyer, Roger Mackenzie, is president of TRA Equities Inc. Mackenzie is evasive about the true owners of TRA and says that he does not know if Cuenca is involved in the firm. Mackenzie connected with Graham & James, the San Francisco-based legal firm which represented a number of Marcos cronies.

The two office buildings on Market St, together with the annex on Montgomery St., are valued at $10.3 million in 1983.

NEW JERSEY

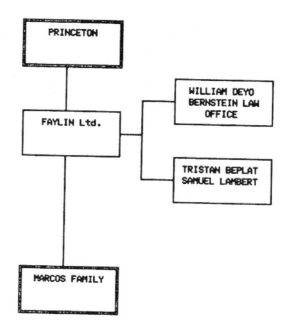

NEW JERSEY

A set of expensive houses were bought in New Jersey for the Marcos children when they were studying in Princeton and the Wharton Business school.

Imee, Marcos' eldest daughter, was given an 18th-century estate to live in while she was studying in Princeton. The estate, located on 3850 Princeton Pike, Mercer County, Lawrence, Princeton, New Jersey, was purchased on October 26 1982. It includes a historic mansion and 13 acres of land lying beside the battle field of Trenton. The historic mansion had been owned for generations by the Johnson family of New Jersey.

It is estimated that the Marcos family spent approximately $3 to 5 million in furnishings and improvements on the property. The mansion and the 13-acre grounds were later sold for $1 million m October 1987.

A shell corporation based in the British Virgin Islands, Faylin Ltd. Corp., was used to acquire and hide the ownership of the property. The registered address of Faylin was listed as the Bernstem law office:

c/o William Deyo Esq.
Bernstein, Carter & Deyo
29 W 57th Street
New York, NY 10019

All papers dealing with the Princeton property and Faylin Ltd. were to be sent to the Bernstem law office. William Deyo, a partner of the Bernstein law office, represented Faylin Ltd. in the purchase of the property and also served as the notary in the sale.

Marcos'only son, Ferdinand Jr., was given a house in 19 Pendleton Drive, Cherry Hill, New Jersey when he was studying in the Wharton Business School of the University of Pennsylvania. The house was bought for $119,000 on April 1985.

A second house was bought in the area for the servants and the security men serving the son. The second house, located at 4 Capshire Drive, Cherry Hill, New Jersey, was purchased for $90,000 on 23 November 1978 by Julian L. Antolin Jr. Antolin, a lieutenant colonel in the Philippine Army, was a military attache assigned to Philippine Mission to the United Nations in New York. The title to the house was later transferred to Irwin P. Ver on November 26 1979. Irwin headed the Philippine Presidential Security Command, a battalion of 15,000 men personally loyal to the dictator, and is the son of Marcos' Chief of Staff, General Fabian Ver. Antolin and the younger Ver were classmates at the Philippine Military Academy and were close mends.

Tristan Beplat played an important role in the purchase of all of these houses in New Jersey. Beplat was a former senior vice-president at Manufacturers Hanover Trust Co. and was in charge of the Overseas (Asian) Affairs for the bank. He enjoyed a cozy relationship with the Marcos family, receiving such honors as a presidential medal from Marcos, the Golden Heart Award, in 1971. Beplat was also included in Marcos' guest list when the dictator was honored at the White House during the Marcos State visit.

Beplat served as the broker and agent for Faylin Ltd. in the purchase of the 13-acre Princeton estate. He was also the agent for the nouse at 19 Pendelton Drive.

Beplat was also associated with another house in New Jersey linked to the Marcoses, the residence at 231 Dodds Lane, Princeton, New Jersey. This house, initially used by Imee Marcos, was listed under Beplat's name and was purchased with the help of Samuel Lambert III Esq., the lawyer used by Beplat to acquire the property. Beplat maintained andf received the bills for the Dodds Lane residence, as well as the other Marcos New Jersey properties.

OLYMPIC TOWERS

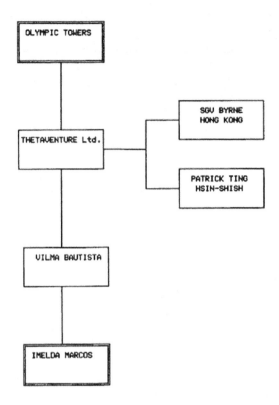

OLYMPIC TOWERS

A total of five expensive Manhattan condominiums are known to have been bought by Imelda and Floirendo at the Olympic Towers. The Olympic Towers, located on 5th Avenue, New York City's central thoroughfare, is a luxury high-rise building in the center of New York and is right beside Saint Patrick's Cathedral, one of the city's most famous landmarks.

Three adjacent condominiums on the 43rd floor of Olympic Towers were bought in [1981]. The walls of all three condominiums were torn down to form a gigantic L-shaped apartment covering almost a whole city block. The resulting three-in-one condominium gave a panoramic view of New York City ana its suburbs from its north, south, and east sides. From this height, other famous city landmarks such as the Empire State, World Trade, PanAm, and Newsweek buildings, seen so closely through the floor-to-ceiling glass windows, give an appearance of being part of the apartment's furnishings. Right in front of Imelda's bedroom is a majestic view of Central   Park   and the Crown Building she owned. (The contents of the apartment which remained after it was cleaned out by Floirendo were partially described in Chapter I.) Typical of all Imelda's houses, the condos in Olympic Towers were renovated to have marble-tiled bathrooms, complete with gold-plated faucets. Imelda's personal bathroom was redone with her favorite pink marble and was complete with a jacuzzi, while the other bathrooms had beige-colored marble.

These three condominiums were officially bought by Thetaventure Ltd., a Hong Kong based shell corporation. Thetaventure lists its address at the SGV Byrne Hopewell Centre in Hong Kong and names Patrick Ting Hsiun-snish as one of its directors and subscribers. Vilma Bautista, Imelda's personal secretary, is the authorized agent for Thetaventure. Floirendo also admitted to fronting for Imelda for these apartments.

The three condominiums were purchased for a total of $688,000. The remodeled three-in-one condo was later resold for $3.75 million.

Another condominium at the Olympic Towers on 641 5th Avenue was Apartment H on the 29th Floor. The condominium was purchased by Floirendo on September 1976 for $270,000. It was bought through his Philippine automotive marketing chain, United Motors, which also had an office at 210 West 70th St., New York City.

A fifth OlympicTower apartment associated with Marcos and his cronies was bought, and this was resold on February 1985 for $1.1 million.

The last two apartments were bought by Sugarbush Corp. NV, a shell company based in tne Netherlands Antilles, but it was Floirendo's brother-in-law, Rodolfo del Rosario, who signed the papers. The shell corporation has appointed del Rosario and Floirendo with full power of substitution throug a special Power-of-Attorney. Floirendo organized a shell corporation to front as the formal owner of the apartments and that this front has in turn given Floirendo and del Rosario legal power to act on its behalf. Legal work was done by the law office of Rosenman, Colin, Freund, Lewis & Cohen.

LINDENMERE

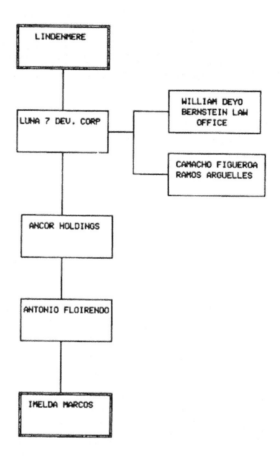

LINDENMERE

Imelda also acquired her own resort, a private enclave of 13.5 acres on the southern shore of Long Island with a superb view of the Atlantic Ocean.

The Lindenmere Estate in Center Moriches, Suffolk County, Long Island, sixty miles east of New York City, was originally a private hotel and resort, but was transformed by Imelda into her own beach hideaway.

The upper floor was reserved for Imelda's security detail, while the other rooms were renovated for Imelda and her guests. While Imelda rarely visited the place, she nevertheless had a staff of twenty full-time employees working on the estate. The bathrooms were likewise renovated and retiled with marble, and the original faucets were replaced with gold. The old swimming pool was transformed into a reflecting pond, while a new one, complete with a gazebo, was constructed fronting the Atlantic Ocean. There was also a huge pagoda adorned with marble tiles near the pool, and hand-carved life-size animals such as giraffes adorned the premises. Inside the pagoda was a barbecue pit large enough to roast a whole cow.

The whole resort was estimated to be between $19-20 million after improvements were done. Renovation of the property, estimated to be $3 million, were carried out by Ernest Hoffstaetter. Tne renovation was paid by personal checks from Vilma Bautista or from Luna 7 Development Corp., a corporation registered in New York, which acquired the estate in 1981.

Apart from Imelda, other investors in the Lindenmere Estate included Augusto Camacho, an architect who served as the corporation's president; Jorge Y. Ramos, another architect who served as vice-president; Dr. Pablo Figueroa; and Miguel Arguelles, who served in the Philippine Consulate in New York. Figueroa was a close friend of Ernesto Pineda, the Philippine Consul General in New York close to the Marcoses. Camacho admitted in February 1984 that Imelda "was and is the dominant party of interest of Luna."

Ownership of Lindenmere was transferred on 23 December 1982 from Luna to Ancor Holdings, N.V., a shell corporation based in the Netherlands Antilles. The transfer was handled by law office of Bernstein, Carter & Deyo. The Bernstein law office represented both Luna 7 and Ancor Holdings, with William Deyo acting as the notary in the deed papers transferring the estate from Luna to Ancor.

Floirendo, one of the two managing directors of Ancor Holdings, first claimed that he was the beneficial owner of Ancor but later admitted that he that acted as Imelda's nominee in Lindenmere.

EAST 66TH TOWNHOUSE

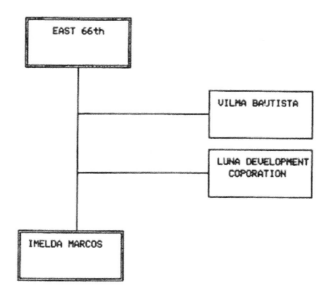

EAST 66TH TOWNHOUSE

The Townhouse at 13-15 East 66th, New York City, is different from the rest of the Marcos East Coast properties because it was not purchased through a shell company but through the Philippine Consulate and the Philippine National Bank. The property was initially purchased for the use of the Philippine Consulate in New York and the Philippine Mission to the United Nations, thus avoiding the need to pay expensive New York taxes on the purchase, but it was later turned into Imelda's personal disco pad and the depository for the expensive art works we discussed in the first chapter.

The East 66th Townhouse is a luxurious residence located in the East Side of New York City. The Townhouse's location in the East Side, described as "one of the most elegant residential and shopping districts in the world," was well suited for Imelda who regularly toured the nearby shops whenever she was in New York. The 6-story Townhouse, built around the 1920's, had a total of 30 rooms and had a mixture of architectural styles. Ernest Hoffstaetter, who worked on the Lindenmere estate, also remodeled the Townhouse. Again, typical of Imelda's tastes, the bathrooms were remodeled with marble and 24-carat gold faucets, with pink malachite marble for her personal bathroom, while beige-colored marble adorned the rest.

The third floor was reserved for Imelda's use, and a secret passage connected her room with an adjoining guest room. The fourth and fifth floors were for her children, staff, and other visitors, while the sixth floor was converted into a private disco, complete with an adjoining fully-carpeted room where the guests can romp and play with giant pillows. Serving to divide Imelda's disco pad from the adjoining residence of Bob Guiccone, the publisher of Penthouse magazine, was a solarium which had nothing but plastic trees and stuffed birds [126], All the six floors were served by an elevator which was specially constructed for Imelda.

While Imelda always rented whole floors at the Waldorf-Astoria whenever she visited New York, the Townhouse served as her playground where she would entertain her guests in her discopad. It was also a place where the pianist Van Cliburn could play on the four Steinway pianos for Imelda.

As we saw in the first chapter, the Townhouse was also served as the hiding place of the expensive art works Imelda collected over the years. Frustrated from not being able to buy a condominium because of concerns of the neighbors, Imelda settled for its contents, the Leslie Samuels Art Collection, which she purchased for $5,950,000 via Tantoco. The collection of antiques were then deposited at the Townhouse for safekeeping. Gliceria Tantoco, her brother-in-law Hector Tantoco, and the Sanmar Export Corporation of which Gliceria was president were later indicted by a grand jury in a "scheme to defraud" the City and State of New York City of sales taxes in connection with the purchase of the antiques. Sanmar later pleaded guilty to these charges, while Tantoco remained abroad and was pronounced a fugitive.

While the Townhouse was purchased directly using Philippine government funds, the cost for renovations were shouldered by Luna Development Corp. and Thetaventures.

HERALD CENTER

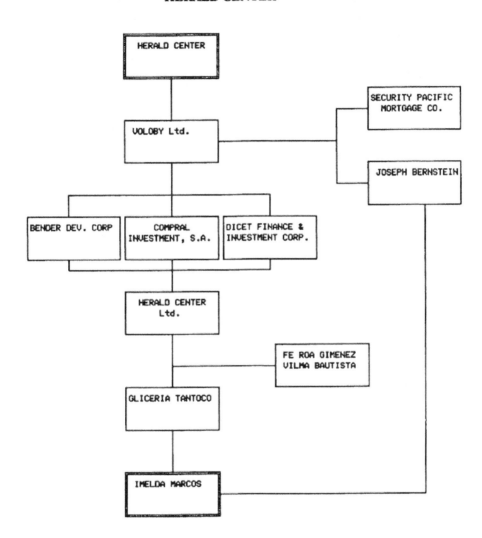

HERALD CENTER

Imelda, the quintessential shopper, soon outdid herself: not content with her shopping sprees around the world, she ultimately bought her own shopping center in New York.

Imelda and her nominees acquired the old Korvette Building in Manhattan and renovated it into a modern shopping mall with shops specializing in brand name products. This move was perhaps an effort to cash in on the popularity of Macy's, reputably the biggest the department store in the world, since this new acquisition was right in front of Macy's and was strategically located on the intersection of 34th St., the Avenue of the Americas, and Broadway, three of the busiest streets in New

York.

The purchase was made in February 1982 through Voloby Ltd., a corporation based in the British Virgin Islands. The directors of Voloby were Tantoco and the Bernstein brothers, although one existing document names Joseph Bernstein as its sole director who is to act in the interest of the shareholders. The Voloby shares were later transferred to three other shells based in Panama:

Bedner Development Corporation
Compral Investment, SA.
Dicet Finance and Investment Corporation.

The Voloby shares were equally distributed among these three Panamanian companies. The shares of these companies were then issued in bearer form and given to Tantoco, and the shopping mall and the corporation holding the lease to the property was then renamed Herald Center Ltd. in 1983. The Herald Center Ltd. listed its office with New York Land Co., the realty company owned by the Bernstein brothers.

Money for the shopping mall came from both the Philippines and from credit sources in the US. There is evidence that at least on three occasions, millions of dollars were transmitted from the Philippines for the purchase of the Herald Center. These three transmittals, for which Imelda and Tantoco were indicted for wire fraud, occurred on November 1981, January 12,1982, and February 16, 1982. These wire transmittals involved the following amounts:

$19.3 million   November 1981
$4.8 million   12 January 1982
$2 million   16 February 1982

These wire transmittals were carried out through telex messages from Manila to New York. The Herald Center was estimated to cost around $70 million.

The names of Bernstein, Floirendo, Tantoco, Gimenez, and Bautista also surface in connection with the purchase of the Herald Center. There is evidence to indicate that Floirendo personally delivered a $600,000 check to Bernstein in 1982 as a deposit for the purchase of the Herald Center. A report to Fe Roa Gimenez from Vilma Bautista prepared on March 1984 shows that $9.5 million was transferred to Voloby Ltd. in connection with the purchase of the Herald Center. Apart from looting the Philippines, funds for the shopping mall also came from a $29 million mortgage from Security Pacific Mortgage Co., a California bank. Henry Bullock, a vice-president of the bank ana manager of its North California office, was the loan officer for the mortgages to the Herald Center as well as the Crown Building.

The Herald Center was inaugurated on 29 March 1985, with Imelda making a discreet visit to the place a few days before.

200 MADISON

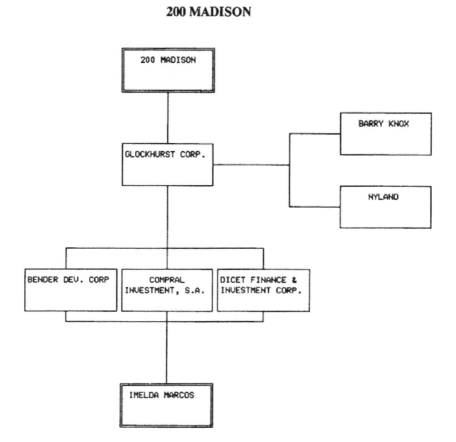

200 MADISON

Another office building in New York, 200 Madison Avenue, was acquired on 22 November 1983 for $50 million. The building was bought from Harry Helmsley, the New York real estate magnate, using Glockhurst Corp. N.V., a shell corporation based in Curacao. Tantoco, acting for Glockhurst, directed that its shares be issued to the same Panamanian corporations which controlled Voloby, the shell company used to purchase the Herald Center:

Bedner Development Corporation
Compral Investment, SA.
Dicet Finance and Investment Corporation.

Glockhurst lists its office as NYLand. Barry D. Knox, the signatory for Glockhurst, was authorized to borrow $57 million for the building's renovation. Knox, who served as a director of the Manila-based Rizal Banking Corporation when it was owned by the Tantocos [127], also arranged funding from the Security Pacific Mortgage Corp. Knox was also involved in the financing of the Herald Center and the Crown Building.

Imelda and her associates were indicted for wire fraud for moving the following

amounts in connection with the purchase of 200 Madison:
    $55 million
    $9 million
    $5 million   4 November 1983

    A report to Fe Roa Gimenez from Vilma Bautista on March 1984 shows that $4.3 million was received by "Blackhurst (sic) -11/4/83" in connection with the purchase of the property.

CROWN BUILDING

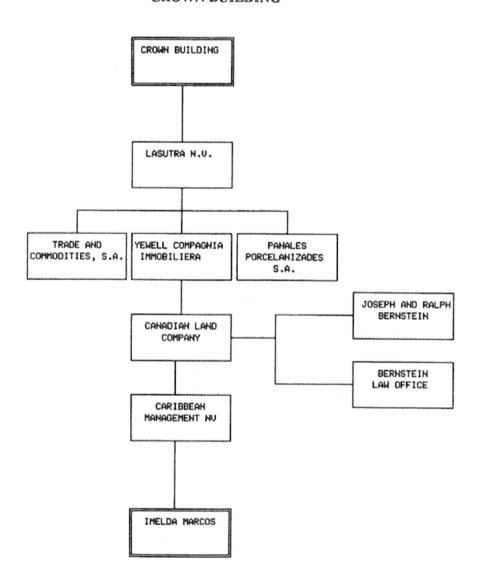

CROWN BUILDING

The Crown Building, a large edifice located at 730 Fifth Avenue, New York, was purchased by Imelda in 1981 using Lasutra Corp. N.V., a shell corporation based in the Netherland Antilles. It is said that Imelda pleaded with Marcos in 1981 to allow her to acquire the property. Formerly the Hecksher Building, the Crown Building is a huge office tower right beside Central Park and is strategically located on the comer of 5th Avenue and 57th Street.

The Crown Building was purchased in September 1981 for $51 million using Lasutra as a front. Around $15 million was initially planned for renovations. The shares of Lasutra were owned by three Panamanian corporations through bearer shares:

Trade and Commodities, SA
Yewell Compagnia Immobiliera
Panales Porcelanizades, SA.

Bernstein served as a director of Lasutra from 1982 through 1984. Ownership of the shares were later transferred to another shell corporation, the Canadian Land Company of America, N.V. The two Bernstein brothers, Joseph and Ralph, are listed as the sole directors of Canadian Land. Both Lasutra and the Canadian Land Company list their address as the same suite at the New York Land Co. of the Bernstein brothers. A third shell corporation based in Curacao, Caribbean Management N.V., controls Canadian Land Co. and provides a third layer of anonymity. The Bernstein law office, Bernstein, Carter & Deyo, handled the legal aspects of the purchase of the Crown Building. The building is managed by the Bernsteins.

Part of the funding for the purchase of the Crown Building came from a $34 million loan by Banque Paribas to Lastura Corporation N.V. arranged by Stephen Cattaui.

Imelda and her nominees have been indicted for wire fraud for transferring approximately $48 million around August 1981 from the Philippines to purchase the Crown Building. Henry Bullock of Security Pacific Mortgage Corp. handled further loans for the building.

40 WALL ST

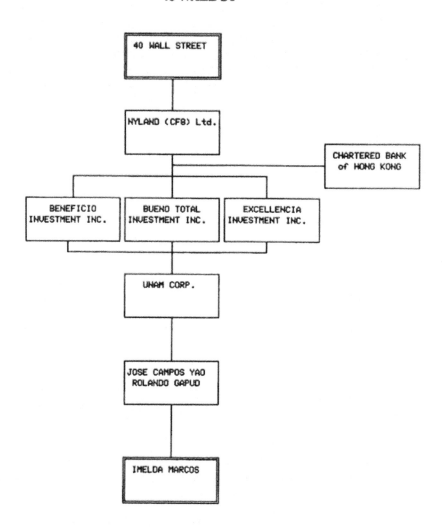

40 WALL ST

Imelda and her confederates also acquired 40 Wall Street, a large historic building in New York's financial district. This building formerly housed the stock exchange and for a time was the largest office building in lower Manhattan. The building, a 70-story tower offering a million square feet of office space, is now considered to be the second largest office building in lower Manhattan.

The purchase was made through NYLand (CF8) Ltd., a shell corporation based in the Netherlands Antilles. It was purchased for $71 million on 20 December 1983. Renovation costs were initially estimated at $15 million. NYLand (CF8), formerly known as Ainsville, N. V., in turn issued 2,000 shares to three other shell corporations based in Panama:

Beneficio Investment Incorporated

Bueno Total Investment Incorporated
Excellencia Investment Incorporated

The Bernsteins and these three Panamanian companies were listed as the sole directors of NYLand. These three corporations then later issued bearer shares. These Panamanian companies were organized with the help of Rolando Gapud and were controlled from a trust account from Chartered Bank, a Hong Kong bank which Marcos used extensively to launder money. The correspondence of these three shells were mailed Unam Corp., a Netherlands Antilles firm controlled by Campos. Contracts and supporting papers for the buildings were left in the presidential palace in a brownenvelope marked "PFM's Copy," Marcos' initials.

Imelda and her associates were indicted for the transfer of $55 million on October 1983 from the Philippines to purchase 40 Wall Street.
* * *
The Marcos real estate network knew that good relationships with local politicians would helpful for their operations.

The Bernstein brothers therefore contributed to local New York politicians. Mayor Edward Koch received $10,000 for his 1985 campaign from through NYLand and an affiliate. Though technically not a political contribution, the Bernsteins also invested $250,000 of the $440,000 used to produce *Mayor,* a musicale on the life of Koch, through their firm NYM Partners, making them the major financier of the production. Andrew Stein, the New York City Council President, got $7,500, while Ken Lipper, who ran against Stein received $10,000. Comptroller Harrison Goldin received $25,000 for his reelection bid. The amount was initially given as a single contribution on 13 February 1984 but had to be returned because it violated the limit on contributions from corporations. The money was then split into five $5,000 contributions from NY Land and its affiliates and redonated on 10 December 1984. The Bernsteins were planning to construct a building on the southwest comer of Sixth Ave. and 46th St. and wanted to add 15 floors to a 45-story office building, thus requiring the air rights over the landmark High School of Performing Arts. The projects needed two separate approvals from Board of Estimate wnich controlled the building and zoning policies of the city. Koch and Golding had two votes on the Board. Given that the Bernsteins had never made any political contributions before, it appeared rather odd that they would make significant contributions all of a sudden. Commenting on the Bernstein's moves, New York State Senator Franz Leichter said "Obviously, these campaign contributions are made by people seeking favor from public officials and, specifically, from Board of Estimate officials." Leichter then asked Koch to return the funds because it was possibly tainted Marcos money. A Koch spokesman said that the funds would not be returned [128].

A more controversial episode involved officials in San Francisco [129].

The old three-story Coleson building on 212 Stockton street by Union Square was razed to make way for a 10-story structure. The demolition was criticized by many since the building was in a preservation district and was considered to have some historic value. Filipinos who have been long-time residents of San Francisco were also attached to the building since it had continuously housed the Philippine Airlines offices since the end of the Second World War.

Adding to the controversy were the extremely liberal exemptions city officials gave the new building:

> • while the demolition was not allowed under city policy, the lawyer for the project, Timothy Tosta, was able to insert special-interest language into an ordinance which permitted it: when "the city Planning Commission finds that the replacement building appropriately maintains the character of the district." According to Tosta, the city Planning Department had said that they would not object if a specific exemption was acquired for the building.
> • exempted from city limits on office space, height, and amount of shadow cast on Union Square Park, the city's central landmark
> • nosignificant environmental study was required, despite the exhaustive environmental analyses that had been asked of Neiman-Marcus and Saks Fifth Ave. when the two department stores started their adjacent projects
> • the leading dock requirement was waived by the city zoning administrator, permitting on-street deliveries at one of busiest intersections, a first in city history
> * Board of Supervisors Ordinance 54-84 imposed an 18-month moratorium on major building permits but exempted the project from it.

The exemptions gave the project significant benefits. According to the *San Francisco Examiner,* the

> *...spate of exemptions not only makes the $33 million project possible but promises additional returns. Combined height and space now permitted will be worth at least another $600,000 in annual income. Lack of a loading dock allows the use of prime retail space on the street worth about $18,000 a year. Avoiding the environmental impact report saved $50,000 for the report and an estimated $1 million in finance charges.*
> *(The project] has benefited from an extraordinary combination of special permits and exemptions that expanded the size of the building by 60% and will generate more than $600,000 a year in additional revenue [130].*

Many attribute the special treatment to the lobbying efforts of Sylvia Lichauco, a Filipina real estate broker based in San Francisco. Lichauco had contributed to San Francisco Mayor Diane Feinstein and almost every member of the Board of Supervisors between 1982 and 1985. As much as $7,000 was contributed to Feinstein, Supervisor John Molinari, and Supervisor Carol Ruth Silver.

> *Another proponent of special exemptions for 212 Stockton St. mu Supervisor Carol Ruth Silver, a dose political associate of lawyer Tosta. She received $4,750 in contributions fiom parties interested in the project and argued strenuously for exemptions from the shadow ordinance, which she signed. She also voted for other exemptions [131].*

A finance committee for Silver's bid as state senator was organized, with Lichauco and lawyer Tosta as members. According to Silver, Lichauco was a "longtime supporter and friend." Adding to the controversy was the revelation that the ultimate source of the contributions was the GSIS, the Philippine government pension fund for government employees headed by Roman Cruz, a close aide of Imelda [132]. Lichauco herself admitted that "I was reimbursed for campaign contributions when it was for the project.... The source of Jamestown (project) funds was GSIS." Jamestown is a California corporations owned by the GSIS. These were potential violations of California and federal law. It is illegal under California law to hide the source of contributions through an intermediary, while federal jaw prohibits foreign governments from contributing to US electoral campaigns.

The ultimate beneficiaries of the caper were identified by the San Francisco Examiner as Roman Cruz, GSIS head, Greggy Araneta, Marcos' son-in-law, and Bongbong Marcos, Marcos' son. Once the new building was constructed, the three had hope to convert it "to their personal property as a source of income."

Cruz organized two shell corporations, Jamestown Co. and Stanway NV, based in California and the Netherlands Antilles, to buy-out the leases of tenants in building and hide the interests at work. Behind the caper was Philippine government money from the GSIS. According to Lichauco, "I can write a check for Stanway or Jamestown. It's the project's money. When I wrote a check... The money was project money, GSIS money." John C. Lyon, the lawyer and a director of Jamestown, also admits that GSIS was the sole owner of the shell corporations.

Lichauco served as the broker when Jamestown purchased the old building in 1983. She then served as its president. Patricia Araneta, Greggy's sister, was Lichauco's partner in a travel agency, while Myra Sulit, a favorite niece of Imelda, was her office assistant. Lichauco also knows Bongbong, as well as Irwin Robinson, a lawyer for Marcos and a former director of the Redwood Bank. Lichauco had at least four accounts in this bank.

Howard Elkus of The Architectural Collaborative (TAC) was hired by Cruz to design the building, valued at $11 million in 1986. Elkus, who was also hired by Cruz to design a new GSIS building in Manila, is known to have helped Jose "Babes" Romualdez, a son of Eduardo, to buy a condominium in the Telegraph Landing development area in San Francisco using a Netherlands Antilles company.

* * *

A Partial List of US Real Estate Properties [133]:

New York
• Apt. 6-P, the Elysabeth, 35-41 East 38th St., $70,000 (September 1981), Miguel Arguelles
• Apt. 14-F, the Beaumont, 30 West 61st St., $92,000 (14 October 1982), Miguel Arguelles
• House, 119 Continental Ave., Forest Hills, Queens, $202,000 (1979), Miguel Arguelles, Jorge Y. Ram06
• Estate, 409 First Neck Lane, Southhampton, Long Island, $1.5 million, Benjamin Romualdez
• Coop apartment, 700 Part Ave., Rodolfo Cuenca
• House, East Islip, NY, (1978), Edna Guiyab Camcam
• Condominium, 402 E 90th St., 1983, Edna Guiyab Camcam
• Three East Side apartments, 80 Park Ave., $441,500, (19 October 1983), Edna Guiyab Camcam
• Apartment, 80 Park Ave. (October 1983) Agusto Camacho
• Apt. 17-M, St. James Tower, 415 East 54th SL, $987,000 (1 Nov. 1982) Kashgar Holdings
Corp./NYLand
• Apt. 17-D, St. James Tower, 415 East 54th St., $680,000, (January 1983), Kashgar/NYLand

• Apt. 16-C, St. James Tower, 415 East 54th St., $485,000, (17 November 1982), Aderito Yujuico, a business partner of Greggy Araneta
• Apt. 11-A, St. James Tower, 415 East 54th St., $716,500, (17 November 1982), Floirendo
• Apt. 11-C, St. James Tower, 415 East 54th St., $460,000, (17 November 1982), Floirendo
• Apartment, 900 Park Ave., $320,000, (December 1979), Aderito Yujuico
* Apartment, 900 Park Ave., $286,000, (January 1980), Aderito Yujuico
• Apartment, 900 Park Ave., $178,200, (April 1980) Aderito Yujuico
• 13-story Webster Hotel, West 45th St., $5.5 million (April 1985), Camacho, Figueroa, Gatan,
& others
• Luxury condominium, Galleria, East 57th St., $159,000, (September 1977), Eduardo & Carmen Reyes
• Four-story commercial building, 304 East 55th St., $950,000, (1 March 1982), Lydia Nicasio
•Three deluxe condos, 43rd floor, Olympic Towers, 5th Ave., $1.1 million, VilmaBautista/ Imelda Marcos
• 27-H, Olympic Towers, 5th Ave., $270,000 (September 1976), United Motors/Floirendo
• 13-15 East 66th Townhouse, Tantoco/Imelda Marcos
• 13.5 acre Lindenmere Estate, Center Moriches, Long Island, $19 million, Imelda Marcos
• Office building, 200 Madison Ave, $50 million (22 November 1983), Imelda Marcos
• Crown Building, 730 5th Ave., $51 million (September 1981), Imelda Marcos
* Office building, 30 Wall St., September 1982, NYLand/Joseph Bernstein
• 70-story office building, 40 Wall Street, $71 million (22 November 1983), Imelda Marcos
• Herald Center shopping center, 34th Street, $70 million (February 1982), Imelda Marcos
* 84 William St., $10.5 million (November 1983), NYLand/84 NYL Partners
* 4-story building, 56 West 57th St., $2.2 million, 57 NYL Partners/Bernsteins
• New York Realty Building, 29 West 57th St., $9.4 million, (March 1982), Shalimar Ltd./NYLand
• High-rise commercial building, 56 West 57th St, Seventh Ave, $104 million, 57 NYL Partners/Bersteins
• 13 acre mansion, Princeton, New Jersey, (26 October 1982), Marcos family
• House, 231 Dodds Lane, Princeton, New Jersey, Marcos family
• House, 4 Capshire Drive, Cherry Hill, New Jersey, $90,000, Ferdinand Marcos Jr.
• House, 19 Pendleton Drive, $119,000, (April 1985), Ferdinand Marcos Jr.
• Apartment, Kingsley condominium, 400 East 70th St., $335,000, (6 April 1984)
• Two condominiums, 80 Park Ave., (1983)

California: Los Angeles
• Condominium, Century Hill, LA, $561,000, (1982), DRM/Velasco
• Mansion, Beverly Hills, $160 million, Imelda Marcos/George Hamilton
• Land of California Overseas Bank, 3710 Wilshire Blvd., LA., Roberto Benedicto
• Office building, California Overseas Bank, 9145 Wilshire Blvd., LA $3.7 million, (1981), Roberto Benedicto
• 107 N Oakhurst Dr., Beverly Hills, Universal Molasses/Roberto Benedicto
• 109 N Oakhurst Dr., Beverly Hills, Universal Molasses/Roberto Benedicto
• Apt., Lo6 Angeles, more than $1 million, (1980),Edna Camcam
• 4-«tory building, (1979), Edna Camcam
• House, 3040 Rivera Drive, Burlingame, Los Angeles, (1978), Edna Camcam
• Three bedroom house, 511 N.Oxford Ave., LA, $319,000, Fortuna Marcos Barba
• Three bedroom house, 2352 Lynn Court, West Covina, $150,000, Fortuna Marcos Barba
• Vacant lot, Lancaster County, LA, $150,000, (1981), Fortuna Marcos Barba
• Condominium/shopping project including 105 acres, Lancaster, Los Angeles, more than half
a million, (1974), Ricardo Silverio
• House, 1161 Barrolthet Dr. [?], Hillsborough, California, $850,000, (1981), Silcor

corporation
• Condominium, 2185 Century Hill, LA., $675,000, (3 June 1982), Velasco
• 10465 Eastbome Avenue #301, Los Angeles, CA, Rodolfo Arambulo
• 1520 South Beverly Glen # 406, Lxx Angeles, CA, Rodolfo Arambulo

California: San Francisco
• Apartment #1104,999 Green St. SF, 9 April 1984, Alfredo de Borja/Velasco
• Luxury condominium, Russian Hill, SF, $400,000, (1984), Alfredo de Borja/Velasco
• Condominium, 660 Davis St, Golden Gateway Commons, SF, $295,000, (October 1982), Adrian S. Cristobal Sr. and son
• Old Clam House seafood restaurant, 299 Bayshore,SF, $50,000, Nemesio Yabut
• House, 501 St. Francis Blvd., Daly City, SF, $520,000, (2 December 1983), Nemesio Yabut
• House, 621 Taylor St., SF, Nemesio Yabut
• Building, 630 Taylor St., SF, $900,000, (1983), Nemesio Yabut
• Two condominiums, 2190 Broadway Heights, SF, $180,000 (for one in 1979), Enrile & wife,
Christina/Renatsac Inc.
• House, 2310 Broadway, SF, $1.9 million, (1982), Enrile/Renatsac
• 2 condos, 1177 California. St., SF, Asia Resources/Disini
⁰ Condominium, 1177 California St., Nob Hill, SF, $348,3400, Disini Jr.
• Condominium, 1177 California St., Nob Hill, SF, Cuenca/TRA Equities Inc.
• Home, 131 Devonshire, SF, TRA Equities Inc./Marianne Cuenca
• 2 office buildings, 625 Market St., SF, TRA Equities, Inc./Cuenca
• Annex, 25 New Montgomery, SF, $10.3 million (price includes proceeding), TRA Equities, Inc./Cuenca
• Coop apartment, 1200 California St., Nob Hill, SF, $800,000, Roman G Cruz
• 10-story building, 212 Stockton Street, Union Square, $33 million project, Roman G Cruz
•Condominium, Telegraph Landing development, SF, Jose 'Babes" Romualdez, son of Eduardo

Other California
• House, 2741 Bcrshire Dr., San Bruno, Cuenca
• House, Santa Monica, $220,000, Cojuangeo/Coastal American Traders Inc.
• 4 lots in vacation resort, Brooktrails Vacation Village, Willits, Mendocino County, $66,014 (1979), Roman C Cruz
• Mansion, 140 Farm Road, Woodside, $1.5 million, Decision Research Management Ltd./Velasco
• Home, 23411 Armita St. Canoga Park, $250,000, (28 March 1984), Concepcion Romual-dcz/Tolosa Resources Corp.
• 9 pieces of property (include two homes), Rancho Murrieta, Sacramento, (1982), Armando T. Romualdez
• 7138 Atheling Way, Canoga Park, CA, Rodolfo Arambulo

Other US
• Two condominium units on Kalakaua Avenue in Honolulu, Hawaii, owned by Yao.
• Helen Knudsen Estate, 2443 Makild Heights, Honolulu, $1 million, Floirendo
• Mansion, 2338 Makiki Heights, Honolulu, $717,000, (14 July 1977), Bienvenido & Gliceria Tantoco
• 11,000 square foot lot, Makiki Heights, Honolulu, Bienvenido & Gliceria Tantoco/New York
Financial Inc.
• Seattle - whole city block
• Texas - more than 5,000 acres
• Spokane - various real estate holdings

THE REST OF THE WORLD

The tentacles of the octopus extended to many other parts of the world. Even the Seychelles, Channel Islands, St. Vincent, ana other places the ordinary person would not normally be familiar with formed part of their world empire.

Imee Marcos took up residence in Morocco. After refusing to testify before a US federal grand jury investigation and being cited for contempt, she was able to inexplicably slip away from the US despite the revocation of her passport and see* refuge in Morocco. The Marcoses have been long-time close friends of Moroccan royalty and are known to have exchanged expensive gifts with each other. It is believed that Imee managed part of the Marcos empire from Morocco.

It is known that Imee has travelled to Singapore where her family has substantial bank accounts. Kokoy Romualdez is also known to have significant bank accounts in this country which were started in the early 1980's.

Manuel Elizalde fled the Philippines after the murder of Ninoy Aquino and built a tourist complex in Costa Rica [134].

Roberto Benedicto is known to have investments in Venezuela and other places in Latin America and now freely travels the world using a South American passport.

Bienvenido and Gliceria Tantoco, fugitives from justice in the US and the Philippines, are now in Italy where they also have run afoul of the law, having been convicted of illegal possession of firearms. They were able to get a suspended sentence because of the connections Bienvenido cultivated when he earlier served as Ambassador to the Vatican. They are now living in a villa in the old section of Rome, Via Appia Antica 247, estimated at $20 million in 1985.

A favorite refuge of many cronies is London. The Mail estimated that Marcos cronies own at least £10 million ($14 million) in real estate and art in London [135]. In the flat of J.V. Cruz, a Marcos newspaper apologist and brother of Roman of the GSIS, is a reported self-portrait of the British painter Francis Bacon, with a possible market value of £500,000 ($700,000). Other items reputed to be in Cruz' home are that of master Filipino artists and expensive English antique furniture. Among the other properties in London owned by Marcos cronies:

* two apartments in the expensive Kensington Court district owned by the Floirendos
* a five-bedroom apartment overlooking Holland Park, West London worth £750,000 ($1.05
million)
* a second West London home
* a house in exclusive Rutland Gate worth £350,000 ($490,000)

As noted in Chapter III, Herminio Disini, Lucio Tan, and other cronies have also gone to Austria either to invest or to settle. Disini became a business partner of Dr. Walther Konrad, a former assistant of the Austrian Federal Chamber of Commerce, forming a Vienna-based export trade company, the ABG (Allgemeine Beteiligungs- und Handelsgeesllschaft) (General Investment and Trade Association). Disini and

Konrad later got investigated by the Austrian public prosecutor in Linz after they got involved in a scandal in connection with the 17% commissions they got from Voest, an Austrian firm which did business with Disini since he was still in Manila. Disini is now
reported to be wallowing so much in cash that, apart from his expensive Austrian villa and the franchise of a local cable television station, he is now purchasing significant shares of public companies listed in the Zurich and Luxembourg exchanges to have an outlet for his money.

Another bank in Austria appears have been used by persons associated with Marcos. The Export-Finanzierungsbank Gesselscnaft mbH [136] lists among the members of its board Eduardo Fajardo, Atanacio Panahon, Efrenilo Cayanga. A military man, Captain Donato L. Guzman, served as vice-president of the supervisory board. Dr. Walter Konrad, Disini's associate, also served in the supervisoiy board, as did Alejandro Melchor Jr., Marcos' Executive Secretary. Michael de Guzman, a financier close to Marcos, served as a managing director. It appears that this is not a regular bank but one which was organized to move funds, attracting   the   attention   of Austrian authorities who have warned the bank. The bank's shares are held by shell corporations, one based in Vienna, Creditmanila Gesselschaft, the other in Hong Kong, Galway Development Ltd. The San Francisco law firm of Graham & James, mentioned earlier in this chapter is believed to have also represented this bank in the US.

Jose Campos Yao, apart from extensive real estate holdings in the Washington and Texas, also has personal and commercial investments in Canada, where he has chosen to settle. His wife, Elizabeth, owns a house in Vancouver, British Columbia, which was assessed at $482,300 in 1982. A $3.1 million building is also among the Yao properties in Vancouver, as well as an investment company, Greenfield Investment Corp., of which he is president.

Yao also boasts of pharmaceutical empire in Asia, owning drug chains in Indonesia and Thailand.

Lucio Tan has extensive interests in baking, tobacco, steel, carpet manufacturing in Guam, Papua New Guinea, and British Columbia.

In Australia, Cojuangco enjoys a multimillion dollar horse ranch. Roberto Sabido, involved with Benedicto, Velasco, and Yulo in organizing a meat cartel, holds leases for 300,000 hectares of agricultural pasture lands. Sabido's leases in Jubilee Downes and Nerimah Downes, 2,000 miles from Sydney, are believed to have been funded with money from the Philippine Ministry of Agriculture [137].

Real estate, stocks investments, and bank accounts in Japan also formed part of the empire [138], Six real estate properties in Japan, in the Tokyo, Kobe, and Kudan areas, estimated to be worth $1 billion [139], were offered by Marcos for sale, despite formal ownership over these properties by the Philippine government. Three of these properties were in the Roppongi, Chiyoda, and Shibuya wards of Tokyo, the world's most expensive real estate area, and were worth several millions each [140]:

• 3,300 square meters located in Roppongi property, one of the most expensive areas in Tokyo (former Philippine Embassy site)
• 3,179 square meters in Fujima, Tokyo, valued at $200 million in 1986 (former Philippine
Embassy site)
• 4,361 square meters at 1-18-1 Fujima Chiyo-da-ku, Tokyo, valued at $60 million in 1986

The *Philippine Daily Inquirer* reported that Marcos had arranged for theprivate sale of more than 830 square meters of land in central Tokyo and Kobe in southern Japan to a Japanese businessman [141]. The three parcels in Tokyo were reported to have been offered at one time for ¥90 billion.

Kiyoshi Wakamiya, the Japanese journalist who travelled with Ninoy Aquino and witnessed his murder, identified Presidential Executive Assistant Victor Nituda and Ambassador Carlos J. Valdes, both individuals personally close to Marcos, as having negotiated sales for these properties since 1982 for a 20% commission [142].

The Kyodo New Service has also mentioned reports that Marcos had around $200 million deposited in Japanese banks [143]. These funds were from commissions gotten from deals resulting in Japanese official commodity loans [144], Marcos is known to have remitted $5 million to a Singapore bank from these Japanese accounts in 12 transactions.

Other overseas interests include reported investments in South Africa. Funds amounting to $12 million from government agencies Imelda headed such as the Ministry of Human Settlements, the Metro-Manila Commission, and the Philippine Tourism Authority were allegedly used by Imelda to invest in the diamond business in South Africa. Using a London-based trading firm as a front, £8 million have ended up in investments in Johannesburg, the world's diamond mining capital [145],

A bank and an apartment hotel in Israel appear to be also part of the world empire.

One piece of property in Israel with reported Marcos links is the Daniel Tower Apartment Hotel. With the exception of one share, all the shares of the Daniel Tower Apartment Hotel Ltd. are held by Dintron Export SA., a shell company incorporated in Panama. The single share is held by the reputed "owner" of the hotel, a possible front, Leon Taman, a resident of the United Kingdom who also has business activities in Switzerland.

Another concerns Jack Nasser, the uncle of the Bernstein brothers and a friend of Imelda. Nasser acquired a controlling interest in FIBI Holdings Ltd, the holding company of tne First International Bank of Israel Ltd. The purchase was made through Palimas Investment Corp., a shell corporation based in Panama. Ran Cohen, a member of the Knesset, the Israeli parliament, wanted to raise the issue in a parliamentary question to the Minister of Finance, but the question was disallowed by the Speaker. Cohen, concerned about the potential political harm Marcos investments could do to the image of Israel, then wrote his questions to the Minister of Finance. In the letter, reproduced below, Cohen inquired about how much the government of Israel knew about the investments and also raised questions about the implications of Nasser's financial support of Ariel Sharon, the controversial Israeli government minister:

The Minister of Finance
Mr. Moshe Nissim
The Ministry of Finance
Jerusalem

Re: The Ties of Mr. Jack Nasser with the deposed dictator Ferdinand Marcos

Dear Sir.

I know about the close times of Mr. Jack Nasser, who has acquired the First International
Bank, with the deposed dictator ofthe Philippines, Ferdinand Marcos, who stole billions
of dollars from the people of the Philippines.

I would like to know:

1. Do the monies raised by Mr. Nasser for the acquisition of the bank have as their source monies stolen by the dictator from his people ?
2. Since Mr. Nasser is customarily required to prove that he has assets of not less than
the value of the acquisition ($21 million) multiplied by three (i.e., at least $63 million), has the nature of Mr. Nasser's financial resources been examined by your Ministry?
3. What did you do and what steps did you take in order to prevent the possible danger
that the First International Bank will become directly or indirectly owned by dictator Marcos?
4. Is it possible that Mr. Nasser is something like a "cover for funds of the deposed dictator and does this not in volve a threat to our political relations with the Philippines ?*
5. Is it correct that the Examiner of Banks, Mrs. Galia Maor, has received secret information confirming the above suspicions?
6. Does not the financial assistance given by Mr. Nasser to Ariel Sharon, and, con-currently, Mr. Nasser's ties with Marcos, to the extent that there exists between them a
secret partnership in the ownership of the bank, cause harm to the Government of Israel
of which Sharon is one of the senior ministers?

Respectfully,

Ran Cohen
Member of the Knesset
13 May 1987
Jerusalem

(translated from the Hebrew original)

What we have discussed in this chapter covers only a small part of the total wealth Marcos and his cronies have accumulated in overseas properties. Many properties and bank accounts still remain unkown.

Marcos and his cronies have employed the techniques of money laundering and dirty money with such great skill that it may not be possible to ever know the full extent of Marcos' overseas empire.

Officials of the Philippine government investigating Marcos' wealth have given varying approximates of how much Marcos' assets may be worth, figures like $5 billion, $10 billion, etc. have been indiscriminately quoted by officials from the government of Mrs. Aquino who have been hard pressed by questions from reporters concerning the net worth of Mr. Marcos. Jovito Salonga, head of the commission tasked with recovering Marcos assets, was quoted on 20 March 1986 as saying that the loot was "more than $ 10 billion" [146]. Less than two weeks later, Salonga was quoted as saying that it was from $5 to $10 billion [147]. Sedfrey Ordonez, then Solicitor-General and a close Salonga friend, reportedly said in April 1986 that Marcos or crony assets worldwide could total $4.9 billion [148j. Raul Daza, another commission member, said he first thought "crony wealth" might reach "hundreds of millions of dollars" but later expressed awe that "it's in the billions" [149]. No definite figure has ever been given by these officials. They have neither explained the inconsistencies in their officially pronounced estimates nor explained how they ever arrived at these amounts. One gets the impression that such figures have been quoted not because they are reasonable estimates but because these officials were embarassed to answer newspaper reporters with the truth: that they do not know, that no one knows, and that most probably no one will ever know the true magnitude of the empire Marcos and his cronies built.

Imelda Marcos was more honest. When she was once asked how much she owned, she quipped, "If you know how much you've got, you probably don't have much."

The real tragedy concerning the overseas properties of Marcos and his cronies is not that we shall never be able to expose and quantify all their overseas assets. The real tragedy is that we shall never be able to recover even those assets which have already been uncovered. Why we conclude the history of Marcos' crony capitalism on a note of gloom is what we shall now turn to in our next and last chapter.

Endnotes

1. "If you see a Swiss banker jump out of the window, jump after him. There is definitely money to be gained in it." We encountered this quotation attributed to Voltaire in Jean Ziegler, *Une Suisse au-dessus de tout soupqon*, but we have been unsuccessful in locating the original reference. We therefore quote Voltaire on Ziegler's authority.
2. David Hume, "Of the Balance of Trade," 1752, ed. Eugene Rowen, *David Hume: Writings On Economics*, (Madison: University of Wisconsin Press), 1970, pp. 60-77.
3. Adam Smith, *Wealth of Nations*, Chapter V.
4. The position of Solicitor General is the equivalent of the US Attorney General. Quoted in Abby Tan, "Marcos denies hidden wealth," *San Jose Mercury News*, October 1985.
5. The global monetarist sees the world as a totally integrated market for goods and capital. The Law of One Price states that commodity prices and interest rates will be the same throughout the world in the long run.

6. Ziegler uses the terms *capital en fuite and Fluchtkapital* in the French and German editions of his book. "J'entends par capital en fuite un capital dont le transfert ne correspond au rfcglement d'aucune dette ou transaction marchande." *Une Suisse au-dessus de tout soupcon* (Paris: Editions du Seuil, 1976), p. 51. "Unter Fluchtkapital verstehe ich ein Kapital, dessen Uberweisungweder der Tilgung irgcndcincr Schuld noch einer Warentransaktion dient." *Eine Schweiz – uberjeden Verdacht erhaben,* (Darmstadt: Hermann Luchterhand Verlag, 1976), p. 49. The French and German terms, devoid of the moralistic overtones of dirty money, literally mean capital in flight or in escape. The French term has the additional connotation of something which is leaking.

7. Guy Sacerdoti & Leo Gonzaga, "Capital Flies From Fear," *Far Eastern Economic Review* 15 September 1983.

8. The operation was christened the Binondo Central Bank since its operations started from Binondo, an old district of Manila. The Binondo operatives bought dollars from families who received dollars from relatives working abroad, US military personnel, tourists, and others at prices higher than the official exchange rate, giving them an advantage over the banks. The accumulated dollars were then smuggled to Hong Kong and deposited in specially chosen banks. Roberto Ongpin, Marcos' Minister of Trade, and General Fabian Ver, Marcos Chief-of-Staff, managed the whole operation which consisted of at least nine dollar-smuggling rings. When six Chinese millionaires were arrested in 1983 for their dollar smuggling activities, Ongpin interceded for them and quickly won their release. After Marcos' downfall, papers two feet high detailing the operations of tne Binondo Central Bank were confiscated. Tne papers showed that the underground operation functioned as a virtual corporation, complete with directors, with Ongpin heading the syndicate.

9. *Wall Street Journal,* 21 March 1986; *Manila Times,* 24 March 1986.

10. *Daily Express,* 31 January 1981.

11. *San Francisco Chronicle,* 3 February 1981.

12. *Wall Street Journal,* 30 January 1986.

13. The takeover of the Security Bank was discussed in the section on Yao and Gapud, Chapter III. The Redwood Bank is discussed later in this chapter.

14. *San Francisco Chronicle,* 3 February 1981.

15. *Far Eastern Economic Review,* 13 February 1981

16. *Daily Express,* 31 January 1981. The careful reader will notice that the $12.7 million ceiling imposed by the Securities & Exchange Commission on Continental Manufacturing already

appears to conflict with the earlier Central Bank rule.

17. *Daily Express,* 31 January 1981.

18. As quoted in the *Far Eastern Economic Review,* 24 May 1984.

19. *San Francisco Chronicle,* 3 February 1981.

20. *San Francisco Chronicle,* 3 February 1981.

21. *Asian Wall Street Journal,* 2 February 1981.

22. *Asian Wall Street Journal,* 2 February 1981.

23. We are not aware that the Mafia intended to play a pun on dirty money when they coined the term "money laundering."

24. Quoted in Ingo Walter, *Dirty Money,* p.119.

25. This is according to the documents Marcos brought with him into exile in Hawaii.

26. Tadeco was a giant banana plantation which was controlled by Floirendo. Produce from Tadeco was marketed by United Fruit. Tadeco received a lot of subsidies from the Marcos government. For more details concerning Tadeco operations, see the section on Floirendo, Chapter III.

27. When some of his overseas properties were exposed, Floirendo claimed that they were acquired with money that was approved for remittance in accordance with the rules of the Central Bank or were legally generated m the US or elsewhere outside the Philippines.

28. This was a special report on the activities of Tadeco prepared by a government team.

29. Tadeco government report.

30. Jerry Esplanada, "Marcos Salted $300 M in HK," *Philippine Daily Inquirer,* 20 May 1986.

31. The Herdis conglomerate initially planned to establish 8 of these overseas offices to export the goods the conglomerate manufactured.

32. *Wall Street Journal,* 21 March 1986.

33. World Bank report No.4912-PHIL released September 1985.

34. Marlen Ronquillo, "$13 billion Philippine earnings since 1965 reported missing," *Malaya,* August 1985.

35. An editorial of the Daily Yomiuri apologized for the role of the Japanese in abetting Marcos' corruption: "We regret that Japan's Official Development Assitance (ODA) was reportedly part of his illicit accumulation of exorbitant wealth. Japan's ODA is given mainly in the form of yen credit, major sources of which are the people's taxes, postal savings, and pension funds." Quoted in *Manila Times,* 15 April 1986. When Japanese politicians are exposed in acts of corruption, they resign immediately and in extreme cases commit suicide in an effort to regain honor. If only Fihpino politicians would do the same....

36. The rapid growth of deposits in US branches of banks owned by Philippine government financial institutions is largely explained by the need of Marcos cronies to move cash out of the country. In the past decade, deposits in these banks owned by the Philippine government rose from $15 million to $277 million. The figure is much higher if we include the deposits in the banks the cronies privately owned. The private Redwood Bank alone had $165 million in deposits.

37. Cariho was given the post of Consul General in Toronto on 16 September 1985 and served the post until the downfall of Marcos in March 1986. Carino is the president and sole authorized signatory for a US firm, Oscarmen Holdings Ltd., which has an account at Republic National Bank in New York.

38. William Scott Malone, "Golden Fleece," Regardies, October 1988. This article offers the best account of Marcos' gold scam. This section owes much to this article.

39. "Marcos network seeking to sell gold," *Japan Times*, 21 July 1987.

40. Among those taken in by Marcos was Steve Psinakis, a Greek-American who was active with US-based opposition to Marcos. Psinakis was a fervent believer of the Yamashita story and wrote profusely about it. The proliferation of these real-life Indiana Jones-types is a testament to the effectivity of Marcos' disinformation campaign. The belief in the Yamashita legend continued until after Marcos was ousted from power. Noel Soriano, a member of the cabinet of Mrs. Aquino, gave special permits to treasure hunters to dig in Fort Santiago, a national historic landmark, leading to much criticism. No gold was found but the historic fort built during Spanish times was damaged. Soriano was later forced to admit having received a substantial sum from the treasure hunters which he deposited in his personal bank account.

41. We originally voiced this opinion concerning the different stories on Marcos gold in an interview with William Rashbaum of the Hearst Publications in 1986.

42. Quoted in Malone.

43. Malone.

44. Malone.

45. Quoted in Malone.

46. Fernandez later recanted this statement and attributed the discrepancy to "incomplete Central Bank data." Cited in Malone.

47. Malone.

48. Malone.

49. Malone.

50. Malone.

51. Malone

52. Malone

53. Philippine Daily Inquirer

54. Hirschfeld quotes Marcos saying that he trusted to gold shipments only with his son and that Bongbong is the only one who knows where the gold is. Cited in Malone.

55. Malone.

56. 1986 TV interview with Adam Smith's Money World.

57. Malone.
58. Manila Bulletin, 15 May 1986.
59. Chit L. Macapagal, "How CB went bust on gold bars," *Philippine Daily Inquirer*, 13 May 1986.
60. Chit Macapagal, "P7.6 B in RP Gold Being 'kept' in 2 Foreign Banks," *Philippine Daily Inquirer,* 11 May 1986.
61. Chit Macapagal, *Philippine Daily Inquirer*, 11 May 1986.
62. Chit L. Macapagal, *Philippine Daily Inquirer*, 13 May 1986.
63. Chit Macapagal, *Philippine Daily Inquirer*, 11 May 1986.
64. *Philippine Daily Inquirer*, 18 May 1986.
65. Malone.
66. *Philippine Daily Inquirer*
67. Quoted in Malone
68. Malone
69. Chit Macapagal, *Philippine Daily Inquirer*, 11 May 1986.
70. Quoted in Malone.
71. Malone.
72. *Ziegler, Une Suisse au-dessus de tout soupqon.*
73. *Ziegler, Une Suisse au-dessus de tout soupqon.*
74. *Ziegler, Une Suisse au-dessus de tout soupqon.*
75. *Ziegler, Une Suisse au-dessus de tout soupqon.*
76. Robert Mayerson, "HK Used to Launder Philippine Capital," *South China Morning Post*, 22 August 1985.
77. Robert Mayerson, "HK Used to Launder Philippine Capital," *South China Morning Post*, 22 August 1985.
78. Robert Mayerson, "HK Used to Launder Philippine Capital," *South China Morning Post*, 22 August 1985.
79. The ambiguity of Mackenzie's answer is interesting. The statement does not outrightly deny that Cuenca is involved, but neither does it admit any connection. Answering "I do not know" greatly decreases the possibility of perjuring one's self while at the same time avoids self-Incrimination. This is similar to the classic answer that Reagan continually invoked when questioned during the Contra-Iran scandal: "I do not remember." It is difficult if not impossible to disprove assertions which depend on what an individual knows or remembers. We are reminded of the epistemological problems Ludwig Wittgenstein grappled with when he discussed "toothaches" in the *Philosophiche Untersuchungen*.
80. *Time*, 31 March 1986.
81. "Wealthy Filipinos Find California Lucrative Territory for Investment," *San Jose Mercury News*, 24 June 1985.
82. The triangle of dirty money is a recurrent theme in the work of Ingo Walter. See his, for example, his book, *Dirty Money*.
83. Credit Suisse also goes under the names *die Schweizerische Kreditanstalt* or SKA, Swiss Credit Bank, and Credito Svxzzero.
84. This is according to Frankfurt police sources. These banks were fined $500,000 for not reporting these transactions to monetary authorities. Walter, *Ibid.*, p. 75.
85. Joachim Preuss, *Der Spiegel,* May 1987
86. Benedicto is known to have ordered payments from this account on behalf of Marcos. Benedicto ordered that the account pay several persons from the account of "Mr. Ferdinand Marcos."
87. "In Search of the Marcos Millions," PBS broadcast over US TV on 26 May 1987; *Daily Express*, 1 October 1986.
88. Laya: "President Marcos had personally intervened in the purchase of Treasury notes by certain Swiss banks. This was in September 1983, in a substantial amount." Quoted in *Business Day,* 17 June 1986.
89. Originally known as Banque de Paris et des Pays-Bas (Suisse).
90. The draft of the letter must have been prepared by the Swiss since we are not aware

that Marcos knows French.

91. Statement of Investments as of 13 November 1983.

92. Statement of Investments as of 14 November 19833.

93. Statement of Safekeeping Account Issued 18 January 1983 with holdings as of 17 January 1983.

94. Statement of Safekeeping Account Issued 13 April 1976 with holdings as of 12 April 1976.

95. Statement of Safekeeping Account Issued 18 November 1981 with holdings as of 17 November 1981.

96. The accountants of Credit Suisse must have goofed up somewhere.

97. Statement of Safekeeping Account Issued 12 December 1974 with holdings as of 6 December 1974.

98. Statement of Safekeeping Account Issued 30 December 1980 with holdings as of 29 December 1980.

99. Statement of Safekeeping Account Issued 28 December 1980with holdings as of 24 December 1980.

100. Statement of Safekeeping Account Issued 29 December 1980 with holdings as of 24 December 1980.

101. Statement of Safekeeping Account Issued 4 July 1978 with holdings as of 3 July 1978.

102. Statement of Safekeeping Account Issued 4 July 1978 with holdings as of 3 July 1978.

103. *Manila Times* 24 March 1986.

104. SASI holds office at 100 Wall Street, New York.

105. Marcos and crony investments in New York were first exposed in "MarcosTakesManhattan," a 1985 Village Voice article written by W. Bastone and J. Conason, while California investments were discussed in a series of articles in the *San Jose Mercury News,* 23 June 1985. This section utilizes material drawn from these two articles as well as subsequent researches made by other investigators.

106. Please see section on Romualdez, Chapter III.

107. Please see Chapter I.

108. Kim Hugcet, "Filipino with Big Bucks Leaves Mark on Sacramento," *Sacramento Union,* 17 March 1986; Kim Hugget, "Hold May Be Put On Imelda's Kin Estate," *Sacramento Union,* 2 April 1986.

109. Quoted in Kim Hugget, "Filipino with Big Bucks Leaves Mark on Sacramento," *Sacramento Union,* 17 March 1986.

110. Quoted in Kim Hugget, "Filipino with Big Bucks Leaves Mark on Sacramento," *Sacramento Union,* 17 March 1986.

111. Please see Chapter III.

112. Ver, Marcos' chief of staff, was implicated in the 1983 assassination.

113. Evelyn Iritani, Duff Wilson, Joel Connelly, "Spokane Property Indirectly Tied To Marcos," *Seattle Post-Intelligencer,* 25 March 1986.

114. Holley Gilbert, "2 Filipinos Involved in Purchase of Land Linked To Marcoses," *Oregonian,* 27 March 1986.

115. The hotel has since gone bankrupt.

116. The full story of Imelda's Manhattan purchases requires another book and is beyond the scope of the present one.

117. Please also see Chapter III.

118. Please see Chapter III.

119. Construction of the building was still in progress at the time of publication.

120. Does not include I. Magnin's or Roosevelt Hotel, both on same block

121. Some sources gave the amount as $51 million. (*Manila Bulletin*, "Campos Agrees to Pay $12 M," 13 June 1986; The Tribune, "Marcos Crony agrees to Pay $12 M," 13 June 1986; *Malaya,* "Crony Pays RP $12 M for FM'sTexas Lands", I3 June 1986; Manila Times, "MarcosTexas estate Dispute Settled,"). Another source gave the figure of $500 million. *Manila Bulletin*, 31 March 1986.

122. John Spclich, "Does Marcos Own Tarrant Land?" *Fort Worth Star-Telegnam,* 5 March

1986

123. The house was bought for $925,000 in 1979. It was estimated at $1.5 million in 1986.

124. Velasco was quoted as saying, "Alfredo de Boija is my nephew, but I don't know anything about his supposedly managing my supposed overseas properties." This statement is similar to Mackenzie's claim that he does not know if Cuenca has any connection with TRA Equities, the company of which he is president.

125. It appears that TRA Equities is also registered in Hong Kong. See Robert Mayerson, "HK Used to Launder Philippine Capital," *South China Morning Post*, 22 August 1985. This report indicates that the company might also have connections with companies based at Commence Consultants in Hong Kong. These reports indicate that among the shareholders and directors of the firm are Patrick Ting, the Hong Kong businessman earlier mentioned, and two nominee companies, Kinship Capital Ltd. and Waitomo Ltd., based in Commence Consultants, Hong Kong.

126. Bob Guirionne's residence on the other hand was completely covered with sound-proof panelling and was guarded by electronic sensors. We cannot say who wanted to hide from whom.

127. *Star*, 20 May 1990.

128. Ron Davis, "Leichter Asks Koch and Goldin to Give Back 'Marcos Money[1]," *New York Newsday*, 28 February 1986.

129. Material for this section is drawn from an investigative article by John Jacobs & Gerald Adams, "S.F. Gave Unusual Lucrative Breaks to Project," *San Francisco Examiner.*

130. John Jacobs & Gerald Adams, "S.F. Gave Unusual Lucrative Breaks to Project," San *Francisco Examiner*

131. John Jacobs & Gerald Adams, "S.F. Gave Unusual Lucrative Breaks to Project," *San Francisco Examiner.*

132. Please see Chapter III.

133. To be able to get a better idea of the value of these properties, we tried to include both the price and the approximate date when the assessment or purchase was made. Names of the cronies connected with these properties are also included.

134. But he was eventually expelled because of scandalous behavior. Please see Chapter III.

135. Quoted in the *Philippine Daily Inquirer,* 3 March 1986.

136. Vienna 1040, Prinz Eugen Strasse 8-10.

137. *Business Day*, 29 April 1986; Malaya, 29 April 1986; Manila Bulletin, 1 October 1986.

138. Luis D. Beltran, "One of the Best Kept Secrets: FM Cronies' Huge Yen Deposits," *Philippines Daily Inquirer*, 16 November 1986.

139. *Philippine Daily Inquirer,* 17 May 1986.

140. *Philippine Daily Inquirer,* 17 May 1986.

141. *Philippine Daily Inquirer,* 16 May 1986.

142. *Philippine Daily Inquirer,* 11 April 1986. Valdes, though, has denied these charges.

143. *Manila Bulletin*, 31 March 1986.

144. *Manila Bulletin,* 31 March 1986.

145. Jerry Esplanada, "Meldy's glitter: P245-M diamonds," *Philippine Daily Inquirer,* 17 April 1986.

146. Quoted in the *Philippine Daily Inquirer*, 20 March 1986.

147. *Business Day*, 2 April 1986.

148. *Far Eastern Economic Review,* 22 May 1986.

149. *Far Eastern Economic Review,* 22 May 1986.

Chapter V

IN LIEU OF A CONCLUSION:
Of Typewriters and Flags

*Un ciudadano salla gritando viva la revoluciSn y llevaba una bartdera Argentina
arrollada debajo de un brazo. Lo detuve en la puerta y le dije que hacfa.
Me contesto: "Lievo una banderapara los muchachos, mi general..." Dentro de la
bandera habfa una mSquina de escribir."*
          — Juan Domingo Peron, un relato escrito sobre la revolucidn del 30 *.

*(•Juan Domingo Peron's written account of the revolution of 1930: "A citizen was leaving,
shouting. Long Live the Revolution, and was carrying an Argentinian flag hanging under his
arms. I detained him by the door and asked him what he was doing. He answered me: 'I am
bringing a flag for the men, my general...Within the flag was a typewriter." Our translation.
Quoted in Eduardo Galeano, Voces de nuestro tiempo.)*
* * *

*Las reformas que vienen de lo alto se anulan en las esferas
inferiores gracias 6 los vicios
de todos, por ejemplo, al Svido deseo de enriquecerse en
poco tiempo y la ignorancia del
pueblo que todo lo constente.*

          — Jose Rizal, Noll Me Tangere, 1886 *

*(•"The reforms that come from the top are rendered useless in the lower rungs, due to the
vices of all, for example, the avid desire to enrich oneself in a short time, all made possible
because of the ignorance of the people." Our translation. Rizal, Noli Me Tangere, p.140.)*
* * *

The first official act of Corazon Aquino upon replacing Marcos was to organize a special commission to recover the wealth Marcos and his cronies had plundered. Mrs. Aquino's Executive Order No. 1, promulgated immediately after her dramatic ascension into office, created the Presidential Commission on Good Government (PCGG) and gave it broad powers to implement its mandate. Among these powers were the authority to sequester properties and temporarily prohibit the overseas travel of suspected cronies.

The speed with which Mrs. Aquino created the PCGG and the far-reaching powers she granted it was a clear acceptance of the viewpoint that cronyism was the defining characteristic of the Marcos regime and that any attempt to dismantle the old order must begin with the eradication of this plague.

Mrs. Aquino named Jovito Salonga, a long-time politician who had served in the Philippine Senate before the Marcos imposed martial law in 1972, as head of this commission. Mrs. Aquino also named four others as commission members, most of whom were Salonga's recomendees. All five commissioners were lawyers.

During his term as head of the PCGG, Salonga never tired of explaining in the many speeches he delivered that the commission had three basic functions:

1. identify, seize, and sequester the assets Marcos and his cronies;
2. return these assets to "the people";
3. prevent recurrence of the corruption that occurred during the Marcos regime.

This chapter evaluates to what extent these objectives have been met. It will be shown that the efforts on the part of the Aquino government to recover Marcos wealth have not been as successful as PCGG officials have made them out to be in their press releases and public posturings. Only a very small fraction has been recovered but the significance of this amount has been magnified out of proportion for the consumption of an uncritical public. Part of the problem lay in the unavoidable difficulty of tracing Marcos overseas assets and marshalling the help of other governments in the recovery efforts. But a large part of the problem was in tne gross incompetence and outright corruption on the part of most of the officials who served in the PCGG and the lack of leadership on the part of the Aquino administration. Economic and political factors operating in Marcos overseas havens coalesced with institutional, strategic, and organizational obstacles operating in the Philippines to ensure that an already tragic national history would conclude with a still more tragic chapter.

THE SWISS WATCH

Clearly conscious of the benefits of a favorable press coverage, officials of the PCGG often gave interviews describing how successful they have been in their efforts to recover Marcos assets. The PCGG public relations campaign was especially noticeable in the case of Switzerland where most of the known Marcos overseas assets are held.

Within a few weeks of PCGG's creation, Salonga was already claiming that the prospects of recovering Marcos assets in Swiss banks were "more than 50 per cent," according to an April 1986 article from the Financial Times of London 11]. The Manila Times, a local daily, also at this time quoted Salonga as saying that "two years would be too long in retrieving the bank accounts of Marcos" [2]. These confident pronouncements were again repeated a few months later, with Malaya, another local daily, quoting Salonga as saying that partial disclosures of Swiss accounts are expected "soon" [3].

Bonifacio Gillego, the first PCGG Executive Director for Overseas Operations, also voiced a similar optimism in a lengthy interview with the Manila Chronicle: "What is very promising is the Switzerland case. In a few month's time, we might be able to recover some of the Marcos deposits in Switzerland" [4].

Later interviews with Salonga, especially those he gave before resigned from the PCGG to run for the Philippine Senate, also show a great deal of optimism. Business Day, for example, quoted Salonga as saying in early January 1987 that

a full disclosure of Swiss accounts may be made within the first half of this year [1987] and the first deliveries of these deposits to the Philippines in the second half of 1987 [5].

A few weeks before he quit his PCGG post to vie for a seat in the Senate, Salonga proclaimed the same message to the Manila Times, declaring that

our Swiss lawyers tell us that by May or June [of 1987], we should opt the full information on the Swiss deposits and that, before the end of the year [1987], we should get a recovery of the first Marcos deposits in Switzerland [6].

Trying to allay the fears of the sceptics, Salonga further noted:

Haven't the Swiss already made themselves clear?.... They have already made him [Marcos] persona non grata -- an unusual move considering that Marcos does not have diplomatic status. They will not even allow Marcos to be present during the hearings on the Swiss accounts [7].

Several years after these auspicious pronouncements a single cent has yet to trickle in from Switzerland to the impoverished coffers of the Philippine government.

A simple review of how the Swiss banking system has reacted to similar requests in the past for a return of money to rightful owners might have led to less sanguine expectations. A thorough review of the literature on the Swiss banking system failed to reveal a single instance where the Swiss had significantly relaxed their banking secrecy rules and returned any substantial sum to their rightful claimants. On the contrary, the literature revealed many instances where the Swiss either adamantly refused to comply with requests from rightful owners for the return of their money or dillydallied with legal procedures until the claimants died or gave up out of sheer frustration. Among the more notable instances of Swiss intransigeance, the following may be noted:

> • **Money** the Romanovs deposited with the Swiss before the Russian Revolution was never returned (8]
> • **Hundreds** of millions of dollars deposited by the Spanish Republican government before Franco overthrew it through the bloody Spanish Civil War have likewise remained in Switzerland (9)
> • **When** Jewish families tried to recover the money deposited with the Swiss during the Nazi period, these banks were given a choice by the Swiss Confederation of keeping the money or voluntarily declaring all funds "without known owners". Compliance with the Swiss "law of restitution" was left entirely on the discretion of the banks [10).
> • **Trujillo**, the Dominican dictator, and his sons 'transferred* more than $500 million in gold and currency to Geneva. Helping Trujillo was his personal banker, Julio Munoz, who later bought Banque Suisse d'Epargne et de Credit in St. Gall and founded Banque Genevoise de Commerce et de Cridit in Geneva. While investigations were going on, Munoz jumped bail of a million Swiss francs and was later sighted in Spain. After more than ten years had passed, the Swiss government finally ruled that, although the Dominican government had a valid case to pursue, further litigation to recover the Trujillo loot would be an unreasonable burden on the Swiss legal system and would

therefore no longer be pursued: The judicial authorities of Geneva are competent to handle the case, but the whole affair is such an inextricable tangle of the penal with the civil that it would take a *juge d'instruction* and a representative of tne public prosecutor a whole year, working full time solely on this case, to unravel it - which is obviously an impossibility" [11]. The Swiss in effect sanctioned Trujillo's plunder of the Dominican Republic.

> • **The Algerian** government has been fighting for the return the 50 million Swiss francs, including the interest that has been accumulating since 1962, which the FLN had deposited with the Banque Commerciale Arabe SA in Geneva. Again, while implicitly recognizing the political and moral aspects of the case, the Swiss again hid behind a strict interpretation of the law and insisted on the "total independence of Swiss courts [12]. Ziegler comments, "But what if the real owner demanded the money back? The federal did not recognize him. Where was the money? The federal tribunal did not wish to know. Who now holds the 50 million subscribed by Algerians working in France? The Banque Commerciale Arabe SA. What happens to the most elementary justice in this case? Banking secrecy is all that matters" [13].

> • **Several other** former dictators and world leaders also maintained Swiss account which were effectively frozen after their demise from power. Evita Peron, Fulgcncio Batista of Cuba. King Farouk of Egypt, King Faisal of Iraq, and Shah Reza Pahlevi of Iran all had Swiss account which either their families or the governments that succeeded them could not recover [14].

The optimism of Salonga therefore does not seem to be grounded on any precedent. Historical precedent, if anything, points to the other direction.

Salonga justified his auspicious assessment of the Swiss banking system by pointing to a freeze order the Swiss authorities issued on March 1986. Hie order, issued under highly unusual circumstances, directed that certain bank accounts Marcos held in Switzerland be frozen. Salonga immediately inter- preted this as a sign of victory and hailed the Swiss move as a legal triumph "unprecedented" in the annals of legal history.

The evidence, however, that has filtered back to the public concerning the nature of these extremely secret negotiations on tne Marcos Swiss accounts did not support Salonga's great faith in the Swiss banking system. The evidence, on the contrary, inexorably forces one to less sanguine conclusions.

From what can be gathered, it appears that Michael de Guzman, a Filipino banker who had run financial errands for Marcos, attempted to withdraw some of the money Marcos maintained with Credit Suisse on 24 March 1986. De Guzman, who co-owned a bank in Vienna with other Marcos associates [15], presented a two-sentence power of attorney signed by Marcos authorizing him to withdraw an initial $213 million [16]. Josef Doering and Gerhard Grob, both of whom were connected with Credit Suisse, and Ivo Beck, a lawyer from Liechtenstein who had earlier dealt with Marcos, appear to also have had a role in the attempted transfer [17]. Credit Suisse, however, balked at the size of the withdrawal [181]. De Guzman was told to come back the next day. An emergency plan was hatched with members of the Swiss Federal Council in the meantime. Kurt Furgler, the Swiss economic minister, the finance minister, the banking superintendent, and other key members of the Federal Council held an impromptu conference [19]. It was decided not to let Marcos withdraw the money. The Swiss then "invited the surprised government of President Corazon Aquino to petition for its return" [20].

It is not at all obvious that one can share the same conclusions Salonga quickly drew from these moves. Many people familiar with the workings of the Swiss banking system were much more skeptical about the motivations of the Swiss and the eventual outcome. The Swiss ordered the freeze not as a response to requests from the Philippine government for judicial assistance but to prevent Marcos or anybody else from taking the money out. Swiss federal authorities were really concerned with maintaining the Swiss tradition of banking secrecy. It is clear that Swiss federal authorities collaborated with the Swiss banks to keep the money in Switzerland. Daniel Zuberbuhler, Vice Director of the Swiss Federal Banking Commission, bluntly admitted over US television that in the wake of the withdrawal attempts precise instructions were given to Swiss banks not to release any funds:

> We told those banks who had funds ...er... would have to give ...er... confirmation in writing that they would not release any funds without prior approval by the Banking Commission [21].

To conclude from the freeze order that Switzerland would repatriate Marcos' loot is a clear case of non sequitur. The freeze order can be explained in a manner more consistent with the history of Swiss banking policy rather than as a "precedent setting" sudden metanoia on the part of Swiss bankers. Indeed, the two moves of the Swiss government — tne freezing of certain Marcos accounts, and telling the Philippine government to petition for its return — can be interpreted with greater consistency as efforts on the part of the Swiss to keep the money in Switzerland rather than return it to the Philippines. It is easier to keep the money in Credit Suisse's coffers if there are two claimants fighting in the courts. Max Soliven, a respected Filipino journalist and former professor of European history, observed:

> ...when there are two or more claimants to money, gold, or jewelry deposited in those super-secret and solid Swiss banks, the Swiss smile at you, allow you to fight it out in their Swiss courts (thus making Swiss lawyers rich also) — but they never, yet, have given any of it back [22].

It would have been indeed precedent setting if the Swiss had frozen Marcos' accounts and returned the plunder. But the second condition was missing. The freeze order therefore did not represent a break with history but ratner a conservative reaffirmation of past historical behavior.

The problem of monetary recovery has nothing to do with the moral values of individual Swiss bankers. The chief obstacle lies in the nature of the Swiss banking system itself and the way it relates to the international financial system. Even if individual Swiss bankers were to miraculously experience a change of heart and try to return Marcos' plunder, they would encounter serious institutional and historical obstacles. Completely lifting the veil of banking secrecy and following it with the repatriation of several decades of plunder would be extremely difficult to implement without creating substantial long-term difficulties for the Swiss banking system.

These difficulties arise because of the nature of economic competition. Economic competition amongst different international financial centers serving as dirty money havens will ensure that any financial center which substantially deviates from the norm will slowly lose its clients and eventually lose its position of dominance.

As was discussed in the previous chapter, the launderer of dirty money seeks to maximize the return on his money, decrease the uncertainty associated with his investments, and maintain his anonymity with regard to these undertakings [23]. Switzerland and other international investment havens therefore compete with each other in terms of providing the international money launderer with the optimum mix of these three elements. A slight easing of banking secrecy might be conceivably compensated for by increases in interest rates or lesser financial and political risks, but under no circumstances can there be a wide and consistent long-term deviation from the standard practice of the centers of dirty money.

The very nature of the Swiss economic system would be undermined if the Swiss were to return Marcos' plunder. Tne issue is not the freezing or return of $213 million, which by any count represents a small fraction of Marcos' Swiss deposits. The real issue is the uncertainty that would be caused with Switzerland's present and future clients. Should the Swiss banking system acquire the image that it can no longer consistently guarantee the safety of dirty money, a great problem would be created for its long-term stability. Any move on the part of the Swiss which might give the slightest appearance that their banking system was not safe or secret would force money launderers to utilize other overseas investment havens. Dirty money will just go somewhere else in search of secrecy. The Swiss therefore cannot simply make up their mind and repatriate Marcos' plunder without substantially eroding their standing as the world center of dirty money. This is true of any other international investment haven. The forces of economic competition ensures that the different centers of international financial capital stay within the norm.

Ingo Walter, a professor of international finance who has written much on dirty money, thus observes:

> All sellers of financial secrecy products have an important stake in doing their best to limit disclosure asfar as possible. Their business depends on it. Any form of discretionary disclosure will damage the value of what they have to sell, perhaps irreparably, given the extreme risk aversion of clients taking advantage of their services....
> ....the international market for financial secrecy is perhaps more competitive than might first appear. Countries see it in their economic interest to offer secrecy products in competition with one another, and institutional arrangements that threaten to erode some of its value are often fiercely resisted [24].

Policy makers in countries which have been used by money launderers are clearly conscious of the problem of competition amongst different financial centers. Robert Carswell, who as US deputy secretary of the Treasury sequestered Iranian assets in the US during the Iranian revolution, states the problem very honestly. While admitting that the US should not be a haven of dirty money, explaining that it would suffer in terms of its image and moral standing, Carswell also recognized that any easing of banking secrecy would have adverse effects in terms of international investments:

> Every time you tried to sift out the illegality, you may well have the effect of scaring other people from investing their funds, but who are sensitive about their privacy or

their ability to move their money when they want to, and so on.
.... if we try to pass statutes that get at the flow of capital where there is no established illegality, where there isn't in the case of most of these - with respect to a lot of capital, we will put ourselves at a significant disadvantage in the world of international finance[25].

Competition and self-interest dictate that centers of dirty money adequately address the banking secrecy concerns of money launderers. Each banking haven therefore has to equal or try to outdo its competitors in the provision of anonymity and other specialized banking services, making it increasingly difficult to recover or even identify the accounts that seek refuge in these monetary centers. In the case of Switzerland, a complex set of laws, procedures, and even historically-defined customs form a formidable wall which effectively keep out threatening inquiries. The Swiss Constitution, Swiss Federal Law, the Swiss Civil Code of Obligations, the Criminal Code, the Banking Law of 1934, and other legislation all ensure that the sacrament of secrecy will not be violated [26].

While it is relatively easy to open a secret bank account in Switzerland, requiring only a minimum of paper work and the requisite amount of money, acquiring information about an account, even if one is armed with a justifiable reason for inquiring, is extremely difficult. Only a minimum of identity documents are requested of prospective clients. These clients, once accepted, can use aliases or the names of foundations and their lawyers for their accounts. Postal addresses suffice for the bank's records. But when a complainant requests for the sequestration of an account, the Swiss banking system requires an unreasonable amount of information, among which are

    1. name and identity of account-holder,
    2. address of bank;
    3. number of account;
    4. approximate amount of money in it [27],

Ziegler reminds us that it is rare to have access to all this information and that even if one had this information it is of no practical use because "it only needs a quick telephone call to the bank from tne account-holder or his local agent to get the number changed or simply move the money elsewhere" [28].

Again, while it is relatively easy to change account names and numbers, access to the information necessary to petition for the sequestration of an account requires a complicated legal process.

The claimant first has to file a formal request for judicial assistance from Swiss authorities. This first legal step is already certain to be fought by the lawyers of the money launderer, as Marcos' battery of 40 Swiss lawyers have done. Swiss authorities cannot and will not take action until disputes are settled in this first round of the fight. Years may pass before anything can be decided in this first step in the legal process.

The legal battle proceeds until the Swiss Supreme Court decides on the matter and authorizes cantonal or Swiss provincial authorities to start questioning bank officials and obtain bank records. This stage is especially complicated because

Swiss federal law allows bank financial disclosure only when Swiss law is violated or when the offenses committed elsewhere is likewise punishable by Swiss law. The latter step may take even more years so that many of the litigants die or give up before this stage is concluded.

After requesting banking records and questioning bank officials, Swiss authorities then decide which of the properties in question were lawfully acquired, and then later decide whether to make the records available to the claimant.

Only at a much later stage will the Swiss Supreme Court decide whether the funds in question are to be repatriated.

Assuming that the litigants even reach this stage, the money launderer and the Swiss banks have a final trump card to play. Not even tne law may have the final say in the matter, and it may turn out that all the complicated procedures were merely an empty exercise to provide money laundering with a legal facade. While the banking secrecy plays a central role in all of these legal procedures, the term has never been precisely defined. Walter writes that "instead of narrowly defining secrecy by legal statute, definition is left to custom and practice, and to judicial discretion" [29]. This ambiguity is a final loophole which allows Swiss authorities a wide degree of discretion in refusing the claimant if by some far-fetched chance he has survived the gamut of legal procedures. Among the accepted factors which allows Swiss authorities to decide in favor of the money launderer are the national customs of Switzerland, and national sovereignty and security - the former condition an implicit recognition that banking secrecy is indeed ingrained in the national tradition of Switzerland, the latter a convenient repetition of that catch-all phrase which has allowed the modem state to commit many crimes against its own citizens.

The many difficulties encountered in requesting information on suspected dirty money accounts, and the still greater obstacles in sequestering the identified accounts, forces one to question whether these technical procedures were really meant to redress grievances or were adeptly-designed mechanisms to silence such grievances. Certainly, the drama of judicial hearings does provide the external trappings of fair play, or at least the observance of proper procedure. But, given the history of how such proceedings have ultimately ended, one is left with the lingering impression that the formal channels of redress found in the Swiss courts function more as a channel to air frustrations rather than as a mechanism to dispense justice. Is it the case that none of the claimants to secret Swiss accounts ever had any valid claims? Yet, no matter how much we research Swiss banking policy, we continue to fail to discover even one instance where banking secrecy was significantly relaxed and substantial amounts of plundered money were given back to their rightful owners.

It is the skeptic who will go further and outrightly say that all of the legal hurdles are but tactics to delay a resolution to touchy issues. Some find proper irony in the Rolex advertisement "Time is the art of the Swiss" and take it to be true of the strategy of Swiss bankers as well [30],

Swiss banks have wielded such great influence in the economy and history of Switzerland that Swiss bankers have enjoyed tremendous influence in the country's affairs. When, for example, a law to withdraw banking secrecy from swindlers and tax-evaders who have been convicted in other countries was proposed in June 1976, the Swiss banks organized a major lobby to defeat the measure.

There are those who believe that Swiss banks really do not have any effective form of external supervision. Ziegler claims, for example, that while there is some nominal amount of legislation to monitor the banks, the supervisory body itself is controlled by the big banks such as Credit Suisse, the Swiss Bank Corporation, and the Union Bank of Switzerland, leading to the anomalous situation where the supervised are therefore still supervising their own supervisors [31].

The effect is that not only is there no external and independent auditing of the banks' accounts by the Swiss government but it also produces the great embarrassment that even the Swiss Federal Council has had to admit that "they do not know how much there is, where it comes from, or where most of the astronomical sums are deposited" [32]. It then leads to the aberration that the Swiss government "does not know or want to know what goes on in its own country."

But such lack of knowledge on the part of monetary authorities seems to be the rule rather than the exception in countries which money launderers use. The US, despite its relatively stricter rules concerning financial disclosure, still has an acknowledged lack of information necessary to supervise money laundering within its boundaries. US Congressman John Bryant, a democrat from Texas who has sponsored legislation for stricter requirements on foreign investments, points out the problem:

> A hodgepodge of 16 different federal agencies collects information on foreign invest-ments here.... But the information is so limited, hidden in bureaucratic quagmires or actually kept secret by law - even from Congress - that we often don't know who is investing here or whether they are from friendly nations, like Canada, or hostile ones, like Libya and Iran. Nor do we blow whether they are legitimate business people or drug traffickers laundering ill-gotten gains.

The linchpin in recovering Marcos' accounts in Switzerland is the recognition of the central role played by the forces of international economic competition. In an effort to attract capital, the different international investment havens attempt to outdo each other in the provision of secrecy, anonymity, and security to their banking clients. Any attempt to recover Marcos' Swiss accounts must take into account the strong presence of these competitive forces. Swiss law and judicial custom operate within a historical matrix which constantly influences the perceptions, concerns, and eventual decisions of Swiss authorities. Salonga, however, in defining the PCGG recovery strategy, operated in a historical vacuum and viewed the recovery of the Marcos Swiss accounts as purely a legal battle to be fought in the courts. Insisting on the purely legal approach, Salonga hired highly-paid Swiss lawyers to lead the recovery efforts. The result of this strategy is that, despite the huge legal fees that have been paid to the Swiss lawyers, a single cent has yet to be repatriated to the Philippines.

ADHERENCE TO DEMOCRATIC PRINCIPLES

Other countries have been equally uncooperative with the efforts to recover the wealth of Marcos and his cronies.

A good example is the United Kingdom. Imelda and other Marcos associates extensively used its Cayman Islands colony to launder their wealth and are also believed to have substantial deposits hidden in London banks. Yet despite the continuing revelations concerning the abuses of the Marcos regime, British authorities categorically declared that the executive branch of the government would not get involved in the efforts to investigate and recover Marcos assets in the United Kingdom. The UK Foreign Office bluntly stated that it was "not their business" and that "the Philippines would have to go through the courts to recover assets" [33].

Japan, where the dictator also had substantial financial dealings, has been equally averse to such efforts. Japanese politicians, particularly those who were closely associated with Marcos, strongly fought attempts to investigate Marcos' activities in Japan, especially those dealing with Japanese loans and aid to the Philippines. Claiming that tne Japanese government was never a party to the contracts funded by these loans, Japanese politicians refused to divulge the list of the companies which Marcos utilized to avail of the funds. Japan had provided an estimated $2.59 billion in loans and aid to the Philippines through 13 loan and aid packages from 1971 through 1986 [34]. Setting the tone for much of the Subsequent investigations, Shintaro Abe, the Japanese Foreign Minister, refused to release official documents dealing witn aid-funded contracts between Japanese companies and the Marcos government. Abe moreover told the opening session of a special Lower House committee that Japan would not take an active part in investigating allegations of Japanese corporate pay-offs to the former dictator. Abe skillfully deflected the investigations by putting the onus of the investigations on the Philippine government, saying that it "should take the primary responsibility in getting the truth out of the allegations" [35].

The more cynical among us might be tempted to utilize conspiracy theories to explain the reluctance of some countries to fully cooperate with the efforts to recover Marcos'plunder. While such a cynical viewpoint might not totally explain the utter failure of the Aquino government's overseas recovery efforts, certain reports which have recently come to light do point to very close personal and financial links between foreign politicians and the Marcos clique.

Details of Marcos' connections with Japanese politicians, for example, surfaced soon after the dictator was forced out of office. The *National Times* of Sydney, an Australian weekly, reported that Marcos had given funds to members of Japan's ruling Liberal Democratic Party through Japanese companies which did business with the dictator. The *Philippine Daily Inquirer* also divulged that part of Japanese aid funds intended for the Philippines had gone to the "campaign chest of Prime Minister Yasuhiro Nakasone [36]. Whether or not the latter accusation is justified, Nakasone later admitted and expressed regret that some funds from the Overseas Economic Co-operation Fund (OECF), the Japanese government-supervised agency which supervises soft loans to developing countries, had indeed been misused. But while lamenting the abuse of the funds, Nakasone also rationalized the arrangements with Marcos, saying "Japan had no choice but to deal with Marcos administration as [he] was the legally recognized head of the Philippines."

Kakuei Tanaka, former Japanese Premier, was another top Japanese politician who was accused of Marcos-related improprieties. It was alleged that Marcos had made a "political donation" of $4.5 million to Tanaka in October 1972 "in return for what is believed to be millions of dollars in kickbacks from ship building contracts" Marcos received. The report cited evidence which indicated that Tanaka would use his influence within the Japanese ship construction industry and "pledged" to pay Marcos 20 to 25% of two contracts for the construction of a fleet of oil tankers for the government-run Philippine National Oil Co. fPNOC) [37]. A front of Kolcoy Romualdez, Marcos' brother-in-law, received the kickbacks, while a former official of the government-owned Development Bank of the Philippines acted as the conduit in the transfer of funds to Tanaka. It was reported that the funds were withdrawn from a government account at the Development Bank of the Philippines and deposited in a Hong Kong account of the official on July 1972. The funds were withdrawn from the Hong Kong account a month later.

Another charge was that Imelda had used $650,000 from the Philippine National Bank for a party she hosted for "a Japanese delegation" at the Waldorf in New York, but Raul Daza, a commissioner of the PCGG, later denied the existence of documents that would support the charge [38]. In an effort to explain the reluctance of the Japanese to thoroughly investigate Marcos' dealings with their politicians and businessmen, a Filipino journalist noted:

> If you are wondering why the Japanese government is so touchy on the matter, one of the open secrets in Tokyo is that the son-in-law of a high Japanese official was involved in kickbacks given to Marcos for a contract to build a dam in the Philippines....
> The Japanese banking system is fully as secretive as Switzerland, and the Aquino officials
> concerned simply stumbled on the fact that there were billions in Yen stashed away in Tokyo by the Marcos cronies. In addition, some Marcos men have considerable stock and real estate holdings. However, the investigation into this form of Hidden Wealth has been temporarily stopped, because the Japanese government has dropped not too subtle hints that it could affect the flow of Japanese foreign aid to Manila [39],

The PCGG promptly "deferred" the investigations on Japanese companies. The PCGG and Office of the Solicitor General then refused to comment on the matter [40].

Whatever value these reports and allegations may have, they at the very least lead us to consider the international political climate under which Marcos dirty money operated. Apart from international economic competition, the political presuppositions of dirty money is equally important in evaluating the adequacy of the recovery strategies of the Aquino government and forms the second major area of concern of this chapter.

Marcos and his cronies clearly understood that a good working relationship must be established with influential politicians and businessmen from the countries they would use as safe havens.

Herminio Disini, the crony discussed in the two previous chapters, for example, successfully wormed his way to local politicians in Vienna and later parlayed his new connections to acquire Austrian citizenship and build new businesses in there.

It was in the US, however, where one is easily tempted to infer that Marcos and his associates engaged in a concerted effort to influence politicians. There have been many reports of instances where Marcos and his cronies made contributions to US politicians.

The New York Times, for example, reported in a study on the impact of foreign investments on US policy that Revere Sugar, the multinational trading corporation controlled by Marcos and Floirendo, had contributed to the campaign funds of some members of the US Congress [41].

More damaging allegations soon surfaced. Among the papers Marcos carried with him to Hawaii was a document detailing contributions to prominent US politicians. The document came from Mabuhay Corp., a San Francisco-based company headed by Dr. Leonilo Malabed, a Filipino physician based in the US West Coast and a long-time Marcos supporter.

Documents revealed that $1 million from Philippine Intelligence Funds of the Philippine National Bank had been transferred to Mabuhay Corp. It appears that Mabuhay Corp. was utilized by Marcos partly to harass the opposition based in the US and partly as a conduit for contributions to US politicians. The Wall Street Journal describes the one-page typewritten memo, dated 15 February 1982, detailing some of the expenses of Mabuhay Corp.:

> *Among the documents was an expense report showing that a company called Mabuhay Corp., based in San Francisco and reportedly run by longtime Marcos friend Leonilo Malabed, had contributed $51,500 in 1980 to the campaign of President Jimmy Carter and $50,000 to the campaign of then-candidate Ronald Reagan.*
> *Spokesmen for both campaign organizations said they didn't knowingly take any contributions from associates of Mr. Marcos. The list also showed other contributions to several California politicians, all of whom made similar denials.*
> *The expense report indicates that Mabuhay had received $1 million from a Philippine government bank for "intelligence" purposes. The report says Mabuhay had spent $762,000 by February 1982, including $506,000 on "special security projects" and $175,200 for "'political contributions" [42].*

While the offices of the mentioned politicians initially denied having knowingly received money from Marcos, Democratic Senator Alan Cranston of California later discovered that Malabed and an associate had contributed $1,000 to his 1980 campaign [43].

The other purposes for which the money was utilized was to try to neutralize the growing anti-Marcos opposition in the US. Malabed also had made some attempts to organize a radio station in California for Marcos. It was these projects which were labeled as "intelligence" and "special security" projects. Other purposes for which the money was used was to harass Filipinos in the US who opposed Marcos. In one incident two Filipino union workers in Seattle, Washington were murdered because of their political activities. A Seattle jury later found Malabed, together with Imelda Marcos, guilty of complicity in the two murders and were ordered to pay millions in indemnities in 1990.

The allegations of political contributions to US politicians appear to violate US Federal law. The relevant part of the Federal Election Campaign Act of 1974 clearly prohibits US politicians from receiving contributions from foreigners:

> *A foreign national shall not directly or through any other person make a contribution, or expressly or impliedly promise to make a contribution, in connection with a convention, caucus, primary, general, special or runoff election in connection with any local, state or Federal public office [44].*

But notwithstanding such prohibitions Marcos not only used conduits but also went as far as personally admitting to having made such illegal contributions. Two Americans, Richard Hirschfeld, a Virginia-based lawyer, and his associate, Robert Chastain, held several meetings with Marcos during his exile in Hawaii and were able to tape some of the conversations. On 21 May 1987, Marcos, apart from talking about the military invasion of the Philippines he was planning, claimed that he had made contributions to US politicians and bragged about the influence he held over them. Malone, the investigative journalist referred to in the last chapter, describes parts of the tapes:

> *What made US officials even more nervous, however, were Marcos' tape-recorded claims of continuing influence over several high-ranking US officials at the Pentagon, the State Department, and the White House. Marcos, according to sources, had even talked about having made illegal campaign contributions to President Reagan himself Hirschfeld will only say that he would rather not discuss that at this time. When Hirschfeld's tapes fell into the hands of Congressman Stephen Solarz of New York, the chairman of a House foreign affairs sub-committee, he was asked by Frank Carlucci who was then Reagan's national security adviser, to postpone a planned hearing for reasons of 'national security.' After one postponement Solarz decided to go ahead with the hearings, but he agreed to delete what he later characterized as 'scurrilous segments' about Reagan and other government officials [45].*

Whatever may have been contained in the "scurrilous segments" edited out of the Congressional hearings, we do know that Marcos and Reagan maintained an extremely close relationship throughout their political careers. The two were already close personal friends wnen Reagan was serving as Governor of California. The Reagans were lavishly entertained as personal guests of the Marcoses at this time. Furthermore, when Reagan's eldest son, Michael, and his wife, Coleen, visited the country in February 1982, Marcos went out of his way to introduce Michael to key government officials connected with the local shipping industry such as Captain Victorino A. Basco, administrator of the Maritime Industry Authority, and also suggested further meetings with Generoso Tanseco of the Philippine Shipyard & Engineering Corp. and officials of the Bataan Shipyard & Engineering and the Philippine Ports Authority. President Reagan's son headed a marine engineering equipment firm which specialized in shipbuilding and repair. Imelda Marcos and Nancy Reagan also maintained a close relationship, at least while the Marcoses were still in power, and there were allegations that Imelda had given Nancy Reagan a $50,000 emerald necklace, but as we pointed out in the first chapter, this charge was later denied by the White House.

The strategic role the Marcos dictatorship played for the US as well as the warm personal relationships that Marcos carefully cultivated with American politicians earned him the unwavering support of the Republican leadership from the Nixon through the Reagan administrations.

American foreign policy strongly supported Marcos from the time he assumed the presidency until the very last moments of his rule. It was largely through the help of American intelligence agencies that Marcos capturerd the presidency of the country in 1965. Tne imposition of martial law in 1972, the ruse Marcos used to impose a dictatorship, was carried out only after consultation with the Nixon administration. It was only after Alejandro Melchor, Marcos' Executive Secretary, had arranged several lengthy exchanges with the US State Department and Henry Byroade, the American ambassador to the Philippines, that Marcos imposed his dictatorship. These consultations with American foreign policy makers were capped with a telephone conversation with President Nixon, where Marcos reportedly asked for his blessing in the imposition of martial law. A February 1973 US Senate Staff Report, written a few months after the imposition of the dictatorship, is typical of the thinking of US foreign policy makers at this time:

> *We found few, if any, Americans who look the position that the demise of individual rights and democratic institutions would adversely affect US interests. In the first place, these democratic institutions were considered to be severely deficient. In the second place, whatever US interests were -or are- they apparently are not thought to be related to the preservation of democratic processes.*

The Reagan administration was especially supportive of the Marcos dictatorship. Not only did it continue the traditional economic and military support that given to previous administrations extended but it also went out of its way to legitimize the dictatorship with the international community. Soon after Marcos had himself declared the winner in a rigged presidential election, officials from the Reagan administration heaped praises on the dictator. Secretary Alexander Haig assured Marcos of continued American support and handed him a personal letter from President Reagan congratulating him for his "reelection." In a veiled apology for the criticisms the Carter administration levelled against the human rights abuses under the Marcos regime, Secretary Haig termed Marcos' reelection as a "wonderful victory" and told him that

> *You are going to find America with you not in a dominating way, not in a pedantic way, but in a true partnership of equality and friendship.... You can be indeed be confident that there is a new America... an America that understands that it must once again bear its burdens that history has placed on our shoulders, to lead and to shore up, when necessary those endangered in the front lines of the great risks we face today.*

And if these were not enough, Vice President George Bush went to Manila to personally attend the ceremonies which formally declared Marcos President for another six years. In his inauguration toast to Marcos, Bush pledged to support the Marcos regime, saying

> *We love your adherence to democratic principles and to democratic processes.... We will not leave you in isolation.... It would be turning our backs on history if we did.*

When Marcos made an official trip to the US in late 1982, Reagan went out of his way to show his support for America's "oldest and most important ally in

Southeast Asia" [46]. Not only did Reagan affirm his support for the dictator but Marcos' deceit was also given an implicit imprimatur when Secretaiy of Defense Caspar Weinberger handed Marcos copies of medals which Marcos had falsely claimed he had earned during the Second World War [47],

Even as the Marcos entourage was looting the country when they left on US Air Force planes, Secretary George Shultz was describing Marcos as a "staunch friend of the US" and "a constructive force" in the Philippines.

The support continued even while Marcos was in exile in Hawaii. Despite the preponderant evidence that Marcos was planning an invasion of the Philippines from American soil and was therefore in direct violation of the US Neutrality Act, there were no attempts to prosecute Marcos for these violations. The most the US did was to warn the former dictator against these violations and to look for another haven for their guest who was quickly becoming an embarrassment. Moreover, inspite the numerous revelations about Marcos' corruption, Reagan gallantly defended his old friend, who was staying in the US as his special personal guest, saying that "as far as I can recall, he [Marcos] was already a millionaire before he came into office."

The special treatment that Marcos received from the Reagan administration led Congressman Chester Atkins of Massachusetts to ask whether the Reagan Administration was "incredibly naive about Marcos" or whether the former dictator had "some sinister hold" over the US government.

One possible "sinister hold" Marcos may have had over certain US officials could be the clandestine ties that he enjoyed with American intelligence agencies which not only supported his dictatorship but also have monitored the growth of his fortune and may also have helped him squirrel it out of the country.

American intelligence agencies were certainly aware that Marcos and his wife were systematically looting the country over the years. Mijares, the former Marcos cabinet member mentioned in earlier chapters, claims that the CIA was aware that Marcos had alreacfy "stolen funds ranging from not lower than several hundred million US dollars to two billion US dollars" by the time he ended his first term as president in 1969.

> The corruption of the Marcos Administration even compelled the Central Intelligence Agency (CIA) to revise its profile on Marcos to include therein an observation that Marcos was "incredibly corrupt," having amassed as of the year 1969 a total asset of cash and other holdings in the Philippines and various foreign countries, including the US and Switzerland, to the tune of TWO BILLION ($2,000,000,000.00) DOLLARS [48].

Mijares cites the revelations made by John Marks, a former assistant in the Bureau of Intelligence & Research in US State Department who had seen a Marcos psychological profile prepared by the CIA. Marks, who later co-authored the best seller CIA - Cult of Intelligence, came across the profile in 1969 while working for the US State Department under Ray Cline, a former Deputy Director of the CIA. At the risk of legal sanctions and a jail term, Marks revealed the classified material in a lecture he gave at a seminar at the Lutheran School of Theology in Chicago on 11 May 1975.

In another study, the CIA concluded in 1976 that Imelda already had taken over a portfolio of four dozen companies. The Imelda conglomerate reportedly included several banks and was worth at least $150 million.

But aside from monitoring the growth of the Marcos fortune, it appears from different reports that the CIA and other US intelligence agencies may have actually helped Marcos ship the loot out of the country. CIA operatives had been certainly active in money laundering schemes for Filipinos and other Asians. One known case is that of Ronald Rewald, whose company the CIA admitted to using as a mail drop and "cover" for some of its operations in South East Asia. Rewald, who was convicted on 94 counts of fraud and perjury by a federal court in Hawaii in 1985, later admitted laundering money for Filipinos and other Asians.

Most of the reports concerning possible links between Marcos and American intelligence operatives revolve around the clandestine shipments of gold out of the Philippines. One account, reported by the Japan Times, claims that a substantial gold cache was brought out of the Philippines by a group composed of

an Australian, a former vice-president of an American aerospace firm, and a former US Air Force officer who was "once a pilot for both Air Force One and Air Force Two," the official names of the jets used by the President and Vice-President of the US [49].

A more revealing connection is that of Frank Higdon, a 67-year-old accountant from Alexandria, Virginia, who some federal investigators suspect as having been a frequent CIA operative [50].

Higdon first attracted attention when he contacted Wells Fargo, inquiring how a large quantity of gold from Manila could be transported into the US. Identifying himself as a CPA who was acting on behalf of a Manila client, Higdon attempted to arrange the transfer of gold bullion, estimated to weigh 75 kilograins per bar, using the facilities of Wells Fargo. Higdon, however, was advised by the bank that it could not deliver the gold to a private residence or a non-financial establishment, frustrating the attempt to ship the cache in this manner [51].

The name of Higdon surfaced again on 24 November 1983, when US Federal authorities held a certain Jose Cruz-Cruzal, later identified as an agent of Marcos' elite Presidential Security Command, for questioning in the Seattle-Tacoma International Airport. Documents in Cruz-Cruzal's possession had caught the attention of US Customs authorities as he disembarked from Northwest Orient Flight 20 from Manila. The documents, contained in a plastic bag, was described by a still-confidential US Customs investigative file as

voluminous documents pertaining to Marcos borrowing billions of dollars from a group of unnamed and/or undetermined banks through an individual identified only as Frank B. Higdon [52].

The documents contained Marcos' plans for obtaining the loans. One document explicitly prohibited banks associated with the International Monetary Fund from being used in the deals. Collateral for the loans would come from "four floors of gold stored beneath a bank in Manila," according to another document.

Both Cruz-Cruzal and his American bodyguard refused to answer any questions from US Customs authorities and insisted on contacting Higdon in Virginia. Malone quotes the parts of the secret US Customs file which describes Higdon's reaction when customs agents contacted him:

> *Upon being advised of the subject matter... Higdon immediately became hostile, saying only that US Customs should not interfere as Cruz-Cruzal's mission in the US was sanctioned by highly placed US government officials and that pursuing the matter would prove detrimental to the US government (and to [the agent's] career). Higdon then abruptly hung up [53].*

The Customs agents then immediately received a call from Higdon's lawyer who told them "that they would soon be contacted by a 'highly placed' US government official advising [us] of the national security involved and instructing US Customs to discontinue its investigation" [54].

The investigation was then officially ended. But the Hong Kong office of the US Customs Service discovered six months later that Hidgon's log of telephone calls included calls to Villacrusis, a trusted operative that Marcos had used in some gold shipments, and his close associate, Jesus Capilli.

Marcos himself later admitted his links with the CIA and Higdon. During the conversations that Hirschfeld secretly taped, Marcos confessed that the CIA was involved in shipping his gold cache out of the country. Malone summarizes the parts of the tape which were edited out of the congressional hearings:

> *In one of the deleted segments Marcos referred to his friendship with Reagan and talked about how the CIA had helped him to ship-and scll-the gold. 'It was those kind of things that astonished me,' Hirschfeld says. 'Marcos had told me the CIA had been involved. This was on the tape also, but they didn't play that excerpt at the hearing. The CIA wanted to use the gold or get the gold and he was going to have them use the gold to borrow cash from banks. He said the banks would have the gold as collateral if there was a default. [Marcos] mentioned this CIA guy in Alexandria, Frank Higdon, "The accountant,' he called him. This guy was involved in that scheme [55].*

The most politically explosive allegation centers on a money laundering scheme Marcos may have launched with Oliver North, the central figure in the Iran-Contra Affair, in cooperation with Israeli intelligence operatives.

It is already established that Oliver North had utilized General Fabian Ver, Marcos' Chief-of-Staff and personal bodyguard, in the scheme to transport military hardware to Iran. After Marcos was booted out of power, the San Francisco Examiner reported that General Ver had helped circumvent the arms embargo by signing fake end-user certificates for arms shipments to Iran. By signing the certificates, Marcos' Chief-of-Staff was in effect claiming that the arms shipment from Israel was going to the Philippines, thus providing an adequate cover for the operation.

But apart from this connection, which would have already been politically damaging had investigators focussed on it during the Iran-Contra scandal, a more politically sensitive Marcos-Ver-Oliver North operation, one dealing with clandestine shipments of gold, also appears to have occurred. Such an operation was so politically sensitive that its details are still kept secret by a US government trying to preempt the potentially damaging effects that a disclosure may cause.

The evidence of a clandestine gold deal come from Oliver North's notebooks. North's notes show him attempting to broker a big gold deal with the help of Richard Miller, a close Reagan aide who played a major part in the Iran-Contra scandal. Malone summarizes the contents of North's note-books:

> According to still-classified government documents, Marcos' 11th-hour machinations to move gold out of the Philippines didn't escape the attention of US intelligence and law-enforcement agencies. Yet the scope of his efforts, and the extent to which Oliver North, various CIA operatives, and others in the Reagan administration may have been drawn into them, still remains mostly a mystery - a story whose final chapter has been stamped 'top secret' by the White House on the grounds of 'national security. '
> Just six months before Ferdinand Marcos was forcibly escorted from his homeland by US military forces, North was ready, willing and apparently able to cut a deal secretly for a share of the Philippine dictator's ill-gotten assets.... North's globe-trotting bagman, Richard Miller, had called from London to outline the proposed transaction, and as he spoke North dutifully scribbled in his spiral notebook: "40 mt. $6 US commission... for Gold - Mtg tomorrow for addl 20 mt. - [code name] has agreed to $2.5M twice for a total of $5M." With a commission of $6.20per ounce on 40 metric tons (44 US tons) of gold - the terms outlined in North's characteristic shorthand - the total take on the deal would have approached $8.7million, and North's operation would have netted at least $5 million [56].

The scheme had its origins in Marcos' attempt to resmelt around 40 tons of gold with the help of some Israelis and reintroduce it to the international market. Malone cites the account of Kevin Kattke, an intelligence agent who had discovered that a large cache of gold was being unloaded in Israel and then contacted the Israelis involved:

> "I asked for two tons," Kattke recalls, 'and he said 'no problem'; they [the Israelis] had a lot more than two tons. The bars were huge - big heavy, and old — supposedly Japanese. But the bars were coming from a Philippine general named Ver. they were scared after the Aquino assassination in '83. The general had something like 40 tons and the Israelis were smelting it to get it back into the [international] system' [57].

Kevin Kattke later relinquished his role to Solomon Schwartz, an international arms dealer based in New York, and Richard Miller, North's associate who handled the funds in the Iran-Contra scandal. Schwartz, who claimed that "people in Washington were interested" in the deal, described the gold in this way:

> The amount was so humongous and the resmelting was a little strange, but when the gold was offered, I had it checked out. They were large, pre-World War II bars with peculiar markings. It was through generals acting on behalf of Marcos or his government. ' [58]

The account are intriguing not only because they involved General Ver but also because the descriptions of the gold fits the unusual characteristics of the gold bars that Marcos had been trying to spirit out of the country at this time.

The deal was apparently big enough involve Richard Miller, who in Schwartz's description "had good contacts at the National Security Council," an obvious reference to Miller's close relationship with Oliver North [59]. Miller had worked for the Reagan-Bush ticket as the person in charge of broadcast services during the 1980 campaign. After being assigned director of public affairs of the Agency for International Development, Miller joined North's clandestine operations in 1983. Miller in fact may have had information on the gold scheme independently of the Israelis due to his close access to North at the National Security Council and presumably to intelligence reports on Marcos prepared by William Casey at the CIA [60].

Studying North's notes, Malone figured that North would have made a huge amount in the deal:

> *Tapping on his desktop calculator, he no doubt found the numbers down-right inspiring: 44 tons equaled 1.4 million ounces, which, at a commission of $6.20per ounce, would work out to the princely sum of $8,729,600 [61].*

North's notes, however, only referred to a sum of $5 million, leaving around $3.7 million unaccounted for. The deal could therefore provide significant funding to the Nicaraguan contras, and as Malone puts it, "there might even be some money left over to compensate the patriotic facilitators for their efforts," the latter remark an obvious dig at the allegations that North had spent some of the money intended for the contras for his personal use.

North and Miller decided to cut the Israelis out of the deal and went directly to General Ver. According to Schwartz, "Rich Miller went to London and met with the contact.... Miller told him point-blank: 'We know the whole thing - give it to us'" [62]. This move then angered Ver who was concerned about keeping the deal secret. According to Kattke, General Ver fumed at his Israeli contacts, screaming, 'What are you doing, telling everybody?" [63]

Malone speculates that North may have been the 'highly placed' national-security contact who Frank Higdon summoned when pressed by Customs authorities. North and Higdon, however, have both declined to comment on the roles they may have played in the Marcos gold deals.

It is not clear if the deal ever went through. But reports concerning the underground activities of a former CIA agent and a Marcos operative in the US West Coast indicate that Marcos gold has already found its way to the US market.

Based on telexes and other documents which US Federal investigators discovered that Marcos had been sending from exile in Hawaii, it was learned that Constante Rubio, described as "one of Marcos' toughest and most sinister operatives," has been active in laundering Marcos gold [64], Rubio's first known deal is a reported sale of $42,000 worth of gold to an American real estate developer. The sale transpired in Hong Kong soon after the fall of Marcos [65]. But Rubio's other transactions, also recorded in the uncovered documents, involve bigger amounts and indicate the possible participation of the CIA. The paperwork pointed to Edward Dewey, the owner of the East Trading Company of Anaheim, California, and a certain former CIA operative who worked from Vancouver, Canada identified by the code name Mary Harper. A participant in a February 1987 related how Dewey and Harper planned to launder the gold by erasing marks indicating its Philippine origin. It was reported that Ms. Harper, now a commodities broker in Vancouver, wanted the 'Philippine hallmark erased completely.' The plan was to move five metric tons a day by "meticulously filing off the hallmarks" and later storing it in an underground vault of a large Southern California bank [66]. The arrangements to launder the gold, which had extremely pure ratings of 9995 and .9999, included the provision of security by the local police. Harper was reported to have admitted in that meeting that "a lot of influential US government officials were involved" in the gold deal [67].

A final nugget is the direct admission from Imelda's lawyer that the CIA and top US officials knew, encouraged, or were directly involved in the laundering of money out of the Philippines. During the federal racketeering trial against Imelda Marcos held in New York in 1990, Imelda's lawyer, Gerald Spence, argued that the CIA was aware of every transaction Marcos made and that then-Vice President Bush had even encouraged Imelda to bring money out of the Philippines and invest it in the US.

It is important to recount the relationship Marcos enjoyed with top political figures abroad because it directly affects the conduct and outcome of the recovery efforts.

At the practical level, politicians who abetted, encouraged, or even collaborated in laundering money out of the Philippines would almost certainly be averse to any form of investigation of the former dictator's accounts. Self-interest on the part of these politicians would almost automatically assure their silence.

But while a conspiracy theory might be a tempting explanation, it is not a necessary one. It is sufficient to show that the cozy relationships Marcos cultivated with overseas politicians have permitted the dictator certain privileges which would have meant jail for many other less-connected individuals. The manner in which overseas politicians perceived Marcos necessarily influenced their decisions towards him [68], It is clear that certain overseas politicians maintained biases which precluded objective judgement when dealing with the former dictator. That Marcos was treated with so much favor is therefore not necessarily part of a conspiracy but merely a consequence of the honest perception that he was a valuable ally and friend. Such biases can obviously affect government policy and the way laws are interpreted.

It is perhaps a consequence of such set notions that allowed the Reagan administration to treat Marcos favorably even when he was already breaking American law. After it was disclosed that Marcos and his entourage had entered Hawaii canying crates of valuables in two US Air Force cargo planes, the Reagan administration unabashedly came to the aid of the dictator. While Marcos had brought in at least $15 million in cash but declared only around $120,000, breaking US Federal regulations that required that any amount greater than $10,000 be declared to Customs authorities, the dictator was quickly exonerated by the Reagan Administration. After the exposes of the vast amounts contained in the Marcos crates, Larry Speakes, Reagan's spokesman, proclaimed to an incredulous public:

> *according to law anyone carrying in more than $10,000 worth of cash or negotiable instruments must fill out a currency and monetary instrument reporting form.... any amount may be declared so long as the form is filled out. We do not release that information unless we find that US law has been violated. At this time **we do not find that US law has been violated [emphasis ours]**.*

Even the interpretation of law can be affected by such bias, as the rulings of federal judge US District Judge Harold Fong have shown. Again inspite of the prima facie evidence of theft that the crates of goods presented, and notwithstanding protestations from the Philippine government [69], Judge Fong showed his partiality to Marcos by ruling that the former dictator could get back, without having to pay taxes, the goods that US Customs authorities held. Fong said that Marcos did not need to pay taxes on the 22 crates because of "a federal law exempting high officials of foreign government and such distinguished foreign visitors that may be designated by the Department of State.

The disclosure of information relating to Marcos' financial operations in the US may have been similarly affected by the political predispositions of US policy makers.

Marcos also brought with him voluminous documents detailing his financial dealings as he carted his crates of valuables and cash into Hawaii. But the manner in which these documents were handled by the US government again raises questions whether US policy makers acted properly or were swayed by other considerations. Despite repeated requests both from the Philippine government and an investigative subcommittee of the US House of Representatives to release the papers, the US federal authorities were less than cooperative. The requests for disclosure were first flatly refused. Then there was a great amount of dillydallying. And when the documents were finally made public, it was later learned that not all of the documents were disclosed and that a lot of editing had taken place. The Washington Post raised the question whether the documents that were made public were not "decoy vouchers for money that was diverted elsewhere" [70]. The concern is quite legitimate. An analysis of the 2,300 pages which were turned over did not reveal anything substantially new about Marcos' finances. The documents covered topics which were already widely known. Moreover, papers which bordered on the trivial abounded, such as a prayer in pidgin Latin which Marcos presumably used. They were hardly the most important papers which a methodological mind such as Marcos would carry when going into exile. Officials of the Reagan administration later admitted that not all of the papers were made public. Those which were considered "personal" were withheld. But, as we have tried to document in this book, the Marcoses no longer distinguished between what was personal and what belonged to the public coffer. Thus, some amount of arbitrariness would have been at work when Reagan administration officials labeled the documents as "personal" and not for disclosure. But a classified document cataloging the papers reveals concerns on the part of US officials which were not directly related to concerns about the privacy of Marcos' personal life: whenever the name of a US official would appear in the index, it would be blotted out. This may explain the reluctance of the Reagan administration officials to release the complete set of documents and the lag of several weeks before they finally released a partial set.

It should be noted that Salonga disappointingly acquiesced to receiving an incomplete set of documents. Not only did Salonga not press the US for a complete set of documents but he even publicly thanked Undersecretary for Political Affairs Michael Armacost, Philippine Desk Chief John Maisto, and Deputy Secretary John Monjo for "facilitating" the turnover of the papers [71], Salonga was later depicted basking in the limelight as newspaper photographs showed him receiving the morsels from US Congressman Stephen Solarz.

US monetary authorities were similarly uncooperative in disclosing information on Marcos' financial activities. While the US government has very strict disclosure requirements on amounts over $10,000, US federal authorities have yet to respond to requests for information concerning the laundering of gold out of the Philippines using American financial institutions. The Federal Reserve Bank in New York, which oversees the activities of the New York banks which Marcos utilized, has not accounted for these transactions or even replied to inquiries from the Philippine government concerning these transactions.

The foregoing considerations reveal another fundamental flaw in the Philippine government's efforts to recover Marcos' loot.

The purely legal approach Salonga and other officials of the PCGG adopted did not take into account that the cozy relationship between Marcos and overseas politicians could aversely affect the prospects of wealth recoveiy. Officials of the Philippine government naively believed that the purely formal aspects of the legal and judicial process would be sufficient to recover the money. Salonga, for example, was quite proud of early judicial victories in New York which placed some of Marcos' properties under a restraining order, rejoicing that "No other country has achieved this much before.... We have won every battle we have had to fight" [72].

But such optimism was not realistic, as the experience of the last years have shown. There is again strong indication that Marcos' past relationship with US officials have influenced how far Marcos would be prosecuted in the US.

A very clear example is the highly-publicized racketeering indictment handed down by a New York court against Marcos and Imelda. Many questions can be raised concerning how much pressure was exerted in the initial investigations, the manner in which the indictment was formulated and timed, and the actual conduct of the trial itself.

Marcos, Imelda, Adnan Khashoggi, and a few of their associates were indicted by a federal grand jury sittmg in the US District Court for the Southern District of New York on 21 October 1988 [73]. The indictment, which indicated that the grand jury had found enough basis to proceed with a trial, charged Marcos and his associates with violating US federal racketeering statutes. The indictment charged Marcos and his associates with several million-dollar transfers of money from the Philippines to purchase New York real estate, defrauding American financial institutions in the purchase of these properties, and the consequent fraudulent transfer of the multimillion dollar pieces of New York real estate they had purchased.

The indictment and the ensuing trial was given wide coverage by the media. But many important facts were overlooked. A recounting of some of these facts largely unnoticed by the public will not only explain the surprising outcome of tne trial but also clarify the political obstacles one faces in recovering Marcos' loot exclusively through the judicial process.

One incident occurred during the investigative phase of the case. When Rudolpf W. Giuliani, the US Attorney who was initially in charge of the case, was gathering evidence for the indictment and was planning to send a team of investigators to Switzerland to gather data on Marcos transactions, he was instructed by the Reagan administration to call off the trip [74]. Giuliani, who was also a member of the ruling Republican party, was told that the trip should not proceed on the grounds that it might jeopardize the 'national security' interests of the US [75].

When Giuliani's work culminated in a potentially strong case against Marcos and his associates for racketeering activities in the US, the Reagan administration intervened once more and "effectively quashed" that broad-based racketeering indictment [76].

Giuliani then redrafted the indictment. The new version pared down the charges [77] to real estate and bank fraud, fraudulent conveyance ofproperty, and the obstruction of justice. The charges were not only limited to the crimes the former dictator committed while he was already in exile in the US but also covered acts where Imelda, rather than Marcos, had played a leading role. There was no mention of the misuse of US economic and military aid to the Philippines, the theft of multimillion dollar loans from US banks intended for the Philippine treasury, the laundering of gold through US financial institutions, the multimillion dollar purchases of expensive art, CIA complicity in Marcos' financial transactions, illegal contributions to US politicians — issues which were all potentially damaging to a Republican leadership which had already been badly tarnished by the Iran-Contra scandal. Malone cites a source close to negotiations as saying

> *The Justice Department got Giuliani down to just three counts.... None of the heavy charges can be brought now. They are trying to make sure it dies a slow death [78].*

But even with the watered-down version of the indictment, the Reagan administration was still reluctant to approve the indictment. The Reagan administration, smarting from the complications brought about by the indictment of General Manuel Noriega of Panama, had earlier issued guidelines to the US Justice Department that any future indictment of foreign leaders should have prior approval of the US State Department and the White House. Marcos, while technically no longer the ruler of the Philippines, was placed under this category, because of tne implications that such an indictment would have on US foreign policy and the individuals who formulated it. The White House then dragged its feet in approving the indictment. Statements earlier made by an official of the Justice Department quoted by the Wall Street Journal explain the reluctance: "We're trying to support the new government without offending Marcos" [79]. The White House approved the indictment only after an exchange of letters between President Reagan and Marcos on 20 October 1988, a day before the actual indictments were handed down. The decision was made only when it was clear that Marcos was already terminally ill and could not possibly survive the long court proceedings. The trial might not have been approved at all if the New York-based Village Voice [80] had not heard of the secret deliberations in the White House and leaked the news to the public, thus embarrassing the Reagan administration into proceeding with the case.

But as the judicial process slowly took its course, Marcos was exempted from the court proceedings on the grounds of poor health, leaving Imelda and the rest to face the charges. This maneuver clearly later influenced the outcome of the trial since a major focus of the indictment was dropped from the case. It also prejudiced the jury since its members were averse to singling out for retribution a person who was depicted by defense lawyers as a poor widow who knew nothing of her husband's activities.

The subsequent acquittal of Imelda and the other defendants was surprising because some oi the accused had already implicitly admitted guilt. One defendant, Rodolfo Arambulo, a Filipino dentist based in Los Angeles who was a close Imelda associate, had already given himself up to US federal authorities after a period of hiding and had agreed to turn witness against Imelda. Roberto Benedicto, the Marcos crony who was included m the indictment, had also sent feelers for a negotiated settlement sometime in the course of the trial. During the trial itself, much was also revealed in cross-examination process. Adnan Khashoggi confirmed that he had indeed backdated documents for the Marcoses, while denying knowledge that it was in violation of an existing court order. Jaime Alberto Arias, the Panamanian lawyer used to backdate the documents, also admitted to participating in the irregularity. So the question that naturally arises is why despite these admissions Imelda and her associates were all unanimously acquitted.

The best explanation can be found with the members of the jury itself. Right before they joined Imelda in a combined birthday and post-trial victory celebration, the individual jurors explained in interviews tneir reasons for acquitting Imelda and the rest of the defendants. The jurors were unanimous in saying that Imelda and the others were acquitted not because they thought she was innocent but because the prosecution performed extremely poorly in proving its case. Here are excerpts from interviews with some of the jurors as reported by different New Yorlc newspapers:

Catherine Balton, jury forewoman
It was a poor case. There was nothing to convince us there was a case — it was poorly prepared." Associated Press phone interview, New York Post, 3 July 1990. There was no evidence. It was a poorly prepared case. Daily News, 3 July 1990. There was no evidence. There was nothing to convince any of us that there was a case. New York Times, 3 July 1990. There wasn't enough evidence to convict." New York Newsday, 3 July 1990.
Llewellyn White
"There was a lot of evidence and key people who were not there, and should have been. For example, the Bernstein brothers." New York Newsday, 3 July 1990. They had access to everything involved in this... The CIA was involved. The FBI was involved. Nothing was hidden from them.... They shouldn't have had any problems bringing any documents or anyone to trial." New York Newsday, 3 July 1990.
Anna Sneed
There wasn't any concrete proof that she knew of any racketeering. Speaking for myself and the others, we had a feeling that she knew about some of the schemes, but the

government didn't prove it" Daily News, 3 July 1990. Their [witness'] memories were very good on Mrs. Marcos' involvement, but when they were asked about dates and times and moneys and what was said in reference to their part in it, they had a lapse of memory" Daily News, 3 July 1990. It didn't feel the government had a case. They had mountains of evidence, but it wasn't against Mrs. Marcos." New York Post, 3 July 1990. "I am wondering why they even bothered and spent all this money bringing them to trial and they couldn't prove anything." Daily News, 3 July 1990.

Thomas O'Rouke

"Was it wasted? That's a very good question... I don't know. They did a bad job, a bad job. And they should have known there was a bad case. And if they knew...." New York Newsday, 3 July 1990. "We thought the government did a terrible, terrible job.... They had half-truths and not the right witnesses. It was at terrible case." New York Times, 3 July 1990.

* lack of good witnesses who never took the stand or those who "just lied and you could tell they were lying" Daily News, 3 July 1990. There wasn't a hell of a lot of evidence.... And what they did [have] had flipped back and forth. Witnesses were conflicting." New York Newsday, 3 July 1990. They did a bad job, a bad job. And they should have known it was a bad case... There was no meat on anything.* New York Newsday, 3 July 1990. "...we figured they had no case against her. They showed us really nothing..... They were

reaching for straws.* New York Newsday, 3 July 1990. "It was an easy decision, really. There were no facts to go by. The government did a crummy job. It was a totally silly case.* New York Post, 3 July 1990. 'it was easy... The first day we took a vote [on] what we thought about the whole thing. It was 10 for acquittal and two for conviction.⁰ Daily News, 3 July 1990. "We do not know why they brought him [AK] into this case" New York Post, 3 July 1990 "Once we found her [Imelda Marccs] innocent on the first counts, we found it hard to find that he [AK] had anything to do with it." New York Newsday, 3 July 1990.

The jury was unanimous in blaming the strategy of the prosecution. One juror, Thomas O'Rouke, called it "a totally silly case" [81]. O'Rouke further charged that Giuliani, who had been preparing to run for Mayor of New York City, as "trying to make a name for himself [82] and that he "needed somebody of higher authority to convict" [83]. The acquittal therefore cannot be taken to mean that Imelda and the otner defendants were innocent of the charges. It just meant that the prosecution did not prove its case.

Neither was the verdict a vindication of the legal prowess of Gerald Spence, Imelda's highly-paid defense lawyer. Spence, who had received the greater part of the reported $4 million Imelda coughed up in legal fees, had encouraged an image with the media as a crafty lawyer and had even once described himself as "the best trial lawyer he ever knew" [84], But Spence had fumbled on many occasions during the trial, was reprimanded by the judge on several instances, and also had disputes with the other defense lawyers. The jurors were not impressed with him. Juror O'Rouke was not impressed with the performance of Spence and contended that the onus of the trial remained on the prosecution [85].

The jury verdict that the prosecution did not present enough evidence and therefore did not prove its case was surprising because the prosecution did have a lot of evidence and witnesses. It presented tens of thousands of documents. Charles La Bella, the US attorney who replaced Giuliani after the latter had relinquished his prosecutorial office to run for City Mayor, had even gone to the Philippines to interview potential witnesses in the trial. The result was that the prosecution had called on several dozen witness to buttress its arguments, setting a precedent in the history of US legal proceedings for presenting the greatest number of witnesses. The claim of lack of evidence is therefore surprising.

The problem lay in the witnesses the prosecution called upon. While the Philippine government had bragged before the trial that it had 200 former Marcos cronies willing to testify, the prosecution did not call upon the most important and most crucial individuals. The prosecution surprisingly did not cll any witness that could directly link Imelda to the charges. Some of the witnesses, while initially presented by the prosecution, actually ended up defending Imelda. There was the case of Jaime Laya, a former Marcos cabinet member. Laya was a witness for the prosecution, but at the end of his testimony the judge instructed the jury to consider his testimony to be in favor of Imelda. Another case was that of the actor George Hamilton. Hamilton had made a deal with the government to turn witness against Imelda. But during his testimony, Hamilton did not testify about the reported financial favors he had received from Imelda but rather recounted that she was instrumental in helping save the life of his mother, a topic which surely touched the emotions of some of the jury members.

The problem also lay in the potential witnesses the prosecution did not call upon to testify. Of these tne following important omissions may be mentioned:

• **The Bernstein** brothers, the agents Imelda used to purchase her New York real estate empire, were central figures in Imelda's purchases. Yet they were not even called upon to testify against her. More surprising was the fact that the Bernstein brothers were not even included in the indictment. This is despite the fact that the Bernsteins had already publicly admitted before the Subcommittee on Asian and Pacific Affairs of the Foreign Affairs Committee of the US Congress, as well as before various court hearings and depositions, that they had indeed worked and fronted for Imelda.

• **Gliceria Tantoco**, one of Imelda's closest confidants who had helped her purchase expensive art and properties in New York, was likewise not called to the stand. Gliceria Tantoco and her husband had already been previously convicted by Italian authorities and were supposed to be serving a suspended sentence in Rome, therefore theoretically making them within easy reach of US law authorities.

• **Roberto Benedicto**, a close Marcos crony who was indicted with Imelda, had sent feelers for a settlement but he was likewise spared from testifying in the trial.

• **Imee Marcos**, the dictator's eldest daughter, was already facing contempt charges in Virginia for refusing to testify before a grand jury hearing charges of misuse of US military aid. Imee Marcos is one of the few individuals who knew about most of her father's machinations, having made a thorough inventory of the assets in the early 1980's. Instead of being jailed for contempt of court, Imee was quietly allowed by US authorities to leave the US and settle in Morrocco where the Marcos family is believed to also have holdings.

• **Bongbong Marcos**, the dictator's only son, could have also been called upon to testify. Marcos himself had admitted that his son was one of the few people who really knew where his gold cache was hidden. Bongbong was in the US as a guest of the government.

˙ **Jonathan de la Cruz,** a close aide of Bongbong Marcos who was reported to have also been involved in the gold deals, is moves freely in Manila and also travels to the US. He could have also been subpoenaed to testify if US federal authorities wished him to.

• **Vilma Bautista**, Imelda's personal secretary who also would have been able to give substantial testimony, was not even mentioned in the indictment. Bautista is known be living in the US and therefore within easy reach of a subpoena to testify.

Given the vast resources US federal authorities spend in the surveillance of its own citizens, and also given the reports that the Inteipol (International Police) had been mobilized to locate Benedicto, it is doubtful that individuals like Benedicto and Bautista would not have located if there were an earnest effort to do so.

Thus Gerald Spence did not even have to present any witnesses for the defense of Imelda. All Spence had to do was to tell the jury that the prosecution had not proven its case. There were no relevant documents presented, and neither were there any witnesses who could directly link Imelda to the purported crimes. Imelda was therefore absolved of culpability without her having to resort to the line of defense which at the start of the trial seemed to be the only feasible one for her - to plead not guilty by reason of insanity.

The decision to call some witnesses and not others may have been the result of either an error in judgement on the part of the prosecution or a policy decision consciously taken. If it was an error in judgement, it then calls the competence of the prosecutors into question. If it was a policy decision consciously taken at higher levels of political authority, then a conspiracy can be charged. In any case, the outcome of the trial is an indictment of either efficacy or seriousness with which US federal authorities prosecuted their former friend and ally.

If the indictment and trial of Imelda failed to prove her guilty, what it did prove was the inherent limitations of a purely legal approach which operates in the abstract, oblivious to the formidable and often hostile political environment in which it operated. Such an outcome leads us to sadly ask whether lip-service pronouncements concerning an "adherence to democratic principles may be in fact the best way to subvert those principles.

TREATIES OF TYRANTS

Given the significant obstacles of economic competition amongst international financial centers and the political dominance in these places of uncooperative institutions, the ideal and perhaps only possible strategy is to use a combination of economic, financial, historical, and legal arguments to prove the case for recovery. Such an approach also requires that the purely legal approach be complemented with a combination of political pressure and diplomacy. This section differs from the rest of this chapter in that in discussing the third level, the strategic, it outlines what may be the only possible way the Marcos loot may be ultimately recovered.

The multi-billion international debt burdening the Philippines is the largely the result of the manner in which Marcos and his cronies incurred loans from international financial institutions. The previous chapters documented how the Marcos gang drew loans from international banks with the sole object of defaulting on these loans and pirating the money to private overseas bank accounts. This practice is the principal cause for the sharp increase in the country's international debt problem.

Marcos and his cronies were able to acouire these loans because the government had certified that the money would be for government-approved projects and because Philippine government banks acted as the official conduits and guarantors of such debts. The loans were possible because government banks shouldered the responsibility for the loans that were being extended to these people. In other words, while the dictator and his friends were benefitting from the loans, it was the ordinary Filipino who was held responsible for the billions in debt, with the national patrimony and the welfare of future generations of Filipinos being offered as collateral.

But very little, if any, of these loans went into productive investments that improved the economic well-being of the country. Most of the loans were designed as a quick method for Marcos and his cronies to raise cash. Disini and the multimillion loans for the non-functioning Westinghouse nuclear power plant is one of most blatant examples of these fraudulent bank loans documented in the previous chapters. As soon as the loans were extended, Marcos and his cronies immediately found ways to get the money out of the country and into their private bank accounts. In some cases, a few book-keeping entries in New York banks — debiting the accounts of the Philippine government while crediting the private accounts of Marcos and his cronies -- sufficed, rendering the actual movement of capital superfluous. Increases in the assets of Marcos and his cronies were balanced off by increases in the debt of the Philippines. The problem of dirty money therefore has as its necessary counterpart the international debt position of the Philippines. Capital flight and tne external debt are but the reverse sides of the same coin [86]. One is the obverse of the other.

The very same banks discussed in the previous chapter as responsible for helping Marcos and his cronies launder money out of the country were also the same institutions which encouraged the increase in the external debt of the country. This was an ideal way for the bankers to earn twice on their banker's fees using the same money. Banks extended loans to the Philippine government, earning money in the process, but at the same time they also encouraged the exit of the money through the mechanisms of "international private banking". The effect of this technique was to increase the assets of the bank because it would be holding a claim against the Philippine government (the loan) while receiving an influx of capital from Marcos and his cronies (the deposit). An economist writing for the New Republic describes the relation between capital flight and international debt, and the complicity of many major international banks in fostering these capital movements:

In some cases, the wealthiest classes of poor countries have actually sent more money out of their countries than foreign borrowing has brought in - and often it's the same money. American banks have promoted, and profited from, both sides of the transaction. Sometimes the money never leaves the US. The entire cycle is completed with a few bookeeping entries in New York. (The money) ...flowed right back out of the door, often the same year or even month it flowed in. Indeed, there are already enough private foreign assets owned by the citizens of major debtor nations to go a long way toward servicing their countries' foreign debts. The most aggressive banks, such as Citibank, have probably accumulated almost as much in assets from poor countries as they have loaned to them. Their real role has been to take funds that Third World elites have stolen from their governments and to loan them back, earning a nice spread each way.

There therefore has been much discussion in some quarters about repudiating the loans Marcos and his cronies incurred. The options considered ranee from a total repudiation of all the loans incurred during the Marcos dictatorship to a "selective" repudiation of the most fraudulent ones. While international bankers often pretend to be shocked with such discussions and pontificate that loan repudiation is totally impermissible, there are ample historical precedents of loan repudiation:

> • *In the late 13th century, Edward I of England drew huge loans from the banking families of Bardi and Penizzi of Florence to finance his wars, promising to pay the debt through the taxes on the export of wool. But this method of payment had a perverse effect since the tax provided a disincentive on exports and thus in the ability to raise the cash for the payments. Edward III upon assuming the throne defaulted on debts, causing the ruin of the Bardi and Penizzi banks and the setting back the development of Florentine banking in general.*
> • ***The French*** *post-revolutionary government repudiated the debts of the royalist regime in 1792, proclaiming in a statement that "The sovereignty of peoples is not bound by the treaties of tyrants."*
> • ***The US*** *also defaulted on its financial obligations to England during the last century. The state governments of Louisiana, Maryland, Mississippi, and Pennsylvania repudiated the bonds they had issued to British investors, causing the investors to organize the British Council of Foreign Bondholders in 1868 and attempt to recover their losses, a venture which is reportedly still ongoing. The repudiation by US state governments of some of the debts owed to the English is what prompted Scrooge in Charles Dickens' A Christmas Carol to fear that his solid British assets had become a mere US security."*
> " ***Substantial*** *foreign investments in Europe were also lost as a consequence of World War I. The losses included not only the direct investments in Europe annihilated in the war, but also the foreign debts that were never paid or were outrightly repudiated. Britain lost 15% of its foreign holdings, while Germany lost all its foreign holdings. Loans amounting to $9 billion the US lent to its allies were not repaid.*
> • ***Perhaps*** *the most famous act of repudiation in history was when the Bolsheviks repudiated all the debts the Czar and the Kerensky governments had previously incurred. The Bolsheviks repudiated an estimated $4.5 billion in debts, a substantial amount in 1918, with the a revolutionary pronouncement that "All foreign loans are hereby annulled without reserve or exception of any kind whatsoever." The Bolsheviks proclaimed that "governments and systems that spring from revolution are not bound to respect the obligations of fallen governments." France, which lost considerable investments because of the repudiation, was further humiliated the Bolsheviks cited the proclamation of the French post-revolutionary government had made a century and a quarter earlier about the priority that the sovereignty of peoples had over the treaties of tyrants.*
> • ***In the*** *Philippine case, the precedent was ironically set by Marcos himself. After mounting criticism concerning the dangers of Disini's nuclear plant, Marcos announced in 1979: "Unless they remove my doubts about the safety of operation, I am going to seek the cancellation of the contract with Westinghouse on grounds that there is a violation of an implied warranty of safety for our people" [87]. Marcos then ordered Finance Minister Virata to stop paying the interest on loans from Exim Bank which then totalled $127,309 a day [88].*

The expropriation of foreign investments is another act of sovereignty which has been exercised by national governments. While expropriations are more common than debtor default, occurring almost after every revolution, the two acts are really vety similar. While expropriation has been historically linked with the confiscation of real assets owned by foreigners, debt default is aimed at the repudiation of the financial claims that foreigners have over the country. In both cases, there is a rejection of claims of foreigners to ownership.

Inflation can be considered a more subtle form debt repudiation. It is a less explicit but nonetheless equally effective form of debt repudiation when the inflation of the currency under which the debt is denominated is rising considerably faster than the rate of inflation of the currency of the debtor nation. The effect is the erosion of the real value of the payments [89].

Debtor default is even recognized in US law. Bankruptcy laws in the US recognize that there may be occasions where debtors may not be able to pay their loans and therefore have to declare corporate or personal bankruptcy. The law provides protection from creditors and opportunities for the eventual rehabilitation of the debtor.

Debt default and repudiation therefore come in many forms and are not as uncommon as most international bankers would have us think.

But Mrs. Aquino's advisers have continually and inflexibly refused to even consider the possibility. Despite clear evidence that international banks not only paid huge illegal commissions to Disini but also actively helped him plan the caper [90], certain Aquino cabinet members continue to commit the country to paying the $2.2 bilhon debt for the non-functioning plant. Interest payments alone for the Disini plant run $300,000 a day. Furthermore, there have been charges that Finance Secretary Jesus Estanislao and Central Bank Governor Jose Cuisia schemed to withhold information   from   Mrs.   Aquino and have at times even acted contrary to her wishes when it came to paying the loans for the power plant, the biggest single foreign debt of the country.

The foregoing discussion of dirty money, international debt, and the possibility of debt repudiation was an important prolegomena to enunciating a strategy for recovering Marcos' assets. If it is accepted that capital flight and international debt are but obverses of each other, then the problem of recovering the loot Marcos and his cronies stashed in overseas banks is capable of a solution. Considered independently of each other, dirty money and international debt are formidable problems in international finance, but when viewed as related issues, it can be argued that one is potentially the solution of the other.

The Philippines would well be within reason if she chose to repudiate all the debts Marcos and his cronies incurred. There would be ample economic, financial, legal, historical, and moral reasons to support such a move. The debts were contracted not by the Filipino people nor a representative government but by a repressive state acting for the interests a few individuals. The sole daim to legitimacy of this state was its repression of its people through military force. The international banks knew tnis to be the case when they extended the loans to the dictatorship. Yet, these international banks, eager to recyde the petro-dollars which was accumulating   in   their   reserves, shed their proverbial conservatism in extending loans and showed very little concern

as to where the money was going. International bankers even went as far as encouraging Marcos and his cronies to avail of the loans, the bankers smug in the belief that Philippine government banks would act as the loans' guarantors. The irresponsibility snown by these banks when they lent to Marcos and his cronies stand in sharp contrast with the great care they took to assure secrecy when these corrupt clients wanted to move the very same dollars out of the country. Such irresponsibility in lending reached unprecedented proportions that Benigno Aquino, the anti-Marcos opposition leader assassinated in 1983, was constrained to publicly warn the banks about their lending practices. Speaking from his exile m the US, Aquino warned the banks in late 1980 that they were risking the possibility of loan repudiation   should
they persist in their financial support of the Marcos dictatorship.

It certainly does not appear right from an economic, financial, legal, or moral point of view to hold an economically burdened people responsible for loans tnat they neither incurred nor benefitted from. Tne contracting parties in the loans were Marcos and his cronies on one hand, and irresponsible international bankers on the other. Drawing a loan from a bank and passing the responsibility of payment to another party is nothing more than an act of banditry. Yet, this is what international banks, complemented with the acquiescence of the Aquino government, are in effect doing when they require the present and future generations of Filipinos to pay for Disini's non-functioning nuclear power plant and the other loans that the Marcos gang contracted. Such considerations make loan repudiation a totally reasonable option. There is more reason to repudiate these loans than the different US states had when they repudiated the bonds they had issued to British investors. There is thus not only ample economic, financial, legal, and moral arguments for loan repudiation, but there is also sufficient historical precedent for such a move.

But it is not necessary to agree with the extremists who argue that loan repudiation is imperative to recover the Marcos loot and solve the debt problem. Another option is possible. The recovery of Marcos' stolen assets can be easily solved by the same book-keeping methods the international banks used to help Marcos launder the money out of the country.

Whenever debtor nations are not able to meet their loan payments, their international creditors institute a debt-equity swap scheme where debts are exchanged for ownership of some asset. Tnis move, similar to the foreclosure of a mortgage where the bank seizes the collateral for unpaid debts, is nothing more than an exchange of one type of asset for another: the claim against a debt is exchanged for the claim against some other form of property. If this procedure is followed in this instance, then the problems of dirty money and international debt can be solved at the same tune. All that is needed is to exchange the claims the international financial institutions have against the Philippines with the claims the Philippines has against the banks which hold a substantial part of the assets that were stolen. This requires nothing more than a few book-keeping adjustments in the ledgers of tne concerned international financial institutions. This is different from an outright repudiation or default of the debt. This position recognizes that a contract existed not between the Filipino people and the international banks but between the international banks and tne dictator and his cronies. As it is they who were the real parties to the loans and it is they who bear the legal and moral responsibility for its payment, not malnourished Filipinos. This option does not mean that the debt is not going to be honored. What it does is clarify which parties are responsible for honoring it. And since Marcos and his cronies have already stashed their loot in the coffers of the very banks that extended loans to the Philippines, all that is needed is for the banks to adjust their ledgers and make the proper adjustments by deducting from the accounts of Marcos and his cronies and at the same tune reducing the loans they hold against the Philippines. It is not inconceivable that the Philippines may end up as a net creditor, not a net borrower, of the international financial system.

This option will of course be fiercely resisted by the banks. They were the ones after all who motivated Marcos and the other crooks to draw the loans, they were also the ones who were responsible for bringing the money out, and they are also the ones who are presently holding the loot, ft is doubtful that the banks will face the consequences of their irresponsible policies on their own accord. Appeals to banking privacy will again be intoned.

The myth of banking secrecy therefore must be totally exposed once and for all. While banks habitually mvoke banking secrecy in tne name of the depositor, it is in reality a convenient ruse for the banks to protect their own interests. Not only is banking secrecy the principal commodity international financial centers use to compete against each other but it is also a weapon banks have used against their own depositors when conflicts of interest occur. The interest of the depositor is protected only while he does not attempt to withdraw substantial amounts of money, but accounts are frozen whenever significant amounts are involved. The example of Credit Suisse earlier recounted is instructive. Credit Suisse blocked the attempts of Italian companies to withdraw their laundered money. Marcos' case is also equally illuminating. When Marcos attempted to withdraw more than $200 million from his accounts through his representative Mike de Guzman, the Swiss banking system simply froze his accounts. Thus, banking secrecy can be and has been used against the depositors — money launderers, yes, but still their bona fide depositors — whenever the interest of the banks required it. The banks cannot do otherwise. The manner in which the international economic system is organized requires it. The structure of the Swiss economy, as well as that of other economies dependent on the provision of services, requires a wide welcome carpet for the influx of capital out exit doors difficult to open when capital attempts to leave the haven.

But the present setup can be used as a double-edged sword to strike against international financial havens such as Switzerland. If the international community begins to perceive that banking secrecy is arbitrarily enforced -- invoking it agamst those who seek to freeze laundered accounts at times, and invoking it against the launderer at other times — then the double-edged nature of the situation can be brought into play. The more money launderers are aware that Swiss banks can also freeze their deposits whenever the interests of the banks are threatened, then this realization will already then be a great disincentive in using these banks for the nefarious activity of money laundering.

An international conference on dirty money would be a step in the right direction in redefining the public's perception of international investment havens such as Switzerland. Such a conference can concentrate on identifying the victims and culprits of dirty money transactions and mapping out a common program of recovery. Since such a conference is to be carried out not as an academic exercise but as a practical step towards recovery, it would be ideal to start with a core of countries which have been most victimized this eviL Apart from the Philippines, other countries which could form such a core might include Chile which has been victimized by Pinochet's rule, Greece which has been attempting to recover the so-called Elgin marbles the British removed from the Parthenon during the last century, Haiti which has been impoverished by the Duvalier family. Such a group should automatically exclude two sets of interested parties from their organization: countries which continue to act as havens of dirty money, and lawyers who salivate at the prospect of high legal fees. Such a group, which can find much common ground with a group composed of the biggest debtor nations, will have a greater chance of exerting pressure and recovering their assets than will an individual third world nation. After getting organized and developing a common program, such an organization of dirty money victims can then enter mto negotiations with the investment haven countries and look for ways to reform the international financial system.

An organization of victimized nations might then be able to pressure the US to invoke the International Emergency Economic Powers Act, a special piece of legislation giving the US president the power to freeze assets in the US of foreign nationals and compel all persons and institutions in the US to cooperate in the gathering of information concerning these assets. The act, which permits the president to "regulate international economic transactions" during times when there is an extraordinary threat to "the national security, foreign policy, or economy of the US [91]," would have been the ideal vehicle for the recovery of the loot Marcos and his cronies stashed in US banks and real estate. Enacted on 28 December 1977, the measure, had it been invoked, would have permitted the quick identification of the assets, prevented their transfer, and would have opened other avenues not available under normal litigation.

The first time this special legislation was invoked was in 1979 when President Carter froze all Iranian assets in the US after the Shah of Iran was overthrown and Americans were taken hostage in Iran. After declaring that a national emergency existed, the necessary condition for the invocation of the act, President Carter then ordered on 14 November 1979 the freeze on all Iranian assets through Executive Order 12170. The pertinent part of the order, entitled "Blocking Iranian Government Property read:

> *I, JIMMY CARTER, President of the US, find that the situation in Iran constitutes an unusual and extraordinary threat to the national security, foreign policy and economy of the US and hereby declare a national emergency to deal with that threat. I hereby order blocked all property and interests in property of the Government of Iran, its instrumentalities and controlled entities and the Central Bank of Iran which are or become subject to the jurisdiction of the US or which are in or come within the possession or control of persons subject to the jurisdiction of the US.*

With a single stroke of a pen, President Carter was able to freeze the millions the Iranian government had in US banks and thus prevent their transfer. Other executive orders followed in the course of negotiating the release of the American hostages. Despite continuing protestations of American officials that they would never negotiate the release of hostages, the International Emergency Economic Powers Act also became an important if not principal bargaining tool in negotiating the release of the American captives. As part of the deal, the US government agreed to later remove the freeze on Iranian assets and allow their transfer, while at the same time decreeing a similar freeze on the US assets of the deposed Shah of Iran. Executive Order 12284, entitled "Release of American Hostages in Iran - Restrictions on Transfer of Property of Former Shah of Iran," was thus issued on 19 January 1981, decreeing that

> *§ 1-102. For purposes of protecting the rights of litigants in courts within the United states, all property and assets located in the US within the control of the estate of Mohammad Reza Pahlavi, the former Shah of Iran, or any dose relative of the former Shah served as a defendant in litigation in such courts brought by Iran seeking the return of property alleged to belong to Iran, is hereby blocked as to each such estate or person until all such litigation against such estate or person is finally terminated.*
>
> *§ 1-103. The Secretary of the Treasury is authorized and directed (a) to promulgate regulations requiring all persons who are subject to the jurisdiction of the US and who, as of November 3, 1979, or as of this date, have actual or constructive possession of property of the kind described in Section 1-101, or knowledge of such possession by others, to report such possession or knowledge thereof, to the Secretary of the Treasury in accordance with such regulations and (b) to make available to the Government of Iran or its designated agents all identifying information derived from such reports to the fullest extent permitted by law. Such reports shall be required as to all individuals described in 1-101 and shall be required to be filed within 30 days after publication of a notice in the Federal Register.*
>
> *§ 1-104. The Attorney General of the US having advised the President of his opinion that no claim on behalf of the Government of Iran for recovery of property of the kind described m Section 1-101 of this Order should be considered legally barred either by sovereign immunity principles or by the act of stale doctrine, the Attorney General is authorized and directed to prepare, and upon the request of counsel representing the Government of Iran to present to the appropriate court or courts within the US, suggestions of interest reflecting that such is the position of the US, and that it is also the position of the US that Iranian decrees and judgments relating to the assets of the former Shah of Iran and the persons described in Section 1-101 should be enforced by such courts in accordance with US law.*

The order against the properties of the Shah of Iran contained all the requirements necessary for the recovery of the assets Marcos and his cronies stashed in US banks and real estate. It prohibited the transfer of the properties of the Shah and his relatives, required all persons who knew about such assets to report them to the Secretaiy of the Treasury and provide the information the government of Iran, effectively precluded potential appeals to sovereign immunity or act of state doctrine that the former Shah might utilize in defense, and declared its position to be that all judgements in Iranian courts should be upheld in US courts. Quite significant is the provision that required all individuals with personal or constructive knowledge concerning the properties of the Shah to report detailed information on its location, value, and circumstances to the Secretary of Treasury within thirty days. The reporting requirement applied to all residents of the US, citizens and non-citizens alike, and covered even business relationships that were lawful.

Had the International Emergency Economic Powers Act been applied in the Marcos case, then the whole matter could have been resolved in a matter of a few months, saving on lengthy investigations and expensive litigation.

The Reagan administration was of course not predisposed to use the powerful act against its friend. There were no hostages being held in the Philippines and therefore no dramatic, television-worthy "crisis" to be addressed.

But while the Reagan administration could not have been expected to act against its former ally on its own, the Aquino administration could have done more to make representations with the US government to apply the International Emergency Economic Powers Act to the case of Marcos. Officials of the Aquino administration could have explained that a potential default of the debts of the Philippines to Citibank, one of the banks which lent most to the Marcos dictatorship, might precipitate a crisis to an important American banking institution which was already having problems with its great exposure to third world debt. Moreover, Philippine officials could have also pointed out that a failure to prosecute Marcos and his cronies might jeopardize the negotiations concerning the future of the American military bases in the Philippines, the largest outside continental US, and the future relations with the US. These are certainly major concerns. Without belittling the importance of American hostages in Iran, these economic, political, and diplomatic concerns appear to dwarf the importance of the Iranian hostage crisis since they affect tne US economy, its national security, and the conduct of its foreign policy, the three areas of concern for which the International Emergency Eamomic Powers Act may be invoked.

But the Act was never invoked. The Marcos clique was then able to transfer most their assets within a few months. An example of such transfers is found in the purported transfer of the expensive New York real estate and art works to Adnan Khashoggi to prevent them from being frozen in the courts. The Philippine government was then left to settle for bones thrown in their way to appease it [92].

It is interesting to note that the failure to invoke the Act and freeze Marcos and crony assets has much in common with the freeze in Switzerland of Marcos' private accounts. While it appears that one country was "freezing" while the other was not, the effect was the same - both had the effect of protecting the competitive position of each country as international investment havens. Switzerland, in ordering the freeze, showed that it was not willing to promptly return the Marcos private accounts to the Philippines, while the US, in not ordering a similar freeze, implied that it was permitting the former dictator to freely transfer his assets within the US. Thus, while there may be superficial differences in the moves of the US and Swiss governments, both had the effect of protecting the national economic interests of each country.

That "double standards" have been applied to dictatorships friendly to the US therefore appears to be true not only in the political support that Marcos received wnile he was in power but also in tne treatment that he received while he was a guest of the US. The treaty with the tyrant continued till the last days of the dictator.

TYPEWRITERS UNDER FLAGS

The utter failure to recover any substantial amount from the overseas hoard of Marcos and his cronies is due less to an uncooperative international environment than to the disorganization, ineptitude, and corruption within the Aquino government. This section analyzes in detail the strategic and organizational problems the PCGG experienced. It will attempt to show that the absence of a clear and realistic strategy, the demeanor of incompetence and corruption amongst those tasked with the job, and the lack of interest and support from the country's Chief Executive are the principal reasons for the pathetic outcome of the recovery efforts.

The failure, for example, to utilize the International Emergency Economic Powers Act as a tool of the recovery efforts lies not only in the friendly posture the Reagan administration had with Marcos but also - and perhaps more so — with the Aquino government. Given that the US was not predisposed turn against its former ally, the Aquino administration still could have done more to declare that the perceived partiality the US government lavished on the former dictator could jeopardize the relations between the two countries and could therefore be a potential foreign policy problem for the US.

The best time to have expressed this position was during the first few months of Mr. Marcos' downfall when Mrs. Aquino had the overwhelming and unprecedented support of the Filipino people and the esteem of the international community. The ideal approach would have been to declare the new government revolutionary in nature, thus freeing it from sterile legalisms, jail all the cronies, and negotiate with them only after they have been given sentences, thus increasing the bargaining position of the government. The key would have been to go after the criminals and not engage in a wild chase after assets. The convicts would then be the ones to lead the government to the hidden assets as part of a lighter sentence. These steps and more were clearly possible with tne declaration of a revolutionary government. They are the necessary consequence of the revolutionary act of repudiating the Marcos regime. The Freedom Constitution, the temporary charter operant immediately after Marcos' downfall, gave Aquino broad political powers for such moves, and her popularity then assured her the support of the people.

Mrs. Aquino could have then utilized her much-applauded speech to the US Congress to remind George Bush of his toast to the "adherence to democratic principles" and request that such rhetoric be turned into practical steps to recover the stolen money that lay in US banks and in real estate. The US Congress surely would have been given it a favorable hearing since Mrs. Aquino still enjoyed at that time the image of a widow who was successful in her peaceful crusade against a corrupt and brutal dictator.

But the proper preparations were not made. Instead of attempting to develop a recovery strategy Mrs. Aquino could have presented to US officials during her trip, members of the PCGG office in New York were more interested in squabbling amongst themselves as to would pose in pictures with the President when she visited New York.

And when the applause had died down after her speech to the US Congress, the discussions concerning the speech centered on the utterly petty -- the subsequent talk was not about issues but bordered on gossip: did Mrs. Aquino actually write the speech she read? One critic insinuated that no Filipino could really have written the speech since it was so good that it actually impressed members of the US Congress. It must have been an American speechwriter who actually penned it. This prompted Mrs. Aquino's Harvard-trained Filipino speechwriter to come forward to answer the critic and claim the authorship of the speech. Filipino honor was thus defended, but we are nowhere any nearer to recovering Marcos' loot.

The opportunity to have hammered out a bilateral agreement on recovering the stolen money was thus lost. The historical moment could have been easily seized and put to good use. If the US had invoked the International Emergency Economic Powers Act against the Shah despite what the counsel for the Iranians described as the "virulent hostility" [93] in the US towards the Khomeini government, then it surely might have given a crusading widow at least a sympathetic ear when she pleaded justice for her people. But the opportunity was squandered. No strategy was developed. The recovery efforts became a costly effort lasting several years and resulting only in token gains.

Mrs. Aquino was content with permitting Jovito Salonga define the recovery strategy in the Philippines as well as overseas. But Salonga had many blind spots from the very beginning, and these lacunae proved to be fatal in the end. Salonga, a lawyer by training, viewed the efforts as a complex legal issue to be resolved in Philippine and international courts. He was also a politician, and his future ambitions appear to have affected many of his judgements while he served as chairman of the PCGG. The dual public personality of Salonga — lawyer and politician -- explains much of the failure of the PCGG's recovery efforts since they determined the recovery strategy adopted and the choice of personnel to serve in the recovery efforts.

Salonga and those who succeeded him chose a recovery strategy which depended on litigation as the sole means of recovery. As early as a month after Marcos' downfall, Salonga had already forsworn any extra-legal or political approach to recovering the assets, continually promising a strict adherence to due process" [94]. This was a path that also found favor with the US since it relieved the Reagan Administration of having to act against a long-standing friend and former ally. The *Financial Times of London* already warned as early as April 1986 that this approach would be an inefficient one:

> [The PCGG] effectively abandoned its attempts to recover through political pressure the fortune stashed abroad...Instead, it has embarked on the long and costly process of recovering the assets through the courts, an exercise likely to take years and one which may yield only a fraction of the estimated $5 to $10 billion believed to have been acquired by Mr. Marcos during his 20 years in office [95].

The result of such a choice was disastrous. Such a strategy permitted the Marcos gang to transfer most of their assets while lawyers squabbled over procedures and investigators groped for evidence that would meet the stringent requirements of the court. It required expensive fees for the lawyers. It also proved to be absolutely inadequate since it dealt with literally only a handful of properties and astonishingly overlooked most of the properties catalogued m the previous chapter.

The PCGG then muddled through both in local and US courts, loosing one case after another. From the very beginning PCGG officials were very lenient with their prey. Raul Daza, a commissioner of the PCGG, even went as far as saying that the government would show "compassion" to any Marcos associate who voluntarily discloses any hidden wealth [96]. Such soft talk failed to produce results. In some cases Marcos cronies bribed officials to avoid prosecution. Even as the administration of Mrs. Aquino is ending, no crony nas ever been sentenced to jail despite the magnitude of their crimes.

There were some limited legal victories achieved in the US within the first few months after Marcos' downfall. The Center for Constitutional Rights (CCR), a New York-based legal organization which had volunteered its services to the Philippines within hours of Marcos' downfall, were able to win preliminary injunctions on four major properties in New York. Lawyers from the CCR volunteered their expertise to the new Philippine government and worked at a hectic pace during the first critical days to prepare the legal groundwork and acquire court injunctions against the transfer of the most important properties in New York. The results were admirable. The lawyers from CCR, who worked for free and under formidable time constraints, prevailed against the arguments of highly-paid Marcos lawyers, won the preliminary injunctions on the properties, and also consequently set legal precedent in law suits against former foreign rulers.

But these initial successes of the CCR were not fully utilized by the Aquino government. Due to the disorganization within the PCGG and the general ignorance of its officials of the long list of properties Marcos and his cronies had overseas, the legal gains achieved by the CCR were not utilized in the recovery of the other properties. While tne precedents the CCR won in US courts could have been utilized to attach other properties, the PCGG again squandered the opportunity. The recovery efforts thus slowly lost steam, and the whole overseas recovery program became a dismal failure.

The first signs of problems emerged when it appeared that some quarters wanted to drive a wedge between tne CCR and the newly-formed PCGG. One indication was an article written by a certain Kirk Johnson for the New York Times entitled "Manila Panel Seeking Marcos Assets Is Faulted by Some Over Its Lawyers" [97]. The article was highly unusual because it did not focus on the litigation record of the CCR in the Marcos cases, which was totally impeccable, but largely faulted the CCR for its ideological position of supporting progressive causes. While the *New York Times* has a tradition of very nigh journalistic standards and is a most respected newspaper, this particular article seemed to deviate from the norm because it tried to crucify the CCR by innuendo and by citing the highly biased views of an ideologically conservative group. An article from *The Nation* described the Johnson article as "a contract on an enemy target" that "some capo or other at *The Times* called" on the CCR and that it was full of "unattributed accusations, invented controversies and sly smears" [98]. Another wedge came less conspicuously when a certain US congressman quietly expressed the view to Salonga that perhaps another law firm less politically controversial than the CCR might better serve the interests of the recovery cases and privately named three such law firms that might be considered. The alarm raised by these curiously interested third parties may perhaps be explained partly because of a Mcarthy-like paranoia of progressive causes and partly because of concerns about potentially lucrative legal fees. The CCR has a consistent policy of taking on cases based on principle and public merit and of never charging legal fees from their clients. Severina Rivera, the chief legal counsel of the PCGG for its overseas operations who worked closely with the CCR, explained that "the whole legal world" was "salivating" at the prospect of the fees to be gained from the Marcos cases. An article from the New York Law Journal also raised the possibility that the "criticism springs from sour grapes over private firms not being retained in a potentially lucrative case" [99]. Despite tne admirable record of successes of the CCR m the initial recovery efforts, and although Salonga later published an open letter with the New York Times expressing confidence with the organization, the recovery efforts progressively came to depend less on the CCR and more on highly-paid lawyers as time went by.

The initial successes of CCR and the close relationship it had with the PCGG took a turn for the worse when Salonga appointed an individual named Rafael Fernando as the Executive Director of the PCGG and head the overseas recovery efforts.

The appointment of Fernando came as a suiprise to many of those involved with the recovery efforts since it appeared that this individual did not have the appropriate background for sucn an important job. Not only did Fernando not nave the proper professional credentials but he also was likewise because he had served as the general manager of Eduardo Cojuangco's trading firm in Los Angeles when Enrile and Cojuangco tried to organize a coconut cartel in the US in apparent violation of anti-trust laws. Fernando, moreover, had even refused to give testimony on the cartel activities of Cojuangco and Enrile when US federal investigators subpoenaed him for his deposition [100], This background is hardly ideal for such a sensitive position as the head of the overseas recovery efforts. Apart from these political concerns, the appointment also did not seem appropriate from a managerial point of view since Fernando was based in Los Angeles and was permitted to continue working there while most of the investigative and lit- igation work was in New York. It appears that theprimary reason that Salonga appointed this former Cojuangco employee was to further his personal political career. Fernando was the chairman of Liberal Party in the US West Coast, the political party which Salonga headed and had hoped to use as a springboard for the Philippine presidency in the event of a Marcos downfall [101]. Because this appointment was done not with the best interests of the recovery efforts in mind but was a blatant act of patronage through which a politician had hoped to further his own career, the overseas recovery efforts suffered irreparable damage.

Fernando's tenure as Executive Director of the overseas operations of the PCGG was fraught with controversy. Upon assuming his post, Fernando made many controversial and questionable moves such as dismantling the many volunteer groups working from Houston, San Francisco, and New York which were investigating and had done an admirable job in uncovering the assets Marcos and nis cronies in the US, spent inordinate sums on lawyers' fees, was extremely loose with the finances of the PCGG, failed to follow-up many important cases covering major Marcos assets, unilaterally made very important policy decisions without consulting the PCGG in Manila.

Soon after Fernando assumed his post, he initiated a campaign to quietly dismantle the different branches of tne PCGG in Houston, San Francisco, and the New York head office. The move appeared totally incongruous with the needs of the situation in the US since major Marcos assets were in these cities and much investigative and legal work was needed to recover them. Furthermore, these PCGG branches were manned by experienced, qualified and well-meaning volunteers from different Filipino communities in these areas who were working in the recovery efforts for free. Some of these volunteers were Filipino exiles who had been active against the Marcos dictatorship and had already done much prior work in researching these properties even before the downfall of the dictator. Many internal memoranda and letters reveal the confusion and deep resentment Fernando's moves caused. Susan Po, who Fernando dismissed as the PCGG head in San Francisco, complained about Fernando's underhanded tactics in a letter to Emmanuel Pelaez, the Philippine Ambassador to the US Fernando likewise dissolved the Coordinating Committee in New York without giving any reason and appointed an individual named Ernesto Medina who was previously associated with Agusto Camacho, an architect who at one time functioned as a front for Imelda in the purchase of the $4 million estate in Lindenmere, Long Island, and Edna Camcam, a close personal friend of General Fabian Ver, Marcos' Chief-of-Staff.

It appeared that these moves to dismantle the groups in Houston, San Francisco, and New York and staff it with individuals whom he could control were just a part of a general program on the part of Fernando to centralize all the overseas operations. In an arrogant show of power, Fernando also curbed the activities of Severina Rivera, who headed the PCGG's legal efforts in the US, issuing strict guidelines under which she would operate. The situation was at the very least curious since Fernando, who had no legal background, was directing Rivera, a Filipina lawyer who practiced in the US and had been active in the recovery efforts from the very beginning, how to conduct the legal battle against Marcos. Fernando then tried to slowly remove the legal initiative from Rivera and the CCR lawyers and shift it to highly-paid lawyers with whom Fernando felt more comfortable. Fernando then used lawyers he personally chose and sued Marcos under Racketeer-Influenced Corrupt Organizations Act ("RICO) statutes. But this case was poorly planned and weakly argued. It failed miserably, ending in a legal defeat for the Philippine side and the payment of huge fees to Fernandas lawyers.

The only known formal study of the overseas operations of the PCGG is a paper presented to Rutgers University by Jennifer Morgan, a graduate student of management. In her paper, written after extensive interviews with many individuals who had served as members and officials of the PCGG in the US, Morgan summarizes the organizational problems of the PCGG and the negative role Fernando played in the overseas recovery efforts:

> The influence of informal groups led to appointments based on political affiliations, not qualifications. Rafael Fernando is a friend of Jovito Salonga. He does not appear to be capable or interested in coordinating a large and diverse staff oriented toward accomplishing the objectives of the PCGG.... Existing leaders have been appointed because of their allegiance to Jovito Salonga. In order to fulfill this qualification, they are necessarily weak and insecure leaders in an organization that needs strong and

secure leaders in order to function. Paul Hersey and Kenneth Blanchard's Situational Theory of Leadership, would state that this situation requires a high task and high relationship style of leadership. Instead, the leadership style worst suited to the situation is presently being employed, that of low task and low relationship.

*Rafael Fernando has what one commission member called a **tingi** mentality [tagalog for small pieces], one that does not look at the large picture, nor grasp the full scope of the mission, nor marshall available resources toward accomplishing the organization's objectives. Instead, he takes little steps, stops, looks around to make sure everything is O.K. with his Manila boss, then moves on. Meanwhile assets slip away, people become disenchanted, and the organization stagnates. His primary concern lies in making sure his ass is covered.... This tingi mentality extended to his dealings with members of the PCGG (US), failing to recognize their reservoir of good will and productive capacity if allowed to participate in running the organization. He employed a non-participative and even secretive style of management, telling PCGG New York members that he was working with them but by his actions clearly working with a hand picked group. Since members are volunteers, these tactics soon engendered deep resentment.*

(Fernando practiced] management styles that exacerbated the given problems rather than mitigating them. Instead of promoting the goals of the organization and subordinating the influence of informal groups, management values and styles served to further weaken allegiance to the organization. PCGG (US) has deviated from its original strategic goals. It is not aggressively identifying more properties, nor actively facilitating the transfer of title for already identified properties, nor selling properties for which it already nos title, nor is it properly transferring proceeds to the Philippines [102].

The result was total disaster. Rather than concentrate on recovering Marcos' loot, PCGG members spent most of their time trying to contain the damage caused by an incompetent leadership. The net cast to recover the stolen hoard, already imperfect to begin with, suffered further gaping holes because of the organizational chaos, permitting Marcos and crony assets to escape.

There was complete failure to recover in all of the major areas where Marcos and cronies had known overseas properties. In some cases, no attempts at recovery were even made. Among these areas are the following:

• New York Real Estate
While the CCR was able to secure writ of injunctions against four major Manhattan properties early in the recovery efforts, the Philippine government failed to sufficiently pursue the matter. Three years after the injunctions were handed down, the Philippine government still did not know what steps to take to resolve the question. The Philippine government could not decide on what strategy to adopt with regard to the properties. The delay prompted US District Court Judge Pierre N. Leval, the presiding judge, to chide the Philippine government, saying that it "has given little assurance that diligent steps have been taken to resolve the case. Leval then increased the bond required from the Philippines to secure the buildings from $6 million to $15 million [103].
Furthermore, banks which lent loans to Marcos have also claimed ownership of the properties in the meantime, further complicating the issue. It turned out that Imelda and her associates had mortgaged the most expensive buildings in Manhattan. This means that even when the Philippine government finally gets the properties, they will not amount much since the mortgages have to be paid. It is believed that Imelda and her

associates mortgaged the buildings to acquire liquidity and place the funds in secret accounts.

Other US Real Estate

The CCR injunction covered only four major real estate properties in New York. But the Philippine government has done very little to recover the other real estate properties listed in the previous chapter, most of which are in New York, Texas, California.

Among the assets which the PCGG never bothered to pursue were the properties of Dovie Beams, the American mistressof Marcos, and George Hamilton, the close friend of Imelda, who was able to transfer some of the properties to the name of Adnan Khashoggi.

Gold

Nothing has been done to recover the gold that Marcos brought out, or even seriously investigate the whereabouts of the gold caches which are still reportedly in the Philippines.

Many intelligence reports were submitted concerning the existence of gold caches and plans to move them, but the PCGG has done nothing to recover them. One report talked about 75-kilogram gold bars in the basement vault of one of the five largest banks in Manila [104]. Another 17 tons of bullion was also reportedly hidden in the southern island of Mindanao [105].

An opportunity which appears to have really been squandered was when the PCGG allowed a cache of gold, estimated to be more than $96 million worth of 75-kilogram gold bars, to remain in an apartment owned by Jonathan de la Cruz, one of the closest associates of Marcos' only son, Ferdinand Jr. The Quezon City apartment of de la Cruz was guarded by the security men of Roque Ablan, a former congressman from Ilocos, Marcos' province, who remained fiercely loyal to the dictator. An informant of the Philippine National Bureau of Investigation (NBI) posed as a buyer, inspected 90 such gold bars on 28 August 1986, and later passed a polygraph test which lent credence to his account, according to a secret report of the NBI [106]. But despite the report, the PCGG still failed to act on the matter.

US Bank Accounts

Nothing was done to investigate and recover the money from hidden overseas bank accounts.

For example, a report prepared by a local PCGG team operating from the Philippines disclosed that a company owned by Floirendo, the crony who dominated the banana industry, was regularly moving money out of the Philippines through a branch of Citibank even after the downfall of the Marcos dictatorship. The report, complete with the Citibank branch and bank account numbers, was relayed to Fernando for action in the US, but Fernando did absolutely nothing to freeze the accounts.

Another example, equally exasperating, was a news account from the Daily News, a New York newspaper, asking Ferdinand Jr., Marcos' son, to pick up his money from a New York bank account which had been laying dormant for the last three years. The account was under Bongbong*s name and had been an inactive account. Even after the account was published in the papers, nothing was done to freeze the account.

Art and Antiques

The CCR had extensively investigated Imelda's art and antiques purchases in New York and secured an injunction against their transfer in early 1986. But beyond this initial victory, the PCGG achieved little in terms of recovering the art and antiques collection which Imelda had accumulated over the years in her New York Townhouse. Within days of Marcos' downfall, two huge container trucks filled with valuables left the Townhouse. The bulk of the art and antiques from the Townhouse has been missing ever since.

The moves taken by the PCGG to recover stolen art and antiques have been again frustratingly inadequate.

Mario Bellini, a prominent art dealer from Florence, admitted to selling many works to Imelda, one of which was a purported Michelangelo [107] which later turned out to be a fake. Since a receipt exists for the purchase, Bellini was guilty of either of two things.

If the painting was a true Michelangelo, then Bellini was guilty of breaking Italian law prohibiting the export of precious art works. If the painting was a fake, then Bellini should be pursued by the Philippine government for fraud. Italian authorities have already questioned and arrested Bellini in connection with the purchase, and Bellini claimed that it was not really a Michelangelo as part of his defense, but the Philippine government has yet to prosecute him and recover the $3.5 million Imelda paid for the fake Michelangelo. Some of the paintings from the Townhouse, (specially those which formed part of the Samuels collection, surfaced later, but the PCGG has done a sorry job at recovering them. It is well-known that Khashoggi played a great part in helping Imelda hide her most important art pieces. In interviews with Australian television, four Khashoggi employees disclosed that a large number of paintings were loaded on Khashoggi's private jet, a Boeing 727, and were flown out of the Butler Aviation Terminal, Newark Airport on 19 May 1986. A second batch originated from Hawaii, where the Marcoses were staying. The huge crates contained 38 works, mostly Impressionist and Renaissance masterpieces, and were first brought to Khashoggi's apartment in Monaco. Seventeen of these paintings, including Rembrandt's Portrait of a Man [108], were later moved to the arms dealers yacht, the Nabila, which berthed near Athens to provide a private viewing of the works for potential buyers. Others were temporarily in kept in his Riviera Villa or stored in a vault at the Sogegard, an art storage agency in France [109]. At least one painting is believed to have been kept in one of his houses in Marbella, Spain.

The transport of these art works occurred between May 1986 to April 1987, right after a Manhattan judge ordered New York auction houses to desist from dealing with stolen art associated with the Marcoses. This clearly makes Khashoggi culpable of violating US law, but the PCGG did not seize this opportunity to nail the arms dealer.

Despite the testimony from Khashoggi's servants and an expose from Australian television station, the PCGG dragged its feet. It delayed seeking an order from French courts to search Khashoggi's properties in France, in the hope that the French authorities would act on their own. Only when it became apparent that the French would not act did the PCGG file for an order. But it was too late. Khashoggi had apparently been tipped off and transferred some of the paintings.

When French officials searched Khashoggi's apartments in Paris and Cannes in May 1987, they found documentation pertaining to the Marcos paintings. Jean-Picrre Sallanic, a lawyer for Khashoggi, said that 31 paintings were actually bought from Imelda. Khashoggi himself gave the number as 38 paintings and claimed that he had not known of the "stolen character" of the paintings. Khashoggi claimed he later sold 20 of these paintings to different collectors for $5 million.

French authorities ordered the seizure of 16 of the 38 paintings found in Khashoggi's yacht. The other 20 paintings which Khashoggi claimed he had already sold were likewise seized by French authorities. It appears that Edwin Meese, Reagan's Attorney General, received 25 of these paintings from French authorities and later formed part of the January 1991 art auction.

But far too many questions about the art works remain unanswered. First, there are varying accounts as to how many paintings the French authorities found in the Nabila. One account says 16, another 17. Given that the 20 other paintings sold by Khashoggi were recovered, this them makes a count of either 36 or 37, depending on the Nabila count [110]. The French turned over only nine paintings initially to the US Justice Department [111], but subsequent turnovers raised the number to 25. There is therefore a discrepancy of either 11 or 12 paintings. If we take Khashoggi's word [112] that there were a total of 38 and not 37 paintings, then the discrepancy rises to 13 paintings. The French have not fully explained the discrepancy nor has the PCGG questioned it. Given the claim that most of the paintings were by French Impressionist masters, it is rather curious that none of paintings the French turned over the US Justice Department were by French artists. The paintings turned over by the French to Edwin Mcese were relatively minor pieces compared to wnat is missing. It is important to keep a close count since even one painting can amount to millions. It is not clear whether the failure in the recovery of precious art works and antiques is due incompetence or a conspiracy. Khashoggi once claimed that the art works arrived in a plane coming from Hawaii. This admission consequently raises questions as to how they arrived in Hawaii. Did they originate from the Townhouse in New York, and if so, how were they transported to Hawaii? Did the Marcoses bring these art works with them from the Philippines as they went into exile to Hawaii? The latter possibility raises further questions as to why these paintings were not included in the properties US Customs authorities listed as being brought in by the Marcos entourage. Did US Customs authorities provide an incomplete list of properties? What further complicates the picture is the fact that the FBI has been conducing intensive investigations on the art works but has not made any of their findings available to Philippine authorities nor has it made any arrest or seizure in connection with the paintings.

Extremely intriguing was the comment of Richard Pichler, a well-respected professional Swiss art dealer based in New York, concerning Marcos stolen art. When shown the list from the PCGG was using to track down the art works, Pichler, who is extremely knowledgeable with both the European and US art market, commented that "whoever prepared this list either did not know what he was talking about or deliberately tried to mislead investigators. The way that this list is constructed makes it impossible to recover any of the art works. Many of the paintings listed here form parts of a series, or there are several versions of the same portrait. This makes it difficult to identify and find if no other information is provided. Is someone trying to mislead investigators?'

Dewey Dee, Herminio Disini, Roberto Benedicto, and others
Nothing has been done to pursue key Marcos cronies who left the country or even recover the assets they stole.

Dewey Dee, who almost brought about the collapse of the country's financial system after embezzling between $70 to $100 million, has found refuge in Canada, where immigration officials have refused to divulge any information. The Aquino government has not done anything to bring him to justice or reclaim the money he stole.

Herminio Disini, the Marcos crony who received an estimated $50 million in illegal commissions for a non-functioning Westinghouse nuclear power plant, is now enjoying a comfortable life in Austria, where he owns several businesses. Again, the Aquino administration has done nothing to bring him to justice or recover the millions he criminally obtained. Instead, government bureaucrats from the Aquino administration pontificate how morally right and economically proper that the Philippines continue to pay for the international debt acquired by the Marcos administration. Roberto Benedicto, the man who controlled the sugar industry, roams around the world, free to enjoy the millions he accumulated at the cost of great hardship on the part of poorly-paid sugar plantation workers. Benedicto was a defendant in the New York trial of Imelda but never made an appearance. Since Salonga has met Benedicto in Hong Kong [113] and other PCGG officials have met with him on other occasions, it appears that the immunity that Benedicto enjoys is not due to an ignorance of his whereabouts. If the Aquino government wants him back, a request for Interpol assistance would surely bring results. But Benedicto continues to roam free.

Hundreds of these former Marcos cronies continue to enjoy immunity from prosecution. Despite the decades of corruption the countiy had to endure, not a single Marcos associate has been convicted or put in jail by the PCGG.

Swiss Accounts
As was noted earlier in this chapter, nothing has been recovered from the Marcos accounts contested in the Swiss courts despite huge fees paid to Swiss lawyers [114]. Moreover, there are other accounts in Switzerland, Liechtenstein, Austria, Hong Kong, London, Singapore and other places which remain secret. Furthermore, secret withdrawals have been made from these accounts. Joseph Bernstein, the New York real estate broker who fronted for the Marcoses, confided that Karl Peterson, Khashoggi's lawyer, was able to withdraw "some dollars" from the Marcos accounts on

November1989 despite the "freeze" order imposed by the Swiss government on all Marcos deposits.

Not only have these major assets escaped the reach of the PCGG but Salonga and Fernando have also inexplicably let former Marcos associates escape while they were within easy reach of the law or granted them extremely liberal compromise conditions.

An example is that of the properties of Armando Romualdez in Rancho Murieta, Sacramento, California (see Chapter IV). The properties had already been under an injunction obtained by lawyers working closely with the CCR. Romualdez, who could not prove how he acquired the money to buy the property, except with the vague claim that it was through the sale of "stocks" m a corporation he formed and made profitable [115], The case was practically won. All that had to be done was for the PCGG to formally argue its case and the property would have been returned by the California court. But Fernando inexplicably caused the case to be dropped, claiming that there was no evidence against Romualdez:

In US courts, you have to establish the money was moved through a government source X, Y, and Z to establish a linkage... Until such time as we can clearly establish that, we will not pursue this any further [116].

It would have been a simple matter for the PCGG to sequester the papers of Armando's firms in the Philippines and show that funds from these firms went to purchase the Sacramento properties. Two companies owned by Romualdez were known to have benefitted from government money. Armando's Highway Builders Inc. got overpriced construction contracts, while his Golden Country Farms received generous loans from the government. A judgement could have been acquired in the Philippines which could then have been easily presented to the California court. No such attempt was made. The property was not recovered. Other PCGG workers in the US found out that the case was dropped only through the newspapers.

Other questionable deals were also arranged during the last months of Salonga's stint with the PCGG. Salonga, already preparing to leave the PCGG to run for the Senate in early 1987, was anxious to capitalize on his work with the PCGG to win votes. But since no substantial gains in the overseas efforts could be shown, Salonga and Fernando worked out deals with two Marcos cronies which contained very questionable terms. The first deal was with Jose Campos Yao, who built a fortune in the pharmaceutical industry. The terms were extremely beneficial for Yao. Yao turned over properties which were primarily Marcos', such as real estate in the Philippines and a list of paper corporations, but was permitted to retain his pharmaceutical empire which was built through the nelp he received from the Marcos government. Yao was furthermore permitted to retain most of the land in San Antonio, Corpus Cristi, Fort Worth in Texas discussed in the previous chapter, worth an estimated $51 million inland [117], after giving up land in the area worth $12 million [118]. Yao was furthermore given absolute immunity from all forms of suits and legal prosecution [119].

The second deal Salonga entered into was with Floirendo, the banana crony. Like Yao, Floirendo turned over some properties he had held for Marcos but retained most of the money he had acquired during the dictatorship. Among properties Floirendo turned over was a house in Honolulu and a condominium in the Olympic Towers in Manhattan. But Floirendo was permitted to retain another condominium he owned at the Olympic Towers, without thoroughly inquiring about the source of funds for the place. Furthermore, Floirendo turned over Imelda's condominium only after it had been emptied of its contents. Those who spirited away the contents of Imelda's Olympic Towers were given ample time to clean the place up before Salonga received it from Floirendo. The only things that were left were a valuable painting which was hidden under a bed and was inadvertently overlooked, an indication that the condominium was used as a depository for the missing art works, and objets de vertue which could no longer be carted away. Floirendo also turned over $12 million, a paltry sum compared to the hundreds of millions he acquired through his control over the banana industry and the trading of sugar. Floirendo's acquisitions from the international trading of sugar and his control over the banana industry were never scrutinized by Salonga. Salonga, nearing the start of the campaign for the senatorial elections, personally announced the turnover of the token sum he received from Floirendo, claiming credit, bragging "I worked out the compromise settlement" [120], Salonga at this time also justified his "compromise" with Floirendo by claiming that it would have an "extremely favorable effect" on suits against the Marcoses [121]. But if one of the conditions of the deal was that Floirendo would participate in later cases against the Marcoses, it is surprising that Floirendo was never called to the witness stand nor even mentioned in the trial against Imelda in 1990. As discussed earlier in this chapter, the jury hearing the case against Imelda had complained about the lack of witnesses. It is therefore rather peculiar that Floirendo who was to have had an "extremely favorable effect" on the trial was never even called to participate as a witness. When Salonga later tried to explain Imelda's acquittal, he conveniently omitted mentioning Floirendo in his speech.

Later compromises with other cronies were equally questionable. A compromise between the PCGG and Jose de Venecia, a front Marcos used in oil exploration companies, was blasted by Sandiganbayan Justice Romeo Escareal as having benefitted the Marcos couple that further proceedings would be "an exercise in futility" [122]. In the case of the California-based Redwood Bank, the PCGG settled for merely 43% of its assets, despite admission from Marcos' nominees that most of the assets were owned by Marcos, thus providing a clear windfall for them. When the details of a proposed compromise with Benedicto leaked to the public, it was found to be so lopsided that a senator threatened to go to court against the PCGG in his capacity as a private citizen should it persist with the deal.

There also has been talk of a compromise with Imelda and lift the world-wide freeze on her assets imposed by a US court. The PCGG has kept the details of these negotiations secret, but reports say that the government's offer is to drop the $5 billion suit against Imelda in exchange for $250 million [123], Later reports said that the amount the government is willing to settle for went down to $50 million [124], a paltry sum compared to Imelda's estimated net worth.

Salonga's compromises with Yao and Floirendo were clearly motivated by his need to claim results before he relinquished his PCGG post to run for the Senate. Yao and Floirendo retained most of their properties and received immunity; Salonga got publicity [125].

Salonga made other questionable decisions during his tenure at the PCGG. For example, instead of prosecuting Enrile, Marcos' Minister of Defense who controlled the coconut industry, Salonga, who maintains a cordial personal relationship with Enrile, offered the former Marcos defense minister five board seats to the United Coconut Planters Bank (UCPB), the bank which controlled the coconut industry, when it was reorganized. Another curious case involves the negotiations for the Swiss accounts of Marcos. When Michael de Guzman failed in his initial attempts to withdraw money from the dictator's Swiss accounts, he attempted to withdraw the money again, the second time claiming that it was no longer Marcos who had authorized him to withdraw the money but Sedfrey Ordonez, then serving as the country's Solicitor General and a close associate of Salonga. De Guzman was trying to convince the Swiss to release the money to him by depositing it in the Export-Finanzierungsbank, the Austrian bank discussed in the previous chapter. Ordonez even went as far as going to Europe in the hope of persuading the Swiss that it was safe to allow the transfer using this private Marcos bank. The Austrian finance ministry then decided that it did not want to get involved in such an operation [126]. The attempt was surprising since Ordonez was in effect trying to convince Swiss and Austrian authorities to release Marcos funds to another Marcos bank, a move highly irregular for a government trying to recover Marcos' stolen loot. Salonga later claimed that he was the one who actually stopped the operation but did not explain why his associate Solicitor Ordonez got involved in the first place. Salonga refused to give an account of the events when a congressionalpanel later investigated the fiasco. The motivations and circumstances behind the operation were never fully clarified.

A comparison of the costs of the overseas recovery efforts with its benefits raises the question of whether the whole effort was worth the trouble. Bonifacio Gillego, who headed the overseas operations of the PCGG before the appointment of Fernando, claimed in 1986 that there was an estimated $900 million in Marcos assets in the US:

> When we say properties - we mean real estate, bank accounts, stocks, bonds, and a lot of other properties that may have been held by cronies who have executed deeds of trust or declarations of trust - we would have something like close to $900 million in the US alone [127].

Gillego did not explain how he arrived at the figure. But whatever may have been the motivation behind the statement, an analysis of what has been actually recovered throughout years of attempts show that less than 1% of this purported $900 million has been recovered. Comparing the amount of money recovered from Marcos and crony assets in the US with the associated costs reveal managerial bungling of colossal proportions.

The limited number of Marcos assets recovered after several years pale in comparison with the extensive list of Marcos and crony properties enumerated in the previous chapter. The only properties which have been recovered from tne time the recovery efforts stated to the end of Fernando's administration are the following:

• **Princeton** Estate

(see previous chapter for description)
° **Lindenmere**
(see previous chapter for description)
• **Olympic Towers**
(see previous chapter for description)
• **East 66th** Townhouse Auction
The remnants of the East 66th Townhouse, catalogued in the first chapter, were auctioned on August 1986. While PCGG officials bragged in Manila newspapers that the auction was able to raise a total of $900,000, the actual amount was much smaller, grossing only $610,000. Some $20,000 of this amount was not turned over to the PCGG by the auctioneer who managed the auction.
It should be emphasized that the objects in the auction were the bones that Imelda and company left in the Townhouse after they had moved out two container truck loads. Nothing of the objects taken out with the two trucks have ever been recovered.
• **Tristan Beplat** and Theresa Fernandez
Cash from two bank accounts, totalling $479,033, were turned over in 1986 (128).
Teresa Fernandez, a niece of Imee Marcos' husband, Tommy Manotoc, on her own volition turned over $320,980 in cash she held in a New Jersey bank for Imee Marcos. Another account was also turned over on September 1986.Tristan Beplat, the international banker mentioned in the previous chapter, was ordered by a New Jersey judge to tum over $158,053 representing the proceeds from a prior sale of a house in New Jersey owned by the Marcoses.

This is a short list comprising relatively minor properties which Marcos and his associates did not contest in court. They cover only a small fraction of total number of the overseas properties discussed in the previous chapter. A week before the New Jersey properties were turned over Salonga bragged in a speech to graduate students at the University of the Philippines that "the govemment is likely to recover some $100 million worth of real estate and bank assets of Ferdinand Marcos in New Jersey" [129]. The Princeton Estate was worth around $1 million, while the combined bank accounts were $479,033, totalling $1.4 million, a figure which by any stretch of the imagination is nowhere near Salonga's figure of $100 million. Furthermore, these were properties which the Marcoses did not contest in court — they were the bones left in the Townhouse and bank accounts and real estate held by other people. Apart from the fact that properties such as Lindenmere and Olympic Towers form part of deal earlier noted as having dubious merit, these properties were also relatively minor compared to the others enumerated in the previous chapter. It is therefore rather presumptuous for the PCGG to claim victory in the recovery of these properties. In the two areas where significant Marcos funds were involved, the case on the major Manhattan properties and Swiss accounts, have not brought any significant positive results. In these cases, the PCGG has had to fight Marcos lawyers.

Further complicating the issue was the manner in which Fernando spent the money that was recovered. As soon as the New York branch of the PCGG had raised the money from the auction, Fernando, then the newly-appointed PCGG head in the US, directed that the money be transferred to him in Los Angeles, claiming that he immediately needed it to pay some lawyers. Fernando claimed to have sent $75,000 to three Swiss lawyers and $275,296 to a law office in Los Angeles. Within a short period of three months, from October through December 1986, Fernando spent all of the funds from the New York auction. By January of 1987, he was frantically asking the PCGG office in Manila for more funds. In a period of three months, Fernando further received a total of $300,000 from the PCGG in Manila, $100,000 each month from January through March of 1987.

The request caused concern amongst many quarters. PCGG workers from the New York office who raised the money from the East 66th Townhouse auction were of the opinion that the money should have gone directly to the Philippines rather than pay for the expenses of Fernando in Los Angeles. Moreover, the administrative and financial officer of the PCGG in Manila also raised the point that the transfer of $300,000 to Fernando in the first quarter of 1987 was clearly illegal since the presidential decree authorizing the organization of the PCGG did not make any provision for the transfer of funds overseas. The $300,000 was nevertheless sent to Fernando, largely because of the personal intercession of Salonga.

The expenses appeared to be incongruous with what the public knew. Clearly, notning haa been achieved with the Swiss accounts so the $75,000 for three Swiss lawyers did not appear to make sense. Payments to the Los Angeles law firm of Munger Tolls & Olsen also caused concern. Fernando had chosen this law firm all by himself and went on to file a RICO (Racketeer-Influenced Corrupt Organizations) suit against the Marcoses. People who kept a close watcn over the recovery efforts were surprised by these moves. They wondered why Fernando chose to file the case in Los Angeles while most of the most of the Marcos real estate and bank accounts covered in the suit were in New York. While federal RICO statutes were being employed in the suit, permitting the case to be filed in Los Angeles, it seemed more appropriate to file the suit be filed in New York since legal arguments concerning forum non conveniens [130] could be countered more easily because New York was the place where most of the crimes were committed. Furthermore, it also appeared odd that Fernando chose to pay large fees to a private law firm in Los Angeles in a racketeering suit, while the CCR, which had already made significant legal gains for the Philippines, had been working for the Philippines for free. The RICO case, handled by Richard Kendall of the law firm of Munger Tolls & Olsen, was subsequently lost, giving Marcos a boost in the overall fight for stolen assets.

Fernando also hired Sills Beck & Cummis, a law firm based in New Jersey, for legal work in connection with other Marcos properties. Compared to the work the CCR had previously done, the work assigned to Jeffrey Greenbaum of Sills Beck & Cummis did not appear as complicated. From what is known, it dealt primarily with the Princeton property, which was uncontested in court, and the legal work for the transfer of tne condominium at Olympic Towers, again something which the Marcoses did not contest. But large fees were paid to the firm. From what is known, Sills Beck was paid witn a check for $140,000 on 17 August 1987, and that upon receipt of the check Sills Beck office had promptly called the PCGG office in New York asking about a balance of $317,038.11. The Coordinating Committee of the PCGG in New York, concerned about the mounting expenses of Fernando, attempted to make sense of the payouts. Working with newspaper accounts to piece together the whole picture, Dennis O'Leary, a member of the Coordinating Committee who had administered the Princeton property for the PCGG, noticed an inconsistency in the figures. In a smart piece of detective work, O'Leary discovered that the $158,053 Tristan Beplat was ordered to turn over could not be accounted for. A check with the administrative and financial officer of the PCGG in Manila showed that the money had not been received. Beplat on the other hand claimed that he had complied with the court order and had turned over the money to Fernando sometime in September 1986. Since there were no records of the money either with the New York or Manila offices of the PCGG, members of the Coordinating Committee in New York confronted Fernando about the discrepancy. Fernando snapped at the Coordinating Committee members, saying "the money has been turned over directly to President Aquino. If you want to verily this, you can check with Manila!" But it was already known that only $300,000, primarily the money from the bank account of Teresa Fernandez supplemented by money from the New York auction, had been given to Mrs. Aquino when sne visited the US on 22 September 1986 [131]. After further investigation, it was discovered that Fernando misspoke during the meeting and that the $158,053 from Tristan Beplat was paid to Sills BecK without the official knowledge of the PCGG. At least $615,091.11 was paid to the law office of Sills Beck for properties which the Marcoses were not even contesting. Fernando later dissolved the New York Coordinating Committee and in turn assigned an individual which had previous links with Edna Camcam, General Ver's close friend, and Agusto Camacho, the architect who fronted for Imelda in the Lindenmere property.

Morgan's Rutgers University paper on the operations of the PCGG also analyzed Fernando's financial operations:

> *Absence of Financial Controls: Fernando did not set up any financial controls and Manila did not insist on them. The movement of money seemed to be purposely obscured. PCGG (US) members did not know where funds were nor what they were being used for. Members of PCGG in Manila did not even know that proceeds from the auction had been sent to Los Angeles at the same time that it had been told to send funds to Los Angeles. Questions concerning the whereabouts of all this money, that is, $882,000, or how it was spent remain unknown to PCGG members in New York.*

The other expenses incurred by Fernando caused further concern. Fernando had also directed the New York office to send him the objects from the East 66th Townhouse which remained unsold, claiming that he planned to hold a similar auction in Los Angeles. But Fernando never gave an accounting of these properties. Another legal expense Salonga and Fernando chalked up was $25,000 sent to Abram Chayes of Harvard University for providing legal advice to Salonga. The PCGG also spent $20,000 for "closing expenses of Olympic Tower," but it is not known whether this amount went to Sills Beck. Concerned that the fight against crony capitalism was leading to lawyer capitalism within the PCGG, the COA attempted to audit the overseas operations of the PCGG. Teofisto Guingona, who then headed the COA, wanted to verify that money was indeed going to the lawyers. But Fernando refused to submit and asked Salonga to intervene with Guingona to scrap the audit. The audit was never conducted by the COA even until after Fernando left the PCGG to join Salonga's staff in the Senate.

The kinder critics explained the actions of Fernando as merely the effects of a bungling, incompetent, and insecure man whose sense of power and personal esteem was easily threatened. But Dennis O'Leary, who had the chance to observe Fernando closely, believed that something more sinister was at work: "Looking back at how Fernando worked and the results of his actions, the only explanation I have was that it was a deliberate act of sabotage."

It is really difficult to say whether the failure of the recovery efforts were due to incompetence or sabotage. Both explanations appear to have a basis. There were many instances of total incompetence botn in the overseas as well as Philippine operations of the PCGG. But the influence of many people formerly associated with either Marcos or his cronies over many of PCGG's activities also lend weight to the conspiratorial theory.

A catalogue of the instances where the incompetence of PCGG officials led to the escape of assets would fill a book and would most interestingly parallel A Concise History of Economic Bungling, a curious book which documents the instances of incompetence in economic policy. On one occasion, PCGG officials in Manila brought a suit against a dead man. The man, Sulplicio Granada, a former official of the organization which controlled the coconut industry, had apparently died without informing the PCGG. On another occasion, officials of the PCGG were suing another man, Francisco Eizmendi, describing him as "whereabouts unknown," while other officials of the PCGG had helped him get elected president of San Miguel, one of the country's largest firms [132], And while two commissioners of the PCGG, Raul Daza and Mary Concepcion Bautista, were squabbling over turf, the bank vault containing many important documents about over which they had been fighting disappeared under their noses [133]

The recovery efforts were also "stymied by presence or participation of former aides of known Marcos cronies" [134]. Mary Concepcion Bautista, a commissioner who had a veiy controversial record within tne PCGG, was a charter member of "Friends of Marcos" [135]. Salvador Hizon, the person Salonga chose as the chief of legal division of PCGG, had worked with Rodolfo Cuenca, the Marcos crony who controlled the construction industry. Hizon was the legal counsel of Philfinance and CDCP, the Cuenca company which bilked the government millions. Hizon was also later hired by the Los Angeles-based Century Bank, owned by Marcos cronies. Critics charged that the appointment of Hizon to head the legal division of the PCGG had resulted in a "discriminatory pattern" in the prosecution of Marcos cronies [136], a reference to the fact that Cuenca, Hizon's former boss, was never adequately prosecuted. And when the PCGG was being revamped, Mrs. Aquino strangely appointed Adolfo Azcuna as the Officer-in-Charge of the PCGG, a dummy of Kokoy Romualdez, Imelda's brother. Azcuna had served as president and chairman of Trans Middle East Phil. Equities Inc., a firm owned bv Kokoy Romualdez, and was an incorporator of PNI Holdings Inc., a firm which was apparently used to move the shareholdings of Romualdez in 36 firms right after the downfall of Marcos. Azcuna was about to be included as a respondent in die ill-gotten wealth case filed against Romualdez before the Sandigan-bayan (Ombudsman) before Mrs. Aquino appointed him as Officer-in-Charge of the very body which had prepared the charges against him. When this was pointed out to Mrs. Aquino, she still expressed confidence in him, saying that his activities with Romualdez involved merely the regular functions of a lawyer. Mrs. Aquino said that her appointee did not act as a dummy and was quoted as saying:

> *You know, they prepare the papers for their clients and initially they are made the incorporators. But then, once everything is ready and finished, they turn over all of the stocks. He was never a dummy... The way I've been told, this is regular practice among*

lawyers.

Mrs. Aquino apparently did not realize the contradiction in her statement. It is an exact description of the activities of dummies and crony nominees.

A *New York Times Magazine* article quoted John Caroll, an American Jesuit priest and sociologist who has lived m the Philippines for many years, in his opinion of Mrs. Aquino: "she is not a conceptual thinker" [137]. Mrs. Aquino's tendency to commit lapses in thought, such as the above justification of the appointment of former Marcos cronies to sensitive positions, may not necessarily justify Imelda's description of her as "a coconut." But it certainly is a valid cause of concern. The problem, however, is not so much the inability to think as the refusal to learn. An article from the Philippines Free Press aptly zeroed in on the problem when it described Mrs. Aquino as "incapable of appreciating any advice except the kind that reinforces her ignorant prejudices' [138].

The most plausible explanation of the failure of the recovery efforts is the corruption and greed of many of those who served the PCGG. The very people tasked with recovering stolen property were accused of the same kind of wrongdoing which was Marcos' trademark. A Wall Street Journal article summarizes the work of the PCGG:

> ... the commission has yet to prosecute a single crony. Worse, some of the commission officials themselves are now being accused of pocketing the remaining assets which they were assigned to protect. Some have resigned. Others have been removed from their posts [139].

Salonga, who has carefully cultivated a public image of honesty, has been sensitive about talk of corruption within the PCGG. He is particularly touchy when the talk centered on the activities of his son, Steve. While he did not officially hold any position within the PCGG, Steve nevertheless was an influential presence within the organization, being tasked by his father with sensitive assignments. When Salonga was led to believe that his deputy information officer in Senate, Ching de las Alas Montinola, had "Dad-mouthed" Steve by claiming that his son had accumulated houses in Alabang, a wealthy suburb, and enjoyed a garage full of expensive cars, she was summarily dismissed. But talk about the activities of his son persisted. Jose Luis Alcuaz, former deputy commissioner of the National Telecommunications Commission under tne Aquino administration, for example, publicly accused Steve Salonga of "coddling a reported business associate of former Chief-of-Staff Gen. Fabian Ver." Alcuaz was referring to Steve Salonga's relationship with Raymord Moreno, who was under investigation by the US government for allegedly receiving "commissions" from military supplies the Philippines bought from the U.S.

Whether or not the charges against Steve have any basis, there were many other accusations of corruption within the PCGG. A sampling of the charges:

   • **thousands** of head of imported cattle and 14 airplanes sequestered by PCGG could not be accounted for.
   • **a PCGG** fiscal agent, a former military officer, who was assigned to oversee companies of cronies which had been sequestered, was able to buy a $900,000 house in the exclusive village of North Forbes and spend a further $50,000 remodelling it. The

house was bought under the name of his common-law wife.

• **The Far** *Eastern Economic Review* reported that Federico Macaranas, the Deputy Executive Director of Fernando, was forced "to resign in 1986 after an internal commission audit uncovered 'financial anomalies in connection with the purchase of a computer."* [140]

• **Quintin Doromal**, a commissioner personally close to Salonga who once held the position of PCGG vice-chairman, was arrested and detained for graft. Francis Garchitorena, the Presiding Justice of the Sandiganbayan, the country's ombudsman, accused Doromal of using his position as PCGG Commissioner to obtain a multimillion peso contract with government corporations through the Dorormal International Trading, a family corporation where Doromal is president. Doromal was charged with violating the 'conflict of interest' provision of the Anti-Graft and Corrupt Practices Act because he "willfully and unlawfully" participated in the bidding sponsored by the Department of Education, Culture, and Sports and National Manpower Youth Council. The $3 million contract involved the supply of educational supplies and electronics equipment.

Another clear case involving Doromal involves the lobbying activities he exerted on officials of the PCGG to buy a used minicomputer from his associates. Doromal railroaded the purchase of a $40,000 DEC (Digital Electronics Corp.) PDP-11 minicomputer on January 1987. No public bidding, comparison of prices, or a study of the appropriateness of the computer was involved. The computer was an old, used refurbished model which had already been phased out by DEC A newer, more powerful model from DEC would cost only $10,000. The minicomputer never worked, but the PCGG could not complain to any other body since it involved one of their own commissioners. Doromal has not yet been made to account for this anomaly.

• **Fernando** assigned a real estate broker in New York, to head an important committee in the overseas operations. All parties interested in buying the Marcos properties that approached the PCGG were instructed by the broker that all proposals for the properties should be coursed through her and that they were not to talk to anyone in the PCGG except her, a violation of the rules of the PCGG that the disposition or sequestered assets must always be done through public bidding and must always be open to the scrutiny of the public. In one occasion, the broker told a potential buyer for the Princeton property that she could facilitate the sale of the property if "a gift" were to be given to her. Surprised at the offer, the potential buyer tried to clarify what was meant by the term "gift." The answer of the broker was, "you know, a gift, like what you give to the doorman at Christmas when he opens the door for you".

• **The brother** of a top official of the PCGG involved with the overseas recovery efforts was facing possible deportation from the US because his visa was about to expire. The official used his office to request the Philippine Ambassador to the US that his sister-in-law be given a position in one of the offices connected with the Philippine diplomatic mission, reasoning that his sister-in-law was performing a service essential to the recovery efforts. The request was granted. The brother and his family acquired diplomatic passports and were allowed to stay in the US

• **The son** of a top official of the Aquino administration secretly met with the son of one of the richest cronies of Marcos in Hong Kong on the weekend of 7 March 1987. A reported $2-$4 million changed hands. The crony was given lenient treatment and was never bothered again.

• **During the** hearings of the Philippine Senate on the operations of the PCGG, it was revealed that one of the commissioners, Mary Concepcion Bautista, had twice suggested to another PCGG official in July 30 1988 that he that he raise money for her personal use, arguing that it was alright "since most at PCGG are making money" [141].

• **Mrs. Noemi** Lirag-Saludo, the Officer-In-Charge assigned by the PCGG to manage De Soleil Apparel Marketing Corp. and American Interfashion Corp., two garment firms connected with the Marcoses, was accused of attempting to use her position to cam "commissions" from companies' garment exports. Pioneer Texturizing

Corp., another textile firm owned by Lirag-Saludo's financier Juliano Lim, were given 25% ot the two firm's export quotas for garments. The government is estimated to have lost $50,000 [142].

• **Two groups of** PCGG workers assigned to manage Baseco, a ship-building facility owned by imelda's brother, accused each other of anomalies. One group entered into two contracts which permitted the sale of metals from the facility falsely labeled as "scrap." The Supreme Court had to intervene on October 1986 and direct the PCGG not to implement the contracts.

Juan Domingo Peron had an interesting and relevant anecdote about the revolution in Argentina in 1930. In the anecdote, quoted at the start of this chapter, Peron related how he saw a man was leaving a building carrying an Argentinian flag wrapped under his arm, shouting, Long Live tne Revolution! When Peron detained him and examined what was inside the flag, the Argentinian leader saw a typewriter wrapped under the flag.

The story is relevant in this context since much has been made about the corruption of Marcos and the need to overthrow him because of that corruption. In the name of justice, in the name of nationalism, many criticized and fought Marcos. But under the guise of the same cry of social justice, nationalism, and revolution, some unscrupulous individuals have tried to advance their own personal fortunes. Many persons within the PCGG who were supposed to have been trying to rectify the legacy of corruption were the very ones who were perpetrating the social cancer. The typewriters in Argentina in the 1930's have now given way to computers in the post-Marcos era. But both have come wrapped under the guise of nationalism and revolution.

It is then little wonder that the recovery efforts in the Philippines have also proved to be a failure. PCGG officials, especially those who had ambitions for public office, tended to exaggerate the accomplishments of the Commission. The data regularly released were most often incomplete or misleading. PCGG officials, for example, were always quick to point out the number of real estate properties and companies they were able to sequester. But there is not much credit to be had in "recovering" real estate. No one, including Marcos, can carry a subdivision or a gold mine with him into exile. Real estate titles may be prove to be worthless if the property is in deep mortgage. The same is true with companies. For example, Benguet Corp., a large Philippine gold mining firm listed with the New York Stock Exchange, was sequestered from Marcos and his cronies, but it turned out that the firm was in deep mortgage with four commercial banks for almost $20 million [143]. Thus, similar scrutiny must be devoted to PCGG proclamations that they had sequestered a total of 218 Marcos and crony companies and had made a total haul of $750 million within the first 100 days of operations. But the reality was not as positive as the impressions created by tne newspaper headlines. A study of the fine print reveals that just 10 of these sequestered companies already a "negative equity position" of $80 million, while 108 companies, representing almost half of tne "haul," did not have any financial statements [144]. The 1986 Year-end PCGG report claimed that 268 companies and $1.1 billion had been recovered. Doromal, the PCGG commissioner who was later arrested on charges of corruption, gave a higher figures, saying that the sequestered and recovered assets was something like" $1.5 billion [145]. But again the figures need to be placed in context. It was later reported that of the 268 firms sequestered, only 67 had financial statements [146]. Moreover, the assets that were recovered and could be disposed ofwere only $90 million in cash and cash items and $5 million in Treasury bills, according to Ramon Diaz, the Vice-Chairman of the PCGG [147]. Another report revealed that the PCGG had recovered $5.4 billion in "non-performing assets" which had a market value of only $1.19 billion [148]. This means that the PCGG recovered only 22% of the real or former value of these corporations. This is hardly a cause for celebration. It is a far cry from the extremely optimistic figures that Salonga bragged about early in the recovery efforts. Most of the Marcos and crony companies the PCGG had recovered in the Philippines were either paper corporations which led to overseas assets beyond the reach of the Philippine government or were corporations which were heavily in debt to commercial banks and therefore had no real value to the government. But PCGG officials were still quick to seize the opportunity and claim victory in the newspaper headlines.

The blame, however, cannot be placed at the doorstep of merely the PCGG. The blame equally lies with an mcompetent national leadership which headed a bureaucracy whose members were quick to place their personal interests above the welfare of the country. The general political atmosphere during the Aquino administration is hardly ideal for an effective recovery program.

Many officials of the Aquino administration conducted themselves in a manner diametrically opposed to the rhetoric of reform Mrs. Aquino mouthed. An idealistic activist who struggled against the Marcos dictatorship related the shock and disappointment sne experienced when she accidentally saw some of Imelda's jewels missing from the Presidential palace in the dresser of an individual with close ties to the new administration. The activist, who was a trusted worker of the new owner of the jewels, tried to keep her discovery a secret so as not to unduly discredit the new government.

The story is merely one of many accounts concerning the administration of Mrs. Aquino. Many other accounts of how those close to the new administration have conducted themselves in their newly-acquired positions of power bear much similarity with how Marcos and his cronies operated. A sampling of reports of how persons close to the administration of Mrs. Aquino have conducted themselves leads one to question whether it is indeed a government committed to reforming the social ills that Marcos left behind:

* **Emmanuel V. Soriano,** the National Security Adviser, was involved in a scandal where he deposited $115,000 from a private company, International Precious Metals Inc. (IPMI), into his personal bank account. The company was involved in a controversial search for the purported Yamashita gold treasure and had excavated part of a national historical landmark despite much public protest. Soriano acted as the "comptroller" for the company, disbursing at feast $73,0u0 from his private account for the company. Soriano claimed that he deposited the funds in his bank account for "safekeeping." According to the Special Prosecutor who investigated Soriano, the act was "tantamount to violation of the constitutional provision on conflict of interest," referring to the provision that prohibits cabinet members from having interests in private corporations. Upon further investigation, it turned out that International Precious Metals had a questionable background in the US and that the excavation might have been a front for some other operation. The case against Soriano, however, ended in a whitewash where he was declared to have "no criminal liability" in the matter, with Mrs. Aquino merely

telling Soriano 'not to do it again."

Soriano was also not held liable for taking pari in the desecration of Port Santiago, a national historical landmark which the Spanish started building in 1591 [149], La Real Fuerza o Castillo de Santiago, now popularly known as Fort Santiago. The Spanish fort was the center of life in the country from the end of the 16th until the end of the 19th century. Soriano furthermore asked the office of the Ombudsman to censure and reprimand the government official who exposed the irregularity.

Raul S. Manglapus, Mrs. Aquino's Secretary of Foreign Affaire, was criticized by members of Congress for using embassy and consular officials in five US cities in a campaign to promote a 'Filipino Car.' Manglapus was reproached for using the embassy and consular offices in Washington, New York, Chicago, San Francisco, and Los Angeles to promote the Filipino Car to be manufactured by the Filipino Car Foundation, a company where Manglapus had a reported stake. Congressional members charged that "embassy and consular officials were instructed by Manglapus to push the promotional campaign by inviting members of the Filipino communities in the US or sympathetic Americans to $100-$200-a-plate fund-raising lunches where the foreign secretary allegedly collected $250,000."

The critics demanded an explanation of the project and "the propriety in law and in public ethics of the foreign secretary organizing a private enterprise, his spearheading a fund-raising campaign for such enterprise utilizing embassy and consular personnel and resources, and his having a direct hand in the administration of these funds." They said that they were "intrigued by Manglapus' excursion into the field of car manufacturing. If it were a personal hobby, the opposition would not mind it at all. But to use embassy and consular officials to raise funds for his dream car is another matter" [150]. The supporters of Manglapus defended the car project as a "patriotic" venture. The appeal to patriotism has a strong resemblance to Peron's story of the typewriter under the flag.

* **Philip Juico**, the Agrarian Reform Secretary, was involved in what has been called the "Garchitorena land scandal" where there was an attempt to sell overpriced, undeveloped land to the government. The scheme was justified by claiming that 1,808 hectares of unirrigated land in the province of Camarines Sur was going to used by the Department of Agrarian Reform in the Comprehensive Agrarian Reform Program (CARP). But it was common knowledge in the area that the land in question was not arable and used merely for grazing cows.

A private firm, Sharp Marketing, originally purchased the property for $190,000 on 29 December 1988, then an attempt was later made to resell the land to the government for $3.1 million, representing a mark-up of 1,531.58% within a few weeks.

The increase was justified by presenting figures where the regional office of the Department of Agrarian Reform in the province of Bicol assessed the property to first have a value of $1,450per hectare, later scaling it down to $1,250, and later further raising it to $1,650. At $1,650 per hectare, the total price would come to $2.9 million, but the Department of Agrarian Reform agreed to pay $3.1 million. The prevailing prices of land in the area were between $100-250 per hectare for irrigated lands and $50 tor unirrigated lands. If the price for unirrigated land is used as a basis for comparison, then the price at which the Department of Agrarian Reform was going to buy would be at least 3,200% overpriced.

The scam involved not only the personnel of the Department of Agrarian Reform but also apparently had the knowledge and participation of the head of the Department, Agrarian Reform Secretary Philip Juico, who 'not only signed a deed of sale, but also protested when the President of tne Land Bank refused to agree to the sale" [151]. When the deal was exposed by the media, Mrs. Aquino stepped in, quickly cleared him, and directed him to investigate the proposed sale, prompting a journalist to comment that The presidential order was reduced to a case of Juico investigating Juico, which most will agree is ridiculous."

Emil Ong, who enjoyed a cabinet-rank position as head of the National Food Authority, at one time had two cases filed against him with the government prosecutorial body. A Wall Street Journal article describes how "...a tugboat captain hired to transport two barges of the agency's rice turned up in port saying the boats had vanished on the high seas. He spoke of strong winds, but his tale grew shakier and shakier the more he told it. Many suspected that Mr. Ong may have had something to do with the disappearance of the rice, worth some $850,000.

A Senate panel investigated. It found no evidence to suggest the rice had been stolen, but it unearthed enough administrative problems to declare Mr. Ong unfit to manage the agency. President Aquino dismissed him. The very next day, he was appointed to a new post with the rank of undersecretary and no cut in salary" [152].

Jose Concepcion Jr., the Aquino cabinet member who promised "I will put a soul and the fear

of Goa" [153] in the Department of Trade & Industry, also came under fire. While cabinet members are required by law to divest themselves of their interests in corporations upon assuming their posts, it was not clear if Concepcion and his wife, Maria Victoria Araneta, had actually divested themselves of their shareholdings in their family corporations when he assumed his cabinet post on 14 March 1986. Concepcion claimed that he had executed an "irrevocable" trust agreement with Citytrust Banking Corp. covering his stocks in Republic Flour Mills (RFM), the giant mill his family owns, but did not actually provide proof of his claim. Members of the Senate, headed by John Osmena, charged conflicts of interest and required him to provide the documentation and show trust agreements on divestments and statements of assets and liabilities from 1986-1989. Concepcion refused. Mrs. Aquino permitted Concepcion to leave for a US trip during the investigations. Concepcion never provided the required documents.

The Concepcion family has extensive interests in flour milling, appliances, and banking. A Wall Street Journal article asks further questions on the conflicts of interest of this favored Aquino minister "Could it be mere coincidence, for example, that in this hot climate, the state controls imports of air-conditioner compressors, and that the family of the minister of trade and industry, Jose Concepcion, is in the air-conditioner business? Or that a handful of flour millers enjoys the protection of import controls on flour — in a country where many people still go hungry, their incomes averaging roughly $600 a year according to the World Bank?" [1M].

The sale of the Philippine Air Lines Building in San Francisco (see previous chapter for description) was one of the earliest scandals to blemish the Aquino administration. The building was sold for a reported $7 million, with some sources saying that it was as low as $6 million, while there while there was an offer of $14 million [155], defrauding the country of $7-8 million. The sale, negotiated by unauthorized persons, was conducted in secret and with undue haste. The legal requirement of a public bidding for the property was ignored.

A Senate panel which later investigated the deal declared in a carefully worded statement that they could find no proof that money had "lined public officials' pockets." The principal person behind the deal was indeed not a public official but was an individual who enjoyed do6e ties with the Aquino administration.

Ernesto Maceda, who served as Aquino's natural resources minister, was accused of attempting leave the country with an estimated $350,000 to $500,000 dollars in an attache case on Cathay Pacific flight CX 900 for Hong Kong on 16 May 1987. A sharp guard noticed the package, aborting the trip. Maceda's brother, Boying. has also been accused of participating in a forgery syndicate and issuing fake permits for the hauling of logs. A woman testified that Maceda's brother offered a permit to haul logs worth $65 million in exchange for $100,000. Mrs. Aquino later personally supported Maceda's candidacy when he ran for a seat in the Senate.

Hernando Perez, the Transportation & Communications Minister, was accused by one of his

subordinates, Jc»e Luis Alcuaz, the deputy commissioner of the National Telecommunications Commission (NTC), of inhibiting the investigation of two communications firms, Liberty Broadcasting Network Inc. (LBNI) and Radionet Inc., owned by Raymond Moreno, an associate of General Ver implicated in the misuse of US military funds.

The accusations of Alcuaz led to further revelations concerning Perez' interest in the companies. It was discovered that an individual, Agnes V. Torres-Devanadera, a managing partner of Perez' former law firm, Balgcs & Perez, was a director of one of the firms, LBNI, and owns 3,200 shares of it. Torres-Dcvanadera admitted that she was a nominee for a client which some quarters believe was Perez, charge Perez denied. A Perez relative, Ramon Gutierrez, also a law partner in Balgos & Perez, is corporate secretary of LBNI. When confronted by journalist Belinda OHvares-Cunanan, Perez admitted that he was a lawyer and director of another Moreno-owned company, Electromex Inc., a sister company of LBNI and Radionet, the two companies Perez prohibited Alcuaz from investigating.

• **Jose Fernandez,** Mre. Aquino's Central Bank Governor, is a hold-over from the Marcos dictatorship. The previous chapter documented the role of the Philippine Central Bank in smuggling the gold out of the country. Most of these transfers were done during the term ofFemandez as Central Bank Governor. He therefore is in the best position to try to solve the mysteries surrounding the disappearance of the gold from the national reserves. But he refuses to open the books of the bank or release the internal report on the "$600 million that disappeared through 'figure inflation' in October 1983 [156]. Moreover, government prosecutors have recommended the filing of graft charges against him for his activities with regard to the closing of Banco Filipino during the Marcos regime. It is said the Office of the President intervened to prevent the filing of the charges. Furthermore, his term as Central Bank Governor was extended when he reached the compulsory age of 65. Fernandez is related to Mrs. Aquino [157].

Even with this short and incomplete catalogue, one can readily see that this culture is hardly the ideal atmosphere to prosecute Marcos and his cronies. Consistency and credibility require that a reforming government does not practice or is not accused of the evils it intends to reform. This lack of consistency and the concomitant lack of credibility is a major factor why the government of Mrs. Aquino failed dismally to recover Marcos' loot ana has had to settle for bones.

The instances where members of Mrs. Aquino's cabinet held positions in private firms or had a clear interest in them is a clear and direct violation of the constitutional provision against conflicts of interest.

But Mrs. Aquino does not appear to object to her cabinet members holding other jobs. She even promulgated Executive Order 284 which allowed her cabinet members, undersecretaries, assistant secretaries, and other appointive officials to keep two more posts aside from their primary jobs. This presidential order, signed into law two days before Congress opened and she lost her law-making powers, was clearly in conflict with several provisions of the constitution [158]. Yet Mrs Aquino persisted in promul- gating it, arguing that the executive order was "in keeping with the interest and spirit of the Constitution" and that her cabinet members needed to "live above the level of corruption."

The order further required that at least one-third of the board members of the hundreds of existing government firms be members of the cabinet or their deputies. This allowed one Aquino cabinet member, Franklin Drilon, an ACCRA lawyer who had worked for Cojuangco and was later assigned as Aquino's Labor Secretary, later Justice Secretary, and still later Executive Secretary to accumulate at least 17 directorships in such firms at one time. To live "above the level of corruption" means that cabinet members receive, apart from their regular government salaries and per diems, commissions from the government corporations which range from a low $150 a year to a high $500,000 a year, depending on the government corporation mvolved. The directorship at the Asian Development Bank which is acquired through the nomination of the Office of the President is a particularly coveted position amongst cabinet members since it carries an annual salary of $90,000. Justifying Mrs. Aquino's move, Sedfrey Ordonez, then Mrs. Aquino's Justice Secretary, declared that "public interest is safeguarded in a [government] corporation which requires the participation of a Cabinet member." Ordonez's remark implies that cabinet members are more morally trustworthy than ordinary citizens, a position which is neither metaphysically nor historically tenable.

Congress, ideally the institution which could provide the needed corrective, has equally been disappointing. It is a little more than a debating club, with the discussions often degenerating into petty squabbles over who will chair which strategic committees. During its first session after the downfall of Marcos, Congress was able to pass merely 15 bills during the eight months that it was in session, a dismal average of less than two bills a month [159]. Moreover, it spent an average of $195,000 for every member in 1988, increasing the average per head to $285,000, a jump of 46% in a year. On one occasion, the Senate ordered 35 new cars for its members while there were only 23 Senators. Members of the House of Representatives, on the other hand, have been accused of spending tax money in pointless junkets abroad, implicated in smuggling ana stock market scams, and other charges such as the possession of illegal drugs.

Mrs. Aquino has often been criticized for being indecisive. Both her critics and her friends attribute most of the shortcomings of her government to this fault. But Mrs. Aquino has shown this assumption to be false on at least two occasions.

Both instances concern how Mrs. Aquino has reacted when individuals working in her government got into conflict with her relatives and other people close to her.

The first case involves the treatment of Gerardo Esguerra, a special assistant of the Customs Commissioner working at the Manila International Airport. Before serving in this post, Esguerra had made great personal sacrifices to bring about reform in the country, working as early as the 1970's during the period of student activism, until the last years of the Marcos dictatorship when he had to go underground because a price had been placed on his head for his activities. Even an Aquino relative, Congresswoman Teresa Aquino-Oreta, admits that Esguerra is a person "of unquestionable character. But a certain Myra Cruz, a lawyer who worked witn the presidential office, picked a quarrel with Esguerra and used the presidential media facilities to curse and hurl obscenities at him over television. While the reasons for Cruz's picking a quarrel with Esguerra were never publicly clarified, what infuriated a lot of people was the idea that Ms. Cruz would use the presidential press office to shout four-letter words during a presidential press briefing to attack Esguerra. A newsman who was in the press briefing later wrote that Ms. Cruz

... is something else. She had the gall to use the harshest Tagalog dirty word before the microphones and the cameras. The one which goes "p— na mo." Really - they should cut

off her tongue.

Ms. Cruz then used her influence to have Esguerra dismissed from his job. Mrs. Aquino did relieve Esguerra of his airport job but offered him other government positions. Esguerra, a man of principle, declined the offer to further work with the Aquino administration.

The other occasion shows more clearly how Mrs. Aquino reacts when it concerns her relatives. Jose Luis Alcuaz, who served as Telecommunications Commissioner, was fired only a few hours before he was to testify at a Senate investigation on alleged graft in government on November 1987. Alcuaz was trying to break up monopolies in the telecommunications industry but encountered what he described as "undue influence from three presidential relatives." Alcuaz complained that two sons-in-law, Eldon Cruz and Manolo Avellada, were interfering with "the functions of government" through their "political appointees." Alcuaz charged that Cruz recommended one Aloysius Santos, while Abellada recommended one Florentino Ampil for positions in the Department of Transportaion and Communications, and that both appointees had tried to stop the approval of the applications of Philippine Global Communications (Pnilcom) to operate an international gateway that would have broken the monopoly the Philippine Long Distance Telephone (PLDT) enjoyed. The PLDT is owned by the cousins of Mrs. Aquino. Alcuaz claimed that Cruz, the presidential son-in-law, had deputy NTC Commissioner Aloysius Santos to hold the applications of other firms. Alcuaz further charged that another presidential relative "intends to be a stockholder" of Radio Philippines Network or Inter-Continental Broadcast Corp., two firms which had been sequestered by the government from the Marcoses. Alcuaz said that he was willing to reveal under oath before Congress what he regards as interference of presidential relatives. But before he was to go before Congress, he was summoned by Mrs. Aquino and was told to just concentrate on his job as NTC commissioner. When Alcuaz insisted on testifying, Mrs. Aquino terminated him. Alcuaz' superior, Transportaion and Communications Secretary Rainerio Reyes, then askeid the Senate committee on public services, transportation, and communications to cancel the scheduled hearing, a request promptly granted by the senators.

The reaction of Mrs. Aquino was dismaying because it was a move that one would have expected of a Marcos but not of a widow who had come to power seeking reform. There are at least two laws which are relevant in this context. Administrative Order 94 bans members of the Aquino and Cojuangco families, including persons who invoke the names of these families, from soliciting favors, concessions, or privileges from government officials. The Anti-Graft and Corrupt Practices Act (Republic Act 30191, Section 5, likewise bars relatives of the President within the third degree of consanguinity or affinity from intervening "directly or indirectly in any business transaction." As as been documented in this book, these rules have been continually broken during the Marcos regime. To what extent these rules were observed in practice will determine the credibility of Aquino's claim that she is a moral improvement over Marcos.

But some who have had the chance to closely study the Aquino administration have already made their judgement. Joaquin Roces, a highly respected figure in Philippine journalism who had consistently supported Mrs. Aquino from the beginning, charged a month before he died that the Aquino administration was characterized by "self-aggrandizement and service to vested interests, relatives and friends" [160]. A member of the Japanese parliament, Upper House Dietman Hata Yutaka, observes how Japanese business recognizes that while individuals in power have changed little has changed in basic patterns of behavior:

> *Though the Marcos empire has collapsed, it has not been eradicated. Japanese enterprise, including the nine major trading houses, are redrawing thepower map of the new administration and urgently tracing new personal connections [161].*

An article from the Manila Chronicle summarizes the feeling of many Filipinos about the Aquino administration:

> *Pretty soon, however, the President began to disappoint even her most avid supporters. For when talk of her relatives making hav and raking in profits from businesses that are either illegal or acquired through the undue use of influence, flourished, she demanded proof of wrongdoing. Like a passive observer, she ordered investigations and let justice take its course. One official investigation she ordered on alleged misconduct by her relatives resulted in what looked like a cover-up instead [162].*

The most damning criticism has come from Ramon Diaz, the successor of Salonga as head of the PCGG. Diaz tried his best to fulfill the job given to him, despite the chaos and problems Salonga and Fernando had left behind. But he encountered many problems in performing his job and finally resigned in bitterness. He complained that not only had he not received any support from the President but also that presidential relatives had constantly attacked the PCGG. The grievances Diaz aired was but an echo of an earlier New York Times article which reported that

> *A number of wealthy Filipinos who are social friends of Mrs. Aquino... have been applying increasing pressure against the [Presidential] Commission [on Good Government]'s action in freezing the bank accounts and seizing the assets of some Marcos associates, the investigator said. We're not getting any support from the Government, we're just being told to slow down,' he added [163].*

The resignation letter of Diaz not only contains his criticism of the Aquino administration but also highlights one of the major reasons for the failure of the recovery efforts. Diaz sent two resignation letters to Mrs. Aquino. The Office of the President chose to make public only one of them, possibly the less politically damaging of the two.

In the letter that was made public and in a later press statement, Diaz complained about how both the office of the Ombudsman and the Solicitor General had not brought to trial the cases the PCGG had prepared against the cronies, of how the old fiefdoms of cronies were prevailing, and of how presidential relatives attacked the PCGG. Complaining about the mcompetence of the government prosecutors, Diaz stated:

> *All 39 cases filed with the Sandiganbayan in July 1987, and handled by [Solicitor General] Chavez, are deeply mired in atrophy, with Chavez leading in asking for postponements, and with the lawyers of cronies just playing around him. blot one of*

these cases is anywhere near trial, and more importantly, the principal defendants, Mr. and Mrs. Marcos, have not yet been summoned a year and two months after the complaints were filed.
Chavez is proving true to the estimate of PCGG's panel of international law experts who, after one day of conference with Chavez last year, told me they believed that Chavez does not have the competence to handle the PCGG cases, [from press statement]
Both the Sandiganbayan [the Ombudsman] and the Solicitor General [Chavez], instead of concentrating on the main issue of ill-gotten wealth, were easily led astray by opposing lawyers so much so that until now, one year later after the PCGG filed the complaints, the principal defendant has not yet been served with summons, and for that matter no crony has yet been tried, [from letter]

Diaz's resignation letter also complained that the new plan concerning Meralco, the national power utility, had the "makings of a gigantic rip-off and of how shares in the PLDT, the phone company, were not sequestered "despite adequate evidence showing the shares actually belong to Marcos" (please see Cnapter III). Diaz further claimed that most of "the cronies still lord it over their old fiefdoms and have wisely availed of the legal services of well-related practitioners." Diaz's letter to Mrs. Aquino also talked about how

unwarranted interference of the Solicitor General [Chavez] was simply the last straw in a series of interventions by interested and well-connected parties in the biggest cases,
from San Miguel to PLDT to Bulletin -- interferences that have been repeatedly relayed to Your Excellency.

The most damaging part of the letter was when Diaz referred to a "concerted effort to have me removed as chairman of PCGG" and that the "PCGG never got any support from the President in face of constant attacks from relatives.

THE SOCIAL CONSTRUCTION OF POVERTY

Rene Saguisag, a member of the Senate and an ally of Mrs. Aquino, tried to defend her administration by saying "corruption is an age-old way of life in the Philippines that is not likely to be eased within this generation" [164]. The reasoning is strangely similar to the justification that Cesar Virata, Marcos' Prime Minister, gave concerning cronyism under Marcos. At the height of the economic crisis in 1984 and the amidst the demands to dismantle the crony monopolies, Virata justified Marcos' administration by saying that cronyism was a natural fact of Philippine life:

Crony capitalism goes lo the Spanish times and the American times.... All the presidents of the Philippines have had their so-called 'identified friends' that have been able to get projects and things like that, and it's probably true for any other nation [165j.

Both arguments are specious. They both imply that since corruption has existed throughout different historical periods it is then a natural, unchangeable fact of life. The reasoning is totally false on both historical and philosophical grounds.

The assumption that corruption has existed in the Philippines throughout her history — in Saguisag's term, "an age-old way of life — is historically false. It was precisely this perversion of historical facts by those who wield power that led Jose

Rizal, the Philippine national hero, to immerse himself in historical studies and attempt to correct historically inaccurate statements about the Filipino character. Spanish friars had continuously maligned Filipinos of the previous century, labeling them indolent, stupid, etc. Rizal combatted these calumnies through his historical researches and showed how they were historically false. Concerning the assertion that corruption has continuously been existent in Philippine history, the historical research of Rizal shows that the position is untenable. Rizal refers to the work of Chao Ju-Kua, a 13th century Chinese geographer who visited the islands which later comprised the Philippines. Chao Ju-Kua wrote that the inhabitants of the islands were an honest and hard working people and that they always paid their debts, even when the traders who lent tnem money would be gone from the islands for long periods of time and had already practically forgotten the debts [166].

One may also point out that ordinary Filipinos, especially those who still remain uncorrupted by city life, are generally honest and respectful of the rights of others. It is difficult to accept the proposition that corruption is a national trait of a particular race. It is more plausible to view corruption as a behavioral pattern ingrained in the government bureaucrat who foists it on the rest of a victimizedpopulation.

The important question is not whether cronyism has been present in different epochs in Philippine history but to understand the historical process by which it came about in different periods. Pointing to the presence of corruption and cronyism in different historical periods without explaining how it has come about in each of those periods leads to the myopia that corruption is a natural state rather than a historical phenomenon. But this is philosophically wrong. It confuses historical occurences with a natural state of affairs.

Working within the tradition of the sociology of knowledge, Peter Berger and Thomas Luckmann have shown in The Social Construction of Reality that all social institutions are products of human action. While we experience social institutions most often as a given and immutable objective reality, the truth is that they are products of the actions of men. In the words of Berger and Luckmann, society is an objective reality, but it is also a social product. If it is accepted that institutions in society are products of men, that they are social and historical products of human action, then the clear implication is that they do not belong to the natural state of things and can therefore be changed by men. Earthquakes are natural occurrences, but the deaths resulting from the collapse of buildings constructed by corrupt contractors are not. There is a clear distinction between the natural world and the social world. The former is given and immutable, the latter is subject to human action.

The discussion then brings us full circle and we arrive at our starting point at the beginning of the book. We intended not only to document the history of Marcos' crony capitalism but to also show how the culture of corruption brought about the extremes of poverty and wealth.

It is hoped that we have adequately documented how the pursuit of wealth during the Marcos dictatorship has brought about the great poverty of the country. It is hoped that we have sufficiently exposed the economic and political mechanisms employed to create great wealth on one hand and extreme poverty on the other. It is further hoped that we have fully backed the assertion made in the first chapter that wealth and poverty are causes and effects of each other.

One only needs to recall the sections of the third chapter which documented how workers in the sugar, banana, and coconut industries were forced to live in abject poverty andperform hard labor to create fortunes for Marcos and a handful of cronies. It is not difficult to understand that the hemorrhage of capital we documented in the previous chapter would have a direct and adverse effect on the overall level of economic activity - the country's level of national income and output, its pattern of income distribution, its rate of savings, capital formation, and investment, its balance of payments and exchange rates position. Clearly, the outflow of money would have an immediate adverse effect on the economy and bring about greater poverty for an already suffering people.

Poverty is therefore not an unchangeable state of affairs, an immutable fatum to be perpetually suffered, but a historical condition which can be changed. Poverty is a product, a social product, brought about by institutions created by men.

MONTAIGNE AND THE DOUBLE MAN

The Aquino administration has done little to recover the assets of Marcos and his cronies. It has done nothing to alleviate the poverty of its people.

The term revolution has often been used to describe the overthrow of the Marcos dictatorship. Many, mesmerized by the drama of the peaceful transition, often refer to it as the 'People Power Revolution.' But since the opportunity to launch a real revolution of the social system was squandered, and the promises of reform have become merely the convenient slogans of politicians, the overthrow of the Marcos regime is a revolution only in the most limited sense of the word. In classical mechanics, a revolution occurs when an object executes a 360-degree turn and returns exactly to its initial position. Since the very ills for which Marcos was overthrown are not being addressed by the Aquino administration, this particular definition of revolution might be the most appropriate one to apply to the transition from the Marcos dictatorship to the Aquino administration.

Some quarters argue that the administration of Mrs. Aquino is a clear improvement over that of Marcos. This is a most pathetic argument. It uses as a standard of comparison one of the most corrupt dictators the world has known. A better standard would have been what is possible, of what lies within the human potential, of what is morally ideal. It may well be that Mrs. Aquino's administration can come out ahead of Mr. Marcos' dictatorship. But the fact that we have to use such an abominable standard to measure our behavior and achievements is in itself already an admission of our failure.

And what of the treasure that lies abroad? We have already failed in our attempts to retrieve it. And this failure may be a blessing in disguise. The way Rizal concluded his second novel *El Filibusterismo* is instructive. It will be recalled that Simon, the main character, returns to the Philippines after a long exile, ready to wage a revolution against Spanish tyranny. He comes disguised as a wealthy jeweler who uses his money to finance the revolutionary efforts. His plot is however discovered, and Simon is forced to flee. Woundea, he reaches rr. Florentino, a wise old Filipino priest, in the mountains. As Simon lies dying, Fr. Florentino delivers his famous soliloquy. In the end, the old priest takes Simon's cache of jewels and pushes it to tne sea, saying that the jewels would not be for the use of the present generation and will be retrieved at the proper time when they can be put to better use:

¡Que la naturaleza te guarde en los profundos abismos, entre los corales y perlas de sus eternos mares!.... Cuando para un fin santo y sublime los hombres te necesiten, Dios salva sacarte del seno de las olas... Mientras tanto, alli no haras el mal, no torceras el derecho, no fomentaras avaricias!... [167]

Given the way the Aquino administration has conducted itself, the present defeat in the recovery efforts may be the best solution. Since we cannot be assured that a return of the money from the Swiss banks at the present moment will be used for the betterment of the people who suffered most under the Marcos regime, we may perhaps take a cue from Fr. Florentino who threw the cache of jewels into tne sea and hope it will be retrieved when it can be best utilized. Since the political institutions in the Philippines are still rife with corruption, any return of these assets from the Swiss banks will most likely end up lining private pockets and back in overseas accounts. The best thing therefore is to keep the money there, place the Swiss on notice that we have a moral and legal claim to the assets, and work on strengthening the political institutions so that when the assets are finally returned, they can be put to the best use. Since the constitution guarantees that the right of the state to recover unlawfully acquired properties will not be barred by prescription [168], there is no point in rushing into an ill-defined, costly, and potentially-fruitless attempt to get at the Swiss accounts at the moment. If the mechanisms to receive and utilize the returned assets are not in place, then any return would be pointless.

Soren Kierkegaard, the Danish philosopher, once talked about philosophy as the confessor to history. By this he meant that philosophy should closely listen to what history says, interrogate it, hold it in judgement, and give it its penance.

But at the end of our account of Marcos' crony capitalism, we find that while we have closely interrogated history, we cannot come to a conclusion and render a judgement. Rather than a confessor which summons the divine for judgement, we feel more like Gothe's Faust, who after a long life of study, asks himself of what use was all of his studies in medicine, law, and philosophy, and tries to make sense of his life. We suffer a deep uneasiness after taking great pains to document a story, only to find out that the conclusion points to a typewriter hidden under a flag. Our original purpose was to document the corruption within the government of Mr. Marcos and have taken great efforts to achieve this goal, but in the end we find it not only difficult to conclude about the regime of Mr. Marcos but also find ourselves asking fundamental questions about human nature. Recalling that those who served in the government which vowed to reform the evils of tne Marcos dictatorship were tnemselves accused of corruption, we have strongly resisted coming to the same conclusion as Montaigne:

It is not possible for a man to rise above himself and his humanity.... We are, I know not how, double in ourselves, so that what we believe we disbelieve, and cannot rid ourselves of what we condemn.

Endnotes

1. *Financial Times*, 25 April 1986.
2. *Manila Times,* 17 April 1986.
3. Ellen Tordesillas, "PCGG Spreads Dragnet over Treasury Raiders," *Malaya*, 4 June 1986.
4. *Manila Chronicle,* 24 September 1986.
5. *Business Day*, 19 January 1987.
6. Max Soliven, "The Marcos Billions and Switzerland," *Manila Times,* April 1987.
7. *Business Day,* 19 January 1987.
8. Max Soliven, The Marcos Billions and Switzerland," *Manila Times,* April 1987.
9. Max Soliven, "The Marcos Billions and Switzerland," *Manila Times*, April 1987.
10. Ziegler, Une Suisse au-dessus de tout soupqon.
11. Ziegler, Une Suisse.
12. Ziegler, Une Suisse.
13. Ziegler, Une Suisse.
14. Philip Lustre, Tilting At Windmills: Fighting the Swiss Banking System," *Philippines Free Press,* 19 October 1991.
15. Please see Chapter IV.
16. June Kronholz, "Much Marcos Wealth, Still Carefully Hidden, Eludes Investigators," *Wall Street Journal,* 11 February 1987.
17. Alexander N. Gilles, "How Marcos Built a Secret Empire" *Manila Times East,* 24 June 1987.
18. June Kronholz, "Much Marcos Wealth, Still Carefully Hidden, Eludes Investigators," *Wall Street Journal*, 11 February 1987.
19. Alexander N. Gilles, "How Marcos Built a Secret Empire", 24 June 1987
20. June Kronholz, "Much Marcos Wealth, Still Carefully Hidden, Eludes Investigators," *Wall Street Journal*, 11 February 1987.
21. "In Search of the Marcos Millions," PBS broadcast over US TV on 26 May 1987.
22. Max Soliven, The Marcos Billions and Switzerland," *Manila Times,* April 1987.
23. Please see Chapter IV and also Ingo Walter, Dirty Money.
24. Walter.
25. Adam Smith interview
26. Ziegler, Une Suisse.
27. Ziegler, Une Suisse.
28. Ziegler, Une Suisse.
29. Walter "Dirty Money" article.
30. Max Soliven, The Marcos Billions and Switzerland," *Manila Times,* April 1987.
31. Ziegler, Une Suisse.
32. Ziegler, Une Suisse.
33. *Financial Times*, 25 April 1986.
34. *Bulletin Today,* 15 April 1986.
35. Carla Rapoport, Tokyo starts gingerly to prove the steady flow of bribes," *Financial Times,*
25. April 1986.
36. *Philippine Daily Inquirer*, 24 April 1986.
37. *Philippine Daily Inquirer*, 26 April 1986.
38. *Manila Times,* 29 April 1986.
39. Luis D. Beltran, "One of the Best Kept Secrets: FM cronies' huge Yen Deposits," *Philippine Daily Inquirer,* 16 November 1986.
40. *Manila Bulletin,* 18 November 1986.
41. *New York Times*, 30 December 1985.
42. *Wall Street Journal,* 21 March 1986.
43. *Time,* 31 March 1986.

44. Section 441 (e).

45. William Scott Malone, "Golden Fleece," *Regardies*, October 1988.

46. *Newsweek,* 13 Sept. 1982

47. Marcos' fake medals were exposed in a 1985 *New York Times* article.

48. Mijares, p.90.

49. "Marcos network seeking to sell gold," *Japan Times*, 21 July 1987.

50. Malone

51. Malone

52. Malone

53. Malone

54. Malone

55. Malone.

56. Malone.

57. Malone.

58. Quoted in *Malone.*

59. Quoted in *Malone.*

60. Malone

61. Malone

62. Quoted in Malone. According to *Malone,* Miller's presence in London is what accounts for North calling it the "British gold transaction" in his notebooks.

63. Quoted in *Malone.*

64. Malone

65. Malone

66. Malone

67. Malone

68. This is really an epistemological problem as much as it is a political one. Psychology talks about the selective nature of our perception; the sociology of knowledge has shown that our knowledge is sociologically conditioned; and epistemology, the branch of philosophy which deals with the nature of knowledge, acknowledges the perspectival and historical nature of our thought.

69. The Philippine government argued that the export of currency in pesos or US dollars without an export license was subject to confiscation.

70. Dale Russakoff, "Anatomy of a Looting: ExPresident Marcos' wealth Traced in Depositions, Confessions," *Washington Post,* 30 March 1986.

71. Ellen Tordesillas, "Given for no reason at all: $40,000 for Imelda's flowers," *Malaya,* 7 April 1988.

72. *Business Day,* 19 January 1987.

73. Among those charged were Ferdinand E. Marcos, Imelda R. Marcos, Gliceria R. Tantoco, Bienvenido Tantoco, Sr., Adnan Khashoggi, Roberto S. Benedicto, Rodolfo T. Arambulo, Bienvenido Tantoco, Jr., Karl Bock Peterson, Jaime Alberto Arias, California Overseas Bank.

74. Malone

75. Malone

76. Malone

77. Malone

78. Quoted in *Malone*

79. *Wall Street Journal,* 17 March 1986.

80. Article by J. Conason.

81. *New York Times,* 3 July 1990.

82. *New York Post*, 3 July 1990.

83. *New York Newsday,* 3 July 1990.

84. Spence made this remark in a TV interview.

85. New York Newsday, 3 July 1990.

86. A very good discussion of the topic is to be found in James Henry, "Where the Money Went," *New Republic,* 14 April 1986.

87. *Washington Post,* 16 June 1979.

88. *Associated Press*, 13 November 1979; Washington Post, 14 November 1979. It would have been totally within the character of Marcos to have used this as a tactic to blackmail Westinghouse to give him more commissions. The payments were later resumed.

89. International banks are clearly aware of this and therefore most often denominate the payments in a stable international currency.

90. Warner Hutchins, an executive director of Citicorp, and Robert Cushman, a managing director of Asia Pacific, met several times with Disini to plan the financing the plant.

91. Section 1701

92. Should the failure to use the Act in the Marcos case while invoking it against the Shah tempt us to conclude that hostage taking was worthwhile? Its application in the case of the Shah was premised on the existence of a "national emergency" - i.e., the hostages in the American embassy in Iran. In the Philippine case, however, there were no hostages but moreover involved another former ally who was careful to develop ties with the Republican leadership. The events seem to imply that those who choose the way of litigation would end up wasting a lot of time and money in investigations and litigation but end up with nothing, while those who take hostages are met with more success.

93. *Wall Street Journal,* 17 March 1986.

94. *Manila Bulletin*, 8 April 1986.

95. *Financial Times,* 25 April 1986.

96. *Philippine Daily Inquirer,* 18 April 1986.

97. *New York Times,* 22 May 1986.

98. The Nation, 14 June 1986.

99. Daniel J. Komstein, "Guilt by Lawyer?" *New York Law Journal,* 10 June 1986.

100. Please sec Chapter III.

101. Fernando then served as part of Salonga's staff when Salonga became President of the Philippine Senate.

102. Jennifer Morgan, Case Analysis: Administrative Analysis, Spring 1987.

103. Paul Moses, "Swiss Jail Saudi Jet-Setter," New York Newsday, 19 April 1989.

104. Malone

105. Malone

106. Malone

107. Please see Chapter I.

108. William Sherman, "The Marcos Collection," *ARTnews,* October 1990.

109. William Sherman, "The Marcos Collection," *ARTnews,* October 1990.

110. Another account says that 15 paintings found in Paris warehouse in early 1988, while 9 were turned over by Khashoggi, making a total of 24. Far Eastern Economic Review, 29 September 1988.

111. *New York Times,* 8 January 1988.

112. William Sherman, "The Marcos Collection," *ARTnews,* October 1990.

113. *Business Day,* 19 January 1987.

114. An exception is a small amount which was returned because a crony firm in the Philippines had been sequestered and its Swiss account was consequently closed. But this has nothing to do with the major Marcos Swiss accounts being fought out in the Swiss courts where issues of banking secrecy are raised.

115. *Sacramento Union*, 3 October 1986.

116. *Sacramento Union*, 3 October 1986.

117. Wall Street Journal, 21 March 1986.

118. "Campos Agrees to Pay $12 M," Manila Bulletin, 13 June 1986; "Marcos Crony agrees to Pay $12 M," *Tribune,* 13 June 1986; "Crony Pays RP $12 M for FM's Texas Lands," *Malaya,* 13 June 1986; "Marcos Texas estate Dispute Settled," *Manila Times,* 13 June 1986.

119. *Manila Bulletin*, 20 May 1986.

120. *Manila Bulletin*, 8 March 1987.

121. *Philippine Daily Inquirer and Manila Times,* 9 March 1987.

122. *Manila Bulletin*, 6 December 1989.

123. *Philippines Free Press*, 8 December 1990.

124. *New York Times,* 3 November 1991.

125. Fernando, on the other hand, was aiming to fill the position of PCGG commissioner Salonga vacated. Since he had already aroused the concern of the other commissioners, Fernando did not get the position. Fernando then served in Salonga's staff in the senate.

126. Alexander N. Gilles, "How Marcos Built a Secret Empire," June 1987.

127. Interview with the *Manila Chronicle,* 24 September 1986. Our italics.

128. *Philadelphia Inquirer*, 13 September 1986.

129. *Philippine Daily Inquirer,* 5 September 1986; *Manila Times*, 4 September 1986.

130. Legalese for appropriate place or venue to hear the case.

131. *New York Times,* 23 September 1986.

132. Max Soliven, "Sueing a dead man and a 'missing' president," *Star,* 3 August 1987.

133. *Manila Times*, 30 June 1986.

134. *Tribune,* 11 July 1986.

135. "Wild Mary Keeps on Charging," *Star,* 3 August 1987.

136. *Tribune,* 11 July 1986.

137. *New York Times Magazine,* 19 August 1990.

138. Mikael G. Aquino, "The Danding Coup," *Philippines Free Press,* 16 February 1991.

139. *Wall Street Journal,* 24 October 1988.

140. *Far Eastern Economic Review*, 17 September 1987.

141. *Manila Bulletin,* 23 September 1988.

142. *Tribune and Bulletin Today,* 18 November 1986.

143. *Malaya,* 15 July 1986.

144. *Manila Times*, 10 June 1986.

145. *Business Day,* 19 January 1987.

146. *Business Day*, 19 January 1987.

147. *Business Day,* 19 January 1987.

148. *Manila Bulletin*, 4 March 1987.

149. "Por una carta del estado militar de Filipinas sabcmos que en 1591 estaba ya comenzado (la fuerza de Santiago]," Maria Lourdes Diaz-Trechuclo Spinola, Arquitectura Espahola en Filipinas (1565-1800), (Sevilla: Escuela de Estudios Hispano-Americanos de Sevilla, 1959).

150. *Manila Bulletin* 19 July 1988

151. Ninez Cacho-Olivares, "Favored Big Fish," *Philippine Daily Inquirer.*

152. *Wall Street Journal*, 24 October 1988.

153. *Business Day,* 5 March 1986.

154. 7 February 1990, *Wall Street Journal*

155. *Manila Times,* 18 June 1986.

156. Malone

157. Malone

158. Section 13, Article VII is an absolute prohibition against high government officials holding more than one office. Section 7, Article IX-B, which covers appointive officials, and Section 8, Article IX-B, which covers additional, double, or indirect compensation may also be relevant provisions.

159. *Philippine Daily Inquirer,* 3 April 1988.

160. *New York Times*, 17 October 1988.

161. Shukan Post, 21 March 1986, reprinted in *Business Day*, 25 March 1986.

162. "The Cross Cory's relatives must bear," *Manila Chronicle,* 11 October 1988.

163. Fox Butterfield, "Marcos Crony Returning Despite Fraud Evidence," *New York Times*, 24 March 1986.

164. *New York Times,* 17 October 1988.

165. *Washington Post,* 16 August 1984.

166. "Los malayos filipinos, antes de la llegada de los europeos, sosteman un activo comercio, no s61o entre si, sino tambi£n con todos los paises vecinos. Un manuscrito chino del siglo XIII, traducido por el Dr. Hirth (Globus, Sept. 1889), y del cual nos ocuparemos en otra ocasion, habla de las relaciones de China con las Islas, relaciones puramente comerciales, en que se hace mencien de la actividad y honradez de los mercaderes de Luz6n, quicncs tomaban los product os chinos, los distribuian en todas las Islas viajando por nuevc meses, y volvian despu6s para pagar reliaosamente hasta las mercanrias que los chinos no habian crcido dar..." Nuestro 6nfasis. Jose Rizal, "Sobre la indolenria de los Filipinos," Escritos Politicos e Histdricos, (Manila: Comisi6n Nacional del Centenario de Jose Rizal, 1961), p. 233.

167. "May nature hide you in her depths, amongst the corals and pearls of her endless seas!... And when men should need you for a holy and noble cause, God will know how to rescue you from the waves that cradle you. Meanwhile, there you will do no harm, you will not pervert what is right, you will not engender greed...." Our translation. Rizal, El Filibusterismo, p. 286. For those who have read the novel in its entirety, it will be clear that the cache of jewels is a metaphor for revolution. We are not yet ready since the social, educational, and institutional preconditions to make a political revolution successful are sadly not yet in place.

168. Article XI, Section 15 of 1987 constitution. In other words, there is no time limit capping the right to recover.

ABOUT THE BOOK

Some Are Smarter Than Others is the expanded and updated version of the now-classic pamphlet of the same title published in 1979.

This book documents in detail how state pover was used to intervene in the economy during Marcos' rule. It focuses on how privilege and wealth were created for a few individuals while the country was inexorably pushed into increasing underdevelopment and the majority of the Filipinos were consigned to live in abject poverty.

Like the 1979 pamphlet, the present book draws its title from a statement attributed to Imelda Marcos. Parrying criticisms of relatives who became overnight millionaires after her husband assumed absolute powers in 1972, Imelda countered: "Sometimes you have smart relatives who can make it... My dear, there are always people who are just a little faster, more brilliant, more aggressive."

COMMENTS ON THE 1979 STUDY

"... the best overview of the cronies and their activities."
                                        Raymond Bonner. Waltzing With a Dictator

"... impressively documented."
                                        John Oakes, The New York Times

".. the most explosive document to have rocked Manila."
                                        Ninoy Aquino, December 1979.

COMMENTS ON THE PRESENT WORK
    " ... a gold mine."   Edward Pound, Wall Street Journal

"... a gothic novel."   Rafael Cecilio, literary critic and Educator

> *"... this book is without parallel. Extremely scholarly as well as relevant,*
> *this book sets a standard for scholarship and committed writing.*
> *Philippine political historiography will never be the same.*
> *This is the definitive work on the topic. Henceforth, anything written*
> *on the subject will be mere commentary on the present book."*
>   Dennis O' Leary, veteran journalist specializing in Asia

THE AUTHOR

Ricardo Manapat authored the 1979 study of the same title. He was harassed and persecuted by the Marcos regime for his activities and had to go into exile in 1980. He invested close to 11 years to complete the present work. Totally devoting himself to the research and writing of this book, he spent these years as a semi-hermit and recluse.

Appendix
Books by Dr. Hilarion M. Henares, Jr. (Larry Henares)

Make My Day Series: Essays on Phils. 1980's-90's
Book 1: Make My Day
Book 2: Nice and Nasty
Book 3: Cecilia My Love
Book 4: Sweet and Sour
Book 5: Saints and Sinners
Book 6: Villains and Heroes
Book 7: Tough and Tender
Book 8: Light and Shadow
Book 9: Give and Take
Book 10: To Be or Not to Be
Book 11: Cash and Credits
Book 12: Rise and Fall
Book 13: Swans and Swine
Book 14: Touch and Go
Book 15: Life and Death
Book 16: Kiss and Bite
Book 17: Good and Evil
Book 18: Beast and Beauty
Book 19 Beggar and King
Book 20: Trash & Treasures
Book 21: Wear and Tear
Book 20: Trash & Treasures
Book 23: Pretty Ugly
Book 24: Salvation & Damnation
Biographical Books: 1980's-90's
1) Hilarion G. Henares: Life and Times, (Larry's Father)
   co-author Edith Perez de Tagle
2) Don Daniel Maramba: Life and Times, (Larry's father-in
   law) co-author Edith Perez de Tagle
3) The Moving Finger Writes: Love Letters (Larry & Cecilia)
4) Search for Antonio Luna's Descendant
Special Books:
1--Opus Dei and the CIA, 2017
2- Opus Dei Pirates and Parasites, 2017
3- Ipis Dei: Cockroach of God, 2017
4- Magnum Opus Dei – Of God and Greed – co-author
   Dr. Esteban Luis Latorre. 2017
5- The Dawn of Great Civilizations: Heralding
   the Return of the Mother Principle, 2017
6- The Sinatra Songbook, 1,300 lyrics, 2000
7- The Milk Wars, 2017
Older Books:
1-Behold the Radiance, 1966
2-Sun and Stars Alight, 1976

(All books in paperbacks – searchable &
available at amazon, kindle and online sellers)

ooO0oo

Made in the USA
Las Vegas, NV
15 May 2022